T.H. MEYER was born in Switzerland in 1950. He is the founder and publisher of Perseus Verlag, Basel, and editor of the monthly journal *Der Europaer*. He is the author of several books including *D.N. Dunlop, A Biography*; *Rudolf Steiner's Core Mission*; *The Bodhisattva Question*; *Clairvoyance and Consciousness* and *Reality, Truth and Evil*, and editor of *Light for the New Millennium*. He has written numerous articles and gives seminars and lectures around the world.

CW01499641

LUDWIG POLZER-HODITZ
A European

A Biography by T. H. Meyer

TEMPLE LODGE

Dedicated to the memory of Menny Nita-Schwarz-Lerchenfeld
who passed away on 2 November 2004

First published in Great Britain in 2014

Temple Lodge Publishing,
Hillside House, The Square
Forest Row, RH18 5ES

E-mail: office@templelodge.com

www.templelodge.com

Originally published in German by Perseus Verlag, Basel, in 1994. This translation is based
on the second edition of 2008

© Perseus Verlag 2008 www.perseus.ch
This translation © Temple Lodge Publishing 2014

Translated from German by Terry M. Boardman

Facsimiles of handwritten notes and letters have been reduced in size

A catalogue record for this book is available from the British Library

ISBN 978 1 906999 64 3

Cover by Morgan Creative
Typeset by DP Photosetting, Neath, West Glamorgan
Printed and bound by Beforts Ltd., Hertfordshire

Whoever cannot give an account to himself
of the past three thousand years,
remains in darkness, without experience,
living from day to day.

Wer nicht von dreitausend Jahren
sich weiß Rechenschaft zu geben,
bleib' im Dunkeln, unerfahren,
mag von Tag zu Tage leben.

Goethe, *West-Eastern Divan*

Je me suis assez vite aperçue
que j'écrivais la vie d'un grand homme.

Marguerite Yourcenar, *Mémoires d'Hadrien*

Contents

IV. YEARS OF WANDERING

V. THE TESTAMENT OF LUDWIG POLZER-HODITZ

VI. APPENDIX

Foreword to the English Edition

Ludwig Polzer-Hoditz (1869–1945) is but vaguely remembered by most older anthroposophists in the English-speaking world. The younger generation, though, may not have even heard his name. This book tries to make up for this double lack.

Polzer was a close pupil and friend of Rudolf Steiner and played a key role in the unfolding of the threefold movement in and after 1917, together with W.J. Stein* and Count Otto Lerchenfeld. He established personal links to a number of public figures like Masaryk and Benesch. He played a key role as a mediator in the tragic events which befell the Anthroposophical Society after Steiner's death. At the Society's Annual General Meeting in April 1935, he delivered a clear-sighted speech showing the necessity of finding a genuinely new style of working within the Society based on individual trust and without any institutionalized spiritual leadership.

Polzer had clear insight into the opposition forces working against anthroposophy and threatening the real task of Middle Europe from two sides—from the decadent masonic stream in the West as well as from the inner core of the Catholic Church—both increasingly cooperating in this opposition. He became one of the few pupils of spiritual science who understood the long term strategies inherent in these opposing movements. That is one of the reasons why a deeper knowledge of his life and striving may help illuminate all those who seek clarity in the midst of our present day's confusing and belligerent events.

It is fortunate that this book is published at the same time as the new English edition of my biography of Daniel N. Dunlop. Polzer had formed a particularly strong link to this outstanding anthroposophist and founder of the World Power Conference (now World Energy Council). His important speech in April 1935, read by Dunlop before his premature death in May 1935, forms a central part of another parallel publication entitled *The Development of Anthroposophy Since Rudolf Steiner's Death*.†

It is with deep gratitude to Terry Boardman for his painstaking and meticulous translation of this book that I'd like to wish a benevolent reception for it from its English-speaking readers.

27 August 2014   T.H. Meyer

---

* It was W.J. Stein, who had emigrated to London, who first published an English version of Polzer's memories of Rudolf Steiner in his journal *The Present Age* in the 1930s.

† Compiled and edited by Paul V. O'Leary. To be published by SteinerBooks (Great Barrington, MA).

Foreword to the New Edition

Why a new edition?

Fourteen years have passed since the appearance of the first edition of the present book. In the middle of this period occurred the catastrophe which since that time has changed the face of the world: the attacks of 11 September 2001.[*] We are living in the time of the global 'War On Terror' and of China's rise to become a world power. If the biography of Ludwig Polzer-Hoditz is now republished in a revised and extended form, this is not least in the hope that it can offer today's reader constructive viewpoints to make sense of world events.

Hardly any other student of Rudolf Steiner was as concerned as Ludwig Polzer-Hoditz to understand and gain an overview of the *great patterns* of historical processes. To these belonged what would make it possible for Europe and the world—inspired by spiritual science—to realize a dignified future for humanity, and to them also belonged on the other hand, everything that works against this effort. These counterforces include, for example, those impulses evident in the so-called Testament of Peter the Great. Certainly, the Testament is, viewed in external terms, a fabrication, but the ideas presented in it are still *effective* today! These are ideas which have as their goal the elimination of the European Middle and which led in the East to the installation of the socialist experiment instead of a threefolding of society.[†] They are ideas which instead of a world economy in a brotherly sense brought to power a globalizing elite (dominated by the West). They are ideas which would make Europe into an American vassal state, the spirituality of which is to be that of the Church of Rome.

The tragic events of 11 September 2001 are only in an external sense something very new and 'incomparable'; in truth, they represent the most dastardly and mendacious example in world history of the effort to push through age-old group interests at the cost of thousands upon thousands of lives, when one adds to 9/11 the wars which followed it in Iraq and Afghanistan.

---

[*] See T.H. Meyer, *Reality, Truth and Evil—Facts, Questions and Perspectives on September 11, 2001.* Temple Lodge Publishing, London 2005.

[†] How far this experiment was carried out under the direction of western circles is clear from the role played by Alexander Kerensky as Prime Minister of the Provisional Government in the summer of 1917, when the advance of the Bolsheviks could still have been stopped. See the article by Elisabeth Heresch in *Der Europäer*, #10, No. 2/3, p. 13ff.

One who tries to gain an overview of the great formative movements of history will soon recognize how far the catastrophe of 2001, as well as most of the developments and events of the *present* catastrophic world situation, are linked to intentions which are directed against the awakening of the *individual's* spirituality in modern humanity. Where there is a struggle for spirituality, there is also a struggle for the sense of truth, for only the individual thinking human being can be the bearer of this sense of truth.

It is precisely because negative political, economic, and spiritual developments have intensified enormously in recent years that a book that can sharpen one's perception for the deeper forces behind these developments and which was published many years ago should now once again be made available to the public.

Additions to the first edition

I would like to refer here to the most significant additions to the first edition:

—From a sketchbook found in Vienna can be gleaned how close in his youth Polzer was to Sophie Chotek, later the wife of Archduke Franz Ferdinand, who was murdered at her side in 1914.

—In relation to the last part of the book, which reaches into the present, events after 1994 have occasionally been taken into account, including events in the Anthroposophical Society and movement, such as the 'Chantilly Experiment', the noising abroad of, and the dilettantish defence against, the accusations of racism against Rudolf Steiner or the alleged 'occult imprisonment' in which the Anthroposophical Society had been placed, according to Manfred Schmidt-Brabant, the first President of the General Anthroposophical Society, who died in 2001.

—In relation to the *so-called* 'Class Lessons' affair, an important document has been placed in the appendices (p. 579) which shows Polzer's stance in this matter in a manner which is both of the greatest clarity and also still highly relevant. The comments of a witness of Polzer's way of reading Class Lessons are also printed in the appendices.

—Accusations that the notes of conversations between Polzer and Rudolf Steiner had been falsified had been raised before the first edition of this book was published but became available in detailed form only after publication. These notes became known after the death of Polzer's friend Paul Michaelis. From letters of Polzer to Michaelis which were discovered subsequently, it became clear how deep the relationship of trust between the two men had been and how highly Polzer thought of Michaelis. Only a complete discontinuity in Michaelis' personality, combined with a real mastery in the production of a historical hoax, could somehow justify the claims of falsification that have been raised against him as well as the accusations against his person; there exists no evidence of either. I have investigated in detail the claims held to be valid by, above all, the President of the Albert Steffen Foundation and those spread on the Internet and have published my findings in the appendices. The actual validity of these claims is virtually zero. In addition, the new-found correspondence between Polzer and Michaelis makes much clearer the significant impulse of the two men in the area of the dramatic arts: with Polzer's co-operation, Michaelis wrote a series of dramas, amongst others one with the title '1917', which has unfortunately disappeared.

—With regard to autobiography, after the first edition of this book appeared Polzer's *Schicksalsbilder aus der Zeit meiner Geistesschülerschaft* [Images of Destiny from the Time of My Spiritual Pupilship]. They originate from the year 1943 and were published in 2000. Polzer here presents the high points of his anthroposophical life and, amongst other things, discusses his conversations with Rudolf Steiner as well as the Hadrian experience of 1928.

Menny Nita-Schwarz-Lerchenfeld—In memoriam

On 2 November 2004 the last person who was deeply bound in friendship with Ludwig Polzer crossed the threshold: Menny Nita-Schwarz-Lerchenfeld. She was ten years younger than her sister Sophie Lerchenfeld, with whom Polzer also had a deep friendship. Menny Lerchenfeld had wanted to be a pianist but later turned to painting. She loved travelling and sometimes led an adventurous life. She married the radio editor and novelist Victor Schwarz (d. 1967). She married again in her 80s in order to enable a Romanian asylum-seeker to gain citizenship.

The writer first met Menny Nita-Schwarz-Lerchenfeld at the beginning of the 1990s at her family estate of Köfering near Regensburg, where she lived during the warmer times of the year. She practised Yoga and astonished her visitor with her spiritual and physical agility. Anthroposophy, which she had encountered in her parental home as the daughter of Count Otto von Lerchenfeld, appeared now to have receded into the background of her life. In 1992 the author had an intensive, friendly exchange with her, with occasional visits to her winter residence in Schwabing, Munich. Towards the end of her eventful earthly life, Menny Nita relived once again in her feelings in the most intense fashion the relationship of destiny and friendship with Ludwig Polzer that had, in a certain sense, previously slipped into the periphery of her consciousness. For the first time in decades she went deeply into the many—despite frequent changes of residence—well-preserved letters from her fatherly friend and adviser. And she experienced how only then did many a sentence, many a word she read, come home to her. Something of this is expressed in her memoirs[*]. She began writing them in 1992, 'by coincidence' on 23 November, the same day when, exactly 100 years ago (23.11.1908), Ludwig Polzer first heard a lecture by Rudolf Steiner. She was one of the few people who knew of Polzer's connection to the Roman Emperor Hadrian. This fact and the opening this year in London of the largest ever exhibition devoted to Emperor Hadrian led the writer to dedicate the reworked and expanded edition of this book to the memory of Menny Nita-Schwarz-Lerchenfeld.

A Suggestion for the Busy Reader

No one should allow the size of the book to put him off reading it. Those who are especially interested in the dimension of world events referred to earlier can start straightaway with Part V. Those without the patience for a walk through a long portrait gallery can miss out Part I. Those who feel most keenly for the fate of the anthroposophical movement can start with Part IV and if they would like to throw themselves right into the eye of the spiritual storm which tore the Anthroposophical Society apart in 1935, they can begin with Chapter 38.

Those who would like to learn about the newly-found documents can go straight to the appendix.

I have explained the fivefold structure of the whole book in the Introduction (see p. 1ff.) Although the work was conceived architectonically as a unity, readers can nevertheless start their exploration of this large building from whichever standpoint suits them best.

Basel, 6 September 2008　　　　　　　　　　　　Thomas Meyer

---

[*]Menny Nita-Schwarz-Lerchenfeld, *Erinnerungen und Erfahrungen* (Reminiscences and Experiences) (out of print). A second, extended edition appeared in 1998 with the title *Reflexionen und Gesichte* (Reflections and Appearances) in the Reimann edition and today can only be found at antiquarian booksellers (www.zvab.com).

Foreword to the First Edition

Many people have contributed to the appearance of this book. First, I would like to thank my friend Kurt Berthold, who at the end of the 1970s and in the early 1980s was able to trace many threads in the life of Ludwig Polzer.[*] Hilde and Kurt Berthold had studied the childhood and youth of Rudolf Steiner for years, and on my visits to them in the Ameisenbergstrasse, Stuttgart, conversation soon came round to Ludwig Polzer, his wife Berta, the Building Association (*Bauverein*) and many other events and people related to the life of Polzer. To speak with Kurt Berthold about Polzer or Marie Steiner or Ita Wegman meant to enter upon areas of research together; it threw up questions, or led one to ponder inconspicuous details. One sought the reasons for the relationship which Polzer had with his friend and teacher Steiner and appreciated the way in which Polzer took care of Steiner's siblings. In Steiner, Polzer saw not only a spiritual researcher but also an earthly human being with earthly bonds of human relationship. During the often very extensive conversations in the Berthold household the motivation to write this book first emerged. Kurt Berthold entrusted to me many of Polzer's notes, above all, the plan notes for his lectures in the years after Rudolf Steiner's death. If the character of the noble Count occasionally wanted to come alive in conversation, so later silent contemplation of the harmonious lines of his writing had a similar effect.

Many other helpers soon appeared on the paths which led to this book. Those will be mentioned first who Polzer himself knew and of whom we know from what he remembered of them.

Christward Johannes Polzer, Ludwig Polzer's grandson, was able to provide valuable pictorial material in addition to notes from Polzer's last years, for example, his dream diary.

On repeated visits to the Vienna apartment of Elisabeth Polzer and Maria-Christine Koutny, two daughters of Ludwig's brother Arthur Polzer, the two sisters spoke in a most lively fashion for hours on end of their father and uncle; they displayed watercolours and oil paintings by Arthur Polzer as well as his unpublished notes, which were full of detailed descriptions of his personal development and also of the Polzer-Hoditz family, as well as containing a large number of unique photographs. I am very grateful to Maria-Christine Koutny for her generous description to me of the last weeks in the life of their father and uncle.

---

[*] Kurt Berthold died on 28 July 1996.

Anna Polzer, the daughter-in-law of Ludwig Polzer (she was married to Polzer's son Julius) and later occupant of Schloss Tannbach, guided me around the castle which was the most important residence in the lives of the Polzer family.

Not far from her father's estate of Köfering near Regensburg and also in her Munich apartment, Countess Rosa Lerchenfeld (one of the associates and friends of Menny Lerchenfeld) shared with the author things which were previously completely unknown about Menny's friendship with Ludwig Polzer.[*] The many letters which Polzer wrote to her between 1938 and 1943 illuminate a side of his life which would otherwise have had to remain in darkness.

Milos Brabínek Jnr. from Karlsbad and Rudolf Herman from Pardubice were able to relate many significant details. Milos Brabínek's sister Maňa had an important relationship to Count Polzer, while Rudolf Herman was able to tell me about the 'Class Lessons' that Polzer held at the Pardubice branch.

Julie Nováková-Klima from Prague likewise recalled the Count very clearly; with her parents she was able to accompany him, Rudolf and Marie Steiner to Karlstejn Castle; her mother's diaries revealed a number of informative details.

Marta Lauer-Stefanović, Polzer's collaborator in the publication of *Österreichischen Boten* (Reports from Austria) presented me with a copy of the rare first edition of Polzer's *Prager Aufzeichnungen* (Prague Notes) from the year 1937; the copy belonged to her husband Hans-Erhard Lauer. I received it from her with a special feeling of respect in view of the often mysterious paths of destiny, when one thinks of Lauer's connection to Ludwig Polzer that was at first friendly but later tragic.

In Mariensee, which was for almost two decades a kind of place of refuge for Ludwig Polzer, and where he was always hospitably received by Dora Schenker, his often informative entries could be found in the guestbook; Marianne Schenker, the daughter-in-law of Dora Schenker put at my disposal further notes by Polzer, left from his time of refuge there as well as the volume of short stories by Polzer's grandfather, Ludwig, Ritter[†] von Polzer.

In September 1992 my English publisher Sevak Gulbekian brought to my attention the new map of the world which had appeared in *The*

---

[*] Menny Lerchenfeld died on 2 November 2004.

[†] *Translator's note:* The German title 'Ritter' corresponds to the English word 'knight', but 'Sir von Polzer' or 'Sir Ludwig von Polzer' sounds incongruent, as 'Sir' is such an English title, so throughout the text the word Ritter is left in German.

Economist magazine in 1990 (see p. 486). I would like to thank Branko Ljubic for informing me of the role played by quite a number of personalities who played a role in the history of the anthroposophical movement in the former Yugoslavia.

★

Once more I would like to thank my brother Urs Meyer-Hala for proofreading the text; Hans-Jürgen Heitmann for checking citations and footnotes; Madlen Hauser, Salina Saner and Isabelle Sturm for organizing the index; Madlen Hauser also contributed to this book in recent years with bibliographical and other such references. Marcel Jenni once again very kindly took care of production. He himself took many of the book's photographs in Vienna. Without his excellent organization of the progress of the work—as also with the two Moltke volumes in 1993—this book too would never have appeared in time.

Basel, 26 October 1994   Thomas Meyer

Introduction

Count Ludwig Polzer-Hoditz was born on 23 April 1869 in Prague, the German-Slavic heart of the Empire that was Austria-Hungary. In Bohemia the East pushes forward like a bridgehead into the middle of Europe, and Prague, the city on the Vltava (or the Moldau in German), permeated by the sounds of the Germanic as well as the Slavic language element, lies even further west than Vienna.

'Prague' means 'threshold'; first, that between East and West. But more is meant by this word than a threshold in space. Prague can also be experienced as a threshold in time: as the gateway for those cultural impulses of the Slavic East which will be decisive in future times, impulses which today, after the failure of the socialist experiment that was launched from the West 100 years ago, are seeking to bestir themselves freely once more. Not only the East therefore, but even its future seems to press forward in Bohemia like a bridgehead into the centre of Europe.

If Prague, the threshold city of space and time, was the birthplace of Polzer, the year of his birth, 1869, links him to the Eternal City of Rome, the decisive cradle of the occidental civilization of the past. On 8 December 1869 an event had begun to play itself out in Rome which was of far-reaching significance; the First Vatican Council had opened, at which Pope Pius IX pronounced the dogma of Papal Infallibility for statements of all future popes made *ex cathedra*. For Polzer, the Catholic Church was in the first instance the force that represented the continuation of the decadent impulses of the Roman Empire. In the course of his life he strove more and more to penetrate clearly the partly subtle, indirect influences of this world current from southern Europe which have worked into spiritual and political life until the present day.

Whereas the *year* of his birth connects him—*according to his own way of seeing it*—to the ongoing impulses of the former Roman Empire, the *date* of his birth links him with the England of Shakespeare, who was born (1564) and died (1616) on the same date, 23 April. Although no one sees in Polzer a second Shakespeare, and apart from a noteworthy drama about Crown Prince Rudolf, he would make no further efforts in the field of drama, through this 'coincidence' of his birthdate an important motif in his life is sounded: his later preoccupation with that which, alongside the Germanic middle European element, plays such a decisive role in modern times, namely, the Anglo-Saxon world.

In this choice of year, of place and of date, destiny clearly indicated how the the birth of Ludwig Polzer was inwardly connected to great and decisive cultural streams of the past, present and future.

★

With regard to present and future streams in the Anglo-American West and in the Slavic East, attention must be drawn in this book at the outset, in Polzer's sense, to a crucial difference between them: cultural-political elements show themselves in both East and West as essentially two-layered (*zweischichtig*). In what follows, the term 'layer' (*Schicht*) is not used in the narrow sociological sense but in the sense of two quite different spheres or layers of cultural and political impulses; representatives of a sociological layer in the narrow sense can belong both to one or the other of the layers indicated here. In the Anglo-American West there is a stream of a new politics of world domination which has become decisive above all in European and international affairs over the last 200 years. The strongest support for these politics is the modern economy itself; the goal is to gain and retain global dominance in this field. Names such as Cecil Rhodes, Winston Churchill, Averell Harriman and George Bush I and II indicate the effectiveness of these dominant layers in the West today. Under them, however, there is a lower layer which in world affairs today is of less weight but of no less significance. Names such as Wycliffe, Shakespeare and Emerson indicate *this* layer in the West. The situation is similar in the East: during the past few centuries a westernized Slavdom has formed itself over and above the true Slavic element, which has many times been deliberately covered over by the dominant layer (*Schicht*) in the West. We are referring here to names such as Peter the Great, Lenin, or, in our time, Boris Yeltsin or Vladimir Putin. The main deeds of these men ran and run their course entirely in line with the intentions of leading personalities in the dominant layers (*Oberschichte*) of the West. Then again there is the essential lower layer (*Unterschicht*) in which the Slavdom of the future is rooted. A harbinger of this future stream was Dmitri (Czar of Russia 1605–1606). The names of Tolstoi and Solovieff also belong to it.

And finally, also in Europe, especially in its German-speaking regions, a differentiation must be made between the layer of true German culture that is oriented to a cosmopolitan spirit and which, where it really understands itself, will strive towards the universal knowledge and cultivation of the free individuality, and that 'other' German culture which, falling in with the will of the ruling groups (*Oberschicht*) of the West, set itself on the path which led from Bismarck via Wilhelm II to Hitler. In relation to the very much more significant German lower layer, Goethe would, amongst others, have to be named, along with Kaspar Hauser (who not by accident was forced by the power groups of Britain and Rome into a unique captivity of world-historical importance)—and Rudolf Steiner.

Whereas permanent struggles and conflicts rage in the outwardly dominant layers of the West, the Centre and the East, for a genuine peaceful order in the future, one will need to look in all three regions into the concealed lower layers, for these stand in a deeply grounded, harmonic relation to one another. It is therefore self-evident that solid foundations for the bridge-building function of the European middle between the West and the East can only naturally be built up in the middle European lower layer.

When in this book the grandiose—in the negative sense of that word—politics of the power circles of the West have to be repeatedly referred to, and, insofar as they contain the tendency towards total control and the exclusion of the deeper cultural impulses of the East and of the Middle, are repeatedly criticized, an undifferentiated anti-Americanism will in no sense be implied by this; whoever is able throughout to retain his grasp of the whole picture will not find himself nurturing any kind of generalized anti-western feelings or ideas.

A similar impartiality will be maintained in relation to another point. In Anglo-American ruling circles power plays into and shapes much in the course of affairs that never, or at least only much later, *post facto*, comes to public attention, and this fact lies in the interests of those who strive for power. From their standpoint this is quite self-evident. One will not strive for power—and it belongs to the essential drives of the Anglo-American ruling groups to strive for power—and at the same time seek to keep the world informed about one's plans to transform it and the methods being used to realize those plans. Whoever seeks power also seeks to keep secrets. Whoever requires secrecy must take care that that secrecy is not betrayed. Only what is not made public can work effectively to build up power.

Those who seek to guide economic, cultural and political events in accordance with their power-oriented goals must be more active behind the curtain than on the stage of events themselves. Where such goals are aimed at, one finds secret preparations for quite particular things which are then supposed to happen. To work in such ways towards particular goals in public affairs could be called a conspiracy. In such cases one 'swears' to abide by the demand to keep secret the conspiracy's plans and their method of execution. Whoever works in such ways in the course of public affairs is a conspirator. Those who, in attempting to elucidate certain historical or contemporary affairs, immediately have the phrase 'conspiracy theory' thrown at them, should not allow themselves to be swayed at all by such accusations. As with every other theory, it is simply a case of determining whether or not a so-called conspiracy theory is rooted in concrete facts or whether it is merely a fantasy. Certainly, no objections can be made to the theory as such. Was the assassination of Julius Caesar the result of an agitation that had been kept secret from the public? Or the 'surprise attack' on Pearl Harbor? The assassinations of John F. Kennedy or Alfred Herrhausen, the Chairman of the Board of Deutsche Bank? If yes, then there are very particular historical events which cannot at all be explained other than by connection to a 'conspiracy theory'. There is no essential difference whether it has to do with the murder of a single person or with the launching of an entire war. In the power circles (*Machtschichte*) of the West a great deal has been planned in accordance with the principle of conspiracy characterized above and much of it has actually been carried out. In no other way will one be able to make conspiracy theory really superfluous than by setting boundaries to power, which can be done by a threefolding of the social organism. As long as unbounded power is sought by some and even achieved temporarily, then there will be con-spirators, and also silence about their conspiracies will continue to reign within the noise of the media. Those who wish to observe contemporary affairs in a way that reflects reality must therefore also learn to pay attention to 'the intrigues of silence'.

★

To be linked in intimate ways with great cultural streams, as Ludwig Polzer was, also means to be acquainted with counter-streams deep within them that work to destroy cultures; these are evident today in certain Clubs in western ruling circles or the power impulses of Rome that today are manipulated by the West. The destruction—set in train from the beginning of the 1980s—of the socialist experiment by the Holy Alliance of Washington and Rome (co-operation which was at first hidden from the public), and the attempted construction of a New World Order were a classic example in the outgoing twentieth century of the collaboration of such decadent world streams as were indicated above. These world streams are decadent therefore, because ultimately, they want to establish everything according to the old Roman power concepts and to suppress and force back the real development of mankind which strives in the direction of the free spirituality of each human individuality. Indeed, from the perspective of their own stream's essential nature, such decadent forces *have to* force back this free spirituality.

For decades Ludwig Polzer occupied himself with the study of this alliance between Rome and the power circles of the West, and it was precisely out of his knowledge of the specific nature of such decadent world-historical streams that he was able to gain the power to work on the growth and development of true seeds for the future. That he knew how to do this not only with courage and energy but also with an unshakeable consciousness of the goal that was still far distant, he owed to the spiritual science of Rudolf Steiner.

After the decisive meeting in 1908 with the founder of anthroposophically-oriented spiritual science, Polzer's life moved in the sign of the necessary formation of constructive cultural impulses which are bound to work against the hegemony of the ruling power groups of the West (and of the South).

In a very particular way Polzer therefore had to place in his heart the question of the central region of Europe, for nowhere other than in this central region were seeds of true cultural regeneration present in such abundance, even if they were submerged and covered over. A discoverer and developer of these seeds was Polzer's friend and teacher Rudolf Steiner. As an inhabitant of the Danubian monarchy, with its exemplary task of striving for a real harmonizing of peoples and nations in the midst of a rich cultural and ethnic mix, Polzer experienced the realization of this task, which was called for by the times themselves, as a demand of his own destiny. With an unlimited enthusiasm for knowledge, he therefore placed himself in 1917 wholeheartedly in the service of the idea developed by Steiner of the social organism membered in the three relatively autonomous spheres of the economy, of rights and of the free spiritual life. These ideas, forged from reality, would have been able to provide the decaying Habsburg monarchy with a viable path towards the realization of its task which was so vital for the future of Middle Europe. Polzer became the intermediary between the impulse of these healing ideas and those men chosen by world history to be the bearers of external state power in the centre of Europe: the House of Habsburg. A relationship of choice had led him to Rudolf Steiner's side; through his blood he was able to come extremely close to the imperial house, when his brother Arthur was appointed director of Emperor Karl's cabinet in 1916. Through the Polzer brothers, Rudolf Steiner was thus able to convey to the Austrian Emperor the idea of the threefold society as a great and powerful question of that hour of world destiny. It will be a task of this book to show why that attempt failed. The causes of the collapse of the Danube monarchy soon afterwards are without a doubt very much bound up with the failure to accept the impulse of these constructive ideas.

At the end of the twentieth century a comparable collapse appeared to be occurring in the territories of the former Soviet Union and also in the former multi-ethnic state of Yugoslavia. But this collapse was no original process; it was nothing but a collapse resulting from a larger process of decay. It must be recognized that the atomizing, destructive forces in Central and Eastern Europe, which with blind force seek to reduce all comprehensive human relationships to the smallest ethnic-cultural, religious or racial elements, will continue until a consciousness builds in Middle Europe of a viable path for real communication between peoples and nations.

Scarcely had Rudolf Steiner begun to indicate this viable path for the last time in a very public manner at the West-East Congress in Vienna in 1922, when from the same city, Richard Coudenhove-Kalergi embarked on his mission to realize his Pan-Europa concept. He soon found in Rome and Washington loyal supporters while Steiner's public efforts met with an enormous wave of hostility which at the very end of 1922 led to the destruction of the Goetheanum in Dornach. Until the present, the line that has connected Coudenhove with Churchill, Monnet, Schumann, Jacques Delors and today's Euro-architects has been decisive. At the two endpoints of this line are Washington and Rome; all the significant figures who since Coudenhove have done some shovelling on the European building site, have been either devotees of Washington or pilgrims to the South, often both at the same time. Real *European* politics for Europe have been lacking until today and will only arise when those seeds are enabled to germinate which lie covered over in the cultural undergrowth of Middle Europe. That germination will also only occur when those efforts which proceed from the ruling circles of the West are clearly seen through and fended off.

In this regard Ludwig Polzer accomplished essential preparatory work. He laid bare the impulses which inform the so-called *Testament of Peter the Great.* The text stems not from Czar Peter but from a Polish 'visionary' general by the name of Sokolnicki who had the text circulated at the end of the eighteenth century. It is, however, a very precise expression of the western intention to link the West directly to the East *by excluding the Middle of Europe.* It shows the grandiose long-range planning of certain western and southern power elites which have remained active until the present.

European politics of the future that are in accord with reality will contribute to harmony between the German and western Slavic elements without the Vatican (and behind it the White House) having a hand in the game. Today the exact opposite of this is striven for, as for example is clearly evident in the inclination to create of a 'core Europe'—a Paris-

Berlin-Warsaw axis that is intended to lead Europe in the future. From Poland, Catholicism is to be solidly anchored among the western Slavs. To the extent that success is achieved in this direction, the real renewal of Europe will be set back for centuries.

In 1928 Polzer's book *Das Mysterium der europäischen Mitte* (The Mystery of the European Middle) was published; it contained important thoughts about future politics that were really suited to Europe realities. Above all, the book can serve to sharpen the capacity for discrimination so that one realizes that it is not merely a matter of noting where the call for a new Middle Europe comes from, but whether, when one says 'Middle Europe', one has in mind the restoration of old forms of cultural and spiritual life or the seeds of something really new. 'The Mid-European region,' said Polzer in a lecture in London in 1928,

> in which the most various elements from all directions were to be found, in which human souls from all ages and regions are reincarnated [...] is the region where all old forces, all the forces of divine right disappear and lose their effectiveness in order to create a place for something quite new, for something that can ... unfold itself in the future. On the path of return that cultures take from West to East nothing can pass through this Mid-European region without undergoing a complete metamorphosis. All old forces lose themselves on this path towards the East; they cannot go further through this region without renewing themselves out of the spirit. *If they try to press on regardless, they become forces of destruction, they give rise to catastrophes.*

Such a metamorphosis of all old forces of culture and civilization will only seem worth striving for and indeed will only be carried through by those who wish to create out of a really contemporary spiritual life that is to be found in a free way by the individual and who no longer wish to fill their spiritual cups at the exhausted springs of a spirituality that is merely handed down from the past. For those who wish to share in the work of shaping the European house of the future and for its future inhabitants, Ludwig Polzer-Hoditz could be a companion who provides both admonition and counsel.

*

This book consists of four main sections. This structure resulted from that of the first lecture by Rudolf Steiner that Polzer heard, on 23 November 1908. The title was: 'What Is Self-Knowledge?' Steiner showed how it is basically built up in four stages. In the first stage, the influences of 'when' and 'where' on the human being are considered: how different would a human being's development be if he were born in Paris, Bombay or

Beijing; how would he be differently affected by a birth in the eighteenth or the twentieth centuries?

Then Steiner guides the imagination of his audience to consider inherited characteristics and talents—the second stage of concrete self-knowledge.

The third stage concerns itself with those capacities that lie deeper, not in the milieu of the When and Where nor in the inherited qualities but in those which lead back to the individual's previous lives.

And at the fourth stage, self-knowledge is to be gained through the most comprehensive knowledge of the world: knowledge of physical, psychological and supersensible-spiritual world facts.

So profound and of such inexhaustible fruitfulness for Ludwig Polzer's entire life thereafter was this initial experience of 23 November 1908 that it seemed to this biographer objectively justified that the architectural principle of the book should be the four stages of true self-knowledge presented in that Vienna lecture. The reader will therefore find the book organized in four main parts corresponding to the four stages of self-knowledge. Part I corresponds to the second stage of self-knowledge— knowledge of the physical ancestors and of the physical and psychological qualities that stem from them while Part II corresponds to the self-knowledge of When and Where.

Naturally, as in life, in a biographical description of an individual's development no rigid boundaries can be set up between the stages of life and the stages of self-knowledge; they play into each other. This is even more the case with Parts III and IV. This organization of the book in accordance with the 1908 lecture on self-knowledge is therefore not at all adhered to in a rigid schematic fashion.

★

Part V is an attempt to present some of the main lines of development following the death of Ludwig Polzer in October 1945 through the following decades up to our time. How did world events develop, above all in relation to Europe? How did that spiritual stream develop, with which Polzer had especially linked himself so deeply and strongly? What perspectives for the end of the twentieth century and for the new, twenty-first century result from these further developments?

In this last part an attempt will be made to characterize events in the way that Polzer himself always practised, a method which can be termed the *symptomatological observation of history*. This expression, often used by Rudolf Steiner, essentially means the following: instead of seeking to amass and oversee a complete collection of historical events and processes, symptomatological observation proceeds from the basis that there are more and less important events and processes in the course of history. To the important events are reckoned those which relate in a very marked way to particular impulses of historical development over long periods of time. To give an example: when one knows that on 8 December 1854 Pope Pius IX pronounced the dogma of the Immaculate Conception of Mary, that the Vatican Council which would announce papal infallibility to the world began on 8 December 1869, and when one then discovers that the current symbol of Europe, the twelve yellow stars on the blue background was also definitely born on an 8 December and in the Catholic Church is a Marian symbol, then the choice of that day to decide on this symbol is of symptomatological significance. Another example: when President George Bush formally welcomes Boris Yeltsin to the White House as a 'new Peter the Great' then much more is expressed in these words than in thousands of others; they have world-historical dimensions of which, incidentally, one who speaks them does not have to be consciously aware.

It also belongs to a *comprehensive* historical symptomatology that the observer should be in a position of familiarity with ideas that relate to the reality of the supersensible. For someone for whom time spirit (*Zeitgeist*) or folk spirit (*Volksgeist*) are nothing but words, the field for symptomatological observation will inevitably remain restricted: much will remain incomprehensible to him, for in many historical events quite other factors are involved besides those which can be explained on the basis of the sense world alone or from motives present in the human being himself.

In symptomatological observation the question of methodology arises: how does one distinguish the symptomatically significant events from the relatively less significant? The spiritual science of Rudolf Steiner here provides perhaps a rather surprising answer: in that one learns to direct one's attention to a greater degree to what the 'world current' brings to one; what is or is not discovered in the area of symptomatology is always at the same time also a subtle matter of destiny. Certain things of symptomatic significance are continually being brought before every person, but they often naturally remain unnoticed, or the capacity to distinguish what is of real weight may be lacking. The symptomatological observations of various people therefore need to be combined; this is the destiny-laden social component of such a way of observing historical events. The reader of this book will soon see how in his research Ludwig Polzer always allowed himself to be inspired by what the world brought towards him through other people.

Yet one does not wish only to observe the events of past history in this way, but to press on to the pulse of what is in the process of becoming and developing in the present, out of which single concrete facts and happenings coalesce, as it were, and then one soon comes to a boundary of ordinary consciousness and understanding. Through one's reason this assimilates the impressions of the senses and these can only grasp what is already there, what has already happened (in the case of historical study, in the form of documents or other sense-perceptible traces of past events), never the event itself. In this sense, the symptomatological observer of history, no less than the accumulative collector, always and everywhere arrives too late. He always ends up standing before *faits accomplis*. Historical processes in the present therefore at first find no access to the normal state of wakeful, conscious cognition; they are, in the exact, technical sense of the expression, 'dreamed' in the deeper strata of the soul, parallel to the processes in waking consciousness. However, it is possible through a systematic, concentrated and meditative schooling of consciousness, to raise the dream condition to the same degree *above* waking consciousness that it normally lies below waking consciousness. Through such a schooling, that super-wakeful state of consciousness can be cultivated which Steiner calls 'Inspiration'; and only on the basis of such a higher state of consciousness can actual spiritual scientific research into real historical processes be engaged in as they are happening. But there are intermediate stages on the way to this goal. It can happen that some normally occurring dreams attain an unusual degree of wakefulness and that through this, processes that are otherwise ungraspable and dreamed press through into waking consciousness. Ludwig Polzer had many experiences of this kind. With all the care that has to be employed in the interpretation of such experiences, they can nevertheless throw much light on things which present themselves clearly to normal sensory consciousness only later, as *faits accomplis*. In such cases, it is important to note whether a concordance also occurs with outer events, which was frequently the case with Polzer. It is not the experiences in themselves alone that are of significance but the resonance between what arises from within and the facts that come to one from the outside world. The way to the higher consciousness of Inspiration leads through the field of such inner experiences and what corresponds to them outwardly. It is a field of work that is not to be underestimated and which can hardly be avoided by anyone who strives after the essential, conscious preconditions which, out of a symptomatological observation of history, can make a *science* of the process of historical *development*.

★

On leafing through this book, many readers may perhaps experience a mild concern that they will lose themselves in a mass of details and may ask themselves: why go into such detail in the presentation of the life of this man? Yet Ludwig Polzer's life spans in such a unique way the end and fall of a rich, old world and the beginnings and seeds of a really new one, and for those who wish not merely to know about the world-historical upheaval of those times but also to feel it, this becomes possible precisely through the contrast of certain symptomatic details. One only needs to compare the picture of the circumstances of Ludwig Polzer's birth in 1869 with the manner in which his life ended in 1945.

There are also a few, in fact relatively few, major viewpoints from which such details are more easily surveyed. To these belong *first* the already mentioned fact that in the Anglo-American West, supported by Rome in the South, remarkable long-range politics have been pursued which work against the rise of the European Middle and seek to shape the future of the Slavic East in a one-sided manner; these politics, for example, play right into the details of Polzer's biography.

A *second* viewpoint is that behind all external conflicts or wars a struggle is waged between various forms of real spirituality; for a spirituality which advances individual freedom or for one which seeks to annihilate this freedom.

Thirdly, the building of real bridges between the individual and the supersensible world is the precondition for all viable cultural-political links between West and East. This is why certain very subtle processes were included in the book, which often play a significant role in the mostly completely unconscious, ongoing relationships between the living and those who dwell in spiritual spheres adjoining the realm of human history, as would already be noted by purely symptomatological observations. Polzer's life is also instructive in this sense; the inner, regularly repeated individual link made to the realm of the so-called dead is something that in the not so far-distant future may be as much a matter of course as breathing or eating.

Then, *fourthly*, the necessity of the marriage between the German and Slavic cultures must be mentioned.

One who grasps these and other viewpoints and major motifs of this book and keeps them in mind will be able to move around easily in the pantheon of individuals and events without ever losing sight of the unifying dome above them.

Perhaps the reader might object that, here and there, the author has presented an overly hagiographical image of Ludwig Polzer, to which the reply can only be: one who encounters such fruitful deeds, capacities and strivings for the beneficial spiritual and social development of humanity as are actually to be found in the life of Ludwig Polzer has enough to do to present what is important and fruitful in the work of such a man. The author could not regard it as his task to concern himself with Polzer's less important traits or deeds in order to create a so-called 'whole picture'. In his eyes 'the whole' lies not in bringing together a *sum* of the essential and inessential feelings and deeds of such a life; it lies much more in what could remain of this life that is fruitful and significant for the future.

If, despite the symptomatological base in the book's presentation, it seems in general to be organized chronologically, this is because the slow and yet very constant development of Ludwig Polzer could only be concretely expressed in detail in this way. Polzer's inner development really seems to proceed gradually, solely in accord with the calm flow of time. This capacity for constant development, which remained true into old age, seems to be one of his deepest characteristics.

Ludwig Polzer also had a very special relationship to space. Spaces were for him not only geographical regions but also, wherever he went, filled with a soul-spiritual, cultural and historical tincture. What must it have meant for him to find himself in Tannbach, his own actual home, a place *where the ancient Romans had never walked?*

The book thus awaits readers who have both inner space and time. But those too who would like to move through the pantheon quickly with sprightly steps and a deliberate gaze are very welcome visitors.

I. IN THE STREAM OF A RICH HERITAGE

'Nothing disfigures man more than to be a man
without knowing what being a man means.'

Franziskus Josephus Philippus
von Hoditz und Wolframitz

1. Near Habsburg

Ludwig Polzer-Hoditz's father's family comes from Silesia; the line can be traced without a break to the beginning of the seventeenth century, and then, after an interval, back to the time of St Elisabeth of Thuringia[*] (early thirteenth century). The family tree of his maternal family of Hoditz goes back even further, and without any breaks, into the twelfth century, to a family of counts and lords of Bieberstein in the Aargau region, which today is in Switzerland but which from 1173 until 1415 was part of the Habsburgs' lands[1]. Bieberstein Castle, which still exists today, lies barely 20 kilometres from what is the oldest likely ancestral castle of the Habsburgs, the similarly named Habsburg Castle (fig 1.).

The Biebersteins had already moved to Poland and Silesia by the beginning of the twelfth century. In 1109 Wolf of Bieberstein near Raski received from Duke Boleslaus of Kryzywousty of Poland a bison's horn for his coat of arms which led to the origin of the 'Rogalla' family coat of arms (see fig. 2). Descendants of these resettled Rogalla-Biebersteins then moved to Moravia and from the middle of the thirteenth century renamed themselves 'von Hodicz' after their estates and their family castle Hodicz in the district of Iglau. In the sixteenth century the Hoditz family was raised to the rank of Count, and they received from the Emperor the privilege of naming themselves after all their current estates and those acquired in the future. The Hoditz family would make no further use of this privilege than to call themselves from that point on 'von Hoditz und Wolframitz'.

For 700 years the line of the Hoditz family, originally from near Habsburg, drifted on as in a dream down the generations before it suddenly and decisively entered the destinies of Ludwig and especially his brother Arthur Polzer-Hoditz: geographical proximity to the origins of the ruling dynasty now became a destiny-laden closeness to that dynasty's tragic fall.

The long path to this metamorphosed shared destiny through the uniting of the Hoditz and Polzer families was lined by a row of sometimes highly notable scholars, artists or other personalities who deserve attention in a purely human regard. A number of them seem to have passed on to Ludwig Polzer-Hoditz and his brother Arthur valuable talents through the stream of inheritance so they ought not to be passed over even in a relatively fleeting glimpse into the ancestral galleries of the Polzer-Hoditz family.

---

[*] Also known as St Elisabeth of Hungary—*transl.*

2. Count Albert von Hoditz (1706–1778)
Patron of the Arts and Friend of Frederick the Great

Let us turn first to one particular representative of the Hoditz family. According to Arthur Polzer-Hoditz, the Hoditzes were 'always unusually mentally alert, often eccentric, seldom moderate, never stereotypical'[2].In the fifteenth century one Ullrich von Hoditz was sentenced to be tortured and torn in four parts by horses because he had refused to admit to having relations with a high-ranking lady—and thereby saved her life. At the time of the Reformation, some of the Hoditz family became Lutherans, were banished for their stubbornness, left their castle and lands and fought in the Thirty Years' War with the Swedish army. Nevertheless, there arose in this line that descended from Ullrich and which was soon to die out—via the Counts of Kaunitz, family relations to the House of Wallenstein or Waldstein, as it used to be called—a name, which we shall meet again when we come to the years of Ludwig Polzer's youth. The second line of the House of Hoditz, that of the Veits, from which the mother of Ludwig and Arthur came, was 'very different from the first line whose members had been fanatical supporters of Reformation and rebellion; the Veits were just as fanatically conservative, Catholic and loyal supporters of the Empire.'

From this line came Count Albert von Hoditz, who was a friend of Frederick the Great and who transformed his residence Schloss Rosswald in Silesia into a 'fairy palace', world-renowned in its day.

In his young days in Viennese high society the gallant and enterprising Hoditz enjoyed general favour except among the husbands of beautiful women. But life at court did not satisfy him long. He went on his travels, amassed debts and at the age of 28 married the 'somewhat' older, widowed Margravine of Brandenburg-Bayreuth. In 1741 the culturally very active Count founded the first Freemasons' lodge in Vienna, *Zu den drei Kanonen* (the Three Cannons Lodge) of which he became the first Grand Master. In 1742 Frederick the Great conferred on him the honour of command of a regiment of hussars; yet in the following year the Count asked to be released from his position and betook himself to his estate at Schloss Rosswald.

The 'Wondrous Count of Rosswald', as he was generally known, was a great patron of the arts but he also loved, whenever possible, to give rein to his inventive spirit in his own artistic creations. He once delighted his royal friend, who visited Rosswald on his way home after a meeting with

Emperor Joseph in 1770, with a performance of an antique pastoral play in the garden of his baroque residence.

The play extended over the Count's entire fairy palace, and the royal guests were led from scene to scene around the grounds of the estate. The company followed one of the watercourses, emerged from an oakwood into the sunny

> Garden of the Hesperides, populated by the gods and goddesses of anti-quity, who performed the spiciest of scenes before the eyes of the king. By a brook lay the lovely Narcissus, lost in gazing at his own image mirrored in the clear waters, while flirtatious nymphs showered him with pearls of rain. On exiting a group of trees the smooth surface of an enchantingly beautiful lake met the eyes of the astonished guests, who boarded gondolas decorated with colourful flags and rowed by lovely young maidens. The journey passed between the high, uprising Scylla and the raging Charybdis. This was the highpoint of the play. Beautiful young maidens with long flowing locks swam around the king's gondola as nymphs and naiads singing the loveliest songs in varied choruses.

The artfully directed play, which also did not lack satyrs, fauns and seductive arcadian flute music, transported the king into obvious delight and enthusiasm. Of his ancestor's achievement, Arthur Polzer assures us that: 'Böcklin would have thoroughly enjoyed it.' Who would deny it?

But all this was only intended as the hors d'oeuvre for a grandiose banquet. The walls of the dining room were decorated with the forms of Olympus carved in stone, while at the entrance one's gaze was drawn to two marble figures representing the Emperor Joseph and the royal guest. As the king entered the room, a chorale composed by Hoditz began, the melody of which the king later had set to a march. Known as the Hoditz March, it was for a long time a favourite of the Prussian Regiment.

In the evenings there were opera performances which featured such clever manipulation of curtains and stage sets that the king exclaimed that not even in his theatre in Berlin had he seen anything so perfect. During the three days of festivities the famous chess game took place which Frederick and his host played on an artfully laid-out lawn with 64 huge squares of alternating shades. On the commands of the players who sat opposite each other on raised seats 32 people representing the chess pieces moved around the 'squares' in corresponding costumes.

Hoditz could not bear to be surrounded by people without good manners or culture. He therefore had his valets and servants provided with a proper education; he cultivated skills and proficiency in every one of them according to their capacities. When his educative work achieved the desired success after a certain period, he would invite his pupils to eat with him at table. With a certain selflessness, he also uncovered and cultivated those with artistic talent. One of the dance teachers of Empress Maria Theresa's children was a former member of Hoditz's dance troupe at Rosswald.

When Albert von Hoditz, who never travelled driven by fewer than four or six horses, had finally exhausted his financial resources through his extravagant lifestyle, Frederick invited him to move to Potsdam where he presented him with a house. It was there on 18 March 1778 that Imperial Count Albert von Hoditz died. His body was, in accordance with the wishes of the 'Wondrous Count', transported to Rosswald accompanied by a company of the Royal Guard. In memory of his friend, Frederick had the name of the Berlin street where the Count lived renamed Hoditz-strasse, which still runs through Potsdam. The memorial tablet on the Hoditz house in Potsdam relates that this 'patron of all the fine arts' was also the rediscoverer of cremation in the West. However, according to Arthur Polzer, he had opted to have himself interred in the customary manner.

★

It is not easy to form a realistic assessment of this many-sided personality. Certainly, Albert von Hoditz shows many eccentric traits, which Arthur Polzer-Hoditz later regarded as typically Hoditzian, and he was dis-inclined to compromise, not least in the area of financial expenditures. Equally marked in his life was the notable keenness of his mind.

Frederick was not the only one to produce a memorial to the Count; George Sand gave him a new lease of life, albeit with rather vain and dilettantish traits, as the Grand Seigneur in her famous novel *Consuelo*, 'but he was certainly not as mentally insignificant as the Frenchwoman considered him', writes Arthur Polzer-Hoditz: 'If that had been the case, then Frederick the Great would not have had such a high estimation of him', although Arthur judged many of the Count's creations at Rosswald to be inartistic or even mawkish. There are 171 extant letters from the King to the Count which he sent over a 20-year period. When it comes to historical substance, do we go amiss if we too easily prefer George Sand's literary portrayal to Arthur Polzer-Hoditz's own critical appraisal of his ancestor?

3. Franziskus Josephus Philippus von Hoditz und Wolframitz (1669–1727) a Forgotten Thinker

If we now take a small step sideways and backwards in time within our ancestral gallery from the exuberant and ingenious 'Wondrous Count', we find ourselves standing before the figure of his uncle, magisterial, silent, which on closer observation seems to show the signs of a significant thinker: this is Franziskus Josephus Philippus von Hoditz und Wolframitz, fourth great-grandfather of Ludwig and Arthur on their mother's side.

Born in 1669, Franziskus Josephus—who was given his name in this Latin style, like the later Emperor Franz Joseph—was the owner of Busau Castle, which is today one of the greatest sights to see in Moravia. Whereas we know so much about the life of his nephew Albert who later became famous, we know very little about the outer circumstances of the life of this deeply philosophically-inclined personality. He was married three times and seems outwardly to have led the quiet life of a researcher. In 1696 he sold the castle and lordship of Busau to the Order of the Teutonic Knights for a lifelong annuity and retired to Meltsch and later Venice.

Around 1696, the time of the sale of the castle, he wrote a booklet with the title: *Libellus de Hominis Convenientia* (A Booklet on What Befits a Man). He left the manuscript with his brother-in-law, Count Karl Ignaz von Sternberg for determination as to whether it should be published. Sternberg, to whose lands Castle Pürglitz also belonged, left the text in the archives of the Fürstenberg Library in that castle. There it slept like Rip Van Winkel for almost 150 years until in the middle of the nineteenth century it was discovered by Robert Zimmermann, the aesthete and philosopher. He considered the text, which has still neither been printed nor translated into German, as so important that he devoted a chapter to it in his *Studien und Kritiken zur Philosophie*[3] (Critical Studies in Philosophy) under the title 'A philosophical contemporary of Leibniz in Bohemia'.

In his discussion in the *Libellus*, in which his thoughts are developed step by step in a solidly systematic manner and with the greatest care, Franziskus Josephus builds up to the central philosophical question as to the being and definition of man, with the goal of presenting what is truly befitting (*convenientia*) for man in his thinking and acting in accordance with his true nature. He proceeds from a very radical understanding: 'Nothing disfigures man more than to be a man without knowing what being a man means.' Neither Aristotle's definition, 'a reasoning animal', nor that of Descartes, 'a thinking being', satisfy the booklet's author.

Neither of them suffices. For I require of a definition that it determines a man both in relation to what he *is* as well as what he *does*. The first fails in relation to what he *is*. For what does it mean to be 'reasoning'. The second fails in relation to what he *does*, for no one knows, when he hears that man is here in order to think, what he is to think in order to think of what befits a man.

On what does Hoditz build his enquiry into the being of man? He founds it on the clear definition 'Man is the image of God', for this binds together both aspects, 'both that which he is to be and what he *is* created to *do*. For Man is not merely to *be* but also to *act* in accordance with his similarity to God and his godly image.'

Our philosopher supports this definition of the being of Man, received long ago from Moses through divine inspiration, with much incisive reasoning, as he draws the consequences from this definition in the clearest manner for conduct 'befitting' Man, above all in the areas of the life of rights and ethics. According to Zimmermann, Hoditz's achievement in the area of the philosophy of law would, if only developed slightly further, have preceded Leibniz's discovery of the specific difference between justice and morality.

Alerted to the Bohemian philosopher by Zimmermann, another philosophical personality emphasized that the Bohemian Count has 'an enormous significance for those who can see into mankind's history of thought'; this was Rudolf Steiner, who in 1909 devoted a substantial part of a public lecture to a representation of the ideas that Hoditz had written in his *Libellus*.[4]

Steiner found it especially important that Hoditz, who neither had supersensible experiences of his own nor had connections to anyone with such experiences, had managed, *in the lonely work of thinking*, to find his way to a purely spiritual image of the human being through subjecting philosophical and religious traditions to a test of reason.

That he was able to do this he owed to his eminently rational conception of what the human understanding is capable of achieving. For Hoditz, the reasoning mind was the most suitable instrument in which he saw the previously merely revealed 'Image of God' in the act of philosophical self-knowledge through his own effort of thinking. For this human reason is in its intrinsic being already a super-sensible capacity. 'Were it true,' says the *Libellus*, 'that the understanding possessed nothing that was not already there in the senses', an aristotelian thought which Leibniz also challenged and extended it by the familiar 'except for the understanding itself',

then Man would by his very nature only be drawn to sensual enjoyment; he would lack all standards; no action would be good, none bad ... After considering the matter, reason comes to its conclusion in accordance with Man's true purpose; this is provided by the memory; this remembers it and leads it to the human being. Now he *knows* what he has to do; whether he does it or does not do it depends solely upon his will.

For Hoditz, *healthy* human reason is able to perceive the divine, the supersensible and especially the godliness of human being itself. Thus in the 'history of thinkers of mankind' this lonely thinking personality shows in exemplary fashion that even in the time of transition when super-sensible facts *can neither any longer be believed in nor seen*, the human being can grasp the spirituality at the core of his being through the unprejudiced unfolding of his power of reason—in order to think and act in accordance with this core. 'The spiritualization of the intellect' was what Rudolf Steiner would call such an activation of the human power of reason 200 years later.[5] Those who know Steiner's writings only slightly, will soon notice how much value he places on the fact that what is researched by spiritual science can also be fully and completely understood by someone who is not yet able to see in the spiritual sense. Reason must only not exhaust itself in considering the sense world exclusively—that way it would eventually succumb to the dragon of materialism.

★

After Rudolf Steiner had learned of the relationship of this thinker to Ludwig and Arthur Polzer-Hoditz, he remarked to Ludwig Polzer on one occasion that his ancestor's writing also represented in his view the first demonstrable call for a new formation of social relations in Middle Europe.[6]

The personality and the perspectives of this man seemed predestined to play an important role in the life of Ludwig Polzer in many respects. Already long before his first meeting with Rudolf Steiner, Polzer had had a copy of his ancestor's text made. His first meeting with Steiner in the year 1908 would in a remarkable way stand under the star of Franziskus Josephus von Hoditz' central philosophical question, and still in 1932 the great-grandson of this thinker would seek out Pürglitz Castle (Křivoklát in Czech) in the neighbourhood of the more famous Karlstejn Castle near Prague in order to see with his own eyes the valuable text of his ancestor's *Libellus* that was there preserved.

When Archduke Eugen, the last Grand Master and renewer of the Teutonic Order, renovated the former residence of Franziskus Josephus, Busau Castle, 100 years ago, in the great hall of the castle he had the coat of arms of the Teutonic Order placed alongside that of the Hoditz family and beneath them a knight slaying a dragon, and the inscription 'Knight of the Spirit'. Ludwig Polzer was personally acquainted with Archduke Eugen; he got to know him in Basel, where the Archduke was living between 1919 and 1934 in political exile as a member of the Habsburg family.

And when in December 1917, as a consequence of Arthur Polzer-Hoditz' new position at Court, the Polzer family was raised from the status of knighthood (*Ritterstand*) to that of earldom (*Grafenstand*), and thus became equal in standing to the Hoditz family, Earl Ludwig Polzer-Hoditz chose the coat of arms of his significant ancestor Franziskus Josephus Philippus von Hoditz as his personal emblem.

4. Ludwig Ritter von Polzer (1807–1874)
Man of Letters and Art

Let us now turn our attention to the paternal side, to the *Polzers*. As already mentioned, the family originates in Silesia and can be traced back to the seventeenth century. They were then resident in Troppau and were allowed to refer to themselves as 'nobilis'. In the year 1756 a Polzer, whose father was Mayor of Troppau, was raised to the rank of 'Ritter (knight) of noble birth' by Empress Maria Theresa for his services in the Silesian wars.

It is notable that many male members of the family entered the clergy. Baron Franziskus von Polzer became Provincial of the Moravian Province of the Minorites (Franciscans) in the seventeenth century; his brother and his nephew Ignaz entered the Society of Jesus. The latter later became professor of Theology at the University of Olmütz (today, Olomouc). The family also produced two doctors of medicine and an army officer who served in the Imperial army in the campaigns of the Napoleonic era. This was Baron Joseph von Polzer, who later served as a military consultant at army headquarters in Brünn until one day in 1834 when he had to be carried out of the office where he had suffered a stroke.

On this Polzer side of the family gallery—which indeed appears shorter but is no poorer in interesting personalities than the Hoditz side—we shall now take a few steps forward into the future behind the still closed doors of which the birth of the central figure of this biography was already being prepared, however much we would like to hurry on to that important event. Our way leads us past a figure whose very definite features, as evident from a photograph, can make us pause for while. (fig. 5, lower).

Ludwig, Ritter von Polzer—for he is the one of whom we are now speaking—the only son of the above-mentioned Joseph, Ritter von Polzer and grandfather of Ludwig and Arthur Polzer, was born in 1807 in Brünn, where he spent his childhood and youth. After his studies he entered service at the Imperial War Office in Vienna.

Typical of the bon vivant and gallant character of this man is the way in which he made the acquaintance of his wife at the end of his 20s. Arthur Polzer describes the first meeting of his grandparents in the pregnant sentence: 'My grandfather got to know his future wife through an accident, bad weather and a rain shower.'[7] After the end of a theatre performance Ludwig von Polzer was about to step right out into the street—fortunately, armed with an umbrella, for it was pouring down. Then he spotted an elderly gentleman accompanied by a young woman as pretty as a picture and both seemed somewhat at a loss what to do. Without hesitation, the gallant theatregoer walked over to the embarrassed pair and offered them his umbrella. In a tone of laconic satisfaction Arthur Polzer reports the consequences of this gallantry: 'What followed quickly developed in the sunshine of youth and soon led to the couple's engagement.'

Ritter von Polzer's fiancée was extraordinarily musically talented; she had already received a training in singing and had sometimes been accompanied by no less a pianist than the composer Franz Schubert.

Josefine Hauer—for that was the bride's name—was living at the time with her father, who had lost his wife early on: her mother, a French-woman born de Gabillet, had thrown herself into the Danube during a stay at a spa after an unfortunate love affair, aged only 25...

A year after the wedding in September 1833, their first son was born to the couple on 18 November 1834: Julius, later the father of Arthur and Ludwig Polzer.

In the year of revolutions 1847/48 Ritter von Polzer came into two substantial inheritances. He left public service and with his wife and two sons Julius and Alfred moved to Graz, where he bought a house. The family had many servants, owned a coach and horses and maintained a permanent box at the provincial theatre. In those politically troubled years Graz became a kind of haven for many noble families under pressure with whom the Polzers came into the most frequent social intercourse.

Far from falling into the relaxed lifestyle of a bohemian, Ludwig von Polzer knew how to combine a free and easy lifestyle with the most painstaking love of order. His days always followed the same pattern. At breakfast, which he always took with his wife at the same time, he read the newspapers. If he received letters, they were mostly answered by return post. After a stroll and attending to various business matters, around midday he would sit himself before his easel. As an autodidactic painter, he deliberately remained within the limits of his ability and restricted himself mostly to copying the works of old masters. (Most of the excellent copies in the family's possession disappeared in 1945 when the Russians marched into Vienna.) He ate at three o'clock then paid calls or went for long walks. In the evenings Ludwig von Polzer accompanied his wife to the theatre where besides the performances themselves, he loved to visit other people's boxes during the pauses. Supper was an 'unknown' concept for him; he regarded it as unhealthy.

This very regular pattern of life was interrupted, however, by frequent long travels, which were perhaps his greatest pleasure. He therefore came to be regarded as rather unreachable by some of his relatives: his father-in-law never answered the letters he received from him but sent his replies instead to his daughter with the excuse that one never knew which country 'Lui' was in at that point and whether one should address letters to Constantinople, Genoa or America...

The rich experiences of his life found their way into a number of the stimulating novellas which Ritter von Polzer authored in his later years in Graz, which were published in the year of his death, 1874, by Gerold in Vienna under the title *In Mussestunden* (In Leisurely Hours). We shall encounter them again.

5. Julius Ritter von Polzer (1834–1912)
and the Fortifications of the Imperial and Royal Monarchy

Julius, the elder son of this intelligent man of the world and disciplined 'idler' appears to have inherited from his father a firm style of life and an open feeling for life's relationships, and from his mother a love for language and culture of France.

The latter characteristic soon became noticeable. Julius Polzer was according to his own words already in childhood 'small in stature perhaps but a great fan of Napoleon'[8]. At nine years of age he was receiving private French lessons from a friend of his mother's in the neighbourhood. He liked to combine his visits to his teacher with little inspection tours round neighbouring houses. 'Before or after the lessons,' reported the 70-year-old in his autobiographical reflections[9], 'I would go to the nearby houses to ask if a Dr Nerer lived there, of course only out of curiosity, to see how other houses looked inside.' On one such investigative exploration, making imaginative use of his French conversation lessons, he pretended to be a little French boy, who 'doesn't understand German'. The housemaid who came to the door, not understanding French, called the lady of the house to the door 'who was visibly interested in the little French boy and did not want to miss the opportunity to improve her French; she invited me in and conversed with me for a long time'.

Julius Polzer commented on his remarkable performance: 'I can today neither remember nor at all understand how I was able to play the role so well; I only know that I came home very pleased with myself.' The episode was to have a small epilogue: a few days later he was walking with the nanny, who needed to do some shopping, under a vaulted passageway and when he asked the young woman a question, a woman nearby suddenly said: 'That's the little French boy who speaks German very well.' As the servants were very fond of Julius, his parents heard nothing of the affair. 'On my expeditions after that,' he added however, 'I always presented myself as a German...'

When his maternal grandfather—that older gentleman with the umbrella whom we met at the beginning of the last chapter—came to Vienna, he would usually take Julius and his brother Alfred to the Carl Theatre where they could frequently see farces by or featuring the playwright actor and singer Johann Nestroy. They were often also able to see performances by Ferdinand Raimund and the dancer Fanny Elssler. Afterwards, the two boys would go to a hotel for a meal with their beloved grandfather who, besides the theatre, loved simple humour.

It was the time of the *Vormärz* (the years before the revolutions which broke out in March 1848), when Vienna was still surrounded with a wall, fortifications, gates and bastions. Viennese society would gather in the afternoons beyond the Karolinentor for concerts in the park: the ladies in their wide, hooped dresses, from which their upper bodies protruded like lily stalks, their hair in curls and wearing little hats; the gentlemen in dove grey trousers, with high stand-up collars and neck bows that reached up to their chins.

The world of the Habsburg Empire was still 'in good form'...

At the age of eleven Julius, Ritter von Polzer entered the high school (*Gymnasium*) at the famous Benedictine Abbey of Kremsmünster, where, amongst other things, he acquired his mastery of Latin.

In Styrian Graz, where, as mentioned in the previous chapter, his father had moved with his family after the disquieting year of 1848, Julius attended the Engineers' Academy, a military school with a high reputation for its teaching of mathematics in which subject, along with chemistry, he showed himself especially gifted.

In 1854 he was posted to the garrison in Verona as a lieutenant. After completing a higher engineering course in Klosterbruck, he returned after a few years to this town, of which he was very fond. Before his departure he fought his first and, it seems, only duel, which he survived unscathed.

★

During these years the Habsburgs began on the work of upgrading and renovating the fortifications in their Italian territories. When on New Year's Day 1859 it became clear from a remark made by Napoleon III to the Austrian ambassador Hübner that military conflict was coming with the French, who supported Italian efforts for independence, Julius Polzer was sent to Piacenza, where he had been ordered to construct three forts. They were, however, built in vain, for after the Battle of Magenta it was decided to evacuate the forts. With half a company and a large number of wagons and horses he led a dangerous retreat to Mantova that went past Cremona. It was only in faraway Vienna, where he had been ordered to serve on the staff of the army engineers, that Julius Polzer was able to experience the Austrian campaign against the French, who were allied with the Sardinians, and which ended with the well-known, devastating defeat of the Habsburgs at Solferino. Julius' son Arthur would later write of this battle: 'It was the first victory of hostile forces in their war of annihilation against Austria.'

The young *Genie-Ingenieur* (military engineer), as the builders of fortifications were known in those days, was 'very satisfied with his position

1. The Habsburg in Aargau. Print by Matthaeus Merian, 1642

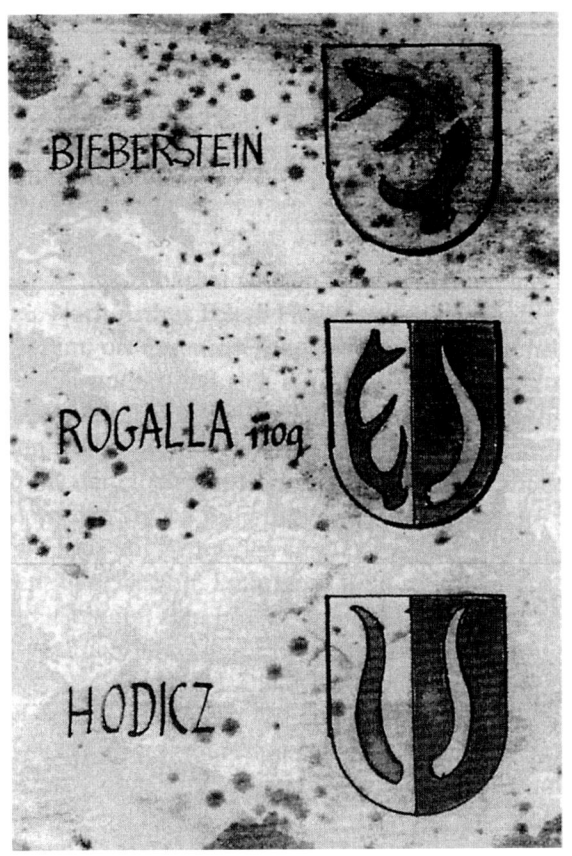

BIEBERSTEIN

ROGALLA ñoq

HODICZ

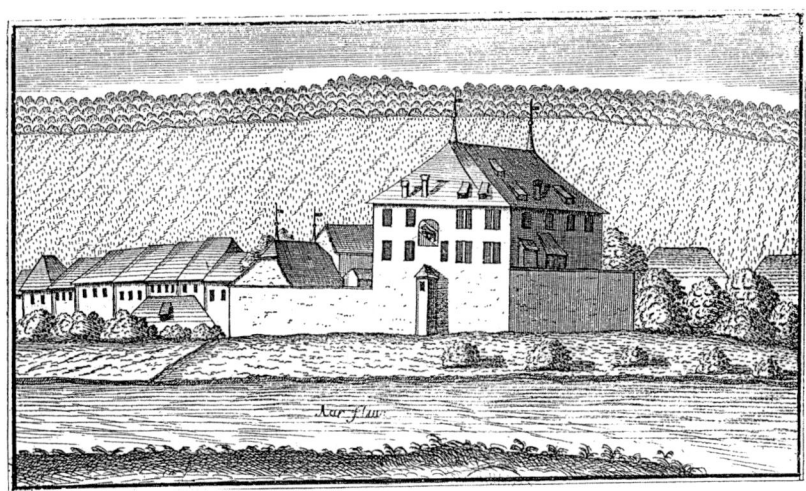

2. The Hoditz family coats of arms; Bieberstein Castle on the Aare

3. Count Albert von Hoditz; Hoditz Restaurant in Potsdam

4. Grandparents Anna and Friedrich von Hoditz

5. Grandparents Sefine and Baron Ludwig von Polzer

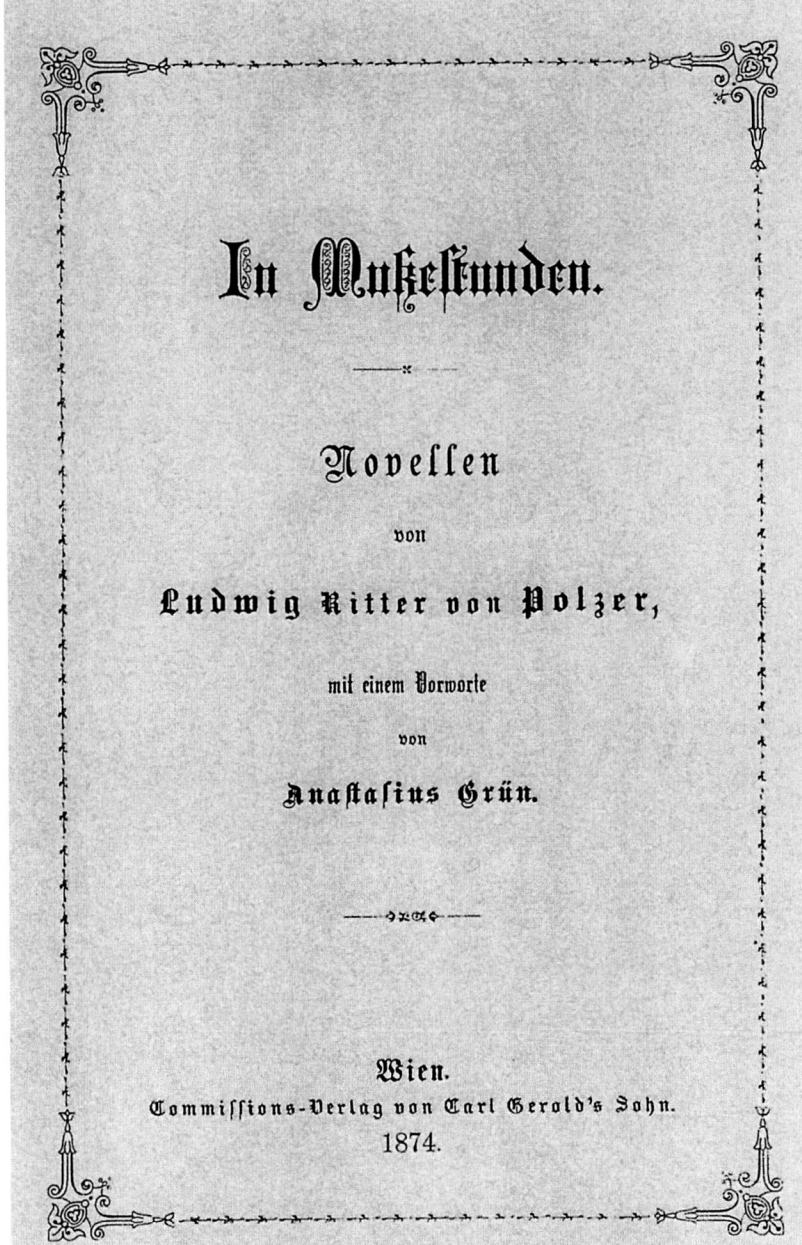

In Mussestunden.

Novellen

von

Ludwig Ritter von Polzer,

mit einem Vorworte

von

Anastasius Grün.

Wien.
Commissions-Verlag von Carl Gerold's Sohn.
1874.

6. *Title page of the volume of novels* 'In Mussestunden' (In Leisurely Hours)

7. *Baron Julius von Polzer and Christine von Hoditz und Wolframitz*

8. Christine and Baron Julius von Polzer

9. Mathilde von Hoditz, Ludwig and Christine Polzer, about 1870

10. Arthur (left) and Ludwig Polzer, about 1872

11. Arthur Polzer, about 1881

12. Ludwig Polzer, about 1881

13. *Robert Hamerling; facade of the Palais Saurau in Graz*

14. Modern. Painting by Arthur Polzer

15. *Wilbraham Tollemache, aunt Mathilde, Blanche Tollemache, Arthur*

16. From left to right: unknown woman, Blanche Tollemache, Mathilde von Hoditz

at the garrison in Vienna'. After a hard day's work as an engineer, he enjoyed as many balls and entertainments in the evenings as his modest military salary allowed.

This pleasurable time in Vienna would, however, soon come to an abrupt end. One day, on orders from his commanding officer, Polzer had to ride into the Prater Park in Vienna with his commanding officer's brother. The riding path was full of riders. After carrying out their orders, the two men were riding back at the gallop when suddenly a woman rode out of the crowd. The two were able to avoid her in time, while the lady rider galloped between them as they shouted 'Watch out! Watch out!' But unfortunately, this was not just any lady, this was the Empress herself! Julius Polzer relates in his memoirs: 'As always, everything was misrepresented and exaggerated and we were said to have ridden the Empress down; in short, the affair caused an unfounded stir in the Prater.' Polzer soon suffered the consequences of this unfortunate affair; while his companion was sufficiently protected by his position to remain unpunished, he himself was posted to Zara in Dalmatia as a result of this breach of form against Her Majesty. How times have changed!

Feeling extremely put out by his ill-fortune and aware that he could not be sent to a worse garrison, from then on, he no longer concerned himself in the slightest with the favour or ill-favour of his superiors. He continued to go about his duties conscientiously, but privately, he 'paid attention to nothing, paid visits to no one [...] and showed [to all] only too clearly that for me everything in Zara was displeasing and distasteful'. He did not shy from deliberately meeting on his strolls the governess who worked for his Engineering Corps Inspector and as the growing sympathy between them appeared to be mutual he accompanied her more frequently and on longer walks. After a short time, on account of so-called 'considerations of duty', he was posted to the Engineers' staff at Cattaro (today, Kotor) and was transferred to the southernmost point of the empire.

★

These setbacks and incidents which seem perhaps insignificant in themselves immediately become more interesting when seen as symptomatic of the inner condition of the monarchy in those days. How much attention was paid in appearance and behaviour to the formalities and etiquette of the court! How important offences against formalities could become, and when considered without concern for individual qualities or capacities, what damage they could inflict on individual destinies! How external all form already appears to have become, how empty of real substance! Was the monarchy not just as much threatened by enemies within, those of formalism and a lack of ideas, as it was by enemies without? Was the old imperial concept still valid and strong enough to provide fruitful solutions to burning issues such as the growing conflicts between nationalities?

In one of his novels[10] Julius' father Ludwig has one of his characters, a Count, express his conviction that 'the ramshackle forms' of the monarchy would, if laboriously preserved, only hold until the next generation: 'The powerful sun of the twentieth century will shine down here only on ruins.' How right he would turn out to be!

The transfer to Cattaro meanwhile worked to Julius Polzer's advantage in every respect. The large port, divided between three large and several smaller bays in which all the fleets of Europe could comfortably have ridden at anchor, as well as the excellent fortifications of the town, all attracted his keenest interest. With his superior Engineering Corps Director Major Mossig he made a six-day journey by mule to visit the defensive posts along the frontier with Montenegro.

Responsible for the coastal fortifications in the district of Castelnuovo the 27-year-old fortifications officer was often impressed by the beauty of the countryside with its many bays and inlets. He spent most of his free time at the house of Major Mossig, who was married to a cultivated lady from Florence.

He was there in the summer of 1860 at the time of the assassination of Prince Danilo of Montenegro when the prince was visiting Cattaro with his wife. The assassin, who was held to have personal motives, was hanged in Cattaro.

At home in Graz, his father, who had doubtless heard of the shots in Cattaro from the newspapers, gradually began to feel a certain resentment in view of Julius' not exactly promising future career prospects in the normally uneventful southern tip of the empire. He proposed to his son that he request a six-month holiday on half pay—which was usually permitted to veterans of the 1859 Italian campaign—and to take a long trip abroad. He would provide his son with any necessary money. Julius was then able to go on an educational trip lasting several months, which took him first to Berlin via Prague and Dresden.

He visited museums and went to theatre performances, but never omitted to visit the more significant fortifications en route. Via Cologne and Aachen he went on to Brussels where he experienced a performance by the 19-year-old Adelina Patti in the title role of Donizetti's *Lucia di Lammermoor*. Patti, whose singing was to make her world-famous, had just returned from New York where she had made her debut in the role of 'Lucia' at the Metropolitan Opera House.

From Brussels his journey went on to the capital of his beloved France where numerous recommendations kept the visitor busy for two months. With his *Bädeker* tourist guide in hand he visited all the main sights in Paris. His excellent French as well as his flawless manners made him a very welcome guest at numerous festivities. The open boulevards with their busy traffic frequently astonished him; Vienna at that time was without its circular Ringstrasse and was still surrounded by its ancient walls.

He often went to the Comédie Française where 'delightful comedies were performed'. Yet in the midst of all these enjoyments and distractions he did not omit to spend time visiting the city's modern fortifications built by Louis-Philippe in the 1830s and in studying the 'great military ideas' that underpinned them. He realized that an army seeking to overcome the fortifications of Paris would have to extend itself over twelve miles, and recalling this visit, he later claimed that in the Franco-Prussian War of 1870/1871, 'without Paris, [France] would have been defeated four months earlier'. Julius Polzer's later descriptions of his experiences in Paris were so much given over to what at the time seemed to him to be the inspired fortifications of Paris that he included in his memoirs a number of very interesting observations about the correct estimation—or, in the case of the Habsburgs, the underestimation—of the importance of forts for the conduct of modern warfare. He mentioned, for example, how unbelievable it had been for him that Austria made peace in 1859 although it was in possession of the four forts known as the Quadrilateral—at Verona, Mantova, Peschiera, and Legnago. He ascribes this failure in the first instance to the Austrian artillery, which since the time of Napoleon's campaigns had increasingly caused the general staff, the army and the general public to place little faith, not only in smaller fortifications but also in large, fortified positions at strategically important points. If the Italian Quadrilateral had been relied on to a greater degree, things would have turned out very differently in his view: 'The French and Sardinian armies would never have taken the Quadrilateral forts; they would have bled to death and would have had to retreat from Lombardy with heavy losses.' Julius Polzer's specialist knowledge as a fortifications engineer does not allow such ideas to be easily dismissed...

After Julius had returned to Cattaro, it was not long before his father once again made his views known and asked his son whether he was thinking of spending the rest of his life in Dalmatia. Without waiting for an answer, he suggested he seek a transfer to a Hungarian infantry regiment. Julius, for whom his father's wish was 'always a kind of order', immediately submitted his application for a transfer to the War Ministry. But the official channels went via the General Inspectorate, which was then headed by Archduke Leopold. Like Archduke Albrecht, Archduke Leopold was the very incarnation of retarding, conservative tendencies within the monarchy. It was because of him that Julius had landed in Cattaro. Instead of forwarding his application to War Ministry, the Archduke highhandedly blocked it by keeping it in his own office. This was the last straw for Julius' father. 'Very capable with a pen and enjoying the confidence of many people', he sent the War Minister a memorandum in which he complained that a letter addressed to the Ministry was not to be put before the authorities. Shortly afterwards followed Julius' transfer to Hungary, which Archduke Leopold finally, after futile objections, had grudgingly to accept; he had been of the opinion that it would be better to keep Polzer in Dalmatia: 'there he would not be able to go riding so often'. Despite this happy change in his fortunes, Julius did not find his departure from the Corps of Engineers easy. In his memoirs he wrote:

> Officers in the Corps of Engineers were educated, comradely, loyal to the service, precise in all their work and completely obedient to their superiors without any kind of servility [. . .] I never later found a better *esprit de corps* than in this branch of the service.

Once he had arrived in Losoncz, barely 100 kilometres north of Budapest, Julius assiduously set about learning Hungarian. But when a year later, 1866, the campaign began against the Prussians, we find him again already in Italy where he was assigned to an infantry regiment in Genoa. Without a certain readiness to travel no military career was possible in the imperial and royal monarchy . . .

A warm friendship was to link him here with his captain, a man of the world and a real charmer, beloved of men and women alike, by the name of Bondi, who at this point was about to be promoted in a very notable manner.

At the outbreak of the war, Bondi decided, on account of his many debts, to forgo his approaching advancement to the rank of Major and request to be pensioned off. He then learned from the official gazette that he had just been promoted Major. He possessed neither the horse nor the weaponry required for this rank. After 14 days' absence in Vienna he returned to his regiment, which was now stationed in Neustadt—and to the astonishment of all the officers, with two horses and equipped for war with the necessary weaponry according to regulations. The new Major explained that he had sought an audience with His Majesty in Vienna, had described to him his difficult circumstances and had asked for his assistance. Astonished, His Majesty had asked him how it had come about that under such circumstances he had been promoted at all, whereupon Bondi, equally astonished, had quickly replied: 'If Your Majesty does not know, *I* certainly do not!'

Emperor Franz Joseph, who was known for his partiality for dry humour and for whom Bondi's open and jolly attitude was very appealing, responded with a smile and ordered that Bondi be given a sum of money.

This anecdote told by Julius Polzer is, even if in a very different sense from the scene in the Prater Park, symptomatic of the inner state of the monarchy, in that it shows that narrow-minded formality did not have the last word in every case. We felt it should not be ignored here since this episode of Bondi's undeserved promotion represents the diametric opposite case to Polzer's hardly-deserved punitive posting to the southernmost tip of the Empire.

Polzer's brigade had to defend the railway line that ran near the Prussian border and had to march back and forth in the region between Trübau and Geyersburg. Because of his relatively low rank 'the reasons for this marching about remained obscure, we were never told anything'. One time he was ordered to advance with his company as far as Senftenberg, but again without receiving any reason or mission. When he met there with a squadron of cavalry, he asked their commander, who also appeared to be without instructions, for orders. Austria's decisions were not always comprehensible even to its higher-ranking officers of engineers—a further symptom of the condition of the monarchy, which even in critical situations began to suffer increasingly from a certain lack of direction. However much this march to Senftenberg appeared to have resulted from no military planning, in Julius' Polzer's personal life the hand of a higher planning would soon be revealed . . .

After the Austrian defeat at Königgrätz on 3 July, Polzer's battalion had to help cover the retreat of the Austrian army. While the Prussians succeeded in partially blocking the line of retreat, they were able to inflict further losses on the Austrians because of the superiority of their modern Dreyse breech-loading rifles.

After six months' leave in Vienna and Graz, Julius reported for duty at the fortress of Theresienstadt. His friend Bondi was serving in the same regiment and had reconnoitred the entire surrounding area in the shortest possible time, with the result that he decided at the next opportunity to pay a visit together with Julius on an elderly Baroness Karg who was living temporarily in Leitmeritz on the opposite bank of the Elbe with her two lovely granddaughters, the Countesses Hoditz.

Normally, Baroness Karg and her two granddaughters resided at the Senftenberg Palace in Prague.

'You must get a good look at the elder one, Christine,' advised Bondi before the visit. 'She would make a lovely little wife for you.' And as if this were not enough to motivate Julius to accompany him, he added: 'I have already worked on presenting you in the best possible light of course and have got the Countess very curious.' Bondi arranged for an excursion by steamer along the romantic valley of the river Elbe. This was the occasion when Julius Polzer made the acquaintance of the then 20-year-old Christine, Countess von Hoditz und Wolframitz. 'The elder of the two countesses,' writes Polzer at the end of his life,

> the Countess Christine pleased me immediately. During the summer we went on many outings in the country. One evening, when I was out alone with my future wife, I took the decisive step; I put the question as to whether she wished to give me her hand. After she said Yes, I told her that the following day I would ask her grandmama, Baroness Karg for her hand.

The Baroness had already made the necessary enquiries, evidently satisfactory, about Julius' past and his way of life with some old friends of hers in Graz. After Julius had obtained his parents' agreement, the engagement took place. Very soon Christine Hoditz, about whom naturally similar enquiries had been made, received words of blessing, advice and enlightenment from her mother-in-law in Graz. 'My beloved daughter,' writes Sefine [abbreviation of Josefine] Polzer to the still unknown bride,

> You ask for our blessing [...] I give it to you with all my heart, with the request that you bear the idiosyncracies of Julius' character cheerfully and patiently. I believe I can assure you, however, that he is in all ways an honourable and brave man [...] But he is intense, very intense and therefore needs a gentle and clever wife [...] Only turn to me in full confidence, make our relationship a sisterly one, restrained by no shyness, and I think we shall manage very, very well with the young master...[11]

Soon, on 18 November 1867, on Julius' 33rd birthday, the wedding was celebrated in Prague. The Catholic ceremony was held in the Church of St Nicholas on the Old City ring, on the same square where the Senftenberg palace residence of the Baroness Karg and the Countesses Hoditz stood.

And so the march to the Senftenberg, to which the officer of engineers had proceeded so utterly without plan or aim during the war, now arrived at its true, destiny-laden goal... For why should the workings of destiny not be permitted occasionally to herald significant events by less significant ones, or sometimes even by preludes that seem completely meaningless?

If Julius Polzer had until now been concerned only for the fortifications of the empire, his attentions henceforward were paid to a similar degree to the fortification of a growing family, which would endure despite all the shocking blows that the empire would soon suffer.

6. Birth in Prague, the Threshold City

When Christine von Hoditz und Wolframitz became Julius Polzer's wife in November 1867 she was 21 years old. Despite the decisive change that had occurred in her life, her thoughts more than once in those autumn days may well have wandered back to her childhood. For at the same age in which she herself had got married, her mother Anna, completely unexpectedly, had suddenly crossed the threshold of death. Born the Baroness Karg and Bebenburg, she was also certainly born with a heart defect but it had been regarded as relatively harmless, especially as she was a very lively, happy being, both as child and adolescent.

In the three short years of her early marriage, with an intimate and ardent love, Christine Polzer's mother had relied on her husband, Friedrich von Hoditz und Wolframitz, who served as a captain in the 12th Regiment of Hussars—which is why he was known in the family simply as 'the Hussar'. 'When I am dead, I shall take him with me within half a year,' Anna von Hoditz had once said.[12] And so it turned out: Friedrich von Hoditz, an original personality with a carefree zest for life, followed his wife to the grave five months later; in Verona, the same city in which, shortly afterwards, his unknown future son-in-law Julius Polzer would often be billeted, Friedrich died early in 1850 from the consequences of a typhus infection that had not healed.

Before making a full recovery, he had returned too early to the circle of his comrades one evening. The following morning he was found completely motionless, a handkerchief in his mouth; it was the one with which he had wiped the perspiration from his wife's brow before she died.

Thus Christine Polzer and her sister Mathilde, two years younger, (we shall learn more about her later) were already orphaned when still very young children. Their grandmother Baroness Karg and Bebenburg, who from 1866 onwards resided at the Palais Senftenberg in Prague, took on the role of both parents to the two infants. Shortly after she had moved to Prague with her two granddaughters she encountered a very unhappy situation, because cholera had been raging in the city since the outbreak of the war against Prussia in the summer of 1866. The sound of bells tolling for the dead was heard constantly. Whole families died. On the other hand, the epidemic brought about the creation of at least *one* new family, because after one of her servants had succumbed to the disease, the Baroness fled with her two granddaughters temporarily to that same Leitmeritz to which Major Bondi, as related in the last chapter, would lead his friend and companion Julius Polzer...

★

What Christine Polzer now desired more than anything else was to be a mother. And during the warm and happy evenings when Julius Polzer and his wife went out to dine after a none-too strenuous day at his military duties, 'many tears fell in the beer glass [...] when she spoke of her distress that she was not yet expecting'.[13]

Sefine Polzer, the mother-in-law in Graz to whom Christine expressed her sorrow in confidence one day, replied in a worldly-wise but heart-warming, uplifting letter: 'You will not bring on what you long for by all this excessive yearning which only creates new agitations,' she advised insistently. 'Be sensible, my dear brave daughter, who is so devout and must therefore hope for God's grace and goodness [...] Make your husband cheerful, not morose, you poor philosopher. Think, you can still have 25 children between 20 and 40.' But her mother-in-law did not only advise greater patience; she followed this with some tried and tested leading thoughts about dealing with men in general and her son Julius in particular:

> You love and are loved in return. You are pious, good and accom-modating. One must hold you dear. So I give you this piece of advice: remain as you are, and you will make others happy and be happy yourself. Only don't take up too much of your husband's time with your concerns. Let him come to you. He should look to you, and let us thank God that he has much work to do, for the busy man longs for home; the man who is not busy longs to be *away* from home. [This is] an old rule, which one can not keep in mind often enough [...] Kiss Julius in my name, today is his name day. Today he is allowed to be in charge. But only today. The other 364 days he should be an obedient husband and consider his wife's caprices as virtues.[14]

Could there be a more exquisite example of a plot than this understanding between a mother-in-law and daughter-in-law ?

★

On 23 April 1869 Christine Polzer's wish was finally fulfilled: her eldest son, Ludwig saw the light of the world. Julius' father, Ludwig, Ritter von Polzer, came to Prague for the baptism. He not only took on to become godfather to the newborn baby but was able—a happy idea of the new parents—to bestow his name on the child, and far beyond the mere blood relationship, a certain inner relationship between grandfather and grandson would even later show itself.

At the time of Ludwig's birth, the young couple were living in

Krakauer Street which opened onto the upper end of Wenceslas Square. In the whole of Prague no better neighbour could have been found for the inner being of little Ludwig than St Wenceslas who made Bohemia a Christian land in the tenth century before he was murdered by his power-hungry brother Boleslav. No place in the whole of Prague would later be sought out by Ludwig Polzer more often with more extensive ideas and deeper feelings than the splendidly bejewelled Chapel of Wenceslas in St Vitus' Cathedral on the Castle Hill.

Prague would become Ludwig Polzer's most beloved and preferred city of cities. His freely chosen destiny tasks would lead him here for many years, to this 'threshold' city, where the marriage between the German and Slavic cultures is constantly sealed anew. It is perhaps no mere accident that the most personal of all his later books, his *Erinnerungen an den grossen Lehrer Dr Rudolf Steiner* (Reminiscences of the Great Teacher Dr Rudolf Steiner), which contains so many social seeds for the future, was published in this city. Besides Prague there were in Polzer's life only two other major European cities of comparable significance: Vienna and Rome.[15] While Prague would remain for him all his life the site of still slumbering possibilities for the future and Vienna would open for him the deeper impulses of the present, he would experience Rome as the echo, as it were, of major cultural impulses from the past. With Rome he would have very critical confrontations in his later years—both with the meta-morphosed continuation of the Roman impulses with the Roman Catholic church and also in relation to his own past.

Just at the time of Ludwig Polzer's birth there was taking place in Rome that fateful Council at which Pius IX promulgated the dogma of Papal Infallibility for papal teachings given *ex cathedra*. Ludwig Polzer, who regarded this as an anachronistic renaissance of the decadent power impulses of the former Roman Empire, felt in his later life that his destiny was linked by the year of his birth to this portentous council and its world-historical consequences. How remarkable this can seem when we read in a novel by Ludwig's godfather and grandfather which stems from the beginning of the 1870s and bears the title '*Reiseerinnerungen*' (Reminiscences of My Travels):

> On one of the last days of the month of October 1869, in lovely weather I arrived in Genoa on the Milan Express [...] As I was already familiar with northern Italy earlier as a soldier, my journey would have led to Rome and Naples, but unfortunately the Eternal City was overflowing with Church fathers from every part of the world who had gathered for an unwholesome Council. News of this gathering came to me like the ringing of a distant funeral bell, and I could not persuade myself to enter the city at the time

when true Christian belief was being so odiously sullied and Catholicism itself—to which I too belonged—so badly wounded, more so than by any Pope since the great indulgences traitor Leo X. Under these circumstances I chose as my destination the Riviera di Ponente, which recommended itself both on account of its natural beauty and the mildness of the climate.[16]

Did the travel-loving Ritter von Polzer take this trip himself half a year after the birth of his godson? It is very probable. At any rate, when he avoided Catholic Rome in the year 1869 the 'novella traveller' was certainly acting in complete accord with his grandson's later ideas...

II. GROWING UP IN
THE EMPIRE OF AUSTRIA-HUNGARY

Nowhere but in Austria could this multiplicity of peoples
be experienced in the same sensitive, spiritual way;
one did not find oneself there in the philistine cell
of an enclosed unitary national state.

Ludwig Polzer-Hoditz, 1937

7. From Prague to Graz

A fortunate destiny allowed me to be born in an environment in which the German cultural life of the previous century was still alive and pulsing, the fire of enthusiasm for it surrounded me. Goethe, Schiller, Anastasius Grün, Hamerling and Grillparzer, Beethoven, Mozart, Schumann and Schubert shone through my youth. That makes the soul receptive to the weaving of the spirit through space and time. It gives the impulse to ask questions about the spiritual background of the world and encourages one [...] to seek for the meaning of life.[17]

With these words Count Ludwig Polzer-Hoditz introduces the brief description of the major impressions and experiences of his youth in his *Erinnerungen* (Memoirs) which was published in Prague in 1937. If the 68-year-old, with good reason, restricted himself in his review of his life to sketching in often broad and swift strokes only the *essential* moments of his rich life, so may the reader with no less good reason expect his biographer to seek out precisely the concrete 'where and when' and to describe the special circumstances in which Ludwig Polzer-Hoditz grew up.[18]

Until Ludwig's seventh year, the requirements of his father's military duties meant that the Polzer family had to change their residence no fewer than four times. In the year of Ludwig's birth even, they had to move to Lemburg, which then was still part of the Austrian Crown territory of Galicia and today (as *Lwów*) is in Ukraine. It was here that on 2 August 1870 Ludwig's brother Arthur came into the world. That he had to be born precisely in this—to what later seemed to him—unimportant city, Arthur Polzer felt 'as a blemish' all his life; all the more therefore was he able to place importance on the *time* of his birth: it was the day on which French troops occupied Saarbrücken. 'So my life began,' Arthur wrote later in his unpublished memoirs, 'on the same day as the war which destroyed the last possibility of a rebuilding of the old German Empire under the sceptre of the Habsburgs[19].'

Soon after Arthur's birth his father was ordered to the History of War Office in Vienna, where the family lived until early in 1872, first in Himmelpfortgasse (Heaven's Gate Lane) and then in Elisabethstrasse. Julius, Ritter von Polzer was then appointed to the general staff of an infantry regiment stationed in Pilsen, Bohemia—and so the Bohemian city became the Polzers' next place of residence.

There is a photograph from this time (fig. 10) which shows Arthur and Ludwig together. Arthur has been planted on a chaise longue and is looking at his elder brother with a dreamy, slightly anxious gaze. Ludwig, with evident self-assurance, stands firmly on the floor with a free, confident air and a steady gaze and seems to be thinking of whether to take a bold step forward or to direct a performance with the rod he is holding in his hand. The picture reveals not only their slight difference in age but also something of the difference in character of the two brothers.

The brothers' first memories both go back to these years in Pilsen. Arthur recalls the house's little garden in the Martingasse which was closed off from the street by a wall. When their father rode home one evening the brothers were lifted up above the wall by their nurse so that they could see the 'lovely brown' that their father rode. Sometimes they were allowed to fly kites with their nurse. One day, when their mother was also with them and they wanted to show off to her, they succeeded with shouts of delight in getting the kites to fly especially high. When they landed again on the ground they had been decorated with sweets that their mother had secretly fastened to the wings. The little angels in heaven had certainly sent the things, she said to the little kite flyers. Sixty years later this scene was still there in all its clarity before Arthur's soul.

The boys' nurse hailed from Switzerland. Did destiny intend by this circumstance to remind Ludwig and Arthur Polzer in their earliest childhood of the area from which their family had originated?

In early 1874 the boys' grandfather, the great traveller in the family, who would only be surpassed in this sense by his elder grandson, embarked on his last journey to the city on the lagoon, Venice. Here he had to see an ear specialist owing to an ear problem he had long suffered; a sudden deterioration of his condition, however, led, despite all efforts to the contrary, to his death on 14 June 1874, after his return to Graz.

So that Ludwig, Ritter von Polzer would at least live yet more strongly in her memory, Sefine Polzer, encouraged by her son Julius, decided to have her husband's stories, which he had written in the last years of his life, published. They appeared, as already mentioned, in the year of his death under the title *In Mussestunden* (In Leisurely Hours), published by Gerold in Vienna. Polzer's novellas, which are still worth reading today, include many autobiographical elements. Thus for example, in a story titled 'Marie—a story from Vienna society' Ritter von Polzer gave literary form to the tragic life of the mother-in-law who had remained unknown to him, who had thrown herself into the Danube, aged just 25. Rudolf Steiner said, when he read Polzer's novellas in 1918, that 'much understanding of destiny lay in them'. [20]

The preface to the small volume came from the pen of Anastasius Grün, a very well-known Austrian poet at that time, whose real name was Count Anton von Auersperg. In it Grün draws a fine miniature portrait of his dead friend. We shall cast a last glance, through the eyes of Grün, on this interesting man, before we turn again to his son Julius and to his own two sons.

Ludwig, Ritter von Polzer, writes Grün,

> was a well-known and much appreciated personality in Graz circles. Never at a loss for topics of conversation which he knew how to match artfully to the inclinations of his listeners, he possessed in addition all the qualities of a pleasant and therefore always welcome member of society. Tireless in his devoted attention to the company of women, he also knew how to be effective in serious conversation and hold the attention of gentlemen through the extent of his knowledge and experience. A sensitive and at the same time acute observer of others' qualities good and bad, he united with a refined sense of tact so much goodness of heart that even his negative judgements were never formed in a manner that was wounding. On the floor of the salon at his own home he moved with pleasure and adroitness, but he was no less at home in discussion of the arts and literature as well as the great problems of politics and society, which an age full of turmoil sets before contemporaries to solve. Unlike the average man who is satisfied by externals and superficialities, his practised eye and cultivated mind knew how to discern the hidden grains of poesy and a deeper, more worthy meaning, even in the phenomena of life of the modern salon. In this sense was clearly displayed the interest and attention which he took care to devote even to the small events and experiences recorded by the daily chronicle of social life.

Scarcely had their grandfather passed away when the life of his son and grandsons was once more on the move. On Three Kings' Day (6 Jan.) 1875 a third child was born to Julius von Polzer and his wife: a girl, who received the name of Marie-Sefine and became the keystone of the architecture of the family.

In autumn of the same year, Julius Polzer was promoted to Major and transferred to Graz. After the various changes of residence of the past years this lovely capital of the Steiermark would provide the family with their longest and most important period of feeling at home. The family's relocation to Graz, a consequence of their father's further promotion, was a special blessing of destiny for the children. For it meant that Ludwig, Arthur and Marie-Sefine could spend their childhood and youth under the encouraging influence of their grandmother, who concerned herself especially with the cultivation of her grandchildren's artistic abilities. And this relocation to Styrian Graz, which took place in the winter of 1875/ 76, was very much in line with the spirit of their late grandfather. For why, after his death, should the soul of this worldly man who possessed such a lively interest in and a gentle, subtle feeling for everything that had to do with destiny suddenly have become blind to the ongoing fortunes of those who belonged to him? During his life he had once followed 'Marie's' path of destiny. Why should he now after death not seek to follow the paths of those living who were linked to him? Had he not already once intervened decisively and helpfully in his son's destiny when he successfully worked to have him transferred away from his hopeless position in Cattaro?

8. 'Austria Would Have Had to be Created...'

Graz on the River Mur, once the place of residence of various Habsburgs and in which Emperor Ferdinand II erected a mighty mausoleum in the seventeenth century, had quite an international ambience in the nineteenth century; according to Arthur Polzer, in the capital of the Steiermark 'almost all the nations of Europe [...] were represented'.

The name of the city comes from the Slovene word *gradec*, which means 'castle' and may indicate an early fortification of the Schlossberg (castle hill) which dominates the view of the city. Because of the many retired people living in Graz (above all, officers from all parts of the empire) the city also bore the nickname Pensioneropolis...

Graz could claim to be 'a city both of the past and the future': it was full of people who had a rich past behind them and a rich future ahead of them. To the present, however, the city appeared 'in a certain sense lost in reverie'. Certainly, Graz had a significant metal industry, and thanks to the southern railway between Vienna with Trieste, a lively traffic in trade; but the great political events of the time appeared only as light or heavier clouds on a distant horizon. Anastasius Grün had extolled Graz as a port of calm amid the storms of a dynamic age. All the more were the balls, soirées, theatre performances and social events of all kinds able to govern the feelings of the inhabitants.

★

At the beginning of 1876 the Polzers moved into lodgings near the Schlossberg in Zinzendorfgasse in order to move shortly afterwards into the neighbouring Beethovenstrasse, where they would stay for the next five years. For the musical and artistic family atmosphere encouraged above all by Sefine and Christine Polzer, there could not have been a better street name.

The new couple in the city on the Mur were not only soon widely known but also widely appreciated. Within a short period of time, the naturally friendly character of Christine Polzer and the convivial nature of her husband had gained for them the highest status in Graz society. Invitations from the Polzers were sought after and if a soirée were held elsewhere, the question was whether Christine Polzer would also be there. At intimate musical evenings, which were arranged in her honour, she was invited to sing, a request with which she gladly complied. Hardly less gifted in the art of singing than her mother-in-law, she practised almost every day with the help of good teachers. Her performances must have been moving. 'When she sang *lieder* by Schumann,' remembered Arthur, 'I thought he must have created them just for my mother. I never heard the *lieder* cycle *Frauenliebe und Leben* (A Woman's Love and Life) sung with such soulfulness and inwardness by anyone else.' He quickly added: 'Many professional musicians shared my view.'[21]

This warm-hearted, artistic woman, who also had certain sensitive and psychic gifts and an intuitive knowledge of character which was seldom wrong, soon discovered what an incomparable supporter of her artistic and family concerns her mother-in-law was. Every Thursday Christine and her husband Julius took care to go to their mother's residence in Radetzkystrasse for dinner. It was a fixture in the family's week at which everything was always discussed that was going on in the Polzer family as well as in the city.

Almost daily, Sefine Polzer attended the Graz regional theatre, where she had her own permanent box. Even with her increasingly weakening eyesight, which eventually led, after two failed operations, to complete blindness, she continued with her beloved habit.

> Punctually, a few minutes before the start of the performance, her coach would roll up at a slow trot. It was already somewhat old-fashioned, everything about it had become old: the coach itself, the coachman, the horses and the servant, who carried a footstool into her box. Every evening she would sit in the theatre, wearing a black or violet silk dress with a little mobcap above her centrally parted hair, dark glasses over her blind eyes, a delicate smile around her mouth, a fan in her hand.[22]

And what was not still performed at that time! How much the theatre-goers still loved the great classics of European theatre! And what wonderful actors of real character were on stage to admire! What a feast when once again the unforgettably great Kainz was performing in a guest role!

Sefine Polzer already took her grandsons to the theatre when they were in their first year at school. Arthur recalls performances of Shakespeare's *Julius Caesar*, and by Schiller *Maria Stuart*, *The Maid of Orleans* and the *Wallenstein* trilogy. It was no wonder therefore, that the Polzer boys soon felt drawn to amateur dramatics groups which were then flourishing in Graz. Naturally, they liked to while away the time in the tastefully furnished rooms in Radetzkystrasse, where they were often invited for meals and where there were so many new things to learn.

Sefine Polzer especially sought to encourage Arthur's talent for painting, for the most fruitful education was and remained in her eyes that of the gentle hand of the arts. They had always helped her to stay young well into old age and she preserved along with her hearty sense of humour a rare intrepidity. When the roof truss of her house caught fire once she did not allow the incident to disturb her composure and looked on with secret enjoyment at the commotion among her frightened servants.

★

While the two brothers were staying with their grandmother or with their sister at the home of their cousins Karl and Lothar, whose house was only a few doors from theirs, their father's attendance at his duties satisfied him less and less by the day. 'What a difference there is between my position in Lemberg and Pilsen and that here in Graz!' he wrote in his notebook in exasperation. In Pilsen he had served under a highly cultivated superior, but in Graz he had to put up with a very weak man.

> After he [his superior, the divisional commander] had come to the end of his petty ideas and calculations, he plagued me with his views of art and showed me some paintings he had done himself. I was interested neither in the one nor the other.

And with rather ambiguous satisfaction Julius Polzer then added: 'Pleasant social relations made up for the many miseries of my duties.'[23]

When in the year 1877 Julius Polzer was once more due to be transferred—and indeed for the second or third time in a year—he began to think seriously about taking the next opportunity offered to retire from the service. He first, of course, obeyed the relocation order—continued to attend to his military duties with great conscientiousness—and moved, at first without his family and without difficulty to Vienna; he then sought out the regimental doctor and had his eyes checked; he was suffering from a growing, very likely inherited, weakness in his vision. Shortly afterwards followed his transfer into retirement, with which the military career of Julius, Ritter von Polzer was finally terminated. He was at this point 35 years old. At once he was free of all the bonds of an occupation and thanks to the continuing inheritance from his father he had the financial means to support his new freedom.

Such a liberation in mid-life from the external obligations of an occupation and from the need to earn money appears, with variations, to be rather typical of many men in the Polzer/Hoditz family. We have seen this signature already in the lives of Franziskus Josephus Philippus von Hoditz und Wolframitz, that solitary thinker of the seventeenth century; it appeared again with the 'Wondrous Count' von Rosswald; later again with Julius Polzer's father, who came into his inheritance and then wrote short stories. It would also play a role in the life of *Ludwig* Polzer.

Thus freed from the burden of his duties, Julius could now turn with all his energies to tasks within his family circle. He gave much careful thought to the education of his sons, who from the autumn of 1876 had to be prepared to enter high school by means of private lessons, which Julius himself partly undertook.

The boys' daily regime was very tightly organized. They had breakfast at 7.30 a.m. At 9 they were to be in the house's entrance hall. Here their father put them through exercises and did gymnastics with them until 10 o'clock. At exactly 10 o'clock Mr Millwitsch arrived to give the boys lessons in various subjects until 12 o'clock. Of Mr Millwitsch's instruction Arthur Polzer records:

> When the bell sounded at 10 o'clock he arrived in our study room in which everything had to be prepared for the lesson. On the desk the textbooks, the writing slates and exercise books, pencils, pens, ink and crayons. The large blackboard had to be cleaned, the chalks laid out, the board sponge moistened. My brother Ludwig and I sat opposite one another. The teacher sat between us at the narrow side of the table. The lesson began with a short prayer calling on the Holy Spirit. Then we had to show him our exercises, which he quickly looked through, corrected and recorded. Mr Millwitsch, who was always dressed in a long black coat, may have been about 40 years old when he first came to us. He had a full, very red face with good-natured eyes looking through his spectacles. He was smoothly shaven and looked like a clergyman. He must have had an excellent method of teaching. With an almost rhythmical regularity he brought us every day a small step forward in our knowledge [...] My greatest interest was in the stories from the Bible. I created in my mind very imaginative pictures which stuck with me. At the end of the hour, actually the hours, for they were two, every day Mr Millwitsch wrote in a fine, neat and tidy calligraphic script a list of headings for the classification of our behaviour, effort, and individual objects of study. The lesson was then ended with a prayer of thanksgiving. We had to show the list to our father before the meal.[24]

Ludwig and Arthur loved this teacher very much. Not least perhaps, because the skilful pedagogue was able to give them the feeling that all the knowledge that he was giving them must eventually lead to that spirit, deserving of all honour, who was called on before every lesson...

The midday meal was then taken at one o'clock. In the afternoons always came a long walk with the French governess and their little sister, which Arthur, at least, did not like very much. The brothers always had to walk in front of the other two and were only allowed to speak French the whole time. The routes were always the same: the Castle Hill, the city park, Schloss Eggenberg etc. The only enjoyable distractions for Arthur and also for Ludwig were beetles, butterflies and minerals, which they were keen to collect.

After returning from the walk they had a snack. Then they were to do their homework. The boys' day ended with a supper, which they took in the children's room. By 8.30 p.m. they were usually in bed.

In the spring they were allowed to stay in the garden in the afternoons and do their schoolwork in the summerhouse.

Much-desired relief from this rather monotonous life came on Sundays and festival days. After breakfast the two boys usually went with their mother to the nearby Gothic Leerkirche church, the oldest church in the whole of Graz.[25] Arthur was always impressed by the stained windows which stemmed from the fourteenth and fifteenth centuries. These visits to the church with their mother—their father preferred to cultivate his religious inclinations in the quiet of his own soul—seem to have pleased the boys no less than the Sunday games with their cousins Karl and Lothar or with other children in the neighbourhood. But the greatest cries of delight always came from the boys when their parents proposed an outing in the countryside. Such a day would be a Sunday of Sundays... 'A carriage would be ordered, a so-called Landauer, that was lockable and so big that we could all comfortably fit in. The greatest fun was to be able sit up next to the coachman on the box seat and occasionally take the reins...'[26]

In the autumn of 1879 Ludwig entered the first class of the Graz State High School (Gymnasium) which was situated in the University building in the Old Town. On his way to school at the beginning of the '80s he often came across the much respected poet Robert Hamerling. Polzer later wrote:

> I always looked at him with interest when he passed me. He made such a friendly impression on me that although I never got to know him personally and somehow never came near him, the image of the man remained indelibly imprinted on my soul.[27]

Hamerling was then at the beginning of his 50s. The unexpectedly great success which greeted his 1866 verse epic Ahasver in Rom, enabled him to give up his teaching work and pursue his poetic intentions. And no city seemed to him more suited to this than Graz on the lovely Mur, where he lived till his death in the summer of 1889.

The Ahasver epic, a widely-loved work at the time is set in Rome in the age of the Emperor Nero and sought to help contemporaries towards a spiritual uplift by contrasting the modern age with the decaying empire of ancient Rome. Ludwig Polzer certainly read the epic by this poet whom he respected during his time in Graz. In doing so, he took into his deeply receptive soul a living seed of all his later studies of and thoughts about Nero and the circle around him.

He later wrote: 'The last heroes of a cultural epoch that has faded today lived in my soul like awakening calls to spiritual duties for a newly beginning epoch.'[28] He will indeed have felt this awakening call while reading Hamerling's epic poem *Ahasver*.

This 'awakening call [...]' came at first only very quietly, scarcely noticeable'. But the feelings of the young high school student were not only able to turn to the awakening influences of *German* cultural life, as they could be experienced through the works of Goethe, Schiller, Grün, Grillparzer and even Hamerling:

> Into this atmosphere led by a German spirituality other individual peoples blended their ethnic qualities and merits as if seeking for a reciprocal expansion to a full image of humanity. Nowhere but in Austria could this multiplicity of peoples be experienced in the same sensitive, spiritual way; one did not find oneself there in the philistine cell of an enclosed unitary national state; one had dealings with everybody and adjusted oneself mutually in freedom. One could experience oneself as *a global child of the middle* and one felt one's homeland to be a place with which everyone was satisfied. One learned English and French and could be equally as enthused by the dramas of Shakespeare as by the novels of Alexandre Dumas, George Sand, Dostoyevsky and Tolstoy; one felt related to the people of east and west.[29]

The experience of a real cosmopolitanism that brings people together can be seen as the best fruit of the Polzer boys' youth in Graz. Looking back to the self-evidently tolerant 'multi-ethnic mood' which today has once again disappeared*, despite the international nature of communications technology, Ludwig Polzer writes:

> Even though I was not conscious of it in my youth [...] one was a member of this many-sided, differentiated ethnic spiritual nature which was uniting and harmonizing; one experienced that one stood in something spiritual that was wanted by the world order itself. That was the environment out of which I was able to understand '*that Austria would have had to be created if it did not already exist*'.[30]

---

* In the context of the Balkan wars of the 1990s—*transl.*

9. The High School Years

Midway through the high school years of Ludwig and Arthur Polzer in Graz came a watershed of a psychological and spiritual nature. If, until their entry into high school, the two brothers had taken to heart the cultural breadth of the multi-ethnic state in a mood of unclouded sunshine, the first shadows now stole into the boys' souls, even if in differing ways.

Arthur, who came top of his first class in the summer of 1881, was suddenly and inexplicably afflicted by feelings of depression. His condition worsened to such an extent that the family doctor referred the case to the well-known psychologist and psychiatrist Krafft-Ebing, who was then working in Graz and who was able to calm the anxious parents. They, however, decided on a period of exclusively private instruction for Arthur. His father took on to teach him mathematics and also continued to teach both brothers projective geometry. For the former engineering corps officer, mathematics was the only exact science, and he taught it so thoroughly and comprehensively that when Arthur returned to school he had already learned almost the entire content of high school mathematics.

Ludwig felt unsatisfied with much of what daily life at school brought him but that dissatisfaction expressed itself less in an outward form; he gradually came to feel a growing mistrust in *the whole way* things were taught at his high school. 'Already in middle school,' he wrote in his Prague memoirs,

> the way things were taught made me feel that the wisdom of the world should not be presented to people in this manner and that another way should be found in another place. I could not grasp it precisely, but the feeling was that the wisdom of the world was being deliberately hidden.[31]

While he had experienced in his life at home and then in his lessons with Mr Millwitsch and his father a feeling of being on the path to this wisdom, Ludwig Polzer now felt in the high school years that followed as if the intention was to mislead him about the wealth of wisdom that was already evident to him.[32] What a contrast!

While only a short time before he had begun his daily private lessons with a prayer to that same spirit which the Catholic church had sought to 'abolish' at the Eighth Ecumenical Council in Constantinople in the year 869—exactly 1000 years before his own birth—he now experienced at high school how much a mechanical non-spirit had permeated the nature of official education in Habsburg Austria. It was as if there had descended 'a nightmare on my soul, a numbing shadow which created fear, which killed the joy of life'.[33] Yet it was like a balsam for his soul whenever he saw the respected Hamerling in the street; a warm pulse of spiritual life seemed still to stream even physically from this man.

In February 1881, in Ludwig's second year at high school, the family moved house again. At 25 Sporrgasse, at the edge of the well-preserved Old Town they were able to rent the first floor of a magnificent building. The house was very close to Ludwig's school, to the Schlossberg and to the Court bakery. The building was the Palais Saurau, built at the end of the sixteenth century, highlighted and described in all the better guide books to the Steiermark. The facade itself presented an unmistakeable sight: the arch of the monumental entranceway, above which was a mighty coat of arms in stone, was closed off at the top by a mighty wrought-iron lattice, while under the gable roof the upper body of a Turk rose into the air swinging a scimitar—a lively reminder of a Turkish occupation of Graz in 1532.

For five years this house was home for the Polzers and provided Ludwig and Arthur with far more than just rest and recuperation from the tensions of their high school education. 'We felt we had arrived in a fairy-tale kingdom,' wrote Arthur. 'The building was for us children the ful-filment of all our dreams.'[34]

The furnishings were of the eighteenth century. The rooms had gold-embellished wood panelling, and were heated by large tiled stoves; they had painted, leather wallpaper and mirrors, fitted with bracket tables, that reached to the ceiling. From the side wing, where the children lived, one could walk into a splendidly laid-out nature park through which a winding path passed by fruit trees up to the clock tower on the Schlossberg—an ideal spot for youthful adventures...

From the drawing room a glass door led into the main garden; in the gravelled area of which, separated off from the dense shrubbery, were garden benches, tables and chairs. Arthur recalled:

> There we would sit in the evenings with our parents when the laburnum trees, wisteria, lilac and later, the roses were in bloom. From the adjoining St Paul's church next door the sounds of the organ and the choir would come over. A special magic, an almost solemn mood [...] spread over this secluded spot.[35]

The first floor is supported at the rear side with columns with Roman-style capitals. On one of the walls of the inner courtyard, not far from these columns, a plaque with an inscription engraved in Latin. This building thus impressed itself on Ludwig's feeling 'for the weaving of the spirit in space and time'[36] in that its whole style and many of its individual features spoke to him of various aspects of epochs past. And if Ludwig Polzer's later interest in the historical past of mankind awoke already in his youth, the Palais Saurau certainly played its part in that.

The area around Graz is very rich in traces of Roman times. Already in the year 15 BC the Steiermark was raised to the status of a province and named *Noricum*. About 30 kilometres to the south of the city there lay at that time a very important provincial town: Flavia Solva. Built on Celtic foundations, the settlement was a main transit point to the Balkans, to Pannonia, Dalmatia and Moesia, as these Balkan provinces were then called. Numerous excavations of coins have shown that there was active trade in the area, while a bust of Mars and a shrine of Isis testify to the existence of religious cults. The town was probably visited by Trajan, under whom the Roman Empire reached its greatest expansion, and it is no less probable that his successor Hadrian stopped in Flavia Solva on the way to Pannonia.

In Graz itself our Polzer brothers, on their way to the theatre, often passed by the special building which, although not of Roman origin, was built in the Roman style and from which a Roman spirit still radiates today: the Mausoleum of Emperor Ferdinand II. Although the building, which dates from the early seventeenth century, is considered to be a prime example of Mannerist architecture north of the Alps and shows a mix of Renaissance and Baroque elements, the overall impression it gives is one of a building from Roman antiquity that would be no less suited to Rome than to Graz. The Graz Mausoleum is not without reason described as a piece of 'Rome in the Steiermark'.[37]

Thus the Emperor's monument on the way to the State High School represented another piece of living history. Its heavy, massive facade may have revealed more to Ludwig Polzer than the history books at school. At any rate, in history class it brought him only a 'satisfactory' mark in the fourth year, which is what he achieved in most other subjects—with the exception of religion, in which he was 'excellent' from the first class onwards.

But it was not only dead emperors that were celebrated in Graz: in July 1883 Franz Joseph paid the city a highly personal visit on the occasion of the celebration of the 600th anniversary of the House of Austria's possession of the Steiermark. This was a special occasion for the Polzer family. The boys' father brought out his long unused parade-ground uniform and took his sons to the station where in *Kaiserwetter*, (literally, emperor's weather)—sunshine and cloudless skies—the Austrian monarch's train was respectfully expected. The great man eventually descended from his saloon car and walked along the red carpet. What then occurred shows how this emperor knew how to make short shrift of excessively formal demonstrations of respect. Franz Joseph walked up to the local dignitaries, who were lined up according to rank and post, whereupon the mayor began to introduce them: 'Herr Council member so-and-so,' and with a hand movement towards the Emperor: 'His Majesty the Emperor.' When the mayor turned to the third man in the line, Franz Joseph said, smiling, 'I believe, dear Mr Mayor, that the gentlemen might know me already.'

Among the dignitaries, who the Emperor greeted very personally, was also Baron Julius von Polzer. 'With pride I saw how he also spoke to my father,' reported Arthur.[38] 'I was most excited for the Emperor was hardly more than two steps away from me.' His brother Ludwig must have felt something similar.

★

In that same summer of 1883 Ludwig Polzer visited his aunt Mathilde in Modern (Modor, in Hungarian) an old small town on the southern slopes of the Little Carpathians, not far from Pressburg (today, Bratislava). The Slovakian capital in those days was part of a county in Hungarian territory, to which Modern also belonged. For the first time in his life Ludwig was now on Hungarian soil. He returned to Graz so excited about the trip that his parents promised to spend the next summer holiday with the children in this beautiful place. Modern was already linked to the Hoditz family in many ways.[39] It would now become the *Polzer-Hoditz* family's favourite holiday destination. In their first stay there they rented a house called 'The Sands', a woodcutter's house in the forest area around Modern.

On the way there, they would stop for a few days in Vienna. Although Ludwig had already travelled through the city the year before, Julius Polzer now took care that this stay would be his eldest son's first real visit to the metropolis, as he knew all the important sights of his own birth-place like the back of his hand. They visited the art gallery in Belvedere, St Stephen's Cathedral, the Hofburg Palace, paid visits on noble families known to them, were thrilled by the acting of Charlotte Wolter and Josef Lewinsky in the old Burgtheater and enjoyed ices at the Dehmel con-fectionary shop, which in those days was near the theatre. And of course they went to the Prater Park and the Wurstelprater amusement park.

They stayed at the Hotel Matschakerhof and breakfasted at a coffee shop on the famous Graben (street) where the children were bought some unforgettably delicious vanilla kipferl (biscuits).

The days seemed to have flown by when the family boarded the Danube steamer. Soon the noise of the city had disappeared and another new world appeared to the children. This new world of the Danube countryside impressed itself all the more deeply on their feelings as the fascinating experiences of Vienna gradually ebbed away. The sight of the Hungarian plain made a strong impression on Arthur. He wrote:

> Until then I had always seen the horizon bounded by mountains and only narrow rapid waterfalls in valleys. Now I was travelling along the sluggish, grey waters of the Danube [...] through the pastures of a huge plain. Everything appeared to me more significant, lovelier and larger than what I had seen until now. A peculiar, unfamiliar feeling came over me when the Marchfeld plain lay spread out before us. I felt I knew what I was looking at, that I had seen it long ago. Pictures from the past arose within me, a glimmering memory of an experience far back in time ...

He added:

> I have no wish to link this special feeling with any philosophical ideas but I believe it has to do with mysterious depths not only of our earthly soul life but of one reaching far beyond it, at any rate, of something more than our school learning ever dreams of.[40]

After a very short visit to a very eccentric Hoditz aunt in Pressburg, the travelling family finally, 'with an unusual amount of luggage', boarded the train for Modern. Here they had been long expected by Mathilde Hoditz and were heartily greeted by her. But the final destination of their summer hopes, the holiday house 'The Sands' was only reached after a long, bumpy coach ride.

The small size of the accommodation and the primitive state of the furnishings appalled Julius Polzer, who had never enjoyed seclusion. But when a neighbour from the town assured them that the female cook they had engaged was very well-known for her skill, Julius was mollified. And when, moreover, at the house of this neighbour, whose fine cello-playing they were soon acquainted with, Julius found that his wife was a connoisseur of Schopenhauer, he soon warmed to their new holiday home.

His two sons only needed to cast a shy glance at the neighbour's lovely daughters to know that *they* had come to the right place. They quickly made friends with the woodcutters in the area and thus discovered the beauties of nature there with which they were so unaccustomed. In the mornings after breakfast their father buried himself in the *Grazer Tagespost* (newspaper) which he had arranged to be delivered. Afterwards he gave Arthur some extra help with his mathematics. One of the neighbour's lovely daughters later stimulated Arthur's interest in learning Greek. He also sat himself from time to time at the easel and painted landscapes.

The boys went along on a hunting party, which made a great

impression on them. And so the Polzer family passed the summer months of the year 1884, in very pleasant occupations and pastimes.

During the holiday the first municipal villa was built in the area and Julius Polzer without hesitation assured his family before their return to the Steiermark that he would rent the comfortable villa for next year's holiday.

★

The year 1885 saw the family's last relocation within the city of Graz. Despite its exclusive status, the house in the Sporrgasse had proved to be uncomfortable in various respects. The family now returned to the Leonhardquartier where they had had apartments twice before. The comparatively modest accommodation was situated right next to the Leonhard Cemetery where, apart from their grandfather who had died in 1874, many well-known personalities in Austrian public life were buried.

The family spent the summer, as planned the year before, in the comfortable villa near Modern. This summer was a special one for Ludwig. Arthur recalled 'My brother, who no longer enjoyed his high school studies and who had a great liking for the cavalry, was preparing himself for entry into the Cavalry Cadets' School in Mährisch-Weiss-kirchen.' Already in the winter and spring of that year he had had riding lessons and had soon begun 'to speak only of horses and of young friends who had chosen the same career'. With an almost envious admiration Ludwig and Arthur looked up especially to two of these friends, Fritz and Cari Wurmbrand. In Arthur's eyes, these brothers were,

> prime examples of élégance. They were a few years older than us, and when we were still at high school, they never carried schoolbooks and, with a certain persistence, failed in their studies. We found this all very swanky and were amazed by it just as much as we were by their elegant short yellow spring coats and their fine cravats.

Once again the summer holidays went by in fine and harmonious mood. Aunt Mathilde had her pianino brought over from her house in Modern 'and so on rainy days we had pleasant musical evenings in which the neighbour they had got to know the previous year played his cello and Christine Polzer sang *lieder*'. Years later Arthur recalled the sounds of those evenings, which were characteristic of the mood of the summer months: 'the heavy steps of the woodcutters coming home from work [. . .], then in the stillness, the sounds of the forest, the long drawn-out call of the owls and often, still late at night the sound of the cello, "Du bist die Ruh" or "Ave Maria" by Schubert.'

Occasionally, someone they knew came to visit who played Hungarian tunes on the pianino. At the end of the holidays there was a wedding at which Ludwig and Arthur had to be groom's ushers and Marie-Sefine a bridesmaid.

How idyllic these years of family life could be in the empire of the Dual Monarchy! And how little the family then even suspected in the magical mood of those summer evenings that another kind of evening twilight was already deepening, which would soon cast its dark shadows over *the entire empire*, plunging it into gloom and blackness . . .

A comparative glance at Ludwig's and Arthur's school reports from this period is instructive. In almost all subjects Arthur was top of his class while Ludwig, with his growing suspicion that 'the wisdom of the world' was more concealed than revealed by school learning, rarely achieved higher than a middle-ranking position in any subject, which can hardly have bothered him. A comparison of his first report, from the summer of 1880, with the later ones, and especially with the last one, which he received in 1885, at the end of his sixth class, reveals something remarkable: there are some subjects in which from the beginning to the end of his studies he only achieved mediocre results; these were the languages—Latin, Greek and German. In only one subject, religion, did he achieve the grade 'excellent' year on year—with one exception, which was 'praiseworthy'. In one other subject, however—and this is of special interest in relation to Ludwig Polzer's school graduation in 1885—his grades improved every year, in Geography and History, which in those days, in view of their interrelationship, were taught as one subject. Here he had begun with an unsatisfactory grade of 'satisfactory' but from the fifth class on to his final report, he had improved it by three grades to 'excellent'. At the point of his departure from school life this double subject Geography and History is the most important for *it is the only one which shows development in his interest in learning*. It may therefore be expected that *after* the end of his school studies, he would remain interested in learning more in this area; perhaps his exit from the world of study can be explained not only by his general lack of interest at school or by his prevalent enthusiasm for horses and cavalry, but rather, was determined by his longing to extend his worthwhile knowledge of geography and history into the area of practical life—before it could begin to gather dust at school.

The development that now followed may in any case not exclude such a motif of a change of course on the part of the 16-year-old. Before school could utterly conceal from him all real wisdom in the important areas of geography and history, he chose instead to go on his own journey of discovery, knowing that wisdom was to be found 'in other ways and other places'.

10. Departures and Visits

As soon as he decided to enter the Cavalry Cadets' School, Ludwig was once again able to feel joy in life. He was filled with anticipation at the prospect of the opening up of new opportunities in life for which he had long yearned, and it soon drove away the nightmare that had oppressed him in high school.

When he set out in the summer of 1886 to step out into the great wide world, Ludwig Polzer really took leave for the first time of his parents and siblings. With this step, as he saw it, the second phase of his life begins,[41] which shows that he regarded the radical change signified by this summer as more important than the family's relocation from Pilsen to Graz or his high school entrance.

Everything that he had experienced until this day had been set in motion, carried forward and settled in a harmonious way by his parents. That was now at an end.

Ludwig's departure was also a signal event for Arthur. Later, he took it as a stimulus to reflect on the relationship which bound him to his brother and which would bind him further in the future:

> We had been brothers for 15 years, and this had now come to an end. Our life paths now divided. We took up different occupations, and had different destinies and in many areas had different ideas about life. But the bond of brotherhood which had bound us tightly as children in our parents' home did not loosen throughout our lives.

We shall frequently find this confirmed.

Of his relationship to his brother Ludwig in their early teens, Arthur writes: 'When we were children my brother was my steward. He was well-suited for that. He always had something new he wanted me to try.'

That was exactly what Arthur sorely missed in the first months after Ludwig's departure. In autumn 1886 he wrote to Ludwig in Mährisch-Weisskirchen in a friendly but critical tone, revealing of his attachment:

> I am very much looking forward to Christmas and I'll be able to challenge you in riding. Then you'll be able to show off your excellent talent as a steward but I'll let it all wash over me and look forward to that time, despite all the inevitable stewarding which you can't do any more now.

Shortly afterwards, there was another leave-taking.

On 4 March 1887 Arthur went to the theatre with his grandmother who had in the meantime become blind. It was a performance of Bizet's

Carmen. After the first act Sefine suddenly said to Arthur: 'I am going to sit on the bench at the back and you sit in my place. I have no idea why I sit at the front—a silly old habit.'[42]

It was the first time in over 30 years that Sefine Polzer did not sit in her usual seat. It was her last evening at the theatre. Shortly after the beginning of the second act she became unsettled and said: 'I don't feel very well, I have pains. Perhaps I should go home.' The nurse who accompanied her immediately agreed, and Arthur hurried to the doorman and had him call a carriage. He led his grandmother out of the theatre and into the carriage and helped her into the carriage. Then he returned to his seat in the theatre as she had expressly bade him do. Just before the carriage left she had said to him: 'It will be over soon.' Three days later, without any great struggle at death's door, Sefine Polzer left the stage of this life; she was 79 years old.

The theatre thus played a key role in the life of this personality who had been so important for her grandson's inner development. Forty years before, after a performance in Vienna, she had become acquainted with her husband 'because of an accident, some bad weather and an umbrella' and now, in the middle of a performance of *Carmen* and in the presence of her grandson, the former singer modestly took her departure from her eventful life at the side of that interesting man. The circle of her life could have rounded itself out in no more suitable manner. 'But art,' declared the *Grazer Tagespost* at the end of a lovely obituary, 'was dearer to her heart than all else.' It was shown even in the manner of her death.

In the Polzer household no partisan discussions of political questions were allowed; and loyalty to the emperor was held to be self-evident. The visit of Crown Prince Rudolf and his wife Stephanie in October 1887 was therefore followed and accompanied with the greatest interest. What had they not heard of Rudolf's extravagant love of the hunt or of his criticisms of the nobility or the clergy, or the gossip about his romantic adventures which Arthur at least imagined more romantically in his fantasy than they had actually been. During the two days of festivities in Graz, to which Christine and her husband were invited, the agile Arthur managed several times to get a close look at the honoured royal pair on their progress through the city. What great hopes many especially in the younger generation had placed on this young heir to the throne, who sought to forge new paths amidst the worsening conflicts between the empire's ethnic groups! Arthur's expectations had been so great, but great too was his disappointment: 'The Crown Prince [. . .] gave me the impression of a tired, bored man,' he stated soberly. 'He sat huddled up in the carriage, was visibly absent-minded in his greetings and did not look up. He seemed to me pale and almost grey.'

Crown Prince Rudolf's physical and psychological health was at that time in fact in a very bad state; the hope of taking on political responsibility alongside his father in the foreseeable future had almost disappeared and he turned more and more to thoughts of suicide. So it was that this visit by the heir to the throne also had about it something of an air of departure as if it suggested Rudolf's approaching end.

Arthur certainly related to his brother all the details of this so disappointingly impressive visit when Ludwig came home to Graz for the Christmas holidays.

In this Christmas period there was another reason for concern about a worrisome atmosphere. After the abdication of Prince Alexander of Bulgaria there was the danger of military conflict with Russia, whose potential aggression against Austria any clear-minded observer of events had had to reckon with since the manoeuvres of the Russian Czar in the Russo-Turkish War of 1853. Arthur recorded that when the Polzer family were sitting in Julius' study on Christmas Eve after their Christmas dinner,

> the conversation was almost exclusively about how a war with Russia would turn out and what consequences it would have. My father was very pessimistic; my two uncles and my brother in the hussars were much more confident. My mother was only worried, and very worried, about Ludwig. His departure at the end of the Christmas holidays was therefore especially hard for her. On 31 December she wrote in her diary: 'I go into the year 1888 with dread. It is still not at all decided whether we are faced with war or peace. Like a nightmare the thought lies on my heart that my beloved child will be drawn into a war at such a tender age.' How great must have been the relief when the danger was once again fended off . . .

In July 1888 Arthur took his final exams at school and was 'happy to have behind me the high school which I had long felt I had grown out of'. Shortly afterwards, Ludwig again had a few days' leave in Graz. He was in the last year at the Cadets' School, in which he clearly felt well and happy. Although at high school he had never had any special achievements to his credit, amongst the more than 60 cadets at the Cadets' School, he was first in class and therefore, in accordance with an old custom, was assured of graduating as a lieutenant, which made Julius Polzer extremely happy. Arthur recalled that Ludwig spent those days in Graz 'mostly on the sofa reading a French novel'. Did he perhaps have in his hand George Sand's *Consuelo* and was he amusing himself reading about the eccentric behaviour of his ancestor the 'Wondrous Count'?

11. 'Austria Will Perish...'

Ludwig Polzer passed out of the Cavalry Cadets' School in Mährisch-Weisskirchen on 18 August 1888—the birthday of His Majesty Emperor Franz Joseph[43]—as the best student in his class and was ordered to report to the *Prinz zu Windisch-Grätz No. 11* Regiment of Hussars, then stationed in Vienna. His entire seven-year long period of service in the regiment would be unblemished.

On 12 October of the same year the 19-year-old saw a performance of *Iphigenia* which made a strong impression on him and which, due to certain circumstances, seemed symptomatically important for him. He writes about it:

> I saw for the first time a performance of *Iphigenia*; it was the last performance at the old Hofburg Theatre in Vienna before it was demolished. The actress Wolter played Iphigenia; the whole experience of the evening was a powerful one. It was the first and only time I was in that world-famous theatre that was adapted to the social circles of the Austrian Court. It was too small and too intimate to be able to cope with modern circumstances. A shame that the whole thing was pulled down. I felt a kind of sadness about it. It was the first stone that started rolling, though I didn't think so at the time, that would end with the whole structure of the Court so soon lying in ruins. Art disappeared from the Hofburg and moved to the Ringstrasse!!

The experience of that evening, which can be compared in a certain sense with Arthur's disappointment with the Crown Prince, awoke in the 19-year-old a particular and fundamental mood that continued throughout his life, which had until then only been slumbering but which lived very strongly in many spiritually striving Austrians of the nineteenth century. Ludwig Polzer put it in the following words: 'Austria will perish...' This mood is the exact complement to that which we encountered in chapter nine: 'Austria would have had to be created if it did not already exist.' Every wakeful person living in the Habsburgs' Empire was familiar with these two polar moods; the tension between them worked over years and decades like a creative disquiet in many people and loosened up the ground for many valuable, cultural creations which Austria was able to present to the world. To do this, however, the poles had to remain in a relative state of balance. As the new century approached, the weight of this balance threatened to move more and more towards the increasingly heavy mood of general decline.

Few events of the time could have contributed more to the spread of *this* mood than the sudden death of Crown Prince Rudolf and his lover Mary Vetsera in the early hours of 30 January 1889. The full circumstances of the lovers' double suicide remain unclear to this day, but Mayerling—Rudolf's hunting lodge not far from Vienna, where the tragedy occurred—was immediately felt in Austria as a real symbol of the looming fall of the entire empire.

Great hopes, especially amongst the younger generation, had, as already mentioned, been placed on Rudolf, as Arthur Polzer's account of his visit to Graz could bear witness. Where constant muddle had become the highest maxim of government under the Ministry of Eduard Taaffe, the Crown Prince, 33 years old at the time of his death, would have been open-minded, liberal and strong-willed enough to promote progressive impulses in Austria, impulses which could both have strengthened and lengthened the empire's grip on life.

Rudolf was very concerned about the problem of the oppression of the Slavs which, since the *Ausgleich* (Compromise) with Hungary in December 1867, with the passing months and years had ominously become a 'Non-compromise' with the Empire's Slavic peoples. He was very critical of the politics of his father, but because of his position was able to express his criticism anonymously in articles, for example, published in *Neuen Wiener Tagblatt* of which his friend Moritz Szeps was the editor. In the Emperor's government Rudolf who, like Empress Elisabeth loved Hungary but not its predominance in the Empire, soon had archenemies who were anti-Slavic and pro-Hungarian. He also thought of effectively limiting, if not breaking, the harmful influence of the Catholic clergy. He thus also created opponents within the clergy. Franz Joseph, conservative and cautious, was concerned to keep his unpredictable son far from the responsibilities of government for as long as possible. It was little wonder that life's prospects seemed ever dimmer to the Archduke!

Many contemporaries could sense something of the world-historical weight of Rudolf's death. Alongside Hermann Grimm, Karl Julius Schröer was the greatest Goethe scholar of his time, and when he heard the news of the deaths at Meyerling, he uttered the single fateful word 'Nero!'[44] Rudolf's death reminded him of the burning of Rome and he felt that the dramatic events at Meyerling were the first act of the clear decline and fall of the whole Empire.

Karl Kraus once described Austria as 'the test case of world decline' and after Rudolf's death the mood indicated by this macabre expression steadily spread among wider circles in the cisleithanian (Austrian) half of the Austro-Hungarian Empire, especially in academic and artistic circles, among people therefore who in their work had formerly borne in themselves something of the polar opposite mood of world *ascent*. One felt oneself imperceptibly to be part of a world of yesteryear; 'today' seemed to recede from view; one no longer dared to speak of a tomorrow which people had once spoken of with earnestness and confidence. One could sense from one's contemporaries on all sides how that Janus-like, fundamental feeling of decline was certainly growing in one form or another.

Just half a year after Rudolf's death another significant Austrian departed this life: the poet Robert Hamerling, who is almost forgotten today and who we met already on Ludwig's way to school. In his poetry Hamerling had once dealt with the age of Nero in his Ahasver epic and had become famous, and Ludwig Polzer loved this poet. While Ludwig himself was serving Emperor and Fatherland, the young Rudolf Steiner travelled to Graz for Hamerling's funeral, standing in, as it were, for Ludwig and for many young people at least to show his respect for the deceased Hamerling, who in life he had only known through letters. With Robert Hamerling, one of the last who strove for a true spiritual life was laid to rest. His death could be experienced as a spiritual sunset following Rudolf's death and the extinguishing of future-oriented *politics*. It was a significant experience for the young Steiner, who was then in Weimar, basing himself on the work of Goethe and conceiving the development of a new realism of ideas based on a living *praxis*.

★

There was no doubt about it: the precarious situation of the double monarchy was in political terms not least due to the constitutional dualism that had existed since 8 December 1867, the so-called Compromise (*Ausgleich*): Hungary now had the privilege of its own constitution and in this respect stood on *equal* footing with the German-Austrians, and that meant, together with the Austrians, constitutionally, *over* all the Slavic nations such as the Czechs, Slovaks, Croats, Serbs and others who were all persistently denied their own parliament. In the eyes of the Slavic peoples, who were pressing for their rights, the Dual Empire seemed more and more like a political stalemate. The dilemma was intensified markedly when at the Berlin Congress of 1878 that followed the Russo-Turkish War, Austria-Hungary received the mandate to administer Bosnia-Herzegovina for 30 years.[45] It is worth noting from which direction this was proposed: it came from Britain's representative in Berlin, Lord Salisbury.[46] It is also noteworthy that at the Congress *on the same day* that the mandate was given to Austria-Hungary, the Great Powers officially confirmed Serbia's declaration of independence; furthermore, that same day was the Serbian national day of the commemoration of the Battle of the Field of Blackbirds in 1389. The Serbs who belonged to the Kingdom of Serbia celebrated their freedom; their brothers in the occupied region fell into servitude. A diplomatic time-bomb of ethnic rights had thus been set on 28 June 1878. It exploded on 28 June 1914 when the Austrian heir to the throne, Franz Ferdinand, was killed in Sarajevo (capital of Bosnia-Herzegovina) which had been occupied and then annexed by the Dual Monarchy. The string-pullers behind the assassination were, amongst others, members of semi-official brotherhoods that served the cause of 'Greater Serbia'.[47]

By taking on the mandate in 1878 and the following occupation of Bosnia-Herzegovina the problem of how to sort out the situation of the Slavs was not solved but considerably worsened. The South Slav question had now become a question of the empire's survival in its existing form—the Austrian Balkans had become Austria-Hungary's powder keg. Here the multi-ethnic state would have to have solved the nationalities problem concretely by the introduction of supra-national rules that would also have taken the Slavs into account. But really new ideas were lacking. Rudolf would perhaps have found them. Even Franz Ferdinand, the next heir to the throne, had decided to solve the Slav problem through positive politics instead of restrictive muddle; instead of a Dualism he was thinking of a Trialism. But Sarajevo put a well-planned stop to his efforts. The Emperor was too old and Hungary too bound. We shall speak later of the world-historical chance for his great-nephew, the monarchy's last emperor. The chance was missed, in any case.[48]

But were such internal weaknesses of the monarchy or failed developments the only cause of Austria's rapid collapse? There are symptoms and indications that Austria's downfall was not only deter-mined from within but that *it had been planned long before outside the Empire, and intensive action had been taken to realize those plans*. Certainly, this occurred mainly through intermediate channels but it was nonetheless all too effective.

In the Christmas 1890 issue of the satirical magazine *Truth* a map of Europe was published (see p. 65) which had the title 'The Kaiser's Dream'. This referred to the German Kaiser Wilhelm II, who was said to have been hypnotized at a distance to tell *Truth* of a dream he had had which vividly showed him the future political and geographical form of Europe. And what did the Kaiser see in the future?

Europe's monarchs had all disappeared and had been replaced by

The Kaiser's Dream, from Truth, Christmas number, 1890

republics. Notably, Germany had even been divided up into numerous 'republics'.

Russia was to remain whole in its post-monarchical form but here too the monarchy had disappeared and on the territory of Russia was written simply 'Russian Desert'. What was meant by that? Certainly not a project to deprive Russian territory of its water supply!

In the context as a whole, by 'desert' can only be meant: in the place of the fallen Czarist empire there would not appear, as in the other former monarchies, an already existing and historically tested form of the state; the Slavic empire in the East was rather to become a test-bed for as yet unproven forms of social life and communal life. That this indication actually corresponds to existing intentions within the politics of the Anglo-American West—which also affected Austria indirectly—will briefly be outlined in what follows.

In 1894 there appeared in London a printed volume containing six lectures which the Englishman C.G. Harrison had given in London in 1893 on the subject of *Occult Science, Theosophy and the Catholic Faith.*[49] In a fundamental sense Harrison's lectures show two things:

1) that international politics has traditionally been practised in the Anglo-American West with long-term perspectives—as has been done otherwise only by Rome
2) that in these politics factors are considered which mean nothing to conventional materialistic natural science.

To these belong the fact that not only the single human being but also whole peoples undergo a real development, from a kind of birth to a decline. There are older peoples who have already fulfilled their main historical tasks; others, who are influential in the present time or who will become so; and finally, peoples who will grow into their tasks and who at present are still at the stage of childhood. For certain Anglo-American circles, it has been clear for a long time that the English-speaking peoples must set the tone in the present cultural epoch. They see the Latin peoples on the contrary as in a state of decadence; the peoples with tasks *for the future* are the Slavs. The fundaments of Anglo-American politics (at least up to the present time!) which has proceeded from a western tradition of occultism can now be reduced to four main maxims:

1. The Anglo-American peoples are destined, *as in ancient times the Romans were,* for world domination.
2. Modern humanity shows the need for certain experiments to be conducted in the social field.

3. Such experiments can only be carried out on a large scale on the Slavic peoples.
4. In order to determine the shape of the future for Slavic peoples, the influence of Central Europe, especially that of Austria, must be excluded.

The exclusion of the European middle was therefore an *indirect* goal en route to the realization of the main aim of point 3.

While the first point was not undisguised in Harrison's lectures, that is all the more the case with the second and above all, the third points. Let us listen to the man himself:

> With the exception of the Slavonic peoples, of whom we shall speak presently, and a small Turanian element which is too insignificant element to deal with[*], the nations of modern Europe and their American and colonial offshoots represent the fifth sub-race of the great Aryan Root Race. [...] Let us turn to the Slavonic people, who belong to the sixth Aryan sub-race, and what do we find? A powerful empire which unites under a despotic government a number of local communes—Russia; the remains of a kingdom—Poland, whose only cohesive force is its religion, and which will be ultimately reabsorbed in the Russian Empire in spite of it. A number of tribes who, oppressed by the alien Turk, have thrown off the yoke, and have been artificially consolidated into little states, *whose independence, will last as long as, and no longer than, the next great European war.*
>
> What are all these but the characteristics of a sub-race in its infancy?

And in relation to the determination of the future of the Slavic peoples: 'Their destiny is to evolve a higher civilization of their own in the future.' And, as it were, the first step towards this consists in the outlooks and intentions sketched by Harrison as follows: 'The Russian Empire must die that the Russian people may live, and the realization of the dreams of the Pan-Slavists will indicate that the sixth Aryan sub-race[†] has begun to live its own intellectual life, and is no longer in its period of infancy.' And just before Harrison changes the subject to speak about very different matters, he makes a concluding remark which provides the key to the true background of the Russian 'Desert' and, as it were, forms the legend of the *Truth* map: 'We need not pursue the subject further than to say that *the national character will enable them to carry out experiments in Socialism, political and economical, which would present innumerable difficulties in Western Europe.*'

According to the intentions of particular Anglo-American circles then, socialist experiments, amongst other things, were to be carried out in the

---

[*] He means the Hungarians—*author's note.*

[†] The *Slavic* peoples—*author's note.*

Russian 'desert'. One only needs to look at the forced abdication of the last Russian Czar in March 1917 and the smuggling of Lenin into Russia which followed a month later (with the help of the German High Command!) to make clear to oneself how real was the force within the intentions indicated by Harrison.

The plans briefly outlined here were self-evidently not conceived at any one time, over night, so to speak. They represent the result of intentions which are centuries old and which already for hundreds of years have in various ways sought to ensure for the Anglo-American peoples dominance over the Slavic East.

A mysterious document, published for the first time in France in 1812 and again in Riga in 1876 also served this aim. It came to people's attention in the fierce debates which raged in the Austrian Diet over the question of approval of massive credits for the occupation of Bosnia-Herzegovina. The document in question was the 'Testament of Peter the Great'.

This much is certain: the testament was clearly *not* written by Czar Peter. And yet, the 13 articles which it contains do give a kind of accurate picture of the main contours of Russian foreign policy since Peter's reign, so for a symptomatological perspective of history, it should not be overlooked.

Peter the Great (1672–1725) is known as the decisive westernizer of the Russian people and of Slavic culture. An admirer of the technical and political achievements of the West, he hurried to introduce both into Russia as much as he could. On his great trip to The Hague and London he came into contact with freemasonic circles, which is why he was also regarded as the first Russian Freemason. The politics he pursued stood, more or less consciously, entirely in the service of western interests. Ludwig Polzer, who was later to concern himself intensively with the Testment of Peter the Great, once characterized it as follows:

> The actual spirit and content of the testimony of Peter the Great aims to erect an Imperialism of the East over against the imperialism of the West *and to annihilate German culture*. The imperialism of western[*] production needed an imperialism which would provide it with passive consumers and which would exclude all economic competition.[50]

Through the intentions expressed in this document, the young, seed-like spiritual capacities in the Slavic peoples were injected with a foreign, imperialistic and militaristic impulse that was alien to its innermost nature and from which until today it has not been able to free itself.

---

[*] Economic—*transl.*

In the debates in Austria about the occupation of Bosnia-Herzegovina various opponents of this dubious foreign policy risk that had been dealt to Austria in 1878 drew attention to the fatal Testament of Peter the Great and especially to its article 5 which contains the following notable passage: 'Austria must be involved in wars, and if that does not work, then she should be handed a piece of Turkish territory that can be taken back from her again later.'[51] With the occupation of Bosnia-Herzegovina that followed, entirely in line with the testament, then according to Ludwig Polzer's later understanding of the issue: 'the basis for Austria's downfall was laid. The occupation of Bosnia [. . .] was the trap which was artfully built for Austria's fall and into which in 1914 it did in fact fall.'[52] Rudolf Steiner, who already at the beginning of the twentieth century had pointed to the document and its world-historical significance stated briefly and succinctly that 'This testament actually brought Austria down.'[53]

But what must not be overlooked is that if much in Austrian politics ran its course to its own detriment in line with this testament then *everything* in the document was arranged to the detriment of a true development of Slavic culture and society, *in line with western plans for domination*. The actual centre point of the testament, article 7, shows clearly where Russian policy is to be directed:

> A firm alliance is to be made with England and with the help of a trade treaty direct relations are to be entered into which will allow her to effect a kind of domestic monopoly[*]. This is a key point, on which the success of this whole plan depends.[54]

Anyone who without prejudice considers this testament alongside the map from *Truth* and the statements of C.G. Harrison will find in front of him the stones of a mosaic-like image which, even if not in a manner that is fully comprehensible, in its essentials brings to expression a *single* grand intention: to direct *from the West,* in the present—and that means for centuries to come—the development of the Slavic peoples, who are only now approaching their world-historical tasks. And to this end the middle of Europe is to be excluded.

★

'Austria must perish'—we can learn to read this saying of Polzer's on three different levels. Firstly, it expresses that general feeling that was so widespread in Austria in those days, the feeling of having arrived at a

---

[*] I.e. inside Russia—*transl.*

cultural turning point where many old forces that formerly carried the culture are denied and no more reliance is placed on traditional values either individually or socially. Secondly, it contains something of the intuition that Austria-Hungary would be bound to face certain collapse if in its last hour it did not raise itself to grasp ideas which could overcome the obsolete principle of the nation state and which were truly new and practical. Finally, it contains a third level: it has within it, even if only in a vague form, a sense of the fact that Austria's downfall had long been *planned for*—more than this, it had been decided on—in western circles and in those circles in the East that are dependent on the West.

This is still hardly noticed today, which is why in these pages we have sought to pay special attention to this third level. How far the intentions which found an echo in this third level, that of the mood of downfall, were also harboured by the Church of Rome will become clear in the last part of this book. At this point only the following preliminary remarks will be made: while Middle Europe was and is seen by the West more as an autonomous economic power that stood in the way of the West's projects for the East, middle European spiritual life, which has as its real basis and aim the free spirituality of the individual, was and is a great thorn in the flesh of the Church of Rome. And as different as these motives are, the free spiritual impulses of Central Europe, on which the Slav-dominated East remains reliant for its own positive development will (apart from the westernized element in the East itself) be strongly assaulted both from the West and the South. Divide and rule, the Romans used to say. For both of these powers that opposed Middle Europe, it suited them that the Austro-Hungarian Dualism,[55] instead of solving the cultural, political and economic problems of the multi-ethnic state, would have to lead to division, oppression of the Slavs, national chauvinism and soon, to the undermining of the middle of Europe. How the world-historical failure of the structure of the Dual Monarchy could have been transformed at the last minute to a threefolded social organism will be shown in a later chapter.

With all this we have apparently come a long way from our biographical path. We left Ludwig Polzer in the autumn of 1888 after that performance of *Iphigenia* in Vienna, after which the old Hofburg Theatre was demolished. And yet, basically, we have only followed the sadness which the young Polzer had felt over this first fallen stone, which then began rolling and would ultimately end in the ruins of the entire Empire. While he followed with keen attention the action on stage, we have only been eavesdropping on certain voices from another performance (in the 1880s only very soft ones) which were stirring *behind* the curtain and which would not remain hidden from Ludwig Polzer's intuitive feelings.

12. A Love in May

While the great European crisis was preparing itself with destructive power in the background of events, a completely different power, one that underlies all existence, appeared on the stage of the 21-year-old Ludwig Polzer—his first love. Its name alone shows that it came from another part of the world—Blanche Tollemache, a name that most likely stemmed from Celtic culture.

Blanche was from an old English noble family and had come to Vienna at the end of the 1880s to study music and singing. She soon became friendly with the artistically-inclined Mathilde Hoditz and it was not long before Mathilde introduced her to her nephew Ludwig, who was then serving with the Windisch-Grätz Hussars in Vienna.

Blanche was six years older than the young officer. Difficult family circumstances had led to her developing a mature, self-contained personality already at a relatively young age.

When, shortly after Easter 1890, Arthur Polzer interrupted his journey to Modern to stop off in Vienna in order to visit Ludwig, who had in the meantime been promoted to lieutenant, it could not have been long before Ludwig opened his heart to him. 'We spent the evenings,' wrote Arthur,[56]

> at the Mansbergs' in Schützengasse. It was always very enjoyable there. During the winter a young Englishwoman, Blanchy, daughter of Lord Tollemache, was staying at the Mansbergs' as a paying guest. She was very musical, played the piano well and had come to Vienna to complete her piano studies. Her geniality met little understanding at the Mansbergs', but all the more with Aunt Mathilde, who took a great liking to her. It was to become a friendship for life.

Something of the discreet charm which both Blanche Tollemache and Mathilde Hoditz exuded can still be felt from the photo (fig. 16) in which the two friends are seen together with one of Blanche's sisters.

At the end of April the two friends went to Modern, where Mathilde had rented a holiday house 'The Sands'. The municipally-owned villa was made ready with loving care and stocked with provisions. On 3 May Arthur and his brother followed 'who was burning with passionate love for the young Englishwoman'. There would only have been a few places near Vienna or in the surrounding region which could have provided such a peaceful and gentle environment as the undulating foothills of the Little Carpathians for what was blazing within Ludwig. The season too made its contribution in bringing its magic to the woods and countryside as if they were waiting in a quiet longing for love. 'The woods were resplendent in festive decoration in the merry month of May. Their splendour was too much for words,' wrote Arthur rapturously.

> Azure blue sky. The young foliage of the beech trees like a light green veil between dark tall pines, the ground strewn with stars of woodruff; on the banks of streams hosts of marsh marigolds and forget-me-nots. The fresh fragrance of woodland air, all the birds singing, the cuckoo calling—the beauty of paradise!

We can thank Arthur Polzer not only for his description of the place where the event took place. In a few brief lines he also drew a portrait of the main actor Blanche. And however much his brother was utterly gripped by the power of love, Arthur's gaze, in calm and clear friendship remained fixed on Blanche. 'Blanchy was a delightful young woman,' he wrote,

> not beautiful, scarcely pretty, but uncommonly warm, intelligent, humorous, and always good-tempered. She also had a quality that I always held to be a criterion of refinement. She always knew how to behave in whatever situation, whether in a farmhouse parlour or in a salon. And she, who was used to a luxurious life in English castles felt happy in the isolation we had to make do with at The Sands.

He added: 'What I also particularly valued in her was her great appreciation of art and her good taste.'

One of Blanche's brothers, Wilbraham, who played excellent violin, accompanied the group for a while. Arthur characterized him as the 'bashful, well-bred type of Englishman, good-natured to the point of naivety'.

While Ludwig spent the week in Vienna and could only travel to Modern at weekends, the three friends enjoyed carefree, happy days. Blanche showed interest in Arthur's passion for hunting and accompanied him on many expeditions, whereas Wilbraham preferred to spend the early mornings in places other than on Arthur's favourite daybreak stalking courses. Time flew by. After evening meals they chatted about their plans for the following day. 'The windows were open,' noted Arthur, 'the crickets chirped, the stars shone into the semi-darkness of the room.'

At the end of this stay at The Sands, the group travelled to Pressburg (Bratislava), where they enjoyed the city's cultural sights and culinary delights.

Considered entirely externally, Ludwig's love for Blanche Tollemache appeared to have crossed none of the borders strictly prescribed by etiquette. Mathilde Hoditz saw to that in clever ways; for example, when Ludwig immoderately wanted to take Blanche to the theatre once again, with presence of mind and full of charm, Mathilde made the invitation herself—and straightaway bought *three* tickets.

Soon, the first love of Ludwig's life receded into the distance. But a piece of his heart followed her, which in secret and in stillness, would not beat for her only temporarily.

Blanche Tollemache was the only person whom Ludwig Polzer encountered in his youth who came from right outside the environment of Austria-Hungary. She was the first pillar of a bridge that Polzer would later, spiritually or physically, again and again build towards the West. In 1910, after repeated invitations from her, he went on his first trip to England. We shall come to speak of it later.

Through his love for Blanche Tollemache, Ludwig Polzer grew up in the full sense of the word. Her departure was also the departure of his own youth.

III. PATHS OF DESTINY

The greatest and most decisive event in my life
was my first meeting with Rudolf Steiner

Ludwig Polzer-Hoditz, 1937

13. With Arthur in Szombathely

Soon after joining his regiment of Hussars Ludwig Polzer made another acquaintance which would become a friendship for life. He got to know Adolf Waldstein, also a lieutenant in the same regiment (see fig. 19). Adolf came from the old Bohemian family which had produced Wallenstein, the famous general of the Thirty Years' War. As their son's best friend, Ludwig was often invited by Adolf's parents to the different residences which the family owned in various parts of Bohemia and often spent time in the Palais Waldstein, which was built by Wallenstein himself. In retrospect, Ludwig described his friend as a 'very modest, undemanding, dear man'[57].

The House of Waldstein became for him a second home.

Polzer was now introduced into Prague's exclusive circles, which enabled him to gain lively insights into the history of Bohemia: 'On many evenings,' he wrote in his *Memoirs*, 'at the beginning of the '90s Adolf and I sat with his Excellency'—Adolf's father—'who was then already over 70 and who told us of his interesting experiences, of events going back to the beginning of the century, which he himself had heard of from eye-witnesses as a child or as a young man.'[58]

A number of major political events had taken place at the residences owned by the Waldsteins, for example, a meeting between Emperor Francis I of Austria and Czar Nicholas I at Schloss Münchengrätz in 1830. The old Waldstein was himself personally acquainted with almost all the personalities who had played a leading role in his lifetime; he had fought in 1848/49 in Hungary and had taken part in the war of 1866 against the Prussians. Ludwig Polzer thus received a very special kind of instruction in history from the House of Waldstein, one which deeply appealed to his nature; he learned very important things about the past from people who had actually lived through them. 'And as I had always liked as a child to listen in when the older people were talking,' he recalled in old age, 'many experiences from their own lives were unfolded by people who had lived before me.'[59] Although he could not always understand all the details of the historical connections, he retained the feeling of the 'the soul mood of that time which lay long before my birth'.[60]

In the autumn of 1890 Ludwig took Adolf with him on a few days' holiday to Peggau, the small property which Julius Polzer, at the urging of his wife, had acquired in January that year not far from Graz. Here Arthur got to know his brother's best friend. He too immediately took to Adolf. 'Adolf was a very nice man,' he wrote.[61]

But what am I writing? The word 'nice' is too banal and applies to so many people. And Adolf Waldstein was far more than what one could say of many other people. He was plain and simple, honest and true, noble in both his appearance and in his whole being. These qualities he possessed in every sense of the word.

After Ludwig and Adolf had left Peggau, Arthur, who had passed his State examinations in October, went walking through the woods in the area, which already bore the colours of autumn. He spent hours in the evenings sitting by the fireplace and fell into a reverie, an inner vision, as though sensing a life long past in which such human sympathies could find their basis and roots. 'The flickering fire conjured up pictures before me in full clarity,' he wrote about such moments.

> But not an active fantasy, rather, one which came about by itself without me doing anything. And therein lay a very special appeal: it was as though I was leafing through a colourful picturebook [. . .] Today I ask myself: were they somehow pictures of a memory of an earlier life?

Such experiences became the new soul inspiration for many of Arthur's paintings at that time.

At the end of that year (1890) Ludwig returned home to Graz for Christmas. According to Arthur, 'he did not feel at all well'. His parents consulted a doctor, who urged him to take several months' rest in Lussin, an Istrian island, about 100 kilometres south of Trieste, and Ludwig requested permission to do so. Was it the separation from Blanche Tollemache who, after such a short time together, he had had to let go again into the distance? Was his heart pulling him towards faraway England? Was he feeling perhaps, from that same England, a breeze in his soul wafting over from those powers whose aim was the downfall of the old monarchies? At the same time that Ludwig was feeling so unwell, there appeared in that Christmas issue of the magazine *Truth* . . . 'The Kaiser's Dream'. (see p. 65)

On New Year's Eve Ludwig set out on his journey to the south. His mother was as anxious as ever. She imagined horror upon horror—he would end up alone and helpless and become really ill in a foreign land! He travelled—met pleasant people, especially a young widow who took care of him. Decades later, Arthur recalled the picture of a young woman that Ludwig had put on his writing desk after his return from the south.

The crisis had lifted; with new courage Ludwig could face his 22nd year of life.

It was not only in the Bohemian but also in the Hungarian part of the Empire that Ludwig looked through the book of friendship. In 1891 his Hussars' regiment was stationed in Steinamanger, which today belongs to

Hungary and is called Szombathely. The city was founded by the Roman Emperor Claudius as Colonia Savaria, later the capital of the entire Roman province of Upper Pannonia, and had a shrine to the goddess Isis, of which remains are still preserved today.

Here Ludwig Polzer got to know Count Emanuel Széchenyi, who was about ten years older, and who at the age of 30 could already look back on a rich experience of foreign travel; he had already served as ambassador in Berlin, St Petersburg, Istanbul and Athens. Ludwig spent many holidays on Széchenyi's Hungarian estates, and when Széchenyi was abroad, the two friends' exchanges continued in long letters.

Through his friendships with Adolf Waldstein and Széchenyi, Ludwig learned to look with understanding at both halves of the Double Monarchy, and now for the first time he became aware of the fundamental sickness with which the Empire had already long been afflicted. He said about it:

> One could experience that the way of thinking and the attitude of prominent people in Hungary was quite different from that in Bohemia. However much the foreign and domestic politics of Austria were influenced, even dominated by that of Hungary, I could already feel at that time that what was really of significance for a future Austria or Middle Europe lay in fact in the *Slavic* lands.[62]

In early 1891 Arthur Polzer visited his brother in Steinamanger in order to take a look at the place where he wanted to complete his one-year, very involuntary 'voluntary service' later that year, in the autumn. His big brother introduced him to Colonel and Baron Wenzel Kotz von Dobrz, the commandant of the Hussars' regiment, who was not only Ludwig's superior but also the uncle of his future wife Berta.

Wenzel Kotz was very close to the Imperial Family. It was through him and also through Ludwig's father-like benefactor Waldstein, that he came into the circle of the heir to the throne and got to know his brother Otto (father of the later Emperor Karl), when both archdukes commanded, one after the other, the neighbouring regiment stationed in Ödenburg (Sopron). Ludwig also made the acquaintance of Duchess of Hohenberg, Sophie Chotek, later the wife of Franz Ferdinand. When she was still a girl, he was introduced to her at a Fasching ball in Pressburg (Bratislava). Later, he made a point of dancing with her at balls in Prague at Fasching and New Year.

Ludwig introduced Arthur to the Széchenyi family and to Emanuel's younger sister, the pretty 18-year-old Jenny in whom, according to Arthur, he 'seemed to be very interested'. And this was also the reason why he did not notice how interested Sophie Chotek was in him. Adolf Waldstein said one day to his friend Ludwig: 'When I was in Pressburg recently, she was asking about you very keenly. You should go to Pressburg more often. She would be a wife for you.' This comes from some of Polzer's notes from the 1930s that were only found after the publication of the first edition of this book. 'I had something else on my mind at the time, Jenny Széchenyi was close to my heart.' Decades later, however, the image of Sophie Chotek still stood clearly before him: 'She was of a slender, beautiful appearance with lovely eyes.' But his love for Jenny Széchenyi made him 'almost forget Adolf's advice'. Sophie Chotek became, as mentioned earlier, the wife of Archduke Franz Ferdinand, whom Ludwig Polzer repeatedly came across, the last time being at St Moritz in 1904. Ten years later Franz Ferdinand and his wife would become the victims of assassination in June 1914. As late as the 1930s Polzer had a notable dream about this: 'I saw that I was walking with a group of people, at whose head was Dr Rudolf Steiner. Berta[*] was also in the group. A woman I knew was walking close to me. Berta asked to be introduced to the Duchess. It was Sophie Chotek.' About this late memory of his early encounters with Sophie Chotek, Ludwig Polzer wrote the words: 'An episode of destiny, which I later learned to understand symptomatically.' Something of the way in which Ludwig Polzer's personal destiny was interwoven with the tragic destiny of the peoples of Austria-Hungary can be sensed in this inconspicuous episode from his time in Steinamanger.

But let us return to the year 1891.

At the end of September life became more serious for Arthur. He moved to Steinamanger for a year. It was the first time he had really taken leave of the parental home in Graz. At the station, Ludwig met his brother, who was to be his assigned subordinate for a year, and installed him in a room above his own at the cavalry barracks. At first, Arthur felt extremely uncomfortable in the unfamiliar surroundings when he was on duty and in his new uniform. 'I did not know how to behave correctly,' he admitted, 'was always tripping over my sabre and could not salute according to the regulations.' Ludwig was now the officer charged with instructing Arthur, and this lent a certain piquant spice to the bond between the brothers, at least from Arthur's viewpoint:

> A brother had suddenly become a superior who would yell at me on duty 'You, annual volunteer!' He mightily impressed me. His stewarding talent that he had practised on me since childhood was now in its element. And yet I was happy when he gave us riding instruction and had us do foot exercises or taught us in the training room. On duty during the daytime he was my superior, to whom I had to show respect and did. In the evenings,

---

[*] Later, Polzer's wife—*Meyer*.

when we relaxed, mostly with Adolf Waldstein, drank tea and smoked cigarettes, he was my brother.

The two hours in the morning at riding lessons, in which Ludwig showed himself to be 'relentless' were literally a torture for Arthur as his 'backside [...] was not yet thick-skinned enough in the proper cavalry manner'. Whoever momentarily bent his back in pain was immediately yelled at to straighten up. All the more refreshing and relaxing was the time after training.

While their supervisor turned a blind eye, the volunteers would pay the orderlies a fee to do their stall duties and would then seek out a place to eat where they could order ham and eggs or a goulash with beer. 'Never did a mid-morning snack taste so good to us as after we'd survived a riding lesson,' Arthur wrote. 'We chatted noisily and were happy as sandboys; we often made a right din.' One day their pleasure was dangerously interrupted. While the company sat happily at table, the noise of horses' hooves was suddenly heard outside. The volunteers jumped to the window and recognized with a shock Colonel Kotz who had just ridden into the courtyard and dismounted.

Arthur's description of what now occurred is not to be passed over and amounts to a priceless portrait of Baron Kotz, who was to play a great role in Ludwig's life.

In the 'Tscharda', as Hungarian eateries were called, there was a panic-stricken scrambling about.

> Each of us grabbed the nearest sabre as fast as we could and put it on, put our caps on and piled out. We stood there like thieves caught red-handed and must have looked like a bunch of simpletons. For the Colonel, smiling, looked at us as we lined up in front of him and saluted smartly. Guiltily, we waited for the storm that would now break over us. Our supervisor had dashed out of the stables, cast poisonous looks at us and wanted to make his report. But the Colonel did not allow things to go so far; he turned to us and said as follows: 'So, how's it going then in the Tscharda? You've probably just had your mid-morning snack. Have the horses been well-attended to?' Our faces lightened up all at once and with a unison 'Yes Sir!', smiling in a most unmilitary manner, we answered in chorus, 'Our most obedient thanks.' That was about the stupidest answer we could have given. But it is remarkable that those were the words that immediately came to all our lips. They expressed everything we felt: thank you for your gracious treatment and for your interest in our horses. Our faces then began to shine when the dear Colonel said the following words: 'Tomorrow is Saturday and Monday is All Souls'. If you wish, you can all go home for two days.' Then he spoke to all of us very warmly—'in an off-duty way', as

we used to call it. He asked after our parents and bade us give his greetings to the parents of this or that man. From that day onwards we certainly rose in our supervisor's estimation.

If Colonel Kotz already appears to us as such a pleasant character in that very warm Austrian way, so one may well wish to get to know his niece, who would later become Ludwig Polzer's wife . . .

On-duty hours continued until about 4 o'clock in the afternoon. The main meal was then about 5 o'clock in the officers' mess. In the evenings, when the Polzer brothers sat together with others and Adolf Waldstein the latest barracks gossip went the rounds. The men told each other stories and talked about hunting and horses. About 9 o'clock a trumpet was sounded to signal lights out.

The young volunteers showed the greatest interest in the oldest officer in the squadron, Henri Baltazzi, the uncle of Mary Vetsera, the former lover of Crown Prince Rudolf. Henri Baltazzi was said to be 'the most elegant gentleman in the Empire'. Arthur was able to gain Baltazzi's affection, which showed itself in that the officer often approached the young Polzer in breaks between exercises and always offered him highest quality, gold-tipped cigarettes—'for us volunteers the epitome of elegance'. The rumour went round that Baltazzi had once struck the Crown Prince with a champagne bottle, which for Arthur was 'naturally nonsense'. But he considered it not impossible that Baltazzi might have played a role in the Mayerling tragedy.

It was a special event when the annual volunteers were given their spurs and rode their own horses for the first time. Arthur, who had none of his own, was allowed to ride one of Ludwig's horses, as Ludwig had three: a wonderful crossbreed Wallach named Livius, who was very hard to ride and sometimes dangerously capricious, a thoroughbred Etoek, and a black named Bango that had the bad habit of turning in the opposite direction from time to time. Arthur chose the Etoek, which had a wonderful stride, but he was only allowed to ride the horse within the riding school.

In December 1891 Arthur became ill. His old stomach problem reappeared. Feeling miserable and desolate, he lay in his room until the doctor diagnosed measles, and Arthur was carried on a stretcher to the barracks hospital's isolation pavilion. It was scarcely an hour later that Ludwig was on the same stretcher heading for the same place, also with measles. 'It was certainly no *schadenfreude* but a real joy that I was no longer alone at least,' admitted Arthur. Ludwig had sent a laconic telegram home—it was just before Christmas—which greatly unsettled their ever-anxious mother.

On 4 January, however, the two brothers, cheerful and back in good health, were able to celebrate Christmas with their family in Graz.

In the spring of 1892 Wenzel Kotz relinquished command of the Hussar regiment to another officer. Arthur, Ludwig and Adolf now often had the afternoons free and they used to ride out into the neighbouring areas of Hégyfalu and Astad, where they often played tennis. Arthur was unhappy that on the way there he always had to ride Bango, which liked suddenly to go off in the opposite direction. Finally, his brother allowed him one day to ride the Etoek over an open field, and Ludwig had to acknowledge with astonishment his brother's unsuspected skill in horse-riding. 'The Etoek was in the best condition,' reported Arthur on his 'maiden ride', 'jumped over all ditches and other obstacles with the lightness and softness that is typical of the thoroughbred. And so I went on a kind of hunting ride, only over short stretches, falling in behind the others [. . .] I rode into Hégyfalu with pride.' Ludwig merely graciously acknowledged that 'You were in luck. The Etoek was on really good form today.'

In the autumn Arthur travelled back to Graz to take up his law studies. And with that, the most important witness to Ludwig's life in the '90s steps for a while again into the background. We learn that at the Fasching ball of the following year 1893 Arthur met his first great love, while Ludwig in April of the same year spent a long time in Peggau but in a very depressed mood.

Jenny Széchenyi, for whom he had felt the warmest interest for two years, was seriously ill with a lung infection. Ludwig travelled for a couple of days to Hégyfalu but returned with the depressing news that the patient's conditioned had only worsened. On 24 April 1893, the day after Ludwig's 24th birthday, Jenny's mother wrote to Christine Polzer: 'Dearest Christine, please prepare Ludwig for everything. My poor Jenny's condition is very bad. I know how hard it will go with him. I embrace you, Your Felici.' A few days later came the news of Jenny's death. She died on 30 April in her 20th year.

In September 1893 Ludwig, accompanied by Countess Felici Széchenyi, came to Peggau for a few days, where Arthur was also staying. 'The poor woman, who had lost her only daughter, made us feel frightfully sad,' wrote Arthur. 'But she bore her pain with great dignity. She remained in frequent correspondence with my mother, in still more frequent correspondence with Ludwig who, so it seemed, she would have liked to have seen as her son-in-law.'

At the end of October Arthur received his official appointment as a probationary clerk in the administration of the Steiermark and soon afterwards entered upon his duties. The careers of the two brothers again began to diverge.

14. 'We Shall See What is to be Done'

It is perhaps no accident that there appear to be no existing accounts of the central years of Ludwig Polzer's military career (1895–1902), either by him or by Arthur. It was rather that his years in the military were for Ludwig hardly more than a stopgap. Since he had firmly turned his back on the abstract manner in which knowledge of the world had been brought to him at school in Graz, an academic career of the kind Arthur was embarking on was closed to him. A military career spared him from dry school learning and offered the promise of encountering real life, and real personalities which could lead him, through concrete experience of life, much more suitably to a knowledge of the world that was present in historical events which were hard to comprehend only intellectually. We have already seen what stimulation Ludwig Polzer gained in this respect from personalities such as the elderly Waldstein or from Count Széchenyi.

Such an uncorrupted seeking after knowledge of the world, and not military ambition, caused Ludwig Polzer to choose his exercise grounds and barracks. These were always, compared with university, the lesser of two evils. His destiny was easier there in that he served in the military in Austria-Hungary and not in Prussia; in Austria military matters were 'fortunately, not taken so seriously'[63], as Ludwig later wrote and as the episode with Wenzel (Wlasko) Kotz and the annual volunteers had shown a memorandum from the year 1939 details a few dates in Ludwig Polzer's ongoing military career in the 1890s: in 1895 he was posted to the Institute for Military Horsemanship in Vienna, which he left after two years, as riding instructor for Brigade Officer Schools. At the outset of his training to become a riding instructor in the autumn of 1895 he was sent as an aide-de-camp to the manoeuvres section at the 'Emperor's Manoeuvres' in Banfy-Hunyad. He took part in the manoeuvres in the retinue of His Majesty the Emperor Franz Joseph. From 1897 to 1900 during the winter he was riding instructor at the Brigade Officers' Schools in Szombathely and Warasdin (today Varazdin in Croatia). In the summer he served with his troop. As lieutenant, he was already commanding a full squadron at infantry division exercises.

So much for a sparse outline of Polzer's military activities in the second half of the 1890s. From Arthur, we are able to fill in the following interesting details: at Christmas 1894 Ludwig was with Arthur at a festive reception, invited by Arthur's superior, the Governor of Graz.

In 1897 Arthur moved to Vienna where he had been called to the Ministry for Culture and Instruction thanks to the recommendation of

Countess Latour, a friend of his mother's. After a long search, Ludwig was finally able to secure an apartment for him in Josefstädterstrasse.

In the spring of 1898 Ludwig once more spent some time in Vienna, according to Arthur, 'in a very companionable mood'. He went to horse races with Arthur and dined with him in the Sacher Garden.* The brothers took part in the Vienna Easter festivities, travelling about by cab.

In September came the shocking news of the murder of Empress Elisabeth. She was stabbed by a so-called anarchist in Geneva, on the open street. The incident must have greatly preoccupied both brothers. Even 30 years later, Ludwig was to pursue extensive studies of Empress Elisabeth and even made her a leading figure in a drama he wrote himself.

The brothers spent Christmas 1898 with their parents and aunt Mathilde at Arthur's apartments in Vienna. There was no lack of champagne.

In the last year of the nineteenth century Arthur suffered a mysterious pair of accidents. During a train journey a stone came through a carriage window and hit him full in the face; shortly afterwards, he experienced a train collision. Ludwig picked his badly injured brother up from Peggau station and was so much in despair about what had happened that his brother had to comfort *him* 'while we were on the way'. These various details might seem to some readers like widely spread-out rocks protruding from a broad river, but they were placed here only to serve as stepping stones enabling us to cross over, even if in large steps, to the firm bank of the twentieth century with dry feet …

★

On New Year's Day 1900 Ludwig Polzer first became acquainted with the person with whom he would spend the rest of his life: Lady Berta Kotz von Dobrz. 'Ludwig is courting Lady Kotz, to Adolf Waldstein's delight,' noted Arthur in March 1900. Julius Polzer and his wife Christine also felt the courtship to be 'suitable and very desirable'. The exact circumstances of the time and place of the first meeting between Ludwig Polzer and Lady Kotz are unknown, but Baron Wenzel Kotz, Ludwig's superior during his early period in Szombathely, even if he had not known of it, had certainly played a role. At any rate, after Ludwig's relocation to Pressburg in spring 1900, Baron Kotz invited Ludwig Polzer to his home, which he shared with his niece Berta. In fact, Ludwig's move to Pressburg was because of his first encounter with Berta, which must have taken place in 1899.

---

* Of the Prater Park—*transl.*

Berta Kotz was born on 15 March 1879 at Schloss Heiligenkreutz in Bohemia. She lost her mother as a young child. Her father had suffered a lance wound in the war against Prussia and as a result, was also psychologically ill with no hope of recovery; he lived in a sanatorium in Vienna. Berta's education was therefore taken care of by her grandmother, Aglaia Kotz. She was brought up in Bohemia, in the home of this good woman at Schloss Heiligenkreutz, the seat of the Kotz family, which was numbered among the most ancient families of Bohemia. When Aglaia Kotz died in 1899, Berta's uncle Wenzel [also known as Wlasko] Kotz took his niece into his home. It was shortly after this that Berta Kotz von Dobrz was introduced to a certain Ritter Ludwig von Polzer ... On 10 April 1900 Ludwig informed his family by telegram that he was going to be engaged to Berta Kotz. The next day, the fiancé travelled in hope to Vienna, where Arthur witnessed his brother's happiness. Well-versed in the service of the State, Arthur quickly prepared the necessary documents, for the engagement was to be celebrated on 15 April, Easter Sunday. The festivities took place in the Pressburg home of uncle Wlasko in a small circle of friends and family. Ludwig's parents had travelled from Peggau with Marie-Sefine. Aunt Mathilde was there, of course, with Arthur. Ludwig's dearest friend, Adolf Waldstein and his wife Sophie Waldstein-Hoyos had also travelled to be there.

It was a very joyful occasion. In the afternoon they went outside and all resolved to go on an excursion to Modern on the 18th and immediately ordered three carriages. 'From the outset the atmosphere was a very happy one,' remembered Arthur, 'to which the fine spring day, the presence of the happy couple and the sparkling, fine humour of Countess Sophie Waldstein greatly contributed.' Arthur's joy at the event was expressed, in his own words, by a real fit of photography ...

Looking back at that first period after his engagement, the happy fiancé wrote: 'With my engagement in Pressburg began a time of happiness with a very special and dear circle of friends. Both Berta and I were much appreciated in Pressburg society, many shared their joy with us and showed it through the most various expressions of friendship. This was also due to the position of the House of Kotz and the fondness with which it was regarded.'[64]

Also in spring that year came the end of Ludwig Polzer's stint at the Brigade School in which he had still been 'very hard-working' until just before his engagement. Afterwards, he 'did not do much anymore, relied on my old knowledge, but was still able to complete my term at the School very well'.

The school courses culminated in a tactical expedition to Kärnten,

Krain, and on to Trieste, where the expedition was to end. Sophie Waldstein, meanwhile, suggested that she and Berta should meet up with Adolf and Ludwig in Trieste and then go on to Venice together as a foursome.

During the expedition our fiancé absented himself for a day to go to Vienna for an audience with the Emperor to seek his prior permission for the marriage. It was the first and last time that Ludwig Polzer had an audience with Franz Joseph. 'Emperor Franz Joseph said to me: "We shall see what is to be done." ' With this promising news Ludwig went off to Trieste.

★

What a signature in Polzer's life! Instructive for the character of the Emperor and instructive too, for Polzer's own path through life: the emperor was ready to lend an ear to one of his subjects' personal plans for a change in his life in the middle of a tactical military expedition! So in Trieste the end of his service at the Brigade School was followed by a renewal of personal relations of friendship. The foursome spent some lovely spring days in the City on the Lagoon, a place which was new to Berta.

The couple stayed in Peggau for two weeks during the summer and then travelled to Heiligenkreutz on 18 August. It was then that Ludwig saw Berta's homeland for the first time; its castle had once been in the possession of the Templars. 'In those days, no trains went there,' he wrote.

> I was picked up in Plan, it took almost four hours [...] The area gave me the feeling somehow that I was fulfilling a destiny, I felt that already at the time. It had a rather sad character; the extensive woodlands really moved me. I remembered the novel by George Sand that I had read in my early teens, Consuelo. Riesenberg castle stood there in this region near Taus.

A deep and earnest sense of destiny gripped Berta's fiancé in her homeland, and this serious mood of destiny became the fundamental tone of the four and half decades they were to spend together.

'Berta loved to show me everything and to make me acquainted with everyone,' wrote Ludwig,

> with the old people in the castle, the servants of the household, the foresters in the woods, the reverend vicar in the village. A lovely, somewhat patriarchal mood lay over the whole place. Everyone's heart was inclined towards Berta. In those days in her home surroundings I first learned from her to know deep, serious feelings; they were two beautiful days, those days of that first visit to her Bohemian idyll.[65]

Meanwhile, Ludwig's humble request, which immediately received the so-called grand signature, had been granted. Right after the end of the cavalry manoeuvres at Kiscell, with the Emperor's august permission, the marriage bond was sealed on 12 September 1900 in Vienna's Votive Church.

On the evening before the wedding came the so-called 'bridal soirée'; it was held at the home of Wlasko Kotz, who at that time had apartments in the house of Archduke Friedrich. Ludwig's witnesses were his father's brother, Uncle Alfred, and Adolf Waldstein; uncle Wlasko [Wenzel] and Count Karl Nostitz were the witnesses for Berta, while Ludwig's sister Marie-Sefine and Berta's pretty cousins were the bridesmaids. After the ceremony a large group of guests were invited to the wedding reception in the Hotel Sacher. After the reception the newlyweds travelled up to the Semmering Pass. Then came the honeymoon, on which they travelled to Innsbruck, Lucerne, Milan and Munich, returning to Heiligenkreutz at the end of September. Here Berta's uncle had prepared for them an especially warm reception.

Ludwig Polzer had rented rooms in Szombathely for the winter on the assumption that he would continue to work in that town as a riding instructor. But then news arrived in Heiligenkreutz that he was to be an instructor at the Officers' Brigade School in Warasdin. So rooms had to be found in haste in the small town in what is today Croatia.

15. Carefree Times

Ludwig Polzer would later describe his time in Warasdin, the newlywed couple's first 'posting', as the beginning of the *third* phase of his life.[66] (The second had begun with the end of his high school years and his entry into the cavalry cadets' school.) It was therefore certainly significant enough, for from that time on, it became ever more evident that 'the conceptions of life that Berta and I had [...] did not correspond to a normal military career'. A loosening in Ludwig Polzer's inner connection to his military activities now became noticeable. It appears that in his new location he became more impartial and more open to the local population and more relaxed in his duties. The couple felt very comfortable in the town, in which many old buildings gave evidence 'of a certain spiritual culture'.

There was a gypsy village nearby, and the gypsies regularly came to the markets in Warasdin. As the couple lived near one of these markets, they followed the activities and conduct of the travellers with growing interest.

The newly-posted officers' riding instructor had nothing to complain about as far as his duties were concerned. However, he soon had to recognize that the commandant of the school was hardly helpful towards his riding pupils. Lt. Col. Dondorf was an aesthete with a developed artistic sense and he liked to paint. Above all, during his service in the army he was devoted to training falcons. 'He did not much like the military,' said Polzer. Those were without doubt not the most favourable preconditions for leading young cavalrymen, especially since not a few of them were really quite hard to handle. Gambling went on in any regiment, which did not always have happy results. As both Dondorf and Polzer had their wives with them, their pupils, when off-duty, were often left to their own devices.

And yet Ludwig Polzer, in looking back to that entire period in Warasdin, could say: 'When I think of that first winter with my dear Berta, everything, even my unpleasant official duties, appears bathed in a beautiful, lovely atmosphere.'

By the time the couple left Warasdin in the spring of 1901 at the end of Polzer's period of duty there, in order to rent 'Harmonie', their holiday house in Modern for the coming three months, Polzer had been promoted to captain of cavalry. But that would have meant much less to him than the approaching birth of his first child. On 22 June 1901 the Hon. Josef Wlasko von Polzer first saw the light of day in picturesque Modern at the foot of the Carpathians.

Aunt Mathilde immediately responded to the arrival of her nephew with touching care. She herself decorated Villa Harmonie for the baptism and laid great emphasis on the need to take the firstborn into the woods as often as possible so that he could breathe the fragrant air of the old pines.

For the young mother—she was then in the 23rd year of her life—this life on the land, as people in Austria used to say, was much more appealing than an existence in town; she herself had grown up on the land and had been brought up according to old traditions in Heiligenkreutz, which in those days was still very secluded, traditions which the local people had maintained. Her extensive education had resulted from more than what she had learned at her school desk; it came from the fact of having read to her blind grandmother hour after hour through the long winter evenings. Should not their own children grow up in similar conditions of closeness to nature and education of the heart? This was the question which the being of little Josef posed to his parents.

So the idea suggested itself 'that we two would also strive to live and work on the land as free human beings', wrote Ludwig Polzer.

But first it was planned, to 'settle for a while', in Steinamanger, where another army apartment stood ready. When Ludwig Polzer was now, against all expectations, suddenly ordered to relocate once again, which seldom happened so often, and this time to the 4th Brigade School, he decided to part company with the army. It was not a difficult decision; in his heart of hearts he had never liked being a soldier and moreover possessed, in his own words, 'rather a weak constitution'. Also, as the result of a fall from a horse, he had had periodically recurring pains in his head. Furthermore, for troop officers there was only a slight prospect of rapid advancement. And finally, the family's financial situation was extremely good. In the spring of 1902, after a military career of 14 years, Ludwig, Ritter von Polzer therefore retired from the army.

★

This sudden change in his life was in the best traditions of his family. His father Julius had given up being an officer at about the same age, took on the education of his children and devoted ever more intensively to his philosophical and cultural interests. Ludwig's grandfather and godfather Ludwig, Ritter von Polzer, that dear connoisseur of life and novelist came into two inheritances in his 40th year, which allowed him the lifestyle that seemed to him appropriate. And finally, one can think of that great-grandfather four generations earlier on his mother's side who at 27 had loaned Busau Castle to the Teutonic Knights for a lifelong rent and had then followed the life of a freelance researcher.

After longer or shorter periods of activity, changes invariably came into the lives of the men of the Polzer-Hoditz family that created a material quiet and favoured the unhindered development of certain capacities, mostly of a cultural nature.

So, from 1902 in the case of Ludwig Polzer too, new forces became available. How would he use them?

★

First, following the death of her father in 1901, Berta bought the house in Peggau from Ludwig's parents, which was a great relief for Julius Polzer; life on the land had never much appealed to him. In March 1902 the couple moved from Szombathely to Peggau. The first great event for them in Peggau was the birth of their second son, Julius, on 4 June.

The estate had its own chapel for which a licence to say masses was obtained, and so Julius' baptism could be celebrated at home.

Ludwig Polzer now threw himself with great enthusiasm into the renovation of the house. The roof was relaid; the side buildings were joined to the main building. While the main work was being done, the family spent the spring of 1903, as they had the previous year, on the Semmering.

After the renovations were completed, they turned to the provision of household needs. A lease was taken out on some land by the river Mur and their first cow bought from the manager of the nearby religious foundation property. Twenty years later Polzer wrote: 'This first one, remarkably, was the best in terms of milk production that we ever had. Without any special feed, she gave for almost one and a half years on average about 20 litres of milk a day.'

They took on a farmer who with his wife took care of what was necessary; the pair lived in a specially built attic room in the stable. Soon the Polzers had three cows, an ox for all pulling work, three or four pigs and about 50 fine, lively hens. The meadows by the Mur were fertile; turnips and carrots were grown.

They often had guests; there was enough space and enough servants. Usually, the family spent autumn with uncle Wlasko in Heiligenkreutz and visited St Moritz twice in summer; it was, for Ludwig Polzer, 'always one of my favourite places'.

In November 1904 the family travelled to 32 Reisnerstrasse in Vienna to celebrate Julius Polzer's 70th birthday on the 18th. He and his wife had moved to the metropolis after the sale of Peggau.

The next day *St Elisabeth* by Liszt was performed at the Court Opera House. The Polzers traced their family back to this saint from Thuringia. The performance made an especially strong impression on Berta. And from this year onwards, it became a family tradition to link Julius Polzer's birthday from then on, whenever possible, to visiting performances of this often-performed work by Liszt. 'I often like to think back especially to those days, which were filled with the memory of my dear father and impressions of those performances,' wrote Ludwig Polzer in 1924. 'I believe that these experiences had a profound meaning and affected us deeply.'

Another, apparently insignificant event occurred in the same year: aunt Mathilde adopted her nephew Ludwig. According to Polzer's own entry in the family chronicle that was always kept by the eldest in the family, 'this adoption had no material consequences, since my aunt had no possessions to pass_on [...] but it happened only so that her name has come to us, as the Hoditz family name is facing extinction'. Until this adoption the unmarried aunt was the last living bearer of the name. 'From then on, we bore the name "Ritter von Polzer-Hoditz and Wolframitz."'[67] We shall have more to say about this adoption later.

★

The quiet time on the land experienced a single disturbance. One afternoon, the cook, jolly as usual, set off for Graz. Shortly afterwards came the shocking news from the railway station that she had collapsed and died there. The shock of this news caused Berta that night to have frightening agitations of the heart. It was decided to call the doctor who diagnosed the condition as 'very severe'. It was the first time that Berta Polzer's health had suffered seriously. Usually, she 'was always somewhat reserved and never one to complain, but this condition of a very fast heartbeat, often day and night' was unsettling. 'She had to suffer it for many years but with great willpower, she returned step by step back to full health.'

In general however, these years passed very harmoniously and were filled with much work lovingly done. Looking back on the years in Peggau Ludwig Polzer wrote: 'The times we lived through there in 1902–[190]5 were fine, pleasant, peaceful and carefree. My parents were happy for our good fortune and our prosperity, the children thrived and brought us joy.'

And yet this was only the exterior, as he himself admits in the same comments: 'If those times caused Berta and me no outward worries, I must nevertheless say that I was often observing very seriously what was going on around us and that these observations gave me cause for concern in my soul about the future and oppressed me.' It got to the point where he had to say of himself: 'I continually had the vague feeling that we were approaching a catastrophe.' While his purely personal life went on very satisfactorily, at a deeper level of impersonal—or perhaps better said, suprapersonal—feeling, what was making itself felt was the approaching European catastrophe. Certainly, many people at that time had similar feelings. But there were only a few who sought to decipher what these inner feelings told them and to be at all aware of their existence—feelings which bore no close relation to their purely personal life, which in Polzer's case, went on very satisfactorily.

Ludwig Polzer often liked to speak with his father about his intimations of the approaching ominous future. Deep down, Julius had similar feelings, but he sought to reassure his son when he became too pessimistic: 'You always believe that everything will go under. But it won't be like that.' He tried to calm him with such words. But Ludwig remembered very clearly *the effect* that such attempts at reassurance had on him:

> I felt that this defence of his was not solid and that in his old age he preferred not to think about it. But it worked strongly, all the same, into his soul. Now, 20 years later, I often have to think about those conversations; of how, when I seemed to overdo it, he would wave his hand, fending off my words. What came about in the end was far more terrible than even I had thought.

This was what was moving deep in Ludwig Polzer's soul in those years in Peggau; intimations of warning rose to the surface of his consciousness, forming a striking contrast to the carefree nature of his outer life.

Meanwhile, the success of the self-sustaining smallholding on the meadow created in Ludwig and Berta the desire to run their own estate. They decided to sell up at Peggau and look for a small estate. That they would also experience various disappointments in the purchase Ludwig Polzer hardly suspected at the time, for the 'situation in Peggau was so favourable. We were in a position to be able to take a loss without much trouble. That the calculations that we made, in that we counted on being able to build on our success, did not of course add up'—was to become clear in the near future.

16. Intermezzi and Contrasts

It turned out not to be so quick and easy to find an acceptable buyer. So, for some diversion Ludwig Polzer took himself off on a trip to Bukovina for some deer hunting; he had been invited by an old friend, Count Vilmos Pálffy. It was the beginning of September 1905.

They travelled in uniform, Count Pálffy, who was much older, wearing a general's uniform, and Polzer the rather more modest uniform of a retired captain. Travelling not only gave Pálffy more pleasure, it also cost him less. The train journey was to Radautz (Radauti in modern Romania); from there they travelled between a number of hunting lodges Pálffy had arranged to be made available. Unfortunately, the weather was not suitable for the trip. The summer heat was very dry, and no deer were to be seen. The situation improved only after some weeks. Polzer spent a night with a Romanian guide in a cabin in the middle of the forest and was told that very nearby 'five deer come together in various impenetrable parts of the forest'.[68] But daybreak brought no sign of them. Far off, he often saw game birds but did not get in a shot.

On 27 September some promising news finally came in a telegram from Berta: 'a certain Count Harrach wants to buy Peggau, is in a hurry and has offered a good price'. So, blessed with little success in hunting deer, Polzer broke off the trip and hurried home towards the sale which promised to be much more successful. A few days later, the property was sold, and in mid-October the family relocated to Pressburg. There, they lived during the winter at No.5 Franziskanerplatz, a pretty house in the Old Town, which still stands.

Winter in Pressburg passed in harmony and calm. Arthur came over frequently from Vienna, and the two infants 'were already beginning to think for themselves', as their father put it, and showed a lively interest in the St Nicholas and Christmas Festivals.

In sharp contrast to the harmony of the family's domestic life was the Russian Revolution in February 1905. Polzer experienced it as a 'serious political storm from the East' and as an event that 'moved him and troubled him deeply' and which he felt as 'the harbinger of difficult, serious times ahead'. Uncertainty with regard to the 'capitalist financial foundations of our existence' made itself felt, and the decision was made to acquire an estate as soon as possible.

The family almost bought a small castle estate by Lake Wörth in Carinthia, Austria. That would have brought them much closer to the war than later turned out to be the case. They spent May 1906 on the

Lido in Venice, and while the children built sandcastles or enjoyed themselves in the sea, their parents engaged in lively conversation with Polish acquaintances. Something particular here occurred to Polzer: these Polish acquaintances, who were gathered around a certain Princess Sangusko, frequently met with Hungarian nobles. Polzer speaks of 'regular political conventicles' in which Prince Saphizka, a papal nuncio, would occasionally be found. Naturally, these meetings could only be directed against the interests of Austria, which at that time still possessed Trentino and Trieste. Italy had entered into the Triple Alliance with Austria and Germany in 1882, which, however, in the First World War, it would soon abandon.

What Polzer was observing here may have been a not wholly insignificant attempt at subversive activity designed to bring Poles, Hungarians and Italians together in understanding and conspiracy against Austria.

In the middle of these conventicles there suddenly took place the visit of the German Kaiser, 'awkward, clueless and swaggering'. William II arrived in the harbour at Venice on his yacht *Hohenzollern* and let off a noisy cannonade of greeting 'which shook the ancient palazzos'. Polzer noted that this 'appearance, like the noisy blare of a market trader, contrasted sharply with the quiet, secretive, clerically-based understandings of the Poles, Hungarians and Italians'. One needs to have an eye for such contrasts; Ludwig Polzer had already developed one early on . . .

To this political contrast was formed in turn another clear contrast in a striking phenomenon which was then strolling on the Lido: the Austrian writer Hermann Bahr, who with his wife the opera singer Anna von Mildenburg, had his beach cabin not far from the Polzers. 'He promenaded in very striking, gaudily-coloured bathing costumes, which often changed colour, and flowing hair and beard, to the great enjoyment of the Polzer boys who dubbed him "the old man of the sea".'

From Modern, where the family once again spent harmonious summer holidays in the Villa Harmonie, Ludwig and Berta travelled on 10 July to Upper Austria to look at a castle property near Gutau (about 30 km. north of Linz) that had been recommended by an estate agency. So it was that they travelled for the first time to Tannbach, which for the following decades would become the actual location of the family's residence. At first, Ludwig Polzer was 'very taken aback' by the exceedingly broad, almost entirely uphill road to Tannbach from the station at Kefermarkt. But Berta 'liked the area and the property so much that we [. . .] soon decided to buy it'. On 18 August the couple signed the contract of purchase; Tannbach became theirs for 160,000 crowns—for Polzer it was 'an act laden with destiny'.

Tannbach was part of lower Mühlviertel, so called because of the many small mills of the scattered farms which were to be seen throughout the region at that time. The family's new homeland, a land of real forested countryside, lay north of the Danube and belonged to the Bohemian granite massif. The Romans had called the extensive forested complex, which had never felt a Roman footfall, the Hercynian Forest. The family were thus settling in an area that had lain quite outside the Romans' former sphere of influence, an area that had long ago been closed off to the South, West and North by a wall of forests and was open only to the East. One who comes to know and understand Polzer's lifelong bond with the Slavic East and his lifelong struggle against all decadent continuations of old Roman impulses in modern times will also be able to feel how very much he felt himself to be in his right place here in Tannbach. Such ethno-historical and geographical circumstances and contrasts are characteristic of the path of Ludwig Polzer's life.

The move to Tannbach was not entirely trouble-free. The furniture removal wagons remained partly stuck in the ground on the Gutau Hill and had to be unloaded onto the road. But thanks to their faithful servant Stefan Vígh, whom Polzer had known since his Hussar regiment days and who had been in his household since 1901, the removal was safely completed.

The family meanwhile spent some time again in Heiligenkreutz, where Arthur arrived, bringing with him as a hunting companion the very young Archduke Karl—later the last Habsburg emperor.

On 6 October 1906 the family came up from Heiligenkreutz and moved into Tannbach.

17. Life in Earnest

'It was only with this purchase that the real earnestness of life began,' Polzer wrote in 1924.[69]

> I went through the first 37 years of my life free of economic cares; I had grown up in a city under the most protected circumstances, I had been through an abstract education and then through a military career, neither of which were suited to provide me with economic and social understanding. So many officers believed themselves to be suited to become landowners because they had been in the military and accustomed to command. Now I know that they must have been unsuited for it precisely for that reason.

Tannbach brought Polzer the opportunity to see through many deceptions and to step all the more firmly into the new realities of life.

It began with a rainy autumn. The harvest was brought in late. The estate was in a much worse condition than it had first appeared. Fortunately, the manager who had worked for the previous owner declared himself ready to continue to serve the estate under its new owner. Polzer speaks of this man, whose name was Ignaz Reichl, with real gratitude and as 'a noble soul who was truly devoted to the estate and to us'. Until his premature death, Reichl represented the interests of his new master 'in a selfless way'.

The whole first year was taken up with building and renovation work. The whole cowshed had to be partly renewed. To select new cows, Ludwig and Berta themselves went to Pinzgau. A further 100,000 crowns were invested, more than half the cost of the purchase of Tannbach itself.

The family spent the summer of 1907 again with Uncle Wlasko in Heiligenkreutz. The time was now approaching for the boys' first lessons. A teacher by the name of Otto Wagner was engaged, an elderly man who was a headmaster in Gutau. Wagner was 'extraordinarily nice and friendly' but proved to be untalented as a pedagogue. Julius especially resisted from the very beginning Wagner's too abstract way of teaching 'as if he inwardly wanted to protect himself against it', as his father thought. Julius was to maintain this resistance against all school learning, which sometimes made his parents feel rather at a loss at what to do about it.

In the spring of 1908 the whole family suffered a heavy blow. Uncle Wlasko lost his wife Henriette Kotz, who was only in her 49th year. Ludwig Polzer had known her since his first days in Szombathely when Wlasko Kotz had been his superior officer. Like Wlasko himself, who was never really to recover from his loss, aunt Henriette had been full of life, always ready to make someone happy. Polzer thought of her as 'the enlivening element in the Kotz household'. She had no particular cultural interests 'yet listened eagerly when someone told her something new which no one had yet heard about'. Soon afterwards, Wlasko's son Heinrich got married, but the sadness of his very lovable father was hardly relieved by his son's marriage.

★

Experiences at Tannbach gradually led Polzer to the insight 'that we live in a time today which, especially on the land, demands to the highest degree that we learn to work in a spiritually educational and devoted manner and to understand the spiritual background of nature and the dynamic forces within it'.

A particular opportunity to enquire into such questions was the discovery of a radioactive spring in the grounds at Tannbach; it came about during an investigation by a specialist into springs at Tannbach. Further stimulus for a deeper observation of the forces of nature may have come from Polzer's many talks with his father, who had for quite a while been interested in Theosophy, read theosophical writings and in 1907 had heard a lecture in Vienna by Rudolf Steiner, then the General Secretary of the German Section of the Theosophical Society. It was certainly thanks to Julius Polzer that his son began to interest himself in Theosophy. In his years in Tannbach Ludwig Polzer occasionally heard theosophical lectures by Franz Hartmann and a certain Herr Böhme. Hartmann was then playing a central role in the theosophical movement in Austria but presented theosophical spirituality, unlike Steiner, in an often trivial, materialistic form. Polzer could therefore 'find no real connection to their presentations', as he himself said. Yet the impressions he gained from such lectures or from the books he read was strong and pushed him towards conversations. His interest in Theosophy gradually deepened 'and always I spoke about this with my dear father'.

So it was that he accompanied his father to a lecture one evening at the Vienna rooms of the Theosophical Society on Mariahilferstrasse where Rudolf Steiner was to speak about self-knowledge.

It was 23 November 1908.

18. 23 November 1908

On the very first pages of his reminiscences of Rudolf Steiner Ludwig Polzer states: 'The greatest and most decisive event of my life was my first meeting with Rudolf Steiner.'[70] From this point in time onwards, he said, a new, *fourth* phase of his life began, which continued until the day of Steiner's death in March 1925. This clearly shows how highly he estimated the importance of Rudolf Steiner for his own life.

Steiner spoke that evening in an unusual way about self-knowledge.[71] He began with Goethe who throughout his life felt a strong disinclination against that form of so-called self-knowledge which proceeds from one or another form of unfruitful self-reflection and brings about the tendency to mystical self-absorption. Steiner was *not* intending to speak about this kind of self-knowledge. Instead of this he urged upon his listeners something quite different in that he showed them that the human being is from the spiritual-scientific perspective a fourfold being and that there are therefore four levels or sides to true self-knowledge. Starting with that which is nearest to us, the lecturer began with the physical sense nature of the human being, the physical body. The first form of self-knowledge, which corresponds to this member of the human organism, must learn to pay attention to how strongly human experiences are determined by the when and where of this physical sense body. Would not very different experiences be felt by the soul of a man if his body had been placed through his birth and childhood in Paris rather than, for example, in Calcutta? Not only would the geographical environment be different; the linguistic and cultural milieu and everything that belongs to it (the folk temperament and so on) would be completely different. Or how different would not everything be in human experience when instead of the body of someone in the twentieth century, one found oneself in that of someone in the thirteenth century? Observing and understanding the specific influences of the when and where of the body on spiritual and psychological development—this leads to the first form of real self-knowledge, that which corresponds to the physical body.

But that is to comprehend only the most external sheath of the human being. For no one *is* his body; one only *has* one's body. Yet the body is *alive*.

To spiritual-scientific observation the life of this body shows itself to be a separate principle; one speaks of an actual 'life body'. That such an autonomous bearer of life exists is finally being claimed here and there in modern natural science in accordance with reason. For spiritual science, the super-sensible presence of the 'life body' can be detected as concretely as the physical sense body can be seen in the physical world.

This first super-sensible member of the human being is amongst other things the bearer of inherited characteristics, tendencies, talents and temperament. One who wishes to pursue self-knowledge at this level will have to interest himself in his ancestors in an objective way in order to differentiate what in him has been received from them and what is determined by the when and where of the physical body. This would be a second stage of concrete self-awareness.

But these two stages by no means comprehend the whole human being either. There are also human characteristics which are derived not from the environment, from education or from 'the spirit of the time' [*Zeitgeist*] nor from the stream of inherited qualities. These other characteristics are rooted in a third layer of the human being. These are, as is very easy to see, more essential, more individual than everything that could already be provided by the two previous stages of real self-knowledge; one might also say: they are more inward. These characteristics are carried over from past lives on earth of the individuality itself in a kind of self-heredity into the present life. Spiritual science speaks of the *astral body* as the bearer of these characteristics. We encounter here the field of the working of destiny through *different earth lives*. The third form of self-knowledge will therefore have to direct its gaze towards the human soul's wandering in the stream of time from earth-life to earth-life in order to see how out of its own past, the soul has woven the character of its present capacities.

And yet this still does not comprise the human being entirely. Within his innermost self there lives something which is raised above all the becoming and fading away of time—his own eternal being. This was once described as the kernel of one's being experienced as something godly and holy—the I AM I. And when the words 'Become who you are' are spoken, then this indicates at the same time the third and fourth layers of our being. 'Become' can only mean: bring to expression within time and space existence what you are and remain in your eternal being—beyond that which arises and fades.

Mystical introspection of the kind that Goethe hated so much can never succeed in truly discovering this I AM. Here self-knowledge means nothing other than complete, comprehensive world-knowledge, and in order to be really worldwide, this must include the spiritual dimension of creation. For like a drop of the ocean the kernel of the I is a part of the spirituality of the world. The I AM is at one with this spirituality of the world and not just one with the tiny little piece of the world that is called our body.

★

Ludwig Polzer was as enthused and moved by what he had heard as was his father Julius. Through this first lecture that he heard by Rudolf Steiner, he felt that 'a seed for a new life had been laid in my soul'. It would be three years before the seed put forth roots and slowly but surely grew into a tree of knowledge on which all the spiritual-scientific knowledge he later acquired was, so to speak, only the fruit.

On the following day Steiner gave a public lecture in the Hall of the Association of Engineers and Architects on 'The Being of Man as the Key to the Secrets of the World'.[72] For Ludwig Polzer, the first lecture he had heard was now in a certain sense extended and expanded. His enthusiasm for that first lecture had led him to hire a stenographer who worked at the parliament and to ask Steiner for permission to transcribe the lecture. Not a word of this new spiritual revelation was to be lost to him!

The presentation of the fourfoldness of the members of the human organism was rendered more precisely in different ways in the public lectures. The spiritual-scientific method of observation shows that a lower member of the organism develops as a condensation of the one above it. Further, it shows that the physical body is the lowest when considered only from one viewpoint because for the individuality it is the *outermost* member of the organism yet from another viewpoint it is the most perfect and harmonious. One may compare the perfect structure of the thigh bone—minimum use of material for maximum weight-bearing—to the relative imperfection of our soul life, the third member of our organism. The physical organism shows itself as the oldest member of our organism, the I as the youngest. Behind the physical body lie four evolutionary periods, behind the etheric body [life body] three periods, behind the astral body [soul life] two periods, whereas the I is in human beings today in the first phase of its inner development. Steiner therefore calls it the baby of all the members of the organism.

Then Steiner explained that the human being was the firstborn of creation and that the animals, plants and minerals were originally the substance of his being which remained behind in development (which means they were incapable of taking into themselves certain higher members) and were therefore placed outside actual human substance so that the human being could advance unhindered in his own evolution. He therefore has to thank the realms of nature that were set outside him for the possibility of his own higher development. An image of this possibility of higher development can be felt in Raphael's Sistine Madonna, with which Steiner had begun his whole lecture.

In this way Rudolf Steiner showed in concrete detail how the human being is, so to speak, an extract of all the other world phenomena, the true microcosm of the entire macrocosm and therefore can be regarded as 'the key to the secrets of the world'.

'From the very first encounter I knew,' wrote Polzer in 1936,

> that this man possessed the key to many mysteries of the world; but I could not guess what an enormous significance this meeting would have for the rest of my life. But I did experience in a flash that a transformation was preparing itself within me and would one day be accomplished.[73]

★

The first two lectures he heard by Steiner appear in hindsight to hold a very special relation to Polzer's inner life. The first one was like the suddenly awakening effect of thunder and lightning; the second was like a powerful rainstorm which brought forth the new seed in the ground of his soul.

19. Transitions in Time

Ludwig Polzer was not a man to rush into things. Despite the deep impression that Steiner's lectures made on him, his activity at home on his estate first continued in a very familiar way. 'Rome wasn't built in a day' is a proverb that also applies in this case. Or as Polzer himself expressed it: 'It took [...] three more years before I recognized that it wasn't only a matter of fine lectures but of a spiritual direction which claimed the attention of the whole human being.'[74]

In these years, with the support of his wife, Polzer worked ever more consciously into the field of agriculture. After every day's work he would have discussions with Ignaz Reichl about the economy of the estate. The serious way in which he sought to secure the family's existence on the land made a great impression on his father, who throughout his life had avoided anything to do with agriculture. It also pleased his father that Julius and Josef were being brought up to appreciate a modest lifestyle and in practical ways of living.

A picture full of allegory impressed itself upon Ludwig Polzer from this time in Tannbach: his father Julius' eyesight was then already very bad and caused him to move about in unfamiliar places only very timidly. 'One day,' reported Ludwig Polzer,

> Julius and Josef, each holding one of his hands, led him to the edge of the forest from where the path went down to Gutau into the ditch at the brook. There both boys stopped and said: 'You can't go down there, Grandpapa, it's too hard for you.' The caring manner in which they said this I found not only very endearing in that moment but I often had to reflect on those words in another sense much later. The scene of the two boys with their grandfather between them holding him back from a danger remained like a symbol before my soul as if a promise of commitment had been made by it which would reach far beyond that moment.

An image worth thinking about! Three generations together on the path—the third walking towards the future which would become an abyss, and the first generation, who was to be spared it. If Julius Polzer still lived in a world in which culture and form still meant a great deal, his grandsons would soon have to experience their complete ruin! And in the middle, bridging between the generations of the grandfather and grandsons, Ludwig Polzer, who retained so much of the old within him that he was to see the need for destruction and to experience and live through the planting of the seeds of what was truly new. Ludwig Polzer thus incorporated a time of transition in his own being.

★

In spring 1909 the whole family paid a longer visit to Berta's aunt Anna Westphalen for the first time in Auersperg, Gyöngyös in Hungarian; she was a daughter of the youngest brother of the Austrian Prime Minister. Aunt Anna, who Berta Polzer loved dearly, had been through a hard school in life. She married a relative against her will, but lost her husband soon after; her only brother was shot in a duel in the garden of the Palais Waldstein in Prague, in which Ludwig Polzer often walked with Adolf Waldstein. Her mother and her sister got caught in the Pressburg Fire when they were getting dressed for a ball and died of burns. She herself had been an excellent rider in her youth and had many times accompanied the Empress Elisabeth on hunting rides in Gödöllö. When the Polzers came to visit, their elderly aunt still had 'great skill with horses', wrote Polzer. 'She herself mostly went about in a bassinet and on trips often took one or the other of the children with her. There was still something of the skilled daredevil rider in her—it showed itself in how she moved about!' It almost sounds as if Ludwig Polzer himself sometimes looked for something powerful to hold onto . . .

With Aunt Anna's daughter and her children—the four 'A's': Anna, Aja, Agi, Alexander—Julius and Josef could at last really enjoy the happiness of childhood friendship.

But Gyöngyös offered another possibility of relationship. Here in 1828 Ludwig Polzer's maternal great-grandfather, Count Friedrich Hoditz und Wolframitz had died when commanding the Palatinal Hussars. The family soon found the grave at the local cemetery. And so Ludwig Polzer moved on this Hungarian trip in a sense to the second stage of self-knowledge in that he found an opportunity to relate to his wife's ancestral stream as well as his own.

His own early military career appeared before him here too; in his aunt Anna's house, in which many officers had used to go in and out, he met his old riding instructor again from Mährisch-Weisskirchen.

What else ought to be noted from this time of transition?

In 1909 Ludwig Polzer's sister Marie-Sefine married Marquis Olivier Bacquehem, who was then a senior Court President. Bacquehem had been Governor of Graz in the 90s; Arthur Polzer had served under him for a while and had in fact played the key role in helping the couple get acquainted.

★

In the autumn of 1909 Polzer travelled along the Dalmatian coast, took an interest in Roman excavations near Pola, visited a nephew there and went on to Ragusa (today Dubrovnik). He would have liked to visit Cattaro (today Kotor) to see with his own eyes the town with its splendid bay where his father during his time with the garrison there had often swum. But the farmwork at Tannbach called him back.

Here he tried out a second breed of cow; Montafoner cows were now added to the Pinzgauers. But after a while the Montafoners bred too fast 'although we always had fine animals' and so the attempt with the Montafoners was finally abandoned.

In the spring of 1910 came another trip to Hungary. It was only to the environs of Steinamanger. Here Polzer wanted to see again his old friends Countess Felici Széchenyi, with whose daughter he had once been much connected, and Count Gábor Széchenyi. The experience he had there is worth noting. He wrote:

> Nothing had altered outwardly; both had become quite old; I had the sad feeling of something fading away, not only these two but a whole era with all its fine sides and its failings. There in Hungary at that time one still saw among the nobility and the farmers the remains of a once really strong agricultural population, a high degree of prosperity and real brotherly hospitality. The Széchenyis of that generation had become very old but were by nature healthy and strong. Already in the next generation this was breaking down. *Perhaps nowhere else could one say that the sudden breakdown of human nature could be so well observed as there.* Those born in the first half of the nineteenth century had strong natures; their sons and daughters less so, and their grandchildren were already mostly decadent and sickly. I could observe that particularly in the Széchenyi and Pálffy families.

So it was that Polzer observed in the example of the great noble families to whom he was close—he had been hunting with Vilmos Pálffy in Bukovina only a few years before—that it was less and less possible to build up something on the basis of genetic inheritance.

After his experiences in Gyöngyös and what he now learned in Szombathely, not only did he become more aware of his connection to his own lineage but the need to draw on much deeper powers of individuality beyond the impulse of heredity became ever clearer to him.

In May and part of June 1910 the family once again holidayed on the Lido in Venice. Aunt Anna Westphalen's grandchildren—the four A's—went with them, to the great delight of Julius and Josef. This time they did not stay in a hotel but rented rooms at the Villa Tami and brought a cook and a maid with them. Even though Berta Polzer had to check the rooms including the ceilings for tarantulas and scorpions before going to bed, the vacation passed very happily, all the more so, when after a while, Ludwig's parents also came to visit. He reserved for them a room at the Hotel

Monaco which still stands today near St Mark's Square, looking out over the sea towards the Lido.

During the daytime Julius and his wife Christine travelled along the Lido or were invited by their son and grandchildren to tea and cakes at the Cafe Florian. Julius Polzer really loved this city, more than Verona. Venice, which had belonged to Austria until 1866, in many of its squares and facades still showed to him the hand of the Habsburgs. And still today the visitor to St Mark's Square will not fail to hear Viennese waltzes ...

In Venice Julius Polzer will have talked over with his son much that he had recently gained from spiritual science. Julius' impressions of Steiner's lecture cycle *Makrokosmos und Mikrokosmos*, given two months earlier, were still deep and fresh.[75] His son was to hear about these lectures, although he regretted that his father had omitted to inform him of the event at the time because he did not want to distract him from his duties at Tannbach. It was the last time that Julius Polzer was in Venice. He was in his 76th year. He would have liked so much to have been able to repeat the visit to Venice the following year, accompanied only by his son.

In August Ludwig Polzer prepared for his first trip to England. This trip too would show him how fragile all old aristocratic culture had become. Blanche Tollemache, his first great love, who we met in Part I, had often urged him to make such a trip. Mathilde Hoditz, who had remained in constant touch with Blanche by letter since the latter's visit to Vienna had already visited her once in England. And so Ludwig Polzer, who had in the meantime become her adopted nephew, decided to travel to make the journey, after he had first improved his English by reading materials in the language with his wife. Polzer was also encouraged to make the trip by Berta's former teacher, Miss Tarnocky who once worked for the Catholic aristocratic Scrope family in Yorkshire.

On 27 August 1910, arriving from Harwich/Ipswich, where he had landed on the ferry from the Hook of Holland, Ludwig Polzer entered Helmingham Castle, about 15 kilometres north of Ipswich. The castle was one of the possessions of the Tollemache family in Suffolk; its gardens are still well worth visiting today. The two-storey brick-built house originates from the thirteenth century and lies in a large park with ancient giant oaks. The park was also grazing land for beef cattle, sheep, game birds and deer.

Blanche came from the old family of Somerset-Stuart and herself lived entirely in the past. The design of the castle, its furnishings, its ancient oil paintings from English history only intensified the impression of the past through its marked lack of any modern culture.

Polzer spent a week at Helmingham Castle. He became acquainted with some of Blanche's brothers, who except for the youngest, whom we encountered briefly in Modern in 1890, suffered from a kind of mental illness.

Almost daily, Ludwig and Blanche travelled into the surrounding area in order to introduce Ludwig to neighbouring friendly families. In the evenings Blanche sang Scottish folk songs for their hosts, and her lovely voice once more conjured up a magical mood of ancient times. Ludwig Polzer was, however, by his own admission,

> often not very comfortable in this house; the atmosphere was one which expressed what remained of the past, there were few people in the entire house, few servants, the stables were empty; everything spoke of loneliness. I had the feeling that time had stopped within this park.

Despite the Scottish ambience life at Helmingham Castle made Polzer think in many respects of the court of Empress Elisabeth.

By contrast, he experienced the following visit to the Scrope family in Yorkshire as more permeated and surrounded by the atmosphere of the Stuarts. The Scropes lived about 40 kilometres north-west of the city of York at Danby Hall, not far from Bolton Castle, where Mary Stuart had been held captive for a time. Danby Hall was built more like a castle out of solid blocks of stone in a hilly landscape, and Polzer felt visibly better in this atmosphere. The region had something light about it; there were young people and children in the house, and the Scrope family treated him, merely due to Miss Tarnocky's recommendation, like an old friend of the family. Moreover, he was able to go hunting, which he still enjoyed, with Henry Scrope, the master of the house.

After this stay with old Protestant and Catholic noble families in England, Polzer spent a week in London to experience something of the country's modern life, again as a guest of Blanche, who owned a property on Grosvenor Road. Here too in London, Blanche touchingly tried to help her guest and friend 'understand how things had once been', as Polzer later wrote. 'I was never in any districts where there was poverty, misery and crime.'

Then our traveller had had enough. He felt the urge to return home. He was not at all used to long journeys without Berta and found them really hard. He therefore stayed in Paris only one and half days, although he had never been there before. He visited the Louvre, the Invalides, Notre Dame and wrote that after London, his impression of Paris was of a city 'uncared for and shabby'.

And so his trip to England, along with all its human and aesthetic experiences, reinforced what he had felt about the Széchenyis: when it came to what could show itself capable of working for the future of humanity, nothing could any longer be expected from the old element of the nobility alone, without a new inspiration from the most modern spirituality. The age of noble dynasties was drawing to a close.

★

A transition of a very different kind showed itself in Ludwig Polzer's activities when he decided to accept the post of representative of the Pragarten District Agricultural Cooperative. It was his first step into the world of politics. For all too soon he would realize how closely agricultural issues were bound up with party politics and how little with actual agricultural necessities. He took on for a time the direction of the cooperative, which consisted of thirteen communities; he held meetings but soon had to recognize 'that these bureaucratic methods could not bring agriculture forward, and that one could achieve nothing ... with material subsidies alone. I could also see how politics was playing a role, how the agricultural council and the cooperatives managed by it were beholden to the Christian Social Party.' And since Polzer the newcomer still had little political credit, and political independents were excluded on principle, he was able to exert very little influence despite his position.

He therefore decided to organize in Tannbach an independent course of instruction in agriculture, in which Alois Reumüller, a capable Swiss colleague was very helpful. As Polzer might well have expected, his undertaking stirred up mistrust among influential Christian Social circles.

In 1911 the first elections to the Imperial Parliament were to be held on the basis of universal suffrage. But the official preparations for the elections 'deeply offended against [Polzer's] concepts of freedom'. In a spirit of noble revolt, he took up his pen and wrote 'Considerations on the Elections', which he had printed and distributed throughout Upper Austria. This pamphlet by a non-partisan autonomous individual led the author to put himself forward as an independent candidate in the elections. Polzer wrote: 'Since the Provincial Governor of Upper Austria, Prelate Johann Nep. Hauser, has been put forward in this constituency by the Christian Social Party, the whole affair has taken on a most interesting form and has preoccupied the public intensely.' Despite prematurely pessimistic warnings, the election results for the unknown candidate were relatively favourable. In the Pragarten area he even gained a strong majority and at the same time the greatest enmity from the Christian Social Party. Now they sought to be rid of him, and in the following way: through 'artificially engineered boundary changes in single communities by the Provincial Cultural Council' the district cooperative, whose representative Polzer had been up to that point, was diminished in size. With great presence of mind, he immediately resorted to the only possible means of countering this move and 'myself divided the three communities of Gutau, Erdmannsdorf and Hundsdorf [...] to which Tannbach belonged, from the rest of Pragarten, in order at least to terminate this reduction manoeuvre myself which had been employed against me'.

From this time onwards, Polzer felt to a much greater degree how uncertain the existence of Tannbach was; he even conceived a plan to look for a post as agricultural correspondent in North America.

★

In opposition to the prevailing tendency for party allegiances, Ludwig Polzer had opted for real human freedom and therefore naturally found little understanding. A few new friends he made at that time wanted to start a new independent party with him. But already in speaking about a programme for such a party Polzer had to confess that this could or should never be the usual kind of party if it was to realize his intentions.

In his will to do something in politics Polzer here came up against a kind of boundary. He formulated it as follows:

> At that time I myself could not find or express the concrete method which could lead to what I felt to be necessary and worthy of human beings. I was often talked about and well-known in the province, but no one really knew what I wanted. To enable me to find exactly what this was, destiny showed me the path to Rudolf Steiner. It was in that very year, after that political episode, that my earnest commitment to Dr Rudolf Steiner began. My political activities were interrupted by this and only later, in 1917, continued in a new form.

It was this will to engage in public, political activity which, through his search for clarity in his aims, only now really led Polzer to seek Steiner out, the man whom he had already encountered three years earlier.

The final decisive factor which brought about the 'earnest commitment' to Dr Rudolf Steiner was Steiner's lecture cycle *The Gospel of St John*[76], which Polzer read with his wife in July 1911 and which gripped Berta Polzer's religiously inclined soul fully and deeply. Until then Ludwig Polzer had always studied Steiner's lectures and works by himself and only occasionally spoken of them with his father Julius.

In his lectures in Hamburg in 1908 Steiner described the world significance of the event of Golgotha. He there presented the transition time of all transition times. Polzer was now ready to work at the construction of a really new impulse for the modern age.

20. A Summer Conference in Munich

The summer of 1911 was of decisive importance for Ludwig and Berta Polzer's engagement with the spiritual science of Rudolf Steiner. The couple decided to travel in August to Munich; it had been announced that a cycle of lectures was to be held there titled *Wonders of the World, Ordeals of the Soul, Revelations of the Spirit.*[77]

But the way to Munich lay via Vienna, where an important family celebration was about to take place: Arthur Polzer, who had been unmarried for many years married Elisabeth Magdalena Jäger on 14 August 1911 in the St Mary Chapel of the Votive Church. Arthur's parents, who only saw the bride for the first time the day before the wedding, were overjoyed; Ludwig was the witness to the ceremony. Shortly before the wedding a telegram arrived from Archduke Karl (the later Emperor) who sent Arthur his best wishes for the couple's 'most intimate happiness and blessings'.[78] This was in Julius Polzer's eyes a very promising omen for the future, both for his private and professional life. After more than ten years working at the Ministry of the Interior, Arthur had since 1910 been First Secretary and Director of the Chancellory of the Imperial Household. On assuming this office he had received the title of Privy Councillor.

For many years Arthur had enjoyed the friendly trust of the archduke, who was 18 years younger than himself. As a doctor of law, he was helpful to the archduke in his studies of the complex problems of rights in the Kingdom of Hungary and advised him in other studies. Already in these early years Archduke Karl resolved to appoint his friend and adviser to the post of Director of the Cabinet one day. Arthur had often spent time as a guest of the archduke at Miramare Castle near Trieste, and on the very same day, three years earlier, that he had first become acquainted with his 'Liesl', the archduke had again sent him a telegram inviting him to Miramare. The future Emperor Karl seemed predestined to play a much greater role in Arthur's life than the reigning Emperor Franz Joseph was playing in the life of Ludwig, who had received the emperor's permission for his own early marriage ...

Since 1907 mystery dramas had been performed at the theosophical summer conferences in Munich; the first had been Edouard Schuré's *Drama from Eleusis* and *The Children of Lucifer*, then from 1910, Rudolf Steiner's own mystery dramas. Berta and Ludwig Polzer did not yet attend the dramas of 1911; 'not yet realizing their greatness'.[79]

They thus found themselves at the lecture which Rudolf Steiner gave on 18 August at the opening of the above-mentioned lecture cycle. Steiner spoke about the origins of dramatic art in relation to the Mysteries of Eleusis and in this lecture spoke about two of the leading figures of the European cultural heritage that had originated in Greece: *Persephone* and *Iphigenia*. He characterized the first of these as the bearer of a power still rooted in ancient clairvoyance, and the second as an image of warning of the necessity to bring certain sacrifices for the religious life in an age of a purely intellectual culture in order to preserve this culture of intellect from degradation. Linking onto this ancient European spirit, Goethe had wanted to bring this same idea to expression in his *Iphigenia*, as the peak of his own art.

Steiner's lecture fell onto well-prepared ground in Ludwig Polzer's soul. Twenty-three years had passed since that unforgettable experience of seeing Goethe's *Iphigenia*, the last play performed at the old Court Theatre in Vienna. It had sunk into his soul in a mood of decline and leave-taking. And now, focusing in his first lecture on Iphigenia, Steiner showed how a renewal of the mystery dramas of antiquity was possible in a contemporary sense. Ludwig may already have felt a mood of sunrise awaken in his soul on hearing this first lecture in Steiner's Munich cycle.

Looking back to those memorable lectures in Munich, Polzer later wrote:

> At that time in Munich I remembered the first lecture I had heard by Rudolf Steiner in 1908 in which the question of the being of man had been so comprehensively addressed and now I felt the question of the destiny of mankind approaching me from the destiny of the many people who were spiritually linked to each other in the anthroposophical community.[80]

This statement shows how deeply the impression of that first lecture of 1908 had lived on within him.

In the course of the summer conference Ludwig and Berta Polzer were personally introduced to Rudolf Steiner by Martha Reif, who would later be a very active Society member, especially in Denmark. Steiner immediately mentioned Polzer's father Julius 'whom he almost always saw at his lectures in Vienna'.[81]

Two women made a very particular impression on the newcomer: the one was Miss Stinde, the President of the Munich branch of the Theosophical Society who 'made the best impression through her clear, forthright appearance, her complete devotion to theosophical ideas [...] without claiming anything for herself and without showing any signs of occult vanity'.[82]

Until her premature death in 1915 Sophie Stinde was President of the Building Association for the 'House of the Word' that was intended originally for Munich but was eventually built in Dornach, Switzerland, according to plans by Rudolf Steiner.

Almost as great an impression on Polzer was made by Countess Pauline von Kalckreuth, who had earlier been one of the empress' ladies-in-waiting and was now putting all her energies into theosophical work.

At a social gathering at the Luitpold Rooms, where the lectures were also held, Ludwig Polzer found himself directed to a seat at a table where he was able to make the acquaintance of Helene Röchling, the wife of a Privy Councillor. She, like Sophie Stinde, was intimately connected with the planned building; she became the most generous donor to the building of the first Goetheanum.

The Privy Councillor's wife from Munich was also very friendly with the wife of the Chief of the German General Staff—Countess Eliza Moltke-Huitfeldt; Polzer would also soon get to know this important individual personally in Berlin.

Berta was directed to a group of Scandinavians with whom she too later maintained friendly relations.

Here in Munich Berta and Ludwig Polzer became members of the Theosophical Society.

For the Polzers this Munich summer conference thus proved to be not only a turning point in terms of knowledge but also socially. 'Until then,' wrote Ludwig Polzer in his Prague Notes,[83]

> we had many relatives and friends in the circles of Austrian, Bohemian and Hungarian nobility whom we visited and who visited us. We went on hunting trips to various castles, met the same people in winter in towns and on trips [...] The people who I had met in my youth and those with whom we associated after my marriage almost all knew each other or at least knew something of each other going back generations. One moved in a rather enclosed circle of people and felt oneself quite comfortable within this as a matter of course [...]
>
> Now it was all different. The change in our circle of acquaintances after 1911 was enormous. Even though we wanted to remain in good relations with our nearest relatives and friends from earlier times and still visited them occasionally, we no longer had the time to devote to the connections with them as intensively as before, and with the circles of people who were somewhat further from us and with the younger generation our relations ceased altogether. So in the course of time there remained only a friendly and faithful memory of them. Common [...] interests, especially those of a cultural kind which grow in a lively way, such as anthroposophy awakens, bind one more strongly than relations which traditionally are formed more externally or on the basis of a community of blood.

And gradually an organ grew in Ludwig Polzer that could sense the background of destiny of these new relationships of choice: 'I felt very soon that the people who I encountered through anthroposophy had been so prepared in earlier lives that at a [...] certain point in time they had had to gather around the [...] teacher.'[84]

Ludwig Polzer—and to a lesser extent this also applied to Berta—thus committed himself quickly to participation in the life of the Theosophical

Society, for in his view one could 'only become an anthroposopher in the full sense of the word' and

> advance to real knowledge of destiny [...] when one engaged with human beings in the same great spiritual destiny [...] Then my interest in the destinies of other people began to awaken; I saw more in my fellow human beings than before [...] Within such relationships of destiny [...] one also stands close to the real impulses in the development of mankind.

We saw earlier how strong Polzer's need to understand such *real* historical impulses was. He added: 'Such a life cannot run in a normal bourgeois fashion.'[85] And indeed, from this point on, *his* own life at least did not run in that fashion.

Berta and Ludwig Polzer's 'earnest commitment' to Steiner's spiritual science which was made in Munich in 1911 was also important for their economic and occupational life. All plans to emigrate were abandoned. Polzer had indicated something of these intentions to Steiner, for he noted the comment that Steiner made about this, most probably still in Munich: 'That our family was too much bound up with European events to emigrate to another continent.' Polzer's own comment on the change in his plans seemed to have flowed from earnest self-observation: 'I am happy about this change in my destiny, for I would have missed out on enormous insights into humanity and life and with my very slight knowledge of business, would certainly not have achieved much.'[86]

Feeling richly endowed with new life goals to strive for across a wide horizon, the couple returned home to Tannbach. Seeing their children again must have been an especially joyful experience. And to the even greater joy of the family, Arthur and his young bride came from Linz to stay in Tannbach for two days at the end of their honeymoon.

The meeting of the two couples, however, did not pass without it becoming clear that there was a strong dissonance between them in how they looked at the world. Arthur wrote: 'Ludwig and Berta showed us the house and farm, and through the stables into the fields and the wood. The rest of the time we spent in Ludwig's study. There they [Berta and Ludwig] took it in turns to read to us from Rudolf Steiner's writings.' And what impression did this make on the visitors? 'What was read to us was certainly full of wisdom, but we, for whom it was all new, lacked an understanding for it.' And now a trait appears in Arthur which not only shows a complete polarity to Ludwig's way of seeing things, but in a certain sense also appears to contradict what lay deeper within Arthur's own soul. Following his comments above, Arthur wrote: 'I am and was always of the opinion that it is not good to seek to research what is unresearchable beyond the boundaries that God has set for human beings.'[87]

Here something of Arthur's spiritually conservative side showed itself, a trait which, however, as already mentioned, appears to stand in an interesting contradiction to his artistic nature and the spiritual tenor of his soul; he had once contemplated, for example, an important personal experience from the viewpoint of earlier earth lives (see p. 55).

★

The new impetus he received in 1911 carried Ludwig Polzer far into the years which followed. In January he travelled again to Munich with Berta to attend lectures by Steiner. On 12 February the Hamerling Branch of the Theosophical Society was founded in Graz in the presence of Rudolf Steiner. The next day, Steiner spoke about this great poet and thinker, whom Ludwig Polzer had often met on his way to and from school.

It may have been on this occasion that Ludwig Polzer was able to have his first private conversation with Rudolf Steiner. 'I still did not know then really how to behave properly and did not even ask for any personal exercises,' he wrote in his Prague Notes. 'I only remember that at that time he spoke to me about my maternal great-grandfather of four generations before, Count Franziskus Josephus [von] Hoditz und Wolframitz.'[88]

A noteworthy signature: the conversation took place in the town where Ludwig Polzer had spent his childhood and where he had first felt within him those deep-rooted impressions of the 'when and where' of life. This leads straight to that man among his ancestors whom we looked at in detail in Part I of this book. So already in this first conversation Steiner placed before Polzer a concrete exercise in self-knowledge, in the sense of the four stages of all true self-knowledge, as he had described them in that first lecture Polzer had heard in Vienna in 1908. He pointed him to the second stage, which is formed of knowledge of the concrete details which are at work in the stream of heredity. And also the following words, which Ludwig Polzer reported from Steiner, contain a call to self-knowledge, even if in a very veiled manner: 'He said to me then that it always appeared to him very remarkable that he[*] had the same names as Emperor Franz Joseph.' Polzer added to this: 'I was unable to understand much about this then; unfortunately, I never came back to it.'[89]

These mysterious words by Steiner were actually pointing Polzer to the *third* stage of self-knowledge, where the thread of destiny, which is woven through earth lives, can gradually be uncovered. This may seem to many readers even more of a riddle that Steiner's remark appeared to Polzer. We shall come back to Steiner's words at a later stage in this book.

---

[*] Polzer's Bohemian ancestor—T.M.

21. Years of Apprenticeship and Travelling

Soon after his conversation in Graz with Rudolf Steiner, Polzer travelled with his wife once again to Munich to attend lectures by his spiritual teacher. If Graz was the city into which he had been guided by ties of blood, Munich became for him and Berta the place they loved to visit where they formed new relationships of choice. For a while this caused a certain amount of discord in the family. It was not felt appropriate that Ludwig should behave like a traveller following after the preacher of a new spiritual teaching, while Arthur, who from childhood on had suffered from chronic stomach pains lay in bed after a stomach (pylorus) operation. It was felt at home that 'we had not cared enough for Arthur during this time', wrote Ludwig Polzer.[90] He freely admitted: 'I must confess that this was the case; but this was because I did not really know what kind of operation was involved and therefore underestimated the whole thing.'

Around the time of Arthur's operation, on 3 March 1912 Ludwig gave a speech[91] as representative of the 'Independent Country Party' that had been founded after his election campaign of June 1911.

At the very outset of his speech he assured the gathering of his supporters that this 'first appearance was no frivolous effort' but was the 'eventual result, in outer activity and appearance, and based on purely idealistic impulses of calm, of honest observation and of the many experiences he had had in life under various circumstances'.

He then spoke, with the pointed clarity he invariably showed on such occasions, against the economic policy of state monopoly which threatened to suffocate the economic self-sufficiency of the single farmer in a 'socialist' state-run and province-run enterprise with a constantly growing army of bureaucrats. 'I do not wish to speak against bureaucracy in general,' he said,

> I oppose only the ongoing increase in the number of officials, which only *appears* to be objectively justified, and which is a consequence of State-controlled enterprise; [I oppose] the creation of more and more new regulations which restrict personal freedom, which require more officials, which unnecessarily threaten autonomy and kill the spirit of enterprise.

He pointed to the absurdity of such politics by mentioning the example of the nationalization of the Austrian Railways, which had become unprofitable.

Polzer denounced the fruitless administrative reforms which were then underway, called for better education and for the people to be much better informed so that 'the inexhaustible powers of the human being can be awakened...in order to be able, equipped with these forces, to engage in a successful struggle for reforms which will make possible the higher development of the single individual and thereby of the whole of mankind.' Here a true individualist was speaking, who only saw the possibility for improvements in social conditions by the liberation and promotion of the single human being who is striving for cultural benefit.

Like an echo of the election campaign of summer 1911 this speech resounded on into the following year. But the Independent Country Party soon petered out lethargically. Where were the people who were supposed to be a position to form a really supra-partisan or non-partisan party as Polzer envisaged? The time was not yet ripe for it.

Arthur's illness was only the beginning of a whole series of illnesses in the family in the spring of 1912 which in two cases ended in deaths.

In April Julius Polzer also fell seriously ill. The diagnosis was calcified cardiac arteries. In May Berta went down with measles. In the same month uncle Wlasko also became suddenly very ill with decomposition of the blood. He died soon afterwards, on 11 June, at his beloved Schloss Heiligenkreutz in Bohemia; Berta and Ludwig were with him.

In July they went once more with the children to aunt Anna's in Gyöngyös. But in the middle of their holidays a telegram came from Vienna which reported a worsening of Julius' condition. The family immediately packed their trunks and left for Vienna. Shortly afterwards, Julius died in his 78th year at his residence in Vienna. It was 25 July 1912, the day of St Christopher and of St Jacob, who is supposed to give assistance to all spiritual pilgrims.

A member of the family had the idea—was it Ludwig?—to bury Julius not in Vienna but in Modern which the family associated with so many happy memories and which Julius loved so much. His grave can still be found at the local cemetery. On the faded gravestone can be read the words:

> *The years come and go.*
> *The bobbin runs busily in the loom,*
> *Humming to and fro.*
> *What the loom weaves—no weaver knows.*

It is a verse by Heine.

Julius' first born later wrote: 'So our dear father was laid to rest in the cemetery at Modern. He lies there now in that notable place, where I always felt the East border on the West. His grave is overgrown with ivy and surrounded with spruce trees.'[92]

On the gentle outlying hills of the Little Carpathians, where Ludwig Polzer's first love for a person from the West blossomed, there now rests the earthly remains of his father, who knew how to light up a *second* love within him which would show itself to be more enduring than that earthly love—the love for the knowledge of the reality of the spirit. It was thanks to *this* love that even death had no power over the living inner relationship between Julius and Ludwig Polzer.

In August we find Berta and Ludwig once again in Munich—at the annual theosophical summer conference. This time they saw the mystery dramas performed. Berta especially was deeply affected by them.

Their circle of voluntary relations also expanded afresh. The first who should be mentioned is Count Otto Lerchenfeld, the nephew of Hugo Lerchenfeld, the royal Bavarian envoy in Berlin. The closest bonds would unite Polzer with Count Lerchenfeld and two of his daughters in the future. Berta and Ludwig also got to know Marie von Sivers, the later wife of Rudolf Steiner, and Julius Breitenstein, Branch leader in Vienna.

As usual, Rudolf Steiner expounded on the performances of the mystery dramas in a cycle of lectures.[93]

The Munich conference had hardly closed when Polzer travelled on alone to Basel in Switzerland to attend a further lecture cycle which Steiner was to hold there on the Gospel of St Mark.[94]

In the Basler Hotel he met Princess Marie Rohan, an old true friend of his father's. She too had come for the lecture cycle. So during those days in Basel there was plenty of opportunity, not only to speak about Steiner's lectures but also to exchange reminiscences of his father.

Had not Julius Polzer ever more frequently sought out gatherings of such people who were united by the same bond of spiritual striving? After the lecture cycle *Makrokosmos und Mikrokosmos*, which he was able to attend in Vienna in 1910, he told Ludwig, 'how much at home he had felt then in [...] the Society, listening to these lectures evening after evening'.[95] So, in the depths of his soul, Ludwig would have wanted to share in the lectures in Basel and also in the conversations at the hotel, with these two people, who like him were united in the sacred cause of the spirit. For who could claim with certainty that Julius Polzer had *not* taken part in the depths of his soul?

In those days Ludwig Polzer knew no theosophists in Basel. So when he had a free afternoon one day, out of a sudden impulse, he just boarded an electric tram and rode it as far as the last stop on the line. There he noticed 'at a small monastery an unusual pyramid of skulls enclosed under glass in memory of the Battle at the Birs'.[96] In 1499 a Swabian army had been defeated by Swiss *landsknechts*. The inscription on the pyramid reads: 'The Lords have to lie with the farmers.' This was a striking saying for Polzer, as he was himself both a lord and a farmer. Later, he learned that on that same day from the same spot at the last tram stop Rudolf Steiner had viewed the piece of land that the Swiss, Emil Grosheintz, had offered for the building that had been intended for Munich. Ludwig Polzer had thus travelled to *Dornach* by accident! 'I was thus drawn at that time by a premonition to the place where until Rudolf Steiner's death the most important events in the anthroposophical movement occurred'[97], he wrote in his Prague Notes. Since the plans for the building in Munich had finally been rejected by the authorities—as Polzer saw it, through opposition from the church—in the following year the foundation stone of the first Goetheanum was in fact laid here in Dornach.

Ludwig Polzer was thus—unconsciously—Rudolf Steiner's first pupil to come upon the place of his teacher's activity in Switzerland.

October began and with it came the outbreak of the First Balkan War. Polzer experienced it immediately as the 'prologue to the coming European catastrophe'. He emphasized: 'It was soon clear to me then that this would be the beginning of a catastrophe for mankind, which I had always expected.'[98] He at least was not to be counted among the army of the clueless, who would soon be shaken out of their historical sleep.

Just a short while earlier he had come upon the building-site of a culture for the future—now in spiritual wakefulness he looked on the coming destruction of the culture of the past, which was no longer viable...

If we look back on this year, alongside his impressions of lectures, his journeys and his new friendships, two events stand out which would be of decisive significance for him in the year to come; one, apparently more personal and one which concerned the whole world. We are referring here of course to the death of his father and to the Balkan War just mentioned. Both would in 1913 be linked to real instruction for Ludwig Polzer by Rudolf Steiner.

★

But first in the spring of 1913 there was a return to the widths and the heights. In May Berta and Ludwig travelled to Helsingfors, as Helsinki was then called, where Steiner spoke on *The Occult Foundations of the Bhagavad Gita*[99]. 'Events were not then as serious as they became later,' wrote Polzer, 'and so, able to devote myself wholly to spiritual science without any great disturbances, without external difficulties or cares, I could hear Rudolf Steiner speak in many cities on the most varied themes of human life on earth and in the spiritual world.'[100]

His travels went via Berlin and Sassnitz to Stockholm, from where he went on a trip through the Skerries with friends and acquaintances. From Abo the journey went on to Helsingfors by train. 'The beauties of the North,' wrote Polzer, 'made a great impression on Berta especially.'[101] They often went into the region around Helsingfors and 'let the landscape work upon [us]'. Ludwig Polzer was so strongly gripped by his experience of nature itself that, although much less practised in handcrafts than his brother Arthur, he was moved to paint a watercolour. Also, in his notes for his memoirs Polzer gives a brief sketch of this visit when he writes:

> We stayed in a hotel opposite the harbour, staffed by Russians. There was almost always a large bread market in front of our windows; the country people came with their four-wheeled wagons, with the most varied products from the land, but bread was especially conspicuous. We were particularly impresssed by the excellent local horses: they were small and sturdy with a huge gait. Already when we went from the station to the hotel, we became quite anxious in the little carriages and the sharp turns round the street corners.[102]

Until then, the couple had only had similar travelling experiences in a rudimentary fashion in Gyöngyös with aunt Anna...

Polzer concludes, 'They were wonderful days we experienced, listening to the lectures and enjoying nature. Such journeys together with so many friends were especially community-building; one felt one belonged to a large, spiritual family.'[103]

Steiner's lectures had such an inspiring effect on the couple that hardly had they returned from the North when, still in June, they were off again to Munich as if to bring what they had experienced to maturity in the city of free relationships.

When aunt Anna came to Tannbach in August she was told in no uncertain terms that her rather brash riding style had some real competition in Scandinavia... It was the last time Ludwig Polzer saw his aunt. She passed way soon afterwards. Ten years later he wrote in the notes for his memoirs: 'My memory of her is extremely vivid; it is as though she is right next to me.'[104]

In the second half of August Berta and Ludwig once again set off for Munich. It was their third and last summer conference before the war. They saw Rudolf Steiner's mystery dramas again. The roles were played by Steiner's pupils themselves, who also prepared the curtains and costumes.

Many new people entered the circle of the couple's friends. For example, the 22-year-old Walter Johannes Stein from Vienna 'who as a very young man at that time at first took up a very critical stance towards spiritual science'.[105] With Stein too, Ludwig Polzer would soon be linked by a firm bond of friendship.

★

This visit to Munich was of special significance for Polzer in another sense. Namely, Rudolf Steiner now began to instruct Polzer, so to speak, in two directions: first, with a reading of material specially suited to Ludwig Polzer's individuality. They linked on to the two events of the previous year already mentioned, which had caused wide ripples in Polzer's soul: the death of his father and the flare-up of war in the Balkans.

In Munich this year Steiner spoke in relation to the mystery dramas on the theme of *The Secrets of the Threshold*.[106] During a pause between lectures in the Luitpold Room it happened that, as Polzer wrote,

> Rudolf Steiner was suddenly standing behind me and tapping me on the shoulder, said, 'Your father has been of great help to us in the spiritual world.' These words were so earnest and spoken with such love that I was as if stunned and shaken to my inmost being.[107]

Certainly, that the dead continued to live on had been something self-evident *as an idea* to Polzer for a long time. But that they lived concretely and could also be described as if they were merely wandering in *spaces near us*: when experienced for the first time, this can naturally be shocking at first—even if, as in this case, indirectly. But Steiner must have had a reason in this regard for not sparing Polzer, who had also been accepted into his Esoteric School in 1912. It was as if he wanted to say to Polzer: 'Take your convictions about the continued existence of the dead after death completely seriously; a great human being has gone on before you. He is more living than many of those who are alive.' Steiner wanted to open Polzer's eyes to this at the right moment.

'From this time on,' reported Polzer further, 'there was hardly a conversation with him in which he did not speak to me of my father.'[108]

From this moment in Munich onwards Ludwig Polzer became more and more aware of the realms beyond the threshold in which our dead dwell, and also more aware of meta-history without which the historical figures active in the physical world remain merely empty, misunderstood spectres. For these are linked by a thousand threads with those other, completely real lives.

Another aspect of Steiner's words should be touched upon. They appear to indicate that after his death the soul of Julius Polzer had become more inwardly united with the striving of spiritual science.

But in this respect, that soul, from its supersensible viewpoint, may have been accompanying with particular interest precisely the steps through life his son was taking in accord with spiritual science as he wandered in the world of the senses—for example, on that free day in September 1912, when Ludwig Polzer was moved to head towards Dornach ...

★

The other basic reading Polzer now undertook, at Steiner's prompting, concerned the background of political events. This too originated in a passing comment Steiner made in the course of a conversation with Polzer: 'As long as Germany goes on politically occupying itself with projects like the Baghdad railway, it will not be able to move forward in Europe.'[109] Polzer wrote the following comment on this:

> At the time I understood nothing of it, but recognized that I still understood nothing at all of the real needs of the development of individuals and peoples in Europe and of the powers that stood against those needs. I asked myself why the building of the Baghdad railway should be something that contradicted German culture. Only in the course of the world war did I learn to understand it.

What had Steiner wanted to awaken in Polzer by his comment about the Baghdad railway? The awareness that not only individuals but entire peoples can stray from their paths when they begin to follow goals that are *foreign to their own being*. And that is indeed what had happened in the Germany of Kaiser Wilhelm II. After the foundation of the Reich, Germany had striven more and more for a position of external power among the nations instead of a spiritual and cosmopolitan development of culture. The Baghdad railway, built by Germany in agreement with the Ottoman government revealed the new Reich's yearnings for power and threw down a completely unnecessary competitive challenge to Britain's trade.

'This comment about the Bagdad railway,' said Polzer finally, 'was the first teaching about world history that I received.'[110] Many more were to follow.

★

The time had now come for Julius and Josef to attend a regular school. For this purpose their parents rented accommodation in Linz at 12

Pfarrplatz, in which a special anthroposophical lecture room was fitted out. The fine, spacious house was in the neighbourhood of the house in which Marianne Willemer, the 'Suleika' in Goethe's *West-East Divan*, had been born and grew up.

Hardly had they settled into their new home when a telegram arrived from Dornach in which Emil Grossheintz informed Polzer of the foundation-laying ceremony of the Johannes Building, as the Goetheanaum was then still called,

For Polzer, who in July had become a member of the Johannes Building Association, there was no hesitation. With real presence of mind, he prepared himself for the trip; he 'had only two hours in which to catch the last possible train and arrived in Dornach by car just before the ceremony began'.[111] It was 20 September 1913. Mercury stood as evening star in the sign of the Scales, when the solemn ceremony, at which only a few people were present, was conducted. Polzer wrote about the moving event:

> On the evening of this day just a few members[*] gathered on the Dornach hill. To sink the foundation stone into the clay soil a circular pit was dug with nine temporary steps down to the bottom where the foundation stone was to be laid. The spot had been calculated such that when the building would be complete, the lecturer's lectern would stand above it. The foundation stone itself had the form of two connected pentagonal dodecahedrons, one larger and one smaller. It was made of copper. The document, which Rudolf Steiner had written to commemorate the ceremony of the laying of the foundation stone, and which was to express the meaning of this moment and of the fact of the building for all time, was enclosed within the foundation stone. Before the ceremony began a pile of wood was burned; rain was pouring down. Some of us held burning torches. We stood packed together in a circle around the pit as Rudolf Steiner approached it. At first he called, one after the other, to all the spiritual hierarchies and in his following address he gave a short cultural historical overview up to the present moment, 20 September, 1880 [years] after the Mystery of Golgotha, that is, 1913 [years] after the birth of Christ [...] Twelve red roses and one white were laid on top of the foundation stone and it was lowered down on belts stretched in the shape of a cross. I remember how I was holding a torch somewhat anxiously, out of emotion and also because drops of fire fell down and we were standing so close together, some holding up umbrellas. The image of this ceremony, illuminated by the burning pile of wood and the burning torches impressed itself deeply into my soul; I knew that I had been allowed to take part in a ceremony that would be of decisive significance for centuries.[112]

---

[*] Of the Anthroposophical Society—*transl.*

But Polzer also knew that 'with this stepping forward of the anthroposophical movement into the open [...] serious opposition against
Rudolf Steiner and the movement began'.

★

Soon after the foundation stone laying Ludwig and Berta Polzer travelled
for the second time that year to Scandinavia. Steiner spoke at the
beginning of October in Oslo on *The Fifth Gospel*[113], that is, on those
phases in the life of Jesus about which the four Gospels are silent and
which can only be read in the Akashic Chronicle, the world memory
accessible to the power of supersensible knowledge. What an experience
for the couple!

For Berta Polzer, it was an unexpected deepening of her religious
striving. For her husband, the incredible thing above all will have been
that here, not on the basis of any traditional physical documents but out of
supersensible knowledge, was a man relating precise, hitherto completely
unknown details of the life of Jesus.

We read in his memoirs:

> To have shared in that meant an enormous enrichment of our experience
> of life on the path to an understanding of the universal human essence of
> man. It seems to me today that what we experienced then was like a
> powerful prelude to everything that came towards us later. An expansion of
> consciousness enabled me to see wider horizons, and new joy for life and
> activity filled my heart.[114]

It was in such an inner mood that Ludwig Polzer now went on to face the
already kindling world conflagration.

22. The First World War

While Ludwig Polzer was holding introductory courses in spiritual science in the autumn and winter of 1913/14 at his Linz residence, the fire in the Balkans was smouldering further. Since the annexation of Bosnia-Herzegovina in October 1908 Austria-Hungary had been highly resented not only by the Ottoman Turks but also by the neighbouring kingdom of the southern Slavic Serbs. And even the Peace of Bucharest after the Second Balkan War in summer 1913 left the Serbs especially extremely disappointed—as Austria-Hungary had denied them the long sought-after access to the Adriatic.

In her book *Mitteleuropa—Bilanz eines Jahrhunderts*[115] [Middle Europe—Account of a Century] Renate Riemeck speaks of 'a war that was thoroughly-prepared and well in advance'. In the chapter 'Austria will perish', we have already detailed some essential elements of this preparation. It will be enough here simply to recall what was mentioned there, as 1914 was merely the historical surface of what, for a long time from within and without, had threatened and undermined the existence of the Dual Monarchy and thus set alight the world conflagration.

In January of the new year 1914 in Dornach, Polzer took part in the second annual general meeting of the Anthroposophical Society that had been founded a year earlier and through it united himself more inwardly and strongly with the destiny of the spiritual stream cultivated by this world Society.

At that time at home Berta often used to read to her sons German or European poetry and thereby enlivened the 'dry, abstract studies that had been drummed into them'.[116] Ludwig also listened in to her readings with great interest; Berta seems to have been a master at handicrafts. In these ways they sought to draw the worst thorns from the unavoidable effects of schooling through a living education of the feelings and the heart.

In April Steiner came once again to Vienna in order to speak about 'The Inner Being of Man Between Death and Rebirth'.[117] Christine Polzer, Ludwig's mother also attended the lecture cycle. She told her son how very much she felt inwardly united with her departed husband, especially during the lectures by Steiner. Such an unassuming expression can throw a light on real spiritual events in the realm beyond the threshold ...

After the lecture cycle Ludwig Polzer travelled for the first time as *a colleague* to the ongoing construction work at the Johannes Building in Dornach. It was intended that there would be architraves in the larger hall of the double cupola building above columns which would show the planets which were particularly involved in the cosmic development of the Earth. According to spiritual science, the development of the Earth itself falls into two distinct phases; a Mars phase and a Mercury phase.

The Mercury phase began with the Mystery of Golgotha; it denotes the future of the Earth permeated by the impulse of Golgotha. For humanity that means an ever greater development of the I, an ever greater individualization of all cultural and spiritual life. The peoples who could promote this I-development the most are those of Middle Europe who, if they remain true to their real path, encourage the drive to individuality, not nationality.[118] These peoples consist of the Germans, Austrians, Hungarians, western Slavs such as the Czechs, Poles, Slovaks, but also the Scandinavian peoples. All of these—despite all their other differences amongst each other—are in a certain sense Mercury peoples. How wonderfully precisely destiny was working when in the spring of 1914 it arranged things so that Ludwig Polzer spent three weeks carving the Mercury architrave which was made of elm wood!

★

The news of the assassination in Sarajevo in Bosnia reached the Polzer family in Traun, Bohemia at a country festival. It was 28 June, the Serbian day of the commemoration of the great Battle of the Field of Blackbirds (1389) at which the Serbs had been wiped out by the Turks; but also the day on which Serbia had become an autonomous kingdom in 1878, when Bosnia and Herzegovina had been placed under Austrian occupation. The murder of Franz Ferdinand and his wife, the Duchess of Hohenberg, (Sophie Chotek) with whom Polzer had danced in the '90s at balls in Pressburg and Prague, was, among other things, financed and organized by the Serbian secret organization The Black Hand. The threads of this assassination lead via Belgrade to St Petersburg and London. This also explains why the purely bilateral issue between the two monarchies of Serbia and Austria-Hungary was not allowed to be restricted to those two countries. In line with the aims of the Testament of Peter the Great, the exclusion of middle Europe and especially of Austria from European politics had been determined on long before.[119] Sarajevo only provided the necessary opportunity, as it did again at the end of the twentieth century, to pursue politics that were hostile to Middle Europe.

In his unpublished notes Arthur Polzer provided an interesting indication with regard to this historical background that has been little researched until today.

A few years before the outbreak of the world war, he reports,[120] a large sealed envelope was delivered one day to the Imperial Cabinet Chancellory; it bore the inscription: 'To His Majesty Emperor Franz Joseph, Vienna, Hofburg'. The sender was not mentioned on the envelope. Inside was a large letter folded several times written in peculiar, calligraphic letters. The clerk of the Cabinet Chancellory was at a loss as to how to proceed in accordance with correct protocol with this peculiar document. He first resorted to having it sent to the Imperial military chancellory, but here too there was no idea as to what to do with it. The script was compared with those of all known living languages; the conclusion was that it could only be a secret code. But as one could not just throw a document addressed to the Emperor into the wastebasket, it was sent to the cipher department of the Ministry of Foreign Affairs. There were scholars there who by their own skilled methods were able to decipher every kind of code. First they turned to two experts in the examination of paper who were to determine the origin of the paper of the document, which was apparently of foreign origin. These two paper experts, without knowing each other, both came to the same assessment, that the paper was of American origin. After months of work the cipher department succeeded in deciphering the script. The content was approximately as follows: the unnamed writer of the letter wrote that high degree Freemasons had decided in a secret sitting at which he had been present, to overthrow the dynasty of the Habsburgs and that of the Hohenzollerns, to destroy Austria and to achieve these aims by sparking a world war. He had been obliged to keep this decision secret but because of the monstrous nature of the plan, could not bring himself to remain silent; he wished to make the threatening danger known to those in authority at least in this, perhaps not entirely understandable form. The paper experts were informed of the content by the cipher department but could not keep it to themselves. They spoke of the peculiar letter here and there; both paid for this with their lives; within a short time they were both apparently the victims of accidents. One was hit on the street by falling tiles, the other was pushed by an untraceable passer-by onto the tracks of a tram and run over.

The warning went unheeded. People did not believe in the seriousness of such secret Freemasons' plans; they held them to be fairy tales and laughed at them.[121]

Today people like to dismiss such matters with the label 'conspiracy theory'.[122] But it was always a tried and tested method of political circles conscious of their goals to spread amongst the masses a theory of laughable 'conspiracies' in order to cover their backs and keep their hands free ...

Arthur Polzer closed his notes about this affair of the letter with the words: 'There were therefore—it became clear through the following fateful events—those who knew, who allowed something to become visible now and again of the threatening plans for world destruction [...]'

Just as unnoticed remained the warning that had been given by the known Freemason Henry Labouchère in 1890 in the satirical English magazine *Truth*.[123] Earlier in this book we looked in more detail at the map from *Truth* magazine and shall come back to the matter again when we discuss the publication of Arthur Polzer's book *Kaiser Karl*, which was published in 1928, in relation to further indications regarding the background issues referred to here. Arthur Polzer also relates what was 'prophesied' about a coming war by a certain Madame de Thèbes in France before 1914 to these power circles whose reach extended as far as France.

'I was very soon aware,' wrote his brother Ludwig, 'that it signified the beginning of hard times.'[124] But he was aware of something else: 'The helper was also standing there—so little known by people—when the catastrophe broke.' This knowledge gave him and Berta strength, and so they decided, precisely in this critical time, to further strengthen their spiritual scientific work. And Ludwig Polzer may have felt it a gentle, unassuming confirmation of this determination when *on the very day of the assassination* in Sarajevo Marie von Sivers informed him in the name of the Central Executive of the Anthroposophical Society that his application to form a new branch of the Society in Linz had been granted. And what did Polzer want to call this branch? 'The Franziskus Josephus Philippus Count von Hoditz und Wolframitz Branch of the Anthroposophical Society.' While the armies of Europe soon began to mobilize, Ludwig Polzer too, in an inner connection to his great ancestor, began to mobilize in a very different way on the battlefield of the spirit... Whether the length of the name of the new branch was a fortunate choice is another matter.

At the beginning of July Ludwig and Berta left for their third trip to Scandinavia in order to accompany Rudolf Steiner to Norrköping in Sweden, where he wished to speak on the theme of *Christ and the Human Soul*.[125] On 17 July the couple travelled back with Steiner to Trelleborg; from there they went by ship to Sassnitz. On this crossing they encountered the warship *La France*; on board was the French President Poincaré, accompanied by René Viviani, at that time Prime and Foreign Minister. They were on their way to St Petersburg in order to assure Russia of France's unconditional faithfulness to its alliance with Russia in case of war.

Only after Poincaré's departure for Russia was Austria's ultimatum to Serbia published on 23 July, which demanded a response within 48 hours. This was after Germany had already assured Austria-Hungary on 6 July of *its own* faithfulness to their alliance in the eventuality of Russian involvement. On 28 July Austria-Hungary then declared war against

Serbia, as the Kingdom of Serbia had not unconditionally accepted the ultimatum, which, amongst other things, demanded that the Serbian authorities allow Austrian participation in the effort to expose anti-Habsburg subversive activities in Serbia. The following day Russia declared partial mobilization and on the 30th, general mobilization. Did Poincaré advise this in St Petersburg? For Russia herself was not at all threatened by the conflict at this point. Russian mobilization led to corresponding orders being issued in Austria-Hungary on 31 July and 1 August. On the last day of July Germany demanded that Russia cancel its mobilization and then issued a further ultimatum, to France, should a Russo-German conflict ensue. Since Russia sent no answer, the German Empire declared war on Russia on 1 August and thereby took upon itself, viewed purely externally, the role of extender of the war beyond the conflict between Austria and Serbia. Since France sought to cover itself behind its commitment to the alliance with Russia, and Britain, for its part, wished to give no declaration of neutrality in response to the express request of the German ambassador in London, the German government declared war against France on 3 August. In accordance with the Schlieffen Plan, which had been devised to deal with the feared war on two fronts, German troops then marched into Belgium. This provided Great Britain with the pretext it needed to enter the war.[126]

It was the Chief of the General Staff, Helmuth von Moltke, who ordered the German army to advance against the West, after the Kaiser on 1 August (!) had expressed the opinion that the whole army should simply be marched to the East. In recent times there may have been only a few people who have been disparaged and castigated as much as this younger Moltke, nephew of the victor of Königgrätz and Sedan, who bore the same name. Polzer once called him 'the last whole man'[127] in the German leadership at the beginning of the war. The tragedy was that there had been no such men in German *politics* for decades ...

Many references have already been made in this book to the decay of Austrian and German politics at that time. These politics are in no way to be defended here. But rather than on the question of German and Austrian 'war guilt', greater value will have to be laid by the historians of the future on the following questions:

1) why, of the Great Powers that were not directly involved in the Austro-Serbian conflict, was Russia the first to order a general mobilization immediately after Austria's declaration of war against Serbia?
2) why did Britain refuse to accept the German offer not to attack France if Britain were to declare its neutrality?

One, however, who knows the western intentions which to a great extent had been guiding European politics for centuries already in the sense of the Testament of Peter the Great, cannot overlook the fact that these intentions, as well as the launching of the socialist experiment in the Russian 'desert' *could not be realized without a great European war.*

★

While the political and diplomatic intrigues on the eve of war were fanning the long glimmering fire, Ludwig Polzer journeyed back from Scandinavia to his homeland. While he travelled with Steiner from Sassnitz to Stralsund, Steiner reminded him of Wallenstein's claim that he would have to take this town—Stralsund—'even if it were bound by a chain to the heavens'. However, it is well-known that Wallenstein was unable to take it in 1628, to his great regret. The unsuccessful siege which went on for months became a turning point in the war, in that Sweden pressed more powerfully onto the mainland. 'Wallenstein's luck ran out in front of this town', wrote Schiller in the second volume of his *History of the Thirty Years' War.*

Steiner made his comment 'with a certain emphasis', Polzer wrote in his memoirs,[128] 'in the way he often did, in order to get us to think further'. What did Rudolf Steiner want to say to Polzer? That they were facing times in which there were similar, high-stakes war aims which would be crowned with just as little success? That a second Thirty Years' War was about to begin, which indeed then happened, the so-called interval of peace between the world wars notwithstanding? After parting from Steiner in Stralsund, and in a very thoughtful mood, Polzer headed on with his wife for Heiligenkreutz in Bohemia. 'After this comment by Steiner', he wrote,

> I realized remarkably that it seemed to be a kind of destiny that we were taking exactly the opposite route, from Eger to Pilsen, that Wallenstein had taken before his murder—from Pilsen to Eger. Since I had already been so close to the Waldstein family in my youth, this comment [by Steiner] made a strong impression on me.

Twenty-five years later, Polzer was still regretting that he had never brought the matter up again with Steiner, 'as in so many other cases'.[129]

★

How many men in Austria-Hungary and Germany who left for the front with patriotic enthusiasm felt they would be 'home again for Christmas'!

One was Otto Wagner, the teacher of Julius and Josef, who left the boys behind only with the greatest regret.

Immediately after the outbreak of war Ludwig Polzer sought to reactivate his military service, while his brother Arthur, as Director of the Chancellory of the Imperial Household, set up a hospital for wounded and sick officers in the deserted Parliament Building. Ludwig Polzer would soon be ordered there as Inspection Officer; he even obtained accommodation in the Parliament Building. Arthur had given command of the army there to Ludwig's old friend Count Wallis, and so during his period of service Ludwig could pursue his studies under a fairly relaxed military regime and was often able to absent himself without any further consequences. At midday he ate with his mother in Bartensteingasse nearby. The evenings he mostly spent sitting in the dining room with the officers. So Ludwig Polzer, who was once his brother Arthur's superior in the army was now his brother's subordinate in the Parliament Building in Vienna and felt it 'quite remarkable to be in command of this House'.[130] Count Wallis hardly commanded at all.

In this very fluid period Ludwig and Berta Polzer wanted their sons Josef and Julius, who meanwhile had become thirteen and twelve years old respectively, to come into closer contact to Rudolf Steiner's movement.

Berta withdrew them from their school and spent the winter with her sons in neutral Dornach. Here a new private teacher was found for them but their main work was in carving the wooden sculptures in the Goetheanum Building.

Polzer spent the first winter of the war with his family in Dornach. 'This first winter of the war,' he wrote, 'where people from all nations were collaborating peaceably on a work with devotion and enthusiasm was an experience for all of us. Day and night we heard the thunder of the guns from the Vosges.'[131]

Polzer writes of a simple Christmas celebration on Christmas Eve and of an address by Steiner which was directed on this evening only to the children; Steiner spoke to them of the conditions of great poverty in which the Jesus child was placed at His birth. 'We adults knew,' wrote Polzer 'that this referred to the poverty which the people of Middle Europe would have to cope with.'[132] To Polzer himself Steiner remarked that real peace could only come from creative thoughts, which would have to lead to a fundamental reordering of all cultural, political and economic relations.

The war drew on. After the dismissal of Moltke in September in 1914 his successor in the German High Command bore not least, on the

German side, the responsibility for enforcing trench warfare. On the domestic front difficulties in supplies began to show themselves.

Ludwig and Berta celebrated Easter 1915 again in Dornach with their sons. In May Steiner travelled to Vienna in order to give two public lectures there. The theme was: '*Supersensible Knowledge and Its Value for the Human Soul—Spiritual-Scientific Considerations with Respect to Our Fateful Times*'. Polzer accompanied Steiner from Vienna to Prague and then to Linz. Steiner spoke here to the public on 17 May and to members on the following day in the lecture room at Polzer's house at 12 Pfarrerplatz. This lecture was of course of quite special significance for Ludwig Polzer.[133] We shall therefore take a short look at the content.

Steiner spoke first about the great wooden sculpture intended for the Johannes Building in Dornach. It portrays the Representative of Mankind, walking between two figures who are eternally unable to bear his presence. In spiritual science they are called Lucifer and Ahriman. The one works in a more dissolving manner that flees from the Earth; the other condenses and binds to the Earth. Steiner then spoke of how, since Golgotha, Christ had worked into the course of history very concretely through historical personalities. The first example he gave was that of a Roman emperor, the Emperor Constantine, who after his victory over his opponent Maxentius raised Christianity to become the State religion. In a dream Constantine was shown that he could overcome the much stronger opposing army if he went into battle under the sign of the Cross of Golgotha. Another example Steiner gave was that of Joan of Arc whose heroic acts were a turning point in the course of European history.

The triad of the wooden sculpture was reflected not only in the course of historical development but also in the affinity of whole peoples to regions of the Earth. While Eastern peoples have more to do with luciferic impulses and Western peoples with ahrimanic impulses, the peoples of the Middle are especially suited to the realization of real Christianity. Steiner drew his listeners' attention to something very noteworthy when he directed them to the connection between the word ICH and the initials of Jesus Christ. Already in this usage by the German language spirit, appears the original Christian character of all true individualism as is exactly appropriate for the peoples of the Middle.

Certainly, of the greatest importance for Polzer will have been Steiner's statements about the physical and spiritual aspects of political ententes. Underneath an alliance between two States on the physical plane could, from a spiritual perspective, be a real opposition between those same two peoples. That was, for example, the case between France and the Russian nation, as showed itself clearly in the behaviour of the etheric bodies of fallen soldiers: the ether bodies of fallen Russian soldiers would dissolve very rapidly while the French would hold fast longer to the form impressed by their folk spirit. Here in Linz Steiner even came to the point of speaking about the potential meaning of the existence of so many unused ether bodies of those who had died early: as on the physical plane, no force is lost on the supersensible-spiritual plane, and due to the countless deaths in battle, immense unused life forces can help to *spiritualize* the convictions and thinking of the coming generations. Only through such a spiritualization of the entire world culture could the enormous sacrifice of life in this war, indeed of all further wars, be offset. Otherwise, this sacrifice would have been absolutely in vain.

Steiner also briefly considered Russia's responsibility for the war and stated that this was the Power that could have prevented the spread of the conflict. The question remains: *which forces* had driven Russia to mobilization in 1914? Was it the *real* Russia that had acted in this way or the Russia that was already corrupted in the sense of the conscious Testament of Peter the Great?

From the thoughts of this Linz lecture Ludwig Polzer must have drawn strength upon strength as from a spiritual well of rejuvenation. Certainly it gave him wings for the lecturing activity he began soon afterwards in Prague. There, in June, in the Künstlerinnen Club he gave what was in effect a debut lecture and then in October went on to give an anthroposophical course of two lectures a month in the Bohemian capital. 'The work in Prague became very dear to me,' he wrote about this new lecturing activity. 'I enjoyed people's trust there and was particularly close to the anthroposophical friends. I felt myself on a path designated by karma.'[134]

His Prague friends at this time included Adolf Hauffen who taught German Studies at the German University, and his wife Klothilde, leader of the Bolzano Branch of the Anthroposophical Society. He also became close to Luděk Přikyl and Ida Freund.

In Prague Polzer usually stayed at the Hotel Zum Blauen Stern (The Blue Star), a well-known, now demolished hotel where the peace negotiations were handled after the Austro-Prussian War of 1866. The hotel stood not far from the Pulverturm (Powder Tower) in the Hybernska-Gasse. Rudolf Steiner too was often a guest there. During one of Polzer's stays there in 1916 Julie Klima sought him out there in order to speak to him about some spiritual scientific questions. She was the wife of Jaroslav Klima, who served in leading positions in the Bohemian and later Slovak police. Both of them from 1917 onwards would play a decisive role especially in Ludwig Polzer's political activity.

Between Whitsun 1915 and summer 1916 the Polzer family were living again in Linz and Tannbach. In autumn 1915 at his own wish Josef Polzer entered the Naval Academy at Braunau; Julius was greatly pained to see him go. The family celebrated Christmas 1915 at Tannbach again but all of them 'had longings for Dornach'. The news from the war became 'ever more serious. Frightful State controls were now added to all the other evils, [...] which caused such awful and unnecessary damage to agriculture.'[135] And as if with a sigh he went on: 'All these bad measures weighed on us all the more when we had the deeper insight into events that anthroposophy afforded us.'

★

In Polzer the desire to return to retirement grew stronger because he saw that he could do more meaningful work within the anthroposophical movement and because 'service on the home front also repelled' him.[136] From the spring of 1916 he therefore turned more to anthroposophical work, alongside his tasks at Tannbach. 'Until then life within the anthroposophical movement had been a receiving, with gratitude and joy, of that for which human souls longed. From now on,' he wrote of the turning point in the spring of 1916, 'it meant struggle and sacrifice.'[137]

It became ever clearer to him through his own observations and through his study of spiritual science that behind the scenes of outer events, advanced by Church and State, a struggle *against the rightful contemporary spirit* was going on which was only to be met with corresponding spiritual weapons.

At the end of June he and Berta travelled again to Switzerland. It had been possible for a whole year to cross the border without a passport, but now there were various formalities to contend with. 'As though freed from a cell', the couple could relax in Buchs, the first station on Swiss territory.

It became still clearer to Polzer: 'This prison had been planned for Middle Europe since the '80s of the last century and its supervision was handed over to the masters of small states created after the apparent end of the war.'[138]

Ludwig and Berta thus travelled to Dornach with Julius and Josef 'to bring back spiritual strength for the struggle for spiritual renewal'.[139]

Hardly had they arrived when they and their sons set to work on the wooden sculptures. Two fulfilling months of hard work went by and then Ludwig Polzer accompanied his sons to Linz where they were to go back to school.

Rudolf Steiner himself was in Dornach from the end of July and only

17. Ludwig Polzer-Hoditz, 1902

18. Marie-Sefine Polzer

19. *Back row, 1st from left: Ludwig Polzer; 4th from left Adolf Waldstein*
2nd row, 3rd from left: Christine Polzer, 5th from left: Sefine Polzer
Front: Arthur Polzer, 1892

20. Emperor Franz Joseph

21. Crown Prince Rudolf, 1892

22. Berta Polzer; Schloss Heiligenkreutz in Bohemia

23. Josef, Berta, and Julius Polzer, 1905

PEGGAU. Schloss-Schüler.

. Schloß   164

24. Schloss Peggau nr. Graz; Schloss Tannbach nr. Linz

25. Archduke Karl, later Emperor, 1904

26. Rudolf Steiner, 1907

27. Julius, Ritter von Polzer, 1906

28. Ludwig Polzer, 1912

29. Berta Polzer, 1912

30. Rudolf Steiner, 1917

31. Count Otto Lerchenfeld, 1930

32. Ludwig Polzer and Sophie Lerchenfeld; the First Goetheanum

shortly before Polzer's departure a month later, did it come to an important private conversation between them. Steiner had just had to experience one of the most bitter and dangerous attacks against himself that he had yet been through. Edouard Schuré, whose work he and his wife had supported tirelessly for many years had in a fit of chauvinist blindness suddenly come to believe that his friend and teacher Steiner was a Pan-Germanic ultra-chauvinist on the basis of Steiner's essay *Thoughts During The Time of War*, which bore the title 'For Germans, and those who do not believe that they have to hate them.'[140] The hate-mongering which Schuré let loose in the French Press could have been very dangerous for Steiner, as an Austrian citizen on Swiss soil then had to conduct himself with absolute neutrality. The authorities could easily have ordered Steiner out of Switzerland. 'I shall certainly never of my own will allow myself to be parted from the building; but forces are at work which can bring this about.'[141] Such were Steiner's own words in this precarious situation.

Out of his current concerns for the building Steiner spoke to Polzer about Sophie Stinde, the former chairwoman of the Johannes Building Association, who had died in November 1915. 'Rudolf Steiner complained that he had so few colleagues and could not really see how to fill the vacant post in the Johannes Building Association: "*If you do not want to take it on, I do not know how best to fill it, but you will be more needed in Austria.*"' Polzer added: 'At the time [*damals*] I had to agree with that last sentence.'[142]

Steiner would certainly have greeted with joy Polzer's willingness to fill Sophie Stinde's post. That Polzer in hindsight even asked himself whether his behaviour was correct seems to be indicated by that one word *damals* [at the time]. And in fact, it would have meant much for the building if the one of Steiner's pupils who had been the first, unconsciously, to visit the property, had now taken the building on. Actually, he bore within him in the background of his own destiny a mystery temple motif, as will become clear in a later chapter.

On 21 November 1916 the Emperor Franz Joseph died in Vienna after a reign of 68 years. 'He resolutely lived his life in the most rigorous fulfilment of his duty,' wrote Polzer in 1936.

> One has to say that as the last representative of the spirit of the Habsburg line, he carried out his duties as monarch with the greatest con-scientiousness. There was a kind of wisdom in him. This wisdom was more useful to lead men and peoples than the later intellectualism, which became ever more abstract but only brings people misery [...] The blows of fate which Austria had to endure during his long reign, his truly honourable

struggle with the nationalities problem, [and] the misfortune in his own family surrounded Emperor Franz Joseph with a mood of decline in which he always bore himself courageously.[143]

Archduke Karl succeeded to the throne in the middle of the crisis of the world war. From the very beginning he strove for peace, but all too soon he allowed his hands to be tied by the anti-Slav forces in the monarchy. Hardly had he become Emperor when, against the advice of his old friend Arthur Polzer, he let himself be crowned in Hungary too, on 30 December, much earlier than was necessary. As the Hungarian coronation of a Habsburg monarch was traditionally bound with a coronation oath to uphold the Hungarian constitution, Emperor Karl had thus in advance himself drastically reduced his own room for manoeuvre with regard to constitutional reforms in the Dual Monarchy.

At the end of December 1916 Steiner, responding 'to the wishes of some friends working at the Goetheanum'[144], embarked on a long series of lectures in which he spoke without reservation and in great detail about the political and occult background to contemporary world events. It was as though his teacher's bold deed in distant Dornach inwardly gripped Polzer's soul, for at the end of the year he too began to write his own *Considerations During the Time of War*. He wanted to draw up an interim assessment of the situation as a contribution to the great spiritual struggle and make fruitful what he had been able to learn from his spiritual teacher in regard to how to make sense of the actual events of the age. 'He illuminated for us the background to the catastrophe,' he wrote; 'through everything that happened in those years we actually woke up for the first time to real life out of a life of illusory dreams in which we had earlier been caught.'[145]

It was in this mood that he entered the Christmas season.

23. The Year 1917

The year 1917 holds a key position in world history. After the failure of
the Central Powers' peace initiatives in December 1916, the war dragged
on and spread further in both East and West. In mid-March Czar
Nicholas II abdicated. Three weeks later, Lenin, who had been smuggled
over to Russia in a sealed train by the German High Command, began his
work in that 'Russian desert' on the injection of the Socialist experiment
which had been discussed in western circles for decades (see map on
p. 65). In the same month of April America entered the war. The
Russian-American power duopoly which would determine the face of
Europe until the end of the 1980s, was now underway.

The world-historical key position of the year 1917 was also reflected in
the activity of Rudolf Steiner as well as in the life of Ludwig Polzer. In this
year it came to an enduring convergence of Polzer's strivings with the
aims of Steiner's work.

In January 1917 Steiner was continuing the course of lectures on
contemporary world events that he had begun in Dornach in December
of the previous year. Meanwhile, Polzer had had his own observations of
world events published just before the end of 1916. He immediately sent
a copy sent off to Dornach. And on the very day it arrived, Steiner
referred to it in his evening lecture on 8 January. After he had spoken in
relation to Fichte's *Speeches to the German Nation* about the 'geniality' with
which the real destiny of German culture had been underestimated and
pushed aside precisely by Germans, he drew his listeners' attention to
Polzer's pamphlet. As his words express something characteristic in Polzer's text as well as his own attitude towards this first cultural contribution
by one of his closest pupils, we shall let Steiner speak for himself:

> I have brought up this matter today because there is definitely a tendency to
> sound a note in the centre, a note differing from that of the periphery. And
> if our anthroposophical work can contribute to this other note, there is no
> reason why we should not say so amongst ourselves. Just today I received a
> pamphlet by our friend Ludwig von Polzer who, as you know, worked
> here: *Thoughts during Wartime*. You see, it is interesting—whether you
> agree in detail with what he says or not—to note that he is not particularly
> concerned with attacking and insulting others but rather with reading the
> riot act to his Austrian compatriots. It is to them he speaks. Obviously he
> has come to be an Austrian as a result of his karma, but he nevertheless reads
> the riot act to his Austrian compatriots. He does not say: We are blameless,
> we never did this or that, we are pure white angels and all the others are

black devils. No, he says: 'Why does mankind hate itself and tear itself to pieces? Are external political differences really the cause of much suffering? Every party to the fray claims to know what it is about, but in reality none of them know.

'A declining decadent culture is fighting its deathly struggle. The Central Powers who are fighting for the first germination of a new culture, have not recognized it as yet; they fight for something they do not know, for something unknown to them; and they are themselves still filled with the convictions against which their own soldiers are bleeding in battle.

'The old degenerate ways must be, as it were, vomited forth and that is why in their final fling they are running so wild. Do we not come up against it amongst ourselves wherever we turn, this attitude of the Entente which bears the old, decadent culture? Has it not infected us as well? We see it on the streets in the latest fashions, it is embodied in modern architecture, it grins down at us from the hoardings, in commerce it runs to orgies, it inflates itself in bureaucratic madness, in its self-important untruthful humanism it lies to itself, our press seeks to outbid its colleagues of the Entente in devotion to the truth, and so on.

'The Entente is here among us, fuming and raging, claiming for our honest soldiers and compatriots, almost all of whom have meanwhile died a sacrificial death.

—All these things running so horrifyingly wild in our own country—let it be hoped for the last time before the collapse—are not *deutsch*.'

So all of those things worthy of censure in his own country he calls 'not deutsch'. His main aim is to appeal to the conscience of his own compatriots. There are further, similar passages in this booklet. It is good that such a thing is said for once in connection with our own endeavours. There is no need for us to be in total harmony with every sentence that is written among us. The most wonderful achievement will be to work on all these things independently, preserving our individuality and taking nothing as dogma or as the word of a higher authority. [...] The main thing we can do to help our age is to work with understanding through the impulses of this age from our viewpoint [...] We should be particularly careful to develop good practices with regard to the proper evaluation and estimation of all that comes to the fore amongst ourselves.[146]

Steiner here had two things in mind. First, that it was really important to be self-knowledgeable and self-critical with regard also to one's own people; then, that his pupils should learn not merely to pay attention to his—Steiner's—words or to swear by them, but also to learn to recognize what individual pupils of his were striving to achieve in the service of spiritual science in working for the impulses of the age.

It must have been a fine and encouraging surprise for Polzer when he later learned of Steiner's comments on his writing.

That his pamphlet had in no way sought to pave the way for any
nationalistic German attitudes is clearly shown by the following words:

> What I want to express in these sentences is that I am not thinking of any
> narrow nationalism, enclosed within itself in order to foster its own egoism
> and pride. German culture has raised itself, has defended itself and now
> comes the time for it to give of itself out of its own hidden depths. To be
> able to do that, a second struggle must be waged within the soul, for those
> who set the tone must not continue to be those who think in English or
> Romance languages but those who understand the true German spirit [. . .],
> who can rouse themselves to give out of this spirit [. . .] And in order to
> destroy any appearance of a narrow nationalistic viewpoint I say that this
> giving is a kind of giving oneself to the other. It is through this giving that
> today's narrow nationalism, stuck fast to externals [. . .] must be overcome
> in Europe.[147]

Setting the direction for Polzer's own direction in practical work in
cultural and political fields in the coming years are the following words
from his text that Steiner commented on:

> The Slavs are not to be treated by the West as the German tribes were
> treated by the Romans. The Germans are fighting so that this does not
> happen; they must prevent it. This is why the Germans stand in the Middle
> between the East and the West. The present between the future and the
> past. German culture has a task with the East. It must not shut itself off from
> this and turn to the decadent West.

It tells us something about Ludwig Polzer that the concrete point of
departure for all his later political activity lies in the direction of *these*
words. What *was* this point of departure?

In November 1915 the sensational trial of the Czech member of
Parliament Dr Karel Kramář dominated the political stage. Kramář was
convicted of activities threatening to the monarchy—high treason. Those
in a position to judge the course of the trial and above all the material
presented to the court against the defendant were, however, united in
their view that this was a highly political, tendentious trial which was
intended to lame the Czech opposition. Ludwig Polzer, on whose heart
the unsolved Slav question had lain at least since his time in Warasdin,
followed the trial assiduously. He wrote:

> The so often unjustified treatment of the Czech people during the war, the
> lack of understanding in Austrian circles for the Czech folk soul angered
> me, and I found it fateful for the Empire. [. . .] The suppression of the Slavic
> peoples on the one hand, the advancement of Hungary since 1867 on the
> other, which became ever more determinant in the politics of the Empire

went along with the destructive will that was directed against Middle Europe. I therefore decided to do something to try to harmonize the German-Slav polarity.

I would like to emphasize that in this connection, I am only speaking of the western Slavs, the Poles, Czechs, and the South Slavs. First I was moved to try to relieve the greatest injustices. Dr Jaroslav Klima informed me about much and I often travelled to see my brother at the Emperor's headquarters to communicate certain facts to him. The treason trial of Mr Kramář had been conducted in such a way that an appeal appeared to me necessary both to calm the Czech people as well as in view of the critical wartime situation. The prosecutions of others, such as Dr Rašín and Dr Preiss, also called for appeals. Emperor Karl wanted justice and felt that without the Slavs, Austria would not be able to go on; he hoped through justice to be able to serve the peace he yearned for.[148]

On 2 July 1917 an amnesty was announced for Kramář and over 2500 others prosecuted for political offences. The text announcing this was presented and formulated by Arthur Polzer who since 1 February had been serving as the Director of His Majesty's Cabinet. The amnesty soon stirred up sharp resistance against Ludwig's brother whose activity as Cabinet Director soon became a thorn in the side of Count Tisza, the Hungarian Prime Minister. The pro-Hungarian Minister for Foreign Affairs at the time, Count Czernin, was from this time on one of Ludwig Polzer's enemies. With the amnesty a certain degree of autonomy for the Slavs was introduced—and that could in no way be in the interests of the Magyars. No less a figure than Thomas Masaryk, later the first President of the Czechoslovak Republic, was at first very taken aback by the Emperor's unusual measure which threatened to endanger Czech resistance abroad or even make it superfluous!

The amnesty urged by Ludwig Polzer and Dr Klima and introduced by Ludwig's brother Arthur and the Emperor thus had very concrete effects. Unfortunately, it was to remain one of the few realistic official actions which the young Emperor, whose hands were tied in almost all directions, was able to undertake.

★

It was his effort to do something for the situation of western Slavs in the empire that led Ludwig Polzer to the clear insight that politically, really new paths had to be found. 'In these first months of the year 1917,' he wrote, 'I knew that something would have to happen if the worst were to be prevented from befalling Middle Europe.'[149] With this insight he headed once more with Berta for Munich, where Steiner was to lecture.

On 19 and 20 May Rudolf Steiner lectured to members of the Society on certain 'Laws of Human Development'. On the 20th he gave an outline of the history of the consciousness of trichotomy in humanity— the consciousness that man is a threefold being of body, soul and spirit. He then showed the effects of the 'abolition of the spirit' at the Eighth Ecumenical Council at Constantinople in the year 869 on modern science and urged the restoration of the lost consciousness of this triad. That the three had been sought after in modern times was evident from the three ideals of the French Revolution—liberty, equality, brother- hood, which, because there was no real knowledge of this triad were all focused in a chaotic manner *on the body*. In reality it is only the ideal of brotherhood that can be oriented to this bodily member of the human organism; freedom is the demand of the soul and equality the law of the spirit. 'This membering,' said Steiner, 'is a demand of of our time and of the near future.'[150] But this demand was still opposed by the old unchristianized impulses of the former Roman Empire, which Steiner clearly linked to the forced initiations of the Caesars such as Tiberius, Augustus and Caligula.

The motif of the Caesars briefly touched upon in Steiner's second lecture is striking and may, as in many of Steiner's other lectures, have been determined by the presence at the lecture of one or more particular individuals.

Steiner also mentioned something unusual in the first lecture, when, in a quite different sense, he shared with his audience that he would be giving no more private conversations as these had led to all too many cases of slanderous opposition. All the more striking is that Polzer was evidently not included in this, for during those days in Munich there was a long important private conversation between him and Rudolf Steiner. Polzer described this in his Prague Notes:

> At that time I had a long private conversation with Rudolf Steiner in which he described to me the seriousness of the world situation. I told him that my brother had been appointed the Emperor's Cabinet Director and enjoyed his complete confidence; that the Emperor longed for peace and that these circumstances could perhaps be used to find ways in which a real peace could be achieved. I remember that Rudolf Steiner was at the time very sceptical and disparaging about the idea that was circulating at the time, of a separate peace for Austria, because through it, the war aims of the Entente Powers, notably the intention to destroy the Habsburg Empire, would not be prevented. He told me that the war was the heavy karma of materialism which did not have its origins in science, but that this scientific materialism was a consequence of the materialism that had proceeded from the church

communities in the previous centuries. People who became further estranged from the spirit could no longer gain any real connection with the spiritual world through the religious confessions, which no longer had anything to do with real religiosity. From the time of the rise of the natural sciences, humanism had striven for a bridge between religion and science; however, for the churches which became ever more external organs of authority, this dualism offered the possibility of a better way of controlling people. They did not want to see faith as the preliminary stage of spiritual knowledge.

In this conversation I felt for the first time the change in the conditions of the world which people were confronting quite unprepared [...] I did not then suspect that spiritual conditions 20 years later would be even more sick and more confused than at that time. Such a thought would have been unbearable for me then. Only slowly can one become accustomed to sinking into what is subnatural and subhuman.[151]

Another, more important aspect of contemporary events was touched on in the conversation in Munich. As Polzer had not been able to attend Steiner's lectures on *Considerations on Contemporary Events* and was only able to obtain a typescript of them that was sent to him in the second half of 1917, he first learned 'in this private conversation something of the fact of an evil form of occultism which was working behind outer events'.

Steiner may for the first time have alerted Polzer in the Munich conversation that spring of 1917 to the Testament of Peter the Great, after he had spoken about it in a lecture to members of the Anthroposophical Society at the beginning of the *Considerations on Contemporary Events* on 9 December 1916.

It is also highly likely that he informed Polzer in Munich of the Socialist experiment planned in the West for the Slavic countries and described by Harrison in London in 1893 (see p. 66ff.). So in this important private conversation, through the deeper background Steiner opened up to him, Polzer learned to make more sense of current events than he had done hitherto. And when he wrote that the Anthroposophers at that time were 'still too bound up in ideological and mystical spheres' then this at least no longer applied to him, at the latest, from that time on when Steiner opened his eyes to the occult background to politics.

★

While Ludwig and Berta Polzer went on with their duties in Tannbach after their stay in Munich, a noteworthy soul drama was going on in the life of another of Steiner's pupils—Count Otto von Lerchenfeld, whom we met already at the Munich summer conference in 1912. Who was Count Lerchenfeld?

Born on 12 October 1868 on the Köfering castle estate near Regensburg, Otto Lerchenfeld had studied carpentry and wanted to become a farmer. The Counts of Lerchenfeld had a family 'seat' reserved for them in perpetuity at Regensburg Cathedral. As the heir to extensive properties, Otto Lerchenfeld also had a seat and a voice in the Bavarian Royal Council. One of his friends from school and studies was Richard von Kühlmann, who became Secretary of State for Foreign Affairs in 1917. Otto's uncle Hugo Lerchenfeld had for a long time been the envoy of the Bavarian Crown in Berlin. Through him Otto Lerchenfeld had become familiar early on with political relationships in the Bismarck Reich.

As a 23-year-old during his studies in Berlin, Otto Lerchenfeld had been invited to a summer garden party held by Karl Heinrich von Bötticher, then State Secretary of the Interior. This opportunity led to the young Lerchenfeld having an experience of decisive significance. In a conversation with a guest, von Bötticher casually happened to make the following remark, at which Lerchenfeld, who had begun to feel bored by the party, suddenly woke up: 'Yes, it is completely clear to me,' said von Bötticher, 'that if in the next 25–30 years the social question is not solved, then we shall fall into chaos. The way in which the parties on the left want to solve the problem is impossible. How the problem can be solved, *I* have no idea. I can only hope that the man will come who can solve it.'[152]

It was a real wake-up call for Lerchenfeld—unforgettable, direction-setting.

Twenty-six years later, in May 1917, he had another opportunity to remember those words. He was visiting his uncle in Berlin and staying in the same room at the Bavarian embassy as before. 'And it was just as before,' wrote Lerchenfeld.

> Just as someone had spoken uninhibitedly in front of the young person, so now again someone spoke in front of the older man. But how different were the words that were spoken! How much hidden anxiety and worry sounded through those words! [. . .] And now the words sound out from that warm June night, and like a black void, chaos stands before me.

In his diary he noted:

> I cannot just stand by and watch this any longer! Everything is at cross purposes: Order—counter order! Cabinet—Imperial Chancellory—the Ministries—the High Command! In our embassy here it's like a pigeon loft—Ministers, parliamentarians, half the federal council, the few remaining diplomats, uncle Hugo is seen only at breakfast. He looks like

he's been hit on the head, totally over-worked. Most of the others who come and go don't look any different, but they are all acting as if they do—with more or less composure. What else should they do? [...] One has the impression from all these men that their tongues are hanging out, and that bleary-eyed, breathless and restless, each seeks ultimate meaning in his own department or little office. For thoughts—no time. Of ideas—no trace! War and victory are reckoned in terms of numbers. To give themselves courage, they ask the military men. *They* dream only of victory, victory, victory. They rarely come to us. [...] Everywhere people who have to deal *ex officio* with things about which they haven't the faintest notion, the small things as well as the great. That is what our parliamentary system breeds. How often I could witness that in the Imperial Council: people voting on matters the basis of which they have no idea [...] A few days ago I met V. Had a long talk with him about these impressions. Was able to draw him out of himself for just five minutes but then he dropped back inside—to his daily routine. This is how it almost always goes, and what is so depressing. I myself am almost more than depressed, I am almost in despair. What can haul us out of this slow but sure grinding mill of fate? A great idea which would have to lead over to others. But where is it? Certainly not in all those which have been active in events thus far.

From this experience of the general lack of ideas and courage, the pain in Lerchenfeld's soul increased to the point where he asked himself the question: 'Who can show the German people the way out of this dead-end? Who—what can help? It was clear to me that only *one man* could do it.'

And out of the question came the deed.

Rudolf Steiner was in Berlin. I sought him out and described the situation to him as I had to see it, but also what in the course of my own political experience had seemed to me to be the result, the principal damage to our public life. He listened to me attentively with only an occasional question or correction now and then. A comprehensive conversation was arranged for the following afternoon. In it, as the answer to my questions, he developed to me as idea the outline of what he then called 'the threefolding of the social organism'. But he thought the idea would first have to be worked out in detail before it could be grasped by life and by the public. Also that day, the directly possible consequences were touched on, and what Rudolf Steiner had to say about that in persuasive logic was such that the mood in which I had come to him was transformed into its exact opposite.

This was followed by a kind of private course in understanding social and political problems in the light of reality. Lerchenfeld wrote:

> More than three weeks of work followed that first conversation, day after day, hour after hour. Weeks of the highest experience, the greatest effort, the most intensive learning; learning, which in reality means the logic of life [...] how logic must reach over into art [...] politics is art, not merely science [...] And then, one fine day, the whole structure stood there, finished, stone on stone right down into all its details.[153]

On one of the last days of this private course Lerchenfeld asked Steiner for 'a kind of short memorandum of his ideas'. Shortly afterwards—it may have been towards the end of June—Rudolf Steiner gave him the first handwritten Memorandum about the threefolding of the social organism.

What is the idea of threefolding in its essentials? To outline the main points briefly: the *spiritual life* must exist in the freedom of the individudal, equality must prevail in the *sphere of rights*; fraternity is the goal of the worldwide *economic sphere* which is to be freed of national political interests. In such a way the ideals of the French Revolution, which were wrongly introduced and related to each other chaotically, must be referred to the corresponding spheres of the social organism before they can work effectively.

Around the same time, at the beginning of July 1917, at the time of the amnesty for the Czech politicians, Emperor Karl offered Arthur Polzer the post of Prime Minister of Austria. He hoped by this to be able to carry through measures he too desired that would increase the degree of autonomy enjoyed by the various peoples of the Empire. Polzer declined the offer because Foreign Minister Czernin and also the Hungarian Prime Minister Tisza were declared opponents of the autonomy programme that he had already drawn up as Cabinet Director. Polzer justified his decision in the following words:

> Such a complete change of course would, when it came to the crunch, set loose a huge storm; the Austrian Prime Minister would not be able to stand alone if the Foreign Minister and the Hungarian Prime Minister were not of one mind with him and the three did not together form an indivisible and unbreakable trio. If this were not the case, I could not guarantee success.[154]

Arthur Polzer later expressed doubts as to the correctness of this decision. He remarked once to his brother Ludwig that he would have accepted the post if he had known of the idea of threefolding the social organism in May, but he only first became aware of it at the end of July 1917. It would have given him the necessary strength for really new initiatives and enabled him to accept the Emperor's offer.

But how did Arthur's brother Ludwig encounter this revolutionary idea? The answer to this question first takes us to his home at Tannbach.

On the afternoon of 10 July a telegram arrived at Tannbach: 'Would it be possible for you to come to Berlin for a few days next Friday? Greetings Rudolf Steiner.'[155] This was the first time Rudolf Steiner had called for a personal conversation with Polzer. 'For a few days...'—that meant something important.

10 July was a Tuesday, so Polzer had to be in Berlin on Friday, 13 July.

After he had obtained the necessary visa in Vienna the next day, with the help of a friend from his youth, he arrived in Berlin as expected, early on Friday. Rudolf Steiner greeted him in his living room/study at 17 Motzstrasse with the words: 'You will perhaps not be able to guess why I have called you.' Polzer answered: 'I guess that perhaps it has to do with conversations I was able to have with you about current events at the time of the Balkan Wars and later.'[156]

Then Steiner told Polzer 'that Count Lerchenfeld had taken the initiative and had come to him with the request for advice as to how Middle Europe could find an honourable way out of the war'. Lerchenfeld was, as previously mentioned, already known to Polzer since the summer conference in Munich in 1913. He had met him again at the foundation stone-laying ceremony at the Dornach Johannes Building in the autumn of the same year; now, four years on, through their mutual, and unsuspected, connection to Steiner's social ideas, a firm bond of friendship began to form between them that was borne by their knowledge of the need for healing impulses in society.

'Count Lerchenfeld,' Steiner went on, 'wanted to arrange a joint conversation of several gentlemen with me, but these have for various reasons contacted me to give their apologies.' They included, according to Polzer, Prince Karl Max von Lichnowsky, the last German ambassador in London, who shortly before the war broke out had asked the British government if Britain would remain neutral if Germany were to march into Belgium; then there was General-Director Albert Ballin of the Hamburg-Amerika Line, Maximilian Harden, the Kaiser-hater and chief editor of the magazine *Die Zukunft* [The Future]. Walter Rathenau, according to Polzer, could also have been invited; Count Johann Heinrich Bernstorff, the last German ambassador in Washington, who Steiner was to meet a few days later in Munich. Due to the regrettable refusals from most of these men, no conversations with them took place apart from with Count Bernstorff. A symptom of the times: in the moment when proposals in accord with reality could have been taken up, in order to respond to the needs of the time, the 'best' of the time had better things to do...

So Steiner first had to restrict himself to instructing Lerchenfeld, and

Polzer, who had been called only recently. 'Straightaway on the day of my arrival,' wrote Polzer,

> Rudolf Steiner began to make me familiar with the idea of the thought of a threefolding of the social organism, which, as he said, should not remain only literature but could only work effectively in the sense of securing peace if it were to be presented from an influential position to which the world looks.[157]

Polzer was, in his way, already well-prepared for the thought of three-folding: Steiner had already, in a lecture in Munich in May, in a sense pre-ploughed the field of Polzer's consciousness with regard to the three-foldness of man and his indications as to the three great ideals of the French Revolution. 'The following days passed in further instruction,' reports Polzer. It was now his turn, after Lerchenfeld, to receive a course of private study. Steiner then gave him the Memorandum that Lerch-enfeld had asked for,[158] which had been typed up in the meantime. Let us at this point take a brief look at the Memorandum.

First, Steiner discusses the question of the causes of the war, so deviously handled by the Entente Powers. He shows that in the summer of 1914 Germany was not ready 'to take the initiative for war'. Further, that Austria-Hungary had itself caused the explosive situation in occupied Bosnia-Herzegovina through its inability to solve the South Slav ques-tion. A timely federalization and granting of autonomy, as required by the circumstances of the nationalities, on the model of the German federal states would have been necessary. Steiner calls on the German govern-ment to make known what diplomatic steps—through Lichnowsky—had been taken on the German side in London in the last minutes in order to forestall a march into Belgium and war against France in the case of an English declaration of neutrality; he calls on the German government to 'show that it would not have undertaken to march into Belgium if the content of the decisive telegram from the King of England had been different'.

By this means, through a clarification of the circumstances at the outbreak of war, Steiner wanted to pave the way for steps to peace that would be in accord with reality, which is what Lerchenfeld had first asked him to do.

Steiner then comes to speak of Britain's *realpolitik*. 'The Russian Empire will fall'—this is a fundamental maxim of British politics—'so that the Russian people can live. And the circumstances of this people are such that one will be able to carry out Socialist experiments for which there is no possibility in western Europe.' This formulation from Steiner's

Memorandum is almost literally the same as the corresponding statement in Harrison's *Transcendental Universe* (see p. 67). It is therefore very probable that Steiner also drew the attention of Lerchenfeld and Polzer to this English occultism in relation to the conversations about threefolding.

The following passage from the Memorandum may have seemed to Polzer like a summary of much that Steiner had indicated to him in years past:

> In Middle Europe one must, without illusion, look in the eye what those personalities have had as their belief for many years—what from their viewpoint they see as the law of world development, namely, that the future of world development belongs to the Anglo-American race and that they are to inherit the legacy of the Latin-Roman race and the education of Russian culture. When this formula of world politics is introduced by an initiated Englishman or American who thinks in this way, it is always mentioned that the German element has no say in the ordering of the world because of its insignificance in global political affairs, that the Romance element does not need to be taken account of because it is dying out anyway, and that the Russian element belongs to the one who makes himself its educator. One could think little of such a confession of faith if it lived in the heads of a few people given to political fantasies or utopias, but it is only English politics that uses an uncountable number of ways in order to make this programme into the practical content of its actual world politics, and from the English viewpoint, for the realization of this pro-gramme, nothing could be more favourable than the present coalition in which it finds itself. A programme for a very long time-frame![159]

At the end of the Memorandum Steiner sketches a 'Middle European Programme' proceeding from a threefolding of the social organism that would have to lead to the creation of the three relatively autonomous spheres of the life of rights, economic life and cultural life. In the execution of such a programme he saw the only possibility to place something real against the ideas of Woodrow Wilson, which were so inappropriate for Middle Europe, and against the superciliousness of British diplomacy. Through such a programme it would be possible to produce 'what is national from [individual] freedom and not freedom from what is national'.

Steiner also told Polzer further that a Middle European foreign policy that reckoned with the goals of western politics that he had described would have to orient itself to the following maxims:

1. *The French idea of revanche would sink into its own pit.*
2. *The Slav question must be solved by positive politics (threefolding).*
3. *Economic competition would have to be seen as a lasting condition; Middle*

Europe would have to remain in a relation of effective competition with England and not allow itself to become economically dependent.[160]

★

On 16 July Otto Lerchenfeld had travelled to Munich in order to make the necessary arrangements for the meeting between Steiner and Count Bernstorff. On 18 July Steiner himself travelled to Munich for the planned meeting accompanied by Polzer. The conversation took place at the Eden Hotel the next day but did not achieve anything. Before his return to Berlin, during a walk in Munich, Steiner made the following unforgettable remark to Polzer: 'He said that the Soul of Prince Bismarck was not at all interested in current political events on Earth.'[161] Another short lesson in metahistory! Apparently, it is possible—for occult research shows the corresponding fact!—that a person who had stood most intensively in the centre of the political events of his time after death turns away firmly from such events. Polzer travelled with Steiner back to Berlin on the evening of 20 July. In the evening of 21 to 22 July Steiner wrote a second Memorandum[162] that was intended for Ludwig's brother Arthur.

In this second Memorandum Steiner deals with the Note which US President Wilson had sent to the Provisional Government of Russia in which he merely masked the policy of the Entente with the fine-sounding phrases 'peoples' rights of self-determination' and 'the liberation of peoples'.

'With the attainment of Entente goals in relation to the forms of the states in Middle Europe,' wrote Steiner,

> real freedom for Europe will be lost. For they can realize these forms of the state because it is in the interests of these forms of the state themselves [. . .]. Anglo-Americanism cannot realize this [Middle European] freedom of peoples because, as long as this freedom exists, it runs counter to the interests of the Anglo-American forms of the state as long as these interests are as they are now and as they have actually put their stamp on this war. The Anglo-American states must come to see that they will have to respect the interests of the Middle European states alongside their own.[163]

'This war,' writes Steiner further,

> is from the Middle European viewpoint a war of peoples when looking to the East and an economic war when looking West—against England and America . . . The liberation of peoples is possible. But it can only be the result of, and not the basis of, the liberation of individuals. When individuals are freed, so peoples become freed through them.

According to Steiner, it was precisely the task of the Middle European form of the state to bring about the liberation of peoples through the liberation of individuals so that 'every unnatural mixing of political, economic and general human interests' should be completely given up. And then he showed what the necessary 'abandonment of the mixing' would lead to. The core of threefolding was and remains the realization of the freedom of the general human spiritual and cultural life. In the second Memorandum Steiner urges that: 'General human relations' (thus everything which does not belong to the sphere of rights and politics or to the sphere of economics)

> and the questions of the liberation of peoples that belong to them require in the sense of the present and the future the freedom of the individual as their basis. On this point, one will be unable to make any start with any proper views as long as people believe that the freedom or liberation of peoples can be spoken of without them being built on the basis of the freedom of the individual human being [...] The human being must be able to associate with a people, a religious community, or any relationship which results from his general human aspirations without the state structure preventing him, in this association, from engaging in his political or economic relationships.[164]

Let us return to the summer of 1917.

Rudolf Steiner was of the view that the Memorandum written out for Ludwig's brother Arthur could serve as the foundation for an Austrian foreign policy that would be in accord with reality. Moreover, he felt that to this end, Arthur Polzer should strive to be appointed Foreign Minister. First and foremost, Steiner had in mind here an offensive of ideas (in the sense of the free spiritual life) with regard to the East. 'In Russia,' he said on handing over this second Memorandum to Ludwig Polzer, 'there are many small spiritual centres spread out. They would understand it and that could become an effective means of bringing about peace; for the East has always listened to ideas from Middle Europe.'[165] How great Steiner's hope was that through Arthur Polzer moves for peace in this direction could be backed by Austria is shown in the following words: 'If the Austrian Emperor were to announce this, then the saying of Prince Bismarck could become true again: "When the Emperor gets on his horse, all his people follow him."' Ludwig Polzer immediately realized how important it was for the survival of Austria to grasp this world-historical chance and was inwardly appalled by the thought of the consequences if it did not succeed. He wrote about this in his Prague Notes:

> When he saw that I was uneasy and anxious about the weight of the responsibility, he said to me in the most caring way: 'Just be calm. One

must also be able to watch how peoples go under.' This was no mis-anthropic cynicism but the statement of a man who saw what unending pain, what a tragic fall the multi-ethnic state was destined to experience if at the last minute realistic ideas could not guide its life onto another path. That was clear enough from Steiner's following words: 'If what I have spoken to you of as a saving possibility does not come about, a series of catastrophes will follow. What cannot be accomplished through reason will still finally have to come about through the greatest upheavals, for it is demanded by the will of the world.'[166]

Now came the so-called coincidence, that just at the time when Polzer was due to travel to his brother with the two Memoranda, another helper appeared on the scene: Walter Johannes Stein, who had been born in Vienna in 1891 and who, while on active service in the army, had travelled to Berlin to speak to Steiner about his PhD research. As it was much easier for military personnel to take written documents across the border, Stein, whom Polzer already knew from summer courses in Munich, immediately offered to take the first typed Memorandum to Austria. 'In an emergency I shall swallow it,' he joked, and his earnest words gave Rudolf Steiner real pleasure. Thus Stein became, alongside Lerchenfeld and Polzer, the third in the group of those who were the first to know of Steiner's threefold ideas. With him too, Polzer would share an unspoilt friendship from then on.

On the evening of 22 July, Polzer travelled to Vienna to his brother Arthur and accompanied the Cabinet Director from there to Reichenau, the Emperor's summer residence. Ludwig gave Arthur the typed first Memorandum as well as the second Memorandum, which he had himself written out. On 26 July Polzer had a conversation with the Prime Minister Ernst von Seidler.

And the Emperor? Would the Emperor of Austria now get on his horse? That naturally depended on how fast and in what manner the Director of his Cabinet would pursue the idea of threefolding. And Arthur Polzer ... hesitated. Not least because just at that time, in con-nection with the amnesty for the Czechs, a malicious witch-hunt against him had flared up, the main intriguer in which was the unscrupulous pro-German, pro-Hungarian Count Czernin. Arthur Polzer therefore believed he should not worsen the situation by presenting the Memor-andum, and he chose to wait. He made a detailed study of the Memor-anda, however, and came to a high appreciation of the value of the documents. In his book *Kaiser Karl—aus der Geheimmappe seines Kabi-nettschefs* [Emperor Karl—From the Secret Files of his Cabinet Director] he wrote, a good ten years later:

I gained the impression that this was a proposal which—unlike so many others—took full account of the practical needs of the encroaching situation. The idea—as far as I understood it—was based essentially on the following: The binding of affairs in political life with those of the economic life and the cultural life, the management of these three heterogeneous areas of life in a unified system has brought about a situation in which not only the circumstances but also the concepts became confused and ultimately a chaos developed, out of which the world catastrophe arose. The three areas of life should no longer be seen and handled as a unity but must be managed separately, as they want to be understood in accordance with different basic principles. Political affairs in the narrow sense, thus legal and political protection, the military and foreign affairs requires, due to its own nature, handling in accordance with the fundamental principle of conservatism in the sense of the maintenance and reinforcement of what has developed historically. Economic matters, in order to flourish, must be managed in accordance with the principle of real efficacy, while human cultural life, in its cultural and spiritual affairs, should be centred in personal freedom, in that the State should allow corporations to form freely that create and manage the whole cultural life, the judiciary, schools and welfare institutions. In the cultural sphere free corporations would therefore have to take the place of State interference and privileging.[167]

It is an unexpected surprise for a historian to see how Arthur Polzer, who kept his distance from Rudolf Steiner's spiritual science, clearly grasped with a sure instinct the potential practical value in Steiner's Memorandum, thanks to his rich experience in politics and his sense for reality. 'I felt I could see,' the Cabinet Director went on, 'that the thought that lay at the basis of the system was in general correct and so I concluded that its realization—however difficult it might yet be—must be objectively possible.' Nevertheless, Arthur Polzer estimated that the expected resistance of the old ways of thinking to the realization of Steiner's idea would be tremendous. He wrote:

> I had from the beginning the feeling that the idea of threefolding, because it was drawn from the spiritual world and signified the ultimate rejection of old conditions, concepts and habits of thought, would be almost universally rejected, especially at a time in which—as was still the case in 1917—it was thought one would not have to dispense so much with what was customary.[168]

Unfortunately, Arthur Polzer proved to be right in this thought too, as the attempt made in Germany at about the same time to realize the idea of threefolding through people in influential positions, showed. At the end of July or the beginning of August a conversation was arranged by Otto Lerchenfeld between Rudolf Steiner and the German Secretary of State, Richard von Kühlmann, Lerchenfeld's friend from his school and university days. The Memorandum was also presented to von Kühlmann. In the course of this conversation Steiner said to Kühlmann: 'You have the choice, either to accept reason now and to heed what is announcing itself in human development, what is supposed to happen, or you will be confronted by revolutions and cataclysms.' It was presumably Kühlmann who, to Steiner's call for an open explanation of the events that had led to the outbreak of the war, objected: 'Yes, if one wanted to realize your very first point, then that would necessarily lead to the abdication of the Kaiser!' Whereupon Steiner had to counter: 'If it led to that, then it would indeed be necessary!'[169] According to Lerchenfeld, who was present at the conversation, Kühlmann 'looked like a fool'; in the spring of 1918, in complete denial of the needs of the times, he went on to organize the forced peace of Brest-Litovsk and helped to strengthen the Bolshevik government by financing its newspaper *Pravda*.[170]

At this time of conversations about threefolding, two appeals for peace were made by the Vatican. Pope Benedict XV or his papal diplomat Eugenio Pacelli (later Pope Pius XII) presented these appeals at the beginning of June and August. Thus alongside the USA in the West and the Bolsheviks who were becoming active in the East, the Church, as the third *Power of the South*, now sought to guide Europe's destiny into the channel which *it* held to be right.

'It would be bad if we had to accept peace from the hands of the Pope,' commented Steiner at the time of the August appeal.[171] But the word of the Middle found no echo. Thus the endeavour to effect a change in the situation, by means of the idea of threefolding, through contacts with influential personalities in the Austro-Hungarian Empire and the German Empire, became stuck when it had hardly begun. A joint visit to Arthur Polzer on 26 September in Reichenau by Ludwig Polzer and Count Lerchenfeld was unable to effect any change.

The catastrophes of which Steiner had warned were not much longer in coming. The October Revolution confirmed the Bolsheviks' domination of Russia, which lay entirely in western interests; the Russian people, who needed something so very different, were shackled for 70 years.

★

Symptomatic of the signature of destiny for the year 1917 are also the intrigues which wove themselves around Arthur Polzer and which decisively determined his hesitant relations with the Emperor. In the autumn of 1917 Arthur Polzer still held it 'to be right in itself',

> that whoever was able to reveal the powers in the west which had secretly worked to unleash the world war and maintained it in a state of permanence, whoever was able to bring to the peoples of the East a peace proposal that would liberate mankind and thus solve the question of peace would find no resistance from the peoples of Middle Europe to the execution of that programme.[172]

But Polzer's powers were already lamed. It was no help that on 11 October he and his siblings were raised by the Emperor to the rank of Count.

With the Austrian victories in Italy in the autumn, the opportunistic Czernin had again begun to count on victory with the Germans and the Hungarians, and efforts for peace and autonomy within the Empire, which were strongly supported by Arthur Polzer and the Emperor, could only interfere: Polzer would have to go. Things were arranged in such a way that the news of his resignation from the post of Director of the Cabinet was presented as a communication to the Press, before the Emperor, who was under pressure from Czernin and the Prime Minister, could inform Polzer of the *merely temporary* step that he felt necessary for a relaxation of domestic tensions.

On 22 November 1917 Arthur Polzer was formally dismissed from his office. 'So Polzer is finished,' a member of Parliament close to Czernin announced to journalists triumphantly.[173] Emperor Karl was angered by the indiscretion of the Press and ordered an investigation. 'Count Polzer has been torn from me by all kinds of intrigues,' he declared shortly after Polzer stepped down.[174] 'The powers of death, which feared revelations, were in a hurry,' wrote Ludwig Polzer over his brother's fall. 'From the occult perspective these details are of great interest.'[175]

Among the grotesque accusations thrown at Arthur Polzer by his opponents was the claim that he had 'once asserted that the danger from the Freemasons was imaginary [and that] there were no Freemasons'. When told of this accusation by the Emperor, Polzer laughed 'and said that it was bizarre that *I* [Polzer] who was better placed than anyone to know of the dangers from Freemasons due to my intensive studies of them should have such a false view ascribed to me and be presented with such tittle-tattle'.[176] He had, for example, taken seriously the coded warning about the fall of the Habsburg Empire that had been received before the war! It is, incidentally, highly instructive that this very passage from Polzer's book, along with all the references to Steiner's threefolding ideas and Steiner himself, were omitted from the English translation of his book *Kaiser Karl*. More of that later.

Only now, in his final leave-taking audience with the Emperor, did Arthur Polzer, whose attitude towards his own fate had been remarkably relaxed, think the time had come to inform His Majesty of the idea of the threefolding of the social organism. 'In the evening and the next day I had audiences lasting several hours,' wrote Polzer, 'during which, no longer bound by the reservations laid upon me by my office, I spoke about the system of threefolding. The Emperor listened most attentively. He fully appreciated the significance of the idea.'[177] Obviously, the idea of the threefolding of the social organism was and is open to much mis-understanding. That was already clear to Ludwig Polzer. He wrote in his notes:

> It was believed, for example, that the proposed economic parliament would create laws, whereas what was actually conceived of was only agreements to make economic arrangements easier for completely unbounded business in an ever larger economic space, because economic life was subject to no hierarchical membering or lawgiving in the political sense. Neither was cultural life thought of as passing laws and orders or that cultural questions should be organized politically. In the sense of three-folding, it had the task of providing new cultural stimuli. While today, for example, the question of school reform in many cases focuses only on school organization and is given political orientation from central government, little thought is given to how to lead the science of pedagogy itself to a higher level. In a threefold social organism in the free spiritual life there will be a continuous competition—which there must not be in the economic life—without any pressure from the State or the Church or even by any indirect economic route, to force people into any cultural group. Everyone will be left quite free, for example, to have his children educated by those in whom he trusts. The most difficult thing today is for people to understand the tasks of the State as being the upholding of rights.[178]

When, after the failure of his attempt to get his brother to present the Memorandum to the Emperor before Arthur's resignation in November, Ludwig Polzer saw Rudolf Steiner again, Steiner said that as Foreign Secretary Arthur Polzer would certainly have been able to accomplish 'what we hoped of him and what could have completely changed the world situation'.[179] For that, however, the Emperor would have had to separate himself from Czernin instead of Polzer, who would have dared to propose such a course of action even less than he would have dared to place Steiner's Memorandum before the Emperor.

★

If in retrospect we look at this first effort to introduce threefolding 'from above', why it was so significant and why its failure therefore *had to* have such fatal consequences, a satisfactory answer can hardly be given without a consideration of specific spiritual facts. One of these lies, for example, behind some words Rudolf Steiner once spoke to Ludwig Polzer: 'The Habsburg family spirit was the force holding the peoples of Austria together. It worked through the individualities of the Habsburgs. This family spirit was of the hierarchical rank of an archangel.'[180] That means that, from a spiritual perspective, one has to do with a very mighty spiritual being. On the other hand, Rudolf Steiner can be seen as a representative of the true modern time spirit, who was in a position to be able to give a really contemporary stimulus in the social field. 'If, through the personality of Emperor Karl,' wrote Ludwig Polzer, 'the Habsburg family spirit had been able to unite with the time spirit [...], the transition into the new era would have been possible without real catastrophes. Rudolf Steiner and Emperor Karl were standing there on Earth opposite each other.'[181] Here, we have also indicated the metahistorical background of the single world-historical chance which presented itself in the year 1917. And against this background one will have to investigate the enormous opposition which, one would have to say, in a flash, annihilated this chance; all the more so, when a similar chance was repeated in the middle of the turning point for Germany that came in the year 1989—but more of that in Part V.

'The last months of the year 1917 were thus filled with extraordinarily painful events and disappointments,'[182] wrote Polzer in his Prague Notes. A further unexpected blow followed: Ignaz Reichl, the family's loyal manager for many years at Tannbach suddenly died in his 49th year. Ludwig Polzer was also in his 49th year. For him too the end of this year in several respects meant departure, conclusion. But the disappointments seem not at all to have drawn Polzer away from his efforts to achieve new, very concrete goals in 1917; he was now much too deep in the spiritual scientific way of thinking. For this science possesses a layer where not only thinking is produced, even if it is a very spiritual thinking, but also where courage and other such moral forces can be won. 'Never work for success', Steiner once said to Lerchenfeld,[183] who followed this advice all his life. Success should never be the decisive factor in the effort to translate into action a decision recognized to be right. Ludwig Polzer too let his own efforts be guided more and more by this incontrovertible principle. It gives one the long breath of real unwavering resolution.

24. The Other Side of the Coin

In Rudolf Steiner's work, the year 1917 was not only the year of planting the seed of the threefolding of the social organism but already at the turn of the year 1916/17 he had begun on a systematic and no-holds-barred exposure and presentation of the occult background of the politics of the English-speaking West. His lectures on this subject were titled *Zeit-geschichtliche Betrachtungen* (Considerations of Contemporary Events), already referred to in this book; the lectures were held in Dornach from 4 December 1916 to 30 January 1917.[184] In Munich in May he drew Polzer's attention for the first time to 'certain facts of an evil occultism'[185] and in the second half of the year sent him the typescript of the *Zeit-geschichtliche Betrachtungen* lectures. Steiner therefore thought it important that Polzer should become familiar with the details of what he had alluded to in Munich. Another typescript of a lecture of Steiner's on 6 November 1917, in which he spoke about the assassination of Empress Elisabeth in connection to certain occult aims also turned up—with evident marks of careful reading—in Polzer's literary estate.

In 1917, on the basis of Steiner's lectures on the topic, Polzer therefore systematically began to build up his knowledge of occult processes behind the curtain of ephemeral day-to-day politics. Much that in his youth had lived in his soul, rumbling on only in the form of a subjective, dull feeling of soul oppression now took on an objective character. Let us recall how Polzer had felt when in 1888 the old Court Theatre had been demol-ished. It had felt to him, symbolically, like an old world falling in ruins. Then, for the first time, he had *felt* the tendencies of decline subjectively; now he learned to know the objective background to his own feelings. Thus one's own soul life can function in much else as the mirror of objective world processes—for one who learns to read it.

Since Polzer took the most important steps in understanding in this regard too in 1917, let us accompany him in this for a while, as it were, and take a look at some of the fundamental motifs in Steiner's explanations.

In his lectures (Dec. 1916–Jan. 1917 GA 173 and 174) Steiner repeatedly characterizes what Polzer once called in relation to the pre-vious centuries 'the single, really political, spiritually effective thought in Europe'.[186] This is the notion of certain Anglo-American circles, already mentioned several times in this book, and also sketched by Harrison, that the English-speaking peoples are called to continue the global domination of the Roman Empire and to this end, would have to render the future-oriented element in Slavic culture submissive to their will, and indeed, they would have to do this with the help of the Latin cultural element that is sinking into decadence. One public statement that expressed this notion was made by the British statesman Lord Rosebery, who was the best friend in his youth of Winston Churchill's father and the much-loved political idol of Churchill himself. Rosebery said in 1893, thus more than 100 years ago:

> It is said that our Empire is already large enough and does not need expansion . . . We shall have to consider not what we want now, but what we want in the future . . . We have to remember that it is part of our responsibility and heritage to take care that the world, so far as it can be moulded by us, should receive the Anglo-Saxon and not another character.*

This was and remains—as far as one also takes into account the American element—the firm, fundamental political doctrine of the West, based on occult insight into the laws of the development of entire peoples; it reckons with centuries of time and not merely with the interval until the next Presidential election . . .

The impulse of Peter the Great served this occult-political doctrine from the seventeenth century onwards; the injection of the Socialist experiment in the East was an important step towards the practical realization of the doctrine and the dismantling of the Socialist experiment in 1989 has to be seen in the light of this doctrine. How the 'doctrine' has been further served by Anglo-American policy since the famous turning point in 1989 will be discussed in Part V.

Fundamental for the activity of occult brotherhoods, which are predominantly active in the Anglo-American world, is that they never limit their activity to a *single* direction. That applies, for example, to the Testament of Peter the Great which served the western doctrine, in which, according to Steiner we see 'two things [in operation] in a [. . .] historically genial way at the same time'. These are: 'sympathy for the Testament of Peter the Great and antipathy for everything western—interpenetrating each other so that this interpenetration can become extraordinarily effective'.[188]

★

A very important point in Steiner's revelations about the brotherhoods in 1917 is his indication of their application of certain techniques to make use of the forces of some of the dead in the service of the goals of the

---

*Rosebery Royal Colonial Institution 1 March 1893, reported in *The Times* 2 March 1893.[187]

brotherhoods' group egoism. On 30 January 1917[189] particularly he went into this dark theme.

Instead of relating to the so-called 'dead' in an inner, active way through spiritual ideas, instead of learning from them how to receive conscious inspirations and how to interpret them knowledgeably, bridges are built to some of the deceased in many lodges through outer ceremonial forms and with a completely materialistic way of thinking. That the modern sense of freedom definitely seeks to avoid bridges *like these* does not mean that they are avoided by *everyone* and are not without their effectiveness.

What is the purpose of the collaboration of the dead that can be achieved through such methods? It bestows on those who come into contact with them a suggestive power—often only indirectly, without the conscious awareness of such lower-ranking people. One would have to learn to distinguish in the case of two politicians or journalists who might in principle talk the same sense or nonsense which one was acting *effectively* in the occult sense and which not. The secret of this differentiation often relates to the kind of lodge activity outlined here.

Are there any signs that lodges of this kind exist? There is much more than that; there are historical examples.

We shall here allow ourselves a short diversion into a later period. One can think of the not entirely unknown and apparently harmless Club at Yale University with the name Skull and Bones, which has existed since 1832 and which until today has taken care to recruit only 15 new members a year. In old photographs of gatherings of members of this club one can see them sitting around a skull. That is certainly the case in many clubs. The question is, however, whether such skulls were actually known to those present as the skulls of former members of the club or whether they were only used as symbolic and anonymous aids to some mystical mumbo-jumbo. In any case, what a contrast, to that cultus of inner spiritual communion with those who have died, which Ludwig Polzer, encouraged by Rudolf Steiner, would practise ever more strongly!

What, in a word, is the technique of such brotherhoods? In order to bring about the eventual New World Order, humanity must be permanently permeated—politically, economically and culturally—by streams and counter-streams so that one can be the master of the results of such self-generated contradictions and be able to cover the traces of one's own actions in the continual to-ing and fro-ing of political events.

A signal service was rendered by Anthony C. Sutton when he showed and proved how a brotherhood like the Skull and Bones Club worked in this contradictory manner into the events of the nineteenth century and still works even more into those of the twentieth century.[190] Mammoth enterprises controlled by Skull and Bones members such as the Guaranty Trust Company or the great investment bank Brown Brothers Harriman & Co have been shown to have acted as the financial godfathers of both ultra-leftist Russian Bolshevism as well as ultra-rightist German Nazism. This appears to be very contradictory, but the contradiction was intended. The historical symptom or result first striven for by means of this dialectical method was, according to Sutton, the construction of the United Nations, with the aim of bringing about Anglo-American world-domination. With regard to this technique that operates far beyond the party political opposition of left and right, Sutton states that it represents in the political field essentially nothing other than the operation of Hegel's notion of the dialectical manner in which all comes into being in the world, and which must always arise in three steps: thesis, antithesis, and synthesis. Thus a core idea of Hegel's philosophy became the fundamental basis of the occult-political actions of certain Anglo-American circles.

Some readers may well ask: did Rudolf Steiner know of this brotherhood? The question appears to be answerable only indirectly. In 1909 Steiner had given a public lecture in Berlin in which he referred to the American multi-millionaire Edward Harriman, who had amassed his fortune through very dubious means and who subscribed to the view, contrary to the spirit of Middle European culture, that no man is irreplaceable in his specific occupation.[191] Harriman's son Averell was admitted to Skull and Bones at Yale in 1913 and until his death in 1986 played a far more important role in American foreign policy than numerous Secretaries of State. Even if, to our knowledge, Steiner never named the Yale society, he must have had brotherhoods like Skull and Bones in mind when on 4 December 1920, in relation to the philosophy of Hegel, he made the following remark:

> Hegel speaks in his philosophy about thoughts and actually means cosmic thoughts. Hegel says: when we look somewhere in the outer world, be it a star on its path, an animal, a plant, a mineral, we are actually looking everywhere at thoughts; it is simply that these thoughts in the outer world exist in a form other than that in our own life of thoughts. One cannot say that Hegel exactly strove to conceive of this doctrine of the thoughts of the world in an esoteric way, but it has remained esoteric because Hegel's works have been little read; but that was not Hegel's intention [...] But it is nevertheless extremely interesting that when one turns to the secret societies of the West, in a certain connection it is regarded as a doctrine of the deepest esotericism that the world is actually formed of thoughts. One

would like to say: what Hegel said so naively of the world, the secret societies of the West, of Anglo-American humanity now see as the content of their secret teachings and they are of the view that this secret teaching is not to be popularized. Grotesque as this might seem at first, one could say: *Hegel's philosophy is in a certain sense the fundamental nerve [core] of the secret teaching of the West.*[192]

To this philosophy also belongs Hegel's idea that thoughts work dialectically in the world, that is, through real contradictions.

The convergence of what Steiner said in his lecture with Sutton's diagnosis of the Hegelian dialectic as practised in the Skull and Bones society is noteworthy, all the more, considering that Sutton speaks as neither philosopher nor as occultist. In the fifth part of this book, we shall return to this Yale secret society, the traces of which in today's American Century can be perceived by any unprejudiced observer.

So much for the present: those initiated into Skull and Bones *in the year 1917* included Prescott Bush, the father of George H.W. Bush, who, like his successor in the American Presidency, Bill Clinton, stands in a clear relationship to those at the peak of the manifest iceberg of Anglo-American occultism.[193]

We are getting ahead of our story, but it seemed appropriate at this point *because 1917 is not only the seed-year of the century with regard to social threefolding, but also in terms of the occult-inspired struggle against this Middle European world impulse.* The forced dismissal of Arthur Polzer—to cite only one example—in November 1917 occurred in this area of conflict. This is, of course, not to say that Skull and Bones was involved in his dismissal, but his departure nevertheless certainly was in tune with the aims of the brotherhood.

The Roman Catholic Church has of course to play the role of (a dualist's) 'second' to the West in this struggle, for while western circles sought to make of the entire East, as already mentioned, a giant department store, for the Church the very idea of a *free* spiritual life was deadly fearful. While in 1917 therefore, the idea of threefolding emerged in Europe, inspired by an occultism that transcended nationality, it immediately called forth the sharpest forces of retardation from the English-speaking West as well as from the Roman Catholic South. From this time onwards, the constant effort to realize the great idea would be combatted ever more ruthlessly by the West, with the aid of the Catholic Church. *Threefolding and the opposition to it from the West and the South—these are, so to speak, the two sides of the same coin.* And Rudolf Steiner wanted Ludwig Polzer to get to know the *whole* coin.

A notable piece of this other side of the coin, or at least symptomatological indications of it, also appears in Arthur Polzer's book about Emperor Karl. The English translation of this book was published in October 1930 in the well-known publishing house Putnam & Sons in London and New York. We have already mentioned the fact that in the English version of the book Steiner's Memorandum as well as all the parts which refer to the idea of threefolding were omitted. The thoroughness with which this was done can be seen from the following passages that relate to February 1918.

Arthur Polzer describes an audience with the Emperor on 14 February 1918. The Emperor says to him:

> Forgive me that I can only receive you for a very short time; I have a frightful amount to do. I would like to ask your view on only one political matter. Count Czernin is now bringing up the issue of national autonomy. Before, when you were pressing for that, it was a crime; now it is suddenly necessary and urgent. It is to be done with an edict. *I was thinking of the proposal that you made to me after your resignation. Unfortunately, I no longer have the pro memoria to hand.*[194]

By *pro memoria* he meant the memorandum written up by Arthur Polzer at the Emperor's request in November 1917, which according to Polzer, essentially repeated the content of Steiner's first Memorandum. The Emperor's last sentences above (in italics) were neatly cut from the English edition of Polzer's book.

Three days later, Arthur Polzer sent the second copy of his pro memoria in a sealed folder to the Emperor, who wanted to give it to his Prime Minister, Seidler. On the evening of the same day, Polzer went to Seidler in order to prepare him for the content of the document which he would be receiving within a few days. Polzer said to Seidler 'I should have told His Majesty about what the idea involves in a long audience I had with him in November 1917 immediately after my resignation, and now the Emperor has come back to it.'

> I had studied the idea of the threefolding of the social organism during my vacation and thought about how it could be executed, so I was in a position this time to make very concrete proprosals to the Prime Minister. Seidler listened attentively and spoke with me very interestedly about the matter.[195]

This passage too was left out of the English version of Polzer's book on the Emperor without any comment or explanation. The English translation appeared in October 1930. *More than twelve years after the historical events described in the book, someone in certain Anglo-American circles had reason to prevent the English-speaking public from reading about the interest in the idea of threefolding shown by the Emperor and Minister-President Seidler.* That must give every serious historian pause for serious reflection... One who might still wish to deny that such omissions amount to much should consider the following, which concerns the very first page of the German edition of Arthur Polzer's book, or more precisely, footnote 1, which relates to this page. It reads:

> I conclude that the destruction of the Habsburg Monarchy had long been a settled matter among those politicians who—by the way—after the collapse of the Central Powers shared out amongst themselves the chief roles in world politics. In this connection may also be mentioned the map showing the division of Europe which the Englishman Labouchère published in his satirical magazine *Truth* in 1890, that is, 24 years before the outbreak of the world war. It is almost identical to today's map of Europe: Austria as a monarchy has disappeared and made way for a republican member of the League of Nations, Bohemia has become an independent state in the incidental form of Czechoslovakia. Germany is squeezed into her present confines and split into small republics. Above the territory of Russia is written the word 'Desert', 'states for Socialist experiments' [see note 196]. The programme would, however, certainly not have been realized so easily if its proponents had not been able to find such willing, mostly unconscious collaborators among the 'statesmen' of Middle Europe.[196]

This whole first footnote in Polzer's book was removed from the English version, which thereby hindered many people in Britain and America from being able to form ideas about the background to the First World War which were in accord with reality! That was obviously to be prevented.

How did the Catholic Church respond to Arthur Polzer's book and to Emperor Karl? Despite Polzer's book, the Church placed the Emperor on the list of candidates for beatification. The process of beatification of this Emperor has been going on since 1949, despite his known interest in the social ideas of Rudolf Steiner, of which the Curia is of course well aware. But perhaps it was precisely this 'weakness' of His Majesty, all too apparently revealed in Polzer's book, which delayed the conclusion of the process and in the end could even block it.[*]

---

[*] Karl I was finally beatified on 3 October 2004 by Pope John Paul II.

25. A Pause for Breath

After the failure of the first efforts to find a hearing in high places for the idea of threefolding, a new phase of inner work began in the life of Ludwig Polzer. His previous experiences and knowledge were reflected on and deepened. In autumn 1917 Polzer had entered the second seven-year period of his anthroposophically-oriented striving and activity since that decisive Munich summer conference.

In those same days in February 1918, when Arthur Polzer again spoke with the Emperor and with Seidler about social threefolding, his brother Ludwig travelled once more to Munich with his wife Berta. Here, on 17 February, in a lecture to the local branch of the Anthroposophical Society, Rudolf Steiner referred to a historical law that Polzer doubtless noted as significant. Steiner spoke of how earlier events are reflected in later ones and indeed in symmetrical distance in time from a particular year that functions as an axial point mid-way between the earlier and later events.[197] Rudolf Steiner proceeds from the year 1879, in which a most important event occurred on the plane of metahistory: the activity of a new Time Spirit began in 1879 after a spiritual struggle that had lasted for decades. This spiritual struggle has entered into the popular imagery of many peoples as the struggle between Michael and the Dragon and is well-known in occultism. C.G. Harrison also speaks of this struggle in his book; it began in 1841. With 1879 as the axial year, the beginning of this struggle of the new Time Spirit with the retarding spiritual powers is mirrored in the year 1917/18. The rapid, sharp resistance to the impulse of threefolding in 1917 may have appeared all the more understandable to Ludwig Polzer in the light of this mirroring principle, even if no less fateful. The resistance was 'in the air'. That does not mean to say that it was *bound to* dominate.

In 1993 there was another mirror relationship to 1841, if we take 1917 as the axis point. The relationship is instructive: as in 1917, the region of the old Danube Monarchy was once again the theatre in which conflicts broke out between peoples, races, religions and nationalities. The only difference was that the retarding forces were even harder at work, and what would only be solvable through an informed differentiation of the social organism was hardened still further through the means of territorial division of ethnic groups, a method which had for a long a time been unusable. While in 1917, with the amnesty in Bohemia, a first step was taken in the direction of a federal restructuring of the Empire, the content of the shower of proposals put forward in 1993 was well *below* the quality of what was striven for in 1917. One can think, for example, of the Vance-Owen Plan that led to the Dayton Treaty, which secured the domination of the USA and NATO in Bosnia, Herzegovina and Croatia.

★

In March Ludwig and Berta Polzer travelled from Tannbach to Berlin, and in April to Stuttgart, Ulm and Heidenheim for further lectures by Steiner and conversations about threefolding. Polzer wrote about this period that 'the public and other lectures became ever greater, in correspondence with that painful time'.[198]

> Lerchenfeld was with me a great deal, and together we tried to get a better grasp of the idea of threefolding down to its details. Rudolf Steiner always emphasized that in trying to carry out the idea, its power of growth and activity would only gradually be revealed in the details of life. What he had written in the Memoranda was no abstract programme but would bear within it formative power if it were set on the road to realization. Only much later did I understand that one could only gradually acquire an inner capacity to apply this thought within developing events and situations; that one could find the right point of entry for it in every situation.

How Ludwig Polzer himself dealt with this in the sense of his understanding referred to in the last sentence above will be discussed later in relation to a Memorandum he himself wrote in 1930 (see p. 542ff.).

Freshly inspired by the new lectures he had heard and also by conversations with Steiner about questions of threefolding, throughout the spring of 1918 Polzer intensified his anthroposophical work in Linz and Prague.

At the end of May he travelled to Vienna, where Steiner gave two public lectures. During his stay in Vienna, Steiner hoped to make the acquaintance of Ludwig's brother Arthur. 'Unfortunately, no meeting came about', Ludwig Polzer remarked, giving no further explanation.[199] Nevertheless, Steiner's intention is noteworthy. To the eye of the historian used to researching symptomatically, it has a seed character.

26. With Rudolf Steiner in Tannbach, Prague and Karlstein

The year 1918 was one of the greatest festive years in the life of Ludwig Polzer and his wife Berta. On 7 June, accompanied by his wife Marie, Rudolf Steiner arrived in Tannbach, after the journey had almost proved impossible. On the same day Otto Lerchenfeld also arrived in Tannbach for the first time.

For civilians travelling on overcrowded trains was often an unpredictable experience. Steiner had managed to obtain the tickets only thanks to a happy accident, as Polzer describes in the Prague Notes: 'Rudolf Steiner told us of this circumstance with a certain emphasis, by which we realized that he wanted to say that his being able to come to us as a result of this circumstance was something approved by destiny.'[200]

From the outset then, the hosts in Tannbach rightly valued the importance of Steiner's coming; they were not under any illusion that it was to be thought of as the sign of a merely personal estimation. From before the arrival of their guests the hosts were filled with expectation of deeper dimensions to this unusual visit.

Rudolf Steiner stayed on the raised ground floor (*Hochparterre*) on the south east side of the house. The following morning at breakfast he asked about the room above which he had slept. Ludwig Polzer told him that it was a storage room for firewood and was not a little surprised when Steiner asked that it be emptied. This was immediately arranged.

The guests were then shown around the environs of the house. Polzer led them to the Waldaist, a delightful mountain stream, the waters of which shimmer golden in many quiet places. The company learned with astonishment from Rudolf Steiner that the stream had been flowing since Atlantean times. It had small amounts of gold in it. He was also shown the strongest of several sources of radioactivity, whereupon the spiritual researcher told them that radioactivity had only been in the Earth since the Mystery of Golgotha.

It was perhaps in the later evening hours of that day that Rudolf Steiner leafed through and began to read the small volume *In Mussestunden* (In Leisurely Hours), the stories written by Polzer's grandfather that were mentioned earlier in this book. Rudolf Steiner felt that 'much understanding of destiny lies in them'. At any rate, according to Polzer, Steiner was reading them in June 1918.

The next day was a Sunday. Rudolf and Marie Steiner accompanied their hosts to Mass at Gutau. This had been Berta Polzer's wish; her religiously inclined soul still highly valued the ritual of the Mass, although she had now long been familiar with spiritual science. How far was this ritual still historically justified? How can the ritual's lost spiritual substance be renewed? Such subjects may have been spoken of on the return to Tannbach. It was like a preparation for what now took place: Rudolf Steiner conducted a ritual of a spiritually real nature in the room that had been emptied the day before. He placed this ritual under the sign of the Rose Cross; the newly revealed room, he told them in a solemn address, had served as a gathering place for Rosicrucians and also later for the Brothers of the Common Life.

In a simple way Steiner then evoked the Rosicrucian *genius loci* of the house and spoke of how already at the beginning of the seventeenth century people in Middle Europe had been ripe to receive a new spiritual impulse—an impulse, moreover, that could have led to the transformation of social life, step by step, in an evolutionary, not a revolutionary way. Steiner spoke of the *Chymical Wedding of Christian Rosencreuz*, that inspired work by the young Johann Valentin Andreae, which remained incomprehensible to its author even in his old age.

Simple too, like the whole ritual, wrote Polzer, was its conclusion: 'At the end he compared the spirit sinking down to Man with the snow which with its purity covers the bare earth in winter.'[201]

Steiner's solemn words went deep into the hearts of all those present—Marie Steiner, Count Lerchenfeld, Berta and Ludwig Polzer and their two sons. 'We felt,' wrote Polzer looking back,

> that the address met the situation in the world because the catastrophe for mankind that had set in with the world war would, despite Rudolf Steiner's life of sacrifice, once again hold up the approach of the spiritual world to human souls, especially those in Middle Europe.[202]

'Tannbach is a place of initiation,' Rudolf Steiner said a few days later to Julie Klima.[203] On that Sunday the new initiation centre had itself been initiated.

The ceremony was followed by a walk in the woods that afternoon, when something special happened that no one noticed except Rudolf Steiner. The group had a police dog with them that was almost blind. Polzer reported,

> He gave a bark when we came to a weather-worn tree-stump, and we wondered whether, in his blindness, he had taken the stump for a human being. When we passed the same spot on the way back, the dog barked at the stump again. Rudolf Steiner said nothing. Years later some anthroposophers told us that in a lecture Rudolf Steiner, without naming names, had described this situation and had told of how he and the dog had seen an

elemental being which was sitting on the tree-stump and saying awful things about us. In the lecture he spoke of how the area had not been so divested of its nature forces by civilization and that the elemental beings had not been driven away from it.[204]

In such ways was Rudolf Steiner able to spend time both in society with his own kind and at the same time 'in society of another kind', without the people who were with him knowing anything about it . . .

During this visit to Tannbach the world situation was of course often a topic of conversation. On one occasion Steiner remarked on the striking similarity between the Imperial Chancellor Hertling, the elderly Munich philosophy professor, and the French Cardinal Mazarin, the successor to Richelieu. Count Georg Hertling had been appointed Imperial Chancellor after the fall of Michaelis in autumn 1917 and would be dismissed in September 1918. Six years after this remark to Polzer, Steiner revealed in a lecture to members the spiritual identity of Hertling and Mazarin (19 Sept. 1924, see GA 238.) Had he already done spiritual-scientific research into this identity in June 1918? Or at the time he made the remark was this research only beginning?

As always through such remarks Polzer could get a direct glimpse as though through a door left ajar into certain destiny questions of spiritual science.

In Dornach the situation was as precarious as ever. Steiner even considered the possibility that the French might march in. Polzer immediately offered to move there in such a case. Steiner demurred. What would have been the use of such a move?

In the same conversation Steiner made the following remark: the whole Gutau region would fall to Germany. Polzer understood this remark as follows:

> With these words Rudolf Steiner was looking into a distant future; he was looking to a Middle Europe which would stand under the cultural influence of the German spirit—in the spiritual-scientific sense—freely acknowledged by people. The question was only whether this would come about after the most severe catastrophes and the most appalling depopulations or after the exercise of moral reason.[205]

Reason did *not* prevail. And it is doubtful whether the most severe catastrophes have yet occurred.

'One felt oneself,' Polzer went on, 'on the eve of a time in which the events of the Thirty Years' War would be repeated in a much more radical way.' *This* time too does not yet seem to be over.

On 11 June—it was a Tuesday—Berta and Ludwig Polzer travelled with Rudolf and Marie Steiner to Prague, while Count Lerchenfeld returned to Köfering. At the station in Prague the travellers were met with great warmth by many anthroposophical friends although the train was three hours late. Both couples stayed at the Hotel *Zum Blauen Stern*, the same hotel in which three years earlier Julie Klima had sought Ludwig Polzer out and had asked his advice. For the following nine days in which the guests stayed in Prague this lady played a fine and a central role. On the day of their arrival Steiner gave a public lecture on 'Goethe's Personal Relationship to His Faust'.[206] Lectures were also planned for two days later and for the Sunday 16 June for after that, Steiner wanted to return to Berlin.

When they did not have lunch with the Hauffens, Julie Klima looked after the physical well-being of the guests with judicious care. Her husband, who was the chief of police in Prague, put a coach at their disposal, which was a real luxury at that time. They were thus able to view Prague's historical sights without effort.

On Sunday they visited the Hradčany Castle and besides St Vitus' Cathedral with its splendid Wenceslas chapel they also visited the council chamber in the old part of the castle. Here they saw the world-famous window where the defenestration had occurred which started the Thirty Years' War. Hardly had the participants in the ritual at Tannbach heard of the spirit-destroying effects of that war than they were standing at *the actual place where that dreadful war broke out!* 'Rudolf Steiner looked so profoundly down at Prague that we stood behind him silently and reverently,' Polzer wrote of the scene. 'We felt how his "seeing" was living deeply into the background of long past events.'[207]

The little group also visited the Strahov Monastery with its wonderful library that same day. Wandering along the ancient aisles of this very special library, Ludwig Polzer confessed to Steiner that he was often overcome with feelings of 'worthlessness' in such places. 'Why?', remarked Rudolf Steiner untroubled. 'You have much of it in you, without knowing it in detail.'[208] Even if one had not read everything that had been written, one was still linked in spirit and soul to the extract of what had been achieved by previous generations of mankind.

When the visitors were shown books which were kept locked away because they were on the Index of forbidden books, Rudolf Steiner exclaimed happily: 'Perhaps my books will be in there too in the future!' Polzer comments: 'That was certainly said in jest, but also in deep earnestness.'[209]

Julie Klima reports that when some handwriting of Jan Hus was pointed out to him, he turned away. 'He intentionally did not look at it.'[210] A noteworthy occurrence, not easily explained. But Rudolf Steiner was not lacking in refreshing humour in Prague. 'We three women,' reported Julie Klima, and she meant by that Countess Polzer, Marie Steiner and herself,

> were not allowed to enter this holy place in the monastery—the male visitors were led into the refectory that was inaccessible for women. When the men came back, Dr Steiner said to us women with his priceless humour: 'You could have gone with us quietly, there was no chance for mischief.'

In the Klima household at this time a moving personal drama was playing itself out. Jaroslav Klima had fallen in love with an attractive actress whom he had to examine in a legal case of *lèse-majesté*. Julie Klima describes in her memoirs how Rudolf Steiner regarded the complications of the situation and what he advised: 'Your case is a tragedy,' he said to Mrs Klima. 'But do you want to experience no tragedies? Only banal people experience no tragedies!' He added the following words of explanation: 'Your husband's temperament needed this. The matter is karmic and has to do with a previous life.' To her husband, of whom Rudolf Steiner was very fond, he gave the following advice: 'One should never suddenly break off such relationships. You must summon up the strength to enable the two women to become friends.'[211] That this was eventually achieved can be counted among the anthroposophically motivated marvels in the private lives of pupils of the spirit.

Jaroslav Klima did not have an easy time with spiritual science. But this did not bother Rudolf Steiner. 'For me the dearest are those who have a hard time in coming to it,' he said to Mrs Klima when she expressed worries about her husband.[212]

Because Dr Klima was often compared in jest to Napoleon due to his characteristic Roman head, conversation at lunchtime one day turned to the Corsican tyrant. Rudolf Steiner said suddenly: 'I could not find Napoleon's soul in my researches anywhere.'[213] It was again one of those utterances that give one something to think about for decades.

On Sunday evening at the Society's Prague branch Steiner held his third and last lecture of this stay in the city. He had thought to depart the following morning with Marie Steiner, but Julie Klima's heartfelt proposal a few days earlier that Rudolf Steiner might also like to visit Karlstejn Castle with the company of friends had moved Marie Steiner to persuade her husband to postpone their departure. What a piece of luck! For there now followed for the small group of travellers the actual high point of Rudolf Steiner's entire visit to Bohemia. The Klimas' young daughter, then 13 years old, who Rudolf Steiner treated with charming courtesy, was also allowed to go along.

On 17 June the group travelled to the castle, which was built by Charles IV. According to Steiner, the monarch, who was of the Luxemburg-Habsburg line, was the last initiate on the throne.[214] In fact, this is borne out by quite specific details of the castle's construction. 'When we climbed the narrow, steep stairway up to the Chapel of the Golden Cross,' relate Polzer's Prague Notes,

> on which both sides are painted frescoes, with the story of St Ludmilla on the right-hand side and St Wenceslas on the left-hand side, my wife drew Rudolf Steiner's attention on the way up to a picture of Wenceslas sitting on a throne in the manner of a ritual. Rudolf Steiner replied simply: 'The Chymical Wedding of Christian Rosencreuz'.

This was certainly a surprising remark for his companions, but definitely also one which could set them thinking. For with it there appeared again on this trip to Bohemia the complementary motif to the Thirty Years' War, namely, Rosicrucianism, and it may have reminded them of the ritual address given at Tannbach.

In the Chapel of the Golden Cross, the visitors were once again astounded. The walls were everywhere covered with the most vivid and colourful precious stones set in gold. From the deep blue cruciform ceiling of the holy place golden stars shone down on the visitors.

A very similar mood settled on the group as on the day before in the Council Chamber at the Hradčany Castle. 'Rudolf Steiner stood bowed towards the altar, deep in thought, and sensing the holiness of the moment, we remained quietly in the background. Of the Golden Cross Chapel he said that it represented a conscious copy of the Grail Castle.'[215] So they had now travelled from one initiation centre to another, from Tannbach's ritual room to the Chapel of the Cross at Karlstejn. It was as though a circle had been closed here.

★

The effects of these experiences with Rudolf Steiner on Ludwig Polzer's inner development can hardly be overestimated. He learned to see the place where he lived, Tannbach, with new eyes. Only now did he rightly understand Prague, the place of his birth. Here the seed was planted for his studies of the history of Bohemia that he would undertake through the works of František Palacký. In later years he would often walk up to Prague Castle and gaze out from there into the distance and from those distances the memory came to him again of those holy experiences. And if his own strong capacity for self-recollection, which he had had since his youth, was blessed at some time and in some place, and purified and enriched through a similar cultic component, then the beginnings of that are to be found in those June days in 1918. *All retrospection on the past can become a sacred act for the soul.* Polzer learned to feel this more and more.

At the same time here in Prague was laid something like a golden ground for all his later activities in the city, indeed throughout Bohemia. For Rudolf Steiner through his stay in Prague in June 1918 had not only cast a light far back into the city's past. On another occasion, he illuminated its distant future. He made the following remark one day to Ida Freund, an early theosophical colleague, at whose home he was lodging in sight of the Hradčany Castle: 'One day up there the first flames of the sixth post-Atlantean epoch will be lit.'[216] These special links to past and future bestowed on Prague's *present* something very special. And in this present, Ludwig Polzer put down ever firmer roots.

27. The Threefolding Work 1919–1921

After such inspiring and significant days with Rudolf Steiner, began the second act of Ludwig Polzer's work for the threefolding of the social organism.

Before the summer vacations Polzer sat alongside Otto Lerchenfeld in a session of the Bavarian Parliament. As a member of the Chamber, Lerchenfeld would have had the right to speak about Rudolf Steiner's radically new social ideas. But despite encouragement by his friend, he was unable to do this. 'The chamber session,' wrote Polzer,

> made the most unsavoury impression on me imaginable. So many people fast asleep to reality in such dire times! A feeling of hopelessness came over me; I was looking at a decaying, utterly decadent culture. People were in positions of influence who were completely devoid of ideas confronted by the challenges of the times.[217]

After this session in the summer of 1918, Polzer accompanied Otto Lerchenfeld for the first time to Köfering near Regensburg and became acquainted with his family. A new thread of destiny now wove itself into Polzer's life. He would form very strong bonds of anthroposophical friendship with two of Lerchenfeld's children, his second eldest, Sophie, then 18, and later to her sister Rosa (Menny), who was then 10 years old.

Before Polzer arrived at the Lerchenfeld estate, Thaddäus Rychter, a painter who had long been a good friend of his and Berta's and who happened also to be staying in Köfering at that time, had already successfully put in a good word for the visitor. 'The atmosphere of the few days spent there was very good and friendly,' reported Polzer, satisfied with a visit that was important for him.[218]

Polzer spent August with his wife in Berlin attending lectures by Steiner. One day they went on an excursion to nearby Potsdam and sought out in Hoditzstrasse, which was still so-named, the house of the 'Wondrous Count', Albert von Hoditz. They found a commemorative tablet to the notable relative and favourite of Frederick the Great. Thus, even in the midst of his earnest efforts in spiritual scientific studies, Ludwig Polzer, made time for reflection on this unusual bearer of his own ancestral stream.

After his return from Berlin, back in Tannbach he wrote down a kind of contemplation of his times that shows how much Steiner's lectures on current events and above all on the special occult background to those events had opened his eyes. It is not merely an echo of Steiner's lectures that one finds in these writings but an individually penetrated and felt view of things, when for example, he wrote: 'The events of the times truly show only too clearly that people could finally see that the power of a trained, hidden spirituality is at work, against which one cannot prevail with cannon and gas bombs.'[219]*

Since then, current events have certainly become still 'clearer', and yet even today, there are still too few who want to know anything about such a 'trained, hidden spirituality'. It was precisely this occult background to contemporary politics that enabled Polzer, trained in Steiner's *open* spirituality, to see ever more clearly.

There were two pillars of the special occultism that was working ruthlessly into all contemporary events which Polzer recognized with increasing clarity: the Freemasonry (FM) that was centred in the Anglo-American West, above all, in the form of high-grade, or irregular, Freemasonry, and Jesuitism (SJ). Both of these spiritual orientations had particular aims, which were in no way for the benefit of the whole of mankind, and insofar as the spiritual science of Steiner was focused on the latter, the two streams could work together against this third spiritual stream, even though, seen from the viewpoint of their lower grades, the goals of the two streams were apparently divergent.

'There is therefore a double power which fights against us,' wrote Polzer:

'1. The English-speaking peoples' will to imperialistic world domination which has been taken over by them from the decayed spirit of Rome, and

2. the imperialism incorporated in the Roman Church.' And further:

> There is a spiritual continuity and thereby naturally a mutual understanding [between FM and the SJ]; even if the one power must be opposed to the other, they nevertheless understand themselves at the same time to be opposed to what represents a new spiritual form that is not part of this continuity, a form which first awakens in German culture and which is to grow into the future.[220]

To Polzer, it had become clear that the strong resistance to the realization of the idea of threefolding, resistance which was opposing it and which would continue to oppose it in the future, was related to the activities of both these two forms of special occultism. For only the emergence of a *free* spiritual life signified a fearful danger for both of these two powers.

---

* The implication here is that things had come to the point where people would be able to realize this *if* they really tried—*transl.*

★

Polzer's writings in Tannbach in August 1918 testify to another note-worthy fact: at this point in time Polzer had been informed by Rudolf Steiner in the greatest detail about the confused, pitiable train of events (already briefly outlined in chapter 22) which played itself out at the highest level in Germany on the eve of the outbreak of war. Steiner himself knew of this at first hand: Helmuth von Moltke, the Chief of the General Staff, who had been so coldly forced from his post in the autumn of 1914, had described it to him in detail. In the spring of 1919 Steiner made the attempt to alter the course of the discussions in Versailles by publishing Moltke's memoirs, which had been kept secret until then, for the writings of the army chief, who had died in June 1916, showed only too clearly how the political leadership in Germany, which has since been blamed for deliberately instigating the war, had actually stumbled into the tragic events in confusion and naïveté. Ludwig Polzer doubtless belonged to the very few to whom Steiner had shared his knowledge of these symptomatically important events already in 1918, if not earlier. 'Such moments can be found,' wrote Polzer,

> as those between 5 o'clock in the afternoon and 10 o'clock in the evening of 1 August 1914, which can reveal how quickly and self-assuredly the actual, hidden string-pullers reached into the unawake, benumbed con-sciousnesses of those in charge; other moments besides these can also be found. When one finds them, one also sees how the spiritual plan is put together which leads the raging fight against human progress.[221]

The last autumn reports from the various frontlines of the war filled Ludwig Polzer with growing anxiety. His nerves were 'strained to the maximum'. The greatest relief for this inner and outer pressure he experienced in the company of Lerchenfeld on several visits to Köfering. At the beginning of October his anxieties about the end of the war made him ill and he was forced to rest in bed. Prince Max von Baden had just had one last chance, in his speech on being appointed Imperial German Chancellor, of speaking out about the idea of threefolding, which had been made known to him, but he had made no mention of it. On 3 October the Imperial German government offered a ceasefire *on the basis of the 14 Points of Woodrow Wilson*. The last hope for a spiritual offensive from official Middle Europe was lost.

A bad attack of influenza kept Polzer in his bed for a while. But he was looked after 'with the greatest care' by his hosts. Polzer participated in the dramatic events of his time in such a strong, intensely personal manner that he was laid low by a severe illness.

After the military collapse of the Central Powers and the spiritual capitulation before Wilson's abstract phrases about the liberation of peoples, Ludwig Polzer became homeless, for the first and most profound time in his life. What was left over of Austria-Hungary for him had 'no meaning any more'.[222] The Habsburg Empire had completely lost the most essential aim of its being—the various peoples that had been united in its territory, without being able to equalize them, without being able to raise them to a more productive harmony. The so-called republics erected on the territory of Austria-Hungary in accordance with a template imposed from the West were for him a mockery of Austria-Hungary's true aims: 'Thus was the intention of particular powers realized.'[223] Nothing fruitful for the future could be expected from the Central European statesmen who had been taken in by the 'double power' of the West and the South.

At this point in time one could only commit one's forces for the sake of 'the condition of humanity in general'.[224] And Polzer now set about doing this with all his strength.

First, however, he had to dedicate himself much more to the Tannbach estate in order to produce the necessary means of survival for his own workers.

Now was the time to introduce the idea of threefolding into the pseudo-revolutionary chaos of so-called public opinion, which consisted, then as now, primarily of little more than the sum of individuals' lack of thoughts. In the winter of 1918 Steiner began to hold public lectures on the subject in various cities in Germany and Switzerland. Really constructive ideas had to be set against the wave of Bolshevism that was breaking over Middle Europe. At the beginning of February, Steiner wrote a 'Call to the German People and the Cultural World'[225] which he wanted to carry the impulse of threefolding to the greatest number of people. To make this call effective, the signatures of well-known personalities in public life were to be appended to the text which would be published in the main daily newspapers. Between 4 and 28 February Steiner gave public lectures in Zurich on 'The Key Points of the Social Question'.[226] He ended one of the lectures by reading out his Call.

One of the anthroposophers listening to him in Zurich was Walter Johannes Stein, who on 7 February sent a telegram to Polzer asking him to come to Vienna for a discussion of a political nature. Polzer set out for Vienna the next day. There, he travelled around with Stein by car gathering signatures. On 11 February the pair were able to report to Zurich that they had collected 93 signatures. Other anthroposophical friends collected many signatures over a short period in Germany and

Switzerland. On 5 and 6 March the Call was then published with the attached signatures in numerous daily newspapers. The signatures from Austria included that of Arthur Polzer-Hoditz.

Meanwhile, in Stuttgart a 'League for the Threefolding of the Social Organism' had emerged on the basis of the Call. A similar group was to be founded in Vienna. On 20 March Ludwig Polzer held the founding lecture with the title 'The Necessity for European Culture of the Upholding and Further Development of German Spiritual Life'; its subtitle was 'The Historical Basis of Dr Rudolf Steiner's Call *To the German People and the Cultural World*'.

It was the first public lecture Polzer had ever held, and given the nature of his own strivings up to this point, it was no accident that this should be its subject. In the lecture, which he also had printed, he gave an overview of the development of German society and culture in the modern period; he showed how this culture had strayed away from the unpolitical goals of its real being, which was focused on knowledge, and had therefore become a victim of western foreign policy which reckoned with the occult facts of the development of peoples. Polzer's lecture was an appeal to the deeper forces within German culture, 'to become conscious of what in reality stands behind social demands and how social instincts can be met'. If true German culture would awaken, then on the basis of threefolding a real understanding with the East would come about and not only a chimera like the forced peace treaty of Brest-Litovsk. But to this end, it had to be recognized that in western and southern power circles nothing was more feared 'than that the Germans and the peoples of the East would find themselves because it was known that nothing would be able to withstand this combined power'.[227]

Instead of this, the intention is that 'the old Roman Empire [. . .] is to be repeated in an Empire of the English-speaking peoples. *For centuries that has been the only really political, spiritually effective thought in Europe.*' Against this thought the impulse of threefolding would now have to be placed openly before the public if the Bolshevism that had been launched from the West was not to stream into the Middle European cultural vacuum.

Polzer's far-reaching lecture, rich in content, is an eloquent testimony of the clarity and depth with which the knowledge of the necessity for social threefolding was alive in him at that time.

While Polzer's friend Stein supported the work with many lectures of his own, the timber merchant Josef van Leer helped through generous financial contributions. Another friend of Polzer's, Hugo Griebsch, a Lieutenant Colonel in the Corps of Engineers, was active in the committee of the League in Vienna. For his part Griebsch was well-acquainted with the Polish General Pilsudski and probably was the linkman who enabled the later contacts between the general and Otto Lerchenfeld to come about.

In April 1919 Berta and Ludwig Polzer travelled to Stuttgart, where the League had its main offices. Both were thus able to witness the first period of Steiner's public work for the idea of threefolding in Germany.

But the visit was to be interrupted and unpredictable. When the couple arrived in Munich late in the evening of 12 April, they were told in the hotel that the last train would be going on to Stuttgart at 5 o'clock in the morning. 'It was the night before the communist takeover in Bavaria,' wrote Polzer.

> We had already had to get out in Gessertshausen, as the train could not be taken further because the tracks between Gessertshausen and Din-kelscherben had been torn up. 13 April was a Palm Sunday. At the place I couldn't get hold of a wagon; the passengers were all waiting for the ongoing journey in a small inn. We went for a walk to pass the time and outside the village soon came across a one-horse carriage which could take a traveller to Gessertshausen. We hired this and got to Dinkelscherben in a few hours. There we had to wait again until the evening. In the station restaurant the waiting passengers were talking politics. Inwardly full of the threefold ideas, I involved myself in these wild discussions and even gave a lecture. We got to Ulm near midnight. There we had to stay overnight again, but were able to set off again for Stuttgart on time in the morning. In Stuttgart we booked into the Hotel Marquardt which was excellently run throughout the whole difficult post-war period.[228]

Polzer and his wife stayed in Stuttgart from 15 April to 6 May. The grand rooms in the Gustav Siegle House or in the Liederhalle were always packed when Steiner lectured. But in the discussions which followed the lectures 'one had to struggle against enormously deep-rooted pre-conceived opinions', Polzer wrote. As for Berta and himself, they were 'completely filled with the attempt to take the great spiritual impulse to the public'.[229]

The response from intellectual and middle class circles to the Call had already shown itself to be surprisingly weak; it was not much stronger in the case of the Stuttgart lectures.

Steiner therefore decided here in Stuttgart for the first time to turn to the workers as well, and so began the *third* phase of the threefold work. First, he spoke to workers at the Bosch Works. The first lectures of this kind were, according to Polzer,

> very well-attended, but soon the workers stayed away on instructions from their leaders [...] It became clear that the leaders did not want the workers

to encounter *real* insight; just like those political circles which supported the [Catholic] Centre Party, they were afraid of them awakening to real knowledge. One could clearly experience the hidden, but common actions of the two big parties.* The main leaders of both parties wanted to maintain their voters' lack of spiritual orientation and their blind following.[230]

Basically, the proletarian leaders wanted nothing other than what they had called for at the beginning of the century, when despite the strong positive response to Steiner's lectures to workers at the Workers' Educational Institute in Berlin, the workers' leaders had insisted on 'reasonable compulsion'.

After a session of the workers' committee of the League for Threefolding, Steiner said to Polzer 'very firmly that there would be no point in continuing to work in this manner if the workers could not free themselves from their proletarian leaders'. And to a more optimistic assessment by Polzer, Steiner said 'very seriously and decisively: "If it goes on like this, I cannot save the workers." '[231]

Certainly, the new government of the State of Württemberg initially showed interest in the ideas developed in Stuttgart for an association of various branches of the economy. But soon opposition was raging against such ideas from the national government in Berlin. Since, according to Steiner, all political or economic upheavals were doomed to failure without a 'real cultural revolution', he tried together with leading members of the League to meet with some professors from Tübingen in June in order to press for the formation of a cultural council. Steiner noted on the journey: 'If we do not succeed in making a breakthough on the spiritual side of the social organism, then we shall also basically have to give up with our economic efforts.'[232] The efforts in Tübingen did not succeed. Confronted with the 'professorial philistines' who only thought to uphold their fixed views, Polzer felt the same hopelessness as he had experienced in the Parliament session with Lerchenfeld in the summer of 1918.

For his work in Vienna, Polzer had asked Steiner to allow him the collaboration of his young friend Stein. Stein had recently gained his PhD in Philosophy and Mathematics and was at the time a free agent. Polzer writes of the vain discussions which he, Emil Hamburger, another good friend who lived near him in Tannbach, and Stein had with 'some communist leaders' in Wiener Neustadt. Stein even travelled to Sopron in Hungary, where communist rule was already established, but soon came 'back very depressed'.[233]

---

* The Christian Social Party and the Socialists—THM.

★

In July 1919 the first issue of the weekly magazine *Dreigliederung des sozialen Organismus* (Threefolding of the Social Organism) appeared in Stuttgart, for which Polzer soon began to write. The articles he wrote in 1919 and 1920 were still appearing in 1920 under the title *Politische Betrachtungen* (Political Observations). They all go straight to the kernel of the issue without frills or inhibitions. These articles too show how much Polzer had not only learned from Steiner but had also understood how to work it through in his own individual way. As to what one could learn at that time from Steiner through being with him, he said:

> The way in which Rudolf Steiner always worked with a given situation without ever losing sight of his goal and without making spiritual compromises, how he taught [us] to be of a mobile spirit was, for all of us who were involved, a training which was to be found nowhere else in the world as with him.[234]

Although the second and also the third phases of the threefolding movement appeared to ebb away without effect, what was intended nevertheless remained in the souls of Polzer and many other helpers who had been there from the first as a present and effective ferment which they would never lose. And in this sense, even what fails outwardly is full of the future. After the three efforts to introduce threefolding to the public, none of those who took part in those efforts looked at politics again in the same way as they had before the efforts were made, least of all Ludwig Polzer. For him, to live through the enormous difficulties which confronted the realization of threefolding became the spur for a powerful deepening of insight into what stood behind real political events. He wrote:

> The appearance on the public stage of those spiritual ideas which were right to seek entry into earthly affairs understandably challenged all the dark forces present and active in the various political camps. But growing knowledge too was strengthened by careful observation of symptomatic events. What was at the beginning only an inner, knowing belief in certain spiritual factors behind events transformed itself in the course of this period of learning into a power of knowledge that could see through events.[235]

Something of this newly-acquired power of knowledge directed Polzer in 1919 very intensively to a study of the Testament of Peter the Great, already mentioned several times in this book. He had already known of this mysterious document for a good two years from Steiner's *Zeitgeschichtliche Betrachtungen* lectures of the winter 1916–1917, and Steiner had spoken of it to Polzer numerous times since then. Polzer thus wrote seven articles which appeared in 1921 in the magazine *Dreigliederung des sozialen Organismus* [The Threefolding of the Social Organism] and as a book in 1922. We referred to the content of these writings in some detail in the chapter 'Austria will perish' and will return to them later, for what lies within the Testament is still extremely active within the foreign policy of the West.[236]

In September 1919 we find the couple from Tannbach again in Stuttgart. The opening ceremony for the first Waldorf School took place on 7 September. The initiative to found the school came from the manufacturer Emil Molt who wanted to create a spiritually grounded school for the children of the workers at his Waldorf-Astoria cigarette factory.

The pedagogy of this school was, according to Polzer,

> wholly based on spiritual-scientific knowledge of the being of the growing human being. Nothing was thought out in a merely intellectual or abstract, humanistic fashion. There were no examinations; instead, the pedagogy proceeded on the basis of an understanding of the growing soul forces of the child. It was built up not on hypotheses but on spiritually perceived facts.[237]

As with the laying of the foundation stone of the first Goetheanum, Polzer experienced with this school-founding ceremony the special meaning of the solemn ceremonial occasion.

In the weeks before the founding of the school Steiner gave a course of lectures for the future teachers, which Polzer's friend Stein from Vienna attended. Polzer would now have to cope in Vienna without Stein.

When Steiner saw Polzer again in Stuttgart, he said to him: 'that it would have greatly pleased him if *I* had also come to take part in the course—"although *you* naturally would not be looking for a position as a teacher".' Polzer added: 'I saw from this comment that Rudolf Steiner wanted me to be present at everything he undertook; for in general, only those were allowed to take part who were aiming for a teaching post.'[238]

After the efforts for threefolding had first proved apparently fruitless, with the founding of the first Waldorf school Steiner laid a permanent foundation stone for the free spiritual life. Until today this stone has been built upon throughout the world.

Like a last outrider of Polzer's contribution to bringing threefolding to the public in 1919 was the visit which he made in November 1919 to the Duke of Braunschweig in Gmunden. The Duke's wife was Princess Viktoria Luise, the only daughter of the deposed emperor Wilhelm II.

'During this visit,' wrote Polzer, 'I spoke very openly about the end of the war, about Anthroposophy and about threefolding. They were pleasant hours which I spent with them and it seemed to me that the couple listened with much understanding for the questions and objections they raised were meaningful and friendly.'[239]

★

Ludwig Polzer spent Christmas 1919 and New Year in the 'threefolding' city of Stuttgart. Here Rudolf Steiner held a course of lectures on natural science, which Polzer did not want to miss. Old bonds of friendship were strengthened; new ones formed. He got to know the Del Montes, whose hospitality he enjoyed. They too were deeply devoted students of Steiner's spiritual science and on later visits to Stuttgart Polzer would often and gladly stay with them. After a short return to Tannbach we find the Count again in Stuttgart with his wife in February of the new year and then off once more to Dornach. The last time he had seen the Goetheanum, as the Johannes Building had been known since 1918, had been three years earlier in 1917. How the double-domed building had changed in the meantime! In many parts it was now almost complete. How fine, how splendid it was to walk about in the building! Its forms had been shaped in such a way that the mighty laws of reincarnation and karma might be able, as it were, to speak gently to the feelings of anyone who visited the building. Obviously, not everyone who spent any time in this House of the Word was able to receive the secret speech of its forms and gestures, but Polzer belonged to this group of 'listening visitors'. He made detailed studies of the geometrical relationships of the building and their inner connections to the past and future cultural epochs of mankind.

From the time of this stay in Dornach, Ludwig and Berta Polzer were often guests for lunch at the Villa Hansi, where Rudolf Steiner lived when he was in Dornach.

'At these lunchtimes Rudolf Steiner was often in a very conversational mood,' recalled Polzer, 'greatly enjoyed himself, and my wife and I always had a very good time and were happy to be able to be with him.'[240] One has the impression that Steiner too enjoyed the Polzers' company.

During their mealtime conversations political events were obviously also often discussed. Even the topic of the Testament of Peter the Great occasionally came up. With quite special affection, however, Rudolf Steiner would often return to speak of Austria. 'When Rudolf Steiner spoke about Austria,' recalled Polzer, his eyes always had a special shine in them; one felt how warmly his heart beat for real Austrian thoughts, which in their purity and freedom recognized so little of anything Roman. Because such thoughts were not understood or because there was no desire to understand them and false ideas were suggested to the populace about them, Austria was robbed of its own mission.[241]

Steiner told Polzer what he was able to experience as a young man in the public gallery of the Austrian Parliament when he listened to the representatives of the various ethnic groups.

Middle Europe had become Roman and overly intellectual. The people were really suffering under this form, which was not suited to their real being but was forced upon them [...] the peoples of the East, West, North and South were speaking past each other and could not find the lost word. The solution of the nationalities problems called for spiritual-historical preconditions that were not present.[242]

From this time Polzer would strive continuously to make people conscious of such spiritual-historical preconditions in regard to Steiner's urgings. In doing this, he contributed to providing the work for three-folding with a deeper spiritual-historical dimension.

On 23 June 1920 Ludwig Polzer spoke in public in Stuttgart about European foreign policy. Rudolf Steiner commented on Polzer's lecture, linking onto it and expanding on it; he spoke about the fierce debates over the occupation of Bosnia-Herzegovina and characterized the difference that can be seen in politics between East and West. Polzer wrote:

English politics did not even think at all in a rationalistic way; there was a spiritual background to its practice. In Middle Europe, the same fundamental ideas, presented by rationalistic liberalizing politicians, were based on nothing; there they were abstractions.

Linking onto this difference, Polzer states instructively:

I learned a great deal at that time about the difference between what is a reality and what is a phrase. It is extraordinarily important to acquire this capacity to discriminate. Rudolf Steiner taught me to recognize that the difference lies not in the words but in whether one is standing within reality or not. The same things spoken in parliaments in London, Berlin or Vienna are always something quite different.[243]

What Polzer learned in all this was useful not only in observing the political events of his own time; he would come to see events within the Anthroposophical Society after Steiner's death in 1925 more and more in the light of this difference.

In August Polzer travelled back to Dornach. He and Berta had decided to bring their two sons to the Swiss centre of Steiner's spiritual science for a long stay. It was a brave decision which was not approved of by all the couple's friends, to say nothing of their relatives. 'Just as other parents sent their sons to high school, we brought ours to the Goetheanum,' wrote Polzer.[244] Josef and Julius were mainly employed in wood-carving work; they also checked the entry tickets at lectures and were active in the fire defences team. They were paid a small amount of pocket money for these activities and were able to attend all the lectures that Steiner held in Dornach at that time. Their parents were obviously of the view that at that period of upheaval in Europe their sons could gain no better education.

The varnish which was first intended to protect the wood of the building proved to be inappropriate and led to weathering. The entire exterior thus had to be renovated. Josef and Julius now took care of the greatest part of this work, standing on the scaffolding with their hammers and chisels. Later, Josef, together with Josef Dubach, an old member of the Society, would push Marie Steiner, who had pains in her feet, in a wheelchair up the hill from the Villa Hansi to the Goetheanum once or twice a day. Thus their parents formed an indirect bond with Marie Steiner, who worked tirelessly for the Eurythmy training and artistic leatures. Criticism by certain anthroposophical friends of this unusual educational phase for the Polzer boys was silenced only when, on the occasion of Josef's wedding in 1923, Rudolf Steiner remarked that their father had done something that was 'very right'.

The unusual far-sightedness of the parents who had the courage to embark on this uncommon educational step for their sons was commented on by Ludwig Polzer himself when he said: 'I know that the content of the consciousness which they encountered at the Goetheanum in these years will last them into their later lives even if they are faced with greater difficulties in life than other young men who today still tread the usual path of study.'[245]

Thus could a man speak who, through his move to the House of the Word, felt himself drawn to take the long view when considering the education of his sons. For it would not be long before those 'difficulties in life' would indeed be encountered.

As Josef and Julius were getting accustomed to their new home, Ludwig Polzer gave his first public lecture at the Goetheanum in one of its rooms on 23 August 1920. He spoke about the significance and consequences of the Testament of Peter the Great, basing himself on his seven articles of 1919. Polzer considered these articles to be so important, even in 1936 when writing his Prague essays, that he incorporated them into his autobiographical essays. This is hardly surprising, for in them he addresses the basic theme of his own spiritual-historical thinking. Anyone who studies these essays learns to understand not only the specific form of politics that rapidly developed in Britain from the time of James I and which knows how to reckon with long periods of historical development; he also learns how to recognize the retarding powers that have continued to work on into our time and which seek in the most radical fashion to prevent the development of the idea of threefolding.

As he had done after Polzer's lecture in Stuttgart in June, Rudolf Steiner added his own lengthy, expansive comments to Polzer's lecture at the Goetheanum. He very much emphasized that one would not be reading history aright if one were always only to seek after the origins of a thing in a philological manner. For the Testament was indeed a fraud in terms of its origin, but in regard to its content, it truly expressed something that was real in the highest degree. The Polish 'visionary' General Sokolnicki, outwardly the supposed author of the document, had meditated in conditions of imprisonment and there had arisen in his soul what the real impulses of Peter the Great were. According to Steiner, the Testament can be conceived as 'a grandiose prelude of what then happened'. In his own words:

> If a spirit had wanted to create what then came about in the twentieth century, he could not have done better to sow the seeds of confusion than to have Peter come to The Hague where various things have always been brewed in connection with European political relations—for from there it is only a short step over to the Anglo-American world. But Peter the Great then went back to St Petersburg and inaugurated there what continued as his Testament, which has worked on in a remarkable way so that those conditions were created which were needed in order to lead on to what came later.[246]

It can clearly be seen from this statement that Steiner was always capable of giving what is grandiose in the *negative* sense in historical events its full due . . .

Incidentally, Steiner evidently took great pleasure in presenting ideas about spiritual-historical phenomena in this way with Polzer. When Polzer, the day before his return to Austria, sought Steiner out in order to take his leave, he was greeted by Steiner in his study with the following words, 'in which there was a friendly satisfaction: "Yesterday we made some great politics together." ' Polzer later commented, quite unflattered, 'Of course, it was only a striving for knowledge, to understand the background to historical events.'[247]

★

Soon after the turn of the year 1920/21 Polzer once again headed for Stuttgart, the Swabian capital. The League for Threefolding of the Social Organism decided early in 1921 to launch a major programme of lectures in Germany to propagandize for threefolding. A larger number of suitable lecturers had to be found and trained for this. To this end, Rudolf Steiner was asked to hold a course for lecturers. It was to be held at the beginning of February.

On meeting Steiner again in Stuttgart in January, Polzer, who naturally wanted to attend the lecturers' course, had his first entirely private conversation with Steiner 'in a personal sense which did not concern the path of pupilship'.[248] In his Prague Notes Polzer shares no more details of the nature of this conversation, but he indicates that it had to do with certain difficulties in life that someone could experience when he had been engaged with spiritual science intensively for a long time and that such difficulties can become noticeable in relation to unusual human encounters. He says only briefly: 'One encounters people who under other circumstances one would not have come across.'

What he indicates here most likely had to do with his relations with Sophie Lerchenfeld, whom he had met for the first time in the summer of 1918 in Köfering and who since then had completed a course of music studies in Stuttgart.

Otto Lerchenfeld was at first reserved about the friendship that formed between his daughter and Count Polzer but later came to oppose it. Although she had a noble character of soul, Count Lerchenfeld feared that Sophie might become too strongly attached to his friend.

It may have been about this situation that Polzer asked for Steiner's advice in that private conversation. He wrote as follows about the effect of Steiner's attitude towards this and other situations of a similar character:

> One found in conventional views of the world and of life an unjustified, life-crippling anxiety of conscience which weakened one from childhood onwards through a false method of education and which created fear. Moreover, it appears to be connected with the wise guidance of destiny that such great difficulties often appear when new tasks approach one.[249]

Indirect confirmation that the situation had to do with complications in Polzer's inner and outer relations with the Lerchenfeld household comes from a letter which he sent to Marie Steiner in the summer of 1921. In the meantime Lerchenfeld was at such a loss as to what to do, in such confusion even, that in a dark moment he even told his daughter that Polzer's real motives were dishonourable, which even Marie Steiner got to know about. The calumniated Polzer thus felt it necessary to say something to clarify the fog that had come to surround the situation. After many years this dark episode in relations between Polzer and Lerchenfeld gave way again to the old understanding between the two men. It would not have been mentioned here had it not been of general interest and indeed mentioned by Polzer himself, namely from the viewpoint that 'such great difficulties often appear when new tasks approach one'. It is therefore instructive in a symptomatic sense that two protagonists in the common threefold work were drawn into conflict of a purely private nature at precisely the moment when it was intended that this work should enter a new, expansive phase. Such a situation can even, in an indirect way, point up the importance of such work.

★

On 12 February Steiner began his course for lecturers. This was, of course, not just a matter of providing the future lecturers with ordinary rhetorical techniques in order to improve the effectiveness of their speeches in the normal sense. The most important precondition for effective speaking about threefolding Steiner held to be:

1. a love for the subject that was carried by sure knowledge, and
2. love for the people whom one was speaking to.

One needed on the one hand to have the greatest possible familiarity with Steiner's ideas about threefolding, a condition that Polzer met entirely, and on the other hand, the capacity to be able to engage with the thinking and attitudes of the listeners in such a way that one did not go over their heads. So that the whole enterprise would have a unified character, Steiner was asked for particular themes 'which were to be dealt with individually'. They were:

1. the great questions of the present time and the threefolding of the social organism;
2. free education and training in relation to the State and the economy;
3. the associative economy in relation to the State and the free spiritual life.[250]

Instead of drills in rhetoric, a very concrete content was given as the material for exercises, for Steiner was convinced that rhetoric that was alive and effective could 'only be nurtured by spiritual content'. Many spiritual-historical aphorisms and witty remarks were scattered throughout the course. In the second lecture Steiner showed the key position which two events in the eighteenth century had had for the entire later constellation of spiritual and economic life in Europe: the Peace of Nystad in 1721 and the Peace of Paris in 1763. The first ensured Russia's long-desired access to the Baltic Sea—a major success of the foreign policy of Peter the Great (and which also bestowed upon him the epithet 'the Great')—which led to a greater flow of Russian cultural life into that of Europe as a whole. The second peace treaty brought to an end the Anglo-French conflict on the American continent. From then on, North America was dominated by Anglo-Saxon culture. Steiner wanted his lecturers to learn to work out of the stream of real historical events.

On 21 February 1921 Polzer spoke on theme number one above to an audience of about 300. He reported with satisfaction that in the discussion following the lecture a communist lecturer expressed himself amazed that 'I as a Count knew of the cultural needs of the proletariat.' His lecture tour then proceeded to Munich, and at the beginning of March to Kiel, Bremen and Hamburg. In the Hansa city Polzer spoke about the theme which he had 'so often discussed with Rudolf Steiner: "World Politics in the Last Century in the Light of Spiritual Science and the Threefolding of the Social Organism".' The following day he lectured in Hannover. At that lecture there were a couple of nationalists who regarded Polzer's speech as treasonous. But he 'was able to refute this accusation factually and energetically'.[251] On this lecture tour, which continued into April, Polzer must have spoken for the idea of threefolding very knowledgeably and soberly; there is little reason to think that Steiner heard anything unfavourable about *his* lectures. However, this was not the case with most of the other speakers, and two years later Steiner made the bitter remark that: 'There was this course for lectures that I gave, before a horde was let loose on the German public. Look at the reaction to what that horde started! What has been concocted out there! It has sometimes been something far beyond the grotesque.'[252]

One consequence of this lecturing propaganda was that attacks on Steiner from German nationalists increased. Doubtless this was sometimes due to one or the other speaker who perhaps made his case too provocatively. Thus on 15 May in the Liederhalle Steiner would probably have actually been physically attacked if he had not been surrounded by the bodies of his friends acting like a protective shield. On the other hand, resistance to threefolding was and is so firmly rooted in the feelings of many contemporaries that it belonged and belongs to the nature of the issue that it provokes hostility. Polzer said about this: 'When one thinks about all these efforts which were made and looks today at the lack of ideas in Europe, then one has experienced the enormous power of the spirits of darkness which oppose any breakthough by living, spiritual thinking capacities.'[253]

★

In July 1921 Ludwig Polzer visited his friend Jaroslav Klima in Kaschau. After his political star had waned following the Czech amnesty of 1917, Klima was appointed Chief of Police and ordered to take up his post in this town in the east of Slovakia. The two friends spoke about the remaining possibilities in the Republic of Czechoslovakia to work for threefolding. On 19 July Polzer wrote a letter to Josef from Kaschau in which he told his son about these conversations. 'In this place Klima has finally become a man who wants to do something and is in a position of authority,' he wrote. 'The whole of eastern Slovakia is under him [...] Perhaps a bridge to the East can be built here.' Polzer also made an instructive statement about his brother Arthur: 'U[ncle] Arthur now wants to get involved with the cause and to subscribe to the threefold magazine. I'm very happy that I've brought him this far, although he still suffers from con[servative] views.'

In August, having returned to Tannbach, Polzer prepared for the first lecture that he was to give in the main auditorium of the Goetheanum. Its theme was: 'The Call for a Free Spiritual Life from the Failings of Old Austria'. 'The awareness that I was standing above the foundation stone was very uplifting,' he wrote in retrospect, 'and I felt the responsibility connected with this, which is why I had chosen the theme.'[254]

Shortly afterwards he took part with Berta in a gathering of members of the Anthroposophical Society in Stuttgart. Of Polzer's appearance at this gathering, Friedrich Hiebel recalled decades later that 'he made an impressive appearance and had the bearing of an officer'. However, Hiebel's memory of Polzer as a speaker was less favourable: 'His laboriously formed way of speaking, accompanied by excessively strong arm gestures made no great impression on us younger ones.'[255] Steiner's younger pupils were more impressed by the lecturing of Polzer's friend Walter Johannes Stein.

★

The year 1921 marked the onset of an important new friendship in Polzer's life. This was Dora Schenker (she had been born in Hamburg). In his Prague Notes Polzer writes that Dora Schenker had done him and his wife 'a great service of friendship' in this year. Mrs Schenker lived on her estate at Mariensee near Aspang and was not without means. One can surmise that this 'service of friendship' also consisted of material support for the Count and his wife. Rudolf Steiner too was concerned for Polzer's material needs. 'When I came to Dornach once at that time,' recalled the impoverished Count,

> he asked me very caringly if I still had any money and wanted to give me some, for he knew how poor Austrians had become who had only cash and owned no property. However, I was always able to come up with what was necessary, especially because my wife sold her jewellery, so I thanked him for his kind offer.[256]

Shortly before his death in 1912 Julius Polzer had foreseen what lay in store for the landed nobility of Austria. 'Have you still got something to eat?' he had often asked. 'They will take everything from you, they will not even leave you your beds.'[257] In 1921, however, things had not yet become quite so bad.

On the last day of October Ludwig and Berta travelled to Dora Schenker's estate for the first time. The wooded estate lay on the so-called Wechselgraben at the foot of the Wechselberg, on the border between Lower Austria, Burgenland and Steiermark. 'Mariensee became more and more for me like a second home,' wrote Polzer, 'and Mrs Schenker a dear friend, who shared much sorrow and joy with me.'[258] In the years that followed, the place would become a kind of refuge for him. He spent some time at Mariensee almost every month, as the many entries in the guestbook show. Dora Schenker made a room available for his private use.

Ludwig and Berta Polzer stayed at Mariensee until 3 November. Berta wrote in the guestbook: 'Erhoffe mir ein Wiedersehn / versprochenen Schmarrn / noch nicht!'

('I hope to return / the promised pancakes / not yet!')

★

In the autumn of 1921 Steiner's interview with Jules Sauerwein appeared in the threefolding newspaper. In it, on the basis of private conversations with the late Helmuth von Moltke, he describes freely and frankly the events that took place at the Berlin High Command on the evening before the outbreak of the war. This led to a new outburst of hostility against him.

At the same time the first conversations took place in Stuttgart which served to prepare a large public congress on the theme of East and West ('the West-East Congress'), which was to be held in Vienna in the spring of 1922. Polzer was to draw up a programme for the congress. It was hoped with this initiative, which was planned on a grand scale, to appeal to 'people of as many nations as possible'. Polzer was inspired by the project. It spoke to the deepest roots of his own strivings. He embarked upon the preparations with the greatest care and prudence and even moved to Vienna for the purpose. At number 6 Köstlergasse, not far from Charles Square (Karlsplatz) he took modest lodgings in the home of Mr and Mrs Breitenstein, where the Vienna branch of the Anthroposophical Society also held its meetings.

28. The West-East Congress and Pan-Europa

The West-East Congress in Vienna represented the highpoint of Rudolf Steiner's public activity after the First World War. It was the second and last 'International Anthroposophical Congress' and was to be held between 1 and 12 June at the Music Association Building (*Musikvereinsgebäude*). While Eugen Kolisko, a friend of Walter Johannes Stein since his youth and his colleague at the first Waldorf School, had been especially involved in the preparations in Stuttgart, in Vienna Ludwig Polzer was strongly supported by the industrialist Jo van Leer.

But the external preparation of the event was by no means enough for Polzer. In March he began to write about the history and effects of the Testament of Peter the Great.

In an expansive manner he shows how the text relates to the East-West question. The main intention which comes to expression in the Testament is slowly but surely to subject the Slavic East to the Anglo-American West's will to world domination and to this end, to exclude the European middle, at least as a political factor in the world. In many details Polzer shows how since the time of Peter the Great, most of his successors on the throne of the Czars, even Trotsky and Lenin, had worked in the sense of the Testament, even if only rarely with any real consciousness of it. He shows how Anglo-American economic imperialism and Roman spiritual imperialism are the two collaborating powers in which the former Roman Empire works on as a hindrance in world-historical development. Polzer also predicts that the Testament 'will certainly continue to work on still further'.[259]

He therefore paints an impressive picture of a process of development from West to East that has been consciously manoeuvred along *false* tracks for centuries—false tracks, that is, seen from the viewpoint of an occultism which seeks to promote the welfare of the *whole* of mankind.

For those in the Anglo-American West consciously conceiving their plans for world domination, one question had become ever more pressing: how was European humanity to arrive at contemporary forms of communal life within the State? The answer was: 'By a world war'. Polzer wrote:

> From the deep knowledge that arises with a new cultural epoch and from the conviction that the English-speaking peoples, through their political and economic abilities, must be the bearers of this new culture, they drew the consequences and concocted a large-scale plan that took into account historical and ethnic forces.[260]

But Polzer raised another question: 'Was there no other possibility within Europe of bringing about *the new world order* without a world war?'[261] The answer to this question about a different form of new world order would have had to be given in Austria-Hungary in a way that was aiming at threefolding the social organism.

Polzer therefore wrote a document about the background of the plans for the false 'new world order' as they were first conceived and since then have been working on until today, and thereby he prepared the way for Steiner, who at the West-East Congress, wanted to show the fundamentals that would be needed for the construction of a true new world order that would serve the well-being of the whole of mankind.

Polzer gave his text the title *'Der Kampf gegen den Geist und das Testament Peter des Grossen'* (The Testament of Peter the Great and the Struggle Against the Spirit). 'It was to be my contribution to the Congress,'[262] its author stated simply. The booklet was printed in April. In June it was in the bookshops in Vienna. A noteworthy review had appeared by then. It came from the pen of Eugen Kolisko, teacher of chemistry and school doctor who had made a profound study of history throughout his life. 'Here history comes alive,' he wrote.

> Polzer has identified a historical phenomenon and has set it in the context of the whole of world history. In each of the pictures that he presents, one has to see great stimuli for further presentations [...] What is worthless for a history based on documents is a significant revelation for symptomatic historical research [...] In Polzer's book one can see the beginnings of a way of looking at world history that is in tune with the times.[263]

In this period of preparations for the West-East Congress occurred the death of the last Habsburg Emperor, Karl I, who had been forced to abdicate on 11 November 1918. He died in exile on the island of Madeira on 4 April. With his death, the last, most important bearer of the hopes for the introduction of threefolding 'from above' left the stage of history to journey on beyond the threshold ...

On 31 May Rudolf Steiner arrived in Vienna. Accommodation had been arranged for him and his wife at the Hotel Imperial. In the Cafe Imperial that belonged to the hotel a friend of Steiner's youth, Friedrich Eckstein, would soon take up residence. Eckstein had become *the* great opponent in Steiner's life with regard to the publication of occult knowledge. He wanted things kept secret—and now, day after day, Steiner walked the few steps from the Hotel Imperial on the Kärntner ring to the Music Society Building in order to reveal, in a last great gesture, knowledge that had been kept secret until then but was now his own and quite new. It is not known whether Steiner and Eckstein ever met during those June days of the congress.

In the printed invitation to the Congress were the words:

> A cultural tension has formed through destructive oppositions between West and East. The release of this tension between the East and the West can be accomplished neither through economic nor through international legal measures; only real spiritual insight into the powers within folk souls will be able to ease it fully in a way that is wholesome for the development of humanity.

It was a festive moment in Ludwig Polzer's life when he opened the Congress at 11.30 in the morning on Thursday, 1 June 1922. He wrote:

> On 1 June I was allowed to open the Congress with a few words and greet Rudolf Steiner and the other speakers and guests who had travelled to Vienna. Anthroposophers had come from many countries, and many people took part who were not members of the Society. The weather was fine throughout the Congress from 1 June to 12 June. Every evening Rudolf Steiner spoke before about 1000 people in the great hall of the Music Society, and they cheered him after each lecture.[264]

While the first Congress of this kind, in Stuttgart in September 1921, had had 1700 participants, the number who came to the West-East Congress was not 1000, as Polzer said, but no less than 2000.

In the evening lectures Steiner unfolded a vast panorama of spiritual-scientific ideas. The first five lectures were titled 'Anthroposophy and the Sciences'; the following five—'Anthroposophy and Sociology'. In his concluding lecture Steiner spoke about 'The Architectural ideas behind Building at Dornach', using slide illustrations.

In the mornings pupils of Steiner spoke on various topics of general interest from a spiritual-scientific perspective. Among the speakers were Polzer's two Viennese-born friends Stein and Kolisko. There were also 'presentations on specialist subjects' for professionals in the audience. In the afternoons artistic performances were put on at the Volksoper (National Opera House). Marie Steiner was in charge of a programme of recitation and two performances of the eurythmic art of movement which Steiner had developed. The programme also included a large celebration of the work of the composer Anton Bruckner.

Friedrich Hiebel, who attended part of the Congress, shared his impressions of it:

> Fortunately it happened that I was standing at the exit of the Music Society Building before the evening lecture where the path led through a quiet

courtyard up to the artists' room. Then Rudolf Steiner came over from the Hotel Imperial, where he was staying during the Congress, with his umbrella and overcoat, accompanied by Count Ludwig Polzer-Hoditz, with whom he appeared to be chatting in a very relaxed manner, as if he had just come back from a very pleasant walk.[265]

So in the middle of a period when he was making the greatest efforts Steiner appeared to enjoy relaxing in Polzer's company...

'Rudolf Steiner expressed himself very satisfied with the Congress,' Polzer himself remarked. 'He complained only that we had given special invitations to official personalities because that had never been our practice before. Since the Congress was to be public, it was natural that everyone who came should be equally welcome.'[266]

The theme of Steiner's actual final lecture on 11 June—apart from the illustrated lecture on the Dornach building the following day—is noteworthy: on that evening he spoke about the 'The Core Issues of the Social Question'. Now the fundamental tone of the entire Congress—the concern for the social future of mankind—moved powerfully into the foreground. Steiner outlined one last time in broad strokes the idea of the threefolding of the social organism, which would have to replace the principle of the unitary nation state.

This last presentation would have deeply impressed Ludwig Polzer for it dealt with the theme of a new world order, the theme which had grown within his heart to become a central question of his own destiny. Another listener in the audience would be reminded of something that was closest to his own heart—his effort for the first spreading of the idea of three-folding in 1917: Otto Lerchenfeld.

We referred to the strong estrangement between the two men which had developed in 1921 because of Polzer's friendship with Sophie Lerchenfeld. That a year later the two men were able to pose in a group photograph together (see fig. 34) must be regarded as a deed. The idea which had originally brought them together and which they both served now brought them together once more, at least in space...

The organizers and speakers had a few meetings with Steiner during the Congress. According to Polzer, Steiner laid 'especially great emphasis to the hope that this Congress, which had achieved so much, would have the right effect amongst the public'.[267] Steiner knew what he wanted; that was shown by what he said a few days later in Stuttgart after the Congress had ended. 'The Congress was a great success, the greatest we have had,' he said at the Teachers' Conference at the Waldorf School on 25 June: 'It was undertaken in such a way that it will certainly cause the greatest damage if it is not made the most of [...] and we should have no illusions that it will not unleash an awful amount of opposition.'[268] About that Steiner would unfortunately be proved right.

With these concerns he left Stuttgart on 15 June and will have spoken further about this to Polzer, who accompanied him as far as Linz. On the way to Linz Polzer made an important proposal to Steiner. He wrote: 'In order to facilitate a small effect in any case, I asked Dr Steiner when I [. . .] accompanied him to Linz, if he could agree that I start a kind of news-paper in Vienna which would appear twice a month.'[269]

★

From Linz, Polzer journeyed home to Tannbach. He was in merry company: his son Josef and Ilona Bögel (later Schubert) a much-loved eurythmist to whom he had recently become engaged; Ilona's mother and her friend Helene Röchling, whom Polzer had known from Munich—they had all been deeply impressed by their experience of the Congress in Vienna and now travelled with him, most of them for the first time, to Tannbach.

'There we spent very pleasant days together in the finest weather,'[270] wrote Polzer. Doubtless Dora Schenker enjoyed the journey; she had also been at the Congress and had decided to join the company. During these 'pleasant days' Polzer gave more and more thought to his plans for a magazine. Rudolf Steiner had already suggested the title: 'Anthro-posophy—Austrian Messenger from Human Spirit to Human Spirit' and had given his permission for the magazine to carry essays by him. And while Polzer was conceiving the details of the project and conversing to his family and friends, it became clear to him that a relocation to Vienna for a while would be unavoidable. He was therefore not to remain long in the peace and quiet of Tannbach in the happy atmosphere of his family and friends.

He determined to rent more spacious accommodation in Vienna and that same summer moved into number 3, Lothringerstrasse where he 'had a very fine room with a view of the Charles Church (Karlskirche) and the Schwarzenberg Palace'.[271] His commitment to making the Congress fruitful in the world had given him a fine new view and not only in the outer sense. His view of the Karlskirche with its two mighty columns might well have gently put him in mind of ancient Rome at the time of the emperors. The two columns were consciously modelled on those of Marcus Aurelius and Trajan. Under Trajan, the predecessor and adoptive father of Emperor Hadrian, the Tenth Legion came to be stationed permanently at the earlier ancillary base at Vindobona and made its camp around today's High Market; Marcus Aurelius, the philosopher on the throne of the Caesars, died in the year 180 in the town he had rebuilt after its destruction by the Marcomanni...

And another noteworthy event: this was the second time in his life that Ludwig Polzer had moved into this house; he had lived there before as a child in 1871 and 1872 before the family's move to Pilsen! With new perspectives and feeling inwardly rejuvenated the 'young' editor eagerly set to work.

★

Polzer's initiative came at a time when Rudolf Steiner ended his own public efforts for threefolding. On 29 August Steiner spoke once more (in Oxford) of the need for a restructuring of society in the sense of this basic idea.[272] On 19 October he made clear that in his view *at the present time* the accent was to be placed on *education* that was in accord with reality:

> It is today almost a waste of time to occupy oneself with all these political matters circulating in the world. Nothing comes of it! If something is to be done, it should be the education of competent fellows once again. That is the only thing that one can strive for. For no one today knows anything [...] Two or three years ago one always had to say: 'Something must happen.' Today it's too late for anything in this direction.[273]

As the failed efforts for threefolding showed, it was not only or not so much a failure of understanding; the 'competence' to be able to realize the new ideas was lacking. So on the one hand people needed to be educated in new ways; on the other hand—and this was Polzer's main concern—more effort needed to be made to sharpen one's view of the realities *behind* the daily facade of politics.

For the *Messenger*, Polzer was able to gain the support of van Leer, who had borne most of the costs of the Congress. Polzer's editorial colleague was the 23-year-old Hans-Erhard Lauer, whom we shall meet again when we come to the 1930s; Marta Stefanović, who would later become Lauer's wife, handled the business affairs. The journalist Ernst Wettreich served Polzer as a judicious source of information. The first issue appeared on 1 November 1922, six full pages long in large newspaper format. Let us take a brief look at Polzer's enterprise. The introduction with its title 'Austria's Spiritual Message' provided the aim of the *messages*: 'The West-East Congress showed,' says the conclusion, 'that there is an urgent need for a spiritual discussion, as spiritual science makes possible and which can show new, viable ways forward. *The Austrian Messenger* seeks to serve this need.'

The first issue included 'East-West Aphorisms' by Rudolf Steiner. Eugen Kolisko wrote about 'Goetheanism'; Walter Johannes Stein about mankind's crossing the threshold to the spiritual world; Josef Polzer contributed an article about eurythmy and Berta Polzer a poem *Schwellengang* (Crossing the Threshold).

Ludwig Polzer himself began the 'West-East' section as follows: 'Under this title views will be regularly expressed on outer, political, world events, as they ultimately all relate to this main theme.'

Polzer called what remained left over of Austria after the war 'a completely impossible, disassociated and deformed state'. As for Middle Europe itself, he wrote:

> Middle Europe has been broken up into a number of impossible, so-called State formations, which imitate the worn-out State formations of an earlier era in a way that craves status and is abstract and bureaucratic and which drags along with it unsolved social and national problems; it [Austria] is doomed to decay because it has been able to realize no new ideas.

To this end 'America and Rome' were working 'together in a common understanding'.

That Polzer did not shy from clearly and pointedly identifying the activities of the opponents of the anthroposophical world impulse is shown in his report of a lecture he had heard that had been given by a Jesuit priest on 6 October in Linz. Under the heading 'The Struggle against the Spirit', he draws the readers' attention to the lecture's discreet but evident, conscious attempt to deny the spirit.

In the third issue (1 December) he comes to speak in his West-East section of a tendency of the times which was, so to speak, the exact counter-picture of the new world order called for by reason. Since this had to do with a counter-stream that is still flowing on with great effect today, we must pause to examine it briefly. Polzer first characterized American politics as follows:

> America lets Europe play with national questions for a while like children, but in terms of economics, it has Europe, and especially the new small states which behave so foolishly, within its power. The way in which England used to treat states in the pursuit of its own politics, America now repeats with continents. Soon the moment will come when it will line up all these militarily against Asia, under the well-known phrases of the Wilsonian variety or perhaps even on behalf of a Christianity that does not yet actually exist. Everything national will then be cleared away and stereotyped by America in a false manner with a demonic technical brutality. *That is how the healing expected from America will actually look.*

Polzer regarded Richard Coudenhove-Kalergi as one of those paving the way towards this dubious 'healing'. Coudenhove-Kalergi sought to weld together a 'United States of Europe' with his so-called 'Pan-Europa' movement. Polzer commented in his *Messenger* on Coudenhove's call, which had appeared on 17 November, prominently featured, in the *Neue Freie Presse* under the title 'Pan-Europa—a Proposal by R.N. Coudenhove-Kalergi'. With sure judgement he immediately stated that this proposal was a case of tasteless old wine in a few new bottles. He wrote:

> The proposal itself calls Europe to defend itself and *excludes England and Russia from this Pan-europa*! Pan-europa is therefore supposed to unite these peoples [of Europe], in which overtly or covertly Fascism blossoms most beautifully. Fascists of all countries, unite yourselves in 'Pan-europa'.

Instead of building bridges between Europe and Russia, a hermetic cordon sanitaire was to be erected in order to make it all the easier for Britain and America to pursue *their own* political aims in Russia without being much disturbed by the rest of Europe: all this was very much in the line of the Testament of Peter the Great.

'In this Proposal too,' Polzer found,

> one hears being sounded the old, boring, mendacious tune of militarism, the elaboration of constitutions, paragraphs about high treason, mass movements, coercive measures, only in a grander, Asian-American style.[*] The trivial question of republic or monarchy is decided with a compliment to the Republic [of Austria].

Then Polzer wrote:

> The concept of this abstractly conceived proposal is therefore uninteresting, but what lies behind the proposal in reality, and of which its author is quite unaware, is highly significant for it is using the author as a tool to help prepare what the Anglo-American peoples want and need.
>
> The focus of the whole proposal lies in a Pan-european military organization with a central defence system directed against the East.
>
> It has been correctly foreseen, and almost anyone today can realize, that if Europe does not become aware, the East will flood in. The Russians are indeed no longer much to fear, but the Bolshevism which has proceeded from the materialist, monist thinking of the West has opened the door to the Mongols. The Russians will, for the time being, have a long sleep under the ice sheet of this Bolshevism and will awaken later to a spiritual culture [...]
>
> Through Coudenhove's proposed Pan-european militarism Europe will not be able to help itself and others, but America needs the Middle

---

[*] Coudenhove-Kalergi's mother was Japanese, and he had many contacts in the English-speaking world—*transl.*

European battleground and Middle European soldiers for its struggle against Asia which, however, will bring as little decisive cultural change as the First World War.

Polzer logically concludes: 'Europe needs something different from this proposal in order to renew itself and its culture, *therefore this proposal cannot be regarded as European.*'

★

From Richard Coudenhove-Kalergi and the Pan-Europa movement that he had called into being, a strongly suggestive effect worked into the world. Let us therefore take a brief look at its originator.[274]

On his father's side, Count Richard Coudenhove-Kalergi, who was born in Japan in 1894, came from an ancient noble family from Brabant who had long been faithful to the Habsburgs. His mother was Japanese, and this interesting 'west-east' mixture explains much in his activities, insofar as these were influenced by the sphere of heredity. All his life Coudenhove felt himself connected to the Christian European tradition without, however, finally embracing real European individualism. His eastern heritage caused the other side of his being to incline to an Asian flexibility that scarcely emphasized anything individual and to a genuine, but rootless devotion to great, noble ideals. Coudenhove considered 'the Catholic Church to be the sole protector of European thought'. He was an outspoken admirer of Wilson's 14 Points.

His book *Pan-Europa* was published in 1923 and became an instant success. In 1924 the Pan-Europa movement received massive support from Louis Rothschild and Max Warburg. The Austrian government put rooms in the Hofburg at Coudenhove's disposal.

In 1925 in his book *Practical Idealism* he briefly touches on Rudolf Steiner's work. In the book Coudenhove speaks (p.194f.) of four main forms of 'Romanticism': 'the Romanticism of the Past', 'the Romanticism of Distance', 'the Romanticism of the Occult' and 'the Romanticism of the Future'. He writes:

> Spengler, Kayserling and Steiner oppose this modern Romanticism. Spengler reveals for us the Romanticism of the Past, Kayserling the Culture of Distance, Steiner the Realm of the Occult. The great effect which these men have on German cultural life can partly be traced back to the Romantic yearning of the hard-pressed German people that looks into the past, into the distances, up to the heavens in order to find consolation there. Fantasy leads into the past, into the distance, into the beyond—deeds lead into the future. Therefore, neither historicism nor orientalism nor occultism are the actual driving forces of our time—but the Romanticism

of the Future; that has given birth to the idea of the State of the Future and with it the world movement of socialism; it has created the idea of the Superman and with it, has introduced the transvaluation of values.

Marx and Nietzsche therefore are for Richard Coudenhove the representatives of this fourth, 'practical' Romanticism. Thus Coudenhove, the 'practical idealist' and 'romantic of the future' considered Steiner's spiritual science, which amongst other things, gave rise to the idea of the threefolding of the social organism, to be 'the Romanticism of the Occult'...

In 1940 Coudenhove held lectures at the Council On Foreign Relations in New York, and after the war, Winston Churchill in his famous Zurich speech (1946), the text of which was later widely circulated and commented on, called for the formation of a United States of Europe and strongly emphasized the efforts of Coudenhove in this regard. In this connection it should not be forgotten that in November 1919 in the House of Commons Churchill had spoken energetically against any association between the German Slavic cultures.[275]

In seeking to further the construction of the House of Europe in the late 1940s Robert Schuman, Adenauer, de Gasperi and other European statesmen were standing in gratitude and recognition on foundations laid by Coudenhove. Coudenhove's efforts made a decisive contribution to the founding of the Council of Europe in 1949 and of the European Common Market. Coudenhove found another eager devotee and promoter of the goals of Pan-Europa in Otto von Habsburg, the eldest son of the last Austrian monarch who died in 1922.

These few indications may suffice to show that both for Catholic Church circles as well as for the Anglo-American efforts to realize the new world order—in their sense of it—Coudenhove was the right man at the right time.

Thus a first stone was thrown into the waters of the historical process, so to speak, which would cause very definite waves in European politics over the coming decades. Expressed half-symbolically, the image of a very notable, real historical parting of the ways: hardly had Rudolf Steiner left the Music Society Building for the last time after making his final appeal for the realization of threefolding in Europe than Richard Coudenhove arrived in the Vienna Hofburg with his unhealthy illusion of Pan-Europa. And while Coudenhove's proposal quickly found praise and support, Steiner, not least through precisely his final public activity in Vienna, was met with the sharpest hostility. What this hostility was capable of would show itself before the end of the year 1922 in the most appalling manner.

29. 'You Should Occupy Yourself with Hadrian'

On New Year's Eve 1922 the First Goetheanum was destroyed by arson. Ludwig and Berta Polzer and their two sons as well as many of Steiner's pupils and friends experienced the tragic event. It was the peak of the hostile activity that the young spiritual scientific movement and its founder were to encounter. In the afternoon of New Year's Eve a Eurythmy performance was presented; it included the Prologue in Heaven from Goethe's *Faust*. At 8 o'clock in the evening Rudolf Steiner spoke on 'The Spiritual Communion of Humanity'.[276] After the last of the audience had left the lecture hall, smoke was discovered and the fire service immediately informed.

Polzer describes the dramatic course of the following hours:

> We were sitting at supper when the alarm was sounded. My sons ran up to the Goetheanum, and we followed. From all the houses friends poured carrying buckets of water and other equipment. Voices shouted: 'Smoke in the White Room!' All the rooms in the South Wing were immediately checked. Smoke was pouring out of an outer wall of the South Wing; the wall was broken through. The structure within the wall was in flames. All the water hydrants were immediately directed against the place of the fire; soon the fire brigades from Dornach and from Arlesheim arrived and later also the fire brigade from Basel. In those hours I witnessed sights of the greatest readiness for sacrifice and helpfulness by many people, especially the younger anthroposophers. Despite everyone's efforts, the fire quickly spread behind the panelling towards the place where the two domes were joined and round midnight burst out between the domes in an enormous blaze. Rudolf Steiner watched the fire in a mood of the greatest calm and gave some directions. Especially when he realized that the building could no longer be saved, he gave the instruction: 'Everyone out of the Goetheanum!' Fortunately, there was no wind that night, so the nearby buildings could all be saved by watering them down [...] The blaze was so great that if the wind had been stronger, part of Dornach and Arlesheim would also have been burned down. The fire burned all night; the great columns and the West Portal lasted upright the longest.[277]

That night Rudolf Steiner lived through the hour of his greatest weakness; it can be compared to Christ's weakness in the Garden of Gethsemane. Thanks to fiery words of encouragement spoken by Ehrenfried Pfeiffer, who found his teacher sitting alone in a room far into the night, the crisis was overcome.[*]

---

[*] See *Ein Leben für den Geist—Ehrenfried Pfeiffer (1899–1961)*, publ. by Thomas H. Meyer, Basel, 3rd ed. 2003, p. 227ff.

The calculations of the opponents did not succeed. On that very night of the conflagration, Rudolf Steiner's spiritual fire of knowledge rose up again intensified, out of the sea of flames. In the background of the fire Steiner saw a second fire: that of the burning of the temple at Ephesus. In the case of the Dornach fire, the destruction had been caused by the envy of *human beings*.

Now the 'karma-awakening-forms'[278] of the Goetheanum were lying in ashes. But only in order to bring Steiner's powerful will for karmic revelation to an undreamed of high point through this very baptism of fire: the night of the fire formed the fiery seed of the overwhelming karma revelations of the year 1924. Without the deed of Judas there would have been no resurrection; without the burning of the Goetheanum there would have been no Christmas Conference in 1923 and no 'Esoteric Considerations of Karmic Relationships' in 1924, in which so many human destinies were followed through various lives on earth and became clearer and clearer.

This world-historical dimension of the fire, which mightily awoke 'karmic vision' was also experienced by one who stood the closest to Rudolf Steiner that night. Ita Wegman, who had been the director of a clinic in Arlesheim since 1920 and was one of Steiner's first and closest pupils, may have been reminded that night of that other fire—at Ephesus, as one of Wegman's friends believes. The intuition arose in her that Steiner 'had already been my teacher in ancient times'.[279] And there grew in her that night the seed which then matured to the point where she put her question about the new Mysteries.[280] From this night on, helping, serving, Wegman put herself at Steiner's constant disposal.

And Ludwig Polzer? His soul too was opened up to deeper levels of knowledge by the painful event of that night. This shows itself indirectly in the conversation that he was able to have with Rudolf Steiner the following day.

Steiner had said very definitely early on New Year's Day: 'We go on with the lectures as planned. The Schreinerei (carpenters' workshop) is to be made ready for them by this evening.' And to Ludwig Polzer he said: 'One other thing. Come to us with your wife for lunch.'

Polzer made detailed notes of Steiner's comments during or after lunch at Villa Hansi. 'When we were with him then,' he wrote, 'and he spoke of the work of ten years that had been destroyed and how the columns had withstood the fire for so long, there were tears in his eyes.'[281]

The conversation[282] turned first, naturally enough, to what was closest, the catastrophe of the night past.

Polzer asked: 'How could this have happened?'

Steiner answered:

> There is too great a difference between [the members'] souls. They want to
> see and hear everything and be present at everything but they do not want
> to wake up. So they have to be awakened by catastrophes and personal
> sufferings. It is not karma that is prevailing in this but only the members'
> lack of wakefulness, and human envy which works even into the physical.
>
> The possibility was given to us of having the Place of the Word, but the
> Place of the Word can only be when it has its counterparts, its living image
> in the human heart, in conscientiousness for the Word, that means, when
> the human being not only listens but wants to bear responsibility, and can
> bear it as a human being who takes responsibility for himself before the
> Word of the world. That was the meaning of the Building. Word and
> answer, Logos and Man.

Then the spiritual researcher laid out the deeper historical perspective:

> In Ephesus we had the secret of the Incarnation of the Word ahead of us. It
> [Ephesus] had to be destroyed; otherwise the counter-forces would have
> been able to develop a significant centre for their activity there, for the envy
> of the Gods was effective as far the atmospheric level. But here, there is a
> reversal.*. The Gods were looking down expectantly to the Place of the
> Word, but the human beings were not there who could protect the
> Building. A possibility was given, but there was no answer from mankind;
> only envy was not silent.

Thus the first of Steiner's pupils who had been inwardly led in 1912 to the
site on which the Building would later stand received a first explanation of
its end. Could this catastrophe have been avoided if I had taken on
Stinde's position which my teacher had offered me in 1915? Polzer may
have been silently turning this question over in his soul on that New
Year's Day 1923. For he felt himself deeply linked to the impulse of the
Building and jointly responsible in a special way for its destiny.

It seemed that Steiner wanted to respond to Polzer's silent inner
questioning, when he went on:

> Look, Hadrian also bore within himself the thought of a Building of the
> Word but it could only be like a caricature of the Word, as he wanted to
> save the old Mysteries. He sought honourably for a renewal of the Mys-
> teries and even came near to Christ. That is why he even went to Egypt, far
> beyond Edfu up the Nile. Egypt caused memories to rise up in his soul but
> they blinded him with the power of the sentient soul's world of images.
> Antinous sacrificed himself [for Hadrian] but he could give him no more
> answers from the other side.

---

*I.e. in Dornach—*transl.*

And then followed the very direct indication to Polzer: '*You should try to occupy yourself with Hadrian and in doing so, think about Egypt.*'

This Polzer would do, but only years later. First, he accepted Steiner's indications about Emperor Hadrian openly and with interest, like everything else that Steiner shared with him. But the question may at the same time have stirred gently within him: Why, after the night of the fire, is my friend and master speaking to me of the building impulse and the deeds of Hadrian? Unconcerned by *such* a question, Steiner went on to describe the Egypt that Hadrian had then encountered:

> There is there [in Egypt] the terraced temple of Hatshepsut where you have deep inside a holy grotto with a representation of Isis and the boy Horus, which works like an archetypal image of the Virgin and the Jesus child. Hadrian too came to this grotto and indeed, immediately after [visiting] On. Here [in the holy Isis grotto of Hatshepsut] there was repeated what he had once experienced more than 1000 years before, in the time of the Thutmoses Pharaohs in the blossoming of the culture of Raphael-Mercury-Hermes the first female Pharaoh reigned and built her wonderful temple. At that time he went as a High Priest of Amun-Re in the entourage of Queen Hatshepsut to the city of On when the Queen brought the architect from the site of the oracle of the Sun initiates.

Steiner did not therefore only speak of Hadrian to his friend and pupil but also of an earlier incarnation of this very significant emperor in the Egypt of Hatshepsut. All of this will have made Polzer wonder more and more. Steiner then finally turned his remarks from Hadrian more to the Mysteries of that earlier time.

★

'All of New Year's Day and the following day crowds of people came up from Basel and the surrounding region to see the site of the fire,' Polzer wrote in the Prague Notes. 'Most of them had never seen the Goetheanum, despite living not far away, but they were interested to see the ruins. That is very symptomatic of the soul mood of modern humanity which is inclined to what is deathly.'[283]

At 5 p.m., in accordance with the programme, the Three Kings' play was performed in the undamaged Schreinerei building.

★

After returning to Vienna, Polzer immediately turned to bringing out the new year's first issue of the *Messenger*. But the catastrophe at the year's end was still working on so strongly and powerfully within him that the New

Year found no place in the *Messenger*. Issue no.1 of the year carried the date '15 January' ...

The Swiss poet Albert Steffen described the Goetheanum fire. Hans-Erhard Lauer, Polzer's colleague in Vienna, wrote on 'The Goetheanum as a Work of Art', while Polzer himself continued the 'West-East' section. He wrote about the memoirs of Helmuth von Moltke, whose widow had had them published in December 1922, before making his own commentary on the Goetheanum fire. Closing his comments, he wrote:

> In these articles attention was repeatedly drawn to the grandiose scale of the work of those forces that wish to lay humanity low and yet which always speak of construction; they will have felt triumphant about what happened on New Year's Eve in Dornach.
>
> Anthroposophers will stand true at the side of Rudolf Steiner, their souls filled with a new strength by the catastrophe and new courage for sacrifice; they will look courageously into the future, and the powerful spiritual-soul form of the Goetheanum will serve their seeing as their guide on the way forward.

For Polzer the first Goetheanum had been a real 'Mystery Centre', a gift entrusted to mankind, but also outwardly

> defenceless against those who hate and do evil. Humanity should have guarded it through Anthroposophers. The anthroposophical movement should have been strong enough to protect it. His [Steiner's] gift was a trial, a test, to see whether mankind was ripe enough to be able to do this during the tests of the war.[284]

Polzer described the very personal consequence that the event of the fire had had for him as follows: 'I felt, more strongly than before the need to remain united with the activity of Dr Steiner in Stuttgart and Dornach. That again required much travelling.'[285]

In addition, he received through certain indications the impression that Steiner was not only working on designs for the new Goetheanum and devoting himself to his lecturing work, but was also 'preparing a new strong impulse'.[286] He was concerned for the future of the Society, which had shown itself to be too weak and was also more and more riven by divisions.

In the first February issue of the *Messenger* Polzer again began a new section: under the title 'World Tendencies, Events, Symptoms and Observations' he brought reports from all over the world and commented on them. At the beginning of March, for example, he commented for the second time on the initiative of Count Coudenhove-Kalergi, the propagator of Pan-Europa. Coudenhove had published an open letter to

Mussolini, in which he called on the Italian Head of State to form a 'United States of Europe' in the face of the danger that was threatening from the East. Polzer recognizes that Coudenhove is bringing forward some half-truths and ideas in an agreeable difference to the barren lack of ideas of the present time but on balance he concludes:

> The ideas are, however, neither European nor Christian [...] His means of defence against Europe's ill fate is borne by eastern illusions. Instead of Christianity, what is rising in Europe is the delusion of Roman Caesarism in an American-Asiatic continental style and it will lead to the complete ruin of Europe.

In March Polzer allowed himself a few days' holiday at Mariensee. Sophie Lerchenfeld accompanied him. A humorous entry in the guestbook testifies to the success of the holiday. Polzer describes himself as 'the chief editor of the human spirit' and Sophie as his 'very important assistant'. These two people, bound by ties of friendship, certainly understood each other very well, and perhaps Polzer told his friend of the private conversation he had been able to have with Steiner on New Year's Day after the fire and which had thrown up so many questions for him . . . Had not Hadrian once been accompanied by a friend and important assistant?

★

At Easter the Count was once again in Dornach, with his wife. On Easter Sunday the couple were again invited to the Villa Hansi for lunch. In the course of their conversation, Steiner said something which touched Polzer very deeply: 'There were spring flowers on the table. Indicating these, he said "the beauty of these flowers makes one sad at the sight of declining humanity".' Polzer added the comment:

> If one values such statements rightly, then one would also have to regard with the deepest seriousness what Rudolf Steiner undertook to anchor the [anthroposophical] movement in a few hearts, and seek to understand it esoterically. *I had more and more the sense that Rudolf Steiner was preparing something that the powers of darkness on Earth would be unable to reach.*[287]

Steiner's will to call his pupils to greater spiritual wakefulness showed itself in an impressive manner at the wedding of Ilona Bögel and Josef Polzer which was conducted by Friedrich Doldinger. The ceremony took place on 4 June 1923 at the Haus de Jaager in Dornach. In addition to the bridal couple's relatives, about 60 anthroposophical guests were invited. Albert Steffen and Max Schuurmann acted as witnesses.

Rudolf Steiner gave the festive address.[288] 'In a very special way,' he said, and turned to the newlyweds, 'your relationship has arisen on the ground of anthroposophical life.' Then he referred their attention to Josef's grandfather, Julius Polzer, who had died in 1912, and described the deep impression made by the 'special, dear character full of goodwill, the extraordinarily distinguished manner of that personality' and emphasized:

> Old Mr von Polzer, your grandfather, was most deeply linked in his soul with the whole spiritual life to which my soul is turned [...] What I experienced with that old gentleman, who has now already been in the spiritual life for a long while, belongs to the most beautiful memories that I have had in the anthroposophical life.

And then, before all those present, Steiner opened a door, so to speak, to that realm which adjoins history and is usually ignored, in that he said:

> I have often been able to say to your mother and father, who are with you here today at your wedding, and may it be today most especially empha-sized on this festive occasion, *because I am of the view, I am quite certain of the intimate love and intimate goodwill with which the soul of the old man is looking down on the festive act which we have just celebrated*.[289]

These were no pretty words intended to lift the general mood of all those present in a special way. It was a simple communication by an eyewitness who was also able to step across the threshold. Steiner's experience of the spiritual presence of Julius Polzer had already once before associated itself with a metahistorical lesson for Julius' son; in that summer of 1913 in Munich. Now the whole company at the wedding alongside him received a metahistorical lesson together. Who could doubt that through this communication the wedding revealed itself to those present to a heightened degree as both a sense-perceptible and supersensible event? And as a clear affirmation that he was utterly serious about this meta-historical remark, Steiner repeated it at the end of his address, when he said to the newlyweds: 'This is what I [...] wanted to say to you in the fullness of love which has always been there for you all the time you have moved in our community, and there for you in community with your grandfather who *is now looking down upon us*.'[290]

The next day Ludwig and Berta were again at the Villa Hansi for lunch. After lunch Ludwig Polzer spoke with his teacher for over an hour in Steiner's study. Polzer did not write about what they spoke of, but his father Julius will certainly not have been omitted from their conversation. Polzer does, however, tell us that 'at the end, he kissed me on my forehead'.[291] We may see in that a delicate gesture of protection for Polzer's spirit-filled striving and at the same time a kind of sealing of what was spiritually experienced during the wedding-ceremony address. Thus it happened that it was *this* pupil of Steiner's who was prepared in a special way for the spiritually real element which would stand in the centre of the laying of the second Foundation Stone at the end of the year.

Back in Vienna, Polzer wrote to deny the slanderous misrepresentation which had appeared in the *Neues Wiener Journal* on 3 June that he had had an audience with Emperor Karl in 1917 and that anthroposophers had presented a memorandum to the monarch.[292] The anonymous author concocted a story about an alleged 'Anthroposophers' State' etc. One can admire Polzer's courage in this case too in refuting a hostile, twisted attack simply by presenting the correct facts without any 'diplomatic' reservations. Polzer wrote in the *Messenger*:

> When anti-spirit stands in a life-or-death conflict with spirit then the main principle of the clever ones—that truth and morality are only for idiots— steps forward with the entire, usual array of tools and describes things in such a way that the well-prepared readership believes the lie and is kept away from that for which it is in reality yearning.

One sees that it fully belonged to Ludwig Polzer's concept of esotericism to step hard on someone's foot if necessary when they sought only to kick at spiritual science.

During 1923 many national societies were founded within the Anthroposophical Society. Steiner had proposed this in order to consolidate the anthroposophical work. He also hoped that it would help the work in the periphery to become more autonomous, more responsible and more independent of Dornach and Stuttgart. He himself was not a member of the Society but only its teacher and adviser. He even considered withdrawing from the Society completely, especially as the steps he had hoped for had not been taken or were embarked upon only very hesitantly. There was in particular on the part of some members a shockingly naive engagement with hostile opponents, as one can read in the volume *1923 The Year of Destiny* (GA 259).

At Michaelmas Rudolf Steiner came again to Vienna. He spoke in three lectures for members about the Time Spirit, Michael.[293] The Austrian national society was to be founded at the same time. The meeting was chaired by the dentist Alfred Zeissig at whose house Ludwig Polzer would be a frequent visitor. Polzer reported: 'The meeting was very unsatisfactory. There was much talking around issues, so nothing could be decided until the last minute. Dr Steiner had to leave in a few minutes and was often looking at the clock; the meeting threatened to end without any result.' Polzer then took the initiative: 'Now I stood up, presented a short motion for the founding of the Society with regard to the formation of the executive council and the termination of further debate and urged those who were in agreement to stand up. The motion had the majority, and the Society was founded.'[294]

Franz Halla, Hans-Erhard Lauer, and Norbert Glas (later replaced by Ludwig Thieben) were chosen to join the previous members of the executive committee of the Vienna Branch—Zeissig, Polzer, and Julius Breitenstein—to form the executive council of the new Austrian national society.

Before the return journey to Dornach, Steiner, accompanied by Polzer, went to visit his brother and sister, who lived in Horn in Lower Austria. 'They were both disabled,' writes Friedrich Hiebel, 'and lived in seclusion in the country. Rudolf Steiner never forgot to provide them with active support. When we learned of this journey, it allowed us to see in a very direct way into the depths of feeling that we had experienced previously through the varied succession of lectures.'[295] Polzer may have felt something similar. He provided for money to be sent to Horn from that point on and he took care of arrangements for them after Rudolf Steiner's death. There was hardly another pupil of Steiner's besides Polzer that could be found who alongside a sense for the deepest esotericism also had a similarly deep sense for heredity and the stream of family ties.

At the end of November 1923 Polzer went back once again to Mariensee. It was like taking a breath before the powerful event of the laying of the second foundation stone, which he had already sensed was coming.

There was already snow on the ground in those 'hospitable winter days'. Polzer wrote a long entry in the guestbook, which began as follows: 'Every year man is reminded of death and rebirth when the pure snow falls.' He thought of the relationship between nature and man and wrote:

> The forest and the whole of nature are used by man; they must serve him, the bearer of spiritual consciousness. He works into matter and spirit, reconciles both and has to lead the whole of nature's life through the death of matter to spiritual birth. He makes her pure like the snow, which reminds him every year to see the light of the spirit in himself.

Polzer's spiritual musings became so inward and intimate that the end of the entry took on a poetic form:

> *Shining snow,*
> *Darkening spruce,*
> *The beech uplifts*
> *Its doméd roof;*

The brightness reminds all
Striving men and women:
'Shine into darkness,
Redeem Natura!'

In such a mood of quiet, reverent, and contemplative awareness of spirit, Ludwig Polzer now experienced the approach of Christmas.

On 15 December he revealed to the readers of his *Messenger* that due to lack of funds the magazine would cease to appear at the end of the year but that it would live on in the form of Hans-Erhard Lauer's *Österreich-ischen Blätter für Freies Geistesleben* (The Austrian Digest for the Free Spiritual Life). And so this important stage in Polzer's activity also came to an end. All the more unburdened, he could now travel to Dornach.

Steiner prepared for the Christmas Conference through wide-ranging descriptions of the Mysteries in ancient times and in the Middle Ages. Polzer experienced at least the last part of these presentations. He may have got to Dornach around 20 December.

30. The Second Laying of the Foundation Stone

With three strokes of a small ceremonial hammer at 10 o'clock in the morning on 25 December 1923, the spiritual researcher Rudolf Steiner opened the solemn act of the laying of the foundation stone of the General Anthroposophical Society. The strokes were in the rhythm of long-short-long, a trochaic rhythm (-u) and an iambic (u-), a falling and rising meter.[296] With this, the conference was placed from the very beginning in the sign of the entire evolution of mankind. The falling meter, which also lies at the basis of the hexameter (-u u) symbolizes the fall of mankind from spiritual heights into the depths of the earth where we were to find ourselves as self-conscious beings; the rising meter speaks of the rise again of the free human I, which has become self-conscious, to those old spiritual heights. Human beings were led down to the Earth from spiritual heights. We learned to stand on the earth. We are again to become beings who perceive the heights and strive for them. *The three strokes of the hammer sounded the three ground phases of the entire evolution of mankind.*

Rudolf Steiner then spoke the 'Foundation Stone Verse', a threefold mantric form that calls on the human being to become conscious of the way he is woven into the world in a threefold way as a being of body, soul, and spirit and shows him the way to 'Spirit-Remembering', 'Spirit-Sensing', and 'Spirit-Beholding'.

So the second foundation stone consisted not of a physical stone but in a structure of words and thoughts which was sunk *into the hearts of those present with a constructive will.* This foundation stone was therefore not originally intended for the planned second Goetheanum; Steiner even emphasized 'that through the spiritual foundation stone, which he laid, there was now a spiritual Goetheanum, whether the external Building was completed or not'.[297]

He did not for a moment think of the reconstruction of the first building. From the beginning the second building had a completely different character from the wooden building that had been burned down; it was 'to place before the world the shame [...] which it had brought upon itself by the destruction of the first Goetheanum', wrote Ludwig Polzer. This time Steiner had no plans for an external laying of a foundation stone.

Many of those present felt something of the turning point of time which the ritual event signified in reality. Behind the veil which appears to separate this 'daily living room' of physical happenings from what lies beyond it, the conference was also experienced beyond the threshold. Rudolf Steiner himself indirectly indicated one who had an experience of this kind. This was Helmuth von Moltke, the Chief of the General Staff of the German Army, who had died in 1916. Steiner was writing down the post-mortem statements of the deceased Moltke in private notes for his widow. On 13 January 1924 he confirmed the following words of Moltke:

> Yes, if that were experienced—'Work at Spirit-Remembering', 'Work at Spirit-Sensing', 'Work at Spirit-Beholding'. But human beings will only hear it when the Michael Spirit succeeds in finding the trail in the astral light that leads to the spiritual altar on which the astral flame is burning that Ahriman fears. This is how it will still be until the end of the century. For the eyes are still not there that can behold the Christ moving in the etheric light. Eyes which are filled with what is divisive in humanity will be unable to come to such vision.[298]

Such were the words spoken from beyond the threshold about the event in the Schreinerei by a soul that was most deeply connected to Steiner's spiritual science. It can hardly be imagined that this has been the only occult commentary on the event. Would Julius Polzer's immortal genius, which had led his son to the site of the future Goetheanum building at the time of Steiner's first visit to Dornach in 1912 and of which Steiner had so often reminded Ludwig Polzer, have remained spiritually silent at Christmastide 1923? Only occult research could provide the answer. But readers who have followed with attention the life paths and spiritual goals of Julius and Ludwig Polzer thus far and have sought to understand them will already be led by *their ordinary reason* to pose such a question.

★

On the day before the foundation stone laying, Rudolf Steiner had presented to the members of the Society the members of the Executive Council (Vorstand) which he had himself formed, that is, he had acquainted those present at the Conference with those with whom he wished to work in the leadership of the Society. As already mentioned, in the Society that had existed since 1913 he had never had a membership card. Now, in the General Anthroposophical Society that he had formed, he himself even took on the presidency. Through this act, he united the anthroposophical movement, the actual spiritual stream, whose representative he was, with an earthly Society. He took a very great spiritual risk in doing this, and did not know before he did so what the consequences would be for his spiritual research by his decision to link it with his leadership of an exoteric society.

During the conference he had a private conversation with Ludwig Polzer in the atelier, as Steiner's work room was then called [today, the Schreinerei]. Polzer wrote:

> Rudolf Steiner said to me when he received me in his atelier: 'I could also have called on other personalities* who can work with me *here*. I shall always take account of the Councils of the national societies. There will be close contact between Dornach and the national societies.'[299]

What are we to make of this? That it was important for Steiner that Polzer should be attentive at the first opportunity that presented itself, that the actual composition of the Vorstand he had formed was not to be seen as something *absolute*, in the sense that the personalities he had appointed— besides the already-named Albert Steffen, Marie Steiner, and Ita Wegman, Steiner also called Guenther Wachsmuth and Elizabeth Vreede to the Vorstand—were not to be regarded unconditionally as *the* most capable or worthy representatives of the anthroposophical cause. Between the lines, Steiner was telling Polzer: 'If *you* were not so firmly bound to Austria, I could also have appointed *you*.' It was already clear from Steiner's evening lectures that from now on 'he was laying the greatest weight on a serious esoteric consideration of karma',[300] as Polzer wrote. In a wide-ranging manner Steiner spoke during the whole conference on 'World History in the Light of Anthroposophy'.[301] He drew attention to the most important, historical karmic relationships with regard to Aristotle and Alexander. *In the intensive lectures on karma, which he continued to give throughout 1924 and steadily increased until his illness in the autumn, he created the main compensation for the loss of the first Goetheanum with its forms that could 'awaken the perception of karma'.*

In 1902 he had wanted to make a general study of karmic considerations but after making his intentions known, he had had to drop the attempt in view of the resistance to it he had felt in the souls of his theosophical audiences. In 1910 he had tried again and held a series of lectures in Stuttgart titled '*Occult History*'[302] in which, among other things, the figures of Aristotle and Alexander played a key role, as in the lectures of 1923/24. But this cycle too did not find the adequate resonance for which he was hoping. Thus from his own experience Steiner knew all the difficulties associated with the opening up of knowledge about karma.

But now, after the unscrupulous attempt, through the destruction of

---

*Besides those in the new Vorstand—*transl.*

the Goetheanum, to at least lame the anthroposophical movement if not to destroy it completely, all reservations had to be put aside. More important things were now at stake. Ludwig Polzer wrote:

> His seer's vision saw what was coming in the future in the most dreadful form and therefore he had to create possibilities for at least some anthroposphers to be able to penetrate spiritual history. He therefore also had to do what he could by using concrete cases of repeated earthly lives in a study of history to ensure that another force could not easily spread nonsense.[303]

And so we see Steiner in 1924 revealing 'the enlightening fiery truth'[304] of reincarnation and karma by means of numerous historical examples: in Dornach, Stuttgart, London, Paris, Amsterdam, Prague, Breslau etc—in short, everywhere he went.

The above-mentioned risk he took did not bind his spiritual tongue; on the contrary, with a much greater freedom and fullness than ever before, he was able to express the unique results of his research. He did not even hold back from saying something about the karma of the anthroposphical movement itself, and amongst other things, outlined the possibility that precisely the souls of anthroposophers would be reincarnated at the end of the century—that is, today—in order to prevent the whole of modern civilization from rolling right into the abyss which threatened it from all sides. Polzer wrote: 'Thus through him, for those who were of goodwill, the post-mortem existence would also be especially prepared so that they could soon return in case the great work should be interrupted for a while on Earth by the spirits of darkness.'[305] We will see later how concretely such words would have to be applied to Ludwig Polzer himself.

★

With the Christmas Conference then, Rudolf Steiner gave, as it were, a strongly intensified esoteric jolt in all his last work within the General Anthroposophical Society that he had founded.

In February in response to the request of Ita Wegman, his colleague in the medical work, who was now leading the Medical Section, he set up the first of three planned Classes within the 'High School'. She was to train in a special way in cognition and ethics those members of the Society who wished to be active in public. Acceptance into this school—it was also called the Michael School—was by Rudolf Steiner himself, while Ita Wegman was designated by him as his 'co-leader' (*Mitleiterin*) in the School.

Alongside this enormous expansion of all karmic and esoteric perspectives of spiritual science, after the Christmas Conference Steiner gave impulses for thorough-going renewal in many other areas. In the spring there were courses for doctors and pedagogical courses; at Whitsun an 'Agricultural Course'; a summer course in Torquay, England; and in September finally a 'Drama Course' and a 'Pastoral Medicine Course': all this besides the total of 82 lectures on karma, countless conversations with individuals and a tireless activity of writing.

One cannot sufficiently imagine the freshness of the new wind that blew through the souls of most of Steiner's pupils after the Christmas Conference. Ludwig Polzer at any rate was more like one newly inspired. He took part in as many courses and lectures in the new year as he could. He met his teacher again in March in Prague, where the Czech national society was founded; Steiner gave lectures for the public and for members.

On meeting Steiner again in Prague, somewhat concerned, Polzer told Steiner about the health of his newborn grandson Christward, who had been born on 3 March, the first and only son of Josef and Ilona Polzer.

How much Steiner's own health was under pressure at this time was noted by Julie Klima: 'His whole bearing was deeply serious, almost sad. He was already seriously ill, but we did not see it, did not want to see it.'[306] Evidently, the new spiritual impulses which Steiner carried into the Society after the Christmas Conference were not received everywhere as they should have been. At any rate, 'a promise' had been made on his part to certain spiritual powers, which in his own words, was to be fulfilled 'unswervingly'.[307] What was at risk since the Christmas Conference, it appears, was nothing less than this: either the members of the Society he had founded would understand the new spiritual impulses more and more and, above all, seek to take up the far-reaching revelations of karma with the necessary respect and earnestness of soul, or else, for having dared to link his own person with the Society, he, Steiner, would have to pay with his health and in the worst case even with his life . . .

A short time before his death he remarked to Ita Wegman that his illness was 'of a peripheral nature'.[308] That means: it was rooted in the pyschological and spiritual behaviour of the members, to whom, through the founding of the Society, he had bound himself more closely than ever before.

After the Prague Conference, on the way home to Tannbach, Polzer made a diversion to Horn. Here he visited Rudolf Steiner's sister Leopoldine, who had an eye problem and yet cared lovingly for her brother Gustav, who was mentally disabled. Polzer probably also brought a gift of money from her brother Rudolf. On 9 April he reported to Steiner by letter:

> Your sister's eye has not become worse, and she ascribes this to your medicament [...] She is satisfied with her brother's condition; he is in good health, is calm and easy to handle. When I told her that you are writing the story of your life in the *Goetheanum*, she expressed the wish to receive this; I shall arrange to have it sent to her via here [...] After your sister gave me a good cup of coffee, I travelled back to Vienna in the afternoon.

In this human, simple and fine manner Ludwig Polzer looked after Rudolf Steiner's brother and sister.

Ludwig and Berta Polzer returned to Dornach in May for the baptism of their grandson. Rudolf Steiner attended the ceremony together with almost all the members of the Vorstand. Albert Steffen and Helene Röchling acted as witnesses, and the ceremony was conducted by Friedrich Rittelmeyer, priest of the newly founded Christian Community. 'During the ceremony there was a crash of thunder, and when we left the house there was a rainbow in the sky.' Steiner always showed a special interest in the boy, for whom he himself had suggested the names Christward Johannes. It pleased him to hear that Christward's baptismal shawl had been worn by his great-great-grandfather, the man of letters from Graz, Ludwig Ritter von Polzer!

At lunch the grandparents from Tannbach ate once again with Steiner, who was 'in the best of spirits'.[309]

★

Ludwig Polzer naturally attended the agricultural conference, which took place at Whitsun in Koberwitz, near Breslau. To the numerous farmers who attended, Steiner revealed 'the most valuable and useful secrets of nature'.[310] He also advised the farmers to avoid the use of artificial fertilizers and told them how they could repair the damage such fertilizers cause. World events were again discussed round the lunch table. Polzer recalled the following statement by Steiner: 'With a dreadful earnestness Rudolf Steiner spoke of the great catastrophe that was facing humanity, there would be a collapse in Middle Europe and only a primitive form of agriculture would remain.'[311] Polzer and other friends confirmed that from this time on, Steiner 'was suffering enormously in body and soul but that the suffering of humanity drove him to tireless activity'.[312] He had special hopes for the work in England which was being so energetically undertaken and promoted by the industrialist, man of the world and friend of humanity D.N. Dunlop.

After his return from Koberwitz, Polzer saw his estate at Tannbach and its management in an entirely new light. Certainly, many difficulties had emerged over the years, but now they were becoming acute. He had already attempted in 1919 to run the estate in accordance with the idea of threefolding, above all in relation to the economic apect in the narrower sense. Hugo Flatz, who had been employed at that time would have been able to put things in order and renew the estate. But an ever-increasing obstacle to such work was showing itself in various places, namely *Berta's* concept of what constituted proper work on the land. Since Ludwig Polzer was repeatedly travelling and for increasingly longer periods, the practical management of the estate naturally passed more and more into Berta's hands.

The contradiction between agricultural goals and the reality at Tann-bach had now become so glaring for Polzer that he decided to share his concerns with Rudolf Steiner. On 25 August he turned to his teacher with the following words: 'In a difficult crisis in my life, which I often feel no longer capable of matching up to and which has so weakened me that I am less and less able to keep a clear head, I am turning to you', and then he described how in addition to Tannbach's 'economic' crisis there was now

> my growing concern about my wife and Herr Flatz [. . .] My wife wants to do everything herself and alone; she isolates herself more and more by this so that I have sometimes become quite anxious that if it comes to an economic collapse, she might suffer a breakdown. Many of her instructions and ways of handling people are, unfortunately, I have to say, often imperfect from the economic point of view and will only accelerate our economic collapse. [. . .] Herr Flatz no longer finds any possibility of being heard. I know how often it has been hard for me to leave that situation because what in earlier times were only trivial economic issues are now issues of survival. Difficult karma appears to lie before us, and only you can help, because my wife would only listen to you.

Polzer then shared with Steiner his thought that he should take Berta more often on trips with him—which would not be possible without financial support from friends—and leave more in Tannbach to the competence of Herr Flatz. 'Often the future looks so bleak,' he wrote, 'it seems to me there is no way out. It is then that I think of you.' Finally, Polzer told his teacher that he wanted to come to Dornach again in September 'for my peace of mind, in order to ask for your help and advice in this situation'.

He arrived in Dornach on 12 September. At this time Steiner was holding a course of lectures on pastoral medicine, another on the arts of speech formation and dramatic art and was speaking in evening lectures to members about the destiny of the anthroposophical movement as well as about particular historical individualities. Several 'Repeat Lessons' of the First Class of the School of Spiritual Science were also given, and it can hardly be imagined that Polzer did not attend these.

It is not known when the personal conversation requested with Steiner took place. Polzer naturally wrote nothing about it in his Prague Notes.

On 17 September there was a performance of Goethe's *Iphigenia*, which reminded Polzer of that other performance he had seen at the end of the 1880s at the Hofburg Theatre in Vienna, shortly before its demolition. The Dornach performance awakened in him the need to go on with the 'Concepten'[313] (Notes) 'for memoirs that I would write later on'. He started on this the day after the performance and in the course of the following two months he filled a whole volume of sketches for memoirs, spanning from that time in Vienna until 1924.

On 24 September a telegram arrived from Baden. Arthur informed him that their sick mother was on her deathbed. Polzer decided to set off for Vienna the next day. Before his departure Rudolf Steiner received him again in his atelier. Perhaps only now did it come to the much-desired conversation about the situation in Tannbach. As always: something much more important was happening. Polzer wrote: 'Never had Rudolf Steiner told me anything as significant as in that conversation.'[314] A remarkable statement, in view of the numerous highly significant communications already made in the course of many years and also in view of the fact that it did not have to do with Polzer's concerns about Tannbach. What then *was* it about?

As so often, it had to do with Polzer's father. Steiner told his pupil:

> I could see in spiritual vision before me a large tablet and on it your father had drawn a kind of cosmic geometry. Then he erased what he had drawn with a large gesture and wrote on the tablet for us a short sentence, which was like a warning.

'Us' could refer to the anthroposophical movement or Society. The sentence could also have been directed to Steiner himself and Julius' Polzer's son. Polzer wrote: 'I can only share this sentence with a few friends verbally because it could easily be misinterpreted if revealed in public.'[315] In handwritten notes from 1943, found after the completion of the first edition of *Schicksalsbilder aus der Zeit meiner Geisterschülerschaft* (Images of Destiny from the Time of my Spiritual Pupilship) [LPS] the sentence appears as follows: 'And wrote on it: *the Church knows no progress.*' And Rudolf Steiner added: 'Yes, my friend, that will already be of significance for the near future. People are sleeping unawares and a hard destiny is so near.' It is understandable that Polzer did not immediately want to circulate this insight from the spiritual life of his father, passed on by Rudolf Steiner.

Newly strengthened by his attendance in Class Lessons, despite the personal hindrances in his spiritual striving, Polzer asked Steiner in this same conversation to allow him to give Class Lessons himself in Vienna, which Steiner immediately agreed to.

Despite Steiner's highly important communication from Polzer's father Julius, he looked to his pupil to be 'tired' and 'disappointed'. Perhaps to show his gratitude to Steiner, Polzer commented 'that through the Vorstand that he [Steiner] had instituted, the continuance of the Society was assured'. But Steiner made 'a hand gesture to me that showed his dissatisfaction as if he had expected something else and had to reckon with various manifestations of opposition'.[316] This was a bleak outlook for the 'unswerving fulfilment' of the promise he had spoken of...

Also, the situation in world events was touched upon again, whereby Steiner spoke about 'the ongoing military struggle against the Bolsheviks' by the Poles and the White armies and expressed the concern that they could be attacked from behind.

Polzer had hardly arrived at his mother's sickbed when a letter came from Josef in Dornach informing him that Rudolf Steiner had fallen ill. As this was the first time Rudolf Steiner had ever cancelled lectures, it certainly had to be something serious. For Polzer, it was a remarkable, very oppressive situation—to experience two people to whom he was so close—albeit in very different ways—seriously ill at the same time.

But he did not abandon anthroposophical activities in Vienna. On 29 September, Michaelmas Day, he gave his first Class Lesson. In a letter to Albert Steffen, witness at his grandson Christward's baptism, he reported: 'There were 21 of us; it was a very good Michaelmas mood.' From another letter to Steffen only two days later, we learn that in those days he was much occupied with Julian the Apostate, especially his 'relation to Bohemia'.

Christine Polzer passed away on 11 October in Baden near Vienna of cancer of the intestine. After the death of her husband Julius she had become a member of the Anthroposophical Society, not least out of a feeling of piety towards him, and in the following years had become friendly with the mother of Walter Johannes Stein, with whom she sometimes discussed anthroposophical questions.

The death of his mother gave Ludwig Polzer a new impetus for a wide-ranging review of his life. In such an earnest mood of looking back on his life, he travelled to Switzerland in November in order to visit Rudolf

Steiner, the other ill person who was so close to him. Steiner called for him on 11 November when he heard that Polzer had arrived. The atelier had been transformed into a sickroom. Steiner received his friend sitting in an armchair. Once again, it came to a long, important conversation. And once again, it began with Polzer's father Julius, across the threshold. But this time Polzer himself was the focus. Polzer put a 'very bashful' but particular question to Rudolf Steiner—something which he later acknowledged he had done far too seldom—about his father's historical-spiritual background. Steiner had lectured in 1924 about Platonism in the Middle Ages, most recently in September, and especially about the great School of Chartres and its far-reaching influence. These lectures now led Polzer to the question of whether there was a connection between this School and his father. Rudolf Steiner replied: 'Your father indeed received impulses from Chartres.'[317]

What followed in that conversation in November is contained in notes of conversations left by Paul Michaelis (see p. 524f.): 'We spoke [...] then about the issue of the Michael School and about the esoteric circle. To my question as to how I should hold the Class Lessons, he answered lovingly: "Do it how you want." '[318] Polzer commented:[319] 'With that, I am taking on a very responsible task. The continuity of the M[ystica] E[terna] is preserved and transformed in accordance with the times. After a long silence I asked Rudolf Steiner whether he was also thinking of establishing a master class in the sense of the old esotericism.' With this question Polzer had in mind the three main degrees of Freemasonry—Entered Apprentice, Fellow Craft, Master Mason. 'He gave me more or less the following answer:

> The classes for the members of the General Anthroposophical Society are, after the establishment [of the master classes], to be put into the hands of Frau Ita Wegman. A Class II for Section leaders and Section members as well as for lecturers and active members who take initiatives, which has yet to be set up, I shall have Frau Doctor [Steiner] lead. Then there will be a final class III, which I shall establish and lead as a kind of master class.

Steiner then spoke of details relating to the establishment of these three classes.

> Then he was silent again for a long time in deep contemplation. Then suddenly his face was overshadowed by deep concern, and Rudolf Steiner sighed, breathing heavily. We spoke about the Christmas Conference and the Constitution of the High School. Further, he spoke about the tasks of Albert Steffen, Frl Vreede and Dr Wachsmuth, whose tasks lay purely in administration. 'They have the places appropriate to them in the sections.'

> Then we spoke about his brother and sister. Before I left, he kissed me again on the forehead.

It is clear from the whole course and manner of this conversation that the future destiny of the Society he had founded was a cause of great concern for the sick man!

Polzer made a second and final visit to Steiner's sickbed on 3 March 1925, the birthday of his grandson Christward. This time too Steiner had called for Polzer to come to him. Now he received him 'already in bed and his speech was rather laboured'.[320] The notes of this last conversation with his friend and master begin as follows:

> After certain difficulties in the Society were spoken about—for example, amongst other things the early death of Sophie Stinde, whose place in the Johannes Building Association I could have taken so that a certain continuity could have been preserved vis-à-vis the western Slavs in relation to the activity of Joh.[ann] Sobieski—the conversation moved on, via Nero–Crown Prince Rudolf, Agrippina and Seneca to Crown Prince Rudolf and Empress Elisabeth. Hadrian and his intermediary role between the mad Caesars were also spoken of again. When I asked the Herr Doctor why he always pointed me to these connections, he replied: '*Because they have directly to do with you. But you have never wanted to know anything of it.*'[321]

It would certainly be wrong to interpret Steiner's remark here as words of censure; they might well have had in Steiner's eyes much more the character of a friendly indication of a still-existing lack of wakefulness on Polzer's part. But it was just these words and the manner in which they were spoken that led Polzer from this point on to take very seriously the questions and personalities that had been mentioned. That would become very clear in relation to his very conscious engagement with the period of the Roman Caesars, with Crown Prince Rudolf and especially with the Emperor Hadrian. So Steiner's final conversation with his pupil bore from the outset the very special stamp of a call to awakening. The next words of Rudolf Steiner, which followed on directly from the above, also showed this:

> Always keep this in mind: the Jesuits have deprived humanity of religiosity, of devotion; they are identical with the power of the Roman State. The battle—that is to say, the sin against the Holy Spirit is the means of power by which they seek to enforce their domination—the only sin which the scriptures say cannot be forgiven. Yet still the spirit cannot be entirely eradicated. But only a few will carry it over into the future.

From these words of Steiner's Polzer would form a key perspective from which to observe historical as well as contemporary events. And though this designation of Jesuitism as denying the spirit was not completely new to him, it may yet have surprised him when Steiner went on:

> This [Jesuit] stream can also be felt in the [Anthroposophical] Society and he hoped to have paralyzed it through the Christmas Conference for it was not without reason that he had sought to safeguard a certain parity of the male and female spirit within the Vorstand, as the tendencies were still there from ancient times that would exclude the female spirit. 'I drew attention to that already in the early days when I spoke about the Temple Legend. But it was not understood and is still a significant undercurrent in the Society. The battle against the spirit has always lain and will always lie in the background of all outer events.

Rudolf Steiner then made certain hard to interpret remarks about the individualities of the painters Fra Bartolomeo and Giotto. In relation to 'the efforts of Roman [Catholic] and western lodges' Steiner emphasized further 'with great seriousness' that it was of very special significance that three tasks were to be solved:

1. The question about the two Johns (John the Baptist and John the Evangelist).
2. Who was Demetrius? [Czar Dmitri of Russia 1605–1606]
3. Where did Caspar Hauser come from?

He specified this by saying: 'It is not who Demetrius was, who Caspar Hauser was that is important but: What was to be achieved by them?'

The close of this thought-provoking conversation led from such broad spiritual-historical perspectives, via an indication as to the importance of *putting the right question*, directly back to Ludwig Polzer's own current tasks.

> Pay attention to what comes to you as questions and how a question is formulated; it reveals much more of the being of a personality than all other outer gestures, deeds and words. It's all about how a question is put. This is an old mystery. In this lies also the very decisive significance of the question put by Frau Dr Wegman, when she asked me about a new esotericism. She did not just want to link on to the old, but she asked me the decisive Parzival question about a new esotericism. Only through this question put in this way did it become possible to establish the Michael School on Earth. In this School lies the kernel of the future as possibility.

And in the following sentence one can still hear, so to speak, Steiner gently pleading: 'If this were only understood by the members, as a possibility!' That means, not as something already realized for them by Steiner! The notes of the extended conversation close with Steiner's advice for [Polzer's] work with the Class Lesson texts:

When and wherever you hold Class Lessons, always keep in mind that during the Class Lesson it is not a matter of reading out a lecture in a teacherly manner but rather that you are taking part in a [ritual] act, you have to accomplish a [ritual] act which can place us in relationship with the Mystery stream of all ages.'

On 21 March Polzer wrote from Vienna that in view of the worsening condition of Leopoldine's eyesight, Austrian friends had decided to 'look in at Horn once a week in turn so that any arrangements that appear necessary can be made'. He emphasized that 'it is to happen uniformly and to be discussed together. We look forward to your special indications.'

Rudolf Steiner's prompt answer followed on 25 March:

> My dear friend Count Polzer,
> I am sorry that the last time you were here with me I did not speak to you about my sister's condition. I had long imagined the time in which something like what has now happened to my sister would have to come. The problem is very stubborn in her case and therefore, unlike in less stubborn cases, cannot be fought.
> I thank you most warmly for the loving and energetic way in which you have taken the matter in hand; it called for urgency. The choice of Frau Wahl, whom I know well, is agreeable to me. I will be most grateful to you, my dear, from my heart for everything you continue in this matter. I beg of you to do what you hold to be necessary.
> You have arranged the remuneration for Frau Barth very well; please let me know when additional payment is necessary.
> My warmest thanks for everything,
> Your
> Rudolf Steiner.

Steiner's letter was sent on to Prague, where Polzer was lecturing at the end of March. At 10 a.m. on 30 March Steiner's letter was in his hand. 'I was glad to see the way in which the letter was written,' he wrote in his Prague Notes. 'It was dated the 25th and written in a firm hand.' Sophie Lerchenfeld, who was also in Prague, sought out her friend in the afternoon and in tears, told him what she had just heard from Frau Eiselt on the telephone: 'Rudolf Steiner *died at 10 o'clock this morning in his atelier.*'[322]

At the same time that Polzer had been reading those last lines written by his friend, Steiner himself stepped silently and suddenly across the threshold of death—it had been feared by many and yet expected by no one—in order to become a completely unhindered contemporary in the sphere beyond history ...

Rudolf Steiner had named no successor and left behind no indications as to what consequences his pupils should draw from his departure. After a temporary liaison with the Society he had founded, he left it to the intentions of his pupils. Too many had leaned on their teacher. Now they had to show how far they could stand by themselves. The only legacy of Rudolf Steiner's was the 'Foundation Stone'. He had wanted to entrust it to their hearts. Would their hearts cherish it?

★

It was immediately clear to Ludwig Polzer that Steiner's death signified a powerful caesura for the society he had founded. 'The universal impulse that proceeded from him can be continued by no human being now living,' he wrote in his memoirs.[323] And looking back at Steiner's last earthly activity, he said:

> When Rudolf Steiner saw that the Society could only continue to exist if he made the sacrifice of taking on the leadership himself, which he did at Christmas 1923/24 he bound his destiny to that of an *earthly* society. When, shortly afterwards, working further on Earth became impossible for him, he died. *In the spiritual world he cannot remain bound to an earthly organization.* He can reach [. . .] individual souls . . . if they are of goodwill in his sense [. . .] A direct continuation of that which only he could keep united must, accordingly, be acknowledged as impossible.[324]

Reasonable and self-evident as this must appear to an historical view of the matter, it hardly became a general guiding principle among Steiner's pupils during the rest of the century from 1925. We shall come to speak of this.

IV. YEARS OF WANDERING

Since the death of Rudolf Steiner my greatest
anthroposophical interest has been turned towards
human beings and their destinies.
The Earth is the stage on which
human souls evolve, to make themselves ripe
to be able to live in other planetary conditions.

Ludwig Polzer-Hoditz 1939

31. Building Bridges

Ludwig Polzer arrived in Dornach on the morning of 1 April 1925. Berta had gone on before him. At his wife's request, he immediately went to see Albert Steffen. Steiner had once said to Polzer that he did not wish to be cremated but buried, and on the site of the Goetheanum Building. But arrangements had already been made to the contrary. It was as if, through this, Steiner's departure from the Society he had founded—though not from individuals who continued to strive onwards in his sense—was to be accelerated.

Over 2000 people came to the funeral. Not all those present had prepared themselves to come to terms with the fact of the death of the great teacher and consider the consequences for the future form of the Society he had left behind.

On the way back from the crematorium to Dornach in the Vorstand car there was the so-called 'disagreement over the urn' between Marie Steiner and Ita Wegman: whether Rudolf Steiner's urn should be placed in the atelier or at Villa Hansi. Certain divergences between the two women which had been in the air since the Christmas Con-ference, and 'which caused Rudolf Steiner serious concern'[325] now came into the open. The day after the funeral, Marie Steiner already wrote a letter to the Vienna doctor and chemist Eugen Kolisko 'that our Vorstand [...] is a nothing';[326] she wanted to give up her Vorstand activities and asked Kolisko to take on the post of President. Like Pol-zer, she too was prepared to draw the consequences from the death of Rudolf Steiner. Could anything in the Vorstand and the Society now remain as it had been? Could a Vorstand set up by Steiner in which there was an altercation already on the day of the cremation be regarded a moment longer as 'esoteric'? Her letter itself gave a clear no to this question. To prevent a split and the break-up of the Society, Marie Steiner's colleagues in the Vorstand asked her to rescind her decision, which she did.

Ita Wegman, on the other hand, began soon after Steiner's death to publish 'Leading Thoughts' for the members and thereby appeared to be continuing the 'Leading Thoughts', the essays which Steiner had begun in the *Goetheanum*, the 'Weekly Magazine for Anthroposophy' founded in 1921. Through these she acted as the pathfinder for another view from that of Polzer and Marie Steiner of the relationship of Rudolf Steiner to the Society he had left behind: the view that the initiate was able after death not only to connect himself to, or better said, to inspire the striving of individuals but also to do the same as before for the whole Vorstand and indirectly for the entire 'body' of the Society.

In this early stage of the difficulties within the Vorstand Polzer sought to mediate by conversations with the different members of the Vorstand. He felt himself really obliged to do this through the fact that he 'had always received from Rudolf Steiner full authorization' that he had asked for in the course of his work, especially 'the permission to hold Class Lessons in the Michael School in Austria and Bohemia in the way I felt necessary and as I wished. This permission laid on me the responsibility to do something so that the Vorstand in Dornach did not split up.'[327]

The psychological preconditions for this were in certain respects not the most favourable, as Polzer acknowledged in his final, unpublished autobiographical writings: 'Marie Steiner was always cool towards the friendship between us [he meant himself and his wife] and Rudolf Steiner. As she said to me once later, she could not find a relation to Berta.' This was for a spiritual student like Polzer at most a reason to free his efforts in mediation completely from all sympathies and antipathies: 'I wanted to remain objective and first sought to support Marie Steiner as she had stood by Rudolf Steiner for so long, helping him, collaborating with him, and she achieved so much as an artist for Eurythmy, for the dramatic arts and for speech formation.' But Polzer was also able to speak of the restraining characteristic of this undoubtedly significant personality: 'Her dominant aristocratic temperament was always breaking through and especially caused difficulties for R. Steiner in his final years.'[328] Thus after Steiner's death, Polzer travelled several times to Dornach where he spoke with Marie Steiner about issues outstanding relating to Rudolf Steiner's estate. During these visits he had conversations with other individual Vorstand members, but hoped in vain for a conversation with the whole Vorstand together. 'The Vorstand as a whole ignored me,' he said.

> I hoped it would call me in order to hear what Rudolf Steiner said to me in the final period and what authorization he gave me. It later became clear that all the members of the Vorstand were quite uninformed about this. They were shy of me in a way, because they knew that Rudolf Steiner had discussed much with me, had even spoken about individual members of the Vorstand.[329]

However much the Vorstand as a whole mistrusted him, Polzer nevertheless enjoyed the confidence of individual Vorstand members.

He learned from Albert Steffen in the year of Steiner's death that Steffen 'could only work with Marie Steiner and not with Frau Dr

Wegman'. Yet both Marie Steiner and Ita Wegman shared some very confidential matters with him. Polzer wrote:[330]

> Both women wanted [...] to speak to me individually in order to justify to me their awareness of the trust Rudolf Steiner had placed in them to continue his work. In no way did I doubt this justification with regard to their areas of Section work. One day Marie Steiner showed me the last letter Rudolf Steiner had written to her. I read it through in front of her. Then Frau Dr Wegman called me. She had a whole pile of papers before her; there may have been some old documents among them. I felt rather awkward. She took out two papers and gave them to me. I read—it was Rudolf Steiner's handwriting. The content was superb, somewhat difficult, [and] to make myself quickly understood, I could not repeat it. There was a lovely, complex interlaced drawing as a heading above the sentences. I was shocked in a way; it made a great impression on me. The letter which Frau Marie Steiner read to me was written with much affection but contained nothing at all of an esoteric nature. It showed how Rudolf Steiner had affectionately struggled to say something to her that he knew she could not understand: 'You have always understood me.' Between the lines, so to speak, he was asking her also to understand that his task on Earth was too many-sided to be linked esoterically with her alone. Such exclusivity was not possible for him. He could not restrict himself in his mission on Earth in a 'bourgeois' way.

Polzer saw the 'perhaps most significant cause of the strife' in the fact that

> various papers and documents from Dr Steiner's writings and possession were in Frau Dr Wegman's keeping. Frau Dr Steiner saw all this as left to her and thought that she alone should be allowed to have it at her disposal. But it is certain that Frau Dr Wegman only took what Dr Steiner had personally given her. As he had also done with the cross that he wore on his breast, so will it have been with other things. Rudolf Steiner certainly would not allow the denial of his right to take certain things from those he owned and present them to his faithful colleague.[331]

A deeper layer to the conflicts at that time and later on showed itself in an event that played itself out between Marie Steiner and Ita Wegman, and the latter herself told Ludwig Polzer:

> Soon after Rudolf Steiner's death, Frau Marie Steiner came to her and wanted to know whether Rudolf Steiner had told her something about incarnations that concerned Frau Ita Wegman. She hesitated somewhat and then Marie Steiner opined that it must be possible among esotericists to come to an understanding of such things. When Frau Wegman then spoke, Marie Steiner stood up and left without a word.[332]

Thus the first line of trust of the three above-named Vorstand members that Ludwig Polzer enjoyed took him right into the field of conflicts between them. And that was to be only the beginning of hard battles! Certainly, he tried then and later on to bridge over all antagonisms. But it is not enough that someone builds bridges; they also have to be crossed.

Polzer's efforts at mediation—as the following years would clearly show—were to bear little fruit. He himself said of them:

> I very soon had to realize that I could achieve nothing, because the Vor-
> stand showed a certain reserve towards me, perhaps precisely because
> Rudolf Steiner had shown so much trust in me and because the individuals
> were concerned about their positions and thought that I could try to get
> into the Vorstand and there become aggressive, which however, in reality
> was completely absent from my mind.[333]

It was certainly not that he achieved *nothing*, but in order to fend off an approaching catastrophe in the Society there would have had to be exactly that real trust in the integrity of Polzer's mediating intentions.

★

While the first dark clouds were forming on the horizon of the Anthroposophical Society, Ludwig Polzer travelled to Venice in the middle of May with Sophie Lerchenfeld for a holiday. Berta remained in Dornach where she had to nurse a very swollen finger.

The two friends stayed at the Villa Tami on the Lido. The Polzer family had lived here in the summer of 1910. Ludwig's father Julius and mother Christine had also come to Venice and had stayed in the chic district, Monaco. It was the last time that Julius would see the city before his death.What stories had he not been able tell his son and grandsons about the city on the lagoon! Ludwig Ritter von Polzer, Ludwig's grandfather, had also visited the city regularly. So the Lido, the city and especially St Mark's Square were full of memories for Ludwig Polzer, and indirectly also for his companion, who was interested in everything that concerned her friend.

Had Rudolf Steiner not said very significant things about Julius Polzer? Here in Venice, surrounded by memories of lovely days long past and in the delightful and heartening company of Sophie Lerchenfeld, Ludwig Polzer made the decision after the passing of his great teacher to turn to his connection to his father across the threshold and to cultivate it con-sciously. Every evening he linked himself in 'Spirit-Remembering' and 'Spirit-Sensing' to Julius Polzer. It became a custom for him, and 15 years later, he stated that he had done this consistently every evening ever since.

At this point let us look once again through Polzer's eyes at his father Julius, the invisible third traveller to Venice. In the last of Ludwig Polzer's autobiographical writings we read:

> My father was a sharp thinker. Mathematics and geometry were the subjects for which he showed a special affection and capability. In the former Austrian Academy of Engineers those were the only decisive subjects for the pupils' progress. Even in retirement he occupied himself with mathematics for a while and taught me during my year of preparation for Weisskirchen in these subjects. Later he turned more to philosophy and in his last years to spiritual science.
>
> The most striking characteristics of my father were his great propriety, his exactitude and his mathematically logical thinking. For him, exact thinking went before all other personal tendencies. In questions of rights or thinking, it was entirely indifferent to him whether he had to do with a family member or someone he hardly knew. He suffered visibly when false conclusions were spoken in his presence or errors in logic were made. One perceived these qualities in him and they were certainly among the reasons why Rudolf Steiner was so interested in him and valued him. He suffered greatly in his soul in his final years; he sensed the coming catastrophe, and this sense was reflected in his concern for the administration of his estate. He was very conscientiousness. He would sit for days working on his tax return striving to harmonize it with his exactitude and the proper requirements. My mother, who was rather lacking in logic and acted more out of feeling, never involved herself in any financial or business matters. They therefore lived together in the finest harmony despite their great differences in character. Yet my father was not only an upright man; he was also good-hearted. He just had a kind of military, rather crashing strictness which I sometimes found very intimidating in my early youth. There was never a real disharmony between us. He loved to talk about his youth, of the severity of his own father, of the order to which he was accustomed [...] He had a very companionable nature and was no friend of reclusive loneliness. The lovely country house at Peggau near Graz which he bought just for my mother and sold to us in 1901, turned out to be only a worry for him, although those worries were actually unfounded and he was happy to be able to give it away. He was in agreement with the practical education our children received, for he sensed that hard times were coming. Above all, he loved Vienna, and liked to tell of how in his childhood in the inner city he knew every alleyway. His lifestyle was very modest, only out of a kind of social vanity did he finally agree to furnish his house in a gentlemanly style. But it caused him much concern when he noticed that his children were at times behaving or living in ways beyond normal expectations. My last memories of him are full of conversations about Rudolf Steiner's spiritual science.[334]

This was *one* consequence that Ludwig Polzer in his individual striving drew from Rudolf Steiner's passing: he united himself all the more strongly with the soul of his father, with whom he felt spiritually related. Those beautiful days in Venice stimulated this very concrete spirit-remembering. This too was bridge-building, in the vertical dimension, so to speak.

★

Following the visit to Venice, feeling himself rejuvenated, Polzer took part in a Whitsun Youth Conference in Dornach. Then in June he travelled to his beloved Prague. The work in the city on the Vltava [Moldau] had always been for him an affair of the heart; now it gradually became more regular and intensive. It increased, and included visits to important personalities. On this trip to Prague Polzer sought out Dr Šámal, the director of President Thomas Masaryk's Cabinet. He 'spoke to him of the need for threefolding' but 'without much success'.[335] But Polzer did not let himself be disconcerted by this; resolutely, he continued to be committed to introducing the idea of threefolding wherever he saw a suitable opportunity. 'Never work for success!' These words of Steiner's to Otto Lerchenfeld also guided Polzer's activity.

Shortly afterwards, Polzer visited Sophie Lerchenfeld in Sestri Levante, where she was visiting the spa. She had suffered from childhood from rheumatism in her joints. Otto Lerchenfeld also visited his daughter there. Polzer doubtless told Lerchenfeld of his conversation with Šámal. They will also have spoken about developments in Dornach.

★

Autumn drew on, the time of far-reaching decisions. Ludwig and Berta Polzer quietly celebrated their silver wedding anniversary. 'Our community began in happiness,' wrote Polzer, 'now we live in constant anxiety.' And almost in a soft wistfulness; he added: 'I thought at that time of my parents' silver anniversary, which they celebrated in a carefree atmosphere. How everything had changed in such a short time!'[336]

The greatest of all their concerns was the economic management at Tannbach. It was decided to call Julius back from Dornach since he, like his brother Josef, had become homeless there since the death of Rudolf Steiner. It was a hard decision for Polzer. On 29 September 1925, Michaelmas Day, he wrote a long letter to Ita Wegman in which he confided to her his concerns about the situation at Tannbach.

It was the anniversary of the first Class Lesson he had held in 1924 in Vienna. The letter therefore first dealt with a matter relating to Class

Lessons. 'I am [. . .] of quite the same opinion as you, honoured Doctor,' he wrote to Arlesheim, 'that especially on the acceptance [into the Class] of young people one should know at least something of them; they would at least have to be known to those who hold the Class Lessons.'

Then he described how his decision to call Julius home to Tannbach had come 'after hard soul struggles' and how he could 'very strongly experience the help and guidance of our dear master Dr Steiner, especially in the last days before the decision'.

> On 3 March the Herr Doctor promised me an answer to the question which was weighing so much upon me, that I feel so torn between my anthroposophical work, which is always so much bound up with historical and political events (and it was just these things that the H. Dr. discussed with me) and my estate, which, financially, is now hardly viable. The first answer that I received from him led me to decide to call my son to leave Dornach and come here.

In other words, Rudolf Steiner's answer to the question that could no longer be put on the physical plane Polzer now experienced as given in a spiritual way. Behind the hard Tannbach decision stood *inspired* advice. That was how Polzer experienced it.

In this way he came to the 'to the insight that I ought not to bury here in isolation the experiences of my anthroposophical work that I had had at the side of the Herr Doctor'. If Julius had not come, he would have had to advise the sale of the estate. Now he placed the management of the Tannbach estate in the hands of his son who was 'to run it in agreement with his mother'. On Berta's relation to the estate, he wrote:

> My wife, who is so strongly connected to the elements in Nature, completely lacks any capacity for business. She *and* Julius, to whom she has always been especially close, should try it; it is what she wants. They are to do with Tannbach what they want. *I will then have my mind free and my path free for my anthroposophical work and can respond to the many calls which always come to me and can develop my political connections. I especially want to focus on Bohemia.*[337]

'It was a really hard decision,' he wrote finally,

> but since I have made it, I feel full of confidence. Now I shall carry on with real energy on my old, new (!) path.
>
> At my age it is somewhat risky to want to take on something. But when one knows that the Herr Doctor stands by one, especially when one seeks to work for his cause, then one must have the confidence that one will be able to acquire the little that one needs in life; one has so many friends.

This letter to Ita Wegman testifies not only in a fine way to the trust that had already grown up between these two in the very short time since they had come to know each other; it reveals an important turning point in Polzer's life, and shows us further something of his loving clear-sightedness with regard to his wife. Above all, it shows how Polzer felt individually still linked to the being of Rudolf Steiner. 'You will not be forgotten', Steiner had said to his pupil at their last conversation in March 1925. Polzer now experienced the fulfilment of those words. The inner connection to his father which he cultivated may in this respect have served also to smooth the spiritual path for him ...

Polzer made prompt use of his new freedom. In October he travelled via Dornach to Locarno where a European security and peace conference was to take place.

The Locarno Pact served primarily as an arbitration treaty to settle Franco-German relations. It is known as the 'Turning Point in European Post-War Politics'.[238] 'I spoke with many of the statesmen who had gathered there,' wrote Polzer, 'at some length with Beneš and Jules Sauerwein, amongst others. I was hoping for something from the latter, because he had also been connected to Rudolf Steiner.'[339] After the turn of the century Sauerwein had been pointed in the direction of his former teacher by Friedrich Eckstein, a friend from Steiner's youth; he became a correspondent of Le Matin in Paris, in which he published an interview with Steiner in 1922 about Helmuth von Moltke. Sauerwein's under-standing of German culture predisposed him for a role in mediation between that culture and France.[340]

As interesting and stimulating as the discussions in Locarno were, Polzer's account of the event sounds very pessimistic: 'The conference gave me the impression of empty phrases; I knew that despite all the gushing mutual praise that went on, nothing would come of it which could bring Europeans inner peace.'[341] He wrote an article which he titled simply 'Locarno'[342] for Lauer's Österreichischen Blätter für freies Geistesleben. In it he wrote:

> The conference therefore had the aim of uniting Europe in line with Anglo-American needs [...] Germany, which had earlier been treated with brutality, was, from now on, to be held in a permanent 'loving' embrace; it was to be brought into a more difficult situation and into still greater dependence, and everything had to be done to prevent Germany from presenting any moral arguments before the world [...] Certainly, one did not hear any of this expressed at Locarno but it was there in the back-ground; if one mentioned it, then one encountered immediate protests that one was touching on some great world evil [...] The absurd phrase 'Si vis

pacem para bellum' [if you seek peace, prepare for war] was circulating like a warmongering phantom at Locarno.

Polzer's article concluded with an address that he naturally did not make at Locarno but which, 'in the sense of the Time Spirit', should have been directed at the British delegation. Amongst other things, Polzer holds the following against the members of the delegation:

> You have gathered in Locarno to maintain peace. With *those* means towards it that you advise, there will be none. Treaties have never been strong enough to guide world history when they have not been formed in accordance with the spirit of development, out of an instinctive knowledge of the forces of becoming. Your diplomats still knew this in the middle of the last century [. . .] Those forces which are now emerging in world history are of an enormous apocalyptic power which will scorch all closed treaties shaped in the old way [. . .] The extent of the catastrophe before us will depend on how large the detours will be on which we can find what is seeking to grow.

In the positive sense, Polzer points out that Britain's real contribution to peace must consist in paving the way to a world economy.

Polzer thus also lived with the events of his time in such a way that he sought to speak, from the perspective of future needs, to leading actors in world events on their own political stages!

★

In the middle of November Polzer spent a week with Sophie Lerchenfeld at Mariensee at the home of Dora Schenker, 'of whom Sophie too had become very fond'.[343] According to the guest book, they went one day to Bernstein Castle in nearby Burgenland. 'How much I had to thank Frau Schenker for all her help and support in the ever more difficult years that now followed,' he later wrote.[344] Dora Schenker's help was not least of a financial nature. 'One has so many friends', Polzer had confided to Ita Wegman in September; Dora Schenker was a prominent figure among these friends of Polzer's.

Ludwig Polzer spent Christmas with his wife in familiar Dornach. In January of the new year (1926) Frau Schenker also arrived, in order to attend the agricultural conference. Their common interest in the practical side of spiritual science could only strengthen the bonds of friendship between Polzer and Dora Schenker.

Polzer had given up his fine room in Lothringerstrasse on the Karlsplatz in Vienna in the summer of 1925. From the turn of the year during his visits to Vienna he would always stay at the home of Alfred Zeissig. For many years thereafter, the Zeissigs' home on Viaduktstrasse became 'an anthroposophical home' for Ludwig Polzer, who also took 'a warm interest in the [Zeissigs'] lovely, harmonious family life and the development of their dear daughters'.[345] A firm soul bond would especially develop between him and Theodora.

In the spring of 1926 Ludwig and Berta Polzer visited their old friends the Klimas in Pressburg [Bratislava], where Jaroslav Klima had become Director of Police. Polzer would be a regular visitor to the Klimas' home in the following years also. Here too he 'found an anthroposophical home in which I felt myself well and safe during my years of wandering'. From Pressburg he travelled one day to nearby Modern, to visit his father's grave; he would make this visit to the grave more often. In the same month of May, in the company of Sophie Lerchenfeld he visited for the first time the spa at Pistyan, [today Pieštàny, Slovakia] which lies not far from Modern. Polzer began to suffer from sciatica and accompanied Klima on a business trip of his to Pistyan in order to gather information. This too would be a place to which he would often return, alone or in company. He was to become a good friend of Dr Reichart, a doctor at the spa and also formed a fine friendship with Reichart's wife and his two daughters.

★

'A positive, right step in the sense of possibilities after his [Steiner's] death was the creation of Rudolf Steiner Hall in London,' wrote Polzer in 1936.[346] The building was created in order to provide the anthroposophical work in England with a worthy site at which public events such as lectures and Eurythmy performances could also be put on. It was the first anthroposophical centre in the world which bore the name of Rudolf Steiner. This certainly stood fully in harmony with the hopes which Steiner placed in England in his last years, and where anthroposophical work blossomed in an especially powerful way through the summer schools at Penmaenmawr and Torquay organized by D.N. Dunlop. Rudolf Steiner Hall was formally opened on 1 June 1926.

Ludwig Polzer was invited to the opening ceremony. He travelled first to Paris to a Eurythmy performance and then went on an excursion to Chartres, 'about which Rudolf Steiner had told us so much'. He was deeply impressed by the cathedral. It was and remained for him 'the most beautiful he had seen'.[347] A month earlier he had visited his father Julius' grave; now he was standing in front of the cathedral in Chartres, the spirituality of which Julius had imbibed much.

In London Polzer stayed with Harry Collison, the then General

Secretary of the English Society. On the day of the opening ceremony he gave an address in German. He included this in his Prague Notes. In it he recalls his first visit to England in 1910 which was made possible by Blanche Tollemache. He described how he had then had the opportunity

> 'to look into history in the most intimate way. I could as nowhere else until that time experience and see the Middle Ages and the present lying next to each other. I saw the positive aspect of standing within the needs of the present, saw the prevalence of the capacities needed by the present cultural epoch and could also experience everything which still worked on from the struggles of that very important time when the Stuarts followed Elizabeth [I].

He spoke of particular homely feelings which could be interpreted through Rudolf Steiner's spiritual science and spoke above all of the spiritual connection between Britain as the main inaugurator of the epoch of the Consciousness Soul and Bohemia as the heart of Central Europe.

> I had absorbed the spiritual atmosphere of the beginning of the fifth cultural epoch as an Austrian can absorb it. I had felt the close, loving spiritual connections of the being of the English people to those of the centre, had come to know the cradle of the message of Wycliffe, the message which found its way to us in the centre of Europe and which introduced the first great emancipation of this fifth cultural epoch from the theocratic and hierarchical element that proceeded from earlier times and was buttressed by the power of Rome.[348]

The fire of spiritual independence that Wycliffe lit in England was carried by Jan Hus, 100 years before the work of Luther, to Bohemia, where Hus strove to spread Wycliffe's writings. This bridge between Wycliffe and Central Europe is the parallel to that other bridge which was and is to be built between Middle Europe and unspoilt Slavic culture. According to Rudolf Steiner, Bacon, Shakespeare, *and the Middle European Jakob Böhme* were inspired from the same source; but also the 'gigantic spirit James I'[349] formed a pillar, so to speak, for the bridge-building between Britain and Central Europe.

'Spiritually conceived, today no earthly souls love each other more than the earthly souls of Middle Europe and the earthly souls of the British Isles,' Rudolf Steiner had said on 15 November 1914[350]—in stark contrast to the outer, warring relationship between the two peoples! 'Spiritually conceived...'! Polzer wanted to build bridges not only to Slavic culture but also this spiritual line of connection between Britain and Central Europe and its harmonizing power. He gave fine witness to this in Rudolf Steiner Hall. What he did there made him, even more than his open personality, the friend of D.N. Dunlop, who also sought to work for this bridge-building from the other end.

Thus this second visit to England and especially Polzer's speech at Rudolf Steiner Hall appears to relate in a mysterious way to Blanche Tollemache. In 1890 Polzer had spent beautiful May days with his friend Blanche in Modern in the circle of his family. Now, *coming from Pistyan and Modern*, he travelled to England for the second time. Had it not been Blanche, the young officer's first love, who had first inspired him to come to the West? The circle of destiny closed in a beautiful way: on 5 June Miss Bailey, a friend of Blanche, brought Polzer in a small car to Alde-burgh near Ipswich on the North Sea, where he 'spent a very fine day recalling old memories with Blanche Tollemache after many long years'.[351]

In the year after Rudolf Steiner's death Ludwig Polzer thus worked in various ways as a bridge builder. In Dornach he mediated between the personalities of the Vorstand that Steiner had established. He began to cultivate consciously his inner connection to his father Julius. He sought in practising 'Spirit-Sensing' the connection to his departed teacher. He approached statesmen, first in Bohemia, in order to work for the idea of threefolding. Finally, he worked to strengthen the line of spiritual con-nection between England and Bohemia. All this bridge-building would in the following 19 years of Polzer's life remain of significance.

32. From Ancient Rome to the Middle of Europe

On 17 June 1926 Polzer travelled with Sophie Lerchenfeld to Pistyan, from where he had left for England. A mudbath treatment and sulphur baths would at least have given him some relief from his sciatica. Dr Reichart put a guestroom in his home at Polzer's disposal. With a week's break the stay at the spa went on till 30 July. The following day he went on with his friend to Prague, where he was informed by Jaroslav Klima to his astonishment that he had come very close to getting into serious political difficulties, from which Klima's high position in the police was still able to guard him. Unfortunately, we do not learn what this was actually about but the matter most likely had to do with Polzer's conversation with Dr. Šámal, the Director of Masaryk's Cabinet, which had taken place in June 1925. As always, Polzer enjoyed the special relief of learning that an imminent danger had been averted, one *of which he had known nothing.*

In August he was again in Switzerland, attending a music conference in Dornach. The weather was very hot, which was hard on Polzer, who had only just come from the spa. He fell ill with flu and a high fever. He moved from the Hotel Vacano to Dr Ita Wegman's clinic at Arlesheim, where he received silver injections. Visits by Berta, Sophie and his friend Eiselt from Prague show how serious the illness was. On 6 October he was again free of the fever. For a 'complete recovery' he travelled with Sophie Lerchenfeld for a week to Rigi-Kaltbad. 'The air there was very good for me,' he wrote.[352]

This severe illness was like a radical intake of breath before the next stretch of his wanderings. For this was to bring very special, deep insights into the background of his own destiny but also that of mankind. 'World knowledge through deepened insight into destiny'—would be an epithet that could encapsulate the following period in his life. A prologue to this can be felt in the branch inauguration which Polzer supervised in Pressburg [Bratislava] on 13 November 1926 after his complete recovery. Following energetic preparatory work by Julie Klima, an anthroposophical branch was founded which received the name 'Karl Julius Schröer Branch'. Rudolf Steiner's great teacher in his student days in Vienna, Schröer himself came from Pressburg, where he taught German Literature. In one of Steiner's last addresses in Dornach he had shared some results of his research with regard to Schröer's previous life,[353] and Polzer knew of this.

Hans Eiselt and Ludwig Thieben both appeared at the inauguration of the Schröer branch.

33. Arthur Polzer's account of the Freemason warning (cf. p. 126 ff.)

34. *West-East Congress, From l. to r.: Alfred Zeissig, Alexander Strakosch, Emil Leinhas, Ernst Uehli, Unknown, Carl Unger, Ludwig Polzer; W.J. Stein, Eugen Kolisko, Count Otto Lerchenfeld, Unknown*

35. Richard Coudenhove-Kalergi, 1931

36. Ilona Bögel and Josef Polzer, Engagement photo, 1922

37. Josef Polzer, Christward Polzer, Ludwig Polzer

Aus den Aufschreibungen de
Hoditz nach Gesprächen mit

1.1.1923

Am Neujahrs-Mittagm nach de
"Wie hat das geschehen könn
Die Differenziertheit der
Wohl wollen sie alles sehe
dabei sein, aber erwachen
So müssen sie an den Katas
Schmerzen wach werden. Hie

II.

11.11.1924

11.November 1924. Heute in Dc
Da Er erfahren hatte, daß ich
er mich rufen. Sein Atelier v
umgewandelt.Er saß damals ers
Lehnstuhl. Wir sprachen von ;
Dann über die Angelegenheit de
und des esoterisc nen Kreise
wie ich in Wien und Prag die

III.

3.3.1925

Am 3.März 1925 Graf Polz
Besuch.Krankenlager.
Nachdem über bestimmte Sc
der Gesellschaft gesproc
über den frühen Tod von S
frei gewordene Stelle ich
Verein hätte übernehmen s
gewisse Kontinuität hätte
den Ranslewen gegenüber.

38. Handwritten Dating of Polzer's Conversations with R.Steiner

stellte, dass diese fast alle eine bedeutende
de Radio activität aufweisen. —
Im Spätherbst dieses Jahres am 21. Nov.
heiratete Butas Vetter Heinrich Bar.Kotz
die Gräfin Gabrielle Trauttmansdorf, die
jüngste Tochter des Fürsten Carl Trautt.
mans dorf. Die Trauung fand in der
Schlosscapelle in Bischofteinitz statt,
ich fungierte mit Carl Auersperg,
Sandor Pallavicini u. Louis Trauttmans.
dorf als Zeuge. —
Heute am 23. November 1924 komme
ich im Schreiben dieser Zeilen zu dem
Tage, der für mein weiteres Leben von
der allergrössten Bedeutung wurde
und es ist sicher kein Zufall, dass
wie
ich eben bemerke, dass dieser Tag
auch der ein 23. November war,
der 23. Nov. des Jahres 1908, an dem
                    Rainueder
ich in Wien im der Theosophischen
Mit diesem Tage beginnt eigentlich mein
vierter Lebensabschnitt u. mit Rud. Steiners Tode
mein fünfter Lebensabschnitt. also 30. März 1925.

39. Account of 23 November 1924 from 'Notes' (LPK)

40. Guenther Wachsmuth and Ita Wegman

41. Albert Steffen and Marie Steiner

42. Josef (above) and Julius Polzer, 1928

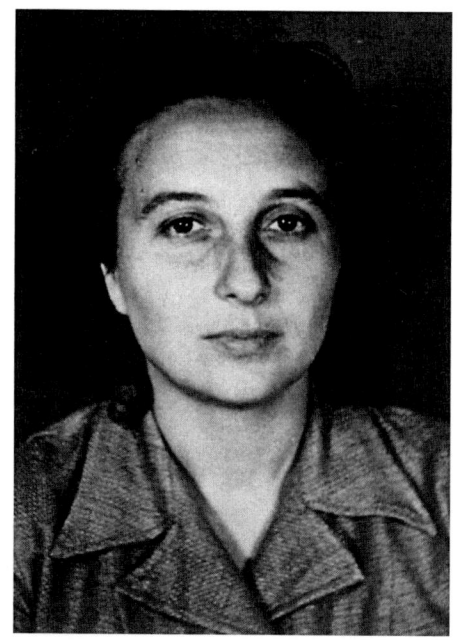

43. Sophie (above) and Menny Lerchenfeld

44. Trajan's Column in Rome

45. Emperor Hadrian (76–138)

46. Julie and Jaroslav Klima

47. Thomas Masaryk (above) and Eduard Beneš

Topolčianky, 1/10 33.

Verehrter Herr Graf,

besten Dank für die freundl. Zeilen y Beigaben.

Alle Gedanken, die Sie vorbringen, beschäftigen auch mich. Heuer war bei mir Herr Ludwig y hat mir viele Fragen gestellt, noch mehr persönliches H.; immer, hin wird sie in Buch interessieren. (Düşfe im Herijaht erscheinen.)

[...]

48. *The beginning of a letter from Masaryk to Ludwig Polzer*

★

In December, after three days of rest at Mariensee with Sophie, Polzer again travelled to Chartres. He then went on to Dornach for the Christmas conference.

He also speaks of many visits he made in 1926 to his brother Arthur and his aunt Mathilde in Baden, near Vienna. He will have been sure to give his aunt an account of his trip to England and his meeting with Blanche Tollemache.

★

The new year began with a completely unexpected shock. On 1 January 1927 Roman Boos, a pupil of Steiner's, disturbed a Class Lesson held by Ita Wegman. Boos accused Wegman of making an unauthorized bid for power in the esoteric sense; however, by his reckless disturbance he quite obviously offended against certain fundamental principles of spiritual striving, to say nothing of the normal rules of outward propriety. Polzer witnessed the intervention. He wrote:

> Frau Dr Wegmann [sic] was holding a Class Lesson. I happened to be sitting near the front that day and could see everything. Frau Wegmann [sic] had just begun. Dr Boos rushed forward from behind onto the podium with a pale, distorted expression and began in accusing words to speak against Frau Dr Wegmann [sic]. It was an attack of the worst kind, a disturbance of a ritual act. After this event, at which other members of the Vorstand behaved weakly, I knew where my place was.

From this dark moment in the history of the Anthroposophical Society after the death of Rudolf Steiner, Ludwig Polzer became a protector of Ita Wegman.

★

At this time Polzer began to occupy himself intensively with Roman history. Three years earlier Rudolf Steiner had indicated the relationship between Crown Prince Rudolf and the Emperor Nero. (cf. lecture of 27 April 1924, GA 236). Polzer had been interested in Rudolf since his childhood. During his schooldays in Graz he had gained a vivid picture of Nero from Hamerling's epic poem *Ahasver*. Then Steiner had shown the surprising connection between the two men. Now, in 1927, Steiner's indication about Nero's destiny bore fruit in Polzer's soul. He began to study the destinies of the circle of individuals around both Nero and Rudolf. On 16 February 1927 he wrote in Dora Schenker's guestbook 'Collaborative Work'. In April we find the even more concrete entry in the same source: 'Five beautiful days with Agrippina and Elisabeth.' By this he meant Nero's mother Agrippina and Rudolf's mother, the Empress Elisabeth.

In this work Polzer had a painful experience. On 11 May news reached him through Frau Zeissig of the death of Dr Klima. He had died on 5 May in Mentone near Genoa after a bout of influenza. Death, which had threatened Polzer himself not long before, had taken a dear friend of his. On the day of his death, Julie Klima had read to her departed husband all of Steiner's Class mantras—more powerful sustenance for his journey she could not have given him.

Klima had once made it possible for Polzer to have an effect on political developments in that he was able to explain to his brother Arthur the injustice in the trials against the Bohemian politicians, which led to the surprising amnesty of July 1917. Polzer and his Bohemian friend had had innumerable conversations about political matters over the following ten years. The fine, richly human times they had shared, some in Prague, some in Bratislava, were now over.

Polzer took inward leave of his friend, aware in his soul that they would meet again consciously in the future. 'We anthroposophers,' he wrote in connection to Klima's death, 'wish [...] to strive *to recognize again consciously* the many friends we lose, not only in the spiritual world *but also in the next life*.'[354] Building a foundation for this later recognition, Polzer would still write twelve years later, 'Dr Klima will always be there in my lasting memories as a beautiful soul' and 'Rudolf Steiner too loved him in his Slavic originality'.[355]

Klima had a Roman profile and in a severe crisis in his life Rudolf Steiner had once recommended he read Boethius who had written his *Consolations of Philosophy* as a Roman prisoner of Theodoric. Klima's death may also thus have stimulated Polzer's study of Rome in a subtle manner. Not unconnected to his work on Rome was Polzer's visit to the Lainzer zoo, which he visited that same month. In that lovely park in Vienna stands the Hermesvilla, a refuge for Empress Elisabeth. Of no little symptomatic interest is the fact that there is a bust of Nero in the Hermesvilla, which when he realized it, was for Polzer a kind of confirmation that his thoughts were moving in the right direction.[356]

In the first two weeks of June came the first fruits of his intensive research on Rome. In the guestbook at Mariensee we read: 'Collaborative work: typewriter clatter'. Dora Schenker typed out seven essays, which have not survived. They formed the basis for lectures given at the end of the year and were also the core of the book *Das Mysterium der europäischen Mitte—eine welthistorische Schicksalsbetrachtung* [The

Mystery of the European Middle—A Consideration of World-historical Destiny].

★

As usual, the second half of the year was richer in outer activities. In the first weeks of July Polzer gave his first lectures in Belgrade, in weather as hot as that in Dornach a year earlier. He stayed with Vitomar Korać, former Minister of Home Affairs. He also got to know Dušan Letica, the later Finance Minister of Yugoslavia on this visit.

He returned to Vienna via Agram (today Zagreb), where he also gave lectures. However, an unexpected incident quickly drove him back downstream, quite literally. Someone set fire to the Palace of Justice, and the trains were all suddenly stopped. On a motorboat like a refugee, Polzer left for Bratislava where he had discussions with Stanislaus Benda, Dr Klima's deputy on this and other, more political issues. Polzer also had some advice to give here: Benda was faced with the choice of becoming Chief of Police in Kaschau or taking a higher post in the police in Prague. Which should he choose? Polzer recommended the latter. Soon afterwards, Benda became the Chief of Police in Prague.

A new friendship developed here for Polzer. On his subsequent visits to Prague he regularly looked Benda up. To his inner gaze, a third was present in these meetings with Benda—the soul of his departed friend Klima.

From his son Josef, meanwhile, there was not much good news. He was going through some difficult times psychologically. After separation from his wife Ilona and his son Christward Johannes, he was supposed to be taking on a job in business, while Heinrich Kotz, one of Berta's cousins, was providing him with material support. However, soon afterwards, Josef had to be accompanied to Buchenbach, where Dr Husemann was leading an anthroposophically-oriented clinic. Polzer too, his steps becoming heavier, would often find himself heading in this direction in the coming years.

After a stay in Pontresina with Sophie, he travelled to a conference in Budapest, which was the initiative of Frau Nagy; Julie Klima went along too. There followed a further stay at Mariensee with Dora Schenker; the pair went on excursions to Burgenland.

In Prague Polzer gave lectures and held Class Lessons. But in November he was again at Mariensee where he prepared his lectures on Rome which he was to give in Dornach at Christmas.

★

It could seem to a superficial view as if Polzer in this and following years was living a life of pleasure and caprice in enjoyment of the senses and the supersensible, doing merely what he liked and avoiding what he found oppressive. But this would indeed be a superficial judgement. How did he himself look back on these years after Rudolf Steiner's death? In 1939 he wrote of them as follows:

> When I write down these days the events of the passing years, which roll past the reader like pictures, it could appear as though my life had played itself out only in a happy way, rich in diversions, as if anthroposophical work was just a series of happy conferences. Certainly I always enjoyed the work itself because it brought me into the most varied situations with people, and there was a common activity with other human beings and with regard to what it means to be human.

Then follows a very noteworthy sentence:

> Only work which is done with joy is worthy of human beings and promotes human development. It was not duty but joy that stood in the foreground. But in the background there was much pain and anxious thoughts. This is how one works within a great, responsible cause for the sake of humanity, and many people come to one with their own soul needs. In the background there are also one's own anxieties about one's own nearest and dearest, and I had plenty of such anxieties. Spiritual work for others works in a liberating way on one's own soul. This should be added to those pictures rolling by.[357]

In the same place Polzer also gives some notable information about the way he went about his historical research. He wrote:

> To this must be added that I learned from Rudolf Steiner to see into what lies behind contemporary historical world events and these are serious enough, and only anthroposophy makes it possible not to lose one's balance and one's courage. One can penetrate to what lies there in the background if one has the will for it and if one raises oneself from a logic of concepts to a logic of facts. *But one must also be able to give oneself over to one's own destiny. This will make it understandable to one in reviewing one's life how one actually stands in life.*
>
> *These symptomatic events, which one needs for one's task, bring one, as Rudolf Steiner said, into the stream of the world, and then one must be able to put them together to grasp reality, even if they often stand far apart from each other in time.*[358]

Polzer's Roman studies, which began in 1927, can already show us in many particulars very concretely how he inwardly linked or lined up his own steps with what came to him from outside. One example is the Nero statue in the Hermesvilla, the existence of which he heard just at the time when he was occupying himself with the karmic background of Crown Prince Rudolf and Empress Elisabeth.

And thereby, the main thread of this chapter is taken up again. But progress cannot be made without small detours; we shall restrict ourselves to those that stand overtly or covertly in relation to the matter of Rome.

'The Mystery of the European Middle in the Light of Karmic History'—that was how Count Polzer titled the three lectures that he gave in Dornach at Christmas 1927. They proceeded, as already mentioned, from those seven essays which were written at Mariensee in the spring and would appear in book form shortly afterwards, further developed and expanded.

Since Polzer based himself on statements of Rudolf Steiner that had been unpublished until that point he had to ask for Marie Steiner's permission—after Steiner's death she administered his literary estate—to cite the corresponding passages. He may have done this during his stay in Dornach in December 1927.

*

On 15 March of the new year (1928) Ludwig Polzer-Hoditz, together with his brother Arthur and their sister Marie-Sefine celebrated the 80th birthday of Countess Mathilde von Hoditz und Wolframitz. Let us recall here that Mathilde adopted Ludwig Polzer in 1904, and the name Hoditz thereby passed over to the Polzer family. Through his aunt Mathilde, the motif of 'adoption' thus became linked to the life of Ludwig Polzer. Let us keep that firmly in mind.

After the celebration, Polzer travelled with Sophie and Dora Schenker to Graz and Peggau and showed his friends some of the places where he had spent his youth. They walked to the imposing Saurau Palace on the Sporgasse and to the Emperor Friedrich Mausoleum, from where came the epithet AEIOU—Austria erit in orbe ultimo: Austria will exist until the end of the world. 'Thus in such pleasant company I was able to refresh my memories,'[359] wrote Polzer in 1939.

After this visit to Graz he travelled once again to his refuge at Mariensee, this time in the company of Frau Schenker. The entry in the guest book is instructive: 'Serious work together on the European Middle and the folk souls, corrections to the book.' The book *Das Mysterium der europäischen Mitte—eine welthistorische Schicksalsbetrachtung* [The Mystery of the European Middle—A Consideration of World-historical Destiny] was nearing completion. The 'work on ... the folks souls' related to Rudolf Steiner's statements about them in his lecture cycle 'The Mission of Folk Souls in relation to Germanic and Nordic Mythology'.[360] The two friends will have given special attention to what Steiner had to say there about the folk spirit of the Romans, but also to his indications about the Greeks' folk spirit, who became the inspirer of exoteric Christianity after the Mystery of Golgotha.

Baden, Graz, Mariensee—the experiences which Polzer had with close friends in these places early in 1928 worked like preludes to his main spiritual experience of this year. It occurred in Tannbach, and that fact too is of importance. For while the first three places were once occupied by Roman soldiers or at least traversed by them, Tannbach lay completely outside the old Roman sphere of influence. On 8 April 1928 here in Tannbach Ludwig Polzer had the following experience:

> On 8 April in Tannbach, on awakening I had the following experience: It was like a picture in the mist. I saw myself sitting in a chair of an unclear type, bent forward and anxious for the empire; that is how I felt it. Two other people were there; sometimes they lifted their hands as if in greeting or in agreement. As the picture faded, I heard a thunderous voice call 'Hadrian!'
>
> I had never before thought of Hadrian. This was why I found the voice and its call so remarkable.[361]

Let us look a little closer at this picture that Polzer describes. It came at the time when Polzer's deep comparison between Rudolf and Nero reached its conclusion. The book that had resulted from this work was complete, although not yet printed. A year earlier, between 6 and 11 April he had lived through 'five beautiful days with Agrippina and Elisabeth'. And now, exactly a year later, came this dream-picture of Hadrian accompanied by the mighty call, like a call to awaken.

If Polzer had 'never before' thought of Hadrian, that does not of course mean that he heard the name of Hadrian for the first time in this dream. He would certainly have become acquainted with him at his high school in Graz, and Rudolf Steiner had mentioned him several times in private conversations; indeed, to Polzer's question why he kept referring to this Roman period, he had even emphasized: 'Because it directly concerns you!' That had been in March 1925. Only now, through his experience in Tannbach, did Polzer feel disposed to go into the matter.

What conjured up this picture before Polzer's soul? From where did the powerful call come? Was this call to his dreaming consciousness from a space adjoining that of actual history to awaken him to the background of his own destiny after he had sought to awaken to what lay in the destinies of others? Questions remain which could only be answered through supersensible knowledge.

Do we not all have dreams relating to what lies in our destiny? Indeed, 'dream' is a word used too often. We are mostly deeply asleep in this sphere. Polzer may often have inwardly been in this state. But now, at one stroke, he had been raised from dull sleep to dreaming of destiny. And now he even decided to awaken from this dreaming.

He wrote: 'In the following period I occupied myself much with Hadrian and read what Gregorovius wrote about him.'[362] The historian known above all for his *Geschichte der Stadt Rome* [History of the City of Rome] had written in his younger days a work that appeared in 1851: *Gemälde der römisch-hellenischen Welt zur Zeit des Kaisers Hadrian* [A Portrait of the Roman-Hellenistic World at the Time of the Emperor Hadrian].[363] Only after that did Gregorovius travel for the first time to the Eternal City that he had described and went on to become *the* writer of its classical history. His book on Hadrian became for him in his own words 'the pathfinder to Rome'. Now Gregorovius' work became Ludwig Polzer's historical pathfinder to Hadrian. This is a remarkable phenomenon, of symptomatic interest in itself.

Polzer did not want to learn only outer historical facts through reading Gregorovius. He was looking for outer correspondences for what he had seen and heard in the experience he had had in Tannbach. 'In one place [in the book],' he wrote, 'it seemed to me that there was a link to what I had seen in the picture in the mist.' For one who knows this work on Hadrian there will be little doubt about which (unmentioned) passage Polzer had in mind. It is the following, which relates to the last year of Hadrian's life; he died on 10 July 138 AD:

> After the Emperor had travelled through his Empire, he found himself again in the palace of the Caesars, tired, aged, and joyless. He continued building his villa at Tibur [Tivoli]; he built his own burial site in Rome. His life's task was complete. With growing illness, he became embittered. *His concern to give the Empire a successor pressed upon him*; for like all emperors before him, with the one exception of Vespasian, Hadrian too had no children of his own.[364]

The question of the imperial succession was a grave concern for the Emperor; he finally adopted Antoninus Pius and demanded that he in turn should appoint the then 17-year-old Marcus Aurelius (his brother) as his successor. With this, Hadrian presented Rome with two of its very best emperors and in doing so, he extended the beneficence of his own reign, so to speak, well beyond his own death. 'Of all his innumerable good deeds, this was the greatest', judged Gregorovius.

The task of adoption weighed heavily upon Hadrian at the end of his reign. He himself had come to power through being adopted by his predecessor and uncle, the Emperor Trajan. It is therefore of symptomatic interest in Polzer's destiny when we come across the motif of adoption in his own life in relation to his aunt, even if this may only appear to be of outer importance.

Through his reading of Gregorovius his inner experience was linked to what was provided by history. Polzer's gateway to Hadrian's achievement was to be found in the last years of the Emperor, who by then had already completed his life's task. Polzer's new preoccupation with Hadrian thus from the beginning had the character of an investigation to clarify a piece of *the past*. With great inner composure he moved from the observation of Nero and Agrippina to that of Hadrian. The fact that his Hadrian experience occurred outside the old boundaries of Roman influence is like a real symbolic sign that the individuality who was once so strongly bound up with Rome had become in his ongoing development very free of anything Roman and could therefore find the place within himself to view the Roman past *in freedom*. Something of Polzer's free view of Emperor Hadrian will be presented later.

Shortly after his Tannbach experience, Polzer spent a week at Mariensee. It can be assumed that he told Dora Schenker of his awakening dream; for why not? It related indirectly to the work on the field of Roman studies that the two friends had been labouring at for the past year. The guestbook entry for 22 April reads: 'Growing understanding of the nature of the ancient Mysteries'. Had the Tannbach experience been the stimulus that led to this theme? Rudolf Steiner had named Hadrian as one of the Roman Caesars who had been initiated in the Greek Mysteries.[365] It is certain that Hadrian spent time at Eleusis to this effect.

★

The course of Polzer's outer life ran on in routine activities. In May (1928) he travelled to Stuttgart for discussions with the Orient-Occident Publishing Company, which was to publish *Das Mysterium der europäischen Mitte*. He went to the theatre with Menny Lerchenfeld, saw Theodora Zeissig and the daughters of Dr Reichart from Pistyan who were attending the Waldorf School in Stuttgart. More reassuring news came from Josef in Prague, where he was working in an anthroposophical company.

In the same month Polzer travelled with Dora Schenker and her daughter Sabine to Belgrade where, at the invitation of friends in the circle of Dr Korać, he was to give seven lectures.

It was decided to travel down the Danube which, on the one hand, Polzer saw as a 'good preparation' for his lecturing work and because 'on the other hand [he] wanted to deepen the experiences he would gain in Belgrade under the impression through observation of the changing landscape along the Danube during the two and a half day-long return journey.'[366]

Belgrade was known as *Singidunum* in Roman times and lay in the province of Moesia, which, along with Pannonia and Dacia, was a favourite province of Hadrian. His initiation had opened the eyes of this peaceful emperor to the fact that the culture of the future would have to develop northeast of the Rhine and the Danube. And so, on his repeated wanderings through his empire on which he stayed for longer periods in Greece and Egypt, he had always returned via the future-bearing provinces of eastern Europe.

And was the spirit of the East not wafting strongly and yet also gently around the small group of travellers on this journey along the Danube?

Yet it was not only the spirit of the East from the future that was wafting towards the travellers; the shadow of the powerful, still existent Roman Empire in the form of the Roman Church showed itself forcefully. On the way along the great river to Budapest, the town of Gran [Esztergom, Hungary] became visible far in the distance. 'The image of the Roman Church militant appeared on a powerful site [on the riverside] in the dome of the Cathedral,' Polzer wrote in his account of the journey. 'It is a monumental statement of the Roman Catholic victory over the West.'[367] On the journey to Budapest Polzer read the drama *Tököly* by Tobias Gottfried Schröer, who was very awake to this Roman shadow, as his poetry shows. His father had once said 'from the depths of his soul': 'Middle Europe must not be Roman'; and now, on his Danube journey, this saying seemed to rise up from the depths of Polzer's own soul, for this truth lived in him no less deeply anchored than in both the Schröers. 'Still less must this be so in Eastern Europe', he could have added to the words of Schröer.

In *Das Mysterium der europäischen Mitte*, which was published at this time, Polzer wrote about the developmental needs of the Middle region of Europe as well as about the dangers that gravely threatened them, and his words reached far beyond the catastrophe of the Second World War which he foresaw, on into our own time and even into an as yet unbroached future.

During and immediately after this time [of the Second World War], the attempt will be made in monastic teaching centres to hammer radical intellectualism in a religious and scientific way into young people of the west, even with occult methods, in order to make them into organs of a mighty European superstate. The domination of this 'holy' Roman Empire[368] will not be able to last long. But then a time will come in which people will reflect; they will seek advice there, where reliable, steadfast hearts will have maintained the Mystery wisdom of the future in relation to birth and death [. . .] In Mystery centres human beings will learn to master situations and keep alive possibilities of founding new, life-enhancing, really social forms. Spiritual beings will work together creatively with human beings in these Mystery centres.[369]

So that the peoples of Middle Europe, who, among others, include Germans, Austrians, Swiss, Czechs, Slovaks, Serbs, Hungarians and Poles and who are disposed to individualization, are able to develop freely, the region of the European Middle must be kept free of all spiritual or economic servitude. Of the specific developmental tasks of this Middle European region between East and West, Polzer wrote the following:

The Middle of Europe is a Mystery space. It requires of people that they conduct themselves accordingly in regard to it. The path of the cultural epoch in which we live leads from the West to the East through this space. *In it the old must undergo metamorphosis [. . .] All old forces lose themselves on this path to the East, they cannot pass further through this space without renewing themselves out of the spirit.* If they seek to do so, they become forces of destruction and give rise to catastrophes. It is in this space which, from human knowledge, human love, and human courage, that must come about which may then proceed in a healing way towards the East.[370]

Accompanied silently and faithfully by these, his own thoughts, which would soon be presented to the public, Polzer travelled down the Danube, on 'the waters of renewal' towards the goal of his journey.

★

On 23 June 1928, in the presence of representatives of the government of Burgenland and many friends, Ludwig Polzer unveiled a memorial plaque in Neudörfl for his teacher Rudolf Steiner. Steiner had spent his child-hood and early adolescence in the station building in the small town. From here he walked daily to the high school in nearby Wiener Neustadt, crossing the River Leitha, the boundary between Transleithania and Cisleithania. The address which Polzer gave on this ceremonial occasion, both warm and at the same time deep, was printed in his Prague Notes. It is noteworthy that the move to erect such a plaque came from the government!

After a period of rest in Mariensee, which was not far away, and where his article about the recent Danube trip was probably written, Polzer travelled to Dornach with Dora Schenker and Margrit Schön, an anthroposopher whom he had met at the conference in Budapest in August of the previous year. From there Polzer, Margrit Schön and Sophie Lerchenfeld travelled to London, where at the initiative of D.N. Dunlop a *World Conference* was to be held.

Polzer saw many familiar and unfamiliar faces here in London. From the Continent came his friend Walter Johannes Stein, Eugen Kolisko and Friedrich Rittelmeyer, to name but three who had been invited to speak at the conference. On 27 July Polzer gave, in German, a lecture he had written out; it was titled 'Middle Europe from the spiritual scientific perspective'. The lecture was a splendid extract from Polzer's spiritual efforts to understand the present and future tasks of Middle Europe and also from the deepened review of his life that he had made in 1928 in the most intense way.

In London Polzer embedded his considerations of the European Middle within a broad overview of Post-Atlantean cultural development. In powerful, striking sentences he characterized the fourth, Greco-Roman epoch, and he slipped in some objective self-knowledge, when he said:

> Let us look for example at the mysterious Roman Emperor Hadrian, who was more of a Greek and an Oriental than a Roman. How he sought to resurrect the beauty of Greece and the grandeur of Egypt! In his soul there was a horror of Roman plainness and lack of fantasy; he knew it must finally end up in a dark, harsh age, lacking in culture. Without insight into the cosmic event on Golgotha that was even the correct perspective of the future, filled with a justified sense of tragedy. Concern for the future lived in him at the end of his life, for the future of the former beauty and wisdom in the world. This decline and twilight of spiritual beings in human consciousness could not be stopped; it was a developmental necessity. But now the time has come when the spiritual background of the world must again be perceived, which will reveal itself to clairvoyant consciousness as a fullness of beings.[371]

Hadrian thus became for Polzer a special eyepiece for the understanding of the entire Greco-Roman cultural epoch and of the new, future age of the Mysteries in the European Middle that was already preparing itself, latent within that earlier epoch.

This region of the European Middle had, according to his idea of it, first of all to solve the great problem of nationalities and not through territorial divisions as has been practised until today, but on the basis of spiritual-scientific knowledge of the nature of peoples and time spirits. For the middle European picture shows us how it would be if the folk spirits would, as it were, give advice in the spiritual world in order to bring mankind that is differentiated in various peoples to a higher stage, to entrust them to guidance by higher beings who can lead them to harmonization. *One sets oneself against the will of the world if one wants to enforce national divisions in Middle Europe.*[372] It will never be attainable and will bring about only confusion. But there are powers who seek this confusion, and who place it in the service of their goals. From the enormous affliction which must result from such attempts to defy the gods, human beings will have to be roused for what is actually necessary.

In *Das Mysterium der europäischen Mitte*, Polzer expanded on this:

> Every single human being today stands before the threshold of the spiritual world; the challenge will be made to many of them to cross that threshold rightfully, not through the means of a dark occultism. Human soul processes always show themselves outwardly in the events of historical life. *The region of Middle Europe contains a threshold problem in that it is charged with the task of solving the nationalities problem on the basis of spiritual insight. This middle region of Europe will yet cause the rest of mankind many anxieties, because until now there has been so little inclination to listen to what world development requires.*[373]

The course of events since the time those words were written appear to give them an even greater weight.

Polzer was happily surprised to see among the faces of the audience at his lecture in London that of Blanche Tollemache! She had travelled from the country just to hear him. 'Such examples of friendship from old times,' he wrote in 1939, 'go deep into my heart and even today when I think of it, I am filled with gratitude and a particular melancholy.'[374]

The experiences in England were worked on further in Pistyan, where he was accompanied by Sophie. As usual, he visited the grave of his father in Modern. A visit was made too to the 'Harmonie' and its manager Frau Nerad. In Pistyan Polzer also prepared the lecture he was to give at the opening ceremony of the second Goetheanum at Michaelmas.

From Pistyan he sent an outline of his Michaelmas lecture to Albert Steffen, the President of the Vorstand of the Anthroposophical Society. Under the title 'Mysteries, Exoteric and Esoteric Christianity', the introduction states: 'Anthroposophical consideration of the past must serve to master the situation of the present spiritually and enable us to find our way into the future in accordance with the will of the world.' Further aphoristic indications included the following: 'Consideration of the Transition from Pre-Christian Mysteries to Exoteric Christianity'— 'Hadrian and the Reception of Exoteric Christianity through the Greek Folk Spirit'—'The Preparation of the Middle European Space' etc.

In August Polzer was in St Veit following the inauguration of the 'Tobias-Schröer Branch' by Hemma and Sigrid Wurzer. Shortly afterwards, at the beginning of September, we find Polzer in Stuttgart. He read through the final corrections to his book at the Orient-Occident publishing house. There was also an important meeting with Menny Lerchenfeld, as we learn from a letter Polzer wrote to her on 9 September from Tannbach. He recommended the 18-year-old, who had a career as a pianist before her, to read *Consuelo* by George Sand. It was a book that had played a great role in his own life and that he now 'after 40 years' himself wanted to read again. Then he wrote to Menny:

> In the next few days I am going to Mariensee. There I have the most peace and quiet to prepare my work [for the Michaelmas lecture in Dornach], fresh air and I am not too bothered by daily concerns. *For the Michaelmas conference lecture something new should be brought and one only gets that when the soul is calm.*[375]

He stayed for two weeks at Mariensee. He wrote up his lecture with the title 'Mysteries, Exoteric and Esoteric Christianity' or dictated it to Dora Schenker to type. The typewritten form with some handwritten comments by Polzer's hand has fortunately survived. We can thus have a very exact picture of the lecture that he presented at the Michaelmas Conference in Dornach, even if he did not, apparently, read it out exactly as written. He reworked it in 1929 and had it published in the February (1930) issue of the magazine *Die Drei* under the title 'Exoteric and Esoteric Christianity'. It is included in that form in the appendix of this book.

In the introduction to the lecture he speaks about the change in the lives of Steiner's pupils that the death of their teacher brought and describes the consequences of Steiner's death for his own strivings. 'I saw myself [...] above all pointed to the question of destiny,' he wrote, 'I had to reflect now in conscientious imaginative review [Rückschau] in time and through observation around me in space.' Do we not recognize in this statement the first three stages of true self-knowledge or at least the first and the third stages? At a time moreover, when Polzer finally began to raise his life's path to the fourth stage, where self-knowledge becomes all-encompassing world-knowledge.

Polzer's work was borne by two supports: an iron faithfulness to spiritual knowledge and an unshakeable confidence in the spiritual form of his teacher. He could thus say to himself:

> Put every form of Philistinism aside and trust that with the help of Rudolf Steiner's instructions weaknesses can gradually be overcome. Do not let yourself be lamed by comfort and the fearmongering question: 'Am I

worthy enough?' and keep advancing with the task that, with the knowledge and aid of Rudolf Steiner, you have set for yourself.

What did he learn from his orienting observation of the environment around him? Polzer put it like this:

'In space I saw in those difficult years the outer shell of the new Goetheanum [. . .] arising, and it became a source of confidence. In my review I saw Rudolf Steiner working on the Mystery Centre that was the First Goetheanum and on the Group of the Representative of Man.' In connection to a true knowledge of space, the following words of his teacher were decisive for Polzer: 'The geography of the Earth is also full of secrets.' For the pupil that meant: 'All previous cultural epochs show this, and the following Post-Atlantean epochs will also show it.'

Polzer handled his comprehensive theme in such a way that he sought to portray Rudolf Steiner's statements about exoteric and esoteric Christianity in connection with the Greek, Roman and Celtic Folk Spirits by means of a very concrete historical example; with the goal 'of making the contemporary situation more comprehensible and of directing anthroposophical activity towards it and on the other hand, of orienting our thinking towards the future'. In this he was attempting 'out of a deepening [of understanding] of the transition from the old mysteries to exoteric Christianity, to produce a guide for the times of the returning Mysteries'. He added: 'I was then helped by the fact that spiritually, an historical personality appeared before my soul; a fleeting image of a situation of an hist.[orical] personality revealed itself.' By this he meant the Tannbach experience of 8 April.

Polzer then describes in broad strokes the passage of the Post-Atlantean cultural epochs. He shows how the third epoch, the Egyptian, repeated at a higher stage what happened in the Lemurian period—the separation of the sexes. Egyptian culture thereby represents the male spiritual pole which therefore had to allow itself to be extended and fructified by the more female spirituality of the cultures of Chaldea and Babylon with their star wisdom.

What is meant by male and female spirituality? What Polzer details, especially in *Mysterium der europäischen Mitte*, can be briefly outlined here: while male spirituality strives in relative spiritual passivity to gain control of the earthly plane and develops art and science, the more active female spirituality is inclined to unite itself intuitively with the divine-spiritual; it was from this that the ancient wisdom of the priesthood developed. One is therefore dealing here with a *spiritual* differentiation within humanity which was developing during the third cultural epoch, a differentiation which is not to be equated with the *physical* differentiation of the sexes that had already developed during the Lemurian period, but rather, represents a metamorphosis of that. In the Bible this polarity appears to us as that between the streams that stem from Cain and Abel. The 'Temple Legend' that gave rise to Freemasonry also comes from this polarity, which will be overcome in the future.

This spiritual duality shows itself also in the Greek and Roman epochs in which the female spiritual pole determined more the Greek culture and the male spiritual pole prevailed in the Roman, which tended towards philistine sobriety and conquest of the outer world. 'Rome became the capital of power, while Athens was the capital of the spirit.'

In this Roman culture, the figure of Emperor Hadrian stands before us in the so-called Roman-Hellenistic middle period; he sought with his soul to embrace both poles. Hadrian therefore incorporates

> in a very real way the Greco-Roman cultural epoch [. . .] at the time [. . .] in which the transition from the old Mysteries to exoteric Christianity was taking place. He stands split between *Stoa* and *Gnosis* and therefore always wanted to unite Rome and Greece, which was impossible in any direct fashion. So he stands inwardly divided between two worlds, one declining, the other arising, and can only maintain himself through knowing something from the Mysteries, through sensing a possible future union: he sought 'the Son', who can harmonize, but could not find him [. . .] But [Hadrian] is one of those personalities in whom world forces are working.

Tragedy breaks into Hadrian's life twice: when in 130 he lost his beloved friend and faithful companion Antinous, who drowned under mysterious circumstances in the Nile; and then on a much greater scale, when he, the Emperor of Peace, was forced into a bloody war of annihilation against the Jews who revolted under Bar Kokhba. But apart from that, the 20 year reign of this emperor was marked by strength and harmony.

The Roman Empire had reached its greatest expansion under Emperor Trajan. Hardly had Hadrian come to power when he set out on a very different course from his great predecessor. He soon abandoned the conquests in Parthia (Iran) and 'wanted to benefit and consolidate his empire'. Stronger still than his sense for beauty and art was his love of peace. 'Hadrian worked in a cosmopolitan way; he was the first to depart from the policy of differentiating peoples. He treated Rome and the provinces equally [. . .] This is clear from his sensing of future development in the North [of Europe]', therefore in those Germanic regions which had not been under Rome's heel, regions which included the later Bohemia, the very heart of Europe's middle region. 'He sees the task of the future less in the Orient, to which all his love nevertheless belongs; his duty he sees in Europe. He is, therefore, the Emperor who was the first to *recognize the significance of the European Middle and who prepares this middle region.*'[376]

It was precisely in this direction that Ludwig Polzer-Hoditz continued the work of this emperor in a unique spiritual-historical manner. In the year 1928 this continuity, in which his own striving stood, awakened to consciousness within him and was recognized.

★

The year 1928 thus came to play a key role in Polzer's life. It was the year in which the main motif of his life—the European Middle—blossomed in the finest way and at the same made visible its root in a Roman past.

Like a crowning of everything that had happened in this year, *Das Mysterium der europäischen Mitte* finally appeared as a book on 17 December.

Noteworthy too is the fact that only a few weeks before another important book was published by Amalthea Verlag in Vienna. This too concerned itself with the European Middle and with an Emperor. It was Arthur Polzer's work—*Kaiser Karl—aus der Geheimmappe seines Kabinettschefs* [Emperor Karl—From the Secret Files of His Cabinet Director]. For Ludwig Polzer it was significant that 'at the same time as my book, my brother's also [...] appeared, which in the appendix published the Memorandum which I brought him from Dr Steiner in July 1917'.[377] Thus, with the publication of the main works of the two dissimilar yet similar brothers, ended the year that fell exactly midway between 1911, the year in which Ludwig Polzer's 'earnest commitment to Dr Rudolf Steiner' was made and 1945, the year of his death.

As dissimilar were the two brothers, so the fates met by their books were also dissimilar. Arthur's book quickly found a strong and widespread echo in the Press. In the 1980s it was republished by Amalthea Verlag and still figures in the bibliography of most works about the end of the Austro-Hungarian Empire. In general, it was very favourably received, apart from a few critical voices in the Hungarian Press. It also received attention outside Europe. The *New York Times Book Review* did a long article on it on 30 December 1928 which carried the tendentious title 'Even a Hapsburg Can Be Human'. At a time when the unceasing plan of certain Anglo-American circles to destroy the Habsburg and Hohenzollern monarchies had, with the help of treacherous forces within Central Europe, finally become reality, even here in the West one could afford to show a smug historical interest in the figure of the last Habsburg Emperor.

It was a very different story for *Ludwig* Polzer's book.

After a stay in Belgrade where he gave lectures and held Class Lessons between 27 December 1928 and January 1929 at the home of Vitomar Korać and after a trip to Venice with Sophie, following his lectures in Belgrade, he arrived at Mariensee on 15 January. He wrote as follows about what then occurred:

> Soon after my arrival at Mariensee, I received a very unfriendly letter from Marie Steiner on account of my book; she demanded its withdrawal. That was impossible, as about 600 copies had already gone public. There followed very unpleasant correspondence between us, because I had told her before publication everything that I had been intending with the book; she then claimed to have forgotten it.[378]

Marie Steiner above all took objection to Chapter IV of Polzer's book, in which he investigates the karmic relationship between Crown Prince Rudolf and Nero and on the basis of a lecture by Rudolf Steiner that was still unpublished. 'Besides the copies that were already out,' writes Polzer,

> I had about 200 in my possession which I gradually gave out to friends. Two parties had formed at that time, one for my book and the other against. Frau Marie Steiner had been influenced from a certain quarter to do what she did; unfortunately, due to other misunderstandings later, this situation was the beginning of further estrangement.[379]

Among those who shared Marie Steiner's disapproval of Polzer's book was also his friend in Prague, Julie Klima, as an unpublished diary of hers attests. Whoever Polzer meant by the 'certain quarter', he was still not saying eleven years later, when he wrote the comments above. But several years after the appearance of this book in 1994, documents were found which throw more light on the reasons for and the background to this sorry affair: a seven-sided letter of Polzer's of 12 February 1929 to the Vorstand of the General Anthroposophical Society and a brief reply by Marie Steiner to him of 12 March, in which she comments on Polzer's letter in the form of remarks in the margins. Both documents are reproduced in the appendix of the present volume.

These writings show that Marie Steiner believed that the part of the book that related to karma and which was based on Rudolf Steiner's Nero lecture had not been sufficiently contextualized beforehand, whereas Polzer felt the opposite. Yet this is only the outer skin of the matter.

After commenting on the outer objections of the publisher and Marie Steiner, towards the end of his letter to the Vorstand, Polzer notes that:

Those are the outer circumstances in relation to the book. *But there are deeper perspectives which led me to write the book as I did, and also there are more deeply rooted factors that lead some people to be opposed to the book.* [Emphasis THM] I shall, however, refrain from bringing those forward now.

Polzer then adds: 'At any rate, it is my conviction that an anxiety, perhaps a fear, that is forever showing itself has no place in the Anthroposophical Society. It would be the worst thing imaginable after the death of Dr Steiner.'

The 'deeper perspectives' in the writing of the book of course had to do with Polzer's own karmic connection to Rome, which he naturally could not speak about directly. What he meant by the 'more deeply rooted factors that led to opposition to the book' is not so easy to clarify, and to this author's knowledge, Polzer never said anything more about it. It may have related to difficulties that had appeared in other human relationships, that is, meeting certain far-reaching karmic experiences of individualities with openness and respect. The difficulties, in a certain sense also those named by Polzer as anxiety or fear, in taking up Steiner's impulse of karmic revelation at the Christmas Conference in an earnest and worthy manner, would play a decisive role in the conflicts of 1935. In a way that was a prelude to the events of 1935, they appear to have played into the resistance against the spread of Polzer's book.

After he himself, and on the basis of his own karmic roots in Rome in the second century, had boldly taken up an important piece of his teacher's karmic history research and carefully worked at it, there came this wide-spread reserve or anxiety about concrete karmic knowledge even among prominent members of the Vorstand. In this sense the affair about *Das Mysterium der europäischen Mitte* was far more than just a sad episode; it mirrored something of the dramatic struggles around the attainment of a modern historical consciousness, which the reality of karma and reincarnation in concrete ways has to encounter.

Polzer closes his letter with the sentence: 'In conclusion, I must say again, as in my first letter, that I have a good conscience in this matter, resting in Rudolf Steiner.' That he was able, *despite everything*, to accept with such calmness the rejection of what for him was such an important work shows something of the esoteric-spiritual stature of this man. If he had insisted on his right, he would no longer have been able, in the years that followed, to engage in the conflicts in the Society in the enlightening and mediating manner in which he did. The destiny of the Society was closer to his heart than one of his own works.

February 1929 brought a wintry cold from Siberia. The Danube froze in Austria, which had never before happened in Polzer's lifetime. What a climatic correspondence to the icy reception of his book among many of Steiner's pupils, as well as the cooling of the relationship between him and Marie Steiner which now set in! In view of the evident misunderstandings in their discussions, Polzer decided to yield to Marie Steiner's will in order to prevent what was basically a private misunderstanding from becoming a conflict within the Society. He therefore travelled to Stuttgart in February to discuss matters with the publishing company. It seems that from that point on, no more copies of the book appeared.

He spent the evenings with Sophie and Menny Lerchenfeld; the three of them went to the theatre several times together. Polzer thus gave way in a difficult, painful affair, and went on with his regular lecturing work in Vienna and Prague.

On 15 March he and Berta celebrated her 50th birthday in Tannbach and on the 19th he was in Mariensee again. He made energetic preparations with Sophie for a trip together that he had long had in view; at the beginning of April they set off for *Rome*.

'It was the first time I had been to this great historical city', we learn from his unpublished notes. 'We stayed for six days and all day long we visited all the old splendid sights,' he reported.[380] These doubtless included the old Roman Forum with Trajan's Column that towered above it. From the window of his room in Lotharingerstrasse in Vienna in 1922 he had been able to look directly over to the two copies of this Roman column, which stood in front of the Karlskirche. Now he was standing before the original! This unique construction and work of art had been erected in the year 113 AD. The band of reliefs that winds over 200 metres up the column portrays Trajan's 'heroic' deeds in Dacia (modern Romania).

Polzer and Sophie no doubt visited the Pantheon, one of the most significant buildings of ancient Rome and one which bears the stamp of Hadrian. Not least was it dedicated to the gods of the seven stars; later it served as the model for the dome of St Peters.

The Castel Sant'Angelo—the mausoleum of Hadrian, the top of which today is crowned by a statue of the Archangel Michael and the interior of which contained so much of world history ... how long did the two wanderers stand on the Via Sacra amidst the ruins of the once magnificent double temple of 'Venus and Roma'? Amor-Roma—for the female-male spirituality of Hadrian this was the *whole* of Rome ...

In the Sistine Chapel the two friends met Hans Voith, an anthroposophical industrialist from Heidenheim and his wife. Voith offered to drive Sophie Lerchenfeld and Polzer to Hadrian's villa at Tivoli.

Tivoli! Hadrian had wanted to preserve here his deepest impressions of his travels in architectonic form. And these impressions were closely linked to the motifs of the mystery centres visited by him. We find there an Egyptian Serapis temple, a piece of the temple in Orphic Thessaly, the Lyceum in Athens, the Academy as well as the Maritime Theatre, and the Emperor's living quarters, which were surrounded by a circle of water.

'Hadrian too had within him the thought of a Building of the Word', Rudolf Steiner had said to Polzer after the night of the Goetheanum fire. In the Villa Hadriana Steiner's words may have appeared to Polzer in a new light, and perhaps more below the dome of the Pantheon.

After seven days the two travellers took leave of the Eternal City, as Hadrian had called the first Rome. Above all the powerful impressions towered the mighty Column of Trajan which instead of the original figure of Trajan now carried a statue of Peter with a halo. Pope Sixtus VI had the statue of the saint erected in 1587. Thus at the time of the Counter-Reformation the Roman Church set itself very concretely on the glorious ruin of the Roman Empire. Since that time this has been its true foundation... Before the return journey the two friends visited Naples and Bari for a few days and then returned via Venice to Vienna. With new strength for his work for Middle Europe Polzer returned to the metropolis on the Danube.

> *Strive for thinking Dying into the All*
> *Strive for destiny Resurrection in the I.*

These words which he had already meditated on for a long time had now become reality in a special way. Much of what had been thought had 'died' on this trip to Rome, even his own thoughts about the *Mysterium der europäischen Mitte*, which in this middle had encountered such strong resistance. There was little more to think there either.

What is the value of a book when the author reads in his own I in the book of destiny?

33. Balkan Impressions

Count Polzer celebrated his 60th birthday at Tannbach with Berta and Julius. Dora Schenker also arrived on the day, 23 April. On 30 April Polzer travelled to Mariensee with his benefactress. Here the two friends prepared for another Danube trip. In the middle of May they took the express riverboat *Saturnus* to Rustchuk[*] and from there went on to Sofia by train. The journey passed through Hadrian's favourite region, the former Roman provinces of Pannonia, Moesia and Thrace. 'This Danube trip and the stay in Sofia,' wrote Polzer, 'was one of my loveliest trips.[381] The countryside along the lower Danube already has a very Asiatic character.'

On the return journey they stopped in Belgrade. Polzer stayed this time with Colonel Leo Knispel, who had taken over Mr Kovač's house. A new friendship began. In the years that followed, Polzer would often visit Knispel and his wife Lou for days or weeks at their castle near Split.

At the end of May Polzer attended as usual the annual general meeting of the Austrian national society [of the General Anthroposophical Society] in Vienna. During these days there was little good news about Josef's condition; he was staying in Prague. Via Linz, where he gave Class Lessons, Polzer returned to Tannbach.

Soon after his arrival, the whole area was hit by an unusual cyclone. 'It uprooted trees and flattened the Zauners' large barn as well as a section of the wood. We could hear it coming with a terrible roar beforehand [...] The tiles flew off the roof and all went dark. Julius was very concerned and had much work to do to repair the damage.' It was like a sign of the dark spiritual storm that would soon sweep through Europe...

Meanwhile he had had a long discussion about his brother Arthur's book published in the July issue of Hans-Erhard Lauer's *Österreichische Blätter für freies Geistesleben*. Polzer emphasized the importance of the fact that his brother had decided to publish the Memorandum he had given him in 1917. He wrote at the end of the review:

> As an anthroposopher, I would like to thank the author of the book that in his true, historical documenting of the facts of such an important period as the year 1917 was for Middle Europe, he included *the pearl of the future*.[382] It goes out into the cultural world through this much-read book and reaches valuable circles of people who otherwise, paradoxical as it may sound,

---

[*] In Bulgaria; Rustchuk is the German form of the old Turkish name Rusçuk; the modern Bulgarian name is Ruse—*transl.*

because of the wakefulness of the retarding powers in the world, would never have come across it.

How those 'retarding powers' took care to ensure that precisely the part of the book that dealt with this 'pearl of the future' and everything that related to it, would be left out of the English translation of the book, has already been mentioned several times.

The unintentional simultaneous publication of the books of the two brothers brought them into regular communication with one another again. Arthur was a guest at Mariensee on 22/23 March for the first time, which was a sign of this new closeness.

Polzer went on his second Danube trip of this year (1929) in September. This time he took Berta with him. 'In beautifully hot summer weather' the couple travelled as far as Belgrade. As there were no more cabins available, they stayed the night on deck under the full moon. In Belgrade the summer travellers stayed with Leo Knispel and his wife.

Knispel brought Polzer again together with Dušan Letica, who later became Finance Minister of Yugoslavia. At the time of the Polzers' visit to Belgrade, Letica was thinking of embarking on a tour of inspection through the whole of Yugoslavia lasting several days. He proposed to Polzer that he accompany him. While Berta travelled back again to Tannbach, her husband happily set off on this new, unplanned trip. It was in a 'heavily built Buick' with a chauffeur. 'The roads around Belgrade were still very bad in those days,' Polzer recalled, 'and full of farmers' wagons taking produce to market. Only when we passed from Serbia to Bosnia were the roads in mountainous parts any better.'

On the first day of the journey, they arrived in *Sarajevo*. The town's Turkish market still looked 'almost as in the old days'. For the first time in his life Polzer saw veiled Muslim women and Turkish mosques. He went to the spot where Archduke Franz Ferdinand and his wife Sophie had been murdered on 28 June 1914. 'This place is really a tight spot,' he wrote. This tight spot had something of a real, symbolic character. Had not the whole of humanity been dragged by those murders into a Moloch-like, tight spot of global dimensions that had demanded countless victims? Franz Ferdinand had had a real understanding of the question of the Slavs in the Empire. If he had succeeded Franz Joseph on the throne, the nationality question would have been handled differently than through vain territorial solutions and there would perhaps not have had to be a second Sarajevo tragedy at the end of the century . . .

On the second day of the trip in great heat they went on to *Mostar* where the travellers saw the increasing devastation of wood which only resulted in new karst formation.

The little group travelled to *Dubrovnik* on the third day. 'The descent to the sea and to the old patricians' town is amongst some of the loveliest landscape in Europe,' Polzer still felt, ten years later. As the town was completely full, the Buick tourers stayed the night in the nearby beach resort of Kupary, which was mainly popular with Czech holidaymakers.

At supper Polzer recognized another guest at the resort as Norbert Glas, a young anthroposophical doctor and earlier colleague from the Vienna Vorstand, who was also on an inspection tour. Glas was looking for a suitable site for a new clinic.

On 13 September the group left for Kotor (formerly Cattaro). Polzer experienced a special mood of reminiscence and expectation. 'On this trip,' he wrote, 'there arose within me all those stories I had heard from my dear father. At the beginning of the 60s of the last century my father was himself at the garrison at Cattaro and loved this place very much. He was in charge of overseeing the small fortifications on the border with Montenegro'. Polzer recalled the story his father had told about the murder of the Montenegrin Prince Danilo in 1860 and much else, as if they had been his own experiences. The great love that Julius Polzer had felt at that time for the romantic landscape stirred within him. Indeed, Polzer's trip to Cattaro perhaps released his father from his spiritual space and made him the fourth, invisible member of the small group of travellers . . .

But what kind of view did Cattaro present in 1929? Polzer wrote: 'Today Cattaro is a deserted place. Many palatial houses on the fringes of the area stand empty; once a merchant town for rich people, with a large merchant fleet, today its splendour has disappeared.'

His impressions of the population and the officials they encountered are also noteworthy: 'The various tax inspectors who accompanied us from one town to the next were warm and friendly men, with whom one could have a very intelligent conversation. For the most part, they were themselves needy and careworn.' Of the population he wrote:

> On the trip we sometimes stopped in small places; there I could see the great poverty of the rural population, I might almost say, the dying out of a rural culture through the excessive foundation of towns which then only become parasitic in various ways. Dalmatia, especially the southern part, has a good warm climate, where the poverty is not so evident.

On the afternoon of the same day they travelled on to *Cetinje*, the former capital of Montenegro. In a collision with a truck on a serpentine mountain road, Polzer broke his right index finger. The decision was taken to have it seen to in Cetinje. Looking back on the following part of the trip, Polzer made the startling observation that 'the view from the Lovcen Road was so splendid that I was able to enjoy it despite my finger'—which was certainly not to be expected, but was characteristic of Polzer's view of life.

In Cetinje the finger was set without the use of anaesthetics. Polzer stayed the night in the town and the next morning was shaved 'more pleasantly and well' than hardly ever before. 'He was a young, brownish Montenegrin,' he wrote, remembering years later still in admiration. 'The blade was perfectly sharp and his sinewy hand remarkably light. How heavy and rough are the hands of such men in our regions, especially when they have done sports.'

Polzer travelled by train back to Belgrade via Herceg-Novi and Sarajevo, while Letica continued the journey without him. Sophie Lerchenfeld, who was living in Belgrade as a eurythmy teacher, met Polzer at the station and accompanied him to the Knispels' home, where he spent the following four weeks until 15 October being 'cared for tenderly'. He 'also held many lectures' and 'enjoyed the lovely autumn'. He was especially happy to look down 'from Kalemegdan [the oldest castle site of the city] and the confluence of the Sava and the Danube, over onto the Hungarian plain where in the evening the sun's fiery red disc would sink'.

On the return journey to Tannbach he made a stop at Hall in the Tyrol where Josef was working under the care of Norbert Glas in his clinic. 'I found him in a reasonably good state of health,' wrote the concerned father in his diary.

★

The last months of 1929 were taken up with lectures in Vienna, Brünn, Prague, St Veit and Linz. He also attended with Menny Lerchenfeld a performance of *Tristan* during a stop in Stuttgart.

But on the last day of the year he was again in Belgrade, the old Singidunum in the Roman province of Moesia, where Sophie Lerchenfeld was waiting for him. In the home of the Knispels he gave a New Year lecture before the lit Christmas tree in front of many guests. Sophie was there too; her own lodgings were nearby.

It was not only the old year that was ending; a dear friendship would now also have to end in its old form. In Belgrade Sophie had fallen in love with a young, poetically gifted anthroposopher from Montenegro, Aleksander Račeta. Polzer's broken finger on his trip in just that place, Montenegro, feels like a prologue to the soul change which was now demanded of him . . .

Sophie's fatherly friend immediately recognized what her meeting with the romantic Montenegrin meant: 'I felt that this was a destiny meeting, which would bring an end to our companionship.'

The Christmas tree was brought to Sophie's room after Polzer's lecture and there the two friends celebrated 'their last Christmas together and the last days of our lovely 12-year-long companionship', as Polzer wrote in 1939. 'They were heavy days for me and also for Sophie.'

But the painful experience changed in a review of the rich years of their friendship. 'She had stood by me despite repeated difficulties with her parents,' Polzer wrote gratefully.

> She wrote for me, helped me on our trips, loved all those who were close to me and felt close to my dead father. My mother and my aunt Mathilde also loved her; Berta invited her many times and often spent much time together with her without me. *Rudolf Steiner was also happy to see us together when we came to Dornach.*[383] There was never a shadow over our companionship.

When Polzer saw that the friend of his heart, who perhaps knew him more deeply than anyone else around him at that time, really loved someone with whom she perhaps also wanted to unite herself for the rest of her life, he resigned himself with all his strength so that in his soul and spirit, he could let her go free. '*For me the freedom of the other is really the holiest thing that I know and especially in the spiritual sense,*'[384] he had written a year earlier in a letter to Sophie's sister Menny.

Without too many words, the Knispels helped to lighten Polzer's heavy days. On 14 January 1930 'with a heavy heart he took leave' of Sophie and travelled to Budapest where he had lectures and Class Lessons to give. And it was natural for the spiritual student and meditator that:

> despite my heavy soul mood the anthroposophical work had to go on. Precisely at such times one must show that the anthroposophical work is the most important and that through it, despite heavy hours, days and weeks, one can find equilibrium again.

During his stay in Budapest he visited ex-Minister Nagy, but recorded nothing of their conversation.

Margrit Schön, who saw to his outer needs, arranged for him to stay in a hotel named *Pannonia*. Would it be surprising that in his room in this hotel while preparing his lectures he reminisced on his bond of destiny with Sophie Lerchenfeld? 'Pannonia'—the name awakened memories of 'ancient, unnameable days' ...

Polzer's Balkan impressions thus closed with a real break in his soul life, which can hardly be understood when one only looks at the surface of what, considered in a purely outer sense, were events of such a kind that also occur in the lives of other people. That something that lay deeper was here making itself felt was shown in what happened after he took his departure from Sophie. Polzer travelled from Budapest to Prague where he was to hold more lectures. In Prague he received a letter from Sophie in which she 'made clear [to him] that she wanted to marry Aleksander Račeta'.

Polzer wrote:

> Now something happened that was quite astounding in terms of destiny. The letter was addressed to Frau Professor Hauffen, with whom I usually stayed [in Prague]; this time I was staying at the Hotel zum Blauen Stern [The Blue Star]. I had visited Frau Hauffen and received the letter from her. On the way to the hotel I opened it and read it as I walked. It was so sweetly written that my heart felt twice as heavy, I almost staggered on the street, my eyesight became blurred, but I walked on with my head bowed. Suddenly I had to stop and lifted my head, and found that in the window of an art shop I was looking directly at a large reproduction of the head of Antinous.

Exactly 1800 years had gone by since Antinous, the youth whom Hadrian loved and who constantly accompanied him, drowned in the Nile in October 130, and now, with Sophie's farewell letter in his hands, the image of Antinous arose before Polzer's soul, awakening spirit-remembering. In the same moment that Sophie finally withdrew into the periphery of Polzer's life, there came to him, as if conjured from the periphery of the world—Antinous . . .

Polzer made no further comment on the scene. And so we too do not wish to disturb any reader's impartial considerations with further comment except to make one observation: like the Tannbach experience of 8 April 1928, this both sensory and supersensible experience occurred in a place where no Roman foot had ever trodden.

Polzer's soul was able to breathe out in Prague in the company of Julie Klima. He then travelled to Mariensee, where Dora Schenker looked after him lovingly, for he 'mostly lay in bed, as his heart sometimes gave way rather'. Letters passed between Belgrade and Mariensee that have not survived.

On 29 January 1930 Sophie became engaged and thereby entered upon a new life that was fully her own. There would of course be other meetings but only on the other side of this deep-rooted, second farewell.

34. Polzer's Two Memoranda and their Consequences

The idea of a United States of Europe that had been taken up and propagated by Richard Coudenhove-Kalergi received a new impulse in 1929. Coudenhove had personally striven for years to influence the statesmen of Europe in favour of his cause, thus far in vain, or so it seemed. Now, in July 1929, the French Foreign Minister Aristide Briand made it publicly known that he would make an effort to work in line with this unifying idea. At one stroke the far-reaching goal of the Pan-Europa movement became known throughout the world.

In September 1929 the first unofficial Pan-Europa conference was held under the auspices of a meeting of the League of Nations in Geneva; 27 government representatives took part. The Pan-European idea was generally acknowledged by European statesmen, for example, by the German Foreign Minister Stresemann and his Czech counterpart Beneš. Only Britain held off from such acknowledgment, while Italy was sceptical. Briand was given the task of drawing up a memorandum.

One may recall that an integral part of Coudenhove's initiative had been and remained the exclusion from Pan-Europa of Russia and Britain—which in view of the world-historical necessity of European bridge-building between East and West indicated in this book was erroneous in the highest degree. Furthermore, Britain itself made no secret of the fact it preferred to work towards European unity from outside rather than from inside.

On 15 February 1930 Winston Churchill was quoted in an article of his titled 'The United States of Europe' as follows:

> The resurrection of the Pan-European idea is generally identified with Count Coudenhove [...] Let Russia, as Count Coudenhove proposes, sink back into Asia and let the British Empire, which is excluded from his plan, fulfil its own worldwide ideal [...] *But we have our own dream and our own task. We are with Europe but not of it.*[385]

In accordance with old tradition, this Briton preferred to rely on the continental game of the balance of power.

Polzer watched the Pan-Europa wave carefully and followed it with growing interest. In September 1929 a critical article about Pan-Europa by him had appeared in the magazine *Anthroposophie*. He still had a lively memory of the beginnings of the movement in 1922 in Vienna. He spoke about Pan-Europa perhaps with Adolf Waldstein, the old friend from his youth, when he visited him in March 1930 and they refreshed their memories; and very probably also with Dušan Letica, whom he met on the street in Vienna by chance at the end of the month. Pan-Europa, amongst other topics, was certainly discussed when he spent two weeks in May at the Knispels' Villa in Kambelovac. He arrived in Split on 15 May. Leo Knispel picked him up and took him to the villa which had been built on a rather exposed site on the coast.

On 17 May, 'Pan-Europa day', Briand's memorandum appeared in the international Press and drew worldwide reactions. It called for the purely political unification of Europe and its integration as such into the League of Nations; it postulated the primacy of politics over the economy. Briand's Memorandum wished to see the principle of the nation state continue to exist completely unchanged. Even Coudenhove himself was disappointed by his supporter, as he writes in his memoirs.[386]

While Polzer was enjoying excursions in the area with Leo Knispel, who shortly before had resigned from his post as Skoda's agent in Yugoslavia, so in the Roman town of Salona, where excavations were then going on, Polzer himself began to 'think about a political Memorandum because those in high positions in the various States ought to be made aware of the threefolding of the social organism'.[387]

That was *his* reaction to the Briand Memorandum that many people found unsatisfactory and yet which once again made the theme of 'European Unity' a hot topic.

On 8 July 1930 Polzer wrote as follows about this Memorandum: 'The Memorandum [...] sprang from a deep urge to try once again to recall to the minds of leading personalities the warnings of Rudolf Steiner. I felt as though apocalyptic times were about to begin.'[388]

After the Annual General Meeting of the Austrian Anthroposophical Society in Vienna, Polzer arrived in Mariensee on 10 June. Here the completed version of the text he had written at the Villa Gambi was typed up by Dora Schenker. Polzer wrote in the Mariensee guestbook: 'Chancellery of the highest concern in connection with the whole of Europe.' Dora Schenker helped in drawing up a list of the addresses of about 80 prominent statesmen to whom Polzer then sent his memorandum, accompanied by a personal letter.

The large format, four-sided memorandum bore the title:

Memorandum

I.   *Helplessness in Europe and useless efforts to provide solutions*
II. *The necessary new shape of Europe required by the development of mankind*
III. *Possibilities of realization*

The title page carried the comment: 'This Memorandum is communicated confidentially to a number of leading personalities, especially in Middle Europe.'

Polzer introduces the first part as follows:

> Much has been said in Europe about the decline of western culture. The difficulties of daily life, especially in Middle Europe, have increased immeasurably. The means applied to relieve these difficulties have only worsened them still more. The way out, which is sought through loans,[389] works like a lethal poison in the social organism. Life problems are seen only as financial and juridical issues. The dominant habits of thought, which damaged the peoples of Europe by plunging them into the war merely for the benefit of a few scheming state machines, have not changed, nothing has been learned. The same thinking operates today on a continental scale that operated earlier on the level of states. Hence the call for a suprastate mechanism, which would, however, only make the powers of the state still more destructive of life.
>
> Today, Europe stands between America and Asia as Middle Europe stood between the western states [England and France] and Russia in 1914. England vacillates undecidedly between America and Europe. [...]
>
> *Pan-Europa, in the way it has been conceived, can at best become the image of a superstate, an organized theatre of war for a mighty conflict between America and Asia.*[390] It remains in debt to America and thereby has become an organ of American will. The possibilities for the lives of the European population who are not dependent on the State will therefore inevitably be further constricted; the peoples of Europe will be sold and sacrificed.
>
> *All the hopes that the European peoples place on America are equally illusionary, as were many of those that were heard in Middle Europe during the war. All the accommodation to America and the attempts to gain its favour are useless, if one does not seek to factor in the role of the Slavs.*[391]

The great support in ideas and material given to the Pan-Europa movement or Coudenhove himself in the 30s and 40s by leading circles in American politics and business—including the *Council On Foreign Relations* and the *Carnegie Foundation*—by itself shows whose interests were actually to be represented through this movement in Europe. It cannot be denied that Coudenhove himself had a certain idealism, albeit flaccid, but this admirer of Wilson's 14 Points operated entirely as an instrument of anti-European interests, while Briand was concerned above all with maintaining France's leading role in a united Europe.

'The rescue of European culture [...] is impossible,' the second part of Polzer's memorandum goes on, 'if, on the one hand, the will for a free spiritual life not privileged by the State, and on the other hand, the will for a world economy independent of political and state life do not become fact.'

After a clear, succinct characterization of the idea of threefolding and its creator Rudolf Steiner, Polzer emphasizes in the concluding part of his memorandum the complete uselessness of hoping for impulses of cultural renewal from old state institutions:

> European culture and civilization can never be rescued through old, exhausted social institutions [...] Preparations for the new should never simply be thrown open straightaway for public discussion.
>
> The beginning of the new social order, that is, the last possibility to save European culture, and with it that of humanity, from the most colossal catastrophes, could only come about if a few leading figures from all the Middle European states were to meet and join together unofficially—men with a higher level of insight into the most pressing necessities—and if, beyond all formalities of state, diplomacy and bureaucracy, they were able to discuss a free, common will impulse. These would then have to work within their States in accordance with this goal.
>
> If this does not happen, then only after the most dreadful catastrophes in which the largest part of the European population will fall victim, will the thoughts laid down in this Memorandum nevertheless come about in later times.

★

This memorandum of Polzer's was, until today, as far as we know, the only attempt made after Steiner's death to awaken understanding among leading individuals for the threefolding of the social organism that the times required. The full text has therefore been reproduced in the Appendix to this book.

In the weekly magazine *Anthroposophie*, Hans-Erhard Lauer, Polzer's former colleague on the Austrian *Messenger* and his Vorstand colleague in the Austrian Anthroposophical Society, wrote in 1930: 'Briand comes before Europe today like a second [Woodrow] Wilson [...] But who today treads in the footsteps of Rudolf Steiner?'

Three weeks before the appearance of these words of Lauer's, Ludwig Polzer was on his way to Brünn, where on 18 June he had a meeting with Thomas G. Masaryk, the President of the Republic of Czechoslavakia, 'this caricature of the Austro-Hungarian Dualism'.[392] Masaryk too had been sent Polzer's Memorandum and had soon responded to it. He was in many respects one of the more culturally autonomous statesmen of Europe at that time, if one ignores his original connection to Wilson's 14 Points. Polzer spoke with him for 'almost two hours' and said, more specifically: 'It was one of the finest and spiritually most significant conversations I have had with a political personality.'[393] It was the beginning of further conversations, some oral, some written, that were, in the end, of a quite different kind.

The response to Polzer's Memorandum from the 60 to 70 personalities to whom it had been sent was astonishing: 'I received answers from almost all of them,' he wrote. 'The best reply came from Dr Schacht, President of the German National Bank; even from Mussolini came a short confirmation of receipt. The reply from Minister Herriot was written on very plain paper which showed something of the economies being made in France.'[394]

On 9 July Polzer wrote in his diary: 'It is nevertheless very interesting that through the Memorandum one can finally see whether there is in any Middle European State any capable person with a sense for the needs of the future. Will *any* of them suddenly realize that these are the thoughts that must be translated into action?' And two days later he wrote: 'The respect for the complex, in reality chaotic, apparatus of administration is simply a spiritual sickness—this must be healed if people do not want to die of it.'[395]

On the day after his visit to Masaryk, on returning to Vienna, where he mostly stayed with the Zeissigs, Polzer heard by telegram of the death of his old friend Adolf Waldstein. He had visited him only two months earlier without guessing in the slightest that this would be the last time they would see each other. A remarkable chain of events: through Adolf Waldstein and his father Polzer had experienced a kind of course of private study in a real understanding of life and history. And now the best friend of his youth died at the moment when, once again, through his Memorandum, he became politically active.

Polzer travelled to Hirschberg for the funeral. He met many friends and acquaintances from the old days; also the old Prince von Thurn und Taxis, the owner of Duino who also gladly discussed anthroposophical questions with Polzer.

In July, for the first time since his departure from Belgrade, he met Sophie and her husband Aleksander Račeta in Vienna. They spent an afternoon in the Prater [park] and in the evening went to an organ concert in St Stephanskirche. The following day they went to the Hofburg and Schönbrunn palace.

'Under the pressure of the many things and all the work that happened since, the first pain had disappeared', Polzer wrote in 1939, 'and lovely memories remained.' On 18 July the three friends went to Linz with Berta, who was glad to see Sophie again and to get to know her husband. 'Then we went our separate ways again.'[396]

Following the celebrations for the 800th anniversary of the founding of Gutau, at which Polzer gave a speech, he went again to Vienna. On 13 August he was with Chancellor Schober 'who received me in a very friendly way and discussed my Memorandum with me'.[397] Shortly afterwards in Karlsbad, he had a conversation with the Romanian Minister Popovici, who was at the spa and to whom he presented a copy of his Memorandum. But the impression that the Minister made upon him 'was very unenthusiastic'.[398]

That was for the time being the last step Polzer took in relation to his memorandum. The unofficial meeting of European statesmen with insight that he had been hoping for did not come about. In September 1930 public discussion about Europe receded after Adolf Hitler's NSDAP was able to chalk up a strong increase in its support in elections to the Reichstag.

The autumn of 1930 went by with short trips to Mariensee, St Veit and Prague, mostly in connection with lecturing. On his work in Prague, he wrote: 'The work in Prague and Bohemia was much closer to my destiny than that in other places; that showed itself ever more clearly in the course of time.'[399]

In November he was in Tannbach for a while in order to help look after Julius who needed intensive care following a heavy fall from an apple tree. Both sons were now a cause of concern, as Josef's psychological condition had worsened; he had had to be taken, as mentioned earlier, to Buchenbach near Freiburg-in-Breisgau.

*

There had also been developments in the Anthroposophical Society had also taken forms in 1930 which concerned Polzer greatly, notably the question of a contemporary leadership for the Society. 'I saw,' he wrote in 1939, 'that after the death of Rudolf Steiner something else was demanded of the Society and the Goetheanum than what attempted rather automatically to push itself through against the great destiny.'

Polzer worked out a second, short memorandum that he wanted to bring to the Extraordinary General Meeting at Christmas. He arrived in Dornach a few days before the meeting of the General Secretaries with the Vorstand on 29 November that was to prepare the General Meeting.

He went to see Albert Steffen, who had been the President of the Vorstand since Christmas 1925. He also had a conversation with Marie Steiner before 29 November meeting; this would not have come about had he behaved other than he had at the time of the objections against his book a year earlier.

He wanted to make especially these two individuals acquainted with the content of his short memorandum ahead of the General Meeting. Why? Because he sensed that it was from objections from these two that he would eventually have to reckon.

What did Polzer propose in his memorandum? He himself put it as follows: 'I [...] said that the individual leaders of the Sections should concentrate on their Sections, and that the leadership of the Section for General Anthroposophy'—in which in Rudolf Steiner's time suitability for esoteric schooling in the so-called Class had been left to him alone to determine—

> should for the time being be left unoccupied. The general, merely administrative affairs of the Society should be dealt with by a management office. No Section leader should be able to place himself above other Sections. No authoritarian tone should rule between the individual Section leaders. If things were conducted in this way then help would certainly come from the spiritual world in due course. The pretension to carry the work forward in such a way that the President or another member of the Vorstand would be considered the representative of Rudolf Steiner would have to be set aside. It would be a presumption because none of them could act out of such universality of knowledge. That was approximately the content of my proposal.[400]

And so as not to appear at the General Meeting with this proposal out of the blue, he discussed it first with Albert Steffen and with Marie Steiner. Of the degree of success he experienced he wrote:

> Both Albert Steffen and Marie Steiner were very reserved about it; Albert Steffen was deeply offended. I thus realized that Albert Steffen really thought that he as President could represent a Society that had been led in such a significant manner before.[401]

Polzer had to resign himself to this realization and left a copy of the memorandum in the hands of Steffen and Marie Steiner. He immediately sensed 'that from this moment on, he was more avoided and feared by the Dornach Vorstand than before'.[402] But perhaps they would be able to discuss his proposals calmly one more time before the conference at Christmas?

He was not present at the twelve-hour-long meeting of the General Secretaries. And at the Extraordinary General Meeting that began on 29 December 1930 he spoke no word. It made upon him 'such an aberrant, hopeless impression'[403] that he attended no more General Meetings in Dornach until the spring of 1935!

Polzer also had clear ideas about the determination of the question of the Class. In 1939 he wrote:[404]

> I hold that after the death of Rudolf Steiner an arrangement of the affairs of the Class is only possible such that the individual who wishes to take on the responsibility before the spiritual world and Rudolf Steiner and who is supported by the wills of a number of individuals shares this with the leaders of the Sections and discusses it with them. I believe that through this, continuity with Rudolf Steiner, which is a requirement, would be preserved.

Polzer therefore naturally disapproved of any centralized conferment of the authority to read Class Lessons. 'A conferment of authority for zealous achievements or acquisition of knowledge would be unacceptable to me; through that we would very soon enter upon on a completely external, authoritarian path.'

And it was to just such a very external, authoritarian-catholic path, unfortunately, that they would very soon come.

At about the time when Polzer wrote his memorandum for the Anthroposophical Society, he made the following observation in his diary:

'The place that R. St. occupied has been left; it does not need to be occupied because R. St. is amongst us when we want to unite ourselves with him in remembrance. He leads us on to the "O Man, know yourself!" '[405]

Polzer built on the bridging power of Spirit-Remembering nurtured by the individual. Others wanted instead or as well, to build on the basis of office and dignities...

Looking back to his second memorandum from the year 1930 and his anthroposophical efforts made in it, which in their essential points have been ignored until today, Ludwig Polzer later wrote: 'I recalled the words of Rudolf Steiner in 1917 in Berlin: "What cannot find its way through in reason, then finds its way through in catastrophes if it is required by the world will." The catastrophe then came in 1935 and led to a series of others.'[406]

35. 'To Be Able to Give Oneself to One's Own Destiny...'

After a flood tide must follow the ebb. What strives out into the world as deed can serve to deepen knowledge in the ebbing phase. We have already confirmed the prevalence of this rhythmical movement in Ludwig Polzer's life path between 1917 and 1922. His realization of the necessity for threefolding was followed by a year-long flood of action; when his outer efforts were blocked by the resistance of old habits of thought, then came a phase of deepening his understanding: Polzer passed from concrete work for threefolding over to a deeper understanding and grounding of its world-historical necessity through consideration of the Testament of Peter the Great.

Something similar happened now in the year 1931. After his attempt to effect something through his political Memorandum and his first important conversations with Masaryk and Beneš, Polzer now turned to an intensive study of the history of Bohemia. Why Bohemia exactly? Because nowhere else did the Slavic and Germanic cultures interpenetrate each other so strongly; Bohemia would have been the ideal starting point for a supranational solution to national differences in the sense of social threefolding. Polzer studied the five-volume *Geschichte Böhmens* (History of Bohemia) by Palacký. But it would be a mistake to imagine that Polzer would only turn to books in an academic fashion. Precisely in historical consideration of a contemporary subject, with him, the concordance of outer events and inner experiences played an important guiding or even empowering role. And these outer and inner events themselves again are related to the many individuals with whom he came into contact. Again and again, specific individuals played a role as catalysts who had something definite to bring into flow in Polzer's research. In 1931, quite apart from the purely human component of the relationships, such a role was played by the Zeissig family and a little later by the Brabínek family, to name only two examples. 'I believe that it is necessary,' wrote Polzer in 1939,[407]

> to write my memories of this year in such a diary-like fashion so that the connections which link us with so many people appear correctly in the course of powerful, historical and sorrowful events and also so that no one will be forgotten. *It is not a matter of indifference under which circumstances and in which events one first encounters people.*[408]

We could add that it is also not a matter of indifference for the interplay between outer experiences and inner strivings that leads to important historical studies. This is why the many people to whom Polzer maintained old ties of friendship or with whom he developed new ones have been and will continue to be mentioned in this book.

But let us return to 1931!

In January of the new year Polzer saw much of the Zeissigs, and Ernst Wettreich, the journalist, with whom he had been in touch since his work with the *Messenger*, and with Klima's successor, Stanislaus Benda. His Prague friend, Hans Eiselt, asked him to accompany him to Ostrau in Moravia in February for the founding of a new 'Plato-Branch', which Polzer gladly did.

At the end of March in Vienna there was a memorial ceremony for Rudolf Steiner, and at the beginning of April in Prague a commemoration of Rudolf Steiner's last visit to the city. On this occasion Polzer spoke about Rudolf Steiner as a man and a teacher. After the conference he visited Karlstejn Castle once more with friends.

Theodora Zeissig, with whom he had attended a performance of *Aida* in Vienna at the beginning of the year, was able to accompany the fatherly friend of the family once more on the evening of his 62nd birthday on 23 April to a performance of the drama *The House of Rothschild* by Sassmann, at the Burgtheater.

Two days later Polzer travelled to Budapest with Alfred and Dorli Zeissig. It was Easter and everything was in full bloom. The three went sightseeing together. After breakfast on Easter Sunder they went to the Matthias Corvinus Church. High Mass was being celebrated. From the choir the solemn sounds of the *Missa Solemnis* greeted the visitors. Dorli Zeissig was overwhelmed by the event. Polzer wrote:

> She stood immobile, it seemed to me, deeply given over to the ceremony and the music, and I experienced a power which united us in some way. On leaving the church we spoke little. We looked down from the Fisherman's Bastion onto the ribbon of the Danube, which is beautifully bordered by the city and the line of hills. I was filled by the mood of history.

Polzer's friend and teacher Steiner had once, with similar feelings, looked down upon the city of *Prague* ...

This scene in Budapest would be continued and crowned in August the same year in a surprising manner. First, it had the effect that Polzer began after Easter to occupy himself, in reading Palacký, with King Matthias Corvinus of Hungary and with his father-in-law, George of Poděbrady, the elected King of the Czechs. Both rulers repeatedly took up arms against Rome and also allowed themselves to be divided by Rome. They were the precursors of a development in the Slavic-

Hungarian region of Europe that sought independence from the might of Rome.

Matthias Corvinus, born in 1443, came to Prague as a hostage after the death of his father John Hunyadi. When he was called from there in 1458 to become the King of Hungary, he was allowed to leave by George of Poděbrady, who in the same year was elected King of the Czechs, under the condition that he marry his daughter, which Corvinus accepted. But the opposing party in Hungary offered the crown to Frederick III (1415–1493), the Holy Roman Emperor, who accepted it in 1459—the year of *The Chymical Wedding of Christian Rosencreuz*. Corvinus fought for his right to rule and secured Frederick's renunciation of the throne in 1462. In 1464 Matthias Corvinus thus became uncontested King of Hungary. He fought victoriously against the Turks and after the early death of his first wife, Poděbrady's daughter, allowed himself to become involved in crusades against his former supporter and father-in-law Poděbrady, who died in 1471. Matthias was victorious against the Poles and fought again against Emperor Frederick when he supported Poland. Corvinus conquered a large part of Austria and also Vienna, and Frederick, from whom stems the saying 'Austriae Est Imperare Orbi Universo' [It is Austria's destiny to rule the whole world], had to be satisfied with a residence in Linz until his own death in 1493. In spring 1490 Matthias Corvinus died suddenly in Vienna. He is supposed to have been poisoned at the instigation of the Church. His scholarly library was destroyed. It is said that among those gathered at his deathbed was also Christian Rosencreuz …

In the conflicts between Corvinus and Poděbrady that were fomented by the Emperor Frederick, who was aligned with the Church, Polzer saw more and more a paradigm for the Church's struggle against the true Middle European spirituality, a struggle that has continued until today. He wrote:

> A devilish political game clearly began, which the Roman Church was playing with the help of its instrument, Frederick III. Now the Emperor is fighting with Poděbrady against Matthias and now with Matthias against Poděbrady. Roman domination hoped to maintain itself by always playing these two against each other. *Middle Europe is not allowed to be at peace. This has been a method used until today, for the spiritual seeds which lie within Middle Europeans are not allowed to come to development.*[409]

Soon after this Easter visit to Budapest, Polzer began to speak in lectures at branch meetings about these events, which were so symptomatic for the obstructed development of Middle Europe.

★

At the beginning of May Polzer was once again on his travels. He went with Dr Eiselt to Olmütz [today Olomouc, Czech Republic], where he gave a lecture on 3 May. Dora Schenker was also able to accompany him to the Moravian town. While they were there, Colonel Dohnal, one of the anthroposophical friends in Olmütz, urged Polzer to go on an excursion with him to the nearby *Burg Busau*. In his lecture Polzer therefore spoke about his ancestor, the former owner of the well-maintained castle, Franziskus Josephus Philippus von Hoditz und Wolframitz. It so happened then, that Polzer had been urged *from outside* to concern himself again with a significant representative of his own ancestral stream. He took this as a concrete opportunity in his lecture to bring in something personal about his relationship to history. 'History had at first always been something dead to me,' he confessed openly, 'with which I could not connect myself inwardly, and so destiny placed me livingly into history through what came to me in life.'[410] So it was too on his visit to Olmütz.

The two wall paintings displayed on both right and left of the entrance to the chapter room of the lovely castle, led Archduke Eugen, the then owner, to say something about them. 'The one on the onlooker's right,' wrote Polzer,

> shows the coat of arms of the Teutonic Knights and under it two mounted knights fighting. The inscription of this picture reads: 'The worldly knights'. The picture of the coat of arms on the left shows the Hoditz coat of arms with the wild bull's horns and under it a rider on a white horse who is slaying a dragon. The inscription reads: 'The spiritual knight'.

★

A few days later the descendent of this spiritual knight came for the first time in his life to give lectures and Class Lessons in Pardubice in Bohemia. The small town, which lies about 80 km east of Prague and 25 km south of Königgrätz (today, Hradec Králové) has a well-kept Old Town quarter with many pretty houses in the Renaissance style. New anthroposophical activity for Polzer began here in Pardubice which would belong to the 'dearest, finest and most successful' work of the following years. 'In the seven years until March 1938'—when the work in Bohemia was suddenly terminated because of the political situation—Polzer wrote, looking back, 'I never experienced anything unpleasant there and never a mis-understanding.' Again he found a new anthroposophical home in the household of Anton Geryšer, the branch leader, and his lovely family. Geryšer was for Polzer 'the most understanding branch leader one can find'.

The day of his arrival in Pardubice is noteworthy. It was 8 May, the death day of Helena Petrovna Blavatsky, the courageous founder of the Theosophical Society, who had also been born exactly 100 years earlier, in 1831. But what did Blavatsky have to do with Polzer's spiritual work in Pardubice? Above all, the following: nowhere else did Steiner's spiritual pupil nurture the element of the *feminine* spirit as he did here in companionship with his esoteric helper Maňa Brabínek, whom he would meet for the first time in December 1932. It was certainly no accident that in the last third of the previous century the first spiritual impetus that modern civilization so badly needed was given through a female spirit. H.P. Blavatsky acted as the intrepid campaigner for the future unfolding of the feminine spiritual element that is so indispensable for a respiritualization of modern civilization. And in view of Ludwig Polzer's esoteric striving to work for the harmonization of the male and female spirits, especially in connection with his work in Pardubice, the date of his arrival in Pardubice had the character of a hopeful omen. It was like a gentle prompting to continue with other means Blavatsky's struggle for the recognition of feminine spirituality which was opposed both by traditional Freemasonry as well by the Church. Here in Pardubice in a ceremony in December 1932 Polzer would bestow upon the already existing branch an esoteric double 'patent' which expressed this striving in a fine way: he named the branch 'Duke [Vojvod] Vàclav and Maid-of-Orleans Branch' in order to promote 'what ought to guide male and female spiritual streams together'.

In relation to this whole special element in Polzer's esoteric striving a general observation may be made at this point: Ludwig Polzer's interest up to this time in Sophie and Menny Lerchenfeld, in Dorli Zeissig, his future interest in Maňa Brabínek and several other women is, apart from a general human fostering of the binds of friendship, to be seen in the light of just this struggle to harmonize masculine and feminine spirituality. One who does not take account of this could easily come to harbour one misunderstanding after another in relation to Polzer's friendships with women.

★

Following his first visit to Pardubice, Polzer travelled with his eldest son Josef for two weeks to the Knispels at Kambelovac. During the day they went on excursions to the island of Lissa, and the evenings were given over mostly to reading anthroposophy together.

In June 1931 Polzer was again in Prague. In Hradec, with Julie Klima, he visited the grave of her late husband Jaroslav; in Modern, with Dora Schenker the grave of his father and *Villa Harmonie*.

In mid-July he left for Venice with the Zeissigs, who were visiting the city for the first time. They stayed at the *Monaco*. On 17 they went on a short excursion to Torcello with its Roman churches and then travelled via Trieste to the island of Lussin [today Lošinj, Croatia]. Polzer had already stayed here once before, at the turn of the year 1890/1891, when he had fallen ill after visiting Blanche Tollemache in England. The Zeissigs rented accommodation for the following four weeks on Lussin Grande, while Polzer, after a few days of Lussin, travelled on to the Knispels. By day he read lectures here with his dear friends, but there was no lack of a joyful mood; they were all 'very cheerful'.

On his way home, Polzer wanted to spend a few more days with the Zeissigs, so on 20 August he took ship to Lussin Grande. The Zeissigs had reserved a room for him nearby. In this room there now continued what had begun at the Corvinus Church in Budapest in April. As already mentioned, since that visit to Budapest, Polzer had occupied himself with Palacký's history of Bohemia, especially with George of Poděbrady and Matthias Corvinus. He therefore had in his suitcase during his stay on Lussin the volume by Palacký 'which dealt with Poděbrady's battles with the Popes and with Matthias Corvinus'. What happened now is highly characteristic of Polzer's way of working on harmonizing inner strivings with outer events. What happened during his stay he himself described as follows:

> The house in which I was staying was very spacious and in the days when Lussin Grande had many visitors, it was a successful pension. But at this time, I was the only guest; all the other rooms, except for those of the owners, were empty. We again spent some fine days together. On some afternoons Frau Zeissig came to me with Dorli. On these visits I read a lecture with them about karmic relationships of particular individuals [. . .] One afternoon Frau Zeissg and Dorli had left after such a reading; I picked up Palacký's book and began to read, but soon became rather tired and easily dozed off. Suddenly I came out of my sleep and heard an inner voice, which said to me: 'Look up at the wall in the corner.' The room was not very bright, and the corner was completely in shadow. The washing table stood there; I had experienced nothing special on the days before. Now I was attentive and saw above the washing table a framed print hanging. It was so dark that with my bad eyesight I could not make the picture out. I took it off the wall and looked at it. Under the picture was the following text in Hungarian [. . .]: 'In Prague they bring to Matthias Hunyadi in 1458 the news that he has been elected King of Hungary.' The young Matthias (Corvinus) stands in the middle before the great magistrates of Hungary who have brought him the insignia of the kingdom. Behind him [is] Poděbrady and his wife with a small girl or boy. With a feeling of devotion

I put the picture back securely in its original place. I arranged to have the picture sent to Tannbach, where it hangs today in my room. That I was living in *this* room by chance and was called from my reading to look at the picture which was related to what I had just been reading about [made] this experience of special significance for me. The experience in the Matthias church in Budapest was completed by that in Lussin.

This experience raises more than a question; first there is the question: what or who stood behind the call that penetrated to Polzer's spiritual hearing? The experience also gave Polzer much to contemplate and think about. It became a pathfinder for his always independently developed method of historical observation as well as for the way in which he came to the themes of his lectures. Eight years later he wrote in relation to the two-part Corvinus experience of 1931:

> Since Rudolf Steiner's death it was always experiences from my own life that led me to lectures about history [...] I never took on to speak on an historical theme without an inner impulse, but it always happened that I found a theme at the right time. Only then did I look up the external historical details. Often I thought I had no theme for the next time and yet something suitable always presented itself in time. That gives one trust in spiritual guidance. Dimly I began to experience real guidance by Rudolf Steiner from the spiritual world. Dreams were never what gave me themes for lectures; [it was] only always attention to an outer event that united itself with an inner will impulse. A good many things also had to be corrected in concrete interpretation. Many things are still struggling today in my soul to be understood rightly.

But this is not yet all. Whoever strives to find in the jumble of facts those that are of symptomatic weight must train quite another capacity which appears—but only *appears*—to have nothing to do with historical research. Polzer formulated it as follows:

> One must be able to give oneself to one's own destiny. This will enable one to comprehend in reviewing one's life how one actually stands in life. These symptomatic events, which one needs for one's tasks are brought to one, as Rudolf Steiner said, by the world current[411] and then one must be able to put them together to grasp reality even when they are often distant from each other in time.

One who wants to work at historical observation in a pragmatic and chronological manner with the unattainably distant ideal of one day being able to have all the facts before the eye of the researcher, will naturally believe he can manage without paying attention to the way outer, so-called coincidences chime with inner experiences. But one who seeks essences in history must learn to follow his own destiny, for only this, and not his abstract thinking, will be able to guide his attention towards things which reveal to a closer observation their symptomatic weight which is at first perhaps hidden.

After this historical-symptomatic experience which gripped him deeply, Polzer travelled for a few days to Italy. Dorli Zeissig, who seemed to be somehow involved in what he had experienced and had contributed to its outer causality at least was allowed to accompany him. From Lussin they went to Ancona and from there for two days to Ravenna, the city of Theodoric. Via Venice the pair, who must have been taken for father and daughter, travelled to Padua and then to Trieste. A car journey to Fiume ended the short trip. Dorli travelled back to Lussin, and Polzer went to Vienna. When Alfred Zeissig, who had returned to Vienna earlier to go back to work, picked Polzer up at the station, Polzer began to tell him of the impressions that he and Dorli had had on their trip. The deepest impression made on Dorli had been the gravestone of Galla Placidia in Ravenna.

In September Polzer spent some time at the spa in Pistyan. Dora Schenker came to visit him here. Then he went with the two Reichart daughters to Tannbach, where they stayed for two weeks. In October he travelled via Prague to Mariensee. Here in peace and quiet he wanted to deepen and extend the most important thing, in the sense of historical destiny, that the 'stream of the world' had brought him in this year. 'Beautiful days—reading Palacký. King Poděbrady and Matthias' was the brief entry in the guestbook.

At the end of the month followed a trip to Dornach, where Polzer saw his grandson Christward and on the way back visited Josef in Wiesneck. But on 6 November we find him once again at his refuge with Dora Schenker. Again he is deep in the history of Poděbrady and Matthias Corvinus. A long poetic entry in the guestbook testifies to this:

> *A bond of destiny*
> *Seeks to enfold the Danube and the Moldau.*
> *Three there were who wanted this,*
> *Who experience themselves in spirit.*
> *The monster in Rome*
> *Gets wind of the spirit,*
> *Divides in strife*
> *Corvinus, Podiebrad, Friedrich*
> *And nurtures the dragon brood*
> *So that new strife splits the peoples.*

But in our time the greatest son of earth
Leaves with spirit-faithful souls
Memory that rises from the twilight.
Time rolls by
And destiny gives its guidance.
Pictures arise,
Releasing powers for the future
And overcome will surely be
The dragon's deadly plan.

While Polzer in Mariensee was occupied in this way with the history of Bohemia and Hungary in the fifteenth century there came shocking news from the Zeissigs. Theodora had gone to a school conference in Stuttgart and had 'there experienced great heartache and had become mentally ill'. A friend for whom she longed had left her. She was taken to Gnadenwald, to the care of Norbert Glas. She had to have a nurse watching her at all times.

The illness of the elder of the Zeissigs' two sisters weighed very much on Polzer's heart; it was most inwardly bound up with what he had been concerned with in the spring and autumn of 1931.

Thus in the late autumn of 1931 he had climbed new, important heights of knowledge only to experience that a young person closely connected to him had fallen into the deepest soul pain. In this autumnal minor mood, 'the circle was closed' that had been opened in Budapest at Easter. 'To be able to give yourself to your own destiny'—even when it is painful—that is what Polzer had to practise in a special way in that dark November time.

36. A Vow in the Chapel of Wenceslas

A major anthroposophical conference took place in Prague between 4 and 10 December 1931. On this occasion the engineer Milos Brabínek senior introduced Ludwig Polzer to his 20-year-old daughter Maña (Maria Magdalena) of whom we have also mentioned in connection to Polzer's first visit to Pardubice on 8 May the year before. Brabínek asked Polzer to accept Maña into the School of Michael, which Polzer immediately did. 'I knew,' he later wrote, 'how Brabínek had raised his children in the spirit of anthroposophy. Maña had also been a year in Dornach after her graduation, So I could immediately accept her and allowed her to come on 6 December.'[412]

In the spirit of his anthroposophical Memorandum of November 1930 Polzer thought it right to act appropriately, autonomously and in a decentralized fashion, and as someone tasked by Rudolf Steiner with the work with the Class mantras he felt he had the right to decide himself who to accept as new members of the School. It is understandable that this was not looked upon favourably in Dornach, where his Memorandum had been met with disapproval by two leading members of the Vorstand.

On 10 December Maña accompanied Polzer to a lecture which he was to give to a small circle on the subject of the idea of threefolding at the request of Maña's father. The invited guests included Dr Schiszl, who was then the director of Thomas Masaryk's Cabinet. According to Polzer, this invitation was 'perhaps a kind of investigation', and even Stanislaus Benda showed himself to be concerned when he went through the list of those invited. But Polzer addressed the theme academically and answered all the questions in such a way that 'no one could be politically apprehensive'. As unsatisfactory as the lecture may have been for the anthroposophical friends in his audience, through it Polzer gained the friendship of Schiszl, who arranged for him to have further meetings with Masasryk. Maña sat 'near me like a guardian angel' during the whole lecture, Polzer wrote, and with this now began the work of this unusual woman at his side, as has already been mentioned.

After Christmas Eve, which Polzer spent with Berta and Julius at Tannbach, he left for Gnadenwald in order to see Theodora Zeissig. Accompanied by the Arlesheim nurse Rosa, he went for walk in the woods with Theodora. But the young woman, who was usually so friendly and happy, spoke not a word and 'was very much changed and shy'.

From Gnadenwald he went to Mariensee. 'Evenings well spent on the *History of the City of Rome*', he wrote in Dora Schenker's guestbook. He was referring here to the classic work by Gregorovius. Alfred Zeissig came to visit for two days. Certainly the three of them would have spoken about Theodora's condition.

From Mariensee Polzer travelled to Bad Saarow to see Dr Erhard Bartsch, who was running a biodynamically farmed estate in nearby Marienhöhe. He met Hemma Wurzer from St Veit again here, who was supported energetically by Bartsch and who soon afterwards married him. 'January this year is unusually mild,' Polzer noted in his diary.

In February Polzer visited Leopold Thurn, an old friend of his grandmother's Karg family, in Choltice. Count Thurn's uncle had been a captain in Polzer's Hussar regiment in Sopron (Ödenburg). He was now 60 years old and interested in anthroposophy.

The Polzer-Hoditz family suffered a heavy blow on 13 March 1932 when their dearly beloved aunt Mathilde died in Baden near Vienna, aged 83. She was buried in the same grave as her sister Christine, Polzer's mother, who had died in 1924.

A conference was arranged in Dornach to commemorate the 100th anniversary of Goethe's death. Polzer travelled there with Hans Eiselt on 20 March. On arriving, first he visited his grandson Christward. The conference, with performances of Eurythmy, *Faust* and music concerts was 'very fine'.

At the Goetheanum he came across Herta Reichart, who was studying medicine in Arlesheim. 'She lightened my lonely, sad mood.' For on his shoulders, like an unseen heavy hand, in addition to his already existing distress, was the riddling destiny of Theodora Zeissig. Bad news arrived from Gnadenwald. Theodora had had to be referred to an asylum for mental patients at Hall in the Tyrol.

At the end of March Polzer gave as usual an address in Vienna in commemoration of Rudolf Steiner. A month later, after a 'week of recuperation' at Mariensee he took part in a large anthroposophical conference in Prague. After the conference he accompanied Albert Steffen, who had come to Prague for the conference, to Karlstejn, and then went with Guenther Wachsmuth, the Society's treasurer, to another conference, which was held in Vienna. If he had not already done so by letter, Polzer may have informed Albert Steffen of the admission of Maña Brabínek and others into the Michael School. Instructive is his observation in relation to Albert Steffen: 'I had the feeling that Steffen felt insecure and rootless outside Switzerland and that he could not really relate to these [other] peoples.'

In May Polzer went to Dornach again, where he had conversation with nurse Rosa who had looked after Theodora Zeissig in Gnadenwald. After an excursion to Seelisberg with Herta Reichart, he went to Wiesneck and then took Josef with him to Tannbach. Shortly afterwards, he took his ailing son to Pilgramshain and placed him in the care of Karl König. Here in Pilgramshain Josef's condition visibly began to improve.

There followed lectures and Class Lessons in Prague. On 17 June Polzer was invited for lunch at the Brabíneks for the first time. He joined the family circle not as a lecturer and teacher but as a man regarded by the family with affection. For Maňa, 'this very special spiritual human being', he had immediately felt 'a very special destiny connection'. But he did not wish to force anything. 'Only when I could no longer avoid the visit, did I decide upon it.' After lunch they all went for a long walk in the *Sarka* in Dejvice, the district of Prague where the Brabíneks lived. The Sarka is a romantic rocky valley, associated with many legends. In November 1620 on the White Mountain, which borders the Sarka, took place that fateful battle which almost completely broke the Hussites' resistance to re-Catholicization. 'It was a wonderfully fine June day,' wrote Polzer. 'The wild roses were in bloom. Maňa plucked a rose, gave it to me and said: "When someone is given a rose, he is also given the key to the soul of the giver, if the gift is to be true, for the rose is a holy flower." ' Polzer wrote of this: 'That was said in a religious, modest way, as if out of an inspiration. She gave me the rose and the trust of her soul as [her] spiritual guide.' Maňa's words said something else to Polzer: '*I heard* [in them] *the Slavic soul speak which recognized the understanding of a German person for this soul.*'[413] On that day in June 'began the short period of the loveliest experience in my destiny which continues in the spirit and always will continue because it stems from ancient times and has received a new consecration with a task for the future'. Of these 'ancient times' and the 'new consecration' we shall soon come to speak.

With the seed of this beautiful June day in his soul, a week later Polzer went with Frau Schenker 'as every year' to Kambelovac. From here he travelled with her at the beginning of July to Cattaro, to see Alexsander and Sophie Račeta. How remarkable that the couple should have settled in that town which bordered Montenegro. Alexsander was close to his own homeland there, while for Sophie, there was the spirit of Polzer's father Julius, to whom she had always felt a strong bond.

The rest of the summer of 1932 passed in quiet diversions in Tannbach, where various visitors came to stay. In mid-August, however, Polzer interrupted his time there in order to visit—as a year before on Lussin— his friends the Zeissigs, who this year were holidaying at St Jacob am

Arlberg, but he did not find Dorli with them. On this visit too her condition will have been the subject of much anxious conversation.

A short time later, he went on a climb from Mariensee out to the Hochwechsel. He 'had a wonderful view in the morning, the Neusiedler lake was shining in the rising sun and reflected back the red of the sun', he wrote in his diary. The light-filled distant view was a balsam for his soul.

As almost every year, in September he went to the spa at Pistyan. With the Reicharts he read the Michael lectures which Rudolf Steiner had given in September 1923 in Vienna. As every year, he visited the graves of his father and of Marie Nerad, the manageress of the Villa Harmonie. 'To all the dear people, with whom I was once there together, I felt so close then,' he wrote about his stay in Modern. During his stay at the spa in Pistyan there began a fine correspondence with Maňa Brabínek which presented his soul with new, far-reaching vistas.

From Pistyan, he went to Prague and Pardubice. On 25 September he was picked up by Brabínek at Pardubice station and taken to Slatiňany, the Brabíneks' main residence. Milos Brabínek worked here as technical supervisor at the fertilizer factory owned by Prince Franz Josef Auersperg and lived with his family near to the factory building at the railway station. As Prince Auersperg was the brother of Berta's aunt Gabriele Windisch-Graetz, Polzer was thus arriving in what was for him both new territory in Slatiňany but also a district with which he already had a certain relationship.

He spent eight days at the Brabíneks' house. During the day, they went to Pardubice for lectures and Class Lessons. In the evenings they returned to Slatiňany and went on walks together in the wooded surroundings. Polzer visited the Auerspergs' zoo several times with Maňa. 'She told me of her dreams which mostly concerned a time long ago in Thebes in ancient Egypt or at a castle, and always the same one, in the late Middle Ages,' he wrote, looking back on those fine days in Slatiňany. He went on, 'Such a pure, spiritual being shone out from her with a loving and reverent enthusiasm for anthroposophy.'

*

Just as Sophie Lerchenfeld appeared to be linked to the Roman layer of Polzer's individuality, so Maňa Brabínek brought the Egyptian and late mediaeval layers of his being to light. In relation to his inner affinity to Maňa's dreams of the Middle Ages the following event is of symptomatic interest. Polzer writes:

> I do not know how it happened that already earlier in Dejvice when I was with her suddenly Frau Wiegand's novel *The Struggle with the Tarnhelm*—

Experiences from the History of King James I of England and His Mother Maria Stuart and her cousin Francis Stuart[414] occurred to me. It was the first book I gave her.

Maña had unlimited trust in her friend and soul guide; she spoke beautifully and freely about what she experienced. 'When we had sat down together on the Waldeshöhe on the rocks and looked down on to the plain, she suddenly said: "I know that we met before in long past times; this memory is connected with a kind of guilt."' Polzer commented: 'The way that was said, very brief, simple and quiet gripped my soul deeply.' Then she told her friend that long ago she had spoken to a young man who she had thought of marrying after finishing her studies; that she wanted children; that she saw her relation to Polzer as spiritual in nature and 'stood higher than merely personal earthly relations'. Then she said: she would not be able to place *all* her forces at the disposal of her friend and spiritual guide. For Polzer, what she said at Michaelmas was 'the beginning of a spiritual companionship [. . .] and the impulse for work together and the taking on of a task which from then on I served anthroposophically and shall serve'. Thus he wrote seven years later.

The deep conversations with Maña gave wings to Polzer's work in Pardubice and Prague in the highest degree. In Pardubice he was also helped by the fact that Anton Geryšer, the branch leader, translated Polzer's lectures ad-lib into Czech with great skill. Polzer usually divided his lectures in three parts so that Geryšer could translate in the pauses. 'It is him that I must thank,' wrote Polzer, 'for enabling my work with the Czech friends to go so successfully.' This success later passed on to the large Prague group. At Michaelmas 1932 Maña once suddenly stood in for the exhausted Geryšer 'and did it very well'.

On 18 October Maña sent Polzer a verse which shows the unlimited trust between the two but makes clear also the consciousness of the spiritual aim with which Maña was filled:

> *To you, friend of my soul,*
> *I send my spiritual love—*
> *Pure through the Word of Christ.*
> *May the word of love help you*
> *When good strives with evil.*
> *May the light of the stars shine through your heart*
> *And make all darkness light.*
> *I send you holy spirit power*
> *Which can change death into life.*
> *I shall never leave you in hardship.*

We step before the great master.
May he give us his blessing,
To you and to me—
That our great yearning
To create harmony
Will in reality be victorious!
In the service of Michael—with HIS aid.
Amen

The friendship between Ludwig Polzer and Maña Brabínek saw its first high point in the last days of October through a fully conscious setting of goals. '26 October,' wrote Polzer,

> was for me and my work in Prague a solemn day of destiny. *At 11 o'clock in the morning in the Chapel of St Wenceslas in St Vitus' Cathedral on the Hradschin [Hradčany] Castle Hill we sealed our companionship with the promise and the will to take on the task of harmonizing German and Slavic souls, of struggling for understanding between Germans and Czechs and to represent this task on into future times.*[415]

To empower this vow in a solemn ritual way Polzer hung a rose cross around Maña Brabínek's neck. Seven years later he wrote: 'This act, by which I hung a rose cross around Maña's neck in the chapel, had its effect in the spiritual world.'

A most important event—at least in the eyes of Polzer and Maña—therefore took place on this day. The significance of the act was enhanced still further by the place in which it occurred. The Chapel of St Wenceslas, wonderfully decorated with precious stones is consecrated to the first King of Bohemia, who is also the patron saint of the land. This ruler, who stemmed from the line of the Přemsyls, was already striving in the tenth century more for a working together of the Czechs with the brother nation of the Germans (especially the Saxons) than with the Papacy in Rome and therefore died by the hand of Rome in the year 929. Polzer wrote:

> Duke Václav [. . .] gave his life for Christ and for *friendship with Germans*.[416] His brother Boleslav, who murdered him, was [. . .] the instrument of a Roman will that fought against the esoteric Christianity of Wenceslas and his grandmother Ludmilla. When Wenceslas was fatally attacked by Boleslav and sought to flee to the nearby church [St Vitus' Cathedral], it was closed to him. The legend tells that Wenceslas' blood had never been washed off the doors of the church. This means that the guilt that the Roman Church took upon itself worked on. His chapel in the Cathedral stands like a constant watcher.

So the place for the ceremonial act was chosen with care. The choice shows Polzer's intention to link the vow he made with Maña Brabínek in the sense of a real spiritual continuity onto the activity of that individual who stood at the historical beginning of collaboration between Germans and Slavs.

In a lecture to anthroposophical friends at that time in Prague Polzer spoke about 'the being of anthroposophy in the history of the present' and amongst other things, urged them to seek out 'the occult factors in modern events'. He emphasized that there was 'still something living in Bohemia which must be fostered so that the unbreakable marriage between Germans and Slavs may harmonize souls'.[417] Representing the few 'couples' of this kind of marriage that then existed and the many more which will have to exist in the future, Polzer himself entered into such a marriage in the symbolically real sense with Maña Brabínek.

In the days and weeks that followed the ceremonial act in the Chapel of Wenceslas, Maña and Ludwig Polzer were often in Dejvice together when they were not in the Waldstein garden or on the Castle Hill. In the St Vitus Cathedral they looked for the graves of the kings, among which was to be found that of George of Poděbrady.

At the beginning of November Polzer went to Karlstejn with Maña and Herta Reichart. Then he travelled with Berta to the Wurzers in Scheifling and held a another branch lecture in St Veit.

At this time Maña wrote him letters which seemed to her friend like works of art, although she had not entirely mastered German. His own letters, he freely admitted seemed to him 'always somewhat philistine, although I am such an enemy of bourgeois rationalistic philistinism'.

Having returned to Prague, he went to the Sarka with Maña and on 20 November to a castle with her again. This time they went to Pürglitz (Křivoklát). Here was kept the document *Libellus de hominis convenientia* that had been written by his maternal ancestor, Franziskus Philippus von Hoditz und Wolframitz. Maña had discovered it in a library catalogue index. It was a copy in octavo format but there was his ancestor's signature. So thanks to Maña's discovery, in studying this document he was able to come a step closer to the being of his ancestor, for it is the soul of a man that is expressed in his handwriting. And one with pure senses can be shown by it, in a perhaps very delicate fashion, the way to this soul, even when that person has long been on the other side of the threshold... Where might it be, the soul of this lonely, keen-thinking 'Knight of the Spirit' who was once the owner of Busau before he left this Moravian castle to the Teutonic Knights? The visitor might have quietly wondered something like this.

'It was a wonderful autumn day,' remembered Polzer, 'some of the trees had lost their leaves, and the ground was covered with their gold. We sat for a long time facing the castle with our historical thoughts and feelings, which united us.'

Soon after this enjoyable visit to Pürglitz Castle, the pair extended the arc of remembering further back into the past. On 3 December they saw a performance of *Aida* at the Prague Opera House. Had Maňa not spoken to her friend of a time long ago in Thebes that had appeared to her in a dream?

*

In all the following *political* efforts that Polzer made in Bohemia the soul-spiritual marriage with Maňa Brabínek worked as something that inspired him and gave direction. This was true for the second meeting he was able to have with Masaryk on 16 December thanks to the good offices of Cabinet Director Schiszl. He visited the 83-year-old President of the youngest caricature of the shattered Habsburg monarchy in his library at the Hradčany and later wrote of the meeting:

> He said a lot about the unnecessarily long period of time young people spend studying at university and said: 'When they are finished, they can't even sharpen a pencil'; he spoke of the professors' lack of a sense of reality and the need for a new pedagogical method, whereupon I told him about Rudolf Steiner's pedagogy. I had the impression of a lonely man who would like to do something different from what was going on around him. I also had the feeling that he spoke with me differently than with other people, that he felt he could trust me.

That Polzer did not also speak about the need for a connection between German and Slavic culture that would be completely independent of Rome was due to the political circumstances at that time: in view of the rise of Hitlerism that consumed all true German culture in scorn and derision and hate, to raise this theme would have run the risk of causing frightful misunderstandings. Yet the first and most direct step to realize the vow for German-Slavic understanding led from the Chapel of St Wenceslas to Masaryk's library. And there too Polzer was following Maňa's thoughts.

*

He also tried in other ways at this time in his work in Bohemia to link on to the deeds of Wenceslas. When he was asked by the friends at Pardubice to give the branch an esoteric name he conducted a second consecration of the branch on 29 December 1932 in which he said the following words:

I place myself in your service, great Teacher in the spheres, in the sign of the Rose Cross:

E.D.N.
J.Ch.M.
P.S.S.R.

We live, my friends, in the spiritual guidance which adds a new circle of life to the cross and out of which the Rose (of resurrection) blooms. That is what is to guide together the masculine and feminine spiritual stream, and so I call two great pure souls and ask them to become the twin sponsors of this branch of the anthroposophical movement:

You, the man: Duke Václav—
You, the woman: Maid of Orléans.—

You, who lived a pure life, you, the accomplisher of brave deeds.

To you, whose lives were lives of sacrifice, I call and ask that you may keep watch: that wisdom may guide this branch, that beauty may grace it, that strength may be its deeds. 'Duke Václav and Maid of Orléans' branch in Pardubice.

Polzer thus made the figure of Duke Václav [Wenceslas] fruitful in a double relationship: the one for the bridge-building between Germans and Slavs; the other for the reconciliation between the spiritual poles of man and woman. Closer consideration now shows that the two tasks relate to each other most inwardly. Is not the spirituality in Slavic culture more of a feminine nature? Here we must of course have regard for the true Slavic nature, in contradistinction to the corrupted Slavic stream represented by the Testament of Peter the Great; when Slavs incline to this second stream in a more Cain-like, masculine way then that can indirectly show up the more Abel-like, feminine character of all true Slavic culture.

Maña Brabínek and Ludwig Polzer did not only make a vow for the marriage between Czechs and Germans; in Pardubice they also created a model for the second marriage, which is closely connected to it, that between the feminine and masculine human spirits.

Following the new consecration of the branch, Polzer conducted an 'esoteric rite' after a Class Lesson. While, according to a witness, at least in Pardubice, he always read the Class Lesson texts out word for word, we do not know with certainty of what the esoteric rite may have consisted. Polzer probably made use of some esoteric mantras which Rudolf Steiner had used in the Esoteric Lessons he had held in the Theosophical Society.[418]

Polzer spent the first days of the new year 1933 with the Brabíneks in Slatiňany. He read a great deal with Maňa. During the day they would go for walks in the woods. In the evenings they would sit before the Christmas tree and read a lecture. On 6 January, after the last holy night, they celebrated the birthday of Joan of Arc, the guardian of the newly consecrated branch. With this, they built the other pillar of the arch of consecration which was begun in October of the previous year in the Chapel of St Wenceslas.

After the weighty experiences and ceremonies in Prague and Pardubice, Polzer allowed himself a quiet week at Mariensee in January. The Knispels also visited there for the first time. They spent fine, cheerful days, followed by a jolly evening in Vienna where the friends enjoyed gypsy music at Patacky's wine cellar. They also saw the popular musical drama *Sissy* about the life of Empress Elisabeth, which was performed every evening.

On his monthly visits to Prague Polzer never neglected to visit St Vitus' Cathedral and the St Wenceslas Chapel with Maňa. The lectures which he held at the Prague Group led by Julie Klima, were interpreted by Maňa. Her fiancé sometimes attended, but his interest in spiritual-scientific questions was at that time only slight. From one of these Prague lectures (in March) there is a sketch which Polzer as a rule drew on single sheets of A5 size paper. On this occasion he spoke of the pathology of the human soul in relation to the different members of the human being, basing himself on statements made by Rudolf Steiner in 1917.[419] It was certainly not without inner concern for the condition of Theodora Zeissig that Polzer had wanted to deepen his understanding of these results of spiritual scientific research, and had been able to do so. But at the end of his lecture, the main motif of the past year emerged when he spoke of the necessary 'harmonizing of the disturbed communal life of German and West Slavic peoples' and added: 'This Michaelic impulse must sound out loudly into the world!'

★

A book of dreams in octavo format provides some insight into Polzer's vivid dream life between 1933 and 1940. Over 100 dreams are described, most of which with great clarity and lucidity. People, both alive and dead, with whom Polzer was inwardly related, appear in them. Some of these dreams comment on contemporary events, some are even prophetic, as we shall see.

Polzer speaks in his dreams with his father, with Berta, with Otto Lerchenfeld, Albert Steffen or Masaryk. But most frequently it is Rudolf Steiner who figures in them. Before visiting Masaryk for the third time in April 1933, he noted on 24 April in this book: 'Dr Steiner said to me: "Do it well!" ' Polzer related the dream to the approaching conversation with the President and the meeting with Beneš, the leader of the Czech National Socialist Party (only the name was similar to the German Nazi Party) and Masaryk's right hand, which would be following immediately afterwards.

Maňa too had dreams in which Polzer's mediating efforts figured which were directed toward the goal of the German-Slavic vow. Before his meeting with Masaryk, she dreamed she was a captive of Mussolini. And she saw 'a great face in the sky and above it, the swastika'. It was a few weeks after Hitler's wanton seizure of power. Polzer immediately took note of Maňa's experience and was a few degrees more wakeful when in the 'very intimate' conversation Masaryk asked the question: 'What do you think? I wanted to write to Mussolini that Fascism is not acceptable and not applicable to us.' Polzer said:

> that Mussolini had said that himself and that the effects of this Italian Fascism nevertheless reached us as imperialism through the Roman Church, but that Middle Europe and its methods should not be Roman. I also said that in Mussolini there worked a 'will' against which one could achieve nothing with arguments.

Polzer went further in their confidential conversation: 'We spoke about the damaging effects of the Jesuit-led Roman Church which consciously follows an anti-Christian line by secret methods. I could not go further; but he did not really understand what I meant about Mussolini. And yet what I said had an effect on him.'

Unfortunately, this was the last time that Polzer was able to meet the President. 'Those around him did not want that I should meet with him further,' he wrote, 'and the Departmental Head Schiszl confirmed this to me when he said "The president is always rather disturbed after discussions with you and this is not good for his health." ' It was held to be more healthy that until the end Masaryk would travel on the old tracks that had been laid out for him . . .

But Masaryk could nevertheless arrange for his visitor to meet with Eduard Beneš. This happened on 28 April 1933. Polzer wrote:

> Masaryk was [. . .] too old and a prisoner. Now I tried to gain an understanding with Beneš. With him too I quickly found trust and was able to speak with him not at all in an academic way but wholly and appropriately

in relation to the present situation. He wrote down much of what I said to him. There were difficulties with Hungary at that time. The advice I gave him made sense to him but his efforts to win the President's chair made him too careful; he did not have the courage I asked of him, although it would have served him better than his fear. With all my love for many old Hungarians and dear Hungarian friends, I had nevertheless recognized for a long time that Hungary as a Middle European State was only a tool for dark Jesuit and Jewish Freemasonic forces.

It is questionable whether Polzer would have included the adjective 'Jewish' if the extent of the coming persecution and murder of those belonging to this people had been clear to him. If one is surprised at this negative judgement of certain Jewish circles, one can find a key to understanding it in the chapter 'From Ancient Rome to the European Middle' which deals with Polzer's own Roman past.

This conversation with Beneš was continued on 8 June. 'At the end of this visit,' wrote Polzer, 'he said to me: "I promise you I shall not go to Rome." It was normal at the time for so-called statesmen to go on pilgrimages to Mussolini in Rome [...] Beneš kept his promise.'

But his path to Beneš was also soon to be blocked. This happened, as Polzer himself said, due to a lack of foresight on his part. He had felt his connection with Maña Brabínek to be 'like an inspiration'. He wrote in retrospect: 'The Czech folk soul which—perhaps only temporarily—worked through her in a pure way and remained esoteric held out a promise for the future.' From this experience he wrote two articles about Prague and the royal tombs in St Vitus' Cathedral where, amongst others, George of Poděbrady is buried. Polzer's articles were written entirely in the sense of this promise. Polzer wrote them 'only to seek out people in whom the Czech-Slavic folk soul had upheld itself purely and consciously'. Yet it was lacking in foresight to offer the articles to the *Prager Presse*. They were declined on grounds of lack of space.

Polzer spoke of this—admittedly in 1935, for until then he had had more meetings with Beneš, about which he reported nothing in detail—to Beneš's secretary, and also gave copies of the articles to this man. The consequence was that he was no longer allowed to meet the Secretary. Polzer suspected that the man whom he called 'the philistine Professor Krofta', who Beneš had called into the government as his Minister for Foreign Affairs, blocked any further conversations with Beneš. From this point on, according to Polzer,

> there was a complete change in the internal guidance of foreign policy which even paralyzed Masaryk through Roman-Vaticanic forces and prepared the way for everything that occurred later. Masaryk and later

Beneš [who replaced Masaryk as President in 1935] were only more manoeuvred personalities. The spiritual awakening of the people was hindered and everything sailed on wholly in accordance with the will of western f.m. [freemasonry] and the Vatican. Without seeing through this community of interests in its goals and methods, the ahrimanic powers cannot be kept within their bounds.

Polzer's activity for a mediation free of Rome's influence, between Czech and German culture, began again to ebb in the summer of 1933; that is, it had to be continued again for a while on the soul's inner field of work. It would be short-sighted, however, to regard his outer efforts to have been entirely unsuccessful. He himself always saw these things from the following viewpoint:

> *I know that the failure of spiritual efforts informed by Michaelic spiritual science does not prove them to be wrong. Such efforts must always be continued. Everything that one does with consciousness on these paths works on further in what is unseen and strengthens the esoteric Michaelic force in mankind as a whole.*[420]

★

In mid-June Polzer came to Prague again, this time with Berta. They dined with the Brabíneks in Dejvice,and Berta got to know Maña. Julie Klima joined them from Hradec. On 17 June, the day on which, exactly a year earlier, Maña had given Polzer the rose, he walked with Berta and his friend to the Visehrad, the legendary birthplace of Prague. In the evening he held a Class Lesson at the Brabíneks' house at which Maña sat next to Berta. Two days later Polzer and Maña were in the St Wenceslas Chapel on the Castle Hill for the last time. Then they went to the Sarka valley again. The wild roses were again in bloom. Their friendship had been sealed under the sign of the rose and under the sign of the rose the two friends now went their increasingly separate ways. 'The gradual outer withdrawal of my esoteric helper Maña,' wrote Polzer in 1939, 'was not allowed to break the work we had undertaken together. The pains of the soul now became our helpers. The work did not suffer at all, on the contrary, it became ever more successful among the Czechs and also strengthened me in my autonomy vis-à-vis the declining Vorstand in Dornach. I had to learn to stand alone when destiny required it.'

Polzer had ended his first essay about the royal tombs in St Vitus' Cathedral with the following words; they show in a beautiful way the connection between the motif of St Wenceslas and the motif of destiny observed in this chapter—how significant it is for a symptomatic study of history:

Two people, one older man, one younger had spent some time at the royal tombs in St Vitus' Cathedral. They left the Cathedral; the last rays of the sinking autumn sun lay over Prague. They looked to the Visehrad, the birthplace of this threshold city. The lovely saga of Libuše and Přemsyl was alive in their souls. The young person asked: 'What can we do so that the promise in this saga can be fulfilled? The enormity of the task overwhelms me.' The older one answered: 'One who earnestly seeks to know how human destiny is advancing and who gives himself to this destiny will find that the world current will bring to him the thoughts and symptoms that he needs in order to incorporate his esoteric work for the development of mankind rightly into the stream of human becoming.'

37. Travels, Wonders, Surprises

In June 1933 Polzer went on a trip to Venice and Dalmatia with his brother Arthur's eldest daughter. For Christl (Maria Christine), it was her first time to see Venice and the sea. The weather was wonderful, and so uncle Ludwig and his niece went to the Lido and spent happy days on water and on land. They visited Venice's churches, the collections of paintings in the Academia and would certainly have enjoyed eating out together. They also went on a short excursion to Torcello. 'They were lovely days,' wrote Polzer, 'Christl is a pleasant travelling companion, enjoys everything so much and is very grateful for everything.'[421]

At the end of July they went to Dubrovnik, which in those days was called Ragusa. The sea there was very calm, so Polzer was spared seasickness and could even enjoy the crossing. From Ragusa they travelled on by bus in more beautiful weather to Kotor and over the Lovcen to Cetinje in Montenegro again. Then the travellers responded to the invitation of the Knispels and spent some fine days in Kambelovac. Frau Schenker and her daughter Sabine were also guests of the Knispels. There is a photo which shows the small group of friends and acquaintances in a happy mood (fig. 49). After a few days Polzer travelled to Graz with his niece and showed her the places where her father and he had spent their youth. They climbed the Schlossberg, stood in front of the Renaissancehaus on the Sporrgasse, visited the grave of Uncle Alfred, the brother of Christl's grandfather Julius.

When the pair arrived in Baden at the end of their long journey, on which they had not had a single day of rain, they were joyfully welcomed by Arthur's family. Marie-Sefine especially was overjoyed to have her niece back again looking so healthy. They all spent a happy evening together. Christl, whose health had benefited from the trip, danced for them a little.

The two brothers, who were both so similar and yet so different, became closer again as a result of the trip. Ludwig wrote that 'our old brotherly relationship, which had suffered somewhat due to our different destinies, was restored to its original untroubled nature and has remained so since'. The brothers decided to visit Modern for two days. On 25 September they went to visit their father's grave, then the old monastery mill, where they had used to play as children and which Arthur had since acquired. They went to The Sands, to the Holzhauer cemetery and visited a cousin, who invited them for a meal. 'How fine I felt our old brotherly bond in those two days,' wrote the elder brother of their stay in Modern.

From that time on the brothers exchanged views more and more on political experiences and memories. One day Arthur read to Ludwig from writings that came from Empress Zita which made clear that Emperor Karl had ordered that Foreign Minister Czernin be arrested before his resignation but that the head of the police had hesitated to carry out the order. Ludwig said of this:

> This shows that there was a well-concealed conspiracy against Emperor Karl, who had placed Czernin at his disposal at Brest-Litovsk [...] The Empress was not well-disposed towards my brother—I can well understand that—and yet she fought like him against Czernin [...] the Empress at that time was an instrument of the Roman Church authorities, and Czernin the instrument of the German military.

★

At the end of September Ludwig Polzer travelled to Dornach for the Michaelmas Conference. Rudolf Steiner's fourth mystery drama, *The Soul's Awakening*, was performed. For lunch he went to the house of Erna Bögel, the mother of his daughter-in-law Ilona, with whom his grandson Christward was growing up in a quiet, well-cared-for manner.

After the conference he went to Geneva, where the League of Nations had its centre. He wanted to speak to Beneš but was unable to meet him. He received a letter from Masaryk on 5 October. It was dated 1 October and had been written in Topolcianky, where Masaryk regularly went for his health.

During their last meeting in April, Masaryk had urged Polzer to write to him, which Polzer very soon did. Now the old President wrote back:

> Honoured Count,
> My warmest thanks for your friendly words and the additional materials.
> All the ideas which you bring forward I have also been concerned with [...] I occasionally reflect on how far the expansion of which you speak is caused by overpopulation. I ask myself this question in regard to Hitlerism—more important than the racist mythology is the call for territory—where? In the East. Thus Poland and Russia are much more important [for Hitler] than the Germans in the neighbouring states. This also applies to the drive to the east, which began from the Hamburg area. I shall speak to Dr Beneš about some more of the ideas in your philosophy of history.
> With best greetings: T.G.Masaryk

Polzer had apparently spoken to Masaryk about the problem of 'Lebensraum', the great illusion that domestic political conflicts could be solved by territorial expansion. Besides the Nazis' racist mythology, the old President underestimated the danger of expansion of the Germans 'in[to] the neighbouring states': On the same day he wrote his answer to Polzer, the 'Sudeten Germans' Home Front' was formed, led by Konrad Henlein. Exactly five years later, on 1 October 1938, following the signing of the Munich Agreement, German troops occupied the Sudeten German regions of Czechoslovakia with the dubious blessing, amongst others, of France and Britain. In a certain respect, the lamentably cunning Munich Agreement resembled the decision of 28 June 1878 at the Berlin Congress when, at the urging of Lord Salisbury, the Austrians were advised and allowed to occupy Bosnia-Herzegovina, with similarly evil consequences.

But let us return to the autumn of 1933. Masaryk fell ill soon afterwards, and Polzer's answer had not been sent by the time of Masaryk's death in 1937. We shall come to speak of Polzer's answer later on.

When Polzer received Masaryk's letter, he was thinking of leaving for Zermatt, not least because that part of Switzerland was unknown to him. On 6 October he climbed the Riffl-Alm from Zermatt and the following day returned to Austria via Basel.

In October he had another meeting with Theodora Zeissig, whose psychological illness, as Polzer himself said, weighed very much on his heart. 'Like a miracle', she had recently been completely cured by a magnetopathic treatment. 'I saw her again in October after a long while. She has become a strong healthy girl.' Deeply indicative of his idea that, from across the veil of history, it was possible for Rudolf Steiner to accompany the destiny paths of those who were united with him, are Polzer's words: 'I am sure that Rudolf Steiner helped towards this destiny's fulfilment.' Polzer's own study of Steiner's characterization on 14 January 1917 of the three basic types of psychological illness (GA 174) may at least not have hindered the favourable course of Theodora's case . . .

A weight of destiny fell from Polzer's heart. Its weight can be surmised from the relief that sounds through his words:

> What was in many respects a heavy year also brought me a pure, light joy. Theodora Zeissig, who was apparently completely mentally disturbed at the Federal Therapeutic Institute at Hall near Innsbruck has been healed by a magnetopathic treatment. It is like a miracle.

Six years later, he was still able to say: 'Her health has remained steady; six years have gone by since she recovered and there has not been the slightest sign of illness.'

Shortly after this news which enabled him to breathe out, as it were, he went on a short trip. Margrit Schön had invited him to Budapest for lectures. Once again, he took one of his nieces with him, this time Arthur's youngest, Hannerl.

On 15 November he lectured at the Hotel Bristol to an audience that consisted of members of the public as well as of the Anthroposophical Society. His title was: 'The Fifteenth Century and the Present in the Light of Anthroposophy'. With Hannerl he visited the daughter of his old hunting friend Vilmos Pálffy who before her marriage had been a lady-in-waiting to Empress Zita. Aimée Pálffy also came to Polzer's Budapest lectures.

One afternoon he was asked to call on the infirm Countess Andrássy, the wife of Géza Andrássy, who had expressed a wish to learn from him something about anthroposophy.

The next day he and Hannerl went to a performance of *Tristan*. Géza Andrássy too was sitting next to Aimée Pálffy and a man from the Austrian embassy when Polzer lectured on the two Elisabeths on 19 November, the saint from Thuringia (to whom the Polzers traced their line) and the Empress of the same name of whom the Hungarians were so fond. He observed, 'This is always an attractive theme for Hungarians.' On the way home to Baden, they stopped in Pressburg [Bratislava], where he gave a lecture to Society branch members.

★

'My health is beginning to cause me more problems, and political and economic affairs fill me with concern.' Polzer began the year 1934 with this observation, but throughout the year his lecturing activity went on undiminished.

In Prague in January and February he saw a lot of his friends Lou and Leo Knispel who were spending a long holiday in the city. They were staying at the hotel *Hybernia*, where Polzer too would stay in the coming years, after the demolition of the old familiar hotel *Zum Blauen Stern*.

On 12 February there were street battles in Vienna after Chancellor Dollfuss had banned the 'Nationalist Party' the previous year. Polzer noted in his diary: 'A heavy, dark mood hangs over Austria. I consider that in this situation it cannot go on; [Austria] it can only become an object of booty.' Four years later, this became the case.

In Prague he spoke at the end of February again on the two Elisabeths of whom he had spoken in Budapest. Maňa Brabínek, who had married Zdeněk Kalva on 12 February came again when she could to Polzer's lectures in Prague and Pardubice.

'Today, as in the fourth cultural epoch,' he warned in his lectures in February in Pardubice, Prague and Vienna, 'the attempt is being made to establish a universal empire with a rigid, spiritually-mechanized centralism, the most appalling display of power and blind subjugation. The call for a dictator goes through the whole civilized world because humanity has lost the sense for life, the dignity and meaning of the human being.' Polzer pointed to Steiner's warning (in the seventh Class Lesson[422]) of the intention of certain circles to resurrect 'the Holy Roman Empire of the German Nation in order to bring under their domination precisely those peoples and individuals that bear in themselves the spiritual seeds of a later culture'. Then he spoke about Dostoyevsky's *Grand Inquisitor*, in which the attitude of theocratic domination towards a new Christ revelation is made clear, even though Dostoyevsky represents this new revelation as something entirely physical. Polzer titled his lecture 'Caesar or Christ' and based himself on Steiner's lecture cycle on the Fifth Gospel.

*

In February and March 1934 he made two short visits to Mariensee. After the February visit, he wrote in the guestbook: 'Ludwig Polzer, the poorly invalid', but on 9 March: 'Ludwig Polzer reactivated.' This was fortunate, for his newly gained forces would soon be needed for a new task: new regular lecturing activity began in the same month. From this point on, Polzer travelled once a month to Graz, where he stayed with Frau Neumann in Heinrichstrasse. He continued this work until the fatal General Meeting of the Anthroposophical Society in spring 1935. Following a warning given by Rudolf Steiner, he often spoke in 1934 about historical individuals in the time of the twilight of the fourth cultural epoch and the transition to the fifth: Cola di Rienzi, Dante, Charles IV, Joan of Arc. But also the struggle between the Popes and the Emperors, the Guelfs and the Ghibellines was a basic theme of this period of his lecturing.

On 30 March he led the Pardubice Branch in its commemoration of his friend and teacher Rudolf Steiner.

Hardly had he arrived at the home of his friends the Knispels in Kambelovac and begun to relax when a telegram arrived calling him to Baden. His sister Marie-Sefine lay dying. When he arrived in Baden on 14 April he learned that his sister had died the day before of a carcinoma.

A few days later, the traveller was once again in Prague.

On 20 April he went to a performance of *Boris Godunov* with Herta Reichart. Perhaps this gave him the impetus to take up the problem of Dmitri[*] which Rudolf Steiner had indicated to him in 1924?

---

[*] Czar Dmitri of Russia, the so-called 'False Dmitri' 1605–1606—*transl.*

After a further excursion with Herta to the beloved Karlstein, he gave a lecture to members of the Anthroposophical Society in Vienna on 8 May and the following month again in Prague. The outline sketch of this June lecture in Prague includes a very interesting key idea which was to carry ever more weight in Polzer's own view of the growing problems within the Anthroposophical Society. '*The Church built its external power and domination on the ruins of Rome.—Principle of the centralization of power.*

'*Esoteric Christianity will build an all-human world on the ruins of the bourgeois world by [the] principle of freedom-decentralization.*'[423] He added the notes: 'Rudolf Steiner told me to go out and speak to people. Not being able to carry things through showed itself.' This comment may be applied to Polzer's decentralizing steps in public outlined in the fourth chapter as well as his actions within the Anthroposophical Society from the General Meetings of which, as already mentioned, he had stayed away from since 1929.

At the end of June he went for his last visit to the spa in Pistyan. He read lectures by Rudolf Steiner together as usual with Herta Reichart's parents; he also gave lectures himself to the small circle.

With his forces renewed, after a few weeks he took up again his stay in Kambelovac which he had interrupted. He went with Leo Knispel to the island of Korcula where Dora Schenker was holidaying. There was also a Yugoslavian foreign ministry official there by the name of Alfieri. The small group studied lectures by Rudolf Steiner from the year 1917. Thus was decentralized freedom within anthroposophical work practised concretely.

Only in August did Polzer once again spend a period of some weeks continuously in Tannbach. There is a passage from a diary from this period that speaks of his unbroken inner relationship to Berta:

> Berta, you dear true companion of my life, you destiny comrade in both good and hard times! So strong and brave is your great soul, but I feel it is also in a hard struggle. I know and also learned to be silent. And you are a blessing for children, first for your own and then for all those you meet [...] What your influence can do for children, I experience in a dear child's soul who has been a guest at Tannbach for a few years now. A good destiny led her to you.

It is not clear who Polzer meant by this 'dear child's soul', but his deep appreciation of Berta's nature becomes all the more evident when he goes on: 'When I take up any of the poems of my dear Berta they are so liberating in all the difficult situations in life; through them I even feel the effectiveness of Rudolf Steiner working individualized in a way that is so close to me in destiny.'

Polzer also spent much time in Tannbach with a book Maña Brabínek had given him: the novel by Agnes Günther—*Die Heilige und ihr Narr* [The Saint and her Fool]. 'When my heart feels heavy, when a kind of fear grips me then I take up this book these days [. . .] and then something is relieved in my soul.'

So, in these days in Tannbach two meaningful books played an essential role for Polzer—Günther's novel and Berta's volume of poems—books from two people who were so close to him, albeit in very different ways.

During a two-week-long stay in Mariensee the incessant wanderer climbed several heights. In the guestbook on 26 September he wrote: 'Enjoying the lovely autumn with a newly-awakened wanderlust.' But a very grave event occurred at this time. It came in dream on awakening. Polzer wrote: 'On 21 September at Mariensee I had an experience in the morning as though someone would say to me that King Alexander I of Serbia was in danger of being assassinated.' We would wish to leave the reader to ponder as to the question of the origin of this voice; let us instead follow Polzer's words further.

'King Alexander had heard of anthroposophy from one of his military adjutants and had also read Steiner's *Occult Science—An Outline*.'[424] The adjutant was Branko Naumović, who later fought against Tito and then emigrated to America. Alexander 'strove for a Balkan league out of the forces of the Balkans and its own peoples and individuals. He represented the real, remaining Slavic soul in opposition to that which was corrupted by the West.' For Polzer he was therefore one of the very few figures in the western Slavic countries who was in a position to be able to build a counterweight to the corrupted Slavic stream that was swayed by the Testament of Peter the Great.

Alexander was due to make a State visit to Marseilles at the beginning of October. There he was to discuss with the French Foreign Minister Barthou a projected pact between France and the Balkan countries proposed by Barthou.

Polzer, who over many years on the basis of many similar experiences had developed the ability to be able to discriminate well between truth and illusion even in the area of inner experience, acted, as so often in decisive moments, very fast and resolutely. He immediately wrote to Leo Knispel, who just then happened to be hosting Col. Vujić (see Fig. 49) at his home. Vujić was acquainted with Naumović, and so Polzer hoped that his advice to cancel the planned trip to France would come at the right time thanks to Vujić's intervention. But unfortunately, his letter was 'not taken seriously enough'. On 9 October 1934 Alexander I was assassinated in Marseilles at the instigation of the Croatian Ustasha movement. Polzer wrote: 'When the assassination happened soon afterwards I was myself very shaken and Col. Knispel no less.' He made further comments about what lay behind this assassination: 'Alexander was in the way of all the leading political power groups, including those in his own country. The same forces were active in the background as with the assassination of Michael Obrenović in 1868, the assassination of Franz Ferdinand and others.' These others also included the last Obrenović, King Alexander Obrenović who was assassinated with his wife Draga Mašin in Belgrade in 1903.

These victims of destiny who preceded Alexander I strove in various ways to solve the Serbian Question independently of western and Roman interests. To an even greater degree was this true of King Alexander who was assassinated in 1934.

> Alexander wanted to be free of the influences of the West and of Roman [Catholic] countries—to which his Marseilles visit was in a sense opposed—[he] did not agree with Soviet Russia's entry into the League of Nations and was against any Balkan Federation that would be under the influence of a Great Power yet he did not perceive what was working against him and was therefore unable to recognize effective ways and possibilities of avoiding the destiny that befell him.

Polzer pointed to a fundamental problem in throwing light on such political assassinations in the following words: 'The real figures behind this assassination are well-disguised by the general clouding of human souls' spiritual insights.'

Real contemporary processes are not normally experienced more wakefully than in dreams. One could just as well say: 'than in feelings'. For even the reality of feeling we normally experience only in a state of dreaming. That we are awake in relation to our *ideas* about dreams and feelings and contemporary processes is another matter and should not be allowed to disguise the fact that the real effectiveness of the phenomena in question, which is independent of our ideas and which concerns the level of consciousness with which we grasp it, is nevertheless *dreamt through*.[425]

Only a spiritual training can *awaken* one from the dreaming of real historical impulses so that certain events are not grasped only as *faits accomplis* (post factum) but in *statu nascendi* (as they are happening). This is what we can state was the case with Ludwig Polzer at this point: an awakening to the real powers of becoming that are at work in very definite outer events and that would otherwise be, if not entirely slept through, then dreamt through.

By this dream experience Polzer felt both shattered but also strengthened in that his capacity for realistic understanding of actual historical growth forces was developing positively, even if they appeared to be giving him at first only insight into very negative phenomena. So despite its shattering nature it marked a milestone on the path of his inner development. And only if people become more and more conscious of the real impulses that form history—which also include the worst retarding forces—can the philistine 'science of history', with its unsuitable methods of understanding and which is always and everywhere too slow in its conclusions, be transformed step by step into a higher form of research of historical and contemporary events.

★

Following the murder in Marseilles, Polzer once again gave thought to statements by Rudolf Steiner that could have made a real contribution to the awakening in question here. He wrote:

> How often Rudolf Steiner warned that if the living spirit is unable to enliven the thinking of considerable numbers of people in Middle Europe, then brutalization, barbarism, the worst cruelty and destruction will take hold in Middle Europe such as have never been known in human history. How clearly recognizable this is! No one, however, should say that not enough was done to alert the public in time. The 'soul sleep' was so deep that even the cruelties of the First World War could not bring mankind to an active recognition of the spiritual world in art, science and religion.

And not only in the waking-dream anticipation not only of a single murder but of the already approaching murder of whole peoples, he warned at the time of writing these notes (LPE; spring 1939):

> The absurd phrase 'liberation of peoples' which during the First World War was used by the West to justify the war, is now sounding again from the Middle. How can one want to liberate something directly on Earth, which is only a nominalistic concept on earth and does not actually exist in reality? One can only liberate *individual human beings* on Earth and can only grasp peoples through doing this. *On Earth the highest is the individual human being; his liberation can only be a spiritual deed. All wars, acts of violence, and outer revolutions cannot accomplish that. A revolution of the spirit is necessary.*[426] Spiritual comfort, lack of spiritual courage, fear and hatred of the spirit must be overcome. *Humanity slept while the initiator was here and will have to bear the consequences,*[427] until a new opportunity presents itself. The paths of individuals' destinies and that of society, of humanity, have become intertwined and confused. We must learn to find our way within this

complexity. All cleverness in political economy—to use this monstrous phrase—and juggling with lies ultimately is of no help at all today.

★

In that same autumn when Polzer had penetrated a level deeper, so to speak, into the fluid, real fundaments of historical events through the murder in Marseilles that he had experienced prophetically, the 69-year-old Archduke Eugen returned to Vienna from exile in Basel.

The last Grand Master of the Teutonic Knights, as already mentioned in an earlier chapter, between 1895 and 1905 had renovation work carried out at the Order's castle at Busau, which had once been owned by Polzer's maternal ancestor. On that occasion, as described earlier, he had had the paintings of the worldly knight and of 'the knight of the spirit' moved to the lobby of the Knights' Hall. Polzer immediately called on the archduke, whom he had known personally from the time of his exile in Basel. The archduke knew Rudolf Steiner and had attended many events at the Goetheanum. Like Masaryk and King Alexander, Archduke Eugen, with his liberal views and his spiritual interests, was for Polzer someone in whom he could have political hopes. 'I place some hope in him,' wrote Polzer.

> Not in the legitimist sense[*] but in the spiritual sense. Linking on to the conversation I had with him, I wrote him a very long letter in which I shared with him some insights I had gained from Rudolf Steiner in relation to the present concrete situation. He promptly replied with a very warm, personal letter which gladdened me. He was political and cultured, but still a prisoner and too old to remove his shackles.

Nevertheless, Polzer thought he could say of him: 'He was one of the Habsburgs who had maintained some spiritual autonomy, one of those few that there have always been over the centuries.' Archduke Eugen's eventful and interesting life still awaits its biographer.

★

In October 1934 Polzer went to Karlsbad to visit his friend Hans Eiselt who was suffering from a severe stomach and liver illness. The friends spent two fine days together without suspecting that Eiselt only had a few years left to live. In Polzer's eyes, Hans Eiselt was the soul of the German-speaking anthroposophical work in Bohemia.

Soon afterwards, on 1 November, he gave a lecture at a branch

---

[*] The cause of the Habsburg dynasty—*transl.*

meeting in Prague. Maña was also in the audience. In this lecture he gave an overview of the history of Serbia, from Michael Obrenović to King Alexander I. He referred to the Testament of Peter the Great and emphasized that Alexander too had wanted to 'bring the South Slavs together', for which goal Michael Obrenović and Archduke Franz Ferdinand had striven before him. This was why he had 'the whole world against him'.

Polzer thus made fruitful the experience that he had had in connection with the murdered king in that he incorporated this murder into his observations on the modern history of Serbia and the whole of European politics.

The following day the inveterate traveller went once more to Karlstejn with the Reichart daughters. How often he had been to this place, where first he had gone with Rudolf Steiner! 'Without him perhaps we would never have gone there,' he writes in his notes in 1939, and later we read in them: 'It was often such an encouragement for me, as if he had led me in an earlier phase of destiny.'

Let us recall Maña's dreams of Karlstejn, and of a very particular late mediaeval castle, in which her friend and teacher played a role then it becomes understandable why Polzer always felt drawn back to Karlstejn. Not that he felt a link to an earlier incarnation of his own at this place; Karlstejn always made him feel, however, a very special affinity with *the period* of the approaching modern age ...

Shortly after this excursion to Karlstejn, news reached Polzer, who had gone to Heiligenkreutz with Berta, of the death of his friend in Vienna, Jo van Leer, without whom the West-East Congress of 1922 would not have been possible. Van Leer had died on 3 November in Baku in the Caucasus after suffering an angina attack.

In December 1934 Col. Dohnal arranged a conference in Chocen. Polzer spoke on 'World History in the Light of Anthroposophy' and focused again on the period of transition from the fourth to the fifth post-Atlantean cultural epochs and on certain representative personalities from that period.

He spent Christmastime with his family at Tannbach until 4 January. They were the last calm days before the heavy storms that 1935 would bring.

38. 'Do You Know the Jesuit?'

Around the turn of the year 1934/35 Ludwig Polzer composed another memorandum, nine pages long, for Central European statesmen. Although it is not known in this case who he sent it to and how it was received, it ought not to remain unmentioned in any biography of Polzer, particularly when, in Polzer's sense, even acts of thinking that are unrealized in immediate practical life become effective in the course of history, perhaps in later times.

Polzer began his memorandum with the words: 'The entire population of Europe stands before momentous events and decisions'[428] and went on to characterize a central factor in recent international politics:

> Imperialism has worked over centuries and in its present form stems from the mentality of the old Roman empire and has been continued and carried further by the Roman [Catholic] Church in such a way that, in order for it to maintain itself, it has to—systematically and very consciously—play the German and Slavic peoples off against each other. It does this to its own advantage and to the damage of the development of Middle European culture. It has made use of the most various methods, including covert means, and also historical resentments which have arisen in the tragedy of Middle European history and others which have resulted from them. *This centralizing, Roman imperialistic idea which, proceeding from the peoples of the Mediterranean, ever sought to establish itself in northern Europe has in the last few centuries based itself on the economic capabilities and potential of the English-speaking peoples and has influenced these capabilities in a political and strategic manner. Consequently, the economic capabilities of these peoples have not been for the benefit of general human welfare and progress but only for the egoistic development of the power of a single group of States which has believed that it alone can provide the culture needed for the future, while in reality what was driving it were economic and egoistic power motives.*
>
> *The Anglo-American Empire became the economic support for the Catholic Church's dominance which it was increasingly unable to maintain by spiritual means. As the old Caesarism has conserved itself in the Roman Church in a pseudo-democratic form, it has always set itself against the development of the human spirit and soul and has emphasized the immutability of human souls.*[429]

A consequence of Roman-Anglo-American politics was that among the Slavs *two* streams formed, which have already been referred to several times in this book, one that is corrupted by the West and is, as it were, obedient to the West, and another that is the still uncorrupted, but largely submerged, second stream, that of true Slav culture. This second 'stream of the Slavs must not be wholly exterminated; it is awaiting its salvation'.

Efforts for such salvation would have to take their start from the harmonizing of relations between the Germans and the Western Slavic regions—wholly in the sense of the vow that was made in the Chapel of St Wenceslas.

> Mankind can only go forward to a future worthy of human dignity and really begin to build up Europe—to use this much abused expression—if a spiritual and cultural marriage takes place between German culture and western Slavic culture. Only from this can proceed the beginnings of a general human, truly social, new order which will serve the progress of the culture of mankind as a whole.
>
> Russia belongs to a much later period of cultural development, for which Middle Europe and not England must create the preconditions. Cultural communities must therefore not be conceived as intended by western powers, namely that a boundary is to be fixed in Europe between German and Slavic culture [...] The boundary for the Middle European cultural community would therefore have to run between the Russians and the western Slavs.

This idea that serves general human cultural progress was opposed from the Anglo-American side and transformed into a gigantic counter-concept: that of the dominance of the Anglo-American peoples, who are also called to take in hand the cultivation of the Slavic peoples. The idea of Anglo-American imperialism is expressed in a grandiose style, as already mentioned, by Lord Rosebery, British Prime Minister in the 1890s, who was close to the circle around Cecil Rhodes. Rosebery was a close friend of Winston Churchill's father and was much admired by Winston Churchill himself, who wrote a memorial to Rosebery in his *Great Contemporaries*.[430]

Orienting itself ever more strongly towards cooperation with the Church of Rome,

> Anglo-American politics [increasingly directed itself] in accordance with the following guidelines: Romanness is in decadence; on its ruins we seek to build the economic imperium of the English-speaking peoples and the power of the Vatican. We seek to establish the universal empire of the old Rome by means of economic power as a universal empire of economy, politics and a formal ecclesiastical power *opposed to the spirit*, which will mechanize people and thus make materialism into the truth of life.

'A real symptomatological study of the history of recent centuries and its spiritually hidden background,' said Polzer near the end of his memorandum, 'could show the necessary paths and possibilities by which the peoples of Middle Europe can be rescued. This rescue is only possible when one allows oneself to be guided by the principle: "Middle Europe must never become Roman!'' And in the broader context that means: never Anglo-American-Roman.'

With the thoughts in this memorandum Polzer had cast his eye on two powers which obstruct all real human progress, one more in the economic sphere, the other more in the spiritual sphere. At the beginning of 1935 he had first turned to the activities of this double power on the macro-scale and through this had prepared himself to look chiefly into *one* side of this double power—which was now approaching the high point of its destructive effectiveness—within the spiritual stream to which he himself felt connected. It hardly needs to be said that both powers of obstruction are always only in a position to work indirectly, through consciousnesses that are fast asleep or deeply dreaming, until finally, the individual's sleepiness itself opens the doors to them . . .

In his notes for a lecture he gave in Prague in January 1935 is written: 'My effort: to awaken from small personal affairs to the great seriousness of the times. Anthroposophy: not for the playground and also not for philistines. Mankind in the greatest spiritual struggle [that] has ever been.' From the struggle the Anthroposophical Society was not to be spared.

In his writings from the year 1939 Ludwig Polzer introduces his account of the split in the General Anthroposophical Society (G.A.S.) and of the breakdown of its Vorstand in the following simple words: 'This year was decisive for my relationship to the Vorstand at the Goetheanum and to a part of the Anthroposophical Society.' What was decided?

Let us relate the process of events.

In the night of 18 to 19 February 1935 Polzer had a very special dream. He wrote (LPE):

> I dreamt that I was in a gathering in a lecture hall in which there were some empty chairs. Dr Steiner stood at the podium and addressed a question to me: 'Do you know the Jesuit who wishes to bring jesuitic methods into the Society?' I answered, somewhat confusedly: 'No, Herr Doctor.' There was agitation in the room. Then I awoke and could not understand what it could have meant.

On 6 March a confidential letter arrived for the Vorstand of the Society in Vienna. It was addressed to Hans-Erhard Lauer, Polzer's Vorstand colleague and co-worker from the time of the *Austrian Messenger*. Lauer read out the letter from Dornach. It contained the motions which some of the Vorstand of the Society in Germany wished to present to all the members at the Easter General Meeting.

> These [motions] were concerned to exclude Frau Dr Wegman, Frl. Dr Vreede [from the Vorstand] and to exclude a number of older members

who had been much esteemed by Dr Steiner [from the Society] because they did not wish to submit to the will of a part of the Vorstand. The opposition to Frau Dr Wegman, to whom he had entrusted the Medical Section and whom he had appointed Recorder to the Vorstand—opposition which was already there when Dr Steiner was alive—had now broken out openly.

The other candidates for exclusion, all of whom were members Rudolf Steiner had valued, included Jürgen von Grone, who worked more than any other to give an objective account of the life and work of Helmuth von Moltke; Eugen Kolisko, Willem Zeylmans van Emmichoven, the General Secretary of the Society in Holland, and Daniel Dunlop, the General Secretary of the Society in Great Britain.

Reading this communication from Dornach worked like a destructive elemental force within the Austrian Vorstand. Polzer wrote: 'Since the founding of the Society in 1923 we had worked together harmoniously. In this session the Vorstand split apart as if struck by lightning.'

And looking back on that Vienna Vorstand session of 6 March 1935 eight years later, he wrote:

> In my soul I had the impression of an elemental catastrophe due to the enormous agitation that showed itself. Until then, we had been 'in Austria' and now we were seized by powers of destruction. Dr Lauer, Dr Thieben and Herr Breitenstein declared themselves for the motion; Herr Alfred Zeissig, Prof Halla and I were opposed.[431]

The same lightning strike which split the Vienna Vorstand in two groups that day suddenly threw light for Ludwig Polzer on the peculiar dream he had had in February. Now he knew what the experience of that night had prepared him for! He understood the dream, however, not in the sense of a call to recognize particular members of the G.A.S. as Jesuits but as a call to awaken to how the *Jesuit spirit* could work through various personalities: 'So it was the Jesuit spirit! This indication became for me a guideline for my later observations within the Anthroposophical Society; the struggle against the spirit always lay and still lies in the background of all outer and inner events, especially since the Thirty Years' War.' Polzer added to this: 'Since then it has been my aim to penetrate this in detail. The experience that night* before the General Meeting showed me how I should work in order not to lose my connection with the great teacher.'[432]

If one seeks to characterize this Jesuit spirit in a few words, then one can

---

* In February 1935—*transl.*

say: it strives for the establishment of a centralizing spiritual power, for 'Papacy' not only in the Church but in every other spiritual stream. The papal principle advanced by the Jesuit spirit is always accompanied by the faith in a central authority. These two Jesuit principles by themselves regard the 'ethical individualism' of spiritual science—according to which the individual can himself find his own principles of thinking and acting—with utter scorn. A third attribute of the Jesuit spirit lies in the principle of divide and rule (*divide et impera*) which was practised by the pre-Catholic Roman Empire.

This Jesuit spirit burst upon the G.A.S. in 1935 as if through a broken dam, with the widespread force of an epidemic. People spoke of the 'correct method' and began to think in terms of this one correct method. Others insisted on the authority of some members of the Dornach Vorstand and above all on authorization by the President of the Vorstand.

Though Polzer had worked in a collegial and friendly manner with Hans-Erhard Lauer until the mid-1930s, suddenly the letter from Dornach opened up an abyss between the two men. The motions did the same in all the Vorstands of national societies in the G.A.S. and from the Vorstands these fissures spread like an earthquake throughout the entire membership.

★

Polzer immediately decided to try to block the disastrous effects of the elemental catastrophe unleashed by the exclusion motions as quickly as possible.

After he had attended the funeral of Dorothea Teutschmann, one of Dora Schenker's daughters, on 8 March in Linz, he travelled to Dornach. Here he wanted above all to speak to Albert Steffen, who had been a witness at the christening of his grandson Christward, in order 'to ask him not to proceed with his intention to have the motions printed in the Goetheanum Newssheet'.

How did Albert Steffen react to this request?

Polzer wrote:

> Herr Steffen was astonished that I had come. I did not hold back from explaining that this [the exclusion motions] would cause a fateful split in the whole Society and that I could in no way vote for it at the General Meeting. Steffen appeared to me to be quite helpless and said that he would have to take account of the attitude of a working committee which had formed for this purpose and which was publishing a *Memorandum*. He advised me, to speak with some other gentlemen, that is, with those who were writing this Memorandum, which I promptly and energetically said I would not do.

The *Memorandum* Steffen referred to here was an 'attack piece' which appeared only three weeks before the General Meeting and sought to create a climate of support for the exclusion motions by a mixture of truths, half-truths and untruths. (It was reproduced in the third volume of *Wer war Ita Wegman?* [Who Was Ita Wegman?] by Emanuel Zeylmans van Emmichoven).

It is not our intention to present a comprehensive analysis of the complex processes which led to the split in the Society. The interested reader is referred to the available literature. Only one aspect will be recalled here (cf. the chapter 'Building Bridges') which to us seems essential: the impulse of karma revelation, which emerged after the Goetheanum fire of 1922/23 between Rudolf Steiner and Ita Wegman in a very conscious fashion and which was also of decisive importance for the Christmas Conference in 1923 as well as for Rudolf Steiner's karma revelations in 1924. All the difficulties, divergences, and splits within the G.A.S. stood directly or indirectly in relation to this central aspect of the Christmas Conference. When one thinks about the far-reaching nature of karmic considerations, then it is scarcely to be wondered at that, especially when they go into concrete details and immediately fall onto hard 'soul ground', they can easily lead to strife and division. For nothing stirs up the lower, unrefined nature of the human being more than observations that concern his true, eternal nature which has passed through various incarnations. The ego that is bound to the current physicality of *one* incarnation has through its earthly nature the impetus within itself to fear, doubt or scorn the supra–earthly character of the true individuality and its *repeated* earth lives.

The *Memorandum* of spring 1935, in a way, brought to expression all these difficulties in a manner that is as instructive as it is shocking. Although, for example, no author of this attack piece claimed to have researched the karmic background *out of his own knowledge*, one finds in the text sentences such as the following:

> Some members, partly through their study of Dr Steiner's lectures, but also partly, as they said, on the basis of their own karmic research, had come to a conviction which made a deep impression on some others. This conviction was that the individuality of Alexander the Great, described by Dr Steiner a number of times and especially at the Christmas Conference of 1923, had incarnated amongst the membership. Not only was this supposed to be the case but it was claimed that Alexander's entire company had also reappeared and indeed among these very members who were doing this karma research. All these great figures were now clustered around Frau Dr Wegman herself. And thus for this circle the question of the ongoing

leadership of the Anthroposophical Society was solved [...] Since, beside this, Dr Steiner had spoken of the significance for spiritual life of the historical individuality concerned, those circles believed themselves able to devote themselves to the thought that after Dr Steiner's death, a second leader of the Anthroposophical movement was active in earthly life. From the combination of the *apparent* reincarnations of so many former military leaders with their so-called esoteric tasks [...] there developed an attitude of soul which proclaimed on the one hand, that everything that Frau Dr Wegman and some of her colleagues did was infallible in word and deed and on the other hand, demanded from the members followership and obedience rather than *judgements based on one's own reason.*[433]

One can observe the underlying scorn, the mockery even, which is evident in some of these phrases. The tone and style employed here could have been employed in a serious manner at most, if one had wanted to test or even had been able to test the truth of this 'apparent' karmic knowledge or only karmic supposition objectively—instead of the a priori way in which it was here regarded with an aura of scorn—and if then, as a result of such testing, it had been found to be of no value at all. However, in the entire text there is nowhere any evidence of any such testing or even of an *intention* of testing such 'apparent' reincarnations. This fact alone gives the Memorandum the character of unserious superficiality and shows, in crass contradiction to what the authors of the Memorandum call for, a shocking lack of *judgements based on one's own reason*. This of course is not to say that on the part of those who were genuinely striving for understanding and knowledge of particular karmic relationships, there had not been mistakes made or carelessness in regard to the question of the right time or place for communicating certain things.

After the fruitless conversation with Albert Steffen on 11 March, Polzer went to Ita Wegman for a confidential talk with her and to inform her of his own standpoint. Then, 'without having achieved anything', he returned to Vienna.

On 17 March the ill-fated motions appeared in the *Nachrichtenblatt* [Newsletter].[434] They can be found in the third volume of *Wer war Ita Wegman?* by Emanuel Zeylmans van Emmichoven, along with the uncut reproduction of the Memorandum.[435] The first motion was concerned with the exclusion of the two Vorstand members Wegman and Vreede; the second with that of the above-mentioned prominent members of the Society; the third with the non-recognition of the United Free Groups, which had first formed themselves in Germany following the Vorstand members' difficulties in working together. The motions were followed by an 'Explanation and Reasoning'. This stated that:

For years the impossibility of collaboration in the Vorstand in view of the actual and open opposition of two Vorstand members [Wegman and Vreede] has been evident. This opposition has led to unsolvable problems for the Society, because it has to do not only with differences of opinion but with the fact that members of the Vorstand have, through their insincere behaviour and continuous obstruction, brought the Vorstand, as the leadership of the Society, ad absurdum.

From Polzer's perspective, things looked rather different. He wrote:

In recent years this step [the motions for exclusion] has been prepared by Marie Steiner, Herr Albert Steffen and Dr Wachsmuth by continuous hostility towards the other two Vorstand members and towards Dr Kolisko, Dr Walther Johannes Stein and against English and Dutch friends. This made it especially difficult for English friends *because attention was paid only to the centre in Dornach and not at all to the work in the periphery.* The consequence of this was that very little came from the side of those disinclined to Dornach, who did not recognize that a divided Vorstand was esoterically justified in presenting such motions. The Middle European national societies, especially those of Austria and Slovakia, were split. In Austria, more leaned towards Frau Marie Steiner; in Bohemia, especially the Slavic element, more towards Frau Dr Wegman.

In Polzer's view a *centralizing ethos* had more and more gained the upper hand—one could even say: a Jesuit ethos. This gave rise in the first motion to a very particular formulation: there was mention of 'acts' [*Handlungen*] by both Vorstand members 'that bore the character of self-exclusion'. Emanuel Zeylmans noted: 'Steffen's use of the term "self-exclusion" [*Selbstausschluss*] is, as it were, the anthroposophical counterpart to the *excommunication ipso facto* of the Catholic Church: a person who denied defined dogmas of the Church thereby excluded himself.'[436]

In defending Ita Wegman (and Elisabeth Vreede) Polzer was not acting from personal motives but felt himself obliged to do so for very definite objective reasons; indeed, for the same reasons that had led him to try to mediate between the two Vorstand members in 1925. He wrote:

Frau Dr Wegman must [...] be supported [...] at the General Meeting. Since I received from Dr Steiner the authorization to hold Class Lessons in the Michael School and Rudolf Steiner designated Frau Dr Wegman as being in the closest relationship with the Michael School, I saw it as my task to defend Frau Dr Wegman and to stand by her.

From a letter sent by Ita Wegman on 2 April to the art dealer Wilhelm Goyert in Cologne, who was linked to the curative pedagogy work through his wife Ingeborg, it is clear that Polzer wanted to mobilize as many members as possible who would vote against the exclusion motions planned for the General Meeting on 14 April and that he had been successful in this regard in England and Holland but not in Germany. Wegman's letter also expresses in a remarkable way her inner composure in the face of the appalling situation. She writes:

> Dear Herr Goyert!
> A while ago Count Polzer was here from Vienna to speak to me about Society matters. He told me that he had felt called spiritually by Dr Steiner—he told me of a dream that he had had—to do something for the Society to protect it from the particular machinations by spirits that seek to destroy Rudolf Steiner's work by taking over unsuspecting people as their instruments. In the Vorstand of the Austrian Society he has, along with two other members of the Vorstand refused to sign the motions for the exclusions of the two [Dornach] Vorstand members and of the six other individuals. He now wants to gather together those people who wish to defend themselves against what is going on, because he finds it a disgrace for the Anthroposophical Society and contrary to the principles of Rudolf Steiner. He also asked me what I thought of it and I answered that if I were in his position I would do the same but that naturally, as a member of the Vorstand, I cannot do other than quietly await what the members themselves want.
>
> Count Polzer is also of the view that if one cannot oneself come to the General Meeting, one can at least protest and make one's voice heard, and although we do not believe that it will be of use, given the general mood, it may yet be valuable for *the history of anthroposophy* to have voices of protest [...]

To this end, Polzer composed a short, formulaic protest statement, but either the voices of protest from the periphery faded away very quickly or else, which is more likely, one wanted in Dornach only to acknowledge the voices of those members who were actually present at the General Meeting and not views that were sent in. At any rate, in the formal voting procedure on 14 April there was no mention of such views having being received.

Near the end of her letter to Goyert, Wegman showed her considered, impersonal attitude to the threatening situation very clearly once more when she wrote:

> If you now ask me what I think of the whole situation, then I can tell you: personally it would not bother me if the Anthroposophical Society were to exclude me and the other individuals from the Vorstand or from the Society. *I regard all such things as a maya.* It looks differently from the spiritual world, and it can also be that the destruction of a form has to be thought of

in the same way as the Goetheanum had to be thought of: it is sad but it is an earthly thing that has been burned down; *the spirit cannot be harmed and it will work all the more strongly*, indeed one can even speak of a symbolic burial which could well be followed by a resurrection.[437]

While Ita Wegman herself therefore decided to do nothing and to await calmly what would come, Polzer decided to do the opposite: to do everything so that no one would be hurt by the consequences of a deed that had been planned. To put it in aristotelian terms: Wegman acted according to the category of *passion* (passively enduring the actions of another) whereas Polzer acted according to the category of *action*; each acted in accordance with the *position*—another of Aristotle's categories— in which *he* found himself. The way Polzer and Wegman related (to name another of Aristotle's categories, that of 'relation') was therefore properly directed to the situation in which they found themselves.

This complementarity in Ludwig Polzer's and Ita Wegman's behaviour of acting and enduring stands out as something unique in the G.A.S. in 1935.

After visits to Bratislava, Prague and Pardubice to give lectures, Polzer arrived at Dora Schenker's house in Mariensee on 30 March. Here, on 3 April, he had another experience in the night. He wrote: 'A voice said to me: "Ask to speak in Dornach, otherwise you will not be able to speak." I did this immediately on awakening.'

Now he prepared a speech to the General Meeting. Dora Schenker typed it up for him. It is reproduced in the appendix. On 9 April he went to Vienna to take part in

> the 'Members'-Struggle-Meeting' there, which was very turbulent. Two who would destroy the Society brought forward much that was unobjective and spiteful. I was able to experience very vividly the Jesuitic attitude of two of the main agitators against those on the [Vienna] Vorstand who were opposed to the exclusion motion.

On 12 April he travelled back to Dornach accompanied by Franz Halla and a few friends from Prague, among them Milos Brabínek. He had with him 50 signatures of members opposed to the exclusion motions. It was painful for him that Hans Eiselt did not go with them, as he had other views on the exclusion question. The friendship between the two men did not suffer however, according to Polzer, and it continued until Eiselt's death in May the following year.

Because opponents of the motions did not, with a few exceptions, turn up at the General Meeting and because Polzer's proposal that people should be able to send their views to Dornach had evidently been declined, the proposers of the motions had an easy time to put together a majority in favour of the motions at the Meeting itself. An open letter from English members, drafted by D.N. Dunlop, sent two weeks before the Meeting was *not* published in the Newssheet for Members. By these methods one was able to get together 'all those members especially who lived not far from Dornach and those who lived in Dornach itself and to influence them' [to support the motions]. Quite a large number of supporters also came from Stuttgart. Rudolf Steiner had frequently had to recognize a certain tendency to dogmatic and fundamentalist attitudes in this city, in which so much of importance had happened for the anthroposophical movement. He coined the phrase 'the Stuttgart system' because of it. Polzer was also of the view that it was due to this Stuttgart tendency that 'he [Steiner] had never held lessons of the Michael School in Stuttgart, although it was not far' [from Dornach].

On Palm Sunday, 14 April, there were about 1400 members in the Great Hall of the second Goetheanum when the General Meeting began at 10 a.m. Almost all of those present were in favour of the motions and made up 95 per cent of the Meeting yet formed only a small minority— 8.5 per cent—of the total number of members worldwide (20,000). This General Meeting was therefore hardly in a position to represent adequately the views of the entire membership!

Ludwig Polzer therefore had a strong pro-motion mood around and against him when he went up to the lectern at about 11 o'clock to do his spiritual duty. And if he had not applied in writing to speak beforehand, he would hardly have been able to speak and perhaps not at all. For he saw that 'everything had been arranged to the last detail so as not to let the opposite side speak'. Whoever had been behind that voice in the night at Mariensee, had given him good advice.

Albert Steffen and Günther Wachsmuth were sitting at the Vorstand table; Marie was listening from behind the curtains on the fully occupied stage, sitting on an easy chair, as her legs were giving her trouble.

Polzer began his speech:[438]

> If I engage actively at this time in the strife of these events in the Society it is because I feel myself justified in doing so not only on the basis of my experiences and observations over many years but also because I feel obliged to do so. I know that I am confronting a majority that over years, especially here in Dornach, has in a certain direction formed a judgement that comes to expression in the *Memorandum*. So I am conscious of the difficulties I am facing here when I counterpose my own judgement to that majority judgement and on the basis of my judgement must say 'No' to what a majority of the Society in Dornach now wants to do. But I rely on

the force of the decisive facts with which I acquainted myself over many years because I always met them without sympathy or antipathy and remained open and honest with both parties in the dispute.

In what followed, Polzer did not at all conceal that there were problems on both sides, above all in connection with the leadership of the so-called High School. With regard to this, he recognized that 'impossible pretensions', had appeared 'first from one side and then, somewhat less emphatic, from the other side'. Therefore, 'in accordance with reason and in view of the absence of a spiritual leader, a new, freer, more ambitious basis for the Society could not be found'. And what, he went on, could not be accomplished through reason would be accomplished later anyway, but through catastrophes. He outlined his own view of the question of the leadership of the Society in the following way:

> For me, Rudolf Steiner is even today still the only leader of the High School, if this still has its esoteric character. The [leadership of the] Section for General Anthroposophy can be occupied by no one and taken on out of an earnest, real responsibility. Because of this, the possibility for the Section leaders to meet esoterically still does not seem to me to be an illusion today *if one of these personalities does not claim the leadership in some kind of succession, which is not at all the case here*—Rudolf Steiner did not name a successor. But that this happened after Rudolf Steiner's death I have always regarded as a mistake and said so at the time.

The Section 'for General Anthroposophy' is, amongst other things, responsible for controlling the affairs of the Class. In Polzer's view, after Steiner's death, this could no longer be managed centrally—in any Jesuitic-centralistic manner—but only in a decentralized way in accordance with destiny, which is why he proposed that no leader of this General Section be nominated, a proposal that Albert Steffen had already felt was offensive in 1929; he and his supporters were meanwhile *de facto* claiming the leadership for him.

'A control of Class affairs,' Polzer went on, 'after the death of Rudolf Steiner I hold to be possible only if the person who wishes to take on the responsibility to the spiritual world and to Rudolf Steiner and who is carried by the wills of a number of [prominent] individuals communicates this to the leaders of the Sections and speaks with them about it.' Polzer therefore held it to be improper and damaging that the Class Readers were appointed by a central leadership of the General Section, a leadership that, legitimately, was not at all any longer in existence, and he emphasized that it had to do with *a responsibility towards the spiritual world and Rudolf Steiner*, not towards an earthly administrative centre! 'A granting of authorization [to be able to read Class Lessons] because of diligent 'achievements' and the acquisition of a great deal of knowledge would be unacceptable to me; that way, we would very soon be travelling on an entirely external, authoritarian path.'[439]

Polzer then criticized the 'outrageous, moral calumnies' which had been spoken out, especially against Ita Wegman and dismissed them as being 'directed against the will of Rudolf Steiner'. He spoke of a 'resentment [among some] in the last years of Rudolf Steiner', which had remained mostly unconscious, at the fact that Ita Wegman had received new esoteric authority in connection with the Christmas Conference and therefore was the *second* significant personality beside Marie Steiner to stand close to Rudolf Steiner. In objective impartiality, he then emphasized at the same time 'that Frau Dr Steiner, who worked for so long with Rudolf Steiner'—also in the area of esoteric ritual—'is spiritually the one who has advanced the most'. Nevertheless, she sometimes lacked, in Polzer's view, 'a will for friendly understanding' in relation to Ita Wegman.

Clear and not over-sensitive, free of all Jesuitic diplomatic manoeuvring, Polzer drew his conclusions from what he had said:

> It is for me an impossibility to grant to a part of the broken Vorstand the right to put all the blame on the other part and on the basis of repeatedly uttered concepts that have for a long time now become slogans—such as 'method', 'lack of method', 'forming a judgement', 'achievements'—to proudly state that 'we are the only ones justified and capable of continuing Rudolf Steiner's work.'

Finally, Polzer expressed some remarkable ideas about the relationship of the first to the second Goetheanum. He said:

> The first Goetheanum was built as a Mystery Centre; it was taken from us because inside it we spoke purely intellectually. There was no one there who could have protected it. *Rudolf Steiner was not allowed to protect it because he gave it to mankind as a test of its maturity.* Then Rudolf Steiner [at the Christmas Conference 1923] laid the Foundation Stone [the Foundation Stone Meditation] in the hearts [of the members]. The Foundation Stones, which rest in strong hearts are no longer bound to one place and one building. They must become the Foundation Stones for the Mystery Centres of the future in various places. Those who will plant the seeds for these Mystery Centres can only be called to do so directly by the spiritual world through their destiny. This calls above all for esoteric courage, not subordination and uniformity.
>   The second Goetheanum was built entirely for the public—for the activity of 'the little book' from outside, as is shown in the fourth

apocalyptic seal [presented during the Munich congress of the Theosophical Society in 1907]. But the continuation of the Mysteries will come
from the 'the little book' that works from inside. The most important
requirement of the anthroposophical movement and Society is therefore
trust in people, not resentment of them. Trust that is first *given* from
Dornach, not trust that is first claimed.[440]

Polzer closed his speech, which lasted about 40 minutes with the sentence: 'I think that also financial catastrophe for the Goetheanum will not
be avoided if the call for greater freedom is not met with reason.'
  Eight years later, looking back at that hour of destiny he wrote:

> I was very calm and yet, while speaking, I was carried by the audience. I felt
> an inner satisfaction about this; despite the great pro-[the motions] majority
> there was repeated applause. After the first quarter of an hour my mouth
> was so dry that I asked for a glass of water. The interruption was only very
> short. Dr Wachsmuth, who brought me the water, made an inappropriate
> joke in that, smiling to those roundabout, he put the bottle under the
> lectern. At the part where I said that soon after the death of the Rudolf
> Steiner Steffen indicated to me that he could only work with Marie
> Steiner, he jumped up and wanted to know the date of that day. I could
> only say that I had not made a note of the day and that it was quite
> unimportant as the fact showed itself right after Rudolf Steiner's death. I
> went on calmly and in almost 40 minutes was able to say everything I
> intended. After that, some spoke briefly and very personally against me.
> Soon after 12 o'clock the General Meeting was paused until 3 o'clock in
> the afternoon. During the lunch break, they armed themselves against me
> and discussed how to oppose me.[441]

No doubt there were many present who regretted that Polzer's name was
not also on the list for exclusion. Could this still be done?
  In the afternoon session Polzer's former colleague on the Vienna
Vorstand, Hans-Erhard Lauer, stepped up to the lectern as the main
speaker. He made a name for himself with his slanderous remarks against
Polzer. Even supporters of the motions criticized Lauer's stance. 'The
Jesuits among the members were silent.' Since Polzer did not regard it as
proper that new members should be admitted centrally at that time, but
argued instead for decentralized admissions through the national societies,
which would then report new admissions to the central administration in
Dornach, he had, according to Lauer, departed from the ground of the
Christmas Conference: 'Count Polzer therefore has no longer any right to
refer himself to Rudolf Steiner [...] Through the way in which he has
acted for years in the esoteric area, Count Polzer has lost the right to set
himself up as judge in matters of esotericism.' Lauer went further:

At our upcoming Vienna General Meeting we shall have to come to a new arrangement and we shall then need to draw conclusions from what Count Polzer has said today about his idea of the Society. I now only wish to say that I do not consider it possible that Count Polzer should continue to exercise functions in the Society any longer [. . .] It will also no longer be possible for us, as you will understand, after the views that Count Polzer has expressed with regard to the former leadership of the Goetheanum, to extend to him that trust that is necessary for a person from whom one is supposed to receive Class Lessons.[442]

The weapon Lauer used for his attack Polzer later characterized as a 'Michael sword made of wood'[443]—a fitting description; it points to the Jesuitic illusion that one ought to fight in the sign of a higher spiritual power for 'the one true method'—the aim of healing of the Society 'sanctified' the exclusions—but showed only spiritual weakness.

After a few other votes, those managing the event moved the Meeting to the main vote on the exclusions. The result of this vote was that 1691 members voted for and 76 (!) against the motions and 53 members abstained. The Meeting closed at 5 p.m. For Ludwig Polzer,

> the esoteric character of the Vorstand was forfeit. Thirty-three years from the beginning of Rudolf Steiner's anthroposophical activity, the last endeavour of his life [the Anthroposophical Society with the esoteric Vorstand instituted by Steiner], on which he placed such great hopes, was buried. The hope that the exclusion of the two Vorstand members would be in the Society's best interests was not fulfilled. The struggle in Dornach was not calmed, the Society was divided in two. One could still speak of an anthroposophical movement but no longer of a 'Society'.[444]

This then was Polzer's commentary on the result of the vote.

★

Polzer spent the evening with Ita Wegman and with friends 'very pleasantly' at the clinic in Arlesheim. Probably, in this occasion he gave Ita Wegman a copy of his speech; she had stayed away from the General Meeting. He recalled a saying by Rudolf Steiner: 'Nothing real of course comes from majority decisions, only a *dominant phrase*.'[445]

That night Polzer had a dream. He recorded the experience in his diary as follows:

> I dreamt that many people were up on a high tower, a storm came and the tower was swaying. Some of us fell off. Then a picture opened up below us: I saw men gathered for a ritual. Some names were called out which were chosen. Finally my name was called and I was chosen as a member of the

inner circle or committee. I had a feeling—a feeling went through my body as though I had been consecrated.[446]

An experience in the night had drawn Polzer's attention to the spiritual storm which sought to split the Society; another experience in the night had spurred him to seek to speak at the General Meeting in Dornach. A third experience in the night gave affirmation of the esoteric action he took, that is, action out of his own spiritual insight, from a higher Vorstand. At the same moment that he was forced out of the building that only still bore Goethe's *name*, he felt himself accepted in a higher Society. Empowered and as though revivified, he continued his wanderings through the world and through life. From that night on, he felt that he now belonged to the inner circle of a true Tower Society, as we know it from Goethe's *Wilhelm Meister*, a community of active and free spirits, constructing humanity's social building of the future.

39. Between England and Bohemia

In the Easter week after the General Meeting Polzer went on a short trip with his grandson Christward. They travelled to Lucerne and Seelisberg and enjoyed the towns and the countryside and each other's company. The trip was like a sign of hope for Polzer that his grandson would 'understand later on what he had been through'.

Changes were underway in Tannbach. Hugo Flatz, the manager who had been a true adviser to Julius and Berta for many years was looking for surety on a property, as his brother wanted to expand a salt business that was going well. The Polzer family went along with his proposal, and from then on, Julius received a commission for the surety which he found very welcome. Flatz was a great connoisseur of herbs, folk remedies and other aspects of traditional folk culture. The bond between Flatz and the Tannbachers became ever stronger.

In May Polzer made a start in Pardubice on the new organization of anthroposophical work in Bohemia. The Czech groups he had been taking care of now worked completely independently of Dornach. The main Prague group 'Studium' joined in and received a new branch statute. Luděk Přikryl and Method Bauer, two longstanding anthroposophers, were very helpful to Polzer in this work.

On 14 May he held his first lecture in the new Studium Branch. With this, the connection with the Czech national Society, which, according to Polzer, 'always showed itself to be very anti-Czech [...] and completely subject to Albert Steffen' was effectively terminated. Painful personal experiences accompanied this step; along with Hans Eiselt, Julie Klima too now took a separate path from Polzer in the anthroposophical work. But he never allowed personal relationships to prevail when it was a matter of drawing consequences from spiritual knowledge. 'Since Rudolf Steiner's death,' he wrote,

> various things are demanded of his pupils, according to their talents, potential and karmic relationships. That this was not understood in Dornach led to a necessary split. Since the death of Rudolf Steiner those working outside the German-speaking countries had not at all been understood and not as well taken account of and supported as was necessary. *The idea of centralization which is at work in humanity showed itself here too, strongly and without understanding.*[447] I had to draw the consequences from what I knew, if I was not to be wholly excluded. The good progress my work had made on the one hand, and on the other, the increasing disassociation of countries from one another proved me right in the future.

A few days after the ceremonial refounding of the Studium Branch Polzer travelled to his friends the Knispels in Kambelovac and shared with them his decision to work independently of Dornach in the future. The two friends immediately concurred with this.

About this time a letter came from Dornach in the name of the rump Vorstand (Marie Steiner, Günther Wachsmuth and Albert Steffen) which demanded that Polzer return the texts of the Class Lessons and that he cease his reading of Class Lessons. One can imagine how Polzer reacted. He replied 'only briefly' that 'I could not acknowledge the esoteric character of the present tripartite Vorstand and that it was not justified in seeking to take from me an authorization that stemmed, not from it, but directly from Rudolf Steiner.'[448] After this, he came to an understanding with Ita Wegman and agreed to send on to her from then on all applications for membership that were directed to him.

It might have been around this same time, when he arrived in Bratislava on a lovely Sunday in spring 1935 when some German friends invited him to give a lecture. Zdena Šmídova writes in her memoirs of the impression which Polzer made at that time. 'I remember how he had appeared among our regular guests one Sunday in spring 1935, a tall, slim grey-haired gentleman with sparkling eyes who greeted everyone in a lively manner. After his departure, someone said that one could imagine J.W. Goethe to have been like that.'[449] This is a noteworthy remark. It is as though the initiation experience of the night after the General Meeting was still evident in what radiated from Polzer... As if the new distance from the Goetheanum had become perceptible as a closeness to *Goethe*, a closeness to the mysterious Tower Society. The perception of this closeness to Goethe will be mentioned later in a surprising way.

At Whitsun Polzer actually wanted to travel to London. He had been invited to an internal conference by anthroposophical friends and already had his tickets bought in Split. Then a telegram reached him that Daniel Nicol Dunlop had died on 30 May, Ascension Day. Since the Dornach General Meeting, Dunlop had been excluded from the G.A.S. but had remained the General Secretary of the national Society in England which, like the Dutch Society, had distanced itself from Dornach. The London conference was cancelled. George Adams-Kaufmann, one of those English friends, had translated Polzer's speech to the General Meeting, and Dunlop had been able to read it. But this great man, who Rudolf Steiner once called 'brother' answered the self-amputation of the Anthroposphical Society with his early, unexpected death.

Dunlop had 'great trust' in Polzer, and if further cooperation had been possible between them the two men would, with their energy and far-sightedness, doubtless have achieved significant things for the lively progress of the anthroposophical cause along the important line of spiritual connection between Britain and Bohemia.

Polzer therefore stayed longer than planned with the Knispels and travelled to Prague and Pardubice in order to continue the work in Bohemia. In June he lectured in Hochenmauth near Pardubice on Psychoanalysis with reference to Steiner's lectures on this subject from 1917. He also spoke about the Brothers of the Left who make use of old spiritual knowledge in their strivings for power. He described the struggle of these dark brotherhoods against the new Christ Event and emphasized the necessity of the struggle against evil in the fifth post-Atlantean cultural epoch. He spoke also of the dead who were ever more present and who worked as centres of destruction in the earthly sphere due to their materialistic mindset in their former lives and were thus able to be used by the above-mentioned brotherhoods. He spoke of Ireland, where luciferic forces were able to work less effectively.

In this way Polzer shared the truths of spiritual science and acted according to Rudolf Steiner's insight that today the most important thing is the *communication* of spiritual knowledge, as in the age of freedom one must not work directly on the will of others.[450] People are then left free to act as they see fit having received those truths in the form of ideas.

Following the small conference Polzer met his wife Berta in Vienna at the end of June. In the lovely weather they travelled together up to the Kobenzl, went walking on the Kahlenberg and returned in the evening through the vineyards to Grinzing. Later the couple met Herta Reichart and then they went to listen to the Wiener Sängerknaben [the famous Vienna Boys' Choir]. Polzer had been on few excursions of this kind with his wife. All the more therefore could he say: 'I enjoyed this day with Berta immensely.' He also went with her to Mariensee and with Dora Schenker they went on a drive into the Burgenland region. Ita Wegman in Arlesheim was one of those who received postcard greetings from this trip.

On 9 July Ita Wegman wrote a lovely letter in reply which was at the same time an answer to earlier, unanswered letters from him and which shows her view of the situation after the General Meeting as well as the trust which had grown more and more between her and Polzer. She wrote:

> Dear Count Polzer!
> I thank you warmly for all the lovely letters and postcard greetings you have sent me. As I myself have so unbelievably much to do, I was not able to write, although I would have liked to write to you. The illness and subsequent death of Mr Dunlop came so unexpectedly that one had a great

deal to do to get through everything that came to one. It is really very sad that we have had to suffer such a loss. But the work will go on in England as it has done until now. I am glad that you have also decided to go to the Summer School in Harrogate. We will have possibilities there to speak with one another and to talk about the future.

I am sorry that you have been attacked so much after you had sought to do what was right and proper, and it is noteworthy how everything that has or should have a meaning for a particular time is always made use of at a later time in a false way. The present administration at the Goetheanum like to do that on a colossal scale, always putting confusing things in the world and in such a way as to make out that they have the greatest right to do so. Hopefully you too will have a quieter time. It was good and fine what you did at the General Meeting!

We are able to work on very well here at the clinic, and I am actually inwardly relieved to a certain extent that I no longer have the heavy tasks that come with a Section. I can now deepen my work here in peace and quiet, which satisfies me very much. This work can be continued quite undisturbed. Just as in earlier times, we have our courses, our patients and at the Sonnenhof our public curative pedagogy seminar. So we wish to await calmly what the future brings to us and work intensively.

With friendly greetings also to your wife and to Frau Schenk[er], who signed a card that you sent from Burgenland. My warmest thanks!

Looking forward to good collaboration,

I remain

Your I. Wegman Dr med.

Before his departure for Harrogate (Yorkshire), Polzer spent a few days with his niece Christl in Modern at 'Harmonie'. They ate lunch with the cousin from Megyesy and had fine conversation with her. Here in Modern news reached Polzer of the unexpected early death of another cousin, Marianne Stürgk who had died on 14 July.

Perhaps this death or perhaps the letter from Ita Wegman contributed to his wanting to seal another death: his undermined relationship to the Austrian national Society on the Vorstand of which he had been active for twelve years.

On 24 July 1935, the day before the birthday of his father Julius, Ludwig Polzer-Hoditz resigned from the Austrian national Society.

*

Now it was time for preparations for his trip to England. The Summer School in Harrogate to which he had been invited took place from 12 to 25 August. On 5 August Polzer travelled to Paris, where he stayed for two days. Then he went to Calais where, as in Dover, he intended to spend a night 'in order to gain an impression of these ports'. And what were his impressions? 'Calais made a dreary, unpleasant, communist impression. Dover was very different.'

Seven years after his last stay in London, Polzer then arrived in the new Rome of the West. But this fourth visit to England stood under a new sign for him. Polzer wrote: 'The old connection with Blanche Tollemache and aunt Mathilde is dead and gone.' For Blanche Tollemache too had died meanwhile and indeed, just two days after D.N. Dunlop, as Polzer only learned during his stay in London; he had wanted to visit her.

Polzer had now lost three friends in a short period, and these friends had belonged to different phases of his life: the blood-relationship with his recently deceased cousin, the personal relationship of the heart with Blanche Tollemache, and the relationship of free choice with D.N. Dunlop. But stronger than the pain that they brought, these deaths were felt and experienced by Polzer more strongly as heralding new bonds of friendship.

In London he stayed as a guest at Kent Terrace, a property acquired by Ita Wegman for the medical work in England. In Regent's Park the guest from the Continent saw a performance of Shakespeare's *Midsummer Night's Dream*. What a healing and a stimulus for his feelings was the dramatic humour of the atmosphere of this play! The following day he visited Hampton Court which made a great impression on him.

On 12 August he travelled with many friends to Harrogate, which was at that time one of England's main seaside resorts. He saw many old friends again, above all, Walter Johannes Stein who was now living in London, and got to know many new ones. In his notes from the year 1939 he included the names and addresses of every one. Three names can be given here which will stand for many: Montague Wheeler, Eleanor C. Merry and Dorothy Osmond. Through these three Polzer learned to know Dunlop better, with whom all three had been well-acquainted.

Fig. 57 shows Polzer with George Adams. Polzer's humorous but earnest gesture seems to say: 'If you Jesuits think you've finished with us through the exclusions, you've made a big mistake!'

And in his memoirs he writes: 'Seldom have I experienced so much sincere trust and so much evidence of friendship as in this month in England.'

On the first evening there were several greeting addresses. Polzer spoke too—after George Adams had helped him with his draft—for the first time in English. He recalled the late Daniel Dunlop with warmth when he said:

Before coming to this Summer School in the North of England out of the midst of Europe there often has stood before my soul the picture of our dear friend Mr Dunlop. Only lately through Mr Kaufmann and through what Dr W.J. Stein wrote in memoriam of Mr Dunlop in the *Mitteilungen* I learnt something more about his active and successful life.[451] This combined with my own remembrance of personal meetings and gave me the impression of a most lovable and beautiful human soul.

In Dunlop's invitation to him to come to England, Polzer saw the spiritual guidance of Rudolf Steiner at work from beyond the threshold:

I think that Rudolf Steiner has guided the threads of fate so that we can find each other to tie nearer relations between anthroposophers here and anthroposophers living in the Eastern part of the heart of Europe. And he saw in the gathering in Harrogate a possibility to link the Anglo-Saxon element, via middle European mediation with the future-bearing Slavic culture: Anglo-Saxon souls led by Rudolf Steiner, living in full light and activity and activity of life nowadays—and over there, in the East of Central Europe, souls of Slavs, bearing germs to prepare mankind for further evolution; they try to meet one another.

Entirely in the sense of these words of greeting Polzer gave an evening lecture on Thursday 15 August in German with the title 'England and Bohemia in the Age of Spirituality—a Study of Destiny in World History'.

He showed in his lecture how one could move from 'spectral history' to a symptomatological view of history, namely, that one learns to leave things to destiny and to complement outer events with inner experiences. He had had opportunity enough to do this in the recent split in the Society, as we have seen. He emphasized that it was no accident that in his last years Rudolf Steiner had spoken so strongly about the two poles of England and Bohemia and had recalled that in 1905 the Czechs had called him to come to them.

In the main part of his lecture he spoke about the 'hidden harmonious relationship between England and Central Europe' (Bacon—Shakespeare—Jakob Böhme—Wycliffe—Hus) on the one hand and between the western Slavs and Middle Europe on the other.

He characterized the task of anthroposphers in the following way: 'They would have to *"gain insight into and prepare both for the end of the century* and also for the sixth epoch"* and they would have to learn *"to survey greater spans of time, as used to be done in the old Mysteries"*.'[452] Between the lectures, which were attended by about 250 people, excursions into the

---

* I.e. the end of the twentieth century—*transl.*

surrounding region were arranged. They went to *Bolton Castle*, where Mary Stuart had been imprisoned for six months and which Polzer knew from his first stay in England in 1910; on another day they visited the ruins of *Fountains Abbey*, the important former Cistercian abbey. 'I never saw anything like it in my life,' reported Polzer full of admiration. 'The wonderful site, the splendid ruins and the scale of it all overwhelmed me and many others.'

On 22 August Polzer gave a brief farewell address, which was instructive in some ways. He said:

> When one has been active in the anthroposophical movement for nearly 30 years and at the end of this time has to go through the painful experiences which have resulted from recent events in Dornach and when one is called upon to play an active part therein, then one is deeply thankful for the days which we have been able to spend together at this anthroposophical Summer School.
>
> I have found again the friendly atmosphere that there was in former times, when Rudolf Steiner was still among us. I have found so many old friends of mine who worked together with Rudolf Steiner. All this has been a great help to me for what we have to do in the future.
>
> So I should like to thank all those who have struggled with the difficulties of the time and have brought about the possibility of this anthroposophical Summer School in such a wonderfull [sic] way.
>
> *Above all, I will give my thanks to our dear friend Mr Dunlop, whose spiritual presence is certainly with us.*[453] Next, to our chairman Mr Wheeler, Mr Kaufmann and all the speakers and those who have helped in the organization here. I must take what I have experienced back again to the East.
>
> There I will tell again how important it seems to me for the position of the anthroposophical movement and for the world that the Englisch [sic] Anthroposophical Society is becoming so strong that from here strength may stream out to the threshold of Europe where Germans and Slavs meet together.
>
> I should like to close with these words which Rudolf Steiner often spoke to us at the end of a gathering: 'Auf wiedersehen—we shall still be together though separated by space.'

Polzer thus ended with warmly felt thanks for a conference which, for him, had taken place in the spiritual presence of Rudolf Steiner and perhaps, even more clearly felt, that of Daniel Dunlop.

After the conference Polzer visited his friends the Scropes in order to renew as well this old friendship and travelled then for a few days to Clent Grove near Birmingham, where Michael Wilson, Fried Geuter and David Clement were running a curative community in the countryside which also had a biodynamic farm attached to it. There 'were many guests gathered there', he wrote, 'some told in the evenings of their first meeting with Rudolf Steiner'.

Then Polzer stopped again in London and saw much of W.J. Stein and Ita Wegman. Stein told him about the Comte de St Germain, with whom he was much occupied at the time and Polzer gratefully took this impulse home with him. He first spent two days in Paris with Ita Wegman and Mien Viehoff before heading for home.

★

For the first time in years Josef spent two weeks at Tannbach in September. His condition had very much improved thanks to the efforts of Albrecht Strohschein and Karl König.

On 18 September Polzer went to Mariensee to Dora Schenker and told her all about his trip to England. 'I am now reading the book about Saint Germain', he wrote on 23 September to Stein in London. 'It contains much interesting information, but I have rarely read such a poorly written book.' This was *Der Graf von St Germain* [The Comte de St Germain] by L.A. Langeveld, for which Stein had written an introduction.[454]

Stein had apparently also introduced Polzer to the book about the Comte de St Germain by the Theosophist Isabel Cooper-Oakley[455] for Polzer wrote in the same letter: 'Frau Schenker is reading the book by Cooper-Oakley for me first. I shall read it after her. Two always read better than one.'

Polzer included in this letter to Stein a copy of his political Memorandum of 1930. In England he had evidently discussed political matters with Stein, with whom he had had a deep bond of friendship since the birth of the threefold movement, a bond that would remain. They had also spoken, partly in Harrogate and partly in London, about the two Johns (the Baptist and the Evangelist), the Youth of Nain, Matthias Corvinus, and Christian Rosencreuz. But the renewal of the bond of friendship between the two men would soon show itself productive in another sense.

There are notes extant of a lecture that Polzer gave that same month in Prague and Pardubice. These show that he still regarded himself as a member of the Society founded at Christmas 1923, even though he had parted company with it since the General Meeting at Easter. 'The membership cards are the historical documents that show we belong to it.' He still then had the hope that the Goetheanum would remain open to the members of the free groups. This hope would not last long. In the new situation, he went on, he must strive 'to gain as much clarity as possible about relationships within the anthroposophical movement and the world situation'. In doing so 'one could easily be misunderstood, precisely because today the circumstances in the world are such that souls are inclined to cleave to parties out of sympathy or antipathy, and when facts are presented, one so easily thinks that one wants to understand things in terms of political parties.' In relation to his English trip he added: 'I did not go to England because I wanted to take the side of England but only because it is especially necessary just now that anthroposophy becomes strong there.'

In Bratislava Polzer was strongly supported by Julius Valenta, in whose house lectures and Class Lessons were held. Valenta worked in the administration of the railways in Bratislava. Together with the bank official Hüttl, he formed the base of the anthroposophical branch work in the city. Zdena Šmídova, who was mentioned earlier in this chapter, and who spoke so finely about Polzer, was Hüttl's daughter. Very satisfied with this branch work in Bratislava, Polzer was able to say: 'They worked very hard for each other [...] with the energy and devotion that is characteristic of Slavic people.'

Thus the first results of the exclusions for Polzer's work were that he put the emphasis of his work on the line that connects England and Bohemia. This was a kind of extension of the 'vow in the Chapel of St Wencenslas': the Germanophile element in England was now brought into the main task of the harmonization of the German and Slavic cultures.

40. The Shadow of the Council of 1869

On 1 November 1935 the Anthroposophical Society in Germany was banned by the Gestapo. Polzer perceived this immediately as a 'harbinger of hard, uncultured times' and he was of the view that this ban was 'even aided by the attitude of the now only three-man Vorstand at the Goetheanum'. 'Rudolf Steiner predicted such official measures if we did not succeed in embracing wider circles and consolidate ourselves in a more cohesive fashion.' They did not succeed, and the effects began to show themselves in contemporary events such as a vehement increase in the anti-anthroposophical forces in Germany.

In the same month Polzer began to occupy himself with the study of the First Vatican Council, which took place in Rome in 1869/70. His friend Ernst Wettreich, the journalist, whom he had known from the time of the *Messenger,* had drawn his attention to a book by Wolfgang Menzel[456], which deals with the period after 1866 and also details of the Vatican Council. It was of symptomatic interest for Polzer that he had come across this book by Menzel just at the time of the ban on the Anthroposophical Society in Germany; he saw Wettreich's indication 'as a sign from the spiritual world for me to concern myself with my behaviour at the General Meeting in Dornach'. The statement might at first seem astonishing. What was meant by it?

Polzer discovered that that council in Rome, at which the dogma of Papal Infallibility was pronounced, had taken place 66 years before the events in Dornach in 1935. Thirty-three years after the Council in Rome had begun, Rudolf Steiner's public activity as a spiritual researcher commenced when, in 1902, he took over as General Secretary of the German Section of the Theosophical Society. Thirty-three years later came the split in the Vorstand that he had formed for the Anthroposophical Society. The historical significance of the 33-year-cycle was well known to Polzer from Steiner's teachings.[457] Every year there is, as it were, a resurrection of the events of 33 years before. The impulses of a very particular year, both the good and the bad, rise up like fruits after 33, and then again after 66 years. Steiner spoke of a 'Christmas year' and an 'Easter year'. The year 1935 was in this sense the second, indirect Easter year since 1869. Linked with the law of historical mirroring (cf. the chapter 'The Other Side of the Coin') the following signature results for 1935: with 1902 as the axis, the year in which Rudolf Steiner began to practise ethic individualism in publishing concrete spiritual knowledge, in 1935 the spiritual events of 1869/70 are mirrored and again become active, but also those of 1902 (1902–1935 = 33 years). Since the spiritual impulses which were set working in the world in the year 1869, exactly 1000 years after that other Council at which 'the spirit was abolished', have been of extraordinary spiritual weight, the question arises with regard to 1935: will the unfree, mighty spiritual impulse of 1869 or the more delicate seed of free spirituality from 1902—the axial mirror year—be of greater weight? That the former would be the case as regards the general public was easy to foresee. Within the anthroposophical movement, the latter might at least have been hoped for.

But let us proceed from Polzer's own first starting point for his research into the matters under discussion here. 'Do you know the Jesuit, who seeks to bring Jesuitic methods into the Society?' By this question that he experienced that night in February 1935 he had been shown a key aspect of the sudden split in the Anthroposophical Society—the Jesuit attitude within the G.A.S. Now, in November, the 'world current' brought him an opportunity to deepen this question in a historical direction and, for this purpose, to study the Council of 1869/70. Let us look more closely at that consequential gathering at St Peter's.

The First Vatican Council was solemnly opened on 8 December 1869 by Pope Pius IX in one of the semitransepts of St Peter's in the presence of 719 bishops. The opening date was no accident. It was the day of the Immaculate Conception of Mary, which had been pronounced as a dogma of the Church by the same Pope on 8 December 1854 on his own initiative without conciliar advice. By this dogma Pius had already in effect demonstrated his infallibility, before it was later to become a dogma itself. Between 1854 and 1869, the Pope issued in 1864 (again on 8 December), the so-called *Syllabus errorum*, a list of 80 'errors' of modernism, which could only dismay everyone, even merely half-rational people, in the European Catholic world.

At that time the ecclesiastical state was threatened with break-up in the course of the Italian independence movement and was kept alive only thanks to a French garrison. In this very precarious situation Pope Pius IX wanted to show a sign of the irrefutability of the power of the Church. But he was clever enough not to launch the intended dogma of the infallibility of the Pope *directly* but to have it thrown into the discussion from another side, as it were, as an objective prompting, a desire coming from outside. He made use of the Jesuit magazine *Cività Cattolica*, founded in 1850, a semi-official organ of the Vatican. In 1865 he formed a 96-man commission to prepare the Council; it consisted of 'ultramontanes', that is, arch-conservatives, advisers who had remained loyal to him and who were also active as the majority of the Roman Curia. Through the commission and the Jesuit magazine, he had his intention to raise papal infallibility to the status of a dogma leaked and spread about. When it sparked strong protests, above all in Germany and France, Pius remained unmoved. He had suffered from epileptic attacks in his youth and even claimed to have had a vision of the Mother of God; he was of the abysmally frivolous view that he had the Mother of God completely 'on his side'.[458]

When the year of the opening of the Council was still unclear, for Pius it was fixed a priori that it would be opened on 8 December, and so it was, in the year 1869.

'It was clear to the pro-infallibility party,' writes August Bernhard Hasler, 'that the dogmatization of papal infallibility could only come about if it was made the central focus of the Council, the most important point of coordination.'[459] The supporters of the new dogma began to organize long before the opponents.

At the Council itself discussion of the new dogma was tightly restricted by means of firm regulation of the proceedings: 'It could not be discussed in smaller groups, the discussions at the Council were not to be published, and the bishops were held under threat of a mortal sin to maintain silence about the proceedings in the Council room,' writes Hasler.[460]

In February 1870 the Council agenda was advanced prematurely: a motion from only ten Council Fathers proposed bringing the debate to a conclusion. The Croat bishop Joseph George Strossmeyer, who along with the canon lawyer Ignaz Döllinger, was one of the weightiest opponents of the proposed dogma, called this decision 'the grave mound of the Council'.[461] 'Important representatives of the minority view were repeatedly interrupted and prevented from speaking further.'[462]

The only thing that the gradually out-voted minority could achieve was that they managed to restrict the dogma of infallibiity to pro-nouncements made *ex cathedra*, that is, from the papal throne: the new dogma would guarantee not 'the Infallibility of the Roman Pontiff' but merely the 'infallible teaching of the Roman Pontiff'.[463] When on 18 July 1870 the 535 participants still present at the Council—the rest had already left for reasons of protest or illness—approved the new dogma with only two dissenting voices, a great clap of thunder sounded over the Eternal City. Hasler wrote: 'The thunder rolled deeply, and the bright flashing lightning threw a ghostly light over the darkness that had suddenly descended.'[464]

Truly a world-historical scene of thunder and lightning! The dogmatization of perhaps the most awful blasphemy in the history of the West represented a kind of higher, or rather, lower octave to the Council decisions of 869 which 'abolished the spirit'. It was the consequence of that earlier Council. After 1000 years of dulling the spiritual activity of the individual members of the Church, one could now move on to postulating the thinking and teaching of a single man as 'infallible'. In this sense the Vatican Council of 1869 was the negative fulfilment of the Council of 869.

★

Polzer had the documents from the Court and State Chancellories in Vienna loaned to him that dealt with the Council in Rome. He studied industriously the reports of the Austrian ambassador to the Holy See, Count Trautmannsdorf, which he sent to Minister of State Beust. Gradually, he gathered from the book by Menzel and from Trautmannsdorf's reports a symptomatic picture, supplemented by the dream that he had, of the inner connection between the events in Rome in 1869 and the decisions in Dornach in 1935. From his studies he came to the following conclusions:

> The way the majority was formed then in Rome was very similar to how it happened in Dornach. At that time no thought was given to the princes of the Church with their great dioceses in the periphery, nor to the deep religious mood and predisposition of the northern peoples in contrast to the more outward Christianity of the Romance Mediterranean peoples with their disposition to imperialism. The majority was formed by drawing on the support of so many church authorities that did not have dioceses and of the many bishops surrounding the centre in Rome; it was prepared beforehand by spiritual and material pressure. *What happened at the General Meeting in Dornach was very similar.*[465]

One could draw further parallels. Let us only recall for example what Polzer experienced when he came to Dornach on 11 March 1935 to see Albert Steffen in order to persuade him not to publish the exclusion motions. Steffen represented them as something that had not come from him but which at the same time he would have to take into account and advised Polzer in all earnestness to speak to the authors of the so-called *Memorandum*. In a similar, even if much cruder, fashion, Pope Pius IX took cover, whenever necessary behind those who *appeared* to express their intentions voluntarily in his favour ...

'The warning from Rudolf Steiner that night six weeks before the General Meeting became ever more clear to me,' Polzer went on.

'*This is why I believe that since then Rudolf Steiner no longer recognized the Society as the appropriate form for the anthroposophical movement.*[466] This certainly has to do with the possibility of its destruction through the [Nazi regime's] ban.'

Polzer's studies had certainly led him to some weighty results.

If one asks oneself further whether the fatal Dornach General Meeting in the spring of 1935, except for the resulting exclusions, did not lead to a result comparable to the Infallibility dogma, the question must undoubtedly be answered in the affirmative.There was the dogmatic conviction, which spread itself further and further, that Rudolf Steiner, was, despite all that had happened, still bound in destiny with the Anthroposophical *Society*, that the Society was therefore still one with the anthroposophical *movement*, and this unity was still presided over by an esoteric Vorstand.

From Polzer's viewpoint such convictions were nothing but Roman, centralized dogmas devoid of any truth; indeed, they were like a kind of mockery of the real situation.

★

That Polzer was able in 1935 to undertake his unique elucidation of what had happened in the Society Steiner himself had founded may be due not least to his own Roman past. This had sharpened in him an ability to identify old Roman impulses that were still working on in later historical periods. For this reason he felt himself so deeply linked to the events of 1869 that he was even able to say: 'That my birth fell in the year 1869 certainly brought me into karmic relationship with this spiritual struggle.' From this deep-rooted destiny relationship to the Roman Empire and its decadent after-effects, it became all the more clear to Polzer how in the Anthroposophical Society at the decisive moment in 1935 was based much more on a Roman-Jesuit ethos than on the spirit of anthroposophy.

Let us recall that other traveller who in the account of Ludwig Polzer's grandfather had decided to avoid going to Rome, because 'the Eternal City was unfortunately overflowing with Church fathers from every part of the world who had gathered for an unwholesome Council. News of this gathering came to me like the ringing of a distant funeral bell, and I could not persuade myself to enter the city at the time when true Christian belief was being so odiously sullied.'[467]

The grandson of this novelist increasingly felt something very similar with regard to another place from 1935 onwards with the difference that he had to listen to the funeral bell of another 'unwholesome Council' from very close up and had been unable to silence it by any words of reason ...

In November and December 1935 Polzer spoke in Vienna, Prague,

Budapest, Bratislava, Pardubice and also at the Arlesheim Clinic 'about the Council of 1869 and the situation of the Anthroposophical Society and the hopes of the anthroposophical movement'. Unfortunately, we have no transcriptions of his lectures; but the list of the places itself where he lectured in the space of a few weeks shows how much his spiritual symptomatic discoveries spurred our traveller's movements.

On 1 December 1935 Polzer wrote a communication for members of the so-called Class.[468] He felt himself obliged to take steps against 'agitations' which were being made 'by individuals over the matter of the Class'. Polzer had been accused of not holding Class Lessons in the way Rudolf Steiner had held them. Before and sometimes after the Class Lesson he spoke certain mantric words that originated with Steiner. To Polzer's question how he should hold the Class Lessons, Steiner himself had simply answered on 11 November 1924: 'Do it how you want to.' Polzer also justified his way of holding Class Lessons as follows: 'That the Classes must be formed in as living a manner as possible and not fixed in anything outwardly dogmatic would have to be clear to every esotericist who does not want the Michael Mystery to go the way which the Roman Church took and which led to the conflicts over dogma at the Councils.'[469] According to Rudolf Herman, Polzer always had a rose cross displayed and three candles lit on ceremonial occasions in Pardubice. In doing so, he certainly did not want to assert any esoteric pretensions of his own in the sense of establishing a 'second Class', as others actually tried to do much later on. It had been clear to him, without any illusions, for a long time already that 'since the death of Rudolf Steiner the Mysteries [. . .] could not be revealed any further in the present time'. But it was just as clear to him that 'the living, *not only the intellectual but also the ritual continuity*[470] with the Mystery content that had been given by him [Steiner] should be further fostered in order to share this with those who no longer knew Rudolf Steiner and yet who seek esoteric and not only intellectual access to him.'[471]

In this way Polzer rebuffed the accusations made against him by means of which it was sought to remove from him the right to hold these ceremonial lessons themselves. When it had to be recognized that he intended to go on working in his way unperturbed, the attempt was made to turn the Class members in Bohemia against each other by declaring that it was not possible to attend Class Lessons both with the National Society and with Polzer; to which Polzer had to urge that this decision must be left to each individual member himself to make. For Polzer these attacks, directed against him as one of the last ethical individualists within the G.A.S., were inspired by the same Jesuit spirit that had been behind the catastrophe at Dornach in the spring. He wrote: 'The constantly recurring objection that I do not hold the Class Lessons like Rudolf Steiner'—who, incidentally, had not himself always held the Class Lessons in the same way—

> is in the spiritual sense untrue and only formally partly correct. This formal rectitude is wholly in harmony with the majority decision, corresponding to merely formal, juridical principles, by means of which the dismissals and exclusions were pronounced at the last General Meeting at Easter in Dornach and through which this General Anthroposophical Society became something other than the one founded by Rudolf Steiner.

With this written communication Polzer's open debate with the functionaries of the altered G.A.S. and their supporters came to an end. This too had taken place completely in the light of his spiritual-historical discovery of November 1935.

As the year ended, Polzer had withstood not only the conflicts and the process of breakdown within the G.A.S.; the deeper background of the split in the Vorstand and its consequences had become clear to him *in its essentials*.

As was so often the case in earlier years, this year in the life of Ludwig Polzer had been far more than just the sum of 365 days on the calendar.

41. Fruits of an Old Friendship

Polzer's public activity in 1935 was followed once again by an 'ebbtide' period of deepening and inner contemplation. Even though the anthroposophical work went on as before unchanged, there was from 1936 onwards a strong mood of looking back. We have to thank the intuition of Walter Johannes Stein, who linked on to this mood of his friend who was 22 years older and took care that it would bear fruit, as we shall soon see. Johannes Tautz evaluated the work of Polzer's friend in this regard in his book *Walter Johannes Stein—Ein Biographie* (Dornach 1989).

In Tannbach meanwhile, economic dificulties had been steadily mounting. It became harder and harder to reconcile tax demands and the possibilities of meeting them, especially in areas with barren land and inclement weather. Julius, who in January had to undergo an appendectomy, suffered very much under this pressure, while Berta 'works courageously on'. Polzer could only help indirectly through his anthroposophical work and the contacts that resulted from it, as had already been the case in the friendship with Hugo Flatz. 'Only through pain and suffering can the human being be healed', he wrote in his diary with regard to these more private needs in his own family circle.

At the end of January 1936 he went again for a week to Mariensee. 'The departure this time,' he wrote, in the guestbook on 28 January, 'means the end of a fine period of my life for which I remain grateful to the dear mistress of this house from the bottom of my heart.' Dora Schenker moved to Linsberg near Erlach, to another of her family's properties, where she hoped to renovate the farm, which had been neglected.

Not long before, Polzer had made the acquaintance of a Russian family, the Makarovs. Mrs Makarov had fled from Russia to Vienna in 1920 with an Austrian prisoner-of-war. She had two pretty daughters who after leaving school had to earn a living and became 'skilled dancers'. Polzer took a special interest in the younger of the two, Tamara. And a small story of destiny unfolded from this. He wrote:

> I was interested in their destiny and I was able to help them with conversations and books. The whole family placed their trust in me. One can also find valuable human talents in such circles. The Russian soul showed itself so clearly. So this acquaintance was in the direction of my interest in Slavic culture and my task to harmonize German and Slavic souls through anthroposophical thinking, feeling and willing. When Tamara asked me to be a witness at her wedding I was happy to do so.

The wedding of Tamara and her bridegroom took place in the church in Gutau.

On the day after the wedding Polzer went for the first time to Linsberg to Dora Schenker where, from then on, an 'especially fine room' was put at his disposal. 'The area is lovely,' he wrote, 'the climate is mild and protected from the wind. In their tasteful solidity, the features of the buildings speak of former wealth. Frau Schenker will certainly be able to put them back in order with just a few means.'

Polzer had evidently made his friend Stein in London aware of Tannbach's material needs. In Easter week Stein sent a letter with 'an enclosure' for which Polzer wrote to thank him very much on 14 April. He wrote to London:

> My dear friend!
> Do you know, I wept tears of joy when I received your dear letter today with its enclosure? It is so seldom in our time that one experiences real active friendship at a distance. It is a balsam for the wounded soul to experience such a dear sign of anthrop. friendship and anthrop. ethos. In this deathly mood of Good Friday which lies over Europe for which the Easter bells will not ring much longer, I felt hopeful that the Easter bells *will* ring and that anthroposophy lives and works. Your letter and the thoughts about your work there, where it is so very necessary, are the Easter bells for me this year.

Stein was mainly working at that time as the publisher of the magazine *The Present Age* which at the behest of the late D.N. Dunlop he had founded in December 1935. *The Present Age* was a unique monthly magazine that dealt with world events, history, natural science but all in a more reserved yet clearer manner in the light of spiritual science. It was the incisive, wide-ranging approach and the boldness of the enterprise which Polzer found persuasive: 'Yes, my dear friend, Berta and I often think of you and are happy that the magazine is *proof of rightly understood a.* [anthroposophical] *work.*'[472]

From the letter it is clear that the conversations in England with his friend had an effect on Polzer for quite some time and spurred him on to various areas of research, for example the circumstances of the death of Matthias Corvinus. Here he had original Latin sources translated at the National Museum in Budapest. 'I was so sorry then in London,' he added, 'that we could not meet again; I would have liked to share some things with you.'

And in relation to Tannbach, he wrote: 'The frightful poverty, the choking demands which are made precisely in poor regions without thought for what is actually possible, must finally bring an epidemic of madness.' One may here be reminded of Polzer's father Julius, who once said: 'Do you all still have enough to eat? They will take everything from you. They will not even leave you your beds.' The situation was now not far from what Julius had feared ... But Polzer raised even such troubles into a higher light when he went on: 'Yes, the faithful will have to go through and experience all such things like Rud. Steiner, when death came to him just in that moment when he was about to embark on such great things. Such interruption is so symptomatic of the times.'

At the end of the letter we read: 'As long as I can, I shall always take my leave of here, which is often hard to do, as I cannot help, because both are stronger souls than me, and I shall go on with my work, which continues, only the infirmities and tiredness of my 67 years often hinder me.'

Little in the year 1936 will have helped Polzer to overcome the tiredness he refers to more effectively than the new bonds of friendship which had formed with the 45-year-old Stein.

After Easter, Polzer gave a lecture in Prague that was spiritually profound. As usual, this time too he refrained from giving any pedantic lecture. He spoke of the seriousness of the world situation, of the fact of the Resurrection, of the need to raise the power of consciousness of thinking to imagination. 'The greatest historical Mystery Event,' he wrote in his notes for the lecture,

> the Mystery of Golgotha, is the starting point for the overcoming of death through life, thus resurrection. Six hundred years before the Mystery of Golgotha the Buddha was teaching. He came from a royal palace and found life. He taught renunciation of the desire for existence. Six hundred years later, men looked, on the contrary, to the body on the Cross and saw in it hope. They recognized in it imaginatively the new sprig from which the roses will bloom. The corpse [is] that which reminds us of the resurrection of life from death. When a Being like the Christ, the greatest avatar, comes down and incarnates on the Earth then something mysterious occurs.

Polzer then described how copies of the I, the astral and etheric bodies of Jesus of Nazareth were created and woven into the corresponding members of the organisms of historical individuals such as St Elisabeth, Joan of Arc and many others. 'The deeper mankind sank down in order to come to its freedom, the stronger were the events that took place in order to experience the active power of the Mystery of Golgotha.' He then spoke about this in more detail on the basis of Steiner's research.[473] At the end of his lecture he emphasized once more how important it is in our time to take up and cultivate a relation to the so-called dead. This must be striven for 'through strengthened thinking, which makes one capable of

Imagination' and not through 'refined intellectualism and the knowing of many facts'. 'Goodwill' is also necessary. Why is this important?

Because the dead 'seek to transform the Earth, for they need it for their next incarnation. We must strive to transform the Earth rightly' and learn to feel ourselves as 'earthly representatives of the dead'.

In such an active Easter mood Polzer wrote another letter to Stein on 30 April in which he told him that one place in Stein's previous letter of September 1935 was still not clear to him and he asked for clarification; also, that he was at that time occupied with St Paul, in relation to Steiner's lecture cycle *Christ and the Spiritual World*.[474] He asked Stein for *his* view on this and on other spiritual scientific questions. Then he made the noteworthy statement: 'As for the world situation, we understand each other very well; it needs no written agreement. *In general anthroposophers are even very naive, and individually lacking in presentiment.*[475] On almost all sides there is the mood of Good Friday.'

In his postscript Polzer added: 'I enjoyed the latest novel by Mrs Krück von Poturzyn *Antoninus und der Grieche*'[476] [Antoninus and The Greek]. Antoninus had been adopted by Hadrian and was nominated his successor. In their oral conversations Stein and Polzer may have talked about the time of Hadrian. A later event makes this still more likely.

At the beginning of May Polzer travelled to Dalmatia to visit his friends Lou and Leo Knispel. On 21 May, towards the end of his stay, he wrote again from Kambelovac to Stein in London:

> I am sorry that you were worried on account of your wife and hope that things will soon improve. But! Should I, at 67, say to you in your forties, that as long as one can crawl along, one should have nothing to do with the gesture of growing old, as you put it. I can assure you that I often have problems on all sides and yet I often feel myself to be so young again that in today's circumstances in the world, so outrageous are they, that I would most of all like to go to battle again.

Polzer therefore appears to have had a good time in Kambelovac! And in fact: 'This is the first time for a year,' he goes on in the same letter, 'that I have stayed in the same place for three weeks. In the period before, there were hardly eight days without moving on.' But once again Polzer recovered his forces not from inactive idleness: 'Here we are now five people, who study anthroposophy together every day for many hours.' Perhaps Dora Schenker and Col. Vujić were in the group?

'You know,' he wrote further,

> that since the death of Dr Steiner, I have been following what has been going on in political affairs with the greatest attention and sought to

make use of various situations in accordance to an indication the Herr Doctor gave me in his last days; every month I have had conversations with a journalist with whom I have been befriended since the publication of the *Austrian Messenger*[477] and educated him in an anthroposophical sense [. . .] In a few days I want to shed light on an event and draw some conclusions from it with regard to the world situation. Everything is lining up, and step by step, everything Dr Steiner said is being borne out.

Polzer also shared a secret of his method of symptomatological research with Stein: 'I am often told things in the night, so I knew 14 days beforehand that King Alexander I of Yugoslavia would be murdered on his trip to France.' So even at a great distance ever finer threads of trust wove themselves between the two men.

After a stay of three weeks in the surroundings of which he had grown so fond, on 25 May Polzer travelled to Graz, where he met his son Julius. He wanted to show Julius the places where he had spent his own youth with his parents and also go with him to Peggau, where Julius was born. Julius, now 34, had last seen the place at the age of three when the family had left it in 1905. Polzer wrote:

It was a great joy for me to show my dear son all the places where I had lived with my parents in my youth. We also went to Peggau. In the house where Julius was born, the former Mensdorf-Schlössel, we were very warmly received by the owner, Dr Stefan Dolinar and his son-in-law General von Trauttenweiler-Strumberg. It was a little painful for me. Almost all the dear people who were around me when the house belonged to my parents have since died. I showed Julius the room in which he came into the world and then we all sat in front of the house under the balcony. It was a very special feeling to see Julius sitting there with the present owners, where I had so often sat with my parents, my brother and sister, and later with my wife and children. All these people, the living and the dead were still there for me in my memory and *I had the feeling that they were glad to see Julius with me here.*[478]

At these places in Graz where he had formerly lived Polzer's mood of reminiscence touched deep roots; from the last words cited above one can see that the power of memory worked so intensively in him that it was becoming a window to those places beyond the threshold in which, amongst other things, the so-called dead are moving . . .

It was in this spiritually real, retrospective mood that Polzer came to make a decision that had been slowly maturing within him. As mentioned earlier, on 24 July 1935 he had resigned from the Austrian national society of the Anthroposophical Society. But he had remained an individual member of the General Anthroposophical Society that was based in Dornach.

After the attacks made in Dornach on his Class work, to which he had replied in December 1935 the time now appeared to him to have arrived when he should also leave the international Anthroposophical Society. He therefore resigned from the G.A.S. on 30 May 1936.

But why just then, in that springtime? A glance at a list he made of the dates of the deaths of those who were close to him can solve the riddle. The man whom he deeply respected more than almost anyone else, Daniel Dunlop, had died on 30 May 1935. Dunlop stood at the other end of the line of connection between Bohemia and England and Polzer greatly valued the far-reaching aims of Dunlop's life. So through his choice of this date on which to leave the G.A.S. he linked to the negative step a much more meaningful, positive gesture, which signified that he wanted to associate his future work along the Bohemia-England line with the individuality of Dunlop who was then on the other side of the threshold. What an enduring loss Polzer's resignation was for the benighted G.A.S.! After it had driven out and lost a great number of its best spirits by the absurd exclusions of 1935 it was now abandoned by one of its finest individuals. Would it ever be able to recover?

On 10 June Polzer gave another lecture in Prague, 'in rooms which were of historical significance for the anthroposophical movement in the Czechoslovak Republic'. Polzer's Prague Group had acquired the former premises of the Prague Freemasonic lodge *Comenius*. This gave Polzer the opportunity to speak, on the one hand about Freemasonry and on the other about Comenius. Free now of all links to the G.A.S., he closed his lecture with words of great hope for future aims, which reach across to the end of the twentieth century:

> Since the lifework of Rudolf Steiner came to its sudden end, we shall have to bear his work ever more quietly, intimately, through death and prepare ourselves for outer activity at the end of the century. Our souls have shown themselves too weak to fight for a new social order in the present. We want to nurture spiritual wisdom so that it can soon unite itself with the fire of enthusiasm. So that it can fuse itself with real michaelic courage in the service of truth [. . .] We must feel ourselves in this creativity linked with all those who have worked and suffered so that continuity during the time without the Mysteries will not cease. We want to take on this space in this esoteric sense and to be active in it.

★

In the same month (June) Polzer was again urged by his friend Stein to write his memoirs. Stein wrote in a letter that his request followed a spiritual stimulus from Rudolf Steiner who had indicated to him that Polzer 'knows and should write' important things.

Polzer, as always after such insights quickly prepared for action, commenced to write up what became his rich, multi-faceted memoirs. They were completed by October and from November began to appear in Stein's *Present Age*, in London, at the other end of the Anglo-Bohemian axis.

The chronic recurrence of his sciatica led Polzer to spend a week in Baden in July where he took a sulphur bath treatment. As a very welcome guest at his brother Arthur's house he had a welcome opportunity to exchange views with his brother on many quiet walks. He certainly told Arthur of his visit to Peggau and Graz with Julius. These days of his spa treatment in Baden were not only of benefit to Polzer's health but were also of benefit to the retrospective mood indispensable for the work on his memoirs.

On 4 August, during his work in Linsberg Polzer wrote to his friend in London:

> When you wrote to me that you experienced Dr Steiner very clearly and that he told you that I know things and should write them down, it was this that was decisive for what I am now doing.
>
> While writing, I have come to understand better what R. St. wanted by this. It agrees with what I experienced in the night after the Gen. Mtg. in Dornach April 1935 in the Clinic at Arlesheim.
>
> *I see what I am writing in a way also as a continuation of the urging that I received from him after the Gen. Mtg.*[479]

These then were the motives for what Polzer was doing—not the widespread personal vanity of so many other writers of memoirs ...

Polzer's memoirs were rendered into English by George Adams who had translated his speech at the English General Meeting in 1935 for Daniel Dunlop. They were published in several further issues of *The Present Age*.

In mid-August Polzer continued his sciatica cure at another location. He went for a week to Bad Hévíz on Lake Balaton. His trip went via Ödenburg (today, Sopron) by bus through a region which 45 years before, had been a dear homeland for 3 years. The bus went through Zinkendorf where the family tomb of the Széchényis was located. 'Old wounds of the heart that had closed up became perceptible again,' he wrote in his diary. On 2 May 1893 he too had been there when his youthful love Jenny Széchényi was carried to her grave here.

Then the journey went on to Hégyfalu and like a sigh there flowed from Polzer's pen the mournful words: 'You beloved place, you beautiful time!'

Hévíz was known for its warm mud ponds, from which lotus flowers grew. Polzer, who bathed in Hévíz daily, was happily surprised to come across Pali Prónay, with whom he had once served in the 11th Hussars. Pali had later married the daughter of another old friend, Vilmos Pálffy. Polzer's time in Hévíz was thus full of diversion and freshly-encountered old memories. After his treatment he travelled along Lake Balaton to Budapest, where he stayed a further eight days as the guest of Margrit Schön. For the third part of his summer spa treatment he went to the baths at Lukasfürdö.

He spent an important, eventful day with Berta in September at Ausee in the Salzkammergut. The couple visited Lili and Eugen Kolisko, who were on holiday there. 'We spent a whole day with them,' wrote Polzer, 'with interesting conversations from morning till night.' From these two friends, who were also close friends of Stein, the Tannbach couple got to know the latest news of his activities in London. He had been able to give an interesting lecture at a recent international Congress of Faiths. Polzer spoke in full acknowledgement of Stein's activities in England in his next lecture in Pardubice, adding that: '*Rudolf Steiner turned not to the Society, but to single anthroposophers who are capable of doing something.*'[480] In the same lecture he sought to describe the preconditions for 'an understanding of the approaching catastrophe'. At this same time he wrote on 22 September in a letter to Stein:

> The awareness grows ever stronger within me that the so-called split [in the G.A.S.] in 1935 was necessary. There are now even different tasks. The work of R. Steiner in his last years in England and Holland meant something other than what is thought of it in Dornach. The Christmas Conference was also so little understood [there].

And of the political situation in the British Empire, he was of the view that: 'A new understanding of India must be brought home to the English. This will not happen without a struggle. The struggle of the spirit will perhaps soon only be able to be led by India.'

Of the contemporary world situation Polzer noted in his diary:

> Spiritual oppression through economic force and impoverishment has yet a way to go! The ideas of Fascism, National Socialism, and the corporate State are only the Bolshevism of the intellect; the thoughts are the same as those which have become fixed in the heads of the workers who want to set up a social order on the basis of today's natural scientific thinking. Thus,

people who do not understand their own spiritual nature end up in the region of subnature and transform Christianity into anti-Christianity.

In another place, he wrote: 'Europe is in agony—people call this the "new age". The new age will only come when the deadly work of those who are now leading the nations will have ended.'

In a lecture on the Templars, which Polzer gave in Prague in November, he came to speak of the approaching catastrophe, the intention of which was 'to make souls tired', which was why the 'fire of enthusiasm as the Templars manifested it was necessary'.

With this new-found fire of enthusiasm he secured a meeting on 14 November 1936 with the Czechoslovak Prime Minister Milan Hodža at the Kolowrat Palace. Polzer gave to Hodža his two small essays which had been rejected by the Press in Prague. Would they get a more positive reception from Hodža? The Prime Minister did at any rate agree to further meetings and urged Polzer to express more of his ideas in writing, but nothing more is known of what became of either of these two proposals.

Polzer was asked by friends in Prague to publish in German his Memoirs from *The Present Age*. Luděk Přikryl arranged for the reproduction of 200 copies, which were rapidly distributed at the beginning of 1937. Thus the German edition of what has repeatedly been referred to in this book as his 'Prague Memoirs' came to be circulated only *in response to the wishes of others.*The German title was: *Erinnerungen an den grossen Lehrer Dr Rudolf Steiner—Lebensrückschau eines Österreichers* [Remembering the great teacher Dr Rudolf Steiner—An Austrian Looks Back at His Life].

At the end of 1936 Polzer, who always regarded people with an open mind, got to know a Dutchman from Java by the name of Buyn, who had spent almost a year in Austria and had joined in the anthroposophical work in Vienna with an enthusiastic intensity. Buyn appeared to possess extraordinary spiritual capacities as Polzer, who was certainly not a credulous person, remarked to Stein. From the correspondence between Stein and Polzer in December, it is clear that they discussed the reincarnation background of the Duke of Windsor who had abdicated in that month [December 1936]. Polzer was to contact the Duke, who after his abdication, was staying at Castle Enzesfeld near Vienna, a Rothschild property. In 1924 D.N. Dunlop had been able to persuade the Duke, who was then the Prince of Wales, to open the World Power Conference which he had initiated. Stein and Polzer now hoped to induce the Duke to take similar steps in relation to the realization of threefolding. Polzer contacted the Duke's secretary by telephone from his brother Arthur's villa in Baden, but on 16 January he received a rebuff by letter. 'His Royal Highness' was unfortunately not able to receive private visits. In a letter to Stein of 27 January 1937 Polzer observed: 'From some things I had been told and learned I was already thinking that he [is] in a kind of captivity. That is also karmically interesting, because R.L. also sat imprisoned in Dürnstein.' R.L. could only refer to Richard the Lionheart, who was 'kidnapped' after the Third Crusade and was imprisoned for a while in Dürnstein Castle near Vienna. In the same month [January 1937] an article about Richard the Lionheart appeared in Stein's magazine *The Present Age*. Whatever may be made of the above-mentioned indications about reincarnation, they show that Stein and Polzer were often engaged in serious discussion of such questions.

At the end of 1937 Polzer travelled to Ostrau Castle near Halle an der Saale to visit his friend Hans Vasso von Veltheim, who was just then being published in *The Present Age*. A few days later, he visited Hildegard Wiegand, the author of an historical novel about James I which had so impressed him. She ran a small guesthouse in Bad Berka near Weimar. The two days he spent there were 'extraordinarily stimulating' for him. He was able to read through an unpublished manuscript of the novel *Götter und Könige* [Gods and Kings] which tells the story of the life of the Egyptian Queen Hatshepsut who ruled Egypt from Thebes c. 1500 BC. This book had been written at the same time as Polzer was working intensively with Maña Brabínek. She herself, as already mentioned, had 'clear experiences from that same period' in Thebes. The first book that Polzer had sent Maña was Wiegand's book about James I—*Der Kampf gegen den Tarnhelm*. And now 'many places in this manuscript' reminded him of the style of Maña's letters! So a delicate circle of pointers to the backgrounds of particular destinies was closed for Polzer here. 'When I read and re-read the novel,' he later wrote, 'Frau Schenker also read it out loud so well—I knew what the real cause of my trip to Germany was.'

★

After Polzer had visited his son Josef in March at the curative home in Pilgramshain and had given an address to the children on 30 March, after his return he set to writing another political memorandum. He titled it 'Today Bohemia holds the Key to Europe'. In broad outline Polzer shows the cooperation between Masons and Jesuits with regard to the economic and cultural oppression of Middle Europe and speaks specifically about the Balkan Federation conceived by these circles. The fruit of his thorough study of the Council of 1869 is the knowledge that 'the map programme of the 1880s, which was probably prepared much earlier, and

the event of the Council of 1869 [are] two events which in many respects
worked on together into later political happenings in Europe and up to
the present'. He shows in his memorandum further how Rome took
revenge for Emperor Franz Joseph's veto against the election to the
Papacy of the anti-German Cardinal Rampolla.[481]

> Rampolla's revenge against Austria was the strengthening of the populist
> movement led by Vienna Mayor Karl Lueger and the creation of the
> Christian Social Party, which was supported by Rampolla and directed
> against all the leaders of the Roman Catholic Church in Austria. Lueger did
> not enter politics for the sake of the workers and farmers; he banded
> together the most egoistic elements of the capital's urban proletariat,
> catholicized them with subsidies and infiltrated them into the younger
> generation of army officers and civil servants. The Emperor's two refusals to
> confirm him originated from insight into these activities. *This party worked
> systematically against German-Slavic cooperation that promised so much for the
> future of the Empire—cooperation that was so feared by Rome*[482] and lowered the
> level of culture; the party was dubbed that of 'the stupid fellow from
> Vienna'.

Polzer thus saw himself called once again to warn against Rome's manoeuvres in the sharpest tone:

> The statesmen of Middle Europe ought to realize that the powers of Rome
> have had the actual political leadership in Church and State as well as in the
> various regions in their hands for centuries and that all the methods
> employed by those opposed to this have until now been useless. In order to
> maintain Roman imperial power the two sister peoples, the Germans and
> the Western Slavs, have for centuries been quite deliberately played against
> each other [...] To confront this evil in the right place is the most
> important task, the most important question that must be addressed.

The task of reconciling peoples which had not been grasped by Austria-
Hungary, still less solved, Polzer saw at that time as falling to the
Czechoslovak Republic. 'The CSR is in a similar position to that in
which Austria formerly found itself. It therefore holds, if only it could
recognize the task set before it, the key to a true culture and human social
order for the future. Its very outer isolation shows this. Through its isolation it is linked to Germany.'

On 30 April 1937 Polzer gave a copy of his five-sided memorandum to
Dr Roda, Hodža's secretary. Two years later Polzer would write on the
original copy of the memorandum near the title 'Bohemia holds the key
position at present' the words: '[she] did not recognize it nor make use of
it—Failure!!'

★

While Polzer was in such ways, amongst other things, once again concerned with the decadent impulses of the Roman Empire, his friend Stein visited for a couple of weeks those places where Polzer's clear insights in this direction had their roots in his destiny: Stein went to Rome and Tivoli. He had been urged by friends to stop his ceaseless lecturing and his work for *The Present Age* for a while and to take a rest. 'I had an opportunity to take a trip through Italy, which the generosity of some friends made possible who had suddenly realized that I must replenish my forces and have a month of complete silence', he wrote in his report of his Italian journey.

He described his impressions of the Villa Hadriana as follows:[483]

> This complex of extensive built structures, gardens, theatres, squares, and schools represents the whole of the world of that time. Hadrian must have been a personality whose need it was to make visible for seeing eyes what others read about in books. We read about the cultures of antiquity, about India or Persia or Egypt. Hadrian built an enormous monument for each of the cultural epochs that was known to him in that he recreated whole scenes, for example, Egyptian buildings and the Egyptian landscape around them and an entire river. Just as we send a picture postcard to a friend and write on it: 'See, this is how what I have written to you about looks', *Hadrian built his memories that he set into the countryside*[484] so that beyond the gates of the institutions where they were educated and were able to imbibe the most valuable ideas of the classical world, the pupils of the schools of philosophy could immediately have before them in visible images what their teachers had been speaking of. He constructed the landscape in such a way that it surrounded him like his personal retrospect over his own life. Others have to wait until the moment of death for their whole life to surround them in living images. Then the human being beholds in a kind of timeless or simultaneous sculpted panorama what he went through in his life [. . .] As a living person *he* [Hadrian] wandered through his own biography. And this life was so comprehensive, of such significance for the world, that others as pupils of great philosophers and worldviews could find in this objectified biography still so much of the breadth of humanity and the comprehensiveness of the world that it became a schooling for them.

After Stein had taken pleasure in his friend's memoirs of his most recent earthly life, he encountered in the Villa Hadriana a deeper and quite different level of those memoirs. After he had wandered through Polzer's memoirs expressed in printed words, in Italy, he wandered through Hadrian's 'memories set in the countryside'.

So as Walter Johannes Stein, awakened through his own retrospective experiences, had taken deeply into himself the destiny backgrounds of Rudolf Steiner, Ita Wegman, Eliza and Helmuth von Moltke, he was now able to do this with his friend Polzer. Not many words will have been exchanged between Stein and Polzer about this, but Stein was very attentive and sensitive—and more and more proficient in being able to surround deeper occult truths with the protective layer of total silence . . .

★

At Whitsun Polzer went travelling. He went to Venice and Trieste with Anneliese Freudenthaler. She was the 17-year-old daughter of the former station master at Kefermarkt station, not far from Gutau, with whose family Berta Polzer was very friendly. From Trieste Anneliese, whose first great journey this was, went alone back to her home, and Polzer went via Rab Island, where he stayed for a couple of days, and visited the splendid Bay of Miotica and then went on to the Knispels in Kambelovac. Here he prepared himself for a conference which his friends in Pardubice had arranged for the holidays 4–7 July and was to be held in Lomnice and Eisenbrod. On these days the lives of four individualities of great significance for Czech spiritual life were honoured: 4 July was the day of St Procopius.[485]

On 5 July both of 'the apostles to the Slavs', Cyril and Methodius, were celebrated. They had been sent to Great Moravia in 863 by Photius, Patriarch in Constantinople and they laid the foundations for the Christianizing of the West Slavic peoples. Photius had been the great opponent of Pope Nicholas I, and so, through Cyril and Methodius, Christianization was brought about from Byzantium, not from Rome.

On 6 July Jan Hus was commemorated, who, 500 years after Cyril and Methodius, reignited the struggle against the spirit of Rome with the weapons of Wycliffe, for which he was burned at the stake at the Council of Constance on 6 July 1415.

All four men worked for a Slavic Christianity free from Rome and therefore stood very close to Polzer's tasks and circle of activity. This was to show itself very clearly in the course of these days in July.

The approximately 60 participants in the small travelling conference left in the afternoon of 4 July by train from Königgrätz to Lomnice, where Polzer was to speak about Prokop, the Hussite leader and about Cyril and Methodius the following day. The journey went by the battlefield where on 3 July 1866, the day before St Procopius' Day, the battle of Königgrätz took place which was so unfortunate for Austria and ended in a victory for Prussia.

Polzer wrote:

The overcrowding on rail lines on those three Czech holidays was huge. Despite the throng I was able to get a seat and found myself sitting next to Major Snítil, who was stationed in Königgrätz and therefore knew the battlefield area well. During the journey he explained to me the various situations of the armies, showed me the direction and the village from which the Crown Prince of Prussia had advanced with his army and won the battle. Then he added, almost casually—it was the day of St Procopius: 'And there is also the village where 400 years earlier (before Königgrätz), Prokop* won his victory [1423] over the Catholic army led by Čeněk of Wartenberg [Čeněk z Vartemberka]. He did not suspect that these words would help me to realize something.

Polzer now went on: 'Like a lightning strike there came from somewhere in me, not through the ear, these words: "So it was not only the needle-gun that was the cause of the Austrian defeat."' The spirit of resistance against the historically invalid Roman theocratic element had actually been the deeper factor which helped the technically superior Prussians to victory at Königgrätz—this was, in short, Polzer's sudden realization. And the form in which it came to him would have to be described as inspired; this time too the question as to the nature of the inspiring spirit would have to be left open. Is it, however, unreasonable, to bring to mind here one of the very living 'dead' just across the threshold with whom Ludwig Polzer had sought to unite himself in meditation for many years and who on 4 July 1866, the day of St Procopius, had in Leitomischl, where he was then stationed, received news of the defeat at Königgrätz? This was of course Julius, Ritter von Polzer, Ludwig's father.

Polzer commented on his sudden realization about Königgrätz as follows:

> Through the Michaelic inspiration of Jan Hus, Prokop, the Hussite leader, the fighter for the first onset of the Consciousness Soul epoch, defeated Wartenburg, who was fighting for the continuation of the obsolete form of Christianity that was Roman Catholicism. The Crown Prince of Prussia was fighting against those who were still fighting in the service of the old Roman Empire and not for their real Christian mission. Neither Prokop nor the Crown Prince of Prussia were actually conscious of what in reality was the determining element that promoted development at turning points in human history. Neither did Wartenberg nor Benedek (the Austrian commander at Königgrätz) know anything of it. One cannot speak in general of blame with regard to any of the commanders. Single individuals act externally out of conviction and a sense of duty: 400 years before—out of religious conviction; 400 years later—out of duty towards the State. Fate

---

*In reality, Jan Žižka—*transl.*

had led the Austrian army into a position in which it could never win. The needle gun and other manifestations of military progress in Prussia were only the consequences of the freer spirit which was prevalent on that side, but the spirit was no more *Christian* on the Prussian side than on the Austrian.

Contemplation of the Austrian/Prussian dualism brought Polzer to a spiritual scientific threefold perspective in which the activity of certain spiritual beings which dominated the two sides became visible to him. He wrote:

> In order to avoid false conclusions, one must be able to distinguish between spiritual beings. A consciousness of Christ can awaken between Austria (luciferic action) and Prussia (ahrimanic action). Four hundred years ago and in the year 1866 there were only admonitions—for the Catholics and for the Hussite Protestants—to recognize the real mission of mankind, and especially of Middle Europe, on Earth. Whether Habsburg or Hohenzollern would extend their dominance was only a minor matter; the real issue was: 'Middle Europe must not become Roman', neither in an ecclesiastical nor in a political form. Neither in the form of a Jesuit Church nor a Jesuit State. It was in this sense that I gave my lectures over the following days.

Thus this conference trip became for Polzer a festival of the joy of knowledge in the best sense. He wrote: 'The harmony of time and space spoke to me, awakening knowledge. It was the simultaneity of the commemorative days of these events and I travelled, during those days through the region in which they had occurred, with an anthroposophical task which related to them.'

Once again outer events were converging with Polzer's inner strivings. 'It therefore happened again that attention to what came to me from outside immediately before I was to speak about a topic related to it complemented my own inner ideas in such a way as to confirm my understanding of it.'

From Lomnice, where Polzer spoke about Prokop [see n. 485] on 4 July and about Cyril and Methodius on 5 July, the group visited Mt Tabor which was closely related to Prokop's activities and also Kozakov, the mountain from which the semi-precious stones originated which were used in Karlstejn Castle as well as in the Wenceslas Chapel on the Hradčany Castle mount in Prague. The journey went on to Eisenbrod [today, Železný Brod], where on the following day, the day of the execution of Jan Hus [6 July 1415] again 'something very peculiarly symptomatic occurred'. At 7 a.m. on 6 July Polzer held a Class Lesson in order to be able to give his lecture on Hus at 9 a.m. He had intended to give a presentation to local members. But with a mysterious rapidity news of his lecture on Hus had spread around Železný Brod. Polzer wrote:

> News now spread in Eisenbrod that I was to speak about Hus; I don't know how that came about. The very large lecture hall was filling to the point where there was soon no more room even to stand. The people could not be kept back. During the lecture, which naturally I had not written down, I had to adjust the content of my lecture to the public. Never perhaps did I speak as easily as on that occasion; I felt myself borne by the audience. Afterwards cheers broke out in the hall.

There can be no doubt: those days were the high point in Ludwig Polzer's lecturing activity; they stood entirely in the sign of that high goal for which he had worked unwaveringly since the solemn vow he had made in the Wenceslas Chapel.

★

When after these eventful days which had given him much to ponder on, Polzer arrived in Linsberg in order to recuperate, a letter from Stein was waiting for him. His friend in London asked if he would like to come in August to the anthroposophical Summer School that was to be held in The Hayes, Derbyshire. Polzer replied that he certainly would if his travel costs and free accommodation could be provided: 'Then that would be very good,' he thought. 'That there are karmic connections between us, but also between me and the English people, is for me certain. It is always my desire to foster these.' Polzer was then invited by Stein to participate in the Summer School for free.

Although his own letters to his older friend are no longer extant on the matter, Stein must also have informed Polzer of something else: after a first meeting with the King of Belgium at the end of June 1937, Stein had succeeded in persuading the monarch to support an extraordinary plan. An economics institute was to be set up in Brussels that would work for the coordination of supranational economic activities. In July there appeared in Stein's journal *The Present Age* an open letter by the King to his Prime Minister van Zeeland in which he proposed the establishment of a permanent 'World Economic Council'. Behind this unusual step by Leopold were Stein's conversations with the unusual monarch.

Polzer wrote to his friend on 29 July: 'Naturally I shall do what I can in this matter. It is very clear to me that it has to do with a possibility that is of the greatest significance which is so intimately related to my own life's task, which I received from the Herr Doctor when he was alive.' Polzer wanted to assist in making this institute known and in finding finance for it and to this end he wanted to contact the journalist Wettreich and the Hamburger and Schenker families. He also thought of speaking to his brother, although he had 'never had any luck' with him in such matters. He himself had to keep in the background: 'In Austria I am so well-known and avoided as an anthroposopher that I am unable to have direct dealings with people in official positions, nor would I be listened to.' He wanted, however, to take steps in Czechoslovakia and Hungary per-sonally, as he was 'not so well-known as an A. [anthroposopher] in other countries'.

However, Polzer was unable to achieve much, and the promising plans for the activities of the Brussels Institute as well as the intended Statistical Institute in the The Hague linked with it at Stein's instigation had to be called off before the beginning of the Second World War. Yet in these steps taken by Stein and King Leopold, which Polzer followed with the greatest interest, we can see significant seeds for the direction of a future world economy.

After a visit from his grandson Christward to Tannbach, Polzer travelled in the second week of August via Arlesheim to England. From Ostend on 17 August he sent a telegram to London giving information about his arrival, only to meet, quite unexpectedly, Stein, accompanied by Frau Lungen, on the ferry to Dover. 'It was a fine meeting,' he wrote later, 'I got to know Frau Lungen for the first time.' She later became Stein's second wife. 'Their friendship came about very quickly, as with people who are supposed to meet in life.' In London he stayed with Miss Osmond, whom he had known since the previous Summer school he had attended in Harrogate; this was also the case with most of the others at the Summer School in Derbyshire except for a 'very dear lively' Indian doctor by the name of Pranananda, who was 'very devoted to anthroposophy'.

Before his return to the Continent Polzer spent many hours in London with Walter Johannes Stein and Yopie Lungen. Then he travelled to the World Exposition in Paris. There was beautiful summer weather when he visited the various pavilions.

Hardly had he arrived back in Tannbach when he wrote a letter to London on 10 September. And while the letter only includes a few details about his stay in England, it gives a clear picture of his inner state of mind after his return:

> Dear friend!
> I arrived here yesterday, and so this letter to you is the first I have written. My time in England, for which I thank you, is for me like a beautiful dream of hope in the midst of an anxious, difficult earthly life. I experienced the friendly anthrop. warmth over there with the greatest gratitude. When one

is lifted out for a time from the situation here and when gentle hopes are raised, one is then always reminded on returning that: 'One must also be able to watch how peoples go under.' Those are the words which HE said to me on leaving Berlin in 1917. And since that time it has been a continuous falling and lifting oneself up again. At 68, the latter is hard, really hard. We in Austria are still traditional and still bound strongly to so much that was once beautiful and worthy. One lives in a house with old memories, here still with the memories of Rudolf Steiner's presence, and don't know what is to happen in the near future. I know that these are small things and yet I cannot quite get over them. But when I think of the great tasks and far horizons which I discussed & experienced with you and look ahead over the next 50 years, then I become calm, certain & full of hope, despite the threatening immediate future before us. However, my thoughts since we met again have been united particularly strongly with all that, that is, with your strivings & tasks [...]

Much love from us all,

Yours faithfully,

Ludwig Polzer

★

From another letter from Polzer which he wrote from Linsberg on 14 September we see that he sent Stein his Bohemia memorandum in which he included a map. 'The text with the map really characterizes our m.e. [Middle European] situation,' he writes in the letter.

> I have to re-experience it again and again, and gradually survey the whole spider's web, from which one can no longer find a way out with the short-term thinking of the present. The striving to find the balance between the city and the countryside has not found, that is, has not accepted the right & possible ways forward.

On his relationship to the Tannbach estate, he writes: 'I am united by such strong bonds of destiny to the two dear people at home & yet I find it so hard to endure the situation there, so I am here now to take a rest & to work. This is all a real heartache!'

Polzer's diary for that period contains some very serious statements with regard to the contemporary world situation. For example:

> Bolshevism has been organized in order to justify the existence of Church and State in their present form in their struggle against Bolshevism, because people suffer from a sterility of ideas and cannot affirm themselves spiritually. The worst is that they do not recognize this sterility and thus act out of fanaticism. Brutality and barbarism advance through technological methods and speak of culture!!

A remarkable contrast to this sharply characterized contemporary situation were the experiences Polzer had on 26 September in the very familiar surroundings of Heiligenkreutz [Holy Cross] Castle. Here a wedding was celebrated in the old style. Gabriele Kotz, Berta's cousin and god-daughter married Baron Adolf Harnier. Berta did not dare to go herself as she had no clothes suitable for such an occasion. Such festivities had become very rare in the postwar period! So Berta had to be represented by her husband Ludwig. 'The day passed very pleasantly,' he wrote of the beginning of the celebration. But it was not only the joy of the occasion that had drawn him there. As on so many earlier visits to Heiligenkreutz, he first went to the cemetery 'where so many dear relatives lie'. Thirty-five years had passsed since he had first visited Berta's homeland. He had then arrived in a mood of great seriousness; it was with a similar feeling in the depths of his soul that he was returning on this day.

In the evening there was a grand reception in formal dress with the obligatory jewellery and decorations. Some of the guests came from faraway and stayed overnight with families who lived nearby. Among them were names such as Czernin, Lobkowitz, Trautmannsdorf, Thun, Kollowrat or Coudenhove. Was the last-named perhaps related to the founder of the Pan-Europa movement?

'One had the feeling that the old times were still here. The wave of destruction had still not reached a good many people,' Polzer wrote. 'I was glad that this was so.'

During the reception in the festive hall all kinds of deputations from the surrounding villages had gathered in front of the castle, from the fire brigade to the local choral society—as in the old days. Speeches were made and there were torchlit processions. The actual wedding did not take place until two days later in the village church. No one was in a hurry. At the high table afterwards Polzer as godfather toasted the couple and expressed the hope that there would soon be another such festive occasion.

Like a last gleam of the culture of the past, this wedding celebration shone into the gathering gloom of the present, which soon, like a Moloch, would utterly devour the old times, skin, bones and all. This was how Polzer experienced the wedding feast at Holy Cross Castle after his stay in England.

On 29 September he returned to Prague in order to continue his anthroposophical work there and in Pardubice. 'Thus I stepped out of the old times once more into the new.'

He had a very similar experience of contrasting times shortly afterwards in another connection. On 11 September, the day after his return from

Paris and England, Thomas Garrigue Masaryk, the first President of the Czechoslovak Republic, had died.

Polzer experienced the funeral ceremonies in Prague in October as a symptomatic event to the highest degree which cast a bright light both on past and future centuries. He had long been thoroughly prepared to comprehend this historical symptom.

He wrote:

> Throughout my anthroposophical activity and especially since the death of Dr Steiner, I occupied myself so intensively with Bohemia's history of suffering that the unique funeral ceremonies for President Masaryk shed light for me on various aspects of spiritual history. It was also not an accident that in recent years I was in England a number of times & made anthroposophical connections there & spoke with Walter Johannes Stein about these. I was living with the greatest interest and empathy into the esoteric relationship which unites England with the heart of Middle Europe. When I write this down, I am certainly not thinking of that which plays itself out externally in the politics of these countries but of a connection in the sense of the deep development of spirit and soul, which is entirely submerged in the materialistic age.

Then Polzer describes the ceremonies themselves.

> The whole spontaneous demonstration of the nation's feeling at the funeral, which was not at all done in a way redolent of power or of the State, was tremendous and astonishing in its immense sincerity. It was an honourable expression of gratitude, a demonstration of sympathy by the entire population. It was something very different from the unworthy, Roman attitude of 'bread and circuses' which is shown today by the Church in Austria and by the State in Germany. Hearts were speaking, not heads. In these days I saw Masaryk as the representative of the whole period from the founding of cities[*] until today in which this has been led to absurdity. [The funeral] was a symptomatic conclusion to this period of bourgeois towns and markets. But intellectuals with darkened souls cannot read symptomatic events. Masaryk's sense for truth also lay in the way this funeral was conducted. The real condition of the human soul expressed itself in the absence of anything cultic. The constitution of the soul, when it gives of itself honourably and shows how it really is, reveals that human souls no longer perceived the spirit active in matter nor the striving for matter in the spirit. The union of the senses in the Last Supper by Christ could no longer be perceived as spiritual. Everything is only abstract thoughts. Spiritual Realism has given way to Nominalism, to disbelief in spiritual being that can be experienced.

---

[*] In the Middle Ages—*transl.*

I felt in these days as if the many people who had streamed past were led by something that lay in their earlier lives on earth. Unconsciously, they were taking leave not only of Masaryk but also of an epoch of time which had run its course, *without the capacities being present that could form a new epoch*: Today, people want to hold on violently and fanatically to the old epoch of the bourgeois city and they create chaos and destruction. There is much talk of *lebensraum* for the peoples but they do not understand how to use space [*Raum*] for living in. Urban centres have expanded to become deathly tumours and the space [countryside] is emptied of people; chaos and madness are on the march [...] The deathly sickness of the cancer in the cities and markets can even be called the madness of the State [*Staatskoller*]. The funeral ceremonies were the apotheosis of an age that had run its course and Masasryk was the inaugurator and terminator of this age.[486]

It can be seen from a longer essay that Polzer wrote in relation to Masaryk's funeral that the expression 'Masaryk the inaugurator' (of the culture of the towns and cities) was meant quite concretely:

One is led to England in the tenth century, to King Edward [the Elder, 899–924], the founder of towns. The towns, which on the one hand were built for defence and also served the purposes of trade and industry, made possible the founding of universities and were indirectly the creators of materialistic economic order and natural science. With the founding of towns the bourgeois social order gradually began. The hierarchical social order became more and more a symbol and finally a phrase. The Holy Roman Empire of the German Nation was the last, merely symbolic manifestation of hierarchical impulses that had once been justified. At the beginning of this bourgeois epoch was struggle and it could only be achieved in ongoing struggle until it finally came more and more into decadence; but the towns and cities lost their moral justification [...] When one looks at cities today, the facts lead one to say that the great cities expand more and more, whole areas of the country are covered by them, small towns become great cities, markets become towns, villages become mar-kets, and for a century now they have been drawing to themselves the forces of the land where actual production originally takes place. In the social organism this no longer works to human benefit but creates sickness. It is like cancer in the human body [...] This one-sided urban culture produces decay; it must make way for a harmonized culture of town and country [...] A culture of the town and country which must form a unity will then be united with a general human social order that can never be organized merely externally by the State.[487]

How much Masaryk had to do with Polzer's knowledge of spiritual history with its contemporary relation to England and especially to his friend Stein can be deduced from the fact that W.J. Stein, who had written his *World History in the Light of the Holy Grail*[488] on the subject of the ninth century, *also intended to write about the tenth century from this perspective.* In outline notes he considered the impulse of the founding of towns by King Edward against the background of the legend of Lohengrin. Stein had doubtless had conversations with Polzer about the impulse of founding towns which had stemmed from King Edward [899–924], the son of Alfred the Great.

On 7 November 1937 Polzer wrote a note on the last letter that he had received from Masaryk in October 1933:

> Because of his illness I could not direct to him any spiritual scientific answer to his question [about the territorial problem of mankind]. Immediately after his death I received, thanks to various spiritually real circumstances, a communication from the spiritual world about his historical personality. Through this it was possible for me to give him the answer after his death. I have the feeling that it was warmly received.

A spiritual conversation therefore followed Polzer's spiritual-historical-karmic knowledge about the individuality of Masaryk. Polzer sought to carry on this conversation with the deceased beyond the threshold.

How does this spiritual answer seem now which he gave Masasryk after his death? On the empty sides of the last letter from Masaryk he noted the main points of his answer. There we read:

> It is not the question of territory which stands in the centre of world history but the awakening to the problem of the spirit. A logic of facts would have to recognize this in many details in numerous events. For example, while one is talking about territory and raw materials, the products of nature are continually being destroyed: land, plants, animals and human beings are rapidly or slowly being killed through chemical ignorance for the sake of what is said to be 'living'. New regions are cleared for cultivation and healthy work in regions which have already been cleared is prevented through false methods of social 'assistance' which proceed from abstract civic or market-oriented attitudes. If the social question can be solved in a generally human way that takes account of the soul and spirit then no territorial question results from any problems of expansion. *It must be recognized that—whether one wants to hear it or not—the age of 'territorial ruler-ships' in the old sense is over.*[489]

Polzer's spiritual-historical knowledge in relation to Masaryk and the problems of land and cities belong to the weightier fruits which ripened on the tree of friendship between Stein and Polzer in the year 1937.

★

On 15 October Polzer wrote to his brother Arthur that Julius would be getting married on 25 October at the Linz parish church. A second wedding thus followed the brilliant and nostalgic ceremonies at Heiligenkreutz, but this wedding was from the outset very different in style and form from the first. Julius wed Anna Stollenberger, a young woman from a farming family. 'When it is hard for us to take the consequences from destiny as it is, I am glad that faithful, noble Julius does that so morally.' Such was Julius' father's comment to his brother Arthur on his son's decision.

On the evening of 24 October the local choir and fire brigade from Gutau came to Tannbach to greet the bridal couple. Ludwig Polzer made a fine speech for the occasion.

'For more than 30 years,' he began,

> we have lived here amongst you in this farming country. We know all the cares and concerns of this most important class as our own. This class is the archetypal image of what a class is. There is an old wisdom which will remain true that when the farmer can live and work, all others will be able to do so. Not one law is needed for that [. . .] Those who would destroy the farmers through exploitation, destroy the State.

And on the relationship between the farming class and the nobility, Polzer said:

> Tomorrow a marriage bond will be sealed at a very solemn time between the nobles and farmers. Long ago the nobility emerged from amongst the farming community. It does honour to itself when it honours the farming community. Knowing this, there are two young people, there is the nobility with its origins [. . .] Much is said about community. Communities arise when moral thinking and moral action prevail. When no moral thinking can find its place, then what follows is disintegration, breakup and a struggle of all against all. The farmer, who stands so close to the realms of nature, always wants to serve work and peace. For this he needs no advice from the city or from Ministries; it lies within his own being which is united with nature. So I thank you for coming to honour this marriage.

Polzer closed his speech with a festive call: 'Long live the people of this farming region!'

In memory of his childhood, Julius wanted the ceremony to take place in the parish church on the church square where the family had lived for two years and from where he had walked to Linz school with Josef.

After the wedding, which took place at 9 a.m., the group of twelve had breakfast at the inn on the same square. Along with the few relatives, the modest festive group included the old friend of the household, Hugo Flatz.

The two weddings of that autumn thus showed the great change of the times that had taken place. Where one was still able to feel something of the glamour of the old age of the nobility at Heiligenkreutz Castle, the second wedding in its earnest simplicity spoke of the need for the nobility to renew their ties to their origins—the farming community.

Alongside such intimate obligations, Polzer was again ever conscious of a certain evil of modern times. This showed itself, for example, in the entry in his diary on 17 December 1937:

'The being of Jesuitism is death. Its thinking is cosmic bigotry. Its feeling is hatred of humanity. Its will is the sin against the Spirit. Whoever allows it into him, must give himself up as a being of soul and spirit. The individual and the community must die without resurrection.'

A further entry in December shows that he was thinking increasingly about the southern European Danube Federation propagated by both the Freemasons and the Jesuits, 'societies united in their hostility to the spirit'.

At Christmas Berta Polzer gave her husband a book about Rákoczy, the Hungarian prince associated with the Comte de St Germain. Polzer read this with great interest, and it may well have called to mind many conversations with his friend in London. From his friends in Pardubice he received a book about Masaryk, which thus, before the year was out, reminded him emphatically of his Masaryk experiences of the autumn.

Many Christmas and New Years' greetings were received from friends and acquaintances. Yet the recipient saw himself obliged to write in reply: 'With heavy thoughts and concerns in this New Year.'

★

The year 1938 began with spiritual refreshment. Polzer had been invited to Arlesheim for a conference which took place between 7 and 10 January. Ita Wegman wanted to bring together a group of people who were active in free anthroposophical work. The group gathered four times a day and studied Rudolf Steiner's lecture cycle given in Kassel in 1909, *The Gospel of St John*.[490] 'There was a high, spiritual scientific mood and a friendly atmosphere,' wrote Polzer, very satisfied.

Strengthened and filled with a new spiritual elan, he went on shortly afterwards to Prague and Pardubice for lectures and Class Lessons.

In February Polzer turned again to Masaryk. He resolved to read to Masaryk's soul in meditation Rudolf Steiner's *Towards Social Renewal*.[491] He thus continued after Masaryk's death the important conversations he had had with him on Earth.

On 23 February he wrote to Stein in London that he would soon like to meet again for a personal conversation, together with a remarkable younger man of whom he had already written to Stein.

> What is happening there through you must be complemented in M.E. [Middle Europe]. The simplest would be if you were to come here, for we could not manage the trip to England and do not know anyone who would finance it. We could perhaps meet up halfway; that would be cheaper, but even that would be hard for us to manage. The affair in Br.[ussels] seems to me to be going rather slowly; the sticking to small state affairs is hard to overcome [...].

Due to the political changes that soon transpired, nothing came of the desired meeting.

At the beginning of March Polzer went to Prague again. He did not suspect that it would be the last time. He again gave to Secretary of State Hodža a short memorandum which he had written in January. In it he diagnosed sharply the sick state of leadership in Europe at that time:

> The leading men in Europe are losing themselves in legalistic strife over definitions and abstract concepts, which kill everything that has life and reality [...] They carry on with dogmatic definitions of nation, state, and homeland, in a way which has nothing whatsoever to do with the reality of the facts from which the actual world events have proceeded. They [...] are moving in a void of soul and spirit, without noticing this void.

The memorandum therefore once more admonished and warned energetically:

> When reason cannot recognize that the only possible way to save culture in Europe is to create a free cultural life that is dominated neither by the authority of the State nor by that of the Church, and an economy that transcends states and thus borders, which means the end of territorial dominion, then catastrophes must inevitably follow, which will mean complete anarchy.

And in relation to the real possibility of solving pressing conflicts in a manner in accordance with reality, the memorandum states: '*What the following centuries need has already been inspired from the spiritual world and is present in the spiritual substance of humanity as a whole. It cannot be improved; it can only be developed.*'[492]

This was the last effort of its kind by Ludwig Polzer, and this time too he did not expect any outward success. Two years later he wrote: 'How was I to be listened to, when the great teacher was not listened to, and yet I know through anthroposophy that all efforts on this path are not in vain but work on. A lack of success is never conclusive for the truth of a spiritual impulse.'

★

While Ludwig Polzer was holding a Class Lesson in Vienna on 11 March the political upheaval began. He wrote: 'When I was walking to the Class Lesson along the Graben* there were still shouts of "Austria", but on my way back, they were shouting "Sieg Heil" and everywhere swastika flags and armbands were appearing.' Polzer went with Dora Schenker by car along the Kreuzgasse to her Vienna apartment where he had been accustomed to stay during his visits to Vienna for the previous couple of years. 'I was silent,' he wrote in 1939, 'and was glad that at least the ecclesiastical, Jesuit direction had apparently suffered a defeat, but in the depths of my soul I could not be glad—and so was silent! How many disappointed hopes and illusions showed themselves so soon!'

To Frau Lungen he wrote two weeks after the upheaval: 'I am busy trying to understand the course of events inwardly and wakefully.'

And already a few months after the Nazi takeover of Austria†, he wrote in his diary:

> One who does not recognize today that the methods and actions of the Jesuits, F.M., National Socialists are all the same, knows nothing of what is going on in the development of mankind. These are all only subsidiaries of one and the same ahrimanic firm. What is going on is the continual destruction of contemporary humanity. How right Nietzsche was when he said: 'The foundation of the German Reich is the extirpation of the German spirit.'[493]

The path to Bohemia was now blocked. Neither would Polzer be able to travel to England anymore. 'This feeling of being fixed is painful,' he wrote to London on 2 April. 'The dear people I know in Bohemia are very sad. One just has to be able to resign oneself to it.' When Polzer here spoke of being resigned, he meant it in Goethe's sense, in the sense of denial as an act of the liberation of creative powers; in the sense also of the title which Goethe gave to the title of the second part of his master novel: 'Wilhelm Meister's Journeyman Years, or *the Renunciants*' [die Entsa-genden]. In the following years Polzer was to have plenty of opportunity for such a positive approach to renunication.

---

* A well-known street in Vienna—*transl.*
† The so-called *Anschluss*—*transl.*

42. 'Goethe in Marienbad'

To celebrate his 69th birthday Polzer travelled to Salzburg with Berta. The following day Berta returned to Tannbach, while her husband made a trip through Germany which lasted four weeks. He stopped first in Regensburg and spent a fine afternoon with Sophie and Menny Lerchenfeld. While he had met Sophie from time to time since her marriage to Alexsander Račeta, he had not seen 'that once so beloved fine girl',[494] as he called Menny, for exactly ten years.

After her studies and a long stay in Paris, Menny Lerchenfeld had made a career for herself in music in Munich. She taught piano, harmony, the history of music and accompanied foreign students to the opera. She had a large circle of friends and enjoyed life in Munich's artistic district.

In her diary Menny described meeting her older friend again:

> Last night with Sophie in Regensburg. L.P. came. A lovely reunion after a long, long time. He quite unchanged. Sat together at *Maximilian*. He spoke a lot about the times and, I believe, very rightly. He spoke about the distorted picture the church (Jesuits) makes of Christ and therefore the disinterest of many people. He related all these questions to the false Dmitri.[495]

Despite the ties of his heart to Sophie and Menny Lerchenfeld, Polzer nevertheless knew how to lead the conversation in an unforced, natural way to essential questions.

While in the past few years it had been Walter Johannes Stein who had supported and accompanied Polzer's lifepath in active friendship, even if mostly from a distance, now in the years that followed and on into wartime it was Menny Lerchenfeld who became his nearest and dearest companion. We shall therefore often encounter in the following pages the gifted pianist and later painter, who was then at the end of her 20s, in the mirror of many surviving letters from Ludwig Polzer to the 'beloved fine girl'.

★

From Regensburg Polzer travelled on for two days to Berlin. He made an acquaintance while travelling, Frau Anneliese Krüger, who showed him round Berlin and Potsdam. They went to Hoditzstrasse and Sans Souci Palace. 'It was the loveliest weather, in the Mon Repos Park all the flowers were in bloom.'

From the window of the Berlin hotel where he was staying, Polzer saw

49. Col. Vujić, Lou Knispel, Ludwig Polzer, Christl Polzer, Leo Knispel, ? [Unknown], 1933

50. *Back row from l. to r.: Rudolf Herman, Anton Geryšer, Col. Dohnal (6.), Miloš Brabínek (8.); middle row: Karolina Geryšer, Maňa Brabínek (3.); front row: Marie Brabínek (2.), Ludwig Polzer. Pardubice 1933*

51. *Ludwig Polzer, Karolina Geryšer, Maňa Brabínek; Karlstejn Castle*

52. Theodora Zeissig; Ludwig Polzer (1936)

53. Ludwig Polzer, 1935

54. D.N. Dunlop, 1925

55. W.J. Stein, 1931

56. Dora Schenker; part of the house on the Mariensee estate

57. George Adams and Ludwig Polzer; account of a dream (see p. 310)

Traumgesicht vom 13. auf den 14. I. 1939.
wahrscheinlich vor Mitternacht. –

Ich fand mich wie in einer Kirche
oder der Sakristei einer solchen.
Ich trat einem Cardinal gegenüber
mit dem ich mich in ein Gespräch
einließ. Wir sprachen nicht mit Worten
sondern mit Augen u. Gesichtsausdrücken
Das Antlitz des Cardinal wurde unend-
lich freundlich u. verständnisvoll.
Dann kam ein zweiter Cardinal hin-
zu. Es wurde mir gesagt es sei der von
Sant Jago di Compostella. Dieser hatte
ein finsteres u. böses Angesicht u.
begann auf den ersten furchtbar
loszuwettern – in höchster Aufre-
gung. Den Inhalt der Gespräche

58. Account of the Santiago dream from 1939

V.

Mein letzter Lebensabschnitt.
Die Zeit nach dem Tode D.ͬ Rudolf Steiners
1925 –

Nach dem Tode R. Steiners empfand ich zunächst
das Bedürfnis Frau Marie Steiner bei der Abwicke-
lung der Verlassenschafts Geschäfte zu helfen und
übernahm die Vertretung der hinterbliebenen Ver-
wandten. In Wien würde ich dabei auch von
meinem Vetter Lothar unterstützt der Sections-Chef
im Justizministerium war. –

In der weiteren Folge der Ereignisse innerhalb
der anthroposophischen Gesellschaft. versuchte ich
anfänglich vermittelnd ni den Streit einzugrei-
fen, der im Dornacher Vorstand zwischen Frau Marie
Steiner u. Frau D.ͬ Wegman latent schon seit der
Tagung zu Weihnachten 1923/24 herrschte u. welcher
Rudolf Steiner schwere Sorgen machte. – Der
Freundschaft welche zwischen uns und Rudolf Steiner
herrschte stand Frau Marie Steiner immer kühl
gegenüber. Wie sie mir später einmal sagte,
konnte sie zu Berta keine Beziehung finden.

Ich wollte aber sachlich bleiben und versuchte
zunächst Frau Marie Steiner zu unterstützen, da

59. First page of the notes from 1939 (LPE)

60. Paul Michaelis, 1965

61. Arthur Polzer, 1940

62. Ludwig Polzer, 1937

63. Berta Polzer, 1937

64. Ludwig Polzer, 1930

Hitler waving his arm about before his departure for Italy. He wrote to Hjalmar Schacht, the Director of the Reichsbank and to Göring, but was only able to speak with one of their representatives. On both evenings he was invited to supper by Anneliese Krüger and her husband.

Polzer's journey then went on to Sarrow and Marienhöhe, where he visited Dr Bartsch and his wife. The next day he went to Pilgramshain and there met Josef, who was on 'really good form'. Three days later, he travelled on to Dresden.

For the first time in his life he now stood before the Sistine Madonna. The sight of the painting reawoke in him the memory of the first two lectures he had heard by Rudolf Steiner in November 1908. In the second of these lectures Steiner had begun by speaking of his own contemplation of the Sistine Madonna. Now Polzer was standing with his consciousness strengthened by that memory before the world-famous work of art. 'I was so clearly conscious,' he wrote,

> that the human being draws art from the heavens [. . .] When that is not the case, then only technique is left and the imitation of nature. The human being is only a true artist when he can experience life with the physical, psychological and spiritual universe which yields itself to him in splendid imaginations.

From Dresden Polzer then travelled to Cologne. Wilhelm Goyert and his wife had invited him to this Rhineland city which had been founded by Agrippina, the mother of Nero. Goyert had been told by Ita Wegman in April 1935 of Polzer's plans in relation to the approaching exclusions, and so there will have been intimate conversation in Cologne about the Dornach majority decision. Goyert invited some friends, and Polzer read from his Prague Notes. The rest of his time in Cologne was spent in sightseeing and visits to galleries. The host and art dealer will certainly have proved to be a very knowledgeable guide. For the first time Polzer experienced the mighty Cathedral with its centuries-long construction history.

Did Polzer know of *Goethe's* stay in Cologne in 1815 and his friendship with the Cologne art historian Sulpice Boisserée? There was also Goethe's visit to the Cathedral at the end of July 1815 and his warm relationship with Boisserée which elicited from him a jocular, light-hearted comment about his relationship to history, especially to that of Rome. 'Goethe spoke of his predilection for what was Roman and suddenly added, *he had certainly once lived under Hadrian.*'[496] That there may have been more behind this comment than Goethe was himself aware of at the time or that his friend Boisserée could grasp is shown by the prominent position given to the Emperor Hadrian in the third book of the *Journeyman Years*. In Lenardo's wanderer speech in which he announces the rules of the world confederation, we find the following passage:

> We have until now at every step known how to do ourselves honour in that we have spoken to the most excellent numbers of active men as our companions and comrades in destiny, so the greatest favour, dear friends, awaits you at the end in that you find yourselves the brothers of emperors, kings and princes. *Let us at first think in blessing of that noble imperial wanderer Hadrian who, on foot, at the head of his army, strode through the inhabited world that was subject to him and thus so completely took possession of it.*[497]

★

Let us accompany our 'noble imperial wanderer' a stretch further. On 16 May 1938 he arrived in Stuttgart. If Cologne had been new for him and held no prior memories, Stuttgart was the exact opposite. What had he not experienced and lived through in this city, part of it with Berta!

Yet because of later developments in the G.A.S. much of what he had once experienced in this place had been overtaken by a gentle melancholy. It was fortunate that Menny Lerchenfeld was able to help him 'overcome melancholy in these days'. Coming from Regensburg, Menny had arrived in Stuttgart on the same day as Polzer. Full of gratitude, she wrote in her diary: 'Soon met Polzer. Had lovely days. How much this man has given me, and how young he has stayed! Goethe in Marienbad!'

'Goethe in Marienbad!'—how much these words express from the mouth of Menny Lerchenfeld! Not only do they characterize the older, respected friend in his inner vigour and the freshness of his soul and spirit, they also sound that motif which sets the tone in Polzer's sensitive affection for the young woman—renunciation. What was apparent already in his relations with Sophie Lerchenfeld and Maña Brabínek now took on a completed form in his relationship with Menny Lerchenfeld. The wanderer had learned to become an ever new 'renunciant'.

'How faithfully and honourably he walks his path,' wrote his friend. 'We spoke a great deal with one another; he came up the old Trauberg and told me of his work in Bohemia, of his hopes and concerns. Once I ate with him at Herr von Grone's and once we were at the Blumes'—for me people I did not know at all.' Jürgen von Grone had been one of those excluded in 1935, and Helmuth Blume was the editor of the *Stuttgarter Nachrichten*. Polzer saw many old true friends again, who von Grone invited. Menny introduced to him the actress Margarete Melzer, who obtained theatre tickets for the two friends.

On free evenings they ate at the *Marquadt* (theatre) and after dinner went for walks in the Hofgarten with its old trees. 'It was so warm and mild—and everyone was in a peaceful mood sitting on benches and looking at us, the birds singing.' This was how Menny remembered it.

Early on 22 May she accompanied Polzer on the train to Munich and happy and grateful, she waved goodbye. Looking back at the lovely days they'd spent together, she wrote: 'The meeting with Ludwig Polzer brought me broad, large thoughts. Everything that comes from him has great meaning. His soul lives from deep romantic images—which live on, endlessly fruitful.'

In Munich, where Polzer hoped to meet Heinrich Kotz, Berta's cousin, his four week trip in Germany ended. 'This journey to visit anthroposophical friends in order to renew old connections was more like a leavetaking journey for me,' he wrote in 1939.

In June Julius and his wife had a baby, who on the day of St Vitus, 28 June, was christened Berta Beata.

In those same days Polzer wrote to his friend in London 'my health is very poor. Shocks in old age are very aggressive'. In regard to his work, he wrote: 'At this time I am very busy in my thoughts with the problem of the false Demetrius [Czar Dmitri, 1605–1606], one can even say with the false picture of Jesus [...] It seems to me to be the problem of contemporary events: Slavs in M.E. [Middle Europe]—Urban carcinomas, democracy etc.' On the changes in Bohemia, we read:

> The work in Bohemia is now broken off. That really strikes me hard & pains me. There are so few Michaelic souls who really see through world events and have sufficient capacity of discrimination, to separate human beings from programmes. At my age it is really hard to wait & and yet it must be learned.

In his diary at this time Polzer noted:

> I am occupied at present with the problem of the false Demetrius in connection with the false image of Jesus, in which the Christ Being was obliterated [...] The guardians of the I [ICH] of Jesus are today still in the catacombs. The S.J. [Society of Jesus] usurped it and denies the creative power of the Christ Being, out of fear of the spiritual development of mankind. The much-abused feudalism was the appropriate form of government for mediaeval society. Democracy and urbanization were the transitional forms for a new age but they have become unusable. Dr R. Steiner provided the new forms. Jesuit-Bolshevistic Imperialism, which is rising up under the leadership of the anti-Christian-Roman-Legalistic Dominion, is the expression of something demonic and is preparing the most terrifying anarchy. This anarchy will ultimately be overcome by really

Michaelic people. Their spiritual capacities are today captive and lamed but will then become free and active.

In the next month we find the wanderer once more on his travels. On 9 July he went to Dalmatia and stayed for a while quite alone on the island of Korcula before visiting his friends the Knispels on his return. On the 27 July he met Alexsander Račeta, Sophie's husband, and travelled with him to Zagreb. Very soon after returning home, in August he visited the family of Hugo Flatz in Ebensee, his business adviser, who had made the Dalmatian trip possible.

★

A dramatic event shattered the autumn of that year: the Sudetenland crisis. Hitler had already declared in May that he would destroy Czechoslovakia on 1 October. The 'liberation' of the Sudeten Germans was for him merely the means to this end; the militarily important fortifications of Czechoslovakia were situated in the Sudeten German region. On 12 September at the Reich Party Conference Hitler gave an inflammatory speech in which he assured the Sudeten Germans in Czechoslovakia of his unconditional support for their striving for independence. On the evening of the same day, disturbances broke out in the Sudeten German areas, which the Czech government was able to bring under control but the Sudeten German negotiators now issued an ultimatum and demanded that the government quit the Sudetenland. The Czech government rejected the ultimatum. Would Hitler now attack and thereby unleash another war?

At this time when war was threatening to break out, Ludwig Polzer drew up a 'Petition for Transfer from Military Retirement Status to Active Service' in order, as an officer, despite his advanced age, 'to make a contribution in the great struggle for German living space [*Lebensraum*] and for Middle Europe's needs'. There can be no doubt that Polzer clearly recognized the will that still existed in certain circles in the south and west to destroy Middle Europe and which had caused the First World War to end in a peace that was unacceptable for Germany. Whether he saw with equal clarity *at that point in time* the demonic will that would destroy whole peoples and which was lurking behind Hitler's territorial claims is another question.

His petition to return to active service was in any case invalidated, and in the following years he did not make another such attempt.

The threatening danger of war was avoided soon afterwards by the Munich Agreement (between Germany, France, Britain and Italy). On 29

September the Czech government was forced to hand over the Sudetenland to the German Reich. The parallel to the Congress of Berlin in 1878 is evident: at that time Austria-Hungary was allowed to occupy Bosnia-Herzegovina, now the German Reich was allowed to annex Czechoslovak territory. Recognized historical research has yet to conduct impartial investigation as to whether there was purely goodwill on the side of the English delegations (at that time the proposal for occupation came from Lord Salisbury; this time the proposal for annexation came from Lord Runciman) to avoid the threat of war by a positive response to Hitler's territorial claims, or whether calculation did not play a role in giving way to the unstoppable dictator so as to animate him into committing further acts of robbery. Renate Riemeck gave a very noteworthy indication on this point in her book *Mitteleuropa—Bilanz eines Jahrhundert* [Middle Europe—The Account of a Century]: 'the Oxford historian [A.J.P.] Taylor lets us know in passing that after Munich some intelligent observers were expecting Hitler's next chess move would be in the direction of the *Ukraine*—a chess move which western statemen looked on with some satisfaction and the Soviets, on the contrary, regarded with fear.'[498]

Another important event in Polzer's life in the autumn of 1938 was of a more private nature. Menny Lerchenfeld wrote to him in September of a serious operation which her father had had to undergo. Polzer immediately set off for Salzburg but was unable to see his old friend Count Otto Lerchenfeld still alive. He had died in the night of 4/5 October. 'Thus one becomes ever lonelier on earth,' Polzer exclaimed, full of sorrow. 'But how entwined destinies are I could experience with particular clarity in my relationship to Otto Lerchenfeld!'

Let us look briefly at the last days and hours of this man, who like his friend Polzer belonged to the same great 'league' of wanderers. On 2 October he had been able to celebrate his 69th birthday. 'Many of us had gathered around him,' wrote his daughter Menny, 'we brought flowers and tears to his bedside. He was happy in his way, but was tired. At that time he asked the doctor how many more days he could still reckon with—and received a clear answer.'[499]

Of her father's last day, she wrote:

> Then he began to speak about the great journey which was before him. Seriously and yet with a constant fine 'godly humour', he spoke each word slowly—it was completely still in the room: 'So, children, now I'm going to a better world over there. Stay all together and may it all go well for you as far as it goes in this world. We'll find each other again.' Then suddenly he looked up and made a gesture upwards as if to say: 'Just follow me' with a

wonderful expression of surrender, of joy. It was like a blessing which was
given to us all from that moment.

Something of that blessing appeared to have been bestowed on the
friendship between Menny Lerchenfeld and Ludwig Polzer. A stream of
letters followed from Polzer to the young pianist, and it could almost
seem as if Otto Lerchenfeld, who had once shown such vehement
opposition to the friendship between his elder daughter and Polzer, and
now beyond the threshold, gradually informed of something better about
the nature of his friend, wanted to accompany the relationship of Polzer
to his younger daughter with all the more benevolence ...

In Linsberg, where Polzer went on to that same month, he sank himself
in the life and works of Novalis. He read *Die Lehrlinge zu Sais* [The
Novices of Sais]. To his relationship, both old and new, with the pianist
Menny Lerchenfeld, Novalis' musical poesy must have seemed really
suited. 'Meeting you again is for me like a confluence of my whole life,
like a musical chord,' he wrote to his friend on 21 October. Polzer's soul
became expansive. He writes in the same letter:

> if I allow my thoughts to run free into the Romantic, my soul expands and
> frees itself from cares and overcomes the confines of the present. Then
> creative fantasy arises and builds future forms and future destinies. It is
> almost as if the present would become one with the past and future. Novalis
> stirs one to such experiences and consciousness. And then you are always
> near, without being able to see anything solid, especially because the
> experiences of the night and of dreams disappear so quickly on awakening.

And in another letter the same day: 'And it is he [Novalis] who can give
you an answer to your question about "love", the mission of the Earth,
and he who understands and seeks the Feminine, yet remains a real man.'

In Linsberg Polzer also studied an early lecture that Rudolf Steiner gave
about Freemasonry, masculine and feminine wisdom, as well as the great
task of the theosophical movement to overcome the physical and
psychological polarity of the sexes instead of reinforcing it, as Jesuitism
strives to do. 'It is hard work,' said Steiner in this lecture in Berlin, 'but it
must be done. It consists in achieving knowledge of the higher, supra-
sexual human being, but it is possible, and it will succeed, it will become
reality.' These were key thoughts which Polzer had in mind in all his
closer relationships with individuals of the female sex; it also applied to the
intimate relationship that now developed between him and Menny
Lerchenfeld.

Polzer had been intending the day before to dictate this lecture to Dora
Schenker in order to send the typescript to Menny, when he discovered

that it had been exactly 33 years before to the day when Steiner had given the lecture on 23 October 1905! He regarded this little 'coincidence' as a confirmatory external echo of his intention:

> One thus receives confirmations, which actually come from the spiritual world. It would be a failing if one did not believe this. This is how one thing follows another. It is no illusion, no mere fantasy, but reality, which one can never look for intellectually—something which comes and came with certainty *before* one thought that the possibility would occur.

In the margin of this letter Polzer added another 'immodest' wish: 'The human being is really immodest—so I even think how lovely it would be if, before the end of my life, I could climb the Acropolis or a pyramid with you.' A yearning for far horizons in space and time was born in him and the need to enjoy them with a very particular person.

This, like many other letters, was signed with a simple 'H'. Why should Sophie Lerchenfeld have not spoken to her younger sister about the conversations and experiences she herself had had with Polzer, in Rome and Tivoli, for example?

Did Polzer want to awaken 'Spirit-Remembering' [*Geist Erinnern*] in his young friend when he sent her the poem 'Rapelle-toi' by Alfred de Musset? Menny herself wrote at this time: 'All the dear lines from L., I lock deep within me. They are full of meaning from another world—for my difficult life. Warm greetings and waves.' Menny's artistic career was still uncertain—she also had real talent as a painter—and she had not yet got over the death of her father.

The two friends wanted to spend the first week in November in Munich together. But how far off that was! And Menny was slow to settle on a final date for the meeting. That gave Polzer the opportunity to write another letter in which he described his experiences on the days of All Saints and All Souls. He wrote:

> [This was] the first time that I really experienced these two days in the inner and outer mood of death and with regard to the resurrection of the spirit, in connection with those many people who have passed over who are so dear to me. Outwardly they were difficult days—I'll tell you about it when we meet—but inwardly there was calm and I felt the help of those beyond who seek connection with us. It was not at all phenomenal, but very delicate and still.

By the expression 'phenomenal' he was referring to the grossly, physically-charged manifestations of the beyond indulged in by certain spiritualists, who omit to pay attention to subtle spiritual experiences of a 'very delicate and still' nature.

'All Souls points to Him who is coming, the Christ in the Etheric, the Resurrection in the Spirit,' Polzer went on.

> That which is material in thinking, feeling and willing will increasingly wane through the love and power of Christ. Christ does not judge (despite the painting by Michelangelo), human beings judge themselves. So at All Souls we must in our thoughts remember especially those human souls in the spheres beyond—that they choose their next earthly destiny so that they can judge themselves. And for that they need the help of people on Earth [. . .] Through Christ we can make it possible to reach our loved ones who have died.

In relation to the seriousness of the times, he added: 'But everything will have to change in the shortest possible time—social forms, science, art, religion, economy etc. Four × 12 will be the leaders called by HIM, and all honest anthroposophers will be able to work freely under them.'

In his last address Rudolf Steiner had said that 4 × 12 individuals filled with the spirit of anthroposophy would be the necessary precondition for widespread activity of spiritual science; it was their united work at the end of the twentieth century that Polzer had in mind here in the letter to his friend. But he was also aware that:

> only very, very few anthroposophers have a proper idea of the scale of the upheaval, because the State and the markets are only opposed in a bourgeois official way, even by those on the land. Comparisons are made with old times, which no longer apply. Therefore even anthroposophers take their small efforts in the old sense more seriously. *But what is necessary first is understanding.*[500]

Polzer therefore turned to his friend's understanding heart.

On 6 November came their reunion, which lasted two days. Polzer had already often been concerned about who could take on his spiritual legacy and also the Class mantras, verses and various notes. Now he had no more doubts: Menny Lerchenfeld! The two days in Munich were spent in the sign of this hope of Polzer's.

'Was with L. at the hotel,' Menny wrote in her diary.

> Sunday morning. He gave me great things. Read to me the Foundation Stone laying lecture and I read another one. A very powerful impression. And I know that I did not receive all this in vain. I listened and read with a kind of reverence. I was given the ideal of life, that which is holiest to an old man [. . .] and shall one day account to him for it. I feel very serious about this.

After these serious, solemn hours, the two spent the evenings in a jollier mood, accompanied by a third person, Jura Gabrichevski, an immigrant Russian painter, and one of Menny's circle of close friends. When Menny later remarked to her older friend that she needed a person of the quality that he (Polzer) possessed, he replied, half in jest: 'It's something to be oneself and not want to leave that to others!' With that he was speaking to his friend, who possessed a distinct sense of independence, really from the heart.

This striving for independence showed itself in her, despite all her respect for her older friend also in her inner relationship to anthroposophy. She wrote: 'He can say: "Only anthroposophy can lead us on." I feel truth behind it, but I also know that *I cannot say that yet*. In my mouth *it would be a lie!!*'

On the next day they met again in the hotel. 'It was lovely and solemn,' wrote Menny in her diary. 'Gave me much that was beautiful again, and there was a good spirit between us.'

Then Polzer gave Menny a present which expressed in a real, symbolic fashion that he wanted to lead over into the new times *through her* an extract of the old times that he had lived through. He presented her with two small red cufflinks in each of which a small diamond was set. He had been given them long ago by the friends of his youth, Sophie and Adolf Waldstein, and had kept them all his life. Trust breeds trust: Menny told Polzer of a dream she had had after meeting him again in the spring. She had dreamed of a mountain on which the light of the sun shone down from the right—around it all was darkness—and in the light she wanted to climb to the peak with two companions. Arriving at the top, the three saw spread out before them a wondrous world of brightly shining mountains, and in the mountains 'profound, magnificent temples' revealed themselves. 'One could see deep inside them through columns and domes where light and colours were weaving. The sight was inexpressible.' She had then awoken with a feeling of happiness such as she had never known. There was a period of deep silence between the two friends. Then Polzer asked Menny to be with him at the hour of his death.

In his next letter to her (9 November 1938) Polzer referred to Menny's important dream:

> Under the spiritual sun the body of the Earth becomes transparent and one sees in it all the metals and the differentiated colours. The metals in the Earth are memories of the planets which were once united with the Earth in a different state [. . .] The transparent body of the Earth under the rays of the spiritual sun is nothing other than the crowning of the work of Hiram [. . .] You saw the macrocosmic 'brazen sea'.

(The 'brazen sea' is a symbolic picture of the future transformation of the mineral realm through human spiritual work.) 'So it was confirmed for me again that I was right to give you 23 October.' In this previously mentioned lecture by Rudolf Steiner of 23 October 1905 there is an account and explanation given of the Temple Legend which speaks of the building of Solomon's Temple by Hiram, the representative of 'the masculine spirit'. Polzer said of this: 'And in the microcosmic human being, according to the person's destiny, the body then becomes spiritually transparent, and that was [your] experience [. . .]'

So sacred for the older friend were the flowers of this love that he was slightly afraid that the time of blossoming could pass by unused or only partly used, so he intimately implored the beloved at the end of the letter:

> Dear, Dearest Menny, do not delay, time is pressing, let me stay with you for a short time in winter at a quiet beautiful place, it will be the last thing I do in my life. You will have time enough for everything else. There should be a beginning so that our bond which must be made on earth, can work together on the work of the brazen sea in the future. HE led us together again; let us make possible a somewhat longer period together and thus lay the foundation for the future. I embrace you most warmly, H.

In her diary from this time Menny held fast to Polzer's explanation of her dream. His wish for a longer time together was unmentioned. She was then living in two worlds. In the solemn spheres of this friendship—and in her artistic world in Munich's Bohemian district to which a thousand threads bound her. And the two worlds could not be so easily harmonized. Had Polzer himself even perceived this objective difficulty in Menny's life, about which she will hardly have spoken?

The following day Polzer wrote Menny another letter, in which he first described his own situation:

> When I also know that many people are thinking of me and are grateful to me, I very much suffer then from being alone. I said to you that actually, no one has time for me, that has its own circumstances, because the few people here have so much to do [. . .] And since my eyes have become weak, I now have many hours in which to think, to remember, to look after myself and to consider possibilities.

Through the meeting with his friend this had now become much easier for him:

> I received so much through you and joy has returned and so the days pass more easily and quickly despite the loneliness [. . .] In nature all is now so still and grey, the trees have lost their leaves, this year they kept them for a long time, but now only the oaks are holding out and still stand there fiery red. The sheep in the meadows give the landscape a peaceful character, but unfortunately, the sound of the shepherd's flute is missing. I often have to

think of the third act of *Tristan*, of the peaceful flute motif which calms the emotional unrest of the wounded, waiting Tristan.

Going on with the letter the following day, he wrote:

> You are now really the only one whom I can tell *everything* without reservation and without embarrassment. It really is so! I believe I can see the fate of the time immediately before us and its necessities [...] as transparently clearly as you saw the mountains [...] *There is to be a continuity with the youth of the next generation, and something has always been missing until now.*[501]

Then he told Menny that he would leave her his writings and notes, of which only two people would know—Berta and Frau Schenker.

> Do with it what you want; my trust will accompany you from the other side without burdening you too much, and I want to help you with it. However you decide to fulfil it will be right by me, it can even happen in a completely different way than I imagine at present. You have already told me so much about yourself, and I have received so much that you did not express. My passing over will then be so beautiful [...] in your dear arms and inwardly with my last gaze upon you.

Such were Ludwig Polzer's thoughts, cares and hopes in those quiet autumn days.

After he had received a 'dear, lovely letter', he wrote on 15 November from Vienna: 'I have no idea what made me worthy of this joy that I am now allowed to experience. I feel so at one with you, so close, and my old, wounded heart beats so strongly and my breath passes in and out. When my meditation goes well, my breath also moves so strongly.'

The next day Polzer wrote another letter. Menny had written in her reply: '[...] *until I too can pass it on to other hands.*'[502] From this he could see that she was ready to preserve the continuity of his work. And he exclaimed: 'Thank you! Thank you! For these words and on this understanding I can now give you everything. Yes, you will one day be able to lead the group, entirely in your own way.'

Now he first gave her extracts from the rich store of his experiences in the anthroposophical work and shared with her 'something very incisive':

> Because Berta and I have been through and experienced all the difficulties in the Society, we have learned almost more than through reading and studying. But the experiences are there and have become a capacity. That is related also to the possibilities for methods of work, quite apart from spiritual content. What one has learned about all this through the errors one has made in various places in the course of many years! How people and groups of people are to be treated who are familiar with anthroposophy

[...] In the work one must distinguish very clearly between: those who are interested, then those who are beginners, then those who already have understanding with certain assumptions as to content; then esoteric work, preparation and the Class, that is, the Michael School. It is a long path, especially for those who had no direct connection to R. St. How many mistakes and illusions did I myself not go through with groups at first! How often in the course of the years did I have to battle against errors, foreseeing that most cases would become a debating club and then would soon come to an end. Only after His Death did I recognize the possibility given me, based on historical karma and his authority for Es[oterics] which he gave me. Only on this ground did success begin, which in the last three years showed itself clearly in Bohemia. And now there are so many unmistakeable signs that it signifies a task—when we found each other in a destiny sense—which we have together and which is still possible but which cannot be deferred.

With regard to the realization of this task, Polzer suggested to Menny that they should work through Steiner's *Philosophy of Freedom*[503] together 'because I saw this common cognitive work as a good accompaniment to Anthroposophy and Esotericism'. She could in principle work through this book with every 'serious, sensible person' 'but not the teaching of the hierarchies and the methods of karmic history [...] What he gave after the reorganization of the Society and movement is precisely that which most people go astray with. And that is also the precondition for the understanding of what is necessary continuity.'

After Polzer had slept on this latest development he told Menny on another day that he had decided to accept her in the First Class immediately so that he could now give her 'what I never believed I would be able to give to anyone as an esoteric legacy'.

He added material to the content of a small cardboard box which Dora had in her keeping in Linsberg and which was to be given to Menny after his death. 'Since I do not need to make any will,' he added, 'there will naturally be no record of it.'

In these days of this very strong mood of 'departure', Polzer travelled with Berta to Vienna for two days, where she had a consultation with the dentist Alfred Zeissig. 'In Vienna it is now frightful', Polzer wrote. In an earlier letter (10.11.1938) he had written: 'Those who are alive will have to take leave of so much, of other people, of homeland (it will all be ruined), things they cherish, which accompany one, in which one felt joy.' Berta had the feeling that she was seeing the city for the last time. She contemplated leaving Tannbach and helping friends out. Arthur Polzer was thinking of opening a shop selling antiquities.

On 20 November Polzer wrote again warning and begging his friend:

> Believe me, dear Menny, we are all standing in front of a monstrous abyss, in both the inner and outer sense. I feel and see that. It is a reality. This abyss cannot be crossed with our present thinking, feeling and willing. All interesting ideas will not profit one there unless one works on one's soul wings which will make it possible for one to go back and forth over this abyss. It cannot be crossed with physical limbs alone. Do not put it off; the possibility of working together on these wings is certainly there because destiny has already made it possible to make a start on it. We have begun and are both prepared!

★

Ludwig Polzer was risking a great deal. Fate seemed to hold its breath at this point in his life. Would his friend respond to his gesture, or would she turn it away? That was the anxious question.

Polzer used the time of waiting to deepen his understanding of Goethe from a lecture by Steiner that had been unknown to him until then.

Why had ten years had to go by apparently unused until his path and Menney's had once again crossed? This question had perplexed him recently. Now it was indirectly answered.

Steiner shows in his lecture that after beginning *Faust* Goethe would have burned up in his soul if he had gone straight on with it. The Duke brought him to Weimar and took care that for ten years Goethe lived through and experienced something completely different, which enabled him to give himself over to sleep with regard to spiritual realities. It was only the meeting with Schiller that led him to go on with *Faust* with new forces.

This lecture helped the wanderer to solve the riddle that lay hidden in his friendship with Menny Lerchenfeld. He wrote to his friend on 21 November:

> Without comparing us with the greatness of Goethe in any way—that was another time and other circumstances of destiny—our case shows that there was a need for this almost ten year interruption so that something can happen between us now which would not have been wholesome at that time. Something had to play itself out in both our lives in a personal and individual nature so that what will yet hopefully be accomplished can be accomplished.

Polzer hoped—and waited. On 25 November he wrote: 'We are standing at the present time in all things at the beginning of a development which can only come in a healthy way through a real connection to the spiritual beings of higher worlds. Very *concrete* ideas [of these beings] must be grasped.'

But the more concrete Polzer became in relation to common esoteric work, the more Menny Lerchenfeld seemed to hesitate. Ten years had perhaps not been long enough *for her* . . .

At the end of November he went to see Josef in Pilgramshain—still without an answer from his friend. 'I don't know if you received my last letter,' he wrote in a postscript on 1 December 'so I must wait anxiously.'

He was then silent for two whole weeks before writing on 18 December from Vienna:

> My dear Menny! It will soon be Christmas and so I want to send warm loving greetings. *Women's souls are so hard to fathom, especially the loveliest.*[504] All beauty must be balanced by pain. The last five weeks were hard. Be assured that on my side everything is unchanged; it is as I expressed it. I really have not the least resentment in my heart about how it has turned out; I have learned to understand what I cannot see through in the moment.

Then he told his friend that he was hoping to travel to the South with his brother 'in order to get through the coldest period'.

Nothing more about the 'task' or about a winter trip together. He had inwardly understood; his friend did not feel herself mature enough for the task, although she had agreed to look after the 'little box', 'Until I can place it in others' hands' . . .

A further letter, which he wrote on Christmas Eve, provides some insight into his daily life at Tannbach:

> It pains me very much that one is becoming more and more isolated anthroposophically and that I have no possibility to go to Bohemia, for correspondence necessarily says very little. Since we have no electric light and only a little kerosene I am, because of my eyes, more in the dark than others. I often go to bed before 8 o'clock because of the cold. So from 6 a.m. I do housework and go on errands to Gutau, all necessary shopping etc. I like doing all that very much and it makes me warm. For the last week snow and especially icy paths have been a hindrance that has to be coped with. This prevents the appearance of any false spiritual pride. That is very good. When I then take a break now and again I enjoy it all the more. This enjoyment becomes ever more primitive. It is of no concern. My life has not much further to last and I feel very calm about what is to come and look forward to it.

On St Stephen's Day Julius suffered an embolism while his wife had fallen ill with gall cramps. 'His illness is dragging on,' Polzer wrote to Menny on

27 December 'so it's probably the end for Tannbach, for I can no longer do heavy labour at 70 years old.'

To a recent letter from Menny he gave a clarifying answer:

> I am so sorry that it's been hard for you. You have completely mis-understood me if you believe I was perhaps angry. I am not even impatient. I know how to test destiny [. . .] I think of you very much with the warmest wishes for your welfare. Yes, soul trials are probably necessary. In old times they were of another kind before one was accepted into the Mysteries. Now the seriousness of anthroposophy is showing itself, and it is much greater than I myself thought. Every one of his words will be fulfilled. You wrote not long ago that much of what I wrote was strange to you. Yes, Menny, we shall more and more stand before what is strange to us and which will then have to become familiar. We must all learn to change our thinking thoroughly, otherwise we shall not be able to fulfil even the first stage of our later task. You know all this yourself already, but I still have to write it. But there is one thing you must not forget, otherwise you will always have disappointments with anthroposophy: it is in the first of the Leading Thoughts, that only those become anthroposophers who have such a need for anthroposophy in their souls just as one feels hunger and thirst [. . .] It is the power, enormously great, of the anti-christian efforts and the cultic activities of the S.J. and the F.M., which destroyed the first Goetheanum, one can only cope with them with difficulty, can only actually make attempts [. . .] it pains me but I have unconditional con-fidence for the future, however terrible it becomes. I have received many loving signs of gratitude these days which strengthen one when one's soul believes it will not be able to go on. My faithful thoughts are with you [. . .] We shall see each other again finally, I leave that to destiny. I neither wish to nor may I force it.
>
> Your L.

★

'A hard year has passed. An even harder one is beginning,' he wrote in his notes for the beginning of 1939.

At least Julius was able to make a good recovery so that Polzer could travel to Vienna and Linsberg for anthroposophical work. Until then he occupied himself with work around the house and attending to the post and read Rudolf Steiner's introductions to the works of Schopenhauer and Jean Paul.

On 12 January he wrote to Menny again from Tannbach:

> I now want to add to my memories of Dr Steiner my outline sketches of the period before and especially after Dr Steiner's death. That will be my last task. If I had not been in such frequent and close contact with Dr

Steiner, I would not do this, for my life has only been interesting because of him.

In April he made a start on writing this record, which he titled: 'The Last Period of My Life—The Time After the Death of Dr Rudolf Steiner, 1925'. It represents the main source for the fourth part of this book.

Sensing what was coming in the new year, Polzer felt the approach of the catastrophe of the age. He wrote in the same letter to Menny: 'Now so many people are standing before the threshold of death that one feels oneself and one's loved ones approaching a mass execution.'

43. The Last Journey to Italy

In the night of 13/14 January 1939, 'probably before midnight', as he himself said, Ludwig Polzer had a special dream, which he described as follows:

> I found myself as in a church or sacristy or some such place. I encountered a cardinal with whom I entered into conversation. We did not speak in words but with our eyes and facial gestures. His countenance was always deeply friendly and understanding. Then came a second cardinal. I was told that he was from Santiago de Compostela. He had a darker face and began to rage frightfully against the first cardinal in great agitation. I could not understand their conversation at all. The one was friendly towards me, the other hostile and also hostile to the first cardinal. I myself was very calm and had the feeling that I was stronger than both of them.[505]

Polzer immediately felt that the dream had something to do with an event within the Anthroposophical Society, but with what, was unclear to him. His friend Stein, to whom he told this dream, offered an interpretation of it, writing from London on 30 January:

> Dear Polzer,
> The one from Compostella [sic] was so angry because at the end of the fifteenth century the Christian writings which had been discovered after the reconquest of Granada, were not returned to [the monastery of] St James but were given to Stephan Rauter, who later became well-known under the name Basilius Valentinus [Basil Valentine] [...]
> I find it beautiful that you have such dreams.
> With many warm greetings
> Your Stein

Stein's very specific interpretation thus related to a historical dispute connected to Santiago, while Ludwig Polzer had in mind something more contemporary. In 1943 he still thought[506] that the dream must have had 'some relation to the tragic struggle in the Vorstand', and he paraphrased Stein's interpretation as follows:

> I was once told that important documents were stolen from the monastery at St James by the Arabs and were recovered from them after the battle of Granada; but they did not find their way back to the monastery. The esoteric situation called for them to be preserved elsewhere. They were the writings of Aristotle. I write this with all due caution, but I want to mention it because it had to do with me externally and internally. One comes to

deeper insights into questions of historical destiny only slowly, through constant effort to penetrate reality.

In the background to this dream may have been the conflict over Rudolf Steiner's will following his death, but also perhaps, Polzer's closer concerns for the fate of his own esoteric legacy. Certainly, Menny Lerchenfeld had agreed to take on the 'little box', but only in an external, not in a spiritual sense.

Such dreams are truly hard to interpret, but one who gives some thought to this difficulty will in this particular case even consider another interpretation which relates to *the future*. This clear, expressive dream appears in any case to have symptomatic weight. In the last part of this book we shall come to speak of it again in relation to the anthroposophical and ecclesiastical efforts to shape the physiognomy of modern Europe.

★

Stein did not only provide his friend with an interesting interpretation of his dream but also arranged for him to visit Rome. The trip was planned for March. Until then, Polzer busied himself with his estate, visited his daughter-in-law Anna after her gall operation in Linz, and wrote letters. He wrote to Milos Brabínek at this time: 'I never forget in the morning when I awake to think of the promise of 26 October 1932 [with Maña in the Chapel of Wenceslas] [...] It will soon be seven years.' Brabínek and his daughter now wanted to continue the esoteric work in Bohemia themselves; Polzer was no longer able to travel there regularly. He replied:

> I want to say something else to you, which is that I am glad about your initiative because I know that it is in faithful hands and that your dear Maña is a guarantee of that for me [...] Perhaps what I have to do in this life is now fulfilled. The living quality of everything that I experienced with you all in Pardubice cannot be weakened by any event.

There was therefore good reason to hope that the work in Bohemia could progress and flourish without Polzer's physical presence.

In March 1939 Polzer set off for Italy. He travelled directly to Rome and thanks to Stein's arrangement, stayed for three days in the Via Cecchini as the very welcome guest of Signora Carmen Tornaghi. 'The old Rome is beautiful,' he wrote, 'and has been incorporated artistically into the new. From the Palatine I enjoyed looking down over Rome at sunset and felt how the old imperialism was still living in the soul of this people. The completely soulless and dispirited Roman Church still lives only as a spiritless fanaticism.' He made the following observation about the churches he visited: 'The monuments of the churches live in the soul only as memories and as interesting constructions, but are quite unreligious. In some smaller churches such as [Santa] Maria in Cosmedin one still feels something religious.' It is no accident that at the entrance of this church can be seen the 'Bocca della verità' [the Mouth of Truth].

From Rome Polzer travelled in a single stretch to Taormina and stayed at the Pension Victoria. It was the first time in his life that he had walked on Sicilian ground.

In the night of 17/18 March he dreamed of Rudolf Steiner 'about Josef—Julius and the lengths of their lives'. His concern for his sons had also accompanied him on this trip to the South; that was clear. Was his own life also to go on longer? Did he not feel that it had arrived at an end, just as he was now at the end of Italy? Was there to be, after the writing of his memoirs, something else to do? Was 'what [he] had to do in this life not yet fulfilled'?

On the following night Polzer had another dream. Three words in his diary testify to the experiences of that night: 'Dream of H.' Who was meant by 'H'? Was it the same 'H' which he indicated by the signatures to many letters to Menny Lerchenfeld?

Despite the cold, unfriendly weather, Polzer took a tour up Monte Zovetto. He made friends with some Hungarians on the tour, with whom he hoped for better weather. But that did not happen, and so, after nine days, our wanderer decided to leave Taormina. He travelled for two days to Palermo and from there on to Naples and the island of Ischia, where he stayed in Porto d'Ischia.

The sea voyage to the volcanic island passed through the northern waters of the Gulf of Naples and the town of Baia that was so famous in ancient times. The area, originally settled by the Greeks, was in Roman times a luxurious bathing resort with the most important thermal baths in the whole empire. The nobility and the emperors owned villas in the city, including Hadrian, who died here on 10 July 138. In his last years he suffered from dropsy; in the hot summer of that year 138 he sought relief from his suffering 'in the balmy air' of the bay after he had handed over the government to Antoninus Pius, wrote Gregorovius.[507] 'But soon, when he sensed his end was near, he had Antoninus called to him.' Dying, he spoke to him the famous verses which were later inscribed on a wall of his mausoleum in Rome:

Animula, vagula, blandula,
Hospes comesque corporis,

Quae nunc abibis? In loca
Pallidula, rigida, nudula,
Nec, ut soles, dabis iocos . . .

Little soul, you charming little wanderer,
My body's guest and partner,
Where are you off to now?
Somewhere without colour, savage and bare;
You'll crack no more of your jokes once there.

And of Hadrian's death his biographer wrote: 'On 10 July 138 Hadrian had the good fortune to die in the arms of one of the most noble human beings whom he himself had named his successor. Antoninus had the corpse of the Emperor solemnly cremated in the Villa of Cicero at Puteoli.'[508]

Polzer had felt a growing mood of death in past months. The only hope for someone who would take on his esoteric legacy seemed to him to be Menny Lerchenfeld. 'My passing will then be so beautiful [. . .] in your arms', he had written four months before to the beloved woman. But it did not turn out as he had hoped. Polzer tried to understand it, remained silent and now had to go on the last stretch of his path, 'wandering restlessly', without her.

And now, once more 'in anticipation of approaching death' exactly 1800 years after the death of Hadrian and seeking relief for his suffering soul 'in the balmy air' of Baia and Ischia, Polzer was passing by the place of his former death.

The premonition of death began to change into spirit-remembering [Geist-Erinnern] of his *earlier* death. Had the 'dream of H.' in Taormina perhaps prepared him for this? The awakening consciousness of his death long ago appears to have given him new life. Here in the Gulf of Naples, not far from Cuma, the location of the Sybelline Oracle, lay the secret source of the last period of Polzer's life.

Feeling himself standing on the threshold of death, the sense of re-encountering the death he had once died presented to him another seven years of life. This is the open secret of Polzer's last long journey to Italy.

★

At the eastern end of the island capital Porto d'Ischia is the fortress, which is of historical interest, but today is only a ruin. In the early sixteenth century a brave woman had held it against the French: Costanza d'Avalos, the aunt of the famous general Fernando Francesco d'Avalos, marquis of Pescara, about whom Conrad Ferdinand Meyer wrote a 'monument' in the form of a novella. The famous condottiero and warrior against the French married Vittoria Colonna at the castle on Ischia 'and was loved by her until his death', as Polzer wrote. After the death of her husband Vittoria wrote numerous important sonnets and became the friend and confidante of Michelangelo.

At the ruined castle Polzer made the acquaintance of a German-speaking tour guide named Kupfer who showed him round the remains of a cathedral near the castle as well as the catacombs of a convent of the Poor Clares, and invited him to his house and 'celebrated the fact that [Polzer] was an anthroposopher'.

On the return to Naples Polzer's gaze may often have sought out Baia and Puteoli one more time, and more in hope than in fact because Polzer's eyesight was no longer of the best. Did he think again of the unhappy Agrippina, the mother of Nero, who was murdered in the year 59 at her villa in Baia at her son's instigation? Polzer made no comment on it. Agrippina would come to play a role in the last task of his own life, when in 1942, he wrote his drama of Crown Prince Rudolf.

On his return journey he stopped off in Rome again. He lodged for a few days again with Signora Tornaghi and befriended her 'young, intelligent nephew' who had just passed his Abitur [school-leaving] examination.

In the night of 1 April he dreamed 'of Dr Steiner' and of a 'task for a short time yet'. The dream may well have been here in Rome.

At the end of the journey was a stay in Venice. Polzer remained there for eight days and 'felt very well'. In the meantime it had finally become warm. He visited the old splendid sights of Venice which were linked to so many memories of his present life. How often he had been here! With his parents, with Berta, and with Sophie and with Adolf Waldstein, with his own children, with his niece Maria-Christine, with Sophie Lerch-enfeld and with Dorli Zeissig. Always in the company of others, but this time alone. But the spirit of the city did not seem to accept that the wanderer would stay here for the first time without some joyful company. When Polzer went to Torcello, he got to know a 'dear young woman from Finland', from Abo, who was going in the opposite direction and was on her way to Rome. Polzer now spent 'three pleasant days' as a guide to the young woman, who only understood a little German. One evening they joined a long gondola serenade party which lasted three hours until 11 o'clock at night. 'They were taken round the Giudecca to "the sound of the loveliest singing".'

And with that ended the last great trip of Ludwig Polzer's life.

★

After about five weeks our wanderer returned to Tannbach in the middle of April. He immediately began to write his last memoirs, which began with the death of Rudolf Steiner and ended with the German invasion of Poland in September 1939. Between April and September he wrote about 250 pages on the events of these 14 years of his life.

Conditions in Tannbach became ever harder. Concerns for Julius 'increased', 'the lack of people has become a huge problem'. Although Polzer received many good wishes for his 70th birthday on 23 April, he felt 'sad and tired'.

He went on steadily with his memoirs and occupied himself also with art and understanding art; this too was a fruit of his trip to Italy. Notable and unusual was the relationship he saw between the confused political thinking of his time and the lack of understanding of art; he wrote:

> Art is no longer understood today; that art was once experienced as the interpreter of nature's mysterious laws—this understanding has completely disappeared. It must return [. . .] Because there is so little artistic spirit, and so much simplistic reductionism, there is so much confusion in methods of social administration and so much demonry in politics.

And on the subject of so-called belief, he wrote after his return from Italy: 'What is currently Christian-Roman faith expresses only fear of the spiritual world and is bound up with hatred and scorn. So thinking, feeling, and willing show themselves as the three evil apprentices of the old freemasonry in the individual human soul.' Concerned about the ongoing development of the lack of understanding for art and true spirituality, he asked: 'How must it look in human souls who quite seriously consider cinema images to be art? The subhuman powers of the mechanical draw human beings into a soulless realm.'

In May Polzer accompanied Berta to Vienna where she had further dental treatment from Alfred Zeissig. Afterwards the couple went to Baden [outside Vienna]. Since the death of her mother-in-law in 1924, Berta had not been back there. Then the couple went up the Kahlenberg, as they had done a few years before, and walked from there to Grinzing. In the evenings they had supper to balalaika music at a traditional Russian-style restaurant 'Boyar'. Berta stayed at the *König von Ungarn* where the couple had often stayed in earlier years, while Ludwig Polzer stayed in the Kreuzgasse, where he had a room at Dora Schenker's. 'It is so rare now,' he wrote about this excursion, 'that I can go somewhere with Berta [. . .] I am glad when I can be together with Berta in this way.'

After a week's stay in Heiligenkreutz, in the period after Whitsun,

Polzer visited Hans Voith in Heidenheim. He certainly told him about his trip to Italy. It had been Voith who had driven him and Sophie Lerchenfeld to Tivoli in 1930. He was two days a guest with the Voiths. He admired the wonderful organically cultivated garden and was shown the great engineering factory run by Voith where 500 engineers worked to produce Germany's largest turbines.

From Heidenheim he went on to Stuttgart. Jürgen von Grone had asked his old friend to visit him again, so he was able to spend two evenings in a circle of friends.

In the pension where he stayed, a letter arrived for him from Menny Lerchenfeld. She asked him to make it possible for them to meet again during the Vienna Reichstheater week, to which she wanted to go with Margarete Melzer. Polzer travelled two days to Vienna and saw Menny again for the first time in six months. So much had happened since then! But their joy at meeting again was unalloyed! Polzer and Menny spent a lovely afternoon at his brother Arthur's house in Baden, where 'Menny played the piano with a magical beauty'. Polzer wrote: 'The whole family was fascinated by her and she too felt very comfortable.'

After the Vienna reunion there was again a brief exchange of letters. Polzer wrote to Menny on 11 June:

> When people meet again in such a happy time [. . .] after a long interval and after so much has happened, including personal things, in the meantime, then you know from your own experience that one mostly says something other than what one had wanted and thought to say. After parting again, I notice that I forgot much or was too embarrassed to say it, because it could perhaps seem too personal. But I know that you are so good, so honest and so dear that I don't need to fear losing your trust.

Then he made an instructive comparison with his relationship to Rudolf Steiner: 'He told me [. . .] how closely bound to him I was by destiny [. . .] I believe I stood *quite* close to him—I am weighing my words—as for example, Hieronymus of Prague stood to Hus in Bohemia. H. of P. stood somewhat nervously near H. but stood by him nevertheless to the end.'

Hieronymus of Prague was not only a true friend of Hus and a great scholar and man of the world; he also loved travelling with a passion and visited England, Russia and Palestine amongst other places. At the Council of Constance he first renounced the teachings of Hus and Wycliffe, but then withdrew his renunciation. He was burned alive at the stake on 30 May 1416.

Polzer also wrote about shopping in Tannbach, which he enjoyed, despite the difficulties of the situation, with his whole heart.

How very often I have returned home with anxiety and a heavy heart. And yet this place has become so dear to me. The most important things in my life have played themselves out here. Because it has been so hard and yet so lovely, it is so hard for me to give up this piece of earth.

And at the end of the letter he expresses open-heartedly his joy at being with Menny again: 'It was so lovely to be with you again! In old age at this time when the soul is grown cold one is allowed to be somewhat sentimental. It is pure love for another being; in this streams the divine nature of the soul.'

Polzer spoke about Tannbach again in a following letter of 18 June. They were thinking of selling the estate in such a way as to acquire a lease from the new owner so that Julius and Berta would be able to remain there. 'We want to avoid what is normally called a sale,' he wrote,

> for T. is not only an economic object for us, but also an esoteric problem of destiny, for He [Rudolf Steiner] held a Rosicrucian ritual here and so we have a responsibility of a kind other than economic, and I want to try as long as I can to avoid a normal sale to someone with whom there is no destiny connection [to Rudolf Steiner].

He also spoke of spiritual scientific matters in this letter; he wrote of Rudolf Steiner's 1924 Rosicrucian lectures and of their remarks about the John [Midsummer] Imagination.

Polzer told his friend in the same letter of the result of his investigations about an eventual further music training in Vienna and could 'seriously recommend' to her amongst others a pupil of Leschetitzky by the name of Sauer.

In a last letter from this time he speaks again of the mood of having to depart from Tannbach: 'You understand that it is not easy to leave a dear place that has almost become your homeland when one does not know where one is going to lay one's weary head [. . .] Perhaps we will be able to live here for a while longer, but then that would only postpone our departure.' But along with this pain of leaving Tannbach he also confesses: 'But I am still hanging on to this beautiful earth; it is the stage on which the human soul has to develop itself in order to become worthy of another stage.'

Looking back to the recent meeting with Menny and her friend Margarete, he added in regard to the spiritual development called for in modern times:

> There is in every worthy soul a longing and a seeking and yet also a not being able to find. The outer resistances are so strong, confusing and distracting. Courage is not strong enough and the body too heavy and too

accustomed to what is bourgeois, for generations now, for a millennium; since the founding of towns and cities. And all of that is now once again running violently out of control. Too few fruits have ripened to pass through metamorphosis.

In regard to the present time, he wrote further: 'Soon the fateful 28 June will be coming round again. I am always attentive to see what it will bring.' It was the day in 1878 when at the suggestion from Lord Salisbury the occupation of Bosnia–Herzegovina was decided on; the day of the assassination at Sarajevo in 1914, the day of the questionable Treaty of Versailles in 1919. 'In this time it is not good to be old. Since my work in B [ohemia] ended, I feel myself mostly superfluous. And at the same time, one becomes so anxious for others; every conflict and every untruth is so very painful.'

What task was he still to take up? It was as yet unclear. But it would have to lie in the direction indicated by the words with which he closed the letter: '*The fact of repeated earthly lives and the question of destiny, as needs of the soul, remain to be addressed. It is in real self-knowledge that the human being comes to quiet, peace and right action, both inwardly and outwardly.*'[509]

Had the Italian journey not provided him with an opportunity for the fact of repeated earth lives to work once again, forming and building, on the construction of his own soul and spirit?

But first the catastrophe, which Polzer felt was approaching relentlessly, was to pile up like a wall of black cloud before his task, the outlines of which were still very vague. At the beginning of the summer, under the heading 'World Symptoms' he sketched out the world situation as follows:

1. The funeral of President Masaryk: the apotheosis of the urban bourgeoisie.
2. The self-destruction of Spain.
3. Japan's grasp for hegemony in Asia, rallying herself for the struggle against America on European territory.
4. The outbreak of insanity in Middle Europe as a consequence of occult powers via the European media. Political parvenus' raging about the State, the cancer in cities and markets. The preparation for the downfall of 100 million people in Europe.

Then the breakthrough of consciousness into the spiritual world and the incarnation of great souls and then, through them, the rebuilding of soul and spirit.

★

The summer of 1939 passed in suffering, anxiety and difficulties. Julius and his little daughter fell ill with severe whooping cough. Ludwig Polzer suffered from intensified sciatica in his femoral joint. He therefore went to Baden for twelve days in August where he took sulphur baths and stayed with his brother Arthur. 'Time passed very pleasantly.'

On 1 September the German army invaded Poland. Could the war again be localized? That was the anxious question.

On 9 September Polzer felt the need to make the following observation:

> It was thoughtless to call the so-called war which began in 1914 a war. It was the first warning to the developed countries as a whole that a turning point in world affairs had arrived. Mankind was told to turn its mind to the spiritual world. The warning was in vain, so what is happening now had to come. In the first mystery drama Rudolf Steiner had the Spirit of the Elements say:
>
>> *Spirits will have to break worlds*
>> *The creations of your age*
>> *Must not bring destruction and death*
>> *To the world of Eternities*
>
> This breaking of worlds is happening now. It is an apocalyptic event, a Mystery that is playing itself out on the open stage of world history and which must be understood.

And on 24 September he wrote:

> The words of the messenger of Michael stand on tablets of spiritual iron:
>
> 1. Statesmen, whose ultimate wisdom is war, are no men of culture.
> 2. War cannot be fought with war; Bolshevism cannot be fought with Bolshevism.
> 3. Peoples and human beings do not make war; states make war.
>
> This is why individual people must limit the activities of states through real ideas.

With this comment Ludwig Polzer brought to an end the writing down of his memoirs, which he had begun after his journey to Italy in April. He added the testamonial wish that they would be passed on to his grandson Christward and expressed the hope that his brother Arthur would also read them. He had the intention of following the memoirs with a 'war diary' that would contain 'what I experienced during the war in spirit and soul'.

44. The Last Years

In the darkness of the world war catastrophe we lose the trail of Ludwig Polzer's life story. It is covered over for long stretches by the silent snow of unknowing. Like islands in the sea, here and there a portion of the path becomes visible thanks to a few surviving letters which Polzer wrote, and even fewer which he himself received. The war diary, which he intended to write, may indeed have been written but it must be assumed to have disappeared. Of what Ludwig Polzer 'experienced in spirit and soul' during the war, standing in as it were for the vanished writings of the war diary are the interpretations of a number of dreams which he had and recorded between 1939 and 1941.

Like erratic blocks standing out in the forlorn landscape of these last years are two completed literary works; the manuscript of a drama *Rudolf, Crown Prince of Austria*, written in autumn 1942, and the small text *In memoriam Frau Dr Ita Wegman*, which he wrote in spring 1943. This last testimony of Polzer's work was written in the anthroposophically-led clinic Heilanstalt Wiesneck where Polzer stayed, often and for long periods, and almost permanently from the end of 1943 until spring 1944, in order to be near Berta who, from 1940 onwards, descended into a darkness of the soul. In Wiesneck Polzer made the acquaintance of Paul Michaelis, the most important companion of the last stretch of his path. Since the appearance of the first edition of this book, some letters from Polzer to Michaelis have appeared which cast some light on the course of Polzer's final years.

Although therefore, much of the last period of his life remains in darkness, the illumined fragments of Polzer's last years do enable a picture to be drawn of his inner development in the time from 1939 until the end of his life. This chapter will now attempt to draw that picture.

★

In the second half of 1939 Polzer had many dreams which can explain how he lived through the events in his personal circumstances but also his experience of world events.

At the end of July he dreamt that he was once again in the large branch room at Pardubice with the whole Group. He conversed with Anton Geryšer and Col. Dohnal. 'It was very solemn.' Since 16 March 1939 all anthroposophical activities in the 'Reich Protectorate of Bohemia and Moravia' had been strictly forbidden. But Polzer's ether body had not yet parted company from the work there that he dearly loved ...

A few days later he dreamt of Rudolf Steiner, before whom he held a lecture. He wrote in his dream diary: '[I] found a confluence of two themes. The link was hard to recognize.'

In the night of 3/4 September he dreamt of Hitler, with whom he was conversing in a room. It was two days after the invasion of Poland.

Two weeks later, he told Mussolini in a dream 'how long I had striven for threefolding'.

If these last two dreams reflected more his living into great world events, the following is an eloquent witness to the state of Polzer's soul and spirit at a time which prevented or at least strongly hindered his spiritual work with other people. In the night of 26 September he dreamt:

> I went to a place, I believe it was Pardubice, with Knispel, we came past a long building. I said: 'That was once a building in which people used to converse. Now it is a ruin.' It was raining, and we had no overcoats.
>
> Then the picture changed. I stepped modestly into a room in which important people were waiting; a lecture was to be given in the next room. I was standing, the others were sitting. Then everyone went into the adjoining room. A friendly woman, one of the most important amongst them, approached me. I said to her as we went in: 'This has actually been my freely chosen independent occupation for more than 20 years.' Then she said that she was always waiting for someone who wanted to work with her spiritually. I asked: 'Do you want to?' Then the dream ended.

Two days later Polzer had another dream. He dreamt of Marie-Sefine, his sister, and of his parents:

> [it was] in an unknown place, then in a house where my father closed the curtains and said to us: 'In our house the curtains are thicker.' [It was] as if one had been laid in a coffin. Then the picture changed. I was walking with a friend, it was as if it was Dr Eiselt. He told me of one the Hoditzes, and I said: 'That can only be Max Hoditz, my uncle.' We were walking up a hill, as if to the Goetheanum. A gentleman came to us who I believed I recognized as M. Hoditz. (I saw his face exactly & the memory has stayed clearly with me.) I spoke to him and said: 'Now we are seeing each for the first time in our lives.' He said: 'One has to be able to see behind events.' I [said]: 'Yes, one learns that up there.' He hesitated, then the image disappeared.

Weighty motifs are formed, it seems, by the dreamer: the motif of the 'curtain', of 'burial', and then, after a change, the motif of seeing through 'the veil of events' ... And all this linked with a 'Goetheanum', which for Polzer continued to exist quite independently of the physical world, as a *spiritual* Goetheanum.

At the end of October he dreamt of his 'dear friend Stanislaus Benda', 'whom he saw in uniform and very happy'. In November Alfred Mee-bold, an anthroposophical friend from Heidenheim, appeared to him in a dream.

This small selection of dreams or fragments of dreams shows how broad the inner horizon of the experiences of Polzer's dream consciousness was: the dreamer is unaware of the threshold between the physical and the spiritual worlds. It is immaterial whether the people who appear on the stage of his dreams are alive or dead, in other words, whether they are in the main room or the adjoining 'rooms' of history. The protagonists of the dream appear in the dream consciousness in both kinds of chambers with equal ease.

Through their clarity and the often dramatic structure of events in them, Polzer's dreams invite closer consideration. 'I find it beautiful that you have such dreams', his friend Stein had written to him in January 1939 in relation to Polzer's dream of Santiago. With all due caution that is called for in the case of such interpretation, one may apply Stein's comment to many other dreams of Polzer's, for they often seem beautiful even before one asks oneself how far they are also true.

Polzer's dreams thus reveal something of the will for beauty that lived in his soul. They are often formed in an artistic way. And it was especially that urge to artistic creativity that belonged to the most important things which in his last years stirred ever more strongly under that quiet snow which covered over the outer circumstances of his life.

★

On 21 December 1939 a Christmas letter arrived from Josef Polzer. With regard to the festive season he expressed his thanks to his parents 'that you, dear parents, found for me such a lovely place for my health and later also for my work'. Josef wrote about a performance of the Oberufer Christmas play in Pilgramshain, which for him was 'a constant source of sustenance'. His parents sent their son a book about Count Albert von Hoditz, the 'Wondrous Count of Rosswald'. After reading the book, Josef wrote on 6 January of the new year (1940): 'Today I finished reading the book about Count Albert Hoditz [. . .] A lot of it I hadn't known at all and other parts reminded me of what I'd been told before. Even though everything is now in the past, it still awakens joy in the present. There is a charitable view of life to be found in it.'

Another fine Christmas letter arrived in Tannbach from Polzer's brother Arthur. Amongst other things he wrote that he too was busy writing his memoirs at that time. 'I am happy that I decided to do this,' he wrote.

Not only because it's the description of a life which played itself out in the change from an old into a new age and therefore perhaps can be of cultural and historical interest because of details which today still certainly appear trifling or even banal, but also as a memorial book for my children to read and think about.

Thus both of these similar and dissimilar brothers were, in 1939, eleven years after the appearance of their main cultural and historical writings in 1928, again working simultaneously on a project in that they were now writing their memoirs. For Arthur it was especially a thank you to all those people who had accompanied and supported him in life and whom he thereby hoped to pay back. 'When I call everything to mind,' he wrote,

> and when the many people who I have met in my life and who showed me so much love pass before me again then I have the feeling that I owe them many, many thanks. And so I believe I owe them a debt of gratitude, even if only inwardly, that I should fulfil in thought; a debt of gratitude that under the pressures of life one all too easily forgets. *And you are also one of these people, and dear Berta too.*[510] And not least my work on the writing of it enables me, at least for some hours, to forget the often unhappy daily life of the present.

Arthur had already written over 1000 pages and had arrived at 1904. There were five large format volumes of manuscript with numerous valuable photographs as well as illustrations drawn and painted by himself. These unpublished volumes formed the prime source for this book, while Ludwig Polzer's memoirs from 1939, as already mentioned, became the most important source for the fourth part of the book.

In a lovely harmony with Arthur Polzer's fond look back at the past his children too wanted 'the Holy Nights to be celebrated as in earlier years', which was not easy to accomplish under the ration card system for daily necessities. Arthur described the same old decorations they had used for festival for decades in order then to remark: 'So the Christmas nights are like the rungs of a ladder of memory which lead back to their very first memories.'

Something very dramatic happened after the first winter of the war, in March 1940. Due to constant overexertion Berta's physical and psy-chological condition made it necessary to have her referred to a mental hospital. Accompanied by a doctor, Ludwig brought his wife to Wies-neck, to the anthroposophic sanatorium led by Friedrich Husemann in Buchenbach near Freiburg in Breisgau. It was the sharpest incision in the couple's last years together.

In a letter to Menny Lerchenfeld six weeks later, Polzer described this incision in the following way:

Dear Menny! How hard destiny is. I could not do anything else but bring Berta here, accompanied by a doctor. Here they still believe that such illnesses can be healed. The last six weeks—caring and struggling day and night to be able to do something for her—were so hard and yet also so beautiful. Between her insane ideas she also has very clear consciousness and when I left, she said to me, sobbing: 'I shall never be able to do anything more for you.' She stood by me courageously and with a holy energy for 40 years & now I feel myself quite exhausted and abandoned. I was afraid to go home alone and I must spend a few days recovering in Gnadenwald. Yesterday, while speaking a lot, she suddenly said to me: 'I won't be able to write to Menny any more either.' The worst moments were those in which she was able to weep. Your unhappy old Ludwig.

Ludwig Polzer visited his wife often in Buchenbach. Dr Husemann provided him with a room in which he could stay for free. The costs of Berta's treatment were taken on by her cousin Heinrich Kotz.

Dr Husemann always treated the Count in the threadbare black suit with great respect and also the co-workers at the clinic felt a kind of awe for the guest who was always benevolent and modest. Berta sometimes had attacks of manic rage which alternated with calmer periods. And 'when she had a good hour again', recalled Erika Warnke, who was then Husemann's secretary, 'he would go for a walk in the park with her, offering her his arm in a gentlemanly manner. She always presented a charming appearance.'[511]

In Wiesneck Polzer, as mentioned earlier, became acquainted with Paul Michaelis. The trained male nurse had only recently arrived at the sanatorium, where he was soon also doing office work. His room became in the following years something of a cultural oasis in Wiesneck. He was also able to obtain coffee, which was then an achievement. Polzer often liked to stay at the oasis. In the spring of 1940 Michaelis was at the beginning of his 38th year; he was going through his second moon node and was wide open for new spiritual impulses. Such a one, for him, was the figure of the 71-year-old man of the world who was now visiting him. For Polzer, weighed down in his soul by his wife's illness, Michaelis with his open enthusiasm was a counterbalance that gave him strength.

Paul Michaelis wrote in the following years under Polzer's supervision a series of dramas, about which there developed an intimate exchange of views in conversation or by letter. They have now partly been lost, some have appeared in private printings, and a few have been published. Some of the titles show how close the themes stood to Polzer's own concerns: 'Master Builder in Egypt', 'Summer 1917', 'Libussa', Caspar Hauser', 'Demetrius'. Polzer had earlier wanted to complete Schiller's fragment of his play about Demetrius himself, as he once wrote to Michaelis. Demetrius [the so-called False Czar Dmitri 1605–1606] must have seemed to him more and more like a spiritual opponent of Peter the Great, like a true pathfinder for the still uncorrupted nature of the Slavs. Now he was glad that someone much more called to the task than him had taken it on. Polzer experienced the meeting with Michaelis as a stroke of good fortune brought about by Rudolf Steiner and he experienced his friend's poetic work which 'lies completely in my line of destiny', as he would write on 21 January 1943. ' So I feel myself deeply united with you in spirit. You are the first man who I have met in this way in my a.[anthroposophical] time.'

Motifs of a common destiny in the past also surfaced in the correspondence between the two men. Rome and Thebes were named, whereby the motif of Thebes was also strongly linked with Maña Brabínek. Then there was the theme (along with England) of Prague in the fifteenth century. Here Polzer several times compared himself with Hieronymus of Prague, who in a similar way had stood as a helper to Jan Hus as Polzer had stood by Rudolf Steiner. 'Between Rome & Prague an episode in southeastern Europe' is mentioned in a letter of 21 February 1943. 'But [I] can't get it all to rhyme,' he confessed to his friend and then closed with the modest but hopeful words: 'My next life will finally bring me some clarity.'

*

Berta was able to leave Wiesneck occasionally. Perhaps she was in Tannbach in the summer of 1940 when Julius' second daughter, Irmgard-Mathilde, was born on 6 August. Apart from this happy event, his work had become much harder as a consequence of his mother's illness. But the family of his uncle Arthur was also going through severe economic difficulties. In order to improve the situation Arthur began to paint and sell picture after picture.

After Berta fell ill, Ludwig Polzer found a room at No. 6 Breitnerstrasse in Baden. Occasionally he went to Vienna. Here in November there was another meeting with Menny Lerchenfeld in November 1940. He spent an afternoon with her. Apparently, it was a very lighthearted time. On 7 November he wrote to her: 'I like to think of that lovely afternoon with you. We were so right to indulge ourselves in that dynamic optimism. And even though I know that you did not completely understand mine, it does not disturb the beauty of my feeling about our being together.'

The conversation seems to have turned to the Christian Community, the movement for religious renewal which had developed out of spiritual science. Polzer wrote: 'The Christian Community is certainly a fine & necessary transition—in relation to feeling—to the new age of a spiritual science which will bring art, science & religion into a unity.' That *he* saw the essential in this spiritual *science* is shown at the end of the short letter:

> Without this spiritual science mankind would have to fall back again into what is old and dead, and culture would have to give way to barbarism. Thinking, feeling & willing will have to change entirely; otherwise, the abyss between the old & the new in consciousness cannot be crossed.
> Warmest greetings,
> Ludwig

★

What do Polzer's dreams in 1940–41 say about his inner experiences? After Berta fell ill in March 1940 he dreamt of a 'cultic ritual' in which he was wrapped with 'a golden coronation cloak'. In the following period, Berta often appeared in his dreams; in June, Lerchenfeld and Eiselt; in July 1940, Ita Wegman and Marie Steiner; and in August a dream of Steffen, about which Polzer provides the following details: 'Explained something of Steffen's behaviour. I thought it was Herr Dr Steiner. Was difficult to formulate. Then someone asked me whether Dr Steiner was there. I answered that *he* would speak and not I.'

Then there is a long gap in his dream diary. The next dreams are from the summer of 1941. In the night of 29/30 July Polzer dreamt:

> At first a friendly meeting and conversation with Otto Lerchenfeld and his wife. Then participation in an Egyptian-style cultic ritual. Stood with crossed arms as a bearer of light. Content [was] in the sense of a Shakespeare drama. Probably an indication of a connection between Shakespeare and Egypt.

With this impressive dream—Polzer shared his birthday with the English dramatist, who had been born and also died on the same day—his dream diary suddenly breaks off.

★

Early in 1941 Josef Polzer was conscripted. Berta was able to leave Wiesneck for a while. But in the spring of 1942 she had a relapse. Until May of 1943 she had to stay in Buchenbach.

At this time it was dangerous to be at the clinic at Wiesneck. The private clinic had about 80–90 patients, some of them soldiers suffering from psychosis, and was considered overcrowded. Erika Warnke remembered no fewer than five visits by the Gestapo.

Dr Husemann's secretary was asked whether letters were sent abroad and if so, where. Once they wanted to go through the clinic's records, and only some money from Dr Husemann was able to prevent them from being taken away. But the worst was that the patients had to be presented for assessment for an eventual 'transfer'. To Husemann and his colleagues it was clear what this would mean: death in a gas chamber, after which their relatives would perhaps be informed that patient X, whose appendicitis was well-developed, had died of an inflamed appendix en route ... As soon as the Gestapo were on their way, the personnel at the clinic hurriedly administered sedatives so that no unruly patient would be reported for 'transfer'. The Husemann clinic was in fact spared this at this awful time. But only after the battle of Stalingrad did the Gestapo's pressure on Wiesneck ease off somewhat.

At this time Ludwig Polzer often stayed at the sanatorium for long periods to be close to Berta, who was endangered and under threat both inwardly and outwardly. His relationship to Paul Michaelis became a friendship. They used the familiar form 'Du' [you] to each other. At the same time Michaelis became Polzer's personal spiritual pupil. On saying goodbye, Polzer would sometimes kiss Michaelis on the forehead as Steiner had done to him. Michaelis now became *the* person who had Polzer's trust.

Not only did his friend Michaelis write dramas in these years, Polzer too felt strongly inspired by his young friend's example to new creations of his own. In September 1942 he wrote 'a kind of drama' about Crown Prince Rudolf. 'One day,' he wrote,'I was inwardly urged to write it; it complements my book *Das Mysterium der europäischen Mitte*,[512] which appeared in 1928', 14 years earlier. That Polzer responded to the inner call and carried it through is doubtless due to the stimulation he received from Michaelis' joy in poetic creativity. Thus he wrote the whole Rudolf drama in one single burst of activity in autumn 1942, as if creating out of a hidden oasis at the end of his destiny-laden life. He called it: *Rudolf, Crown Prince of Austria—Spiritually Real Soul Images of the Destiny Knot of 'Austria' from the Years 1882 to 1889.*

Let us take a closer look at this wonderful creation of Polzer's last years.

45. The Drama: 'Crown Prince Rudolf'

When Ludig Polzer wrote his Rudolf drama in the autumn of 1942 he did it on the basis of a purely inner urge. In 1928, when he wrote about Crown Prince Rudolf in relation to Nero in the central chapter of his *Das Mysterium der europäischen Mitte,*[513] he did this in the awareness that 'out of the knowledge of certain events' he was in a way 'fulfilling a duty to the dead'. Rudolf Steiner's statements about the karmic connection between Nero and the crown prince of Austria (27 April 1924, in GA 236) had been his starting point from a research perspective. Nevertheless, in Polzer's *life* the first seeds of his interest in Nero and Rudolf lie much further back. Hamerling's *Ahasver* already directed his youthful gaze to Nero's Rome in the early 1880s; Ludwig's brother Arthur had experienced the visit of Crown Prince Rudolf and his wife Stephanie to Graz in October 1887; and the tragedy of Mayerling on 30 January 1889, when Rudolf freely chose to leave this world with his lover Mary Vetsera, had greatly moved the Polzer brothers.

In his 1928 book Polzer tried to elaborate on Steiner's indications about Crown Prince Rudolf and the background to his destiny. Polzer cast light on what had been impossible for Steiner in a single lecture—the entire social circle around Rudolf and Nero. He compared Seneca, the advocate of Roman republican principles, to Franz Joseph, Rudolf's father; he drew parallels between Agrippina, the representative of the Roman imperial principle and Empress Elisabeth, Rudolf's mother, as well as between Pallas, Agrippina's trusted adviser, and Andrássy, the Hungarian Minister with whom Elisabeth was friendly. And he asserted that these personalities from Roman times, who probably mostly—like Nero himself—had a further incarnation in the Middle Ages, therefore could appear again in the mid- to late nineteenth century in the same sex as in their Roman incarnations. But he restricted himself, with regard to the karmic aspect in the circle around Nero and Rudolf, very consciously to discussion of the noteworthy *parallels*, 'possibilities' or at most, 'probabilities'.[514] He did this with such care and attention to historical detail that he provided a fine example of how one can work out of Steiner's karma research results and pursue them, rather than just repeating them as they stand or just ignoring them. That Polzer's contribution to the elaboration of Steiner's karmic research has hardly been known of until now, due to Marie Steiner's disapproval of the entire book, is one of the symptomatically significant facts in the development of the anthroposophical

movement; symptomatic namely, not only of the difficulties encountered in engaging with karmic knowledge gained from spiritual
research but also of engaging with it fruitfully. Even less attention has
been paid until now to Polzer's development of his 1928 work on
Rudolf in his drama of 1942, for the simple reason that it never saw
the 'light' of print; indeed, it is almost a wonder that it survived at all.

A glance at the list of the leading characters in Polzer's Rudolf drama
gives one an idea of how in the fourteen years since 1928 the material had
developed and ripened within him. Besides the well-known personalities
of Austria-Hungary who, in the period 1882–1889 in which the action
takes place, act or react on the stage of history, there are also 'the dead,
active only as souls'; these include the souls of Rudolf von Habsburg, the
founding ancestor of the dynasty; Cardinal Rauscher, the archbishop of
Vienna, and Ignatius of Loyola, the founder of the Jesuit Order. Lucifer
and Ahriman appear as 'beings of the spirit world', who are characterized
as follows: 'Lucifer, who seeks to release men in pride from the earth and
lead them away from their earthly tasks' and 'Ahriman, who wants to bind
men entirely to the earth and cut them off in coldness from their original
source'. In the course of the drama there also often sounds a 'voice from
the spiritual world', which appears to sound from higher spheres. From
these elements, as well as from certain particular words and phrases in the
drama it is apparent that Polzer had internalized Steiner's Mystery Dramas
and had worked through them.

Polzer's drama therefore has two layers: in the events in the foreground
earthly history runs its course, as far as was known to historians at that
time; in the background, integrated into the first layer, is a second layer,
where the spiritual dimension of the historical events portrayed is shown.
The subtitle 'Spiritually Real Soul Images...' points to this second layer;
this is the actual special feature of Polzer's drama, although this is not to
underestimate the artistic ability with which the events in the first layer are
connected to each other.

The drama unfolds in 17 'scenes'. The first takes place in the Budapest Parliament where in the summer of 1882 the Prime Minister of
Hungary, Tisza, suggests that Crown Prince Rudolf be offered the
crown of Hungary. This is followed by various dialogues between
Rudolf and Archbishop Albrecht, who is dependent on arch-conservatives and on clerical circles and who in an indiscreet way seeks to
block the coronation of Rudolf (Scene 2); with the journalist Moritz
Szeps, who Rudolf has secretly arranged to have brought to the Hofburg at night (Scene 3). Rudolf speaks to Szeps of the machinations of
the Church (which had itself originated from a single source) and of

political Freemasonry which he knows to be in league with each other and also opposed to his own intentions and whose decadent spirituality he sees through only too well:

> *The one became two;*
> *Decadence, into which they fell,*
> *Split them.*
> *The Godhead held itself back from them.*
> *Divine wisdom*
> *Must now come to mankind*
> *In other ways.*

Through being crowned King of Hungary, Rudolf would have been able, at least indirectly, to gain advantage for the political influence he had been denied by his own father, and he was sustained by the hope of forming, through liberal elements in Hungary, a counter-weight to the continuous muddling of the reactionary politics of Austrian Prime Minister Taaffe; these hopes could only be *feared* by his father Franz Joseph and even more by the Church. There was soon no more talk of a coronation of Rudolf as King of Hungary in official circles.

> *My thoughts are*
> *Turned towards the Balkans and the East.*
> *Austria's future must lie there.*
> *I know little of the West,*
> *They think quite differently from us.*

Rudolf says this about his intentions to Szeps, who advocates closer ties to France. After the departure of his friend Szeps, who has been providing him with information and has been publishing articles by Rudolf, Rudolf says:

> *When he speaks to me,*
> *I feel as though*
> *Expansive thoughts*
> *Arise within me*
> *So that I must say to myself:*
> *He shows the way,*
> *But I see further.*

As here for the first time at the end of the third scene, Polzer shows also in later scenes how the different personalities with whom Rudolf speaks work upon him, mostly in such monologues after their departure from the stage. It is as though the Crown Prince was seeking an after-taste or an after-image of these people and wanted to let those speak on within him who had just been standing before him.

After Rudolf's words about Szeps he contemplates and 'falls into a dream-like state'. In this state 'a voice from the spiritual world' speaks the following to him:

> Your thoughts rise up
> To us in spirit worlds.
> Unite past and present
> In a whole with the future.
> Then you will be able to speak
> To the East and to the Balkan Slavs.
> Your thinking has the power of form,
> And stands close to the West,
> Your heart belongs to the East.
> Lucifer's struggle
> Will be in vain
> Because of your striving,
> And your powers will
> Free themselves in the course of time.
> In his struggling, Lucifer will only
> Serve the Gods.

Through this voice from the spiritual world—and it remains an open question whether the Crown Prince himself hears it—Polzer shows Rudolf to be a man in whom there lives a strong striving for the spirit and a heart-filled understanding of the Slavs.

We find him later, in the 4th scene in Prague, where Rudolf resides for five years on the Castle Hill and becomes popular among the Czechs. Rudolf loves this people too:

> Man's urge for freedom
> Speaks from the people here.
> It will, however, be abused
> By the Church and the nobility.

After a conversation with the Austrian Minister Ernst von Plener, who wants to lead the whole Empire in a western direction and has no understanding for Rudolf's love of the Slavs, Rudolf shows how conscious he is that the task in the East can only be solved through inner self-awareness and a new orientation, and no longer out of the old gabrielic forces of blood and tribe:

> *On this path*
> *The old hereditary forces fade.*
> *One stands there naked*
> *And must come to oneself.*

While Rudolf's thoughts 'are lost in this meditation', the soul of Rudolf von Habsburg appears, who was the founder of the dynasty (and with whom Rudolf at times felt himself strongly connected). It speaks in words which are '*not perceptible*' to Rudolf:

> *You will have to change yourself*
> *And also purify yourself, Rudolf.*
> *Then you will be freed*
> *Of the heavy yoke of destiny.*
> *Only then will the goal*
> *Release you.*

The scenes that follow show Rudolf mostly in Vienna, to where Franz Joseph orders his son to return at the end of 1883 after appointing him commander of a division of infantry. The departure from his beloved Prague is hard for Rudolf. Will he be able to change or purify himself in Vienna?

In the Hofburg the Crown Prince receives the natural science researcher Brehm (Scene 6) with whom he had gone on various journeys. This meeting too prompts him to deep thoughts about the all too 'dull instruments employed by thinkers' in science and philosophy:

> *The dear professors,*
> *They live in a darkness of knowing*
> *And do not notice it.*

He receives a similar after-image of Professor Menger, whose instruction in economy he enjoyed, without ever accepting that economy must be something national. Rudolf speaks to Menger, who had made possible his friendship with Szeps, about the 'Order of Spiritual Knights' which had been an inspiration for him since his youth and which he feels would unite free spirits in all countries, and he speaks of the need to limit the activities of nation states in Humboldt's sense. After the departure of Menger, who had pointed to the resistance the Church would put up against any such Order, Rudolf says:

> *Scientists and professors*
> *They too are distancing themselves*
> *From my kind of spirit.*
> *My isolation is growing.*

Then the 'soul of Cardinal Rauscher' appears, the Prince-Archbishop who had spoken about the need for the close relationship between Church and State at Rudolf's christening in August 1858; he warns against Rudolf's plans for the Order:

> *Rudolf,*
> *The flights of your thinking*
> *Are nothing but pride.*
> *Fight it!*

A second soul appears—that of Ignatius Loyola, the founder of another famous Order. The soul of Loyola says:

> *I once created an Order*
> *Faithful to the Church of Jesus.*
> *It was my idea*
> *Directed in struggle*
> *In noble fashion.*
> *In spirit worlds I then lived but a short time;*
> *I came to Earth again,*
> *Filled with new spirit.*
> *The Order of Jesus*
> *Continued on Earth.*
> *It fell into spiritual death*
> *Because it was leaderless*
> *From the spirit worlds.*
>
> *I had to abandon it.*
> *You will find me soon*
> *In the spirit,*
> *Then shall we, united,*
> *For Christ on Earth*
> *Work onward.*

Rudolf then says:

> *I heard voices*
> *And could not make sense of them.*
> *Cardinal Rauscher*
> *And a monk*
> *Appeared to me in the picture.*
> *Life in the darkness*
> *Is so harrowing.*
> *Yet in the darkness*

Is hidden true light—
My yearning is telling me.

It was a notable inspiration of Polzer's to connect the metamorphosed spirit of Loyola to the Order of Spiritual Knights that Rudolf is striving for in the drama! But it was 'spiritually real' pictures that he wanted to present, and not merely a *fable convenue* on the basis of historical documents ...

The dialogue between Crown Prince Rudolf and his mother which closes this scene shows how much spiritual striving also lived in her—something that could already be known to external history—but, as with her son, lies hidden in darkness. She says:

I know of your soul's need.
We are connected
Through the suffering of our souls,
The powers of destiny would have it thus.
The knot of destiny
Of the House of Habsburg,
The last house
Led by a Folk Spirit—
Is a great tragedy,
But I cannot understand
The meaning of it.
Yet meaning lies in everything
That surrounds us in Nature.
Our seeking too
Creates out of meaning [. . .]

Rudolf speaks to his mother of 'the Order of the Knights of the Spirit':

Since my early youth
I have been thinking
Of a league of spiritual knights.
Does this thought
Come from earlier lives?
The question is so serious for me.
Now I see myself surrounded
By philistines.
They are filled with fear
And hold off from every deed of spiritual heroism.
In scorn and wild hatred
This fear hides itself,

Utterly unreconciled.
Thus is an empire ruled
That demands other things [. . .]
Divine beings have
Laid spiritual treasure
In every human soul.
To let it lie
Seems to me to be
Life's greatest sin [. . .]
Yet when I want to approach it
With my thinking,
I feel everything collapse
That surrounded me in life until now.
Then I fled
And sought to give meaning to my life
In hunting and pleasures.

In the course of the drama, Rudolf's *Faustian nature* reveals itself more and more, and his own individual knot of destiny, as well as the supra-individual one of Austria, are shown to be *threshold problems of consciousness*.

In view of the Serbo-Bulgarian war of 1885 the question comes up in the Austrian Council of Ministers whether Austria agrees to the union with East Rumelia which victorious Bulgaria is seeking at Serbia's cost (Scene 7). Foreign Minister Kálnoky gives the following advice:

To take the side of the Bulgarians
Would certainly mean a break with Russia [. . .]
To intervene strongly for Bulgaria
Would in this situation
Be very dangerous.
Only England is for the union [. . .]
For us there is little
To hope from England,
Either from Salisbury or from Gladstone.
England wants a balance of power in the Balkans,
Not the domination of a single power.
That is more useful to the British.
Then they always stand
Holding the balance.

Austria decides to hold itself back in this case, but in view of the approaching danger in the Balkans, it resolves to strengthen its armaments. Contrary to Rudolf, the War Minister Bylandt believes that the monarchy can still uphold itself with a strong military and that the 'ancestral spirit of the Habsburg still possesses the power to hold out'.

In the following Scene 8 of the drama we see Rudolf in conversation with Count Latour, the most understanding of his numerous teachers. They talk about the current political situation; Rudolf criticizes the policy directed in Austria by the Vatican that is assisted by masonic lodges. Latour encourages Rudolf's strivings for a free spirit with the words:

> *Thought is always,*
> *Through many failures,*
> *The beginning of later growth.*
> *But a failure*
> *Is never a proof against a spiritual impulse*
> *If it really comes from the spirit*
> *And from human love.*
> *Men who love only being*
> *And not becoming—*
> *The world process does not count*
> *On them.*

Through these words of Latour speak Polzer's own experience and ethos, the fruit of many years, in relation to the transposition of 'spiritual impulses' for which *he* had striven. They therefore contain a kind of extract of Polzer's own spiritual ethos in life that he had resolutely maintained.

Rudolf experiences another after-image following the conversation with Latour. He says:

> *I spoke with Latour,*
> *Then thoughts arose in my soul*
> *Which are like friends to me*
> *But I do not know*
> *From where they come.*

After these words, Rudolf falls into 'contemplation', and a voice from the spiritual world, 'audible only in spirit regions' speaks the words:

> *Cosmic beings*
> *Have said*
> *To seekers*
> *Since the beginning:*
> *Over long ages of time*

Spirit powers strengthen
Through errors
And through pain.

A conversation with Kálnoky follows, from which Rudolf seeks to gain insight into the latest state of foreign affairs. The result for Rudolf is an outlook that is not at all promising. He sees that everything is moving in the direction destined for Austria in the 'Testament of Peter the Great'. He concludes:

All this shows
That Austria can only survive
When it can find
New spiritual paths
And learn to speak
To the fiery mind of the East
With newly-won insights in knowledge.

After Kálnoky's departure he says gloomily:

The paths ahead
Are becoming ever darker,
An abyss lies open
Before Austria,
Unavoidable—
And yet I must believe
There is a possibility
It may yet be crossed.

Outwardly he may still have been thinking of the Hungarian coronation, but inwardly he was confronted by the problem of 'crossing' the abyss of consciousness.

The next, 9th, scene shows Empress Elisabeth in angry mood, anxious for her son; then also, the Emperor, who shares her concern and has to confess, resignedly:

I have made him Inspector
Of the Infantry,
To keep him occupied;
But it seems it will not serve
To banish the unrest
In his spirit.

The Emperor, the victim of his own spiritual conservativism—spirit means unrest for him—still places his hopes, like Bylandt, on the ancestral power of the House of Habsburg and sees no necessity for any radical spiritual renewal.

The Empress, left alone, slumbers after a conversation with her friend Ferenczy; 'Lucifer in female form and red costume' appears and speaks:

> *I guided you*
> *Through long ages of time.*
> *You followed me.*
> *But you do not recognize me.*
> *Now you seek yourself*
> *And find me.*
> *The nation that you love*
> *Is also subject to me.*
> *Recognize yourself in it.*
> *Then you will remain*
> *Bound to me.*

Then the Double of (the still living) Count Andrássy is seen and for the time in the drama karmic perspectives from the past earthly lives appear.

> *I remain close to you*
> *When worries weigh upon you.*
> *My people remain true to you,*
> *Because they are close to you by nature.*
> *However, they are going through changes.*
> *The thread of their life is worn out.*
> *It will arise anew*
> *And you will share its destiny.*
> *In ancient times I was already by your side.*
> *Another people was around us then.*
> *It was the right of woman*
> *To be protected*
> *From rough male domination.*
> *I shared your destiny*
> *With you at that time also.*
> *The man who opposed you*
> *As an enemy then*
> *Oppresses you also*
> *In this current age.*
> *In the depths of his soul*
> *He suffers with you.*

At this, the Empress, 'coming to herself', speaks:

What was that?
A being spoke,
One unknown to me,
And yet also a friend.
How can I understand
What was said?

In the 10th scene we witness the growing alienation between Rudolf and his wife Stephanie, who suffers more and more from his lack of attention to her and his involvement in hunting and in love affairs. Then it is announced that the Emperor wishes to speak to him 'about an important matter', at which news Rudolf jumps up and exclaims:

What is important here!
Only form and appearance!
How I would love
To have lived in ancient Rome!
The rulers in those days
Were not prisoners
Of an etiquette
Called ceremonial [. . .]

It is noteworthy how Polzer has Rudolf feel his way towards ancient Rome through *this outburst of emotion*. That already provides half the answer to the question: how far has the Crown Prince since his time in Vienna begun to change and purify himself?

The soul of Rudolf von Habsburg had advised him to do so, but in a way that remained 'imperceptible' to the normal consciousness of the Crown Prince . . .

Rudolf also senses more and more the nature of his destiny link to his mother:

I love her,
Yet something also separates
Me from her.
Is it a soul guilt
From an earlier time?
Thus is one always surrounded by the burden of guilt.

And now Rudolf shows through what follows that he has not advanced far enough on the path of change and therefore must at times be caught by a second spiritual power of obstruction. Directly after his words about soul guilt he says:

> *How would it be if I tore up*
> *This IOU?*

Tired, Rudolf falls asleep, and 'Ahriman appears in a white garb, with a tiara-like headdress, vulture-like, with a bony countenance' and speaks:

> *I have you*
> *Through your arrogance.*
> *I deceive you*
> *And hold you fast.*
> *Brother Lucifer will also*
> *Be of service to me*
> *In holding you thus fixed.*

The service, which 'Brother Lucifer' will soon render Ahriman, consists of getting Rudolf caught up in Hungarian politics at the time of the Defence Bill in 1888, along with his relationship to Mary Vetsera.

Once more, after Ahriman's appearance, comes the soul of Rudolf von Habsburg and says:

> *I see how the empire is fading.*
> *The ancestral spirit,*
> *In stature like a Folk Spirit,*
> *Stood by me*
> *Because the Church which I served*
> *Still stood for Christianity.*
> *But it fell to the powers*
> *That live in cosmic coldness [. . .]*
> *Blood is no bearer anymore.*

Then follows again the warning but now no longer directly to Rudolf:

> *You must transform yourself*
> *Before you can rise anew,*
> *You, Austria.*

In Scene 11 Empress Elisabeth has another conversation with her friend Ida Ferenczy, in the salon of her beloved Hermesvilla in the Lainzer Park; they discuss Rudolf's depressed state of mind and the various problems which have disturbed his behaviour in many places, even back to Rome. Then the Empress shares a dream with her friend:

> *I dreamt recently*
> *That I was in ancient Rome*

Looking down from the Capitol
Upon the city.
It became late,
It was lonely around me,
My heart was empty.
And a frightful calm
Lay leaden over Rome.
The heavy air
Took away my breath.
Then suddenly I saw
The appearence of something red
Which soon became flames.
I heard people screaming
In panic and confusion [. . .]
From out of the din
A voice
Shouted the name 'Nero!'
Then I cried out,
The picture changed.
I saw myself
In my Hungarian homeland [. . .]
Then I awoke,
As if a dear child had called to me.
Why did I dream
Of that fire in Rome
To which I had never given any thought?

Shortly afterwards the Crown Prince appears. He speaks to his mother, full of concern:

Downfall and conflagration
surround my dreams [. . .]
I am not afraid of death
But of life
Which hides its meaning from us.
Meaning lies on the other side
Of this abyss.
How are we to cross it?
I would like to experience
A courageous death.

A voice from the spiritual world closes the scene:

Your wings will grow
If you strive.
To cross the abyss you will need them.
Light will ray out
From the darkness.
Human beings rise to the Earth
With this light.
It lives in you,
The light that is still hidden.
Your powers remain.
They transform themselves in this light
To the Good.

Polzer thus indicates (in harmony with Rudolf Steiner's statements of April 1924) how the tendencies to evil from Nero's time can be transformed to the good and sees this possibility also for Elisabeth, who had been Nero's mother in the Roman period.

Now (in Scene 12) the Roman theme becomes clearer in a conversation between Rudolf and the historian Arneth. Rudolf opens the conversation:

The Julian-Claudian ruling house
In ancient Rome
Stood in the midst of a world struggle
Between the principles of Empire and Republic.
Primus inter pares was the principle
Represented by Seneca,
The teacher of Nero;
Agrippina, on the basis of maternal right,
Upheld the principle of empire.
Woman alone
Could give power and virtue to Caesar;
Blood still carried the capacity to rule.
But Nero wanted to ascribe his ruler's power
To his own divine being.
On Agrippina's side
Stood Pallas the Greek,
Whose ancient wisdom came from the land of Hellas [. . .]
Our law originated there
And also the example of the great State machine
Which kills all life.

> *Christianity is today*
> *As oppressed as it was then.*

Arneth would like to put a damper on Rudolf's comments about Roman history and remarks:

> *We academics*
> *Must necessarily*
> *Stick to documents*
> *The validity of which we recognize.*
> *Belief we leave*
> *To the Church.*

Rudolf only finds that 'very comfortable' and advocates that imagination [*Phantasie*] should have a role in historical research:

> *Imagination is the reddening dawn of souls,*
> *The premonition of a light*
> *Which will bring us the science of the future [. . .]*
> *Insight into the meaning of the destinies*
> *Of peoples and individuals*
> *Must be possible to grasp*
> *Through development*
> *Of the human life of thought.*

Then Rudolf points to the 'Pragmatic Sanction' [1713] which guaranteed the rulership of the House of Habsburg throughout the generations by decreeing that women could also wear the crown, as a continuation of Roman imperial practice. For Rudolf, this went against the tide of history and signified the onset of decay.

Especially impressive and instructive is the after-image which the Crown Prince has after the conversation with Arneth, whose spiritless and desolate 'academicism' makes him shudder, so that because he cannot cross the abyss of consciousness with his own consciousness, inwardly he grasps at escape:

> *Then I seek diversions*
> *In adventures and pleasures.*
> *A lust for murder arises*
> *From my soul*
> *That I can only suppress*
> *Through hunting.*
> *Stephanie does not understand this.*
> *Mary has an eye for me.*
> *She could understand better.*

Countess Larisch, one of Rudolf's cousins and a confidante of his, then appears; under the seal of the greatest discretion he gives her a casket which he commands her to keep safe. In his growing confusion, Rudolf feels he now has only *one* hope:

> *I could still try*
> *With the Crown of Hungary.*
> *I know men from the East of Hungary*
> *Who would be ready*
> *To make the effort from there*
> *To try to reform Europe.*
> *And with Mary*
> *I could start a new life.*

In that moment appears the spirit named *Lucifer* and says:

> *You feel me*
> *But you do not know me.*
> *Your eyes will remain*
> *Closed.*
> *Your soul will then*
> *Be won for me.*

But a voice from the spiritual world immediately counters:

> *Lucifer's struggle*
> *Will be in vain*
> *Because you are striving.*
> *Forces are transformed*
> *In the course of time.*

In Scene 13 the Emperor appears, who is hesitating between the demand from Germany that Rudolf be relieved of his military office and his forbearance with his son, who protests mightily against the pressure from Berlin.

The next scene presents a conversation between Rudolf and Baroness Vetsera, which again shows Rudolf's spiritual striving:

> *I seek to draw*
> *Light from the darkness.*
> *If people's spiritual capacities*
> *Were to grow ever greater,*
> *Ruling would not be*
> *As easy as it is now,*

When thoughts run on mechanically.
Some people are helping themselves now
And behaving very cleverly
In that they say
That only through deception and lies
Are people to be ruled,
And when that does not suffice,
Then with violence [. . .]
You know that I yearn for [. . .]
An Order of Knights of the Spirit
Which certainly already exists
In worlds to which
Normal consciousness
Cannot yet penetrate.
But the time for it is still far off [. . .]
Conflicts of a monstrous kind will have to
Arise and shatter
Our souls
Before we see the true light.

Then Rudolf speaks urgently to his beloved of the hazardous venture that stands before them:

If it succeeds, you will be my wife
And my companion in arms too,
If it does not succeed, then . . .
Mary: I shall stay with you
Even in death.

What was the hazardous venture? Polzer touches on this riddle in his drama only very gently. Rudolf researchers have until today not been able to clarify it, and one has the impression that the longer they have researched, the less they have had to say. In 1941 a book about Rudolf was published by Werner Richter which provides some explanation.[515] Richter claimed that the hazardous venture related to the new Defence Bill which the Hungarian Prime Minister Tisza proposed in Hungary in December 1888 and which included the demand that those aspiring to become officers in the Hungarian reserves would in future have to take a German language test after a year of service, which set off a huge storm of indignation among Magyar nationalists. Richter writes:

> When one tries to make a careful reconstruction of events from the meagre
> materials that are still available today—the systematic destruction of papers

after Rudolf's death was a real masterstroke by Franz Joseph's State—then the following scenario is at least imaginable: A promise was made by Rudolf, perhaps even committed to paper, whereby if the confrontations over the Hungarian Defence Bill should take a violent form, he would have openly stepped forward on the side of the national Opposition—and they for their part would have smoothed the path for him to the Crown of St Stephen. It was an agreement which was just about possible and thinkable, as long as it remained theory in moments of surging emotion. But the closer it came to practice, then it must immediately have revealed to the Heir Apparent the shocking prospect of high treason against the existing State and against his own father. If he did not hold to the agreement and somehow recoiled from it—and perhaps the journey to Mayerling was already the beginning of such a recoil—then that would mean a disloyal break with his fellow-conspirators. A break of faith either with one side or the other was therefore unavoidable. Ever clearer become the traces of that day when Rudolf believed he would have to atone for a crime of honour. He wrote that he had 'no more right to live', and of the 'good name' which 'only death can still save'.[516]

But with this we have jumped ahead in the course of Polzer's drama. It is also indeed very possible that Polzer knew of Richter's book, in which Arthur Polzer is several times mentioned and quoted, and that a reading of it even gave him the impulse for his alternative treatment of the riddle of the Crown Prince.

In the 15th scene of the drama there is a reception at the German embassy in Vienna (a few days before Mayerling), at which Karl Julius Schröer was also present and on whom the peculiar conduct of the Crown Prince made a strong impression. In the next scene we see Rudolf waiting for a telegram from Hungary which is expected to bring the decisive news from Szögyenyi, the close friend of his last years and the man to whom he even entrusted his private papers. This corresponds to the actual situation, known to external history, of 28 January 1889. While waiting, Rudolf says:

> *I asked Szögyenyi*
> *To tell the gentlemen*
> *Not to set conditions for me*
> *To fulfil*
> *Which are not possible for me.*
> *He was also to find out*
> *Whether anything has been betrayed*
> *To our enemies*
> *In order to misrepresent my intentions.*

This delay in the answer
Is worrying.

When the answer comes and he has opened the telegram, he says only:

My life is forfeit.
I am coming, Mary,
Brave child!

He then falls to musing, and 'a voice from the spiritual world', which 'is imperceptible to him but acts' [upon him], says:

As Agrippina fell because of Nero,
So you now fall because of Hungary.
Elisabeth—
She brought it about.
For what you once did against the world
As Nero,
You have now made recompense.
Destiny has been balanced.

Rudolf's last words in the drama are:

I feel divine light
Arise from
The ruins of Europe.

The drama ends with an apotheosis (Scene 17) and shows Empress Elisabeth alone at Rudolf's grave in the Imperial crypt. She says:

Rudolf!
You were so sorely tested!
Your life was a martyrdom,
Self-chosen.
Destiny's heavy burden
Is erased.
Your yearning—
Freedom—achieved.
I must suffer further,
In loneliness of soul [. . .]
The silence of loneliness
Is required of me
To deny the demons
Their insight,
So that the will of the gods[517]

Is not abused.
In loneliness
Shall I be further bound in spirit worlds
Until we two come down
Again to Earth.
Then the Earth will blossom
Again in freedom
And battlefields will become
Places of spirit building.
We shall then be well-prepared.
Great human souls will
Unite themselves with us [. . .]

At the end of the whole drama speaks 'a voice from the spiritual world, *perceptible to Elisabeth*':

What Rudolf did against the world
As Nero
Has been made good.
His death speaks a cosmic speech.
For seekers he will open
The eyes of the spirit for thousands of years to come.
The struggle of Roman principles,
Between the Empire and the Republic,
Will be exhausted
In the Habsburgs' approaching demise.
The Pragmatic Sanction
Was only of short duration.
What now will follow is only its conclusion.
Demons will then come to power
But in their struggle, they will
Serve the gods.

★

Polzer's drama is a true legacy. It draws together, as it were, all the threads of his spiritual striving: rising from understanding of the spirit to spirit knowledge which extends the inner gaze beyond the threshold and can lead to concrete spiritual conversations.

And it reveals an important turning point in Polzer's own development: it is the first time he made use of *an artistic form of expression* in such a way.

There are three sayings of Rudolf Steiner that were pathfinders for

Ludwig Polzer which he returned to many times during the years of his anthroposophically oriented work. The first is: 'We must come, with inner interest, beyond conventional history, to acquire a yearning for that history which must and can be read in the spirit. This history should be nurtured more and more in the anthroposophical movement.'[518] The second saying is: 'It is not a correct principle to want to develop all kinds of abnormal visionary states in nebulous ways. But it is extremely important to attend to what goes on more intimately in the destiny relationships that one can observe.'[519] And the third saying is: 'For the first task and obligation of the spiritually striving human being is to grasp the course of the development of mankind as far as the present and its probable development in the future, in accordance with spiritual orientation.'[520]

If Polzer viewed his journey through life continually in the light of these illuminating words, then in his drama of 1942 they had reached in his soul the highest form of fruitfulness. It is as though they had led him to his Rudolf drama.

The work on the drama, which he began in the summer of 1942, lay exactly in the middle of the period between his Italian journey in the spring of 1939 and his death in the autumn of 1945. We have already indicated that the Italian journey with its visits to Rome, Taormina and the island of Ischia was the probable stimulus for the drama. In a mood of departure from life, Polzer had twice passed by Baia, the place where Hadrian had died (10 July 138), the place where Agrippina also met her end at the hands of Nero's henchmen. That may indeed have brought certain images to mind, if not consciously then in the inner movements of his soul: images from the time of Hadrian . . . There was in Hadrian's life a particular, apparently only external connection to the Emperor Nero. A few years after he became Emperor himself, Hadrian started on the construction of a gigantic 'temple of Venus and Roma' near the Flavian amphitheatre at the eastern exit of the Imperial Fora. For this he required the square which until then had been dominated by the giant statue of Nero, over 30m high, that had stood before Nero's villa, the *Domus Aurea* (Golden House). Hadrian had the 'Colossus Neronis' moved by 24 elephants to the front of the amphitheatre which therefore became known as the *Colosseum*, and he had the head of Nero replaced by a radiant head of the Sun-God Helios.[521] He therefore gave to the Colossus of Nero something sunlike . . .

In a similar way, even if only on the inner stage of his global consciousness, Ludwig Polzer-Hoditz bestowed on the figure of Crown Prince Rudolf, to whom he created a special monument in his drama, a Faustian, sunlike appearance. One who wished to assert that Polzer's image of Rudolf is not realistic could be presented with the question: What is more true—that which has been or that which can still become out of what has been? What did Count Latour say to Rudolf?

> *Men who love only being*
> *And not becoming—*
> *The world process does not count*
> *On them.*

★

Polzer read his drama one evening in Wiesneck in Dr Husemann's room to a small circle of friends, after which, Paul Michaelis sent him the following poem:

> *For you it was no dream of empty hours,*
> *Nor the thoughts of some imagined game;*
> *What from their lives upon you came*
> *Was destiny; you bound yourself to it with all your power.*
>
> *Yet all the hurdles you have now passed o'er*
> *Oh, so many were the dangers and the storms.*
> *But all believed themselves set right upon an aim*
> *And only death they've found to be their door.*
>
> *Now they've been learning, so blind within those worlds*
> *Where only knowledge illuminates the way*
> *And fulfilment comes from deeds of love unfurled—*
> *Until your work turns their night into day;*
> *Heart's warmth arises there in spirit worlds*
> *And light of love, before which blindness falls away.*

Through Polzer's reading of the Rudolf drama and the poem of gratitude he received from Michaelis, the friendship between the two men was strengthened in a new way. Polzer felt himself to be deeply understood in a way he had never before experienced in his last years, while Michaelis was fired to new creative activity. In the summer of 1943 he completed his drama about Kaspar Hauser.

And so we now return once more to the course of Polzer's outer life, where for weeks and months all becomes again quite still and silent.

★

In quite another sense from what Crown Prince Rudolf had once hoped—'with newly-won knowledge'—masses of Germans and other

Middle Europeans were now moving towards the East. In late autumn 1942 began the encirclement of the Reich's army in Stalingrad. At the end of January came the capitulation of the southern and then, soon afterwards, of the encircled northern pocket in the city.

Soon after this, Josef Polzer, 'after proving himself for three months in Russia', came to Bucharest to be trained as an officer. 'He enjoys being in the military, and I am glad about that', wrote his father in the family chronicle in spring 1943. In March of the same year Polzer's grandson Christward Johannes passed his high school leaving exams with distinction. That too Polzer recorded in the chronicle.

At the beginning of that month the sad news reached him of the passing of Ita Wegman. She had died on 4 March at Arlesheim. Deeply affected, he decided to turn, inwardly, once more to this individuality, with whom he had been so deeply connected.

46. The Passing of Ita Wegman

In the summer and autumn of 1942 Ludwig Polzer had occupied himself in the most intensive manner with one of the most notable figures of the nineteenth century—Crown Prince Rudolf. Through Rudolf Steiner's spiritual scientific illumination of the background to Rudolf's destiny, Austria's Crown Prince became for Polzer a real key to an understanding of the relationship of modern European history to Roman impulses. Half a year later, the death of Ita Wegman led him to focus on this personality, who had had such an effect on the anthroposophical movement and Society. Here too, he was inspired by Rudolf Steiner's karmic revelations. Just as behind Rudolf had stood the Rome of Nero, so it seemed, behind Ita Wegman appeared the Greece of Alexander the Great.[522] From a karmic perspective, it can hardly be an accident that Crown Prince Rudolf and Ita Wegman were the two individualities to whom, even if for very different reasons, Polzer's mind was turned most intensively in 1942/43. From Steiner's indications about the deeper nature of these two personalities, there resulted for Polzer a most vivid perspective on how very concrete human impulses and strivings from the Greco-Roman cultural epoch worked on like an extract and had to metamorphose themselves in something new. Just as Hadrian had once travelled across and ruled Greece and Rome, so at the end of Ludwig Polzer's life two figures appeared before the eye of his soul as quintessential representatives of the two spheres of the fourth post-Atlantean epoch—the Greek and the Roman.

As he approached closer to Ita Wegman in the course of his anthroposophical strivings, so she seemed to Polzer in looking back to have been naturally closely connected to the qualities and events of precisely this spiritual stream.

First, however, Polzer had stood close to Marie Steiner, even after the death of Rudolf Steiner, when he offered to take care of handling Steiner's will for his widow. When Ita Wegman had her 'leading thoughts' published at this time, as Steiner had done earlier, Polzer stood on the side of those who disapproved. Now in 1943 he recognized that 'it probably would have been better to give her time and support her with trust'.[523] Then he was taken into the confidence of both women and sought to mediate between them, and also between them and Albert Steffen. These efforts were discussed in the chapter 'Building Bridges'. Then came that dark day when Roman Boos aggressively interrupted a Class Lesson held by Ita Wegman and was not prevented from doing so—

and Polzer then realized that Ita Wegman was in need of a knightly protector. During the events of 1935, Ludwig Polzer had 'acted' while Ita Wegman had 'suffered'. Behind this 'suffering'—seen in an aristotelian sense—was an experience that she had already had in 1934 during a severe illness and of which she wrote to Walter Johannes Stein on 16 January 1935 (in her heart-warming but never quite correct German): 'I was granted a view of the spiritual world, I met Christ and Rudolf Steiner, who sent me back to the Earth and expected me to to do something other than what has happened until now.' After her severe illness she had gone on a trip to Palestine and on her return journey had in Rome developed a 'burning interest in the activities of the Roman Caesars'.

Polzer could feel something of the deep change in Ita Wegman when he spoke with her in March of the following year (1935) in Arlesheim and perceived the equanimity with which she was facing what was then going on. After his speech at the General Meeting at Easter 1935 was rejected by the rigid ideas and still more rigid feelings of the great majority assembled there, he had a wonderful dream in Ita Wegman's clinic and felt himself empowered, liberated and spiritually upheld. He went on holding Class Lessons as before and had Ita Wegman's agreement about those whom he accepted into the Class. It was with deep gratitude that even after his resignation from the G.A.S. on 30 May 1936 he was able to remain united with her in his esoteric activity—*she* had been the one who had asked Rudolf Steiner after the Christmas Conference 'to institute esoteric work again', whereupon Steiner then 'founded the Michael School on Earth, of which he said that it was an institution from heaven'. Rudolf Steiner named Ita Wegman his 'colleague and representative in this esoteric area' from then on. And when Polzer, with Steiner's permission, held his first Class Lesson on Michaelmas Day 1924, he owed this indirectly to that initial question by Ita Wegman.

Until then Marie Steiner had been his 'helper in esoteric rituals'.

> Since the institution of the Michael School, Frau Dr Ita Wegman had become his helper. The times demanded that women must be admitted to the Mysteries. That had been the great difficulty in occult development which had to be overcome. It required sacrifice and pain. We stand in the midst of these today.[524]

This is how Polzer put it in 1943.

But it was not only to the Michael School that Ita Wegman was most inwardly connected; this was also the case with the Christmas Conference. Her becoming aware of this connection with Rudolf Steiner over thousands of years was a *spiritual sine qua non* of this conference. 'The relationship between Rudolf Steiner and me is really an essential element of the Christmas Conference,' she wrote to Stein. 'Many people know this, and this is also why I am hated.' The essence of this hatred she saw in the tendency 'not [to want] to bring people to experience of karma'.[525] We discussed this hatred of karmic revelations and the fear of concrete karmic experience in detail in the chapter 'Do You Know the Jesuit?'

Shortly before her death, Ita Wegman had written a few lines to Marie Steiner; it was a gesture of forgiveness and of looking into the future. One of the last things she said in relation to Marie Steiner was: 'There is nothing more between us that would stand in the way of our work together for Rudolf Steiner in the future.' Polzer did not know of these words, but they would not have surprised him. She also said shortly before her death: 'When I die, you will all have to accompany me!'

And now suddenly, she had set off and had crossed the threshold, and Ludwig Polzer was one of the first who tried to accompany her spiritually.

And so on 4 March 1943 Ita Wegman set out for the second time on the journey to the place of transformation, to where, nine years before, during her illness, she had been allowed to make just a fleeting visit ... She went in order to become prepared and initiated for new work at the end of the millennium.

> *Then will the Earth blossom*
> *Again in freedom*
> *And battlefields become*
> *Places of spirit building.*

These were the words of Empress Elisabeth in Polzer's drama after the death of her son.

And further:

> *Great human souls will*
> *Unite themselves with us*
> *To be called to serve the Gods,*
> *So as to recreate*
> *The dignity of Man.*

Among those great souls was certainly included also that soul which until the spring of 1943 lived as 'Ita Wegman'.

★

At the end of March Polzer was writing down his memoirs and experiences of this strong spirit battler for a new esoteric science and for true 'human dignity'. 'Shocked by the unexpectedly early death of Frau Dr Ita

Wegman, I took up my pen.' With these words he began the memorial sketch with which he wanted at the same time to make 'a contribution to the history of the Anthroposophical Society'. And at the end of it he wrote:

> Now Rudolf Steiner took his dear colleague to him in the spiritual world. In true devoted fashion she spent the years after his death in the service of her Medical Section and of the clinics and institutions which she had called into being, honoured by her colleagues. She walked courageously through life despite all the unjustified persecutions. For people who are of good, esoteric will, her deep and close bond of destiny with Rudolf Steiner is a certainty.[526]

For typing, Polzer dictated his sketch in Wiesneck to Erika Warnke, Friedrich Husemann's secretary and the colleague of Paul Michaelis.[527] We have referred to the ideas in this text, which Polzer did not publish, in various places earlier in this book and are here content to refer the reader to the appendix, where it is presented in full.

47. Departure

In May 1943 Berta Polzer was able to leave Dr Husemann's clinic. 'Hopefully completely cured', wrote Polzer in the same month in one of the last entries in the family chronicle.

The very last entry in his own hand in the chronicle, which had always been maintained by the oldest member of the family, reads: 'My trust in our spiritually guided future is, despite all hardships, unshakeable.' His 'spirit contemplation' [Geist Besinnen] of the personality of Ita Wegman may have increased this unshakeable spirit.

Paul Michaelis completed his Kaspar Hauser drama that summer. The first scene is already remarkable. This takes place in January 1802 and takes the reader to a secret sitting of a 'Lodge of the West'. Disturbed by the spiritual awakening that has begun in Europe with German classicism and the French Revolution, it is decided in the lodge to head off this development by supporting Bonaparte. A messenger from the Vatican appears and tells the brethren that it had been found [through spiritual research] that a Rosicrucian individuality would be born in the House of Baden and that this individuality could unite the gabrielic forces of France with the michaelic forces of Germany. It is decided to place this individuality in occult imprisonment in such a way that it will not be able to live rightly through its childhood nor be able to die in order to hold it in a limbo condition during the decisive time period and to prevent it from being able to seek a new incarnation elsewhere. The collaboration of FM and SJ brought about what was perhaps the greatest and most extravagant occult attack of modern times on the free individuality of a human being.

There can be no doubt that Polzer took an intimate part in the development of this drama, indeed that certain elements such as this first scene, which also speaks of the Testament of Peter the Great, can be traced to his inspiration.

At the same time Michaelis also published his drama 'Libussa'. What *this* drama owed to Michaelis' older friend is clear from a poem that Polzer wrote in gratitude. There we read at the end:

The meaning of East and West,
The powers from which harmony arises
Your work reveals.
You understood Přemysl;
The Greeks named him Prometheus,
And Stephen-Wenceslas,

'The Crowned Ones', in the true sense of the word.
With them you were a thinker of the future
And also a pupil of Michael.

★

While Berta, it appears, already returned to Buchenbach that summer, Ludwig Polzer was until late autumn mostly in Tannbach or Baden. On Michaelmas Day he experienced in Tannbach 'the almost empty house, where everything reminded me of Berta, where the boys grew up, where also the great messenger of our time came and conducted a ritual', as he wrote to his friend Menny in October 1943. 'Berta's rooms remained unchanged, just as they were when she suddenly left four years ago [. . .] A premonition of death gripped me.'

He then went for a week to Heiligenkreutz, to Berta's cousin Heinrich Kotz,

> in the Bohemian Forest, which is so close to me, where 43 years ago I found Berta in the former Templerburg with her deeply religious soul that was so united with nature and art and for which I have so much to thank. Heinrich was for her always a brother and uncle Wlasko was like a caring father. The mood on these visits was not sentimental but serious and sad.[528]

In the second week of October he travelled—to Regensburg. He had written to Sophie Lerchenfeld who had meanwhile returned with her husband and daughter to the family estate at Köfering. Polzer had asked Sophie to meet him in Regensburg. It had, however, 'not only [been] the drama of world-importance that made me call Sophie', he wrote to her sister Menny.[529] By this 'drama' he probably meant the Soviet Army's mounting counter-offensives which were pushing more and more to the West and in September had already recaptured Smolensk. The East was now rolling towards Middle Europe and threatened to smother Germany and Austria; for the armies of the West were also pressing into the Middle European region [Sicily and Italy in 1943] and no one knew how it would all end. So before his own end, on his last journey he wished to see Sophie Lerchenfeld with whom he felt himself so deeply linked. He also had a delicate hope of being able to meet Menny once more, but he refrained from suggesting this himself, a restraint he had firmly held to since his previous experiences. Yet his wish was all too understandable, even reasonable; just a few years earlier, he had seen Sophie's younger sister as the inheritor of his esoteric legacy. In Linsberg the little box was waiting for the future trustee. Or did that have no meaning any more at this point? Had Polzer already made other arrangements? It cannot be said for certain, but it is hard to accept, as the following appears to show: 'On the trip to Regensburg I was always asking myself: "Will she come?!" ' wrote Polzer in the letter to Menny. And then 'it was a sunny surprise, a sound of rejoicing within me, once again a revival of friendship and love'— Menny had come too.[530]

They spent an afternoon and an evening in the city—it is unclear how often they were two, how often three—and walked in the moonlight to the Church of St Emmeram. It was in both the literal and the figurative senses of the phrase truly a 'starry' moment in the final phase of Polzer's life.

Deeply moved and as if rejuvenated, the 74-year-old soon looked back on this meeting in his letter to Menny of 15 October:

> That evening with you I felt deeply united with you, as if our being together would be justified to the end of our lives and may not yet come to an end. I felt an obligation rooted in human-spiritual love that has not come to an end and that has not yet been fulfilled on life's pilgrimage. When we walked through the city in the evening to the Church of St Emmeram as I suggested and you then took the lead as we came to the symbol in stone of a once mighty religious and cultural past, I felt from our conversation that I had failed to take sufficient account of your earnest seeking. But the facts always showed that destiny had created a bond between us. In the twilight and as the moon shone down, we walked towards the threshold in conversation. Yearning arose in me to help you spiritually before I die so that you would be able to find your way, as is your own yearning, through today's thinking, feeling, and willing that is filled with such confusion. How peacefully I would then be able to die in your arms [...] When one is 75 years old then one says as a pupil of the spirit nothing for which one cannot take responsibility. I firmly believe that you have an obligation to the future of Middle Europe for that will be our place of work in our next life. I would dearly love to prepare in this life so that we shall be able to work together in the next. There would be much yet to say about our meeting but I may not do so yet.

These lines, and especially the last, suggest that Polzer even now still wanted to leave open the question whether Menny would not out of herself ask to hear those things of which he was not allowed to speak 'straightaway'. His letter to Menny closed with the words:

> In recent years I have often had premonitions of death. It is not a matter of indifference where one dies. As a spiritual human being, one is bound to a particular place on the earth and remains so after death. Europe remains the heart of the earth between East and West. I want to accompany you in the spirit or in being together in true human and spiritual

love; with these thoughts I embrace you with all my heart and say auf Wiedersehen!

Your old Ludwig

This was to be the last letter which he wrote to his beloved friend before his death.

★

On the day after he wrote this letter Polzer thanked Ulrich Schenker, Dora Schenker's son, from Baden, for 'two boxes' which had just arrived—'help which is very valuable to me'. They most likely contained provisions.

The British Prime Minister Churchill had promised Stalin in the spring of 1942 that a second front would be opened in western Europe, but the Russians had continued to bear the brunt of the war since then. Churchill knew how to keep delaying the second front and instead proposed to the Americans several times an invasion in the Balkans, a second front in southeastern Europe. At the Conference of the 'Big Three' in Teheran (end of November 1943) Churchill spoke openly of a Danube Confederation under Anglo-American leadership. Later, he proposed to Stalin a division of the Balkans into British and Soviet spheres of influence—a continuation of the policy laid out in the Testament of Peter the Great, that is, a policy that strove to exclude any influence from the Middle of Europe on the Slavs living in the Balkans.

Renate Riemeck drew attention to Churchill's policy:

> His intensive efforts with regard to southeastern Europe and the tenacity with which he sought to open a new front in the Balkans lead one to think that he was following more long-term plans than he made out. At any rate, his ideas about the formation of a Balkan federation bear a remarkable similarity to the picture that certain people had formed in England in the 1880s of the future shape of Europe and had incorporated in secret maps.[531]

In that same November when Churchill, Roosevelt and Stalin were negotiating in Teheran, Ludwig Polzer returned to Wiesneck. Except for the month of May, he remained until December 1944 close to his wife. He too now sometimes fell ill and needed physical care.

So he was now once again with his young friend Michaelis, read, reflected, meditated and went for walks with Berta through the park.

Where he spent May 1944 is uncertain, probably once again in Tannbach, Baden or Linsberg. At the beginning of July, Emil Hamburger wrote to Ulrich Schenker that he had just heard from Arthur Polzer's wife that Josef Polzer had been killed at the Romanian front. The news will have arrived at Wiesneck shortly before. Death had claimed Josef Wenzel von Polzer in Constanta on the Romanian Black Sea coast during a Russian offensive on the 11 June 1944, eleven days before his 43rd birthday. He had included a poem he had written in a letter to his mother from Constanta:

If you have fought and striven
In the midst of wild battle riven
By agonies of pain and suffering
And raised yourself from shadows
Of rigidity by renouncing;
And in patience and forebearance
Lived your lives in accord with ideals—
Then from above you will be blessed.
Share out the gifts of grace
Brought down from heaven before your face
Which to you say:
For you is this creation's crown
Take now as reward for your renown
Our being into yourself.

His mother could only reply with a 'call to the dear being of her son':

In the realm of thinking
In streaming life,
In the realm of feeling,
In flowing light,
In the realm of willing,
In kindling warmth,
Where deeds spring up
There beings find themselves
Who wish to unite
To serve all mankind,
When desires have died
That gave rise to selfishness.

Is it not striking how the son's poem turns to the mother and father, while Berta's call spreads like circles of water in which it is hard to find her son?

How Josef's father was doing at this time is shown in a letter which he wrote in November 1944 to Albrecht Strohschein. Strohschein had made an essential contribution to Josef's recovery in Pilgramshain. And since the severe psychological illness which befell him at the beginning of his 30s, perhaps he had never been as healthy as he was at the time when death

took him … Polzer wrote to Strohschein on 20 November from
Wiesneck:

> Dear, honoured friend!
> It was a great joy to hear from you that you managed to get out of Romania
> safely. My daughter-in-law Anna passed on to me dear Josef's package,
> which your wife had kept safe for him. My wife, who has been here, on
> and off, for more than four years already, suffers from relapses in her
> condition and so I have often been here at this time. Since the end of '43 I
> have also often been ill and have been here all the time except for a short
> break in May. *I also have fine work here. Important dramas are being written here
> under my eyes and with my assistance. So I feel myself well in both soul and spirit
> despite the sick and weakened 76-year-old body.*[532] We are therefore more or
> less bound here despite many dangers which threaten so close to the Front.
> In general though, I have every confidence.
> Now I wish you the protection of destiny in the future & my wife and I
> greet you most warmly.
> Your Ludwig Polzer-H.

The italicized sentences in this letter show once more the unshakeable,
fixed-star-like constancy of Polzer's soul and also his urge to, and joy in
creative work for which he was still capable and which could live itself out
in the inspiring and orienteering advice he was able to give to his young
friend, in whom the creative fires were blazing.

Towards the end of the year shocking news arrived at Wiesneck:
Julius had been called up and had to start his military service from
January 1945! That meant: Tannbach now had no one to take care of
it, and Julius' wife and three children urgently needed protection and
help. Ludwig Polzer decided to leave Wiesneck before Christmas with
Berta and return to Tannbach. On 20 December 1944 Polzer took
solemn leave of his friend Michaelis. He presented to him 'his diaries,
notes and part of his Class texts'.[533] From this it was clear that at this
point he no longer saw Menny Lerchenfeld as the guardian of the esoteric texts, for at least Class texts would have fallen under this last rub-
ric. Since October of the previous year he had actually heard nothing
more from Menny, and so he saw no alternative but to alter his last
wish. Perhaps he had already brought the relevant texts, notes and diaries to Wiesneck in May 1944 in order to hand them over to his friend
at the right time. Michaelis then passed them to Dr Husemann, as he
'did not feel justified in continuing the spiritual work of Count Polzer'.[534] As far as is possible, more information will be given in the last
Part of this book about the destiny of these diaries and notes which
Polzer left to Michaelis.

★

On the way to Gutau did Polzer also think of the miserable prisoners who were done to death in *Mauthausen-Gusen* concentration camp? The camp, which was set up soon after the *Anschluss* lay about 15km west of Linz and 20km south of Gutau on the Danube. It can hardly be imagined that Polzer had no knowledge of the existence of the camp. What may have gone on in the depths of his soul in view of the cold-blooded 'Final Solution' aimed at in the Third Reich? The appalling news from such camps may from time to time have penetrated to those layers of his soul which held the memory of the single, really dark chapter in the life of Hadrian—the memory of the bitter war which in the last years of his reign the Emperor had to wage against Bar-Kokhba, the leader of the army of the Jews.

★

On 7 January Julius was drafted.

In February the newspapers reported from the latest conference of the Big Three: Churchill, Roosevelt and Stalin met between 4 and 11 February on the Crimea peninsula at Yalta in order to discuss, amongst other things, Germany's post-war fate: the demand for 'unconditional surrender' was renewed; an 'Allied Control Commission' would replace the German political leadership; Germany was to be divided into zones of occupation. In Yalta, with the exclusion of Central Europe, the long-planned East-West division of the world, which had already taken shape after the First World War, was now to be implemented in full. Hitler's 'Total War' was the excuse for the execution of this old plan, which had appeared in the map from the magazine *Truth* as long ago as 1890. When one does not take into account only Hitler's appalling regime but also focuses on how the leading statesmen of the West had failed to stop Hitler in the early period of his rule of terror—for example in March 1936, when his troops marched into the demilitarized Rhineland, or in autumn 1938, when the Munich Agreement empowered him to annex the Sudetenland,—then it can become clear how far the use of the expression 'pretext' [*Vorwand*] is actually justified. In order to effect the complete political division of the world between East and West, Central Europe had to be laid low more thoroughly than it had been in the First World War, and this had to be done with the help of very many helpers from Central Europe itself. The politics of the German Führer provided the macabre, necessary opportunity for this. The world had first to be made to believe that one was called on by Providence to free the Earth from the ghastly Nazi Terror, which was indeed ghastly. Only a few knew that this terror, quite apart from the support from western appeasers, would never have been able to reach the stage it did *without financial support from the West,* which was then provided. But in affairs of grand politics, both in the 1920s and 30s and also today, it is the actions of these few that are critical. Disraeli had once spoken of 'original Clubs' as the settings in which policies were really born. A representative of such Clubs who knew something about the connection between the Thyssen Bank—to give but one example—with the American Guarantee Trust with which he was affiliated, was Averell Harriman.[535] Like his father Edward, Harriman belonged to the Skull & Bones Club of Yale University, the egoistic, global political aims of which were discussed in Chapter 24. This experienced businessman and (from 1941) US ambassador in Moscow exercised a lasting influence on US foreign policy and at the same time formed an important part of the bridge to the British Establishment; he later married Pamela Hayward, the former wife of Churchill's son Randolph. Harriman was among the American diplomats who flew to Yalta; he had also accompanied Roosevelt to Teheran in 1943.

Thus from the constellation of the main actors at the Yalta Conference an instructive picture, both real and symbolic, emerges: the Anglo-American West dominates, the East cooperates, and the Centre—is missing.

★

Meanwhile, the German policy of total war became ever more insane. What a sense of appalled alienation may have gripped Ludwig Polzer when he read of the Führer's Nero Order [*Nerobefehl*] of 19 March 1945 by which Hitler ordered 'the destruction of all military, transport, news, industrial, and energy facilities'.

On 8 April Julius Polzer was killed after four month's military service in Bohemia. A week later, the Russians marched into Vienna. In May Russian soldiers also forced their way into Tannbach. Anna Polzer left the estate with her children and began a flight for refuge that would last seven months. Ludwig Polzer may have taken his wife with him to Baden.

★

The capitulation of the German army on 8 May was followed on 5 June by the formal takeover of the government of the territories of the former Reich by the three victorious Powers. On 17 July these then gathered in Potsdam—the symbol of Prussian militarism—for another conference. The decisions made at Yalta could now be put into effect. Poland's frontiers were, 'provisionally' extended to the West until a definitive peace deal could be arranged with Germany, which never happened. Thus was Germany—with German assistance akin to suicidal intent— split up into western (British, French, and American occupied) and eastern (Russian and Polish occupied) spheres of influence. The 'German Republics' on the 'Truth' magazine map of 1890 had now become reality. But without the cognitive sleepiness of Central Europeans, who paid less and less attention to how their statesmen were driven into policies of race and power that were ever more alien to a true German nature, the realization of these plans would never have succeeded. The peoples of Central Europe, especially those of the German tongue were given the choice by world destiny of either accepting the spiritual science of Rudolf Steiner and thus the consequences of reason which flowed from it in the sense of the idea of threefolding of the social organism—or of falling for the insanity of Hitler. In the West—naturally not the British or American people as a whole, but in certain leading 'Clubs'—money had been put on the latter choice, and the bet had more than paid off... 'The people slept when the initiate was here and will now have to bear the consequences,' Polzer had written in the spring of 1939.

In July Ludwig and Berta Polzer dared to go to Tannbach. The house was abandoned, the rooms plundered. Ludwig Polzer and Berta made what provisional arrangements and repairs they could. It is not difficult to imagine with what feelings they did this. Both their sons had been killed, Anna Polzer was still in flight with the children. The fate of Tannbach, which like Vienna and Baden,[536] was now in the Russian zone of occupation, was still uncertain. Polzer, who for decades had made such efforts in relation to the real being of the Slavic soul, now had to experience how the mostly unconscious instruments of the *corrupted* Slavic stream occupied Tannbach! The former owners had for the time being been expropriated! 'The great messenger of our time' had once come here and conducted a ritual act, Polzer had written to Menny Lerchenfeld in October 1943.

Overcome by the outer chaos and driven by inner depression, Berta Polzer threw herself from the roof of the house at Tannbach on 23 July. Badly injured—she broke a foot—Berta was brought to the hospital in Freistatt.[537] She died on 24 July 1945 from the consequences of her injuries. At the burial of his wife in Gutau on 27 July Ludwig Polzer was the only remaining member of his own family.

When he arrived in Vienna a few days later, he learned that his brother Arthur had died on the same day as Berta![538] After the occupation of his home by the Russians, Arthur had moved with his family to alternative accommodation in the Breitnerstrasse, not far from his brother Ludwig's last residence in Vienna.[539]

So on 24 July Ludwig Polzer lost both his wife and his brother, the two human beings who had stood closest to him in the circles of blood relationship and freely chosen relationship. To the observer of Ludwig Polzer's life, these two deaths, occurring at the same time, stand like two letters or glyphs in which destiny seems to be written. The day after the deaths, 25 July, was the death-day of Julius, the father of Arthur and Ludwig. Ludwig Polzer owed to his father not only his life but also his discovery of Rudolf Steiner, which had subsequently shaped his own life. That the day of the deaths of the two closest people to him led in such a way to the death-day of his father Julius is another destiny glyph to be read.

★

After the deaths of his wife and brother, Ludwig Polzer was invited by his friend Emil Hamburger to share his apartment in the Kreuzgasse in Vienna. Towards the end of August Polzer travelled to occupied Baden in order to attend to his room in the Breitnerstrasse. He had brought with him from Tannbach the portrait of Berta painted by Hass in Munich (fig. 29). He hung it next to pictures of his sons on the wall. Was *Julius* still alive? Here in Baden he strongly sought to connect inwardly with his wife, striving in contemplation. Turning purely inwardly to Berta, he expressed his thoughts to her in a letter on 29 August:

> My dearly beloved Berta, do I reach you better when I write to you than when I only think? I have been in Baden for two days now and have rearranged the room somewhat. It lacks much but what of it? The large picture of you by the painter Hass is hanging again on the wall and also the pictures of our sons, along with other mementoes. Frau Leschanowski is sweet, friendly and active. Dealing with the Russians and finding food is much trouble for her—provisions are lacking & the cooking primitive. In the evenings I visit Lisl and Hannerl [his sisters-in-law]. I gave your amethyst cross to Hannerl. Your other one, which you always wore, I gave to Christl. I hope that is alright with you.
>
> The picture of Dr Steiner stands before me [. . .] These are outer things & yet are bound to him in spirit. I am sad that I can no longer serve you and I look forward to seeing you again soon. You will surely prepare a sweet reception for me in the spiritual world. I have heard nothing of Julius. Perhaps he is already with you like dear Josef. You dears, I am thinking of you all! Tomorrow I am going to Vienna. Emil is so good, he was also very

ill but is now in the Kreuzgasse again. I found there all the things that I left there one and a half years ago.

In loneliness love grows strong & my gratitude for everything in my long life is always awake.

I am grateful from the bottom of my heart that I met you in life and also for everything that you gave me. I thank you for so much. With your departure my life too has come to an end.

I love you and thank you. Your old Ludwig.

Back in Vienna, Polzer continued his conversation with Berta. On 31 August he wrote:

Beloved guardian of my soul, when I saw you lying there with your foot broken, the sight was so awful that I cannot get away from it in my memory. Today I have had these thoughts about it: The way you walked was always so strong and untiring. And now here in Vienna I walk a lot and am little tired. Perhaps you have given me something of your ether body, of your strong legs. We remain united in love, I with you and you with me. When I came to Vienna, I thought that I would soon starve here & wanted to see my [anthroposophical] friends. But they help me & I can help newcomers [to anthroposophy] and tell them about earlier times, especially 1917.

On 2 September he added the following words: 'You stood so strongly in the spirit that the counterforces wanted to darken you. Now they can no longer approach you. I shall be able to walk the spiritual path to you, and you will make it possible for me to make the right crossing into the spiritual world.'

A few days later, Polzer was suddenly stricken with appendicitis. He was taken to the Oenk Clinic on Spitalgasse and operated on in time on 13 September. The operation was very difficult, and he had to remain a week in the clinic, although, as far as the nursing went, he felt himself to be in miserable hands. On 25 September he wrote from the clinic the last two letters we have from him: one to Emil Hamburger and the second, enclosed in the first, to friends at the Arlesheim Clinic.

In a clear, fine hand he wrote to his friend in Vienna:

Dear Emil,

Please send this [attached] letter via the route you told me of as soon as you can. Herr Dr Salzer told me today that the operation was very difficult and that I should be satisfied with the progress of my recovery. The nursing here defies any description, but the doctor appears to be entirely powerless against the ruling riff-raff; neither do his junior doctors have any further interest in the nursing care and probably also not the slightest understanding of it. I have already written to Dr Wantschura,[540] who is now supposed to have influence in the Department for Health and Nutrition, but doesn't seem to be going anywhere, as with everything in the State.

In my larger suitcase under the desk is a section packed with things of my wife's. That should stay in Vienna. The clothes in the wardrobe should be packed in the case and go with me: i.e. four small cases and a jute pack which has yet to come from Baden nr. Vienna. I shall write to Baden that the few items of laundry that I still have there and a few smaller things like soap and brushes are to be packed there. I think all this is possible with a little will and energy. The red case in the writing desk should be filled with some documents etc. from the writing desk compartments, as many as can go in. Everything else I have already told you about. I am still really helpless at the moment and reliant on others for help. Fr Bittrich helps me where she can, for which I am very grateful.

Warmest wishes,

Your old Ludwig

P.S. There would still be very much to say—of an intimate nature—I hope we shall meet again before my departure.

Polzer was preparing himself therefore for a new, final journey. Feeling that death was near, he wanted to seek out that place where he could die with dignity and where his remains could rest. 'It is not a matter of indifference where one dies,' he had written to Menny Lerchenfeld two years earlier. 'As a spiritual human being, one is bound to a particular place on the earth and remains so after death.'

The second, enclosed, letter revealed where this place of his death was to be. In the letter addressed 'To the Clinical-Therapeutic Institute (formerly of Frau Dr Wegmann)' [sic] he wrote:

Dear friends,

After a very difficult appendectomy I have been in this clinic for three weeks. I lost my wife eight weeks ago and my two sons both fell in the war,[541] my estate was completely plundered and expropriated and recently it was officially sealed up by the Russians. Dr Hamburger took me in with loving friendship. Then suddenly came the appendicitis. It was a wonder that I was operated on and saved by the skill of a doctor. If I had not had a few friends, my personal circumstances would have gone to pieces.

Now I have only one wish: to spend my final weeks or months at your clinic or at one of its branches in Brissago or Locarno. As I am 77 years old, I actually belong to no one anymore, and to my mind, all now depends on the willingness of the Swiss authorities to allow me to enter the country. That possibility depends only on someone's strong will, who does not ask many questions but acts. Since America and England are now in charge, a journey by road would certainly be possible. One only needs to put the facts to people. My grandson, Christward Johannes, has lived in Dornach near Basel since his birth and is studying medicine at college in Basel. A positive response to my request I feel would be entirely feasible, and I hereby warmly request a prompt reply.

With warmest greetings,

hoping to see you again,

Your Ludwig Polzer-Hoditz

Polzer wanted to leave this life at a place where Ita Wegman had worked! Before the threshold then, he was drawn to the circle of life of that person whom he had respected so much and to whom, of all Steiner's pupils, he Ludwig Polzer, *as an esoteric pupil of Rudolf Steiner,* had in time come to stand the closest.

Hamburger evidently did not pass this letter on, as it was found in *his* estate after his death. Hardly had Polzer, who was already on the way to recovery, prepared for this last journey, than at the end of September he suddenly began to suffer circulation problems. His niece Christl and Emil Hamburger were among the very few who knew him that were able to take their leave of him. On the morning of 13 October 1945 Ludwig Polzer-Hoditz died at Dr Oenk's clinic in Vienna of heart failure.[542] Contrary to his last wish, his 'Spirit-Man' was to remain bound to the city in which, on 23 November 1908, he had heard his first lecture by Rudolf Steiner.

It was a Saturday, a Saturn day. His genius had in his last years always enabled him to keep death from his body, even if often only at arm's length; now it brought in the full, heavy, rich harvest of his life.

Until his last breath Ludwig Polzer remained fully conscious and spent the last hours of his life in constant meditation.[543]

When he crossed the threshold, a saying of Rudolf Steiner's may have accompanied him, without the spiritual content of which he never sought to meditate and which still survives in his own hand:

'In the spirit of mankind I feel myself united with all esotericists of the whole world.'

48. Epilogue

The arc of Polzer's life spanned the period from the First Vatican Council in 1869 to the outer devastation and inner self-destruction of Europe. In terms of destiny it played itself out in proximity to the dynasty of the Habsburgs and to the spiritual science of Rudolf Steiner. The later Hoditz family originated not far from *Habsburg*, the ancestral seat of the ruling dynasty. In the epoch-making year 1917 Arthur Polzer and his brother Ludwig found themselves at the centre of world affairs, close to Emperor Karl and to Rudolf Steiner. A new, idealistic sprig could have been transplanted onto the Habsburg tree in that year of destiny through the acceptance of the impulse of social threefolding. The nationalities problem presented to Austria-Hungary by world history would have entered the realm of possible solutions. Only for the sake of this task and the possibility of solving it would Austria have 'had to be created' if it had not already existed. But inwardly, the monarchy slept through and passed by the opportunity, and outwardly, the chance was covered over and pushed away. Austria therefore had to meet its 'downfall'.

'Is it any wonder,' asked Ludwig's grandfather in one of his novellas,

> that where a great thought is lacking, the human being becomes an egoist, and the idea of the State is lost thereby, its rotten forms held together with difficulty and lasting only to the next generation? Certainly, the powerful sun of the twentieth century will shine here only upon ruins.

The 'great thought' which could have metamorphosed the 'idea of the State' in accord with the spirit of the times into the idea of the three-folding of the social organism, had actually come but it was rejected by the darkness in the minds of the leading heads of Middle Europe who believed themselves to be so enlightened. In holding on to worn-out 'rotten forms' of spiritual, social, and economic life, the human being became an 'egoist' in the mass, such as there had hardly ever been before in world history. 'The powerful sun of the twentieth century' did indeed shine down only upon ruins.

On a more individual level, Polzer's life was not only dedicated to friendship, knowledge and action but was also a life of repeated review of the past. In the evenings he would review the day, at the end of the year he would look back on the year, and at the high-point of his life he looked back on another bygone life in Rome in the second century AD.

★

From a symptomatic viewpoint, it is very noteworthy that during Polzer's lifetime a biography of Emperor Hadrian appeared which suggested the motif of review in the title: this was *Mémoires d'Hadrian* by Marguerite Yourcenar.[544] Based on considerable historical knowledge, the book had to do with fictitious memoirs of the Emperor, who did actually write memoirs but they have not survived. Yourcenar began to write her book between 1924 and 1929, in the period therefore, between Rudolf Steiner's first mentioning of this Emperor to Polzer and Polzer's trip to Rome in 1929, with Sophie Lerchenfeld. The authoress destroyed her first drafts as she felt the need to mature with the subject. She took up the project again between 1934 and 1937, only to abandon it again. In 1945—the year of Polzer's death—the image of the drowned Antinous appeared powerfully to her imagination, leading her to write the still unpublished essay *Cantique de l'âme libre*. In 1951 *Mémoires d'Hadrien* was finally completed and was translated into many languages. There are a number of interesting things to note in Yourcenar's notebooks on *Mémoires d'Hadrien*. For example, she writes: 'This second century interests me because it was, for a very long while, *the time of the last free human beings*. With regard to ourselves, we are perhaps very, very far from that time.'[545] In another place she calls her book 'Portrait of a Voice'.[546] Readers of Yourcenar's book in fact become acquainted with a wonderful voice which speaks of the rich life of its bearer in epic detail. One who then reads Polzer's Prague Notes will, perhaps with a slight shock, feel that this other voice somehow seems to have the *same sound* ... To find something of this sound, which also appears to harmonize with Polzer's voice, was apparently reserved for the intuitive power of a feminine spirit to discern ...

But let us remain with Polzer himself: in the course of his life he became a true master of that mysterious power which we call 'memory'. Again and again he even succeeded in breaking through the barriers of memory and to press on to spiritual experience. For the power of memory can, when it is developed rightly, become the power of spiritual vision.[547] But then it is freed from a view of the past alone; in what is remembered of the past seeds of future development can be seen. Many of Polzer's dreams of a prophetic character appear to have this kind of background. What is seen in review [*Rückschau*] bestows a capacity for 'preview' and awakens enthusiasm for building the future. And the three thousand years of the past, of which Goethe called on every man to be able to oversee who did not wish to live only 'from day to day', will one day become three thousand years of preview of the future ...

*

Let us ask once more: how would a spirit like Polzer, at first from beyond history's threshold, have seen and evaluated the course of contemporary events on earth and how would he see the turn of the millennium and the following decades against the background of the future?

That the question is not posed here in any trivial sense but can be formed as a *reasoned hypothesis* in view of the real existence, perceived by reason, of the individualities wandering in spiritual worlds beyond the threshold follows from numerous observations in the foregoing chapters of this book. One who holds such an 'adventure of reason' to be unfeasible may be quite right from his individual standpoint, but no one can claim that it would be *generally* unfeasible. Certain preconditions apply, however, in order to come through this adventure of reason successfully. Menny Lerchenfeld pointed to one of these preconditions in a few words after the death of her father: 'The life of a dead person lives on in each one of us. But to perceive this life, we must be prepared for it.' Whoever, in a state of such inner readiness, turns to the individuality who crossed the threshold of death for a while on 13 October 1945, could, already as a reasoned hypothesis, seek to 'perceive', to hear questions directed by this living being over yonder to all those moving on here in the 'daytime' of history. Questions something like the following:

*How thoroughly will the ruins be cleared out of the way after 1945 in order to build firm foundations of new institutions? How will these new foundations themselves be laid and how will the new arrangements in the spiritual, social and economic fields be made for the second half of the century? After the victory of the German 'Reich' over the German 'Spirit', after the new world order of Wilsonism and the so-called Peace Treaty of Versailles, all of which served as preparers of the journey into the abyss from 1933 to 1945, will people want to build a **truly** new world order, or establish, if it is even possible, a worse caricature of the same? Will mankind at the end of the century want to stand for a third time on the ruins of useless 'new' world orders? What will the contribution of those who belong to the anthroposophical spiritual stream be to this work of construction and what role will the global Anthroposophical Society be able to play in the construction of a new world order? Will people recognize that the middle of Europe will have to be the place for the revelations of the Mysteries in the future, the root space of true individualism? Will the ultimately necessary bridges between real German culture and Slavic culture be built and crossed? How will the impulse of the Testament of Peter the Great be shaped in the future? And what about the ever closer colla-boration between the [freemasons'] lodges and the strivings of the Jesuits?*

In the concluding part of this book the attempt will be made to consider the main outlines of further developments in the decades after 1945 from the vantage point of these questions. In doing so, we shall restrict ourselves to events and facts which are of symptomatic significance in relation to these questions.

Ludwig Polzer left no written personal testament in the usual sense of the word. But the whole strength of his spiritual-scientifically oriented efforts in the social and political realm in the first instance, as well as the lack of fulfilment of those efforts, and finally, the deep earnestness with which he clearly penetrated the counter-movements subsumed under the heading 'the Testament of Peter the Great' which continually sought to block the fulfilment of Europe's true task of the formation of a cognitive and ethical individualism—all this, in our eyes, justifies us in speaking and writing about a 'Testament of Ludwig Polzer-Hoditz', from which the questions indicated above were able to stem. It is in this sense that the last Part of this book is to be understood.

V. THE TESTAMENT OF LUDWIG POLZER-HODITZ

For the individual human being, the
highest is to be found on earth;
his liberation can only be a spiritual deed.
No wars, acts of violence and outer revolutions
can accomplish it
A revolution of the spirit is needed.

Ludwig Polzer-Hoditz

1. The 'Unification' of Europe as the Preliminary Step to an Anglo-American World Government

On 17 April 1945 the founding session of the United Nations took place in the San Francisco Opera House. This new edition of the League of Nations had the declared goal of working to safeguard world peace. From the very beginning, however, the Russians were only very unequally integrated into the new organization. Article 52 of the UN session about 'Regional Treaties', which was added at the last minute, actually served to isolate Russia, as L.L. Matthias clearly showed.[548] Within a short time, the UN became an instrument for initiating the Cold War and for the realization of the East-West division of the world, which had been proclaimed at Yalta and Potsdam.

The dropping of the first atomic bomb on Hiroshima on 6 August 1945 took place without any prior discussion with Stalin, and although he had declared himself ready to cooperate in defeating Hitler's Asian allies by marching his troops into Manchuria. As macabre as this fact is: the bombs dropped on Japan—the second destroyed Nagasaki on 9 August 1945— had as their prime goal that of making clear to the Russians who was going to be setting the international agenda after the end of the war. Stalin had done his duty—now he could be dropped, which naturally does not excuse the atrocities which the ejected statesman now proceeded to commit in his own country.

On 5 March 1946 Winston Churchill gave his famous speech in Fulton, Missouri, President Truman's home state. He spoke of an 'iron curtain' that had fallen in the middle of Europe and stressed the need to erect a bulwark against Russia, with which he had only a short time before been allied. Although Churchill was then only speaking as a private citizen in America—he was voted out of office in July 1945—his speech, in the opinion of Matthias, determined the course of 'post-war politics for decades or longer'.[549] Matthias also wrote of Churchill: 'For him, only the English-speaking peoples had a claim to freedom; all others belonged to second, third and fourth classes.'[550] Or as Churchill himself put it on 1 December 1949: '[...] if there is any race in the world capable of an unbroken effort, it is our British race'.[551]

Six months later, Churchill gave a most significant speech in Zurich.[552] It was on 19 September 1946. A few days before, Count Coudenhove, the initiator of the Pan-Europa idea had been Churchill's guest in Bursinel at Lake Geneva. Churchill revealed to his guest that he was going to speak in Zurich about the unification of Europe and led the visitor to his easel. He was then painting a large landscape of Lake Geneva with an ancient cedar in the foreground. Full of admiration, Coudenhove later wrote: 'His paintings were grand like himself and his style.'[553] What then, were the *ideal* images which he sketched out before the audience of young academics in the atrium of Zurich University?

After the lecturer, esteemed as the important liberator of peoples from Nazi terror, had in a sweeping statement blamed *both* world wars on 'the Teutonic nations in their rise to power'—disguising thereby the at least equal striving for such power in circles within the English-speaking peoples—he demanded briefly and simply that: 'We must build a kind of United States of Europe.'

When this statesman said 'we', it should not incidentally be forgotten what he had written on 15 February 1930 in the English Press: 'We are *with* Europe but not *in* Europe.'[554] After his call for European unification Churchill went on to praise Coudenhove, who had done preparatory work in this direction: 'Much work, Ladies and Gentlemen, has been done upon this task by the exertions of the Pan-European Union which owes so much to Count Coudenhove-Kalergi and which commanded the services of the famous French patriot and statesman Aristide Briand.' Churchill promoted a new partnership between France and Germany as the core of European unification in which he wished France to take-over 'the moral and cultural leadership of Europe'. He held before the Europeans the Four Freedoms of the Atlantic Charter—'freedom of speech, freedom of worship, freedom from want and freedom from fear' and declared that if it was the desire of Europeans to live in accordance with these freedoms, 'they have only to say so, and means can certainly be found, and machinery erected, to carry that wish to full fruition'. But he also presented to his Swiss audience the spectacle of the new Russian danger that he himself had called up at Fulton, Missouri earlier that year: 'But I must give you a warning. Time may be short. At present there is a breathing-space. The cannons have ceased firing. The fighting has stopped; but the dangers have not stopped. If we are to form the United States of Europe, or whatever name it may take, we must begin now.' As the first practical step in this direction, the guest from Britain called for the formation of a Council of Europe.

As in 1930 with Briand's initiative, after Churchill's Zurich speech, the Pan-Europa idea was suddenly again on everyone's tongue. That this fine and grand outline of European unity was in Churchill's eyes only the indispensable means to a very different, higher goal, namely the establishment of a world central government under the direction of the English-speaking peoples—this he did not reveal 'in' Europe, but in

Britain, again six months later. On 14 May 1947 he gave a speech at the *Albert Hall* in London[555]—the 'We' to whom the British statesman here referred is now to be understood in a very different sense:

> We do not of course pretend that the United Europe provides the final and complete solution to all the problems of international relationship. *The creation of an authoritative, all-powerful world order is the ultimate aim towards which we must strive. Unless some effective World-Super-Government can be set up* and brought quickly into action, the prospects for peace and human progress are dark and doubtful. But let there be no mistake upon the main issue. *Without a United Europe there is no sure prospect of world government.* It is the urgent and indispensable step towards the realization of that ideal. [emphasis THM]

Churchill himself pointed to the great similarity of the strivings for power within certain English-speaking circles with those which existed in ancient Rome, when he added: 'We ["we"!] hope to reach again a Europe purged of the slavery of ancient days, in which men will be as proud to say: "I am European", as once they were to say "Civis Romanus sum".' In the light of the conditions laid down by Churchill himself, this can only mean in fact: 'I am a citizen of *the Province of Europe* within the English-speaking world empire.'

The Catholic Church too, incidentally, is interested in re-enlivening the idea of Rome in Europe, even if in the sense of the exercise of *spiritual* power. We shall examine this in the second chapter.

Following the unification of Europe propagated by Churchill in Zurich, Coudenhove was extremely active. He mobilized European parliamentarians and formed the European Parliamentary Union as a preliminary step towards the creation of a Council of Europe. But during this activity he was in some sense excluded by Churchill or by his son-in-law Duncan Sandys.[556] Nothing was further from the Englishmen's intentions than a federalistic European State with a strong parliamentary culture. This part of Coudenhove's efforts was simply sabotaged. When the Council of Europe was then founded in May 1949, it had, contrary to Coudenhove's hopes, retained only an insignificant advisory function. In May of the previous year, Churchill had arranged a European Congress in The Hague, at which 'The European Movement' was founded as an umbrella group for various European organizations; its first president was Duncan Sandys. Through initiatives by Churchill and Sandys, the 'American Committee on United Europe' (ACUE) was founded in 1948, on the board of which sat Allen Dulles, Director of the newly-established CIA. Another board-member was George Franklin, then Director of the

Council On Foreign Relations. Whoever has examined the last-named organization knows that it has (until today) been an influential body in American foreign policy; it has connections to the Skull & Bones Club, for example, through the personality of George Bush Snr. Money from secret funds of the State Department began to flow via the ACUE to the Brussels head office of the European Movement from 1949 onwards. A central aim of this movement, in the view of a connoisseur of clandestine connections in the period between 1949–1953, was 'the campaign to rearm Germany and to solicit support for a European Defence Community'.[557] The first of these aims stood in stark contradiction to Yalta, where the Big Three had decided on the demilitarization of Germany, but also in contradiction to the 'Law Against Rearmament' which the Adenauer government of the Federal Republic of Germany (founded 1949) was to pass in 1950.

With this, we have arrived at the second aspect of Anglo-American efforts for post-war European unity: the economic, or military/economic dimension. The blockade of Berlin by the Russians which began at the end of March 1948 was deliberately drawn out by the Americans (until the end of May 1949) in order to demonstrate to the world the danger of the Soviet Union and to convince the Europeans that this could openly be countered by European rearmament.[558] In the winter 1948/49 discussions were held in Washington on the theme of the rearmament of the future German Federal Republic. 'German generals had been asked whether they considered it possible to set up a German Army,' writes Matthias, 'and whether such an army could be placed under American command. The German generals answered both questions in the affirmative.'[559] This was shortly before NATO was founded on 4 April 1949 by referring to Article 52 of the UN Charter on the possibility of forming certain 'regional agreements' within the UN. Before the founding of this regional organization within the UN, Germany's rearmament had thus already been decided upon, and the decision had come about 'with the agreement of the German generals *at Washington's command*'. [emphasis THM] A notable characteristic of this pressure was the coupling of Marshall Aid for Germany with the required rearmament. On this point, Matthias writes: 'There are even documents which show that if the military demands were not met, sanctions would be threatened. Marshall Aid would be withdrawn.'[560]

Under the deceitful pretext[561] of the Russian threat, business could be done in the following years with a Europe that was rearming, especially with the Federal Republic and naturally not only in the military sphere. Thus behind the Anglo-American promotion of the unification of

Europe—with its distant goal of an Anglo-American world government—there were also blatant economic interests.

These showed themselves in the American support for the later, so-called Schuman Plan (1950), which launched the process that led to the European Economic Community in 1957. It was born as the European Coal and Steel Community (ECSC), the unification of the coal and steel industries of the Benelux countries, the Federal Republic of Germany, France, and Italy and came into force in July 1952. The idea for this came from the French businessman Jean Monnet, who had been an economic adviser to the US government during the war and also to the British and French governments during the First World War. The executive organ was the 'High Authority', the first president of which was Jean Monnet. This first, economic, form of 'the United States of Europe' was enthusiastically welcomed in the USA. 'The 'High Authority' was treated by the USA as a state-like organ, the 'sovereignty' of which empowered it to make decisions which were binding on all the member states of the ECSC. 'It was hoped [...] that with the "High Authority" one would have an instrument capable of shaping a European Union in accordance with one's own requirements over the heads of European governments.'[562] Among the enthusiastic supporters of the ECSC was Averell Harriman and the then US Secretary of State Dean Acheson. Matthias even writes: 'Monnet could even have presented this plan under the name of the American Secretary of State Dean Acheson, who had the keenest interest in it, as did many Europeans, but it was thought better to present it as a European project.'[563] That is what then happened. The French Foreign Minister Robert Schuman became its energetic advocate in France and Europe, and so it was later known as the Schuman Plan.

To avoid misunderstanding: the problem is not that a union in the economic sphere—which in itself is fully appropriate—was undertaken, but that *this unification was from its very beginnings dominated by and shaped in accordance with Anglo-American national economic interests.* American capital dominated the growing United States of Europe more and more. That is it flowed constantly in line with political conditions and specific American interests. The situation did not change with the founding of the European Economic Community in 1957. After the signing of the *Treaty of Rome*, American investments in Europe increased spectacularly. An example of the dominant US economic policy within the EEC zone was the 'chicken war' of 1964: the USA wanted to force its exports of chicken into EEC markets and threatened to raise import duties on VW cars if its demands were not met.

In a truly modern global economy, no national-egotistical or racially-bound factors ought to play any role whatsoever. Yet in place of a supranational global economy, the West has carried on a furious *economic war* in the supposedly post-war era, and an important theatre in that war has been the unifying Europe.

Anglo-American interest in the unification of Europe since the Second World War has thus, at first, essentially had two faces: a political face, oriented towards the establishment of an authoritative, all-powerful world super-government which can only be realized by means of a united Europe, and secondly, a military and economic face which seeks, through the means of a provoked Cold War, to make of the developing global economy a worldwide process determined by western interests. Nothing in this has essentially changed from the late 1940s until today.

It was partly the same individuals that brought about the division of Germany and caused the Cold War who spoke of the unification of Europe and of international peace—and then rearmed West Germany and Europe... At the head of the list was Sir Winston Churchill. Contradictions of this kind are an indicator that behind such policies is the kind of dialectic that was, and still is, practised in Clubs such as that of Skull & Bones. When certain things in the world are only achievable through the strategy of contradiction, as one learns in these Societies— then one can allow oneself no scruples about pursuing the politics of contradiction... Acheson[564], Harriman, Churchill all knew this, to say nothing of the very, very few who stand behind the curtain and of whom no less a statesman than Benjamin Disraeli once said: '...the world is governed by very different personages from what is imagined by those who are not behind the scenes'.[565]

In the dire material straits of the post-war period only a few politicians in Central Europe saw through the unhealthy tendencies in the fatal gifts from the West which were bound to prevent Europe from perceiving its bridging role between East and West. Konrad Adenauer, who had been President of the CDU in the British Occupation Zone since February 1946 had his counterpart in Jacob Kaiser, who was President of the CDU in Berlin and had pointed out to the Soviet Occupation Zone the possibility of serving just such a bridging function. Adenauer voted for the integration of Germany into the West and in doing so, joined the long column of those who have served to undermine the task of Middle Europe.[566]

A few years after the war, the city of Aachen instituted the International Charles Prize [*Karlspreis*] 'for personalities who have rendered distinguished service on behalf of European unification'[567], the first recipient was Richard Coudenhove-Kalergi in 1950. Other recipients after him included Sir Winston Churchill and George Marshall. The capacity of Europeans to reward, with the highest distinctions, those who seek to destroy Europe's spiritual and cultural bridging function between East and West for their dubious services to the so-called unification of Europe is astonishing.

★

Let us follow in broad steps the course of the further development of European unification as far as it has continued under the impress of western impulses. We shall restrict ourselves essentially to symptomatic events from the 1980s, because western efforts to unify Europe gained new strength in that period. If Churchill was clear that without a single Europe there could be no world government, it had become equally clear in the West in the meantime that likewise, a lasting unification of Europe could hardly come about without German unity; neither could it come about without a complete reconstruction of the whole socialist system.

German reunification was prepared or preconceived in the USA in 1955. According to an American intelligence report of 12 July 1955, made public in 1990, Germany-experts in Washington were then occupying themselves with the 'politics and problems of a reunited Germany' and in their secret studies proceeded from the 'assumption' that the unification of Germany would 'then come about if the CDU/CSU were in power in Bonn'. The historian Alfred Schickel, who described this intelligence report in the magazine *Geschichte* [History], writes: 'It was felt that a conservative head of government would be the most reliable to deal with the difficulties of reunification. These problems they saw as including the need for a recognition of the Oder-Neisse Line as the western frontier of Poland as well as the complex economic, adminis-trative, and legal alignments that would be needed between western and eastern Germany.'[568]

Many years had to pass before practical circumstances allowed the intention to be carried through or made it desirable. By September 1981 things had got to the point where Richard Allen, US National Security Adviser to President Reagan and some of the President's most important other advisers met in Bonn for discussions with the CDU leadership around Helmuth Kohl—at a time, then, when the CDU was still *the Opposition party.*

The *Frankfurter Allgemeine Zeitung* (FAZ) reported on these discussions on 10 September 1981 on its front page with the notable headline '*Die Deutschen in einem Zustand der Hilflosigkeit angetroffen*' ['Germans find themselves in a helpless state']; the text read: '*The Germans were almost*

nonplussed when their friends from over yonder recommended a good dose of nationalism. [emphasis THM] Not on demagogical grounds but as something positive.'
The nonplussed German friends were

> also required to hear that Yalta must be revised. The two sides agreed that what was needed was the resurrection of a positive German historical consciousness, and *the American promotion of German nationalism*[569] was indicated in the claim that a country that did not have such a historical consciousness was no good ally.

The correspondent, who was listening to this in some amazement, psychologically struggling for breath as it were, commented at this point:

> After the attempt had been made for three decades, through supranational ties and above all, the integration into Europe, to lead the Germans away from their feared nationalism, now they were being told: There is no country with a foreign policy that does not also have its own nationalism.

It was further revealed to the politicians of the CDU, which was regarded as more capable of bringing about a change of course than the governing party:[570] 'Reunification could certainly be something that western countries would not be bothered about or even oppose, but the Germans would have to take action in this regard.' The new nationalism was then presented to the Germans as follows: It should be 'anti-communist, should keep in mind the destabilization of the Soviet Union, and should pursue a forward-looking strategy'. Finally, in case the Germans declined to go along with the change of course that was to be imposed upon them, they were plainly and simply threatened: 'Were the Germans to take another path, that would provoke American resentment. The warning was expressed very clearly many times.'

The threat was intended to make clear that this starting signal for the desired change of course in German policy was to be taken seriously. It recalls another threat made, at the end of the 1940s in connection with Marshall Aid: No rearmament? Then no Marshall Aid.

The American démarche was no isolated phenomenon; it has to be seen in a wider context. The policy of maximizing tensions that had characterized the first period of the Cold War until the mid-1970s came to be seen in America as having failed or having been abandoned. The American view now was that European efforts in self-defence, and especially those of the West Germans, must be increased, and with mid-range nuclear weapons. When the armaments lobby wants to increase its sales, political 'cover' for this has to be devised. Such was the second part of the 'NATO double-track decision' (December 1979): to enter into negotiations with the Russians about mid-range missile systems. In order to achieve this, one first had to threaten to introduce *more* of these missiles. Richard Allen said: 'We must create an incentive for the Soviets to negotiate seriously.'[571] This incentive was to be created by the first part of the Double-Track: the installation of mid-range missile systems in Germany!

Four months after the German Bundestag had voted in December 1983 for the installation of mid-range missiles despite countless protests about the deployment of modernized systems that gave the Soviets superiority in nuclear weapons, it was noted that a study which, interestingly, was published by the *Federal Agency for Civic Education* (!) in Bonn, considerably downplayed the apparent superiority of the Soviets. The study stated:

> There are numerous contrasts in media reports of numbers of military units, troop numbers and weapons systems. However, the self-evident manner in which such contrasts are presented to the public as reliable statements about the military capabilities of the potential opponents and appear to be accepted as such by the public is in clear contradiction to the poverty of the methodology behind such statements. This method of presenting purely numerical contrasts without any consideration of other factors such as qualitative indicators of weapons, presentations of total potentials, differences in military strategy and tactics, geostrategic initial conditions, let alone factors such as population numbers, economic power and the state of technological development, open the door to gratuitous and arbitrary comparisons [...] the question of the nuclear threat posed by the Soviet Union should not be answered by [...] comparisons of nuclear weapons systems.

The study comes to the following astounding conclusion: '*It can be emphasized that the conclusion of a Soviet "Grand Design" for military expansion towards and subjugation of Western Europe cannot plausibly be substantiated in empirical terms.*'[572]

Apart from economic interests, can there have been other grounds for the German-American deployment of modernized weapons systems for which admittedly flimsy justifications were advanced? The question leads us to an event that paralleled the visit of the Reaganites to Bonn in September 1981.

In March 1981 Richard Pipes, a member of the US National Security Council, had given in advance of his later appearance in Bonn in autumn a parallel start and warning signal to Moscow which called for a radical change of course in Russian politics. Pipes demanded that 'the Soviet leaders must choose between a peaceful transformation of the communist system in the direction of the western model *or go to war*'.[573]

The two American directives of the year 1981, addressed to Bonn and Moscow must be seen in relation to each other. For they are a clear indication that *in leading western circles at this point it was decided to fulfil a decision made many years earlier: the termination of the Socialist experiment in the East*. As it was not expected that the East would simply comply with this peacefully, it was threatened with war. In order to give the necessary force to this threat Europe had to undergo an arms build-up. This is the more *political* background to the build-up demanded by the USA.

The American call for German reunification, expressed in Bonn, and also the arms build-up in Germany must therefore be seen ultimately in relation to this global political aim of the USA—to bring the Socialist experiment to an end. The agenda for American foreign policy in the early 1980s can be roughly outlined as follows: the *first* and ultimate goal, to which all the others were and are subordinated—the establishment of an 'effective world super government', as Churchill had had in mind. For this, *secondly*, the Socialist experiment in the East was to be terminated. *Thirdly*, in order to show the Russians how serious the West was about this political demand, a formidable arms build-up was to commence in Europe. The second and third aims having been realized more or less simultaneously, the *fourth* step was the reunification of Germany. This would help to realize the *fifth* aim—the advance towards the completion of the unification of Europe, which had become stuck. Only through this would the *sixth* step be possible, described by Churchill as indispensable— the comprehensive establishment of a world super government; or as Colin S. Gray wrote in *Strategic Studies* (1982) 'To claim that the United States, a first class super-power, is the guardian of world order is really to do little more than to state the obvious and the necessary.'

In the 1980s the first four points of the programme were to be realized.

Hardly had the future Bonn team been directed in autumn 1981 to take a shot of 'healthy nationalism', which naturally also implied the approval of the arms build-up, than other noises from the USA became audible, worrying about a future reunification of Germany, which was described as 'destabilizing'.[574] That these concerns had to stem from *the same circles* which had just been urging the Germans on to reunification is due to the fact that at that point in time, German reunification was not at all a serious public issue. When one translates such contradictory state-ments—they belong to political dialectic—which again are to be seen in an inner relation to each other when the political actions of the USA are uncoded, then the meaning is this: from now on, German reunification will be worked for at the same time as the destruction of the Socialist system, but this new Germany is not to become too stable, otherwise there would be the danger that a united Europe with a strong and stable Germany at its centre could pull away from guidance by the global world order ...

Only a few months after the CDU took power, the new Chancellor Helmut Kohl announced in the Bundestag in July 1983, with a following wind from Washington: 'We Germans have not come to terms with the division of our Fatherland. We know from historical experience that the reconstruction of the unity of Germany in peace and freedom and can only be realized in the context of a common European order of peace.'[575] In September (1983) in Vienna US Vice-President George H.W. Bush attacked the Soviet domination of Eastern Europe and emphasized that America rejected the idea of a divided Europe.[576] Enough: from the foregoing any unprejudiced observer could see that the 1980s were to be a decade of global political reorganization.

In February 1989, several months before the dramatic events in the autumn, Zbigniew Brzezinski's book *The Grand Failure—The Birth and Death of Communism in the Twentieth Century* was published.[577] As the publisher's blurb for the 2nd German edition emphasized, the book 'forecast the collapse of Communism in Eastern Europe and Russia'. The book had already been completed in August 1988 and had as its subject, according to the first sentence of the introduction, 'the eventual demise [...] of Communism' [p. 9]. Brzezinski gives a short overview of the historical path taken by the 'the Marxist experiment in Russia', and says:

> It was a strange growth, that transplant of an essentially Western European doctrine, conceived in the public reading-room of the British Museum by an émigré German-Jewish intellectual, to the quasi-oriental despotic tradition of a somewhat remote Euro-Asian empire, with a pamphleteering Russian revolutionary acting as history's surgeon (p.15).

Now a new *Operation* was evidently in process and therefore the 'Marxist Experiment' had to be terminated. Brzezinski wrote his book not as the prophet of coming events—events which surprised most Europeans. He had been National Security Adviser during the Carter era on the same National Security Council to which Allen and Pipes had belonged; that means he had an inside view of the long-range foreign policy plans of the USA. How long-range these plans have been will have become clear in what has already been presented in this chapter.

In his third speech on US policy towards Eastern Europe and on national security, US President George H.W. Bush stated, according to a report in the FAZ (26 May 1989): 'We live in a time when we are witnessing the end of an idea—the final chapter of the Communist experiment.' The use of the expression Marxist or communist *experiment* by Brzezinski and Bush is striking. This is the expression used by C.G. Harrison in 1893 when he spoke of 'experiments in socialism'. The circle had been closed; the experiment transplanted to the East in 1917 *was terminated from within that same Anglo-American stream by the successors of those personalities who had introduced it a hundred years earlier.*

★

A symbolic expression of the 'atlanticization' of western and central Europe in the post-war period is what happened on 8 December 1955—the same year in which the future reunification of Germany was conceived—namely, the adoption by the Ministerial Committee of the Council of Europe of the emblem of the circle of 12 yellow stars on a blue ground. It was explained as follows: 'Against the blue sky of the *western* world, the stars symbolize the peoples of Europe in the form of a circle, the sign of unity.'[578]

The emblem of the Council of Europe was later interpreted in a very different way—as a Christian Marian symbol. And with that we arrive at the subject of the next chapter: the influence of the Roman Catholic Church on the development of Europe in the decades after World War II. This chapter too will be something of a symptomatic and aphoristic sketch.

2. Catholic Impulses on the European Construction Site

The influence of the Catholic Church on the so-called unification of Europe has hardly been weaker than that of the West over the past five decades[*]. The Council of Europe emblem adopted in 1955 which, as the symbol of the European Community [EC] since 1986 and then of the European Union [EU] since 1993, has appeared on countless flags, stickers, and posters, betrays not only a western but also a Catholic interest in gaining influence on the course of developments in Europe. In December 1989, under the title 'A Certain 8 December', the following could be read in the magazine *Forum*, an official Council of Europe publication, about the decision to adopt the Council of Europe emblem in 1955:

> A final, amusing detail rounds off the interesting history of the European flag: the official documents give different dates for the final decision. In December 1955 the Ministers' representatives assembled in Paris and were, amongst other things, to make the final decision on the flag. Three days were set aside for the work, and as is normal, the prepared texts bore the date of the last day (9 December). Unusually, the meeting ended after only 48 hours, so the decision about the flag was made on 8 December. In some documents, however, one can find the wrong date of 9 December 1955.

Apparently, a certain value is placed on the coincidence of the 8 December date of this decision, but why?

Let us follow the report a little further:

> It was only a few months before the flag was seen for the first time on an official building. Since 21 October 1956 it has adorned the image of Mary in Strasbourg Cathedral. The glass windows in the apse had been blown out in 1944 by a bomb. The Council of Europe decided to make a gift to France of a composition by Max Ingrand for the reinstallation of the windows. It represents the vision from the twelfth chapter of the Book of Revelation: '*And there appeared a great wonder in heaven, a woman clothed with the sun, and the moon under her feet, and upon her head a crown of twelve stars.*' [Emphasis THM]

The official report therefore first lays great emphasis on a certain 8 December and then on the association of the Council of Europe emblem with the decorative image in Strasbourg Cathedral of the Virgin from the Apocalypse with her head ringed by twelve stars. Is this association only coincidental? Or are we confronted in the starry banner of the Council of Europe with a consciously chosen *Marian* symbol?

---

[*] I.e. until the mid 1990s—*transl.*

Bruno Bernhard Ziegler, author of the booklet *Klaus von Flüe—der Heilige für unsere Zeit* [Nicholas of Flüe—The Saint For Our Time][579] writes in connection with the Council of Europe symbol and the EC:

> It was Christian statesmen such as de Gasperi (Italy), Schuman (France) and Adenauer (Germany) who took the first steps towards reconciliation and friendship. Adenauer repeatedly declared his appreciation of the politics of the holy Bro. Klaus at Nicholas' grave. Since that time the centuries-old self-mutilation of Europe has given way to the will for unity. When the optimism of the hopeful beginnings soon began to wear thin and became limited to technical and economic collaboration, when the egoisms of the different European states opposed and confronted the cause of political unity, it only needed a spark to help achieve a breakthrough of the idea expressed in the flag chosen by the Council of Europe with its twelve stars and blue ground. A biblical, Marian symbol (accepted even by the Turks!) floats above Europe. It wishes to say: 'that it is expected of Christians at this site where the future is under construction that they will commit themselves fully to the work'—such were the declarations that the bishops of Belgium were the first to make on 23 November 1976 in their 'New Impulses for Europe'.

This makes the connections between the EU symbol (which in the meantime has been given the titular varnish of *common symbol of Europe*) and certain 'new impulses for Europe' (though new they certainly are not!) already somewhat clearer.

But 8 December? Did this so conspicuously emphasized *datum* have anything to do with the 'new impulses for Europe'? In fact: 8 December is the date of the Church's celebration of the Feast Day of the Immaculate Conception of Mary. In 1854 Pope Pius IX, in the belief that he had Mary entirely on his side, proclaimed her conception to be 'immaculate' and announced this to be a new dogma of the Catholic Church. This was a prologue for the papal infallibility of the same Pope, which he then declared in Rome at the First Vatican Council on 8 December 1869, Ludwig Polzer's birthday. This therefore is the perspective which opens from the symbol of the twelve stars *towards the South* . . .

It is noteworthy in passing that in the report about the decision to adopt the symbol, the background to this significant Church holy day went unremarked. Evidently, it was not wanted that those who prefer to keep to the more worldly and western side, the reverse side of the coin, should come too close . . .

Numerous events between 1948 and 1989 demonstrate that, in fact, not only in the EU symbol but also in the worldly reality of western and ecclesiastical EU-politics, we have to do with two sides of *one* coin. And just as two sides of one coin are unable to roll in different directions, so these numerous symptomatic events reveal that the western and ecclesiastical impulses were in no sense working only for themselves or independently from one another in this game.

★

While Richard Coudenhove-Kalergi was holding friendly conversations with Truman and Marshall in America at the beginning of 1948, his new opponent Duncan Sandys, Churchill's son-in-law, was seeking the advice and support of the Holy See. At the end of January he had a private audience with Pius XII. The Pontiff showed a lively interest in the European cause and promised 'to do whatever he could to guarantee for the efforts of the European Movement in various countries the benevolent support of the Catholic Church.'[580] A few months later, Pius sent a personal representative to Europa Congress in The Hague, which took place in May. He read out a declaration on behalf of the Pope which recognized and lauded the peace-making strivings towards European unification.

In October of the same year General Marshall also spent some time in Rome in order to seek advice in connection with the Berlin crisis. He had in mind mediation by the Vatican.

It should perhaps be recalled at this point that this Pontiff, as State Secretary Pacelli, had also had earlier occasion to engage in mediation in Germany: he signed the *Reichskonkordat* with Hitler on 20 July 1933. According to William L. Shirer, this had had the following effect: '... coming as it did at a moment when the first excesses of the new regime in Germany had provoked world-wide revulsion, the concordat undoubtedly lent the Hitler government much badly needed prestige'.[581]

On 13 March, two weeks after the Reichstag Fire, Pius XI, under whom Pacelli then served, had praised Hitler 'in open consistory in the presence of representatives of other nations as the first statesman to join him in open disavowal of Bolshevism'. The German bishops later reminded Hitler that Pius XI 'had been the first sovereign to extend to you the handclasp of trust'.

★

With 'deep joy' Pius XII greeted Catholic statesmen in March 1957—among them Konrad Adenauer—and delegates from various European governments who were visiting him in the Vatican on the day before the signing of the *Treaty of Rome*. Their work on the EEC Treaty could therefore be concluded the following day, having received a blessed imprimateur... According to *Osservatore Romano*, the Vatican praised the conclusion of the EEC Treaty as 'the most important and meaningful political event in the recent history of the Eternal City'.[582] And when Robert Schuman, who was then President of the European Movement, held a Europa Congress in Rome shortly afterwards, the Pope, prior to the gathering, emphasized that 'the new community' could also spread beyond the economic sphere 'to realms which foster spiritual and moral values'.[583]

In saying this, the Pope was expressing Rome's central interest in the 'new community': to provide it with that spirituality which alone would be able to place an economic or political and economic community on a really durable foundation. The Church was to permeate the European Community with its spirituality.

Against the background of 8 December 1854, 1869 and 1955, that could naturally only be a dogmatic, authoritative kind of faith-based spirituality, thus, one which, a priori, if it wants to preserve its own life, must combat every form of individual spirituality on *epistemological* grounds. Although this form of authoritarian, dogmatic spirituality can never satisfy the need of the modern human being for true autonomy in his own thinking, allegiance nevertheless continued to be rendered to it by all Euro-Catholics, from Robert Schuman to Otto von Habsburg, the son of the last Austrian Emperor. Thus in his book *Zurück zur Mitte* [Back to the Middle], published in 1991, Otto von Habsburg, President of the Pan-Europa Union since the death of Coudenhove in 1972, declared: 'If we do not find the way back to faith, Europe will not survive. Pope John Paul II made the appeal to our Continent at the Europa celebration at Santiago de Compostela (in 1989): "Find again the way to your self!" '[584] Or, in plain speaking: Back to the bosom of the Church—then all will go well ... This Europa celebration in Santiago de Compostela had had a prologue in 1982, that year which was so important for the Vatican, when John Paul II had called for the evangelization of Europe from Santiago.

But the Vatican was naturally not satisfied with pious hopes or well-wishing recommendations. It was active not only on the spiritual plane but also pursued blatant political goals, as it had done forever and a day. The political plane was also the forum where it could best combine with the economically-oriented statesmen of the West in relation to the form of the coming Europe—at the beginning of the 1980s, which, as we saw in the previous chapter, was decisive in this regard. Seven years before the turning point of 1989, one day in June 1982, the Polish Pope John Paul II received for the first time the American President Ronald Reagan in the Vatican Library. Both had survived assassinations in 1981 and were agreed that communism was a real plague on mankind. According to Reagan, he and the Pope both felt that Yalta and the resulting division of Europe and domination of Eastern Europe by the Communists had been 'a great mistake'.[585] One of the first acts of the Reagan administration had been to recognize the Vatican as a State and 'to make it an ally'.[586] In December 1981, under pressure from Moscow, martial law had been declared in Poland; in October the prohibition of the Solidarnosc [Solidarity] movement would follow.

The 1982 meeting between Reagan and the Pope lasted exactly an hour and took place on 7 June, a Monday; it would be the beginning not only of a new political week but of an entire seven-year period in world politics.

Two years after the fait accompli of the turning point of 1989, one could finally inform oneself fully about that earlier meeting between President and Pope in 1982, the goals and results of which had been veiled in silence. Reagan had been accompanied by, amongst others, Secretary of State Alexander Haig and National Security Adviser William Clark. In the foreground of the various conversations in Rome, in which Cardinal Casaroli and Archbishop Silvestrini also participated, was the Israeli invasion of Lebanon. But in the background, and unknown then to the media, much weightier matters were in train. In *Time* magazine (Feb. 1992) Carl Bernstein authored an important report titled 'The Holy Alliance', which began with the words: 'Both the Pope and the President were convinced that Poland could be broken out of the Soviet orbit if the Vatican and the U.S. committed their resources to destabilizing the Polish government and keeping the outlawed Solidarity movement alive after the declaration of martial law in 1981.'

Reagan and the Pope agreed to undertake 'a clandestine campaign to hasten the dissolution of the communist empire'. Nothing less than that. Richard Allen, Reagan's first National Security Adviser, whom we have encountered already in relation to his appearance in Bonn in September of the previous year, said: 'This was one of the great secret alliances of all time.'

It is noteworthy that the most important operators and middlemen in this secret campaign were, according to Bernstein, 'devoted Roman Catholics': CIA chief William Casey, Richard Allen, William Clark, Al Haig, and Vernon Walters, US ambassador to the Holy See. Walters functioned as the main bearer of news between Rome and Washington, whereby each of his stays in Rome 'did not need to be known about'. Among those who played an important advisory role in the affair was the Polish-born and likewise devoted Catholic Zbigniew Brzezinski, who was also mentioned in the previous chapter. Finally, among many other people not mentioned here, there was also Richard Pipes, through whom Moscow had been given the signal for the radical change of course in March 1981. Pipes too was originally from Poland and was then heading the Eastern Europe and Russia desks at the National Security Council. These far-reaching convergences between physical and religious 'homelands' (Poland or the Catholic Church) doubtless made the unusual campaign of cooperation to end the Socialist experiment much easier.

We shall here refer to a statement by Rudolf Steiner which is of great relevance with regard to what has been mentioned thus far in this chapter. Steiner said on 20 January 1921 (GA 338):

> With regard to world events today, the Church feels that it is still in a position to be able to achieve a real augmentation of its power. It was well aware that leaning on ruling dynasties for support was no longer going to be of much help [...] Against these, the Catholic Church will make use of the strivings of the broad masses of the people in order to increase its power. The Catholic Church makes use of everything it has available to it, and is therefore now also using in its grand world political strategy, which sometimes has a genial tendency to it—genial in the sense that mankind is to become more and more bound by Rome's fetters—it uses something like the nationalizing of the Polish clergy; *and Poland will become an essential part of the game that the Catholic Church is playing.* [Emphasis THM]

Three weeks before his meeting with the Pope in Rome, Reagan signed a secret NSC decision directive. The main aim set out in this document was 'to destabilize the Polish government through covert operations involving propaganda and organizational aid to Solidarity; the promotion of human rights, particularly those related to the right of worship and the Catholic Church; economic pressure; and diplomatic isolation of the communist regime'. A five-part strategy was worked out to achieve these goals in order to 'bring about the collapse of the Soviet Union' and 'to fray ... the ties that bound the U.S.S.R. to its client states in the Warsaw Pact and force ... reform inside the Soviet empire'. One of the goals was the undermining of the trans-Siberian pipeline project, on which the Russians had set great economic hopes; then there was the insane expansion of the 'Star Wars' missile defence system, which was aimed at forcing the Soviets into ruinous competition in defence expenditures.

In the following years technological hardware such as computers, fax machines, cameras, printing presses etc. were poured into underground networks in Poland, while the banned Solidarnosc trade union was financially supported by CIA money and secret Vatican accounts. These operations were so cleverly disguised that the leading members of Solidarnosc were never aware of the real extent of the support they were getting from the Vatican and Washington.

According to Bernstein, 'working outward from Poland, the same kind of resistance was organized in the other communist countries of Europe'.

As Archbishop Pio Laghi, papal nuncio in Washington who arranged Vernon Walters' visits to the Pope, remarked on the difficult manoeuvres of that time: 'It was a very complex situation ... how to insist on human rights, on religious freedom, and keep Solidarity alive without provoking the communist authorities further. But I told Vernon, "*Listen to the Holy Father. We have 2,000 years' experience at this.*"' [Emphasis THM]

★

When one reflects that the Polish Pope was *the* ideal helper for Washington in bringing about the termination of the Socialist experiment in the East; that this termination had already most likely been decided on during the Carter era, when the man with the power of the National Security Adviser had been the 'devout Catholic' and Pole Zbigniew Brzezinski—then one can hardly avoid the very specific question: Was the murder of John Paul II's predecessor also perhaps related to the planned reorganization of the Socialist East? For *if* this reorganization was already on the US political agenda during the Carter-Brzezinski era, then it must have become immediately clear to the agenda planners after the election of Pope John Paul I that this was *not* the man to participate in conversations with Washington and in covert political operations in Eastern Europe using secret Vatican accounts.

★

The plans in Washington and Rome for the reorganization of the East were responded to by the new man in Russia from 1985, Mikhail Gorbachev, with an astonishing swiftness. Even before his appointment as the new General Secretary in March 1985, he paid a visit to the West and visited Margaret Thatcher in Britain. She got to know him as a man whose 'personality could not have been more different from the wooden ventriloquism of the average Soviet apparatchik', as the British Prime Minister wrote in her memoirs. 'He smiled, laughed, used his hands for emphasis, modulated his voice, followed his argument through and was a sharp debater.'[587]

Gorbachev was very well-informed about the West. He knew Churchill's Fulton speech, in which the 'Iron Curtain' had been spoken of for the first time and knew all about Anglo-American world order intentions. Certainly, there were tough conversations at Chequers, the

Prime Minster's official country residence, about the American Strategic Defence Initiative (Star Wars) programme, which Gorbachev strongly criticized, but after his departure, Thatcher later wrote of Gorbachev: 'This was a man with whom I could do business.'[588]

Soon after his first meeting with President Reagan in Geneva in November 1985, where despite their differences, 'a good personal relationship [had] developed' between the two statesmen, Gorbachev announced the new course of 'Perestroika' and 'Glasnost' at the 27th Party Conference.

How much insight did Gorbachev have into the very real, and already ongoing, western efforts in Poland to demolish the 'Building of Socialism' and the western intentions for the reunification of Germany and Europe? The question admits of no easy answer. If he had knowledge of western plans as a whole, he was at any rate not in agreement with every part, for in September 1989 he declared that the Soviet Union was not in favour of German reunification. When Gorbachev was asked in May 1988 in the course of an interview with the Washington Post why he was so convinced that his reform programme would be crowned with success while the reform proposals of his predecessors had always ended in fiasco, he gave an interesting answer:

> Hmm, you have asked the most important question, to which our Soviet people want an answer as much, I believe, as the Americans, since the destiny of both our peoples and countries has brought us to the point where, whether we like it or not, we must learn to work and live together. *The natural precondition for this, however, is that we know each other, above all that we know our plans. They are indeed grandiose.*[589]

This statement is an indication that Gorbachev was at that point in time aware of the full extent of the plans and activities of Washington and Rome that were aimed at the termination of the Socialist order in the East and approved of them in the main, even if when back in Russia, he had to take account of the apparatchiks and could not just drop the established form of Socialism. Thus he will have drawn part of his confidence in the victory of his *perestroika* from the still well-disguised American and papal undermining operations that were going on in the East. For Reagan, despite his various disagreements with the Russians in negotiations over armaments, Mikhail Gorbachev was, in connection with the 'demolition plans', naturally the most important person besides Pope John Paul II. In December, the President of the USA even asked Thatcher whether she thought that at his next meeting with Gorbachev 'he should try to get on first-name terms with the Soviet leader'.[590]

★

The French President François Mitterand, convinced of Gorbachev's will for reform, remarked to Margaret Thatcher in spring 1987 that Gorbachev was of the view that: *'when you change the form, you are on the way to changing the substance'*.[591] This remark can be seen as an acknowledgement of two fundamental elements of aristotelian philosophy in the sphere of practical politics: form and matter (substance), whereby 'matter' is by no means only to be limited to physical-mineral matter. They are present in everything, and 'form' always plays the decisive role.

While the substance of thinking and feeling of people in the Soviet empire for 70 years had been shaped and ruled by the form of socialist, Leninist ideology, now a change of form was taking place. 'Perestroika' means re-shaping, re-forming: within a few years the substance of the thinking and feeling of the East was brought under the new domination of another ideological form originating in the West—that of market economy and so-called democracy.

President Truman would have recognized the distant goal about to be realized in 1989 in that he was supposed to have once said decades earlier: 'The whole world should adopt the American system ... The American system can survive in America only if it becomes a world system.'[592] Even if these words were not actually said by Truman—they perfectly express the way of thinking of the US power elite.

Whether *this* reshaping of the East that was then underway through the ideology of the West was exactly what Gorbachev was striving for may be doubted; that this ideology represented a truly higher form than that of socialism *must* be doubted. For self-evidently, during the de-formation of the socialist countries, a completely different 'form' could have made its appearance in place of the defunct socialism, rather than that of the market economy of the West and the spiritual dogmatism of the South: namely, the form of the threefolding of the social organism.

The following chapter will illustrate how in 1989, the year of the turning point, the chance for a really new contemporary form of society blazed up for an instant and was briefly visible here and there, only to disappear or be covered over again just as quickly. An overview of the present conditions in the former Soviet empire will, however, have to lead to the question of whether the substance of the thinking, feeling and willing of the people who used to live in the former socialist East has developed *to their benefit* as a result of the 'form' since imported from the West or whether that substance is merely supposed to serve to uphold a global system that can only survive *when it becomes the system of the whole world*.

But in saying this, we have got ahead of ourselves somewhat. In conclusion, let us cast a glance briefly back to the time of decision in 1989, which led to the actual turning point in the second half of the year. Are *the traces of Rome* to be found here too, which we have sought to posit in this chapter as the main point of attention? Indeed they are.

Otto von Habsburg*, the son of Emperor Karl, who is of the conviction that Europe can only fulfil its task with the help of a strengthened Catholic element, specifically emphasizes in his above-mentioned book *Zurück zur Mitte* that the opening of the Iron Curtain—the prologue to the so-called reunification of Germany, which was in turn the prologue to the so-called reunification of Europe—was linked in no small measure with the activity of the Pan-Europa Union of which he is the President. 'Those who celebrate the rebirth of Europe or the unity of Germany should not forget that at the beginning [of the process] was the Pan-Europa Picnic on 19 August 1989 on the Austrian/Hungarian border at Sopron/Ödenburg,' wrote the friend and successor of Count Coudenhove-Kalergi. Lukács Szabó, a Hungarian Opposition politician at the time had, according to Habsburg, proposed 'the holding of a border-crossing festival to overcome the Iron Curtain [...] The resulting action was carried out with the help of the Pan-Europa Union and the Democratic Forum.'[593] The consequences of this picnic made history: 661 Germans from Middle Germany [the GDR] were able to escape to Austria through an open door by cutting through the barbed wire. The rest is history... And with regard to the role of form and substance in the processes that followed in the course of the entire revolution: the yearnings for liberation in the East formed events much less than is often assumed; they were to a much greater degree the necessary substance which was forced to accept a new form of servitude in accordance with the wishes of the leading strategists of European reconstruction...

In view of the numerous cases of the demonstrable, at least co-determinant influence exercised by Catholic circles in the re-shaping of European and therefore also global affairs, much more has to be seen in the Catholic moulding or at least usurpation of the EC symbol described at the outset than merely an external playing around with dates and biblical motifs. Symptomatic events and facts such as have been sketched out here can show to every alert contemporary how the European

---

* He died in 2011, three years after the publication of the 2nd German edition of this book—*transl.*

'construction site of the future' has for a long time witnessed the energetic actions of groups that desire to put the stamp of their centralizing Catholic spirituality on the whole of Europe. At the same time, it should have become clear how well these intentions harmonized with certain long-range plans from the West.

3. The Struggle for the Fruits of the 'Wende' [Turning Point] of 1989

An editorial in *Die Zeit* shows how little Germans in 1987 suspected what had been proceeding at full tilt since the 'Holy Alliance' of 1982—the termination of the Socialist experiment, the reunification of Germany etc. In May 1987 Theo Sommer warned patriotic countrymen not to harbour illusions about reunification of the two Germanys any time soon:

> No one can rate the probability of reunification in the foreseeable future very highly; also, what for us would be a dream would, for most of our neighbours, be a nightmare [. . .] More important than the creation of unity must be the easing of the consequences of division. [. . .] We shall not even manage *that* with bigoted solo efforts, let alone reunification.[594]

No one? Those in informed circles in Washington and Rome would have spoken differently at that time . . .

While President Bush was speaking in May of 'the last chapter of the communist experiment'[595] a process in which he had been very personally involved, in the still solitary West Germany there was much discussion of the ideas of a book from the GDR which could not be published on the other side of the Iron Curtain. It bore the heretical title *Der vormundschaftliche Staat* [The Guardian State] with the perhaps even sharper subtitle *Vom Versagen des real existierenden Sozialismus* [The Denial of Real, Existing Socialism].[596] Rolf Henrich, the author, wanted his book 'to stimulate discussion'[597] and for a while it even succeeded. Even *Der Spiegel* showed an unusual interest.[598] The 45-year-old lawyer was a long-term member of the Socialist Unity Party (SED) and was convinced of the superiority of socialist principles to those of the West. He considered the building of the wall in 1961 to have been an absolute ideological necessity, and only the invasion of Czechoslovakia by Russian troops in 1968 had stirred in him the first doubts about the perfection of socialism. With the publication of his book in the West he showed courage as he faced the probability of oppressive measures from his own government. Henrich drew the reader's attention to 'three modern thinkers to whom [he felt] obliged to give special thanks': Rudolf Steiner, Jürgen Habermas and Rudolf Bahro. After an unsparing analysis of the betrayal of the socialist system, the book calls for a radical reorganization of society according to the ideas of social threefolding as they had been developed along broad lines by Rudolf Steiner in 1917. Henrich writes:

> When the socialist state is withdrawn in this way from the spiritual life and from the economy as a force that differs from them in its nature, then the social organism in these two members can step by step create their own forms of self-management. The result will be the emergence of a three-foldness in the three areas that have become autonomous vis-à-vis each other: the cultural life—economy—state. Much in the thinking of the Enlightenment and of Marxism already points to this idea of threefolding. It acquired its most thorough elaboration by Rudolf Steiner at the beginning of this century.[599]

A notable symptom: in the spring air of the year of the Wende [literally, 'change', 'turn'], when the Theo Sommers of the nation still held German reunification to be a utopia for the next millennium and only those in the Holy Alliance were aware of how soon the Iron Curtain was due to be raised, in this period, when the planned reorganization was, as it were, hanging in the air, then the call from 1917 was sounded again. But just as in 1917, events transpired in such a way that this call was soon drowned out—this time by the words of West German Chancellor Helmut Kohl that were so powerfully exported to the East and after a short time, the call of 1917 faded without effect. Certainly, in the first phase of the Wende in Germany, as in the October marches in Leipzig, there was a call for a third way that might find an alternative between socialism and capitalism, there was a demand for 'threefolding' when the call was still *'Wir sind das Volk'* [We are the people].

As soon as the new call sounded out in the second phase—'Wir sind *ein* Volk' [We are *one* people], the turning point had been passed and the chances of a true turning point, a real change for the better, to something really new, fell away and within a year were to be completely spent.

When on 9 November 1989, to the speechless astonishment of the whole world, the unthinkable happened and the Wall fell, it was like the gift of a great Christmastime for Germany and the whole of humanity. And while thousands honourably celebrated this gift, the strategists of reunification hastened on. Now there was no time to lose. The free space which had opened up and allowed millions to embrace each other, had to be dealt with quickly in order to erect the building of German and European unity. There were still dangerous moments. Many members of the Holy Alliance were aware of the danger: it was still called 'three-folding of the social organism'. John Paul II had learned enough of Steiner's Anthroposophy[600] to know what there was to fear in it from the Church's perspective. Henrich, many banners in Leipzig and numerous discussions in the 'New Forum' and then at the 'Round Table' showed only too clearly that in the new vacuum of values Steiner's social ideas were met with great interest here and there. If something had been able to bring down with one blow the American and Roman efforts of the past seven years, it was *the idea of 1917*. At that time the experiment in the East had been presented as an unhealthy alternative to threefolding. Was threefolding to be allowed to have an influence now when the experiment was being terminated? Free spiritual life: a deadly seed for Catholicism; a world economy freed from national interests: a gauntlet thrown against the West. And a political life in Steiner's sense? That would lead to the destruction of the gear levers of political power. Was one to have striven for seven years to achieve a goal through complex and clandestine operations only to see, as the goal was about to be secured, 'victory' gained by someone else? Germany was to be allowed no space in which to take to the idea of 1917. But how *could* it have secured and safeguarded this free space in such a short time? From what revolutionary powers of motivation? 'The revolution that was gifted', people will perhaps call it one day; it was so mild, because it was allowed to take place.[601]

Thus 1989 became a second 1917 but with reversed symptoms: then the experiment in the East was being set up, now it was being dismantled; then the nations of Europe were being fragmented and torn apart, now they were to be shoved together into a 'unity' which would make them easier to steer, within the one Europe, within the great, all-encompassing New World Order... Exactly 66 years after the fading of Rudolf Steiner's activities on behalf of threefolding and the start of Coudenhove's Pan-Europa delusion that obscured them.

Reagan's successor, George H.W. Bush, assumed office in January 1989 and took over the final phase of the termination of the experiment; a communication was made from the Soviet side that 'there would be no interventions made in case of [...] reformist changes in Eastern Europe'.[602] And already in the summer of 1989, thus before the first great hole was made in the Iron Curtain at Sopron, 'there was an order from Moscow that the Red Army, no matter what happened in the GDR, was to remain in its barracks', as Gorbachev confirmed.[603]

How could he have acted otherwise? He did what was human and reasonable, which will do him eternal honour; he spared the lives of many. That was human, for what happened would have happened anyway, even if not so gently; that was reasonable. Gorbachev knew the Holy Alliance plan and had broadly gone along with it.

Therefore all the threefolders from the West came too late, who just a short time before had shared the view of Sommers, like most other contemporaries, in thinking virtually impossible what had already become *reality* since 1982. One brings in vain an idea that is right in itself onto a terrain occupied by opponents who have been preparing to deal with this righteous idea for years. One must know the terrain on which one wants to operate. Only those can do this who have not neglected to familiarize themselves with the long-range plans which are a result of the politics of the South and the West as ice is a result of cold. Nothing else can melt this ice but the sun of knowledge.

Not every man needed to be a fully conscious opponent of the idea of 1917 who was driven by other strivings; by streams that had already been in existence for a much longer time and which already had well-formed channels in which they flowed. Had there not been for a long time already a spiritual life there of the most all-embracing character— 'catholic' means simply 'universal'—taking its start from the greatest turning point of all times? In the form which it had finally assumed since the Counter-Reformation, this spiritual life surged so mightily back and forth through the Brandenburg Gate in the year of change 1989 that one who did not know where else he could find a spiritual standpoint was swept away. Only those few who had abandoned all searching for the spirit, those indifferent to the spirit, could preserve a relatively firm footing on the basis of what was useful and feasible. Why bother with a 'free' spiritual life when one could let oneself be gently uplifted to new soul heights by the warm waves of the faith of Rome that were uniting East and West...?

At any rate, Rome in the 1980s, mindful of what was to come at the end of the '80s or at least at the end of the century, directed its energies not only at the renewal of German spiritual life but at that of the entire continent. In response to a call from the Council of Europe, repairs were carried out on Baroque-era streets in Sicily and Malta that led to particularly important monuments from the time of the Counter-Reformation. The growing united Europe was to be bound into the cultural life that had already flowed for so long and so powerfully towards it... In 1988 the Council of Europe launched the 'Project of a Path of Culture with Baroque flourishes'. Domenico Ronconi, who designed the Council's Project of the Path of Culture, tells us in the magazine *Forum* in December 1989:

> We were on the lookout for a theme with which the 25 states of the Council for Cultural Co-operation could identify in some form, and *we wanted to base ourselves on a cultural phenomenon which in its time, long before there was a European unity, already represented something like a European unity.*[604]

One is keen to know what phenomenon Ronconi had in mind here. He says: 'The first project we decided on was the re-enlivening of the path of St James of Compostella [sic]. Today it is well underway.' Already on 9 November 1982 Pope John Paul II had called for the unification of Europe under the umbrella of Roman Catholic Christian values, seven years before the opening of the Berlin Wall, in the preparation for which, as we have seen, the Vatican played no small part. And in the year of the Wende 1989, another Europe celebration was organized by the Church in Santiago de Compostela, at which John Paul II again called for 'the re-evangelization of pagan Europe'.[605]

In the Middle Ages, especially in the time of the Crusades, when pilgrims to Jerusalem were more and more in danger, Santiago was, along with Canterbury, the most important destination for pilgrims concerned for a true Christian renewal at that time.

In an unsigned article in the same issue of *Forum*, we learn more about the Santiago-related endeavours of the Euro-Catholics:

> With the re-juvenation of the St James' Path (the Camino) to Compostela, the Council of Europe wants above all to raise its cultural significance, without wanting to detract from its religious content. This pilgrim route, which millions of Europeans from all over the Continent took in the past in order to gather at the grave of the martyr apostle St James, is seen as one of the first important steps on the path to a European identity. On the journey, there was a mixing of different peoples and a very special kind of architectural infrastructure: hospices, old people's homes, hospitals, monasteries etc., and all bore the scallop of St James as their emblem. There are still many traces of this and they only need to be reconnected with each other again in order to reawaken them to new life. The project, which is so successfully supported today by the member states, consists of finding these traces, marking them with a special symbol, devising a plan for the restoration of the heritage and providing promotional and instructional materials for tourists.[606]

Thus before and during the time of the Wende, recourse was had again to the spiritual life of the age of faith and of spiritual authority in order to make use of faith and authority for the cultural unification of the emerging collective Europe. Through such manoeuvres, the efforts of those true contemporaries who were fighting for a spirituality of *knowledge* and a *free, individual* spiritual life on the firm foundation of the idea of 1917 were, in advance, forced under water, so to speak, and kept there. But what is today under water will, when the times really call for it, be able to rise anew out of the waves of decadence.

★

To the complex of symptoms relating to the reappearance of the idea of 1917 in the year 1989 and the efforts to renew European cultural life made by the Ecclesia Romana, a third 'factual relationship' can be adduced—that relating to the murder of Alfred Herrhausen, CEO of Deutsche Bank, on 30 November 1989. We say 'factual relationship' because this assassination, which was blamed on the Red Army Faction (RAF), is in fact related to central elements in the current international policy of the USA. How far this policy runs on along a perfectly straight line of the main impulse of the Testament of Peter the Great will be discussed in the following chapter.

Herrhausen, who had become co-chairman for the Board of Deutsche Bank in 1985, had a high, far-reaching aim in mind for his bank: it was to lead West Germany's bid to become a 'global player'. Everything seemed to develop in this direction in the following years. He also proposed to his international, especially American, competitors that the financial institutions of the advanced countries should deal with the enormous debts of developing nations by a massive programme of debt forgiveness. This was an open provocation for the American banks.[607] For while over 70 per cent of Deutsche Bank's credit was guaranteed by its reserves, in the case of American banks the figure was more in the region of a maximum 30 per cent. It was therefore understandable that the American-dominated credit institutions such as the World Bank and the IMF were not exactly delighted by Herrhausen's attempt to move the debt crisis forward. After the fall of the Berlin Wall, Herrhausen fostered *European* plans for the East of the continent. The IMF and the World Bank should in his view keep away from Eastern Europe. Gerhard Wisnewski, one of the authors of the book *Das RAF Phantom*[608] writes: 'The boss of Deutsche Bank imagined a European instrument for the tasks in the East that would gradually develop a stable economic system out of the ramshackle "people's economies" of Poland, Russia and the others.' He was also thinking of the creation of a European, perhaps Polish, development bank in Eastern Europe. And when in November 1989 he signed the contract to buy the great English banking house *Morgan Grenfall*, this also signified that Herrhausen had become a competitor to be taken seriously.

Against this background, it will not be difficult to understand that Alfred Herrhausen's intentions were at cross purposes with certain long-range western aims for the former Socialist East in the post-Wende era. In the circles which had planned and executed the termination of the Socialist experiment were people who had their own ideas about what was supposed to happen in the East after the Wende. The CIA Director

William Webster, for example, on 19 September 1989 at the World Affairs Council in Los Angeles said:

> When the President visited Europe in spring, he pointed out that a historical change was underway. The trend is away from an East-West military confrontation to a global emphasis on economic questions. Economic questions are already a key area of our foreign policy and our tasks relating to national security. There is a multitude of economic questions which directly affect our security [. . .] Among these are Third World debt, trade balances and rapid technological developments.[609]

The authors of *Das RAF Phantom* make the following observation on Webster's statement:

> These statements signify nothing other than that after the end of the Cold War, the USA is beginning to see its economic competitors increasingly as enemies. Webster deliberately and explicitly uses the formula several times that national security can be affected by economic issues. This is not just any formulation, but the statement of a case of—military—defence. That national security is affected is, moreover, the key indicator for the engagement of the CIA.[610]

Herrhausen's alternative to the American credit and interest policy for the developing countries had from this perspective become a matter of the national security of the USA! From a Pentagon paper that became known in 1992 can be seen how seriously American directives were intended to be. According to this paper, the first aim had to be,

> to prevent the re-emergence of a new rival. This is a dominant consideration underlying the new regional defense strategy and requires that we endeavor to prevent any hostile power from dominating a region whose resources would, under consolidated control, be sufficient to generate global power. These regions include Western Europe, East Asia, the territory of the former Soviet Union, and Southwest Asia ... we must maintain the mechanisms for deterring potential competitors from even aspiring to a larger regional or global role.[611]

The magazine specifically quoted US veteran strategist Henry Kissinger: 'Even if there seems to be no European power hostile to the USA today, the mere beginning of some kind of hegemonic behaviour in that region would immediately be perceived by the USA.'[612] There was such a beginning made in the autumn of 1989 and that it was perceived as such is evident from the murder of Herrhausen.

Fletcher Prouty, Oliver Stone's adviser for his Kennedy-movie *JFK*, who in the 1960s served as an Airforce Colonel for Special Operations and who helped to uncover important aspects of the background to the assassination of President Kennedy, said the following in the summer of 1992 about the murder of Herrhausen:

> His loss at this time ... and the startling nature of his loss are without question ... for our day ... the equal of the loss of President John F. Kennedy in 1963. Considering the time ... the enormous train of events taking place in the Soviet Union, in Eastern Europe and particularly in East Germany ... the murder of Herrhausen is an act of enormous significance. It can not be, and must not be swept under the rug as just 'another act of terrorism'. True terrorists do not murder Bank presidents without some special reason. Most terrorists are actually the paid pawns, and 'mechanics' of great power centers. *Some major power center wanted the Chairman of Deutsche Bank removed on that day, in that manner for some reason, and as a lesson to others. There has to be a great message in the act of his death.*[613]

The US message to the Middle Europeans can be summed up as follows: Those who have not sown the seeds can hope for nothing from the harvest.

Herrhausen's murder was planned and then executed with the greatest precision. Yet the preparations for the assassination were carried out, as it were, under the eyes of his bodyguards who were obliged to protect him, and the Federal Police Department's investigation of the case on the assumption that it was the work of the RAF [Red Army Faction] was so dilettantish and full of contradictions that any unprejudiced observer of the circumstances, the background and the details of the assassination would have had to doubt not only the ability but almost still more the willingness of the perpetrator to commit the offence. The greater the effort to attribute the murder of Germany's most important banker at the time of the Wende to an action by the RAF,[614] the more details emerge which argue rather that the head of *Deutsche Bank* was not the victim of some anti-capitalist terrorists but of his own—in relation to existing US interests—'hegemonic hostile behaviour', to borrow Henry Kissinger's words.

The policy of Herrhausen's successor at Deutsche Bank took a completely different direction from the goals of his murdered former boss. The bank was no longer interested either in forgiving the debt of developing countries nor in playing a leading role in rebuilding the economies of Eastern Europe. The 'message' had been understood.

★

And so in 1989, the very year of the Wende, the turning point, many background tendencies of those power circles which had been involved in the termination of the Socialist experiment revealed themselves with particular clarity. For the Catholic Church, 1989 was a year in which it experienced a powerful upsurge in impetus, which can perhaps only be compared with the wave of evangelization at the time of the Counter-Reformation. From every point in Europe pilgrim routes would soon be leading to Santiago . . .

The international economic planners in the West could hardly wait after the Wende until they could feel the market economy they had pegged out for the New World of Eastern Europe under their feet. There would be no Herrhausen to give them problems in that New World. The sowing had been done secretly in a Holy Alliance; at harvest-time one showed quite openly what one wanted to have in the evening in one's own barn.

And the idea of 1917? It will resurrect for the second time when there are enough people who not only see something righteous in it but who can also see through the aggressive tactics employed against this righteousness. And this fight, in which Washington and Rome—considered here as the embodiments of counterforces against everything that is contemporary in a true sense—join hands with each other, is still going on today along the frontline that was drawn by the Testament of Peter the Great.

4. The Modern Relevance of the Testament of Peter the Great

We shall at this point take a look at some aspects of the 13 paragraphs of the Testament, which could be characterized as the expression of the global political intentions of certain Anglo-American endeavours. It reveals—as mentioned in previous chapters—when read in the right light, long-term planning which is essentially aimed at the construction of an unmediated, direct bridge between East and West that excludes the Middle European cultural and economic region. This is not, however, striven for *directly* from the West, but indirectly, in that the Russian people are influenced in such a way that Russian politics runs on in the direction first followed, according to plan, by Peter the Great.

Article 7, 'on which the success of this entire plan depends', reads: 'A close alliance *with England* [emphasis THM] is to be entered into and by means of a trade treaty, direct relations conducted to allow her [England] to exercise a kind of monopoly within [Russia].' We only need to add America to England [Britain] here and we have a political principle that is still effective today, one which even began to reveal its activity unconcealed in and after 1989. The death of Alfred Herrhausen occurred because his actions went counter to this seventh paragraph of the Testament...

Another individual began to work against this same paragraph after the Wende: Detlev Karsten Rohwedder, who was the head of the German *Treuhandanstalt* (Trust Agency) after the dissolution of the GDR. Rohwedder was in favour of a gradual renovation of East German enterprises. This found little response in American economic circles. There, a rapid programme of privatization was preferred. Wisnewski writes: 'Criticism ranged from the time it would take to salvage East German companies to the excess bureaucracy needed for privatization and objections to taking on ecological burdens.'[615] 'In the USA the dark suspicion grew that the Treuhand deliberately sought to exclude foreign businesses from participation in a new economic miracle; in Britain the talk was of "brutal financial self-interest".' After a trip Rohwedder made to the USA in November 1990 the Americans gave him some advice that was basically a warning: 'it would be preferable to engage international investment banks for the privatization of East German businesses'.[616] Detlev Karsten Rohwedder was murdered on 1 April 1991. The murder, which had all the hallmarks of a secret service operation, was again attributed to the RAF and again with amateurish evidence. This was followed by the fact that Rohwedder's successor Birgit Breuel immediately proposed a new course 'which the critics of her predecessor approved to the last dot'. From the middle of 1991 the Treuhand engaged banking houses such as Goldman, Sachs & Co., First Boston Corporation, J.P. Morgan, Merrill Lynch and others with major interests in privatization in the former GDR. These international investment banks implemented entire privatization packages for companies at the Treuhand's request. The great banking house Morgan Grenfell acquired by Herrhausen just before his death notably received no such request. In the upper echelon at the Treuhand the message had also been understood: those who were not there at the sowing had no place at the reaping. Rohwedder too had come up against the effectiveness of the seventh paragraph of the Testament...

In paragraph 11 of the Testament it is emphasized that 'the influence of religion among the [...] Catholics [...] is to be made use of'.[617] We have seen, in connection with the termination of the Socialist experiment how decisive was the role played by Catholics; without the Holy Alliance there would have been no prospect of a foreseeable end to the Socialism that had been transplanted into the East. When one then considers that the end of Socialism was, amongst other things, a precondition for German reunification and this in turn the precondition for the unification of Europe so that the 'one' Europe could become the accurately spinning wheel at the centre of the gears of the American world order—then it becomes clear that the application of this paragraph could serve as the means for the smashing of the European Middle. While the seventh paragraph was attended to in Washington, the eleventh paragraph was more Rome's affair: Rome created nourishment for the hunger of the soul; Washington busied itself with the needs of the body. This was the nature of the fight against *the spirit*.

The following paragraph 12 contains another machiavellian maxim of the greatest relevance to our modern situation. At the outset it states: 'From then on every moment will be valuable: everything must be prepared in concealment in order to lead to the great blow; this must be done in an order, with a foresight, and at a speed *which does not give Europe time to think*.'[618]

It was in accordance with this model that the European Wende and the 'soft revolution' were 'prepared in concealment'. 'The speed which does not give Europe time to think' also belongs to the starkest signatures of the whole period of the Wende. It even seems to have intensified thereafter. After the reunification of Germany were the European nations not hurried into the EU-Moloch one after the other? Insofar as speed kills the level-headedness of calm reflection, the capacity for which is precisely the natural disposition of of Middle Europeans, this paragraph too is directed against a specific characteristic of the European.

Paragraph 9 is also relevant; we only need to replace the word 'Austria' with 'Middle Europe'. It begins: 'One should always *appear* to be the ally of Austria [...]'

★

These are only examples which can show that decisive events in great contemporary affairs play out in most recent history exactly in correspondence with the Testament. There has been until today a concordance between political events and intentions and that peculiar text. That does not necessarily mean that everyone who is engaged in global affairs must be consciously aware of this concordance. The Testament of Peter the Great is originally the expression of a mighty western occult political stream of global dimensions, which makes the western Slavs' culture serve its purposes. In the meantime, this western global current has bound itself to the decadent global current of the South, which is to be seen as its most important undercurrent. Whoever is swimming in this stream is obviously then acting in the direction in which the stream is flowing, whether he is aware of it or not. The impetus of the Testament of Peter the Great is therefore operative today as in the past; the most influential focus of the Testament's ongoing activity today is to be found in the centre and the environment of the Holy Alliance.

★

Let us consider a few more symptoms of recent history which can supplement and consolidate what we have found.

During the process of German reunification there appeared in January 1990 a very noteworthy indication in *The Times* of London. It was prophesied:

> the disintegration of the Soviet Union is now irreversible, and its speed will probably pick up after Gorbachev's return from Vilnius. The Baltic republics will probably become functioning democracies and, in a short while, members of the European Community [...] The disintegration will be an extraordinary and painful process. In each of the potentially independent republics are significant ethnic minorities. It is likely that these will emigrate or be driven out. *The 90s in Europe will see a situation which resembles that of the 90s of the last century.* [Emphasis THM] A united and powerful Germany will be looking eastwards into a great zone of instability but also at economic and political opportunties.[619]

At the beginning of the 1890s decisive arrangements were made in Britain for the execution of the long-range plans for the twentieth century in accordance with the direction set by the Testament; among these arrangements was the preparation of the powder keg in the Balkans. The term 'Socialist experiment' emerged from one of the 'original Clubs' mentioned by Disraeli and made its way into publications available to the general public: C.G. Harrison's *Transcendental Universe* spoke of it; the map in the magazine *Truth* (Christmas 1890) presented a visible, satirical version of the political programme.

After the indication from *The Times*, it was to be expected that 100 years later something similar would appear, that is, that here and there, signs would become visible of how the leading Anglo-American circles viewed the general contours of global political developments *in the twenty-first century*. And so it was. A higher octave of the map from the magazine *Truth* appeared exactly 100 years later in the English magazine *The Economist*.[620] The commentary that accompanied the map was not, as in 1890, something that rather led attention away from it; this time an explanatory essay was provided to go with it. 'The Old Order Passes' was the title on the magazine's cover which showed an Arab with a falcon on his hand. This appeared *after* the clever manoeuvre in which the USA and others had first deceived the Iraqi government and *during* the build-up to the military show-down that was escalated with the aid of an incredible deception of the American public, unleashing the Gulf War.[621] This war had, from a global political perspective, the main function of establishing once and for all the New World Order of the USA, so irreversibly that in the view of certain western circles the disintegration of the former Soviet Union would inevitably follow.

We shall limit ourselves to commenting on a few details of the 'new and accurat [sic] map of the world' shown on p. 486. The five main continents being Euro-America, Euro-Asia, Islamistan, Confuciania, and Hinduland; an integral Europe no longer exists. A channel passes through the East of Europe forming an unbridgeable divide between the Orthodox and the Catholic/Protestant populations of European Christendom. The commentary by Brian Beedham provides a historical justification for this: the main movements of the last centuries of European history—the Renaissance, the Reformation and the Enlightenment—had all occurred without the participation of the Orthodox part of Christendom and the bearers of these three movements would now have to cleave to the cultural roots that belonged to them alone, undisturbed by the Orthodox element. While the western part of Euro-Asia is shown dominated by an Orthodox priest, the East Asian region shows a group of people, some of whom appear to be engaged in a cultic Asian dance. Near Washington a Pilgrim Father is kneeling in the direction of the sun shining in the West (!).

According to Beedham, this map does not represent just 'clumps of land' but ideal 'bodies', cultural regions and ideal continents. The reader is recommended to engage in a 'useful mental exercise' which enables these ideal continents corresponding to the New World Order to become visible. If we ask ourselves how the political programme which lies behind this map was created, we shall only need actually to carry out the 'useful mental exercise' to be able to answer:

1. Europe, as an autonomous Middle sphere of mediation between East and West, is to *completely* disappear;
2. The schism between Rome and Byzantium that became a reality about 1000 years ago is not to be overcome but transformed into an absolutely irreversible chasm;
3. Not only are the two main forms of Christianity to be strengthened in themselves and absolutely isolated from each other, the same is to apply to the three other great religions in the world—Islam, Buddhism, Hinduism. The principle of 'divide and rule' must in the coming millennium be applied especially to these cultural/religious polarities.

The first point of Beedham's programme lies along the continuation of the line that can be drawn from the seventh paragraph of the Testament, which is to undermine Austria's intermediary position (we have but to place Europe in place of Austria). This parallel with the Testament will suffice for now, as it is likely to be the weightiest with regard to the near future of Europe. That Europe is naturally to be a part of the Euro-American continent Beedham shows throughout his essay with the new flag that is seen on every page: the twelve Marian stars of 'the flag of Europe' integrated into the banner of the USA.

A closer look at this 'new' map, incidentally, shows that St Petersburg also belongs to the Euro-American continent. In the sense of the grandiose Testament, how could it be otherwise?

At the bottom left of the map can be read the Latin words: '*Haec tabula mundi vix seria est*'—'This map is hardly serious'. A good old Anglo-American tradition: the deeper octave of this new map appeared 100 years earlier in a *satirical* magazine.

It does no harm—those in the influential Clubs may well say—if *the many* smile at the plans of *the few* which seem to be only fantasy. They are all the less likely to meddle in the execution of plans which they do not take seriously . . .

From: The Economist *1–7 Sept. 1990*

Two years later in *Foreign Affairs*, the official organ of the Council On Foreign Relations, an article was published that was powerful confirmation that Beedham's map and its corresponding political programme was no single phenomenon. In his long essay 'Clash of Civilizations', which stirred worldwide interest (which does not mean that it was taken seriously everywhere), Samuel P. Huntington followed essentially the same line.[622] Huntington too draws the new frontlines after the Cold War predominantly through cultural and religious terrain.

> The fault lines between civilizations are replacing the political and ideological boundaries of the Cold War as the flashpoints for crisis and bloodshed. The Cold War began when the Iron Curtain divided Europe politically and ideologically. The Cold War ended with the end of the Iron Curtain. As the ideological division of Europe has disappeared, the cultural division of Europe between Western Christianity, on the one hand, and Orthodox Christianity and Islam, on the other, has re-emerged ... *The Velvet Curtain* of culture has replaced the Iron Curtain of ideology as the most significant dividing line in Europe. [Emphasis THM][623]

From the Iron Curtain to the Velvet Curtain—Winston Churchill would probably have enjoyed the change of expression...

Huntington too illustrated the main ideas in his essay with a small map; it makes clear that the velvet curtain is to be drawn exactly along the line of the Great Schism of 1054 between Orthodox and Roman Christianity; right through the former Yugoslavia.[624]

★

While on the western frontier of the Holy Alliance such concrete plans for the future were being drawn up, Rome was more occupied, at least outwardly, in exploiting the upheavals of 1989. On the occasion of the 100th anniversary of Leo XIII's Encyclical *Rerum Novarum* in 1891, John Paul II wrote a papal circular of symptomatic significance with the title *Centesimus Annus* (The 100th Year).[625] Not only in the West but also in Rome people were thinking at the same time in terms of centuries...

In the new Encyclical the Pope wanted, amongst other things, to present 'an analysis of some events of recent history',[626] which had been jointly organized to a considerable extent by Rome. The third part of the six-part encyclical dealt with the year 1989. The first chapter of that part is titled: 'The Contribution of the Church to the Change' (Wende). But one should not expect to find in it a detailed account of the conversation between John Paul II and Ronald Reagan in the Vatican Library in June 1982. Instead, we find in the first sentence: 'From the world situation described above and in detail in the encyclical *Sollicitudo rei socialis*, one realizes the *unexpected*,[627] promising extent of the events of recent years.'[628]

Perhaps the claim made in this encyclical of untruth that the upheavals which the Vatican, at Washington's side, had demonstrably been working towards since 1982 had been unexpected would not have been made so openly if the revelations in Carl Bernstein's article in *Time* had been made somewhat earlier . . .

'The struggle which led to the changes of 1989,' the encyclical went on, '[. . .] has in a certain sense developed from prayer and would have been unthinkable without boundless trust in God, the Lord of History, who holds the heart of Man in his hands.'[629]

The unexpected miracle of 1989 would have been still more unthinkable without 'boundless trust' in Washington and in certain Vatican funds.

The encylical went on to expound, with a very particular accent, on questions of Catholic social teachings such as 'the Church and the Labour Movement', 'Land and Labour', 'Exclusion and Exploitation', 'Aliena-tion' and many more. From these titles alone one can see that after the Wende the Church was seeking to operate to an ever-increasing degree as the executrix of the testament of the failed Marxism, which had shaped and trained, if not the intellects then the feelings and attitudes of millions upon millions of human beings, also in the Third World, and therefore in the post-Marxist era this ideological underground of the soul also had to be addressed. The battle against the realization of the threefolding of the social organism was to be continued *also along this front*.

At the end of the encyclical, which was given on '1 May, the Memorial of Saint Joseph the Worker, in the year 1991',[630] we read 'in the third Millennium too, the Church will be faithful *in making man's way her own*'.

On the Catholic side of the European coin there has been since the appearance of this papal encyclical a veritable fever which has spread the political and economic arguments for a united Europe with many references to its being based on and crowned by the renewed Holy Roman Empire of the German Nation.

In particular, astonishing things were heard before the Swiss refer-endum in December 1992 on entry into the European Economic Area (EEA), the 'lobby' of the EU. For example, the Swiss Secretary of State Blankart said: 'Entry into the European Community would be a turning point in our entire history and at the same time would mean a reinte-gration into the Holy Roman Empire, this time of the European Nation. This change is well underway.'[631]

According to the weekly report of a Zurich banking house: 'The coming Europe was spoken of in terms of the heritage of the Roman Empire, or at least[632] of the Empire of Charlemagne, the Holy Roman Empire in the eighth century.' Even if Charlemagne became emperor in the ninth century only and even if the Empire was not referred to as '*Holy Roman Empire of the German Nation*' until the year 1512—this bank report reveals a symptomatic train of thought.

In Germany at about the same time there was formed a German committee for the beatification of Robert Schuman, the 'Father of Europe', that had been announced by the Pope; the committee was also supported by Chancellor Kohl. The former Vice-President of the European Parliament, Hans August Lücker, said in December 1992 that 'the Holy Father has let us know that he is interested in making a solemn announcement of the beatification in 1994 in order to present Schuman to the modern era and especially to those in positions of political responsibility as a personality who invites them to orient their lives spiritually.'[633]

In Washington, the city of Rome's ally, the encyclical found a direct echo. Zbigniew Brzezinski, who speaks in the 1994 German edition of his book *Out of Control: Global Turmoil on the Eve of the 21st Century* (1993) of 'the powerful statement of Pope John Paul II in his encyclical *Centesimus Annus*.'[634] Brzezinski emphasizes in his book that America, which for him is unquestionably called to establish the New World Order, can only play this role rightly when it raises itself to a consciousness of ethical and cultural values. What kind of ethics he has in mind is shown in the penultimate sentence of his book: 'In a world of contingency, moral imperatives then become the central, and even the only, form of reassurance.'[635] In the last sentence he postulates 'the political need of shared moral consensus in the increasingly congested and intimate world of the twenty-first century'. Where imperatives appear, there must be an 'imperator'. According to his unvarnished acknowledgement of the encyclical, it is clear where Brzezinski thinks the necessary moral imperatives are to be drawn from—Rome. Instead of ethical individualism, which could lead to a really free spiritual life—the ethics of authoritative norms. Instead of the threefolding of the social organism—the continuation of the unitary state. Of this, Brzezinski says:[636]

> In our age the profoundest problems that humanity faces have become too great for the nation state, the traditional unity of international affairs, to handle. This does not mean that the nation state has outlived its usefulness [...] The nation state will remain for quite some time the primary focus of civic loyalty, the basic source of historical and cultural diversity, and the

prime force for mobilizing the individual's commitment. However, the world today needs more than the nation-state in order to organize global peace ...

One is keen to know of what this 'more' consists: the nation-states are to be 'encouraged to cooperate in the setting of a larger community ...' Concretely, this means:

to institutionalize the progressive emergence of such a common global community new forms of enhanced cooperation will have to evolve along two major axes: the trilateral relationship among the world's richest and democratic states of Europe, America, and East Asia (notably Japan); and through the United Nations as the wider and more representative framework of global politics ...

To this end, 'the deliberate enhancement of the UN's political role' will be necessary. Then he speaks of a 'gradual redistribution of responsibilities within the trilateral relationship'.[637] The proposal to *continue* the unitary nation-state and at the same time refer to *trilateral* relationships can strike one as unconscious or even conscious mockery of the call, justified by the needs of the times, for a threefold form of society.

And what is the idea that this representative member of the Holy Alliance entertains of the future task of Europe? Brzezinski says of it: 'The message that Europe could aspire to convey to the world—depending, of course, on Europe's further development and unification—could be an extrapolation of the best of *the American way of life* without the worst.'[638] Europe as an exemplary America! Possibly! In other words: the exclusion of the European Middle as a region for the fostering of cognitive and ethical individualism.

That any future bridge-building between Middle Europe and the Slavic East is to be prevented is clear from the words recently expressed like a decree by Henry Kissinger, another American political strategist:

It is not in any country's interest that Germany and Russia should fixate on each other as either principal partner or principal adversary. If Germany and Russia become too close, they raise the fear of condominium. If Russia and Germany quarrel, they involve Europe in escalating crises.[639]

Enough of indications that were intended to show that in the direction of their long-range plans, the perpetrators of the New World Order are now, as in the past, acting in line with the Testament of Peter the Great.

Let us turn in conclusion once more to the question: are there any indications which not only show that the Testament is continuing to be followed but that the anti-European policies of the architects of the New World Order are based on a very conscious connection to the Russian

Czars (who in their turn were steered by the West) and to the impulses that worked through them and after them? There are indeed the following indications.

★

In 1980 a new work appeared in New York about Peter the Great that in the present context is noteworthy for several reasons.[640] The book was awarded the Pulitzer Prize and attracted much attention. It is a scholarly work that is yet well-written and easy to read. Robert K. Massie, its American author, after studying American history at Yale, went to Oxford as a Rhodes Scholar to study European history. One who goes to Oxford as a Rhodes Scholar enters an atmosphere of imperial and commonwealth thinking. Three great 'R's' had been active here and left behind their traces: John *Ruskin*, the art historian and man of letters who in 1870 as a preparer of imperial thinking knew how to inspire his young listeners with the idea of empire; Cecil *Rhodes*, who carried the manuscript of Ruskin's lecture on Empire on his person for the rest of his life, and Lord *Rosebery*—the best friend of Churchill's father—who in 1883 expounded on the concept of the Commonwealth of Nations. One who receives a Rhodes Scholarship, for which very strict preconditions must be fulfilled, enters a sphere of power and activity which is permeated and nurtured by Anglo-American neo-imperialism. The threads which are spun from Rhodes House Oxford via the *Royal Institute of International Affairs* and its American branch the *Council On Foreign Relations* to Washington and from there into the whole world, were followed and recorded by Carroll Quigley, Bill Clinton's teacher at Georgetown University.[641]

Massie based his book about Peter the Great on, amongst others, work by Richard Pipes, who in 1981 gave that indication in Moscow about the coming European reconstruction, which we have already discussed (p. 457).

The resulting picture has a symptomatological quality: at about the time of the western decision to terminate the Socialist experiment in the East, a much-praised biography about Peter the Great, written by a man who is connected to Yale and Oxford and who at least must have enjoyed academic relations with a man such as Pipes, a co-strategist of the plans for the reconstruction of the East. Whether this striking western interest in the Russian Czar *at this point in time* is a mere coincidence, or is to be seen in relation to the world political upheavals that were then in prospect may perhaps not yet be answerable on the basis of what has been adduced thus far.

The following complex of symptoms, however, has more weight.

Although Mikhail Gorbachev had decisively opened up Russia for the market economy of the West, the US planners evidently began to become uncomfortable with him. Instead of continuing to support Russia's perestroika, America favoured the Chinese economy, calmly allowed the former Soviet Union to fall into irreversible disintegration and looked out for a new man in Moscow, who would also be manipulable in the western sense, *after* the Wende. This man was Boris Yeltsin. According to a report in *Der Spiegel*, George H.W. Bush (the former CIA Director) passed on to Yeltsin in August 1991

> the content of telephone conversations [...] which the putsch leaders in Moscow had been having with Soviet generals. *This was how Yeltsin knew that most military units in Moscow were refusing to support the opponents of the then leader of the Communist Party, Mikhail Gorbachev.* Bush then sent a communications expert to Yeltsin's headquarters, so that the Russian President could speak to the generals, without fear of eavesdroppers. The Americans had evidently succeeded in breaking into the most secure communications networks the Soviets had available at the time.[642]

In a speech to the Strasbourg parliament a couple of months before the putsch which resulted in a transfer of power in Moscow, Yeltsin emphasized 'Russia's position in Europe and its cultural heritage that had been influenced by the West'.[643] According to his biographer Morrison, who was another who made repeated use of the work of Richard Pipes, Yeltsin was clearly ranging himself with the 'westernizers and not with the Slavophiles'. 'Perhaps Yeltsin was born three hundred years too late', wrote Morrison after his description of Yelsin's not exactly prissy youth: 'he would have been the ideal partner for another young giant—for Peter the Great, who as a young lad had a similar liking for violent confrontations, scandals and [...] ear-splitting explosions.'[644] Yeltsin, who studied building and construction, also had, like Czar Peter, a strong interest in shipbuilding.

On Yeltsin's next visit to the USA (it was the third in all and the first after the putsch) a grand reception was prepared for him. He was awaited in front of the White House with all the colourful ceremonial reserved for state visits. 'President Bush,' reported one Washington correspondent about Yeltsin's visit,

> in his speech welcoming his Russian guest on the lawn in front of the south entrance to the White House, reached far back in history. *He compared Boris Yeltsin with no less than Peter the Great, who had redefined Russia's role in the world.*[645] As if to appease possible reservations about this bold comparison,

Bush also emphasized that Yeltsin was the first freely and democratically elected head of state in Russian history. The democratic transformation in Russia was bound to become just as successful as the American Revolution 200 years earlier.[646]

When one reflects that George Bush is a member of an occult-political Club based at Yale University[647] which has existed since 1833, one is entitled to regard this public reference to Peter the Great as having more than just an anecdotal value. We should see it much more as a symptom that Bush is speaking on behalf of circles who have long made conscious use of corrupt pro-western elements within Slavic culture and which are also doubtless determined to go on doing so in the future.[648] Bill Clinton certainly fits the bill for someone suited to continue the agenda laid out in the Testament of Peter the Great. He was educated at Georgetown University with its renowned school for diplomats[*]; the university is a Jesuit foundation.[649] From there, he went to Oxford as a Rhodes Scholar in order to complete the law studies he had begun at Yale. And were he to take a wrong turning prematurely, then a more suitable man will be found . . .

★

It should naturally not be concluded in any categorical fashion from everything that has been sketched out and developed in the last four chapters that the source of everything wicked in the world is to be seen in Britain and America, let alone in Rome. Countries and cultures that have produced figures such as Shakespeare and Ralph Waldo Emerson (or Dante) have completely different sides to their nature; but such figures have not been influential in the political, and especially the foreign policy actions of Britain and later of the USA. What has determined Anglo-American political behaviour has been moving—in Britain since the beginning of the seventeenth century and in America at least since the mid-nineteenth century—wholly in line with the impulses of the Testament of Peter the Great.

The European can conclude two things from this. He could increase his striving[650] for a deeper understanding of significant impulses of the English-speaking peoples in the sense of the universal progress of mankind and, at the same time, he could strive to become consciously alert to the enormous shadow sides that have manifested in Anglo-American foreign policy over the last 200 years. For in the end, Europeans have to

---

[*] Clinton attended the Edmund A. Walsh School of Foreign Service at Georgetown—*transl.*

recognize that it is because of their sleepiness that they continually become the victims of tendencies formed and promoted by those—also on European territory, supported by many Europeans themselves—who are 'with' Europe, in order to rule it, without really wanting to be 'in' Europe, to use Churchill's phrase. But to be able to be truly 'in' Europe, a deeper understanding of the capacities and tasks of Europe is necessary than has generally been widespread until now.

5. A Pilgrimage to Santiago de Compostela

We have now outlined the general political developments after Polzer's death in as far as they relate to the present and future of Europe.

Before attempting to present a sketch of *contrasting, more constructive perspectives* which appear to result from Polzer's life, and perhaps to a greater extent, from the unfulfilled *intentions* of his life, we must briefly look, from the point of his death onwards, at the future development of that spiritual stream with which he had united himself so strongly.

Three questions present themselves:

1. How did the *anthroposophical movement* develop after the Second World War?
2. How did the Anthroposophical Society (G.A.S.) develop, which was supposed to be the outer vessel for the movement?
3. Did Polzer's intentions live on in the anthroposophical movement and above all, in the Anthroposophical Society?

It is only possible to speak concretely here of the anthroposophical movement independent of the G.A.S. after Polzer's death to a very limited degree, as outside the G.A.S. there were at most in Middle Europe only very sporadic references to Steiner's spiritual science. This does not mean that only a few people saw anything reasonable and justified in this spiritual science. Here and there it even appeared in universities. The enormous expansion of Waldorf education since the 1970s, which today has even put down roots in former communist countries, doubtless made the founder of Anthroposophy more widely known beyond the circle of the members of the G.A.S. The Camphill movement, the Christian Community, and the growing recognition of medical treatments and certain therapies that have been developed on the basis of anthroposophical knowledge have all made their contribution. But it cannot be claimed that the anthroposophical movement initiated by Rudolf Steiner has by now become a cultural factor that finds widespread public recognition. There are many more symptoms which show that, through today's powerful media, spiritual science still experiences attacks which go beyond anything launched in this direction in the 1920s and 30s. In certain circles in France, in which the old idea of revenge[651] against Germany which is there in the Testament of Peter has yet to disappear, Steiner has for a long time been regarded as a 'Nazi philosopher'. When one looks at the statements based on a completely superficial perception of certain spiritual scientific indications made by opponents who accuse

Steiner of racism, chauvinism and worse, then one must acknowledge that attacks of such a kind which were already made in the 1920s are again on the increase. Neither is it difficult to see that in today's media-oriented public opinion—which bases itself on the lack of judgement of all those unwilling to think—they will play a great role in the future, which will only become greater.

Where is the power of defence against such attacks, when many anthroposophers have in the meantime come to believe that the wave of accusations of racism has been forced back by the Dutch Van Baarda Report? In reality, the supposed 'incompatibility' of certain statements by Steiner with modern views was essentially accepted by such anthroposophers—in a way incompatible with anthroposophy. In February 2000 opponents of anthroposophy were even allowed to make an appearance in the Foundation Hall at the Goetheanum with their dilettantish accusations of 'anti-semitism'.[*]

The reception afforded to the book by Helmut Zander shows that in many anthroposophical circles people have fully accepted the assertion, represented by the opponents of anthroposophy, that Steiner made all kinds of 'incompatible' statements.

Will the friends of anthroposophy as well as the members of the G.A.S. put up a more realistic opposition to such attacks in the future? The obvious lack of defences against such opposition has to do with certain elements in the history of the G.A.S. in the time after Steiner's death.

Since October 1935, the weekly magazine *Das Goetheanum* has no longer carried the subtitle 'Weekly magazine for Anthroposophy *and Threefolding*' but calls itself (after the word 'international' had already been dropped from the subtitle in 1933) only a 'Weekly magazine for Anthroposophy'. This omission is explained by the circumstances of the times; in November 1935 the G.A.S. was officially banned in Germany. The omission is understandable.

But that it remained in force in subsequent *decades* can be seen as a symptom of the fact that the effort to penetrate contemporary world affairs with consciousness receded more and more within the circles of G.A.S. members.[652] Certainly, it has self-evidently never been the task of the G.A.S. to pursue 'politics' in the conventional sense, that is, to support this or that political faction or 'colour'. But *the cognitive penetration* of political processes is one of the most important endeavours for anyone to undertake who earnestly wishes to walk a path of spiritual knowledge. A look at Steiner's *Karma of Untruthfulness* lectures could suffice to convince

---

[*] See *Der Europäer*, March 2000 (www.perseus.ch).

any doubter of the rightness *in Rudolf Steiner's sense* of what has just been asserted.

Without a political consciousness understood in this sense one will be even less awake to the opposition to anthroposophy than in previous decades. To a special degree, one would have to be awake to such a lack in regard to the perception of certain efforts that are ongoing within the G.A.S. itself to counter anthroposophy's spirit of freedom. Grandiose, negative, long-range plans, as manifest in the Testament of Peter the Great, naturally encompass, alongside the political element, also the spiritual element in human evolution, at least indirectly. The paragraph about the use of the Catholic element as well as that about the acceleration of certain processes of which Europe is not supposed to become aware, shows this all too clearly. How could a spiritual stream which values true individualization, reason, freedom, and conscious action on the basis of knowledge be exempt and omitted from such plans? This should even less be the case with a stream which, like anthroposophy, would be in a position to engage in political affairs in a modifying and metamorphosing manner, as will have to be the case increasingly from now on.

If one asks oneself from where this decline in political consciousness within the G.A.S. stemmed from the mid-1930s onwards, one will have to pose a further question: whether this is related to the *increase* in engagement of a very different kind by the Vorstand and the membership? Certainly Albert Steffen, the President of the G.A.S., took care to cultivate political consciousness in the membership in numerous ways after Steiner's death, through his dramas or also through the 'Call to the Swiss People' which he wrote, which reminded the Swiss of the significant impulse of Henri Dunant. The Call was published in the magazine *Gewerbliche Wirtschaft* [Industry] in July 1946, a short time before Churchill's Zurich speech, and was signed by numerous personalities in public life. But on the other hand, and contrary to the hopes and suggestions of Ludwig Polzer in 1930 (see p. 272 and p. 315.), the President also made it possible for a certain spiritual centralization to be established within the leadership of the Society. Even after Steffen's death in 1963 and the return of the English and Dutch national societies excluded by Dornach in 1935, this centralizing tendency only appeared to ebb, at most. But it received new nourishment in the 1970s through questions about the 'Christmas Conference', the 'esoteric Vorstand' and Rudolf Steiner's alleged 'eternal' destiny connection to the G.A.S. These questions were answered at the time—and have been in general until today—in such a way that has made visible how strongly this Society which had proceeded from the principle of *knowledge* had in the meantime come to rest on *declarations and assertions* of all kinds.[653] Declarations, for example, about the irrevocable unity of the G.A.S. with the anthroposophical movement, about the destiny bond of unity between Steiner and the Society (declared to be one with the anthroposophical movement), about the 'esoteric character' of even later Vorstands, which were said to lie in spiritual line of succession to the Christmas Conference Vorstand of 1923 etc. In the dogmatic way in which these issues were presented, a concrete continuation of that element within the G.A.S. shows itself, which Polzer in 1935 identified as 'Jesuit'. One could even speak of a penetration of the G.A.S. after Steiner's death by the spirit of those suggestive parts of the Testament of Peter the Great which have to do with the use of the Catholic element. Although no reasonable grounds could be given as to why, after the failure of the Christmas Conference experiment,[654] and after his premature death, he should link himself not only to individuals who are truly striving spiritually but should link his destiny to that of the earthly Society of the G.A.S. as a whole, this dogma has until today repeatedly been given out as a truth and recognized as such.

In reality, it is nothing other than the weightiest equivalent within the G.A.S. of the infallibility dogma of the Roman Catholic Church. This dogma and its sub-dogmas ('esoteric Vorstand', 'Christmas Conference Society') also determined the practices of the leadership of the Society from the 70s and 80s onwards to a newly intensified degree. Without this dogma, for example, centralized regulation of the 'Class Readership' would have been unthinkable. Without this dogma, a decades-long, Vatican-style 'esoteric protection' of certain records and documents in a well-protected archive (along with several private archives) would have been not only superfluous but without any legitimacy. Quite apart from the fact that secreting away documents of general interest for decades accords not with the principle of scientific enquiry but entirely with that of the exploitation of power. In the Catholic Church such secretive behaviour is a long-preserved tradition.

To what has been put forward thus far, it will be objected here and there that since the end of the 70s or the beginning of the 80s in the G.A.S., much was done in the Society, even by leading figures, namely by Manfred Schmidt(-Brabant[*]) who later became President, to give a new impetus for the recovery of the lost political consciousness of the members.

We shall now demonstrate by means of a symptomatic example how such a new impetus by Schmidt-Brabant looked at the time.

---

[*] On 'Brabant', the second part of the double-barrelled name, see *Der Europäer*, no. 9/10, p. 15.

'Anthroposophy and the Task of Europe' was the theme of a public lecture given by Schmidt-Brabant, then a member of the Vorstand of the G.A.S. in 1979 during a Goetheanum congress in Vienna. (A copy of the lecture, checked by the lecturer, was printed in the March issue of the magazine *Die Drei* in 1980.) Schmidt-Brabant began with Spengler's *Downfall of the West* and contrasted it with the possibility of a new rise for Europe. He then outlined the complexity of the world situation against the background of international politics and referred to 'feeling': 'What goes on there remains largely impenetrable in its reality.' Then he spoke of a threefold fear in modern human beings: fear of 'the impenetrable in the world', fear of 'the all-powerful' and fear of 'hopelessness'.

Immediately after this opening presentation he went on: 'one sees how endeavours are forming themselves in the European Parliament in Strasbourg. The best there ask: What position should Europe adopt in this completely changed world situation in the future? *The answer can at first only be discerned in the seeds of a new fundamental feeling in the European.*'[655] Is there no *more* to contribute from the spiritual science of Rudolf Steiner to the question of the future of Europe than 'seeds of a new fundamental feeling'?

Then—after an interlude about Rudolf Steiner's period of studies in Vienna—he raised the question of Europe's specific task: 'How would the task of Europe look if Europe were to have a specific place as a "middle member" [*ein mittleres Glied*], between America in the West and Asia in the East?' Shortly after this, he drew the attention of his listeners (and readers) to the fact that it is not only in anthroposophical circles that Europe is called the 'heart organ of humanity' and then said: 'in June 1977 there appeared a Declaration from the European Bishop's Conference[656] "Word for Europe". It asked: whether, through services to the world, Europe could not find again and strengthen its will to live, its creativity and the nobility of its soul.'

In order to overcome the threefold fear, the listeners or the readers of these remarks were therefore called upon

1. to look to the efforts of the 'best' in Strasbourg, and
2. in answer to the question about the task of Europe, to pay attention to the words of a bishops' conference and to remember 'the nobility of their souls'.

Referring further to the bishop's conference (which in the eyes of the lecturer was evidently very significant), the audience were then told that 'Europe might create institutions with the help of which it could render especially effective services to the whole family of mankind'. Immediately after this one of 'the best' of Strasbourg (or Brussels) was mentioned:

From other sources Ortoli, the President of the Commission of the European Community, said in the European Parliament in 1973: 'We must create a human Europe which stands in the service of the individual and of humanity.' *Such voices are not sounding by accident; the best in Europe are thinking about what position Europe is to occupy in the world.* [Emphasis THM]

It was thus made clear that the participants at the bishops' conference as well as the French President of the EC-Commission, F.X. Ortoli, all belong to the 'best' of Europe! Once again Schmidt-Brabant spoke of these 'best of Europe' and twice more about Europe's 'nobility of soul'. Three times in total in the whole lecture the nobility of the soul and the best of Europe are specifically mentioned—in relation to a bishops' conference and endeavours of the EC.

What the 'seeds of a new fundamental feeling of the European' which is supposed to put down roots in soil *like this* can contribute to an *anthroposophical* solution to the burning question of Europe is a question the reader himself might like to answer. In the whole lecture there is no word of Steiner's final efforts for threefolding in the Vienna Music Society Hall [West-East Congress 1922] or of the counter-proposals put forward soon afterwards by Count Coudenhove-Kalergi who is well-known to the lecturer and who comes from the old Catholic nobility of Brabant. Two years later in a Swiss lecture Schmidt-Brabant would speak of Coudenhove-Kalergi with honour for his efforts in the cause of European unity.[657]

'"The Downfall of the West", if one looks at what has been determining events in the West,' said Schmidt-Brabant at the end of his lecture in 1979, '[...] "The Rise of the West"—if one listens to the best in a newly awakening Europe, who glean that a new spirituality is forming, beyond nations, beyond frontiers, beyond races.'[658]

A new awakening of the anthroposophical political consciousness? Through their lack of clarity and their repeated obeisances before the trivial, but smooth-sounding, seductive words which the 'best' of Europe say about themselves[659], Schmidt-Brabant's remarks are more likely to have contributed to push any awareness of political and contemporary affairs within the G.A.S. from a condition of slumber into one of deep sleep.

Manfred Schmidt-Brabant later distinguished himself by other, similar acts of genuflection before the endeavours of Europe's 'best'. In 1992 in a public lecture at the Basel Bernoullianum[660] he promoted Swiss entry into the EEA in a roundabout way, which was nevertheless clear enough to those paying attention. In 1994 at the annual meeting of General

Secretaries of the G.A.S. he spoke words of high praise for the European Union.[661]

In relation to the Catholic side of the Europe coin, one learned from him in autumn 1991[662] that the Catholic Church was pursuing the—for the Church, quite obvious—aim of catholicizing Europe completely by the end of the century; at the same time, the lecturer emphasized : 'We do not mean that Europe should be anthroposophical. That would be nonsensical.'[663] In his view, the tasks of anthroposophy included the following: 'Anthroposophy would like to help everything in Europe that has life comprehend itself anew spiritually [. . .] The Catholic Church too *should* [emphasis THM] comprehend itself anew in its fundamentals.'[664] It was thus one of the tasks of anthroposophy to give the Catholic Church a task. Should one not rather leave it to the Church to give itself its own tasks and restrict oneself as an anthroposopher to placing the uniqueness of anthroposophy in the world and waiting to see if the need really awakens in the Church to 'comprehend itself anew spiritually'? No one in fact should deceive himself that the Catholic Church will actually endeavour to 'comprehend itself anew spiritually'—at any rate not in the sense of a self-awareness suddenly informed by anthroposophy.

What Rudolf Steiner said about the relationship of the Catholic Church to other spiritual communities still applies today. On 2 January 1921 he said:

> The Catholic Church will show more hatred to another community to the degree that it finds it similar to itself, or to the degree that it finds that Christian truth is sought in that community. For the aim of the Catholic Church is carefully to avoid Christian truth and to render the power of the Church as great as possible. That is the goal of the Catholic Church. You will not move it by making yourself more and more 'Christian'. You can only reconcile yourself to it when you are simply a person by whom the Catholic Church can swear, as it can swear by a person who belongs to Rome. You can make your peace with it in no other way.[665]

How far Schmidt-Brabant, who became President of the G.A.S. Vorstand in 1984, was already able in the following years to lead a large part of the Society, at least in spirit, along 'the pilgrims' path to Santiago' newly laid by the Council of Europe, was evident for example at the Michaelmas Conference of autumn 1993, 14 years after his lecture in Vienna. The programme promised something unusual. Seven days for the conference and seven 'Mysteries'; from the 'Mystery of the Threshold' to the 'Mystery of Freedom'; for 1000 selected[666] members of the First Class of the School of Spiritual Science. In the preparation phase before this conference, members throughout the world were asked to send in proposals for themes, which duly arrived in great numbers. From the 2000 suggestions sent in, twelve were selected as themes for the conference programme; they were printed at about the same time in the German *Mitteilungen* [newssheet].[667] They were therefore accessible to *all* members and not only to members of the First Class. It can be understood that the selected suggestions were regarded by leading figures as suggestions that were especially representative and to be taken seriously and that *therefore* the intention was to make them known to the membership as a whole.

The text relating to the eighth suggestion read:

> It is often asked whether it is not possible to establish a Second Class. When the reasons for this question are enquired after, one finds a yearning and a need for ritual-cultic work, as was indeed foreseen for the Second Class. Then, what is always referred to is a strict idea of the Class, in the nature of an Order; and always of energetic steps towards a new, living sacramentalism, a true anthroposophical reversed cultus.[668]

What Rudolf Steiner thought about the establishment and content of a Second Class which he himself had intended, he took with him beyond the threshold of death. Certainly, the First Class itself was not completed, but it would have continued in two parts in September 1924 and only then would its formation have been completed.

Nevertheless, in 1993 Schmidt-Brabant dared to use Steiner's expression 'Second Class' in order, either consciously or unconsciously, to conceal esoteric pretensions, against which Polzer already had warned in 1930, and to create the impression that the above-mentioned 'need for ritual-cultic work'—the existence of and justification for which is not to be denied *in Rudolf Steiner's sense* ('2nd Class'!)—*could be* satisfied.

After the so-called Class texts, around which cliques had been formed in numerous places for decades, had been printed and made available— not through careful thought over a long period but due to 'the condition of the times',[669] to use Schmidt-Brabant's expression—there was apparently nothing more pressing than for a few to create, by usurping Steiner's name, a selected, so-called protective substitute for the loss of 'the secret'.

The very fact that the President of the G.A.S. dared to present to the members such a notion as the possible establishment of a '2nd Class' as something really *to be taken seriously*[670] shows the 'esoteric' level that predominated 70 years after the Christmas Conference.

The autumn conference of 1993 had a prelude to it that is of special interest in relation to the theme of the second chapter. The Church in

Rome celebrated 1993 as a Holy Year or Year of St James. In the weekly magazine *Das Goetheanum*, one could read that:

> The Pope had honoured Spain with his visit[671] and Santiago de Compostela received thousands upon thousands of visitors and pilgrims from all over the world. The city was full of life that streamed in and out of the north, south and west portals of the Cathedral which were wide open the whole day—even during Mass [. . .][672]

From 5 to 8 August 1993 the Anthroposophical Society in Spain held a congress in Santiago on the 'Path of St James [the Camino] and the Mysteries of Northern Spain', and this congress 'was imagined as a kind of pilgrim's step to the great Michaelmas Conference in Dornach'. During this conference, Schmidt-Brabant, the President of the G.A.S., lectured explicitly on the Camino, the pilgrim route to Santiago, as a path of soul-spiritual development.

And so very much did many participants at the congress wish to be in inner harmony in their thoughts and feelings with the church's cere-monies at Santiago that after the production of a pilgrims' chorus 'through the *bold* initiative of a Waldorf teacher from Madrid on Sunday, 8 August 1993, they sang pilgrim songs from ancient times on the steps of the altar in the Cathedral of Santiago de Compostela amidst the swirling incense and at the indications of the priests who were conducting the Mass.'[673]

The jesuitical, Catholic Opus Dei incense had evidently befogged the political consciousness of certain members of the G.A.S. to such an extent that they were able to believe such a step in the Holy Year of St James had to be described as something 'bold'. Something from the incense of Santiago Cathedral appears to rise from the words which closed the report of the Prelude to the Michaelmas Conference in Dornach: 'May that which rang out from overflowing, grateful hearts in that noble house of God, have sounded into the great Michaelmas Conference this year.' And so it certainly *did* sound! The Catholic-oriented Euro-architects will certainly have been edified by so much secondary incense wafting over to them shortly before the millennium from the bosom of the G.A.S. . . .

The once so great and magnificent Santiago de Compostela! Of such great significance in the Middle Ages; today an essential source where friends of Europe who are true to Rome follow John Paul II to find refreshment and at the tomb of St James reflect anew on their 'spiritual nobility' in order to pour out over Europe, from the Urals to the Atlantic, a *Catholic* spiritual life instead of one that is really free . . .

★

Can all this not remind us of a dream that Ludwig Polzer once had? In the night of 13–14 January 1939 Polzer dreamt:

> I found myself as in a church or sacristy or some such place. I encountered a cardinal with whom I entered into conversation. We did not speak in words but with our eyes and facial gestures. His countenance was always deeply friendly and understanding. Then came a second cardinal. *I was told that he was from Santiago de Compostela.*[673] He had a darker face and [he] began to rage frightfully against the first cardinal in great agitation. I could not understand their conversation at all. The one was friendly towards me, the other hostile and also hostile to the first cardinal. I myself was very calm and had the feeling that I was stronger than both of them.

We referred to this dream in chapter 43 and in commenting on it, left open the possibility that it may have had to do with a time *that then lay in the future.*

Ludwig Polzer said of this dream in 1943: '*It seemed to me [. . .] somehow to stand in some relation to the tragic struggle in the Vorstand.*' [Emphasis THM.] This tragic struggle has in fact not yet ended. One could describe it as a phenomenon in which truly anthroposophical impulses struggle against a jesuitical cast of mind for the leadership of the Society. It is almost as if in Polzer's Santiago dream there was an element of prophecy.

An intensification of these Catholic tendencies occurred in 1995 when it was announced that the Annual General Meeting of the Anthroposophical Society in France was to be held not, as previously intended, in the expanded centre in Paris but in Les Fontaines/Chantilly, the main Jesuit centre in France, close to Paris. Also in Les Fontaines, interestingly enough, is the Robert Schuman Institute, which is obligated to pursue the Catholic Europe impulse. When questions were raised internally about this 'project', at which Schmidt-Brabant was supposed to speak, it was dropped like a hot potato.[*]

We have arrived at the third question posed at the outset: How have the impulses of Polzer—who had learned with iron patience how to see through these dangers which threaten the anthroposophical movement and Society from the alliance between certain lodges and people with a Jesuit cast of mind, in the widest sense of that phrase, not in the sense of belonging to the Jesuit Order—lived in the G.A.S. since his death?

---

[*] See 'Das Karma der Unwahrhaftigkeit', *Der Europäer*, Vol. 1, No. 9/10, p. 10ff.

6. Symptoms from the History of the G.A.S. and Ludwig Polzer

In view of the fact that instead of an increase in the very necessary consciousness of contemporary world events within the G.A.S. over the past decades there has been a noticeable growth, recurring in waves, of dogmatic, centralizing, ecclesiastical tendencies which appear to have reached a certain high point in 1993, the question as to how the work of an individuality like Ludwig Polzer-Hoditz was met within the anthroposophical movement, and especially within the Society, is not only of anecdotal significance.

First, with Ludwig Polzer's passing in 1945, everything became still and quiet in relation to him. Certainly, there were still people alive here and there who treasured his memory and greatly esteemed his life's work; also people outside the G.A.S. who felt inwardly obliged to Rudolf Steiner. They became fewer and fewer.

In the 1970s interest in Polzer's work gradually grew, not least due to Polzers' writings, which had been preserved by Paul Michaelis, and are included in the appendix to this book, and which in part reproduced conversations Polzer had had with Rudolf Steiner. Above all, Steiner's comments about the 'false (Czar) Dmitri' and Kaspar Hauser have continued to spur many people to do their own particular research. Peter Tradowsky's publications about Kaspar Hauser and Dmitri [Demetrius], for example, are closely related to the existence of such statements by Steiner.

When in 1984/85 Tradowsky was preparing the new edition of Polzer's memoirs that he wrote in Prague, the author of this biography did some accompanying research for it in Dornach and Stuttgart.

The President of the G.A.S., Manfred Schmidt-Brabant, confirmed in response to several enquiries that two files of Polzer materials[674] were extant but that they would contain only administrative papers and that there would be nothing of significance for the publisher of Polzer's memoirs. This was how such questions were dealt with at the highest level.

Originally, it was also intended to publish Polzer's speech to the 1935 General Meeting in the appendix of the above-mentioned new edition of the memoirs. The director of the Verlag am Goetheanum was not allowed by Schmidt-Brabant to do this. These were bad signs for any future new awakening of 'political consciousness' (and also bad for the process of the history of the Anthroposophical Society itself) for which, next to Rudolf Steiner himself, few better sources of inspiration could have been found than—Ludwig Polzer-Hoditz.

In 1989 Polzer's text *Der Kampf gegen den Geist und das Testament Peters des Grossen* [The Struggle Against the Spirit, and the Testament of Peter the Great] was republished in Dornach—in the year of the Wende; it was the right time. But this new edition was ignored, despite the Foreword by Renate Riemeck.

When the author of this biography took up his research again in the same year, he again made enquiries of the President of the G.A.S. with regard to the Polzer papers held by the Vorstand. The enquiries were repeated several times. In January 1994 he finally abandoned all such efforts as hopeless.

This manner of dealing with research enquiries, by the then President of the G.A.S., in relation to one of Rudolf Steiner's closest colleagues was already unjustifiable from a conventional scientific viewpoint. It revealed a special disinterest among the leadership of the G.A.S. in Count Polzer and his work for the spiritual science of Rudolf Steiner. The author of this book cannot at all see in this situation anything relating to his own person; just as little were there grounds in 1984, in relation to the person making enquiries at that time, for seeking to keep Polzer's 1935 speech from the anthroposophical public. In terms of a rebuilding of the awareness of political and contemporary affairs, the publication of this speech could have achieved something considerable, at the last moment, for the processes going on within the G.A.S.!

The reasons for its suppression at that time must therefore be sought in the *content* of the speech. One will recall, for example, the following sentences from the speech:

> The Foundation Stones, which rest in strong hearts are no longer bound to one place and one building. They must become the Foundation Stones for the Mystery Centres of the future in various places. Those who will plant the seeds for these Mystery Centres can only be called to do so directly by the spiritual world through their destiny. This calls above all for esoteric courage, not subordination and uniformity.[675]

Or words such as the following: 'Rather, impossible spiritual pretensions appeared first from one side and then, [...] from the other side. Therefore, in accordance with reason and in view of the absence of a spiritual leader, a new, freer, more ambitious basis for the Society could not be found.'[676] Such words, which had already gone unheeded in 1935 were, along with others, in 1984 once again placed on the Index of the G.A.S....

Although Rudolf Steiner himself 'already said in September 1924 in a significant connection that the attempt to create a High School for Spiritual Science had not been successful',[677] in the following decades his view was cast to the winds, and with growing spiritual pretensions from the 1950s onwards, readers for the so-called Class Lessons were appointed and dismissed, as is carried on in the church with bishops.

It must now actually be concluded that with regard to the rejection of certain impulses and trends of thought in Ludwig Polzer-Hoditz within the leadership of the G.A.S., there could not have been anything personal but rather, only 'material' grounds, which is all the worse, for the materiality of actual motives of suppression lies in the Roman Catholic line that negates truly free spiritual impulses. Instead of these, a sirocco-like south wind blew in, bearing highly dogmatic declarations. Let us again consider two concrete examples of this. The very first sentence of an article produced by the President of the G.A.S. in December 1993 on the subject of the 'Christmas Conference' reads: 'In the coming Christmas time it will be 70 years since that event took place on the hill in Dornach which has until the present determined the life of the Anthroposophical Society *and with it also anthroposophy itself*[678]—the Christmas Conference.'[679]

'And with it also anthroposophy itself'? What could ever guarantee that what determines the life of the Anthroposophical Society—simply because it *once* determined the life of the G.A.S.—must per se and, as it were, automatically 'also determine' *anthroposophy* 'until the present'! Must what goes on in the Church of Rome today also 'determine' true Christianity because there was once an essentially Christian impulse at the outset of the Ecclesia? If there were to be an opponent of Christ ruling the Church today, then, according to the logic of the writer of the article, true Christianity would be duly affected and determined.

Referring to the members of the original Vorstand of 1923, a further declaration from the same article reads:

> What, namely, all the members of the Vorstand sensed, what each one in his way indicated or expressed and *what shines down to us today from the Akasha of the history of this Society like a sun*[680] [is] : in the pains which destiny laid upon the members of the Vorstand [...] in these pains the substance of the Christmas Conference was saved.[681]

The ability to form one's own independent historical judgement within the G.A.S. would have been better served by public access to certain earthly chronicles than by declarations about things that are claimed to exist in the Akashic Chronicle...

And the end of the century, when many students of Rudolf Steiner are supposed to have reincarnated? Shining declarations about this too were made to the members from the Akasha. On the third day of the 1993 Michaelmas Conference which was held under the motto of 'the Mystery of the Akasha' the following could be read in the *Goetheanum* newssheet: 'This day will present the reality of our anthroposophical history. How do we live with our history as a living seed force for the future? Can we take seriously Rudolf Steiner's prediction that many friends from the first period of anthroposophical activity are among us again?'[682] Did Rudolf Steiner ever predict this? 'Among us again'—in this context that means, only too clearly: within the G.A.S.[683] Here too, as we have already seen, a dogmatic suggestion was being made that the G.A.S. is unconditionally one, for all time, so to speak, with the much larger anthroposophical movement.

Let us place the following facts side by side: After the death of Rudolf Steiner, Ludwig Polzer-Hoditz had warned against spiritual pretension in the leadership of the G.A.S. and had proposed that the leadership of the General Section of the School of Spiritual Science be left unoccupied and Dornach be allowed to develop itself as a reasonable and effective administrative centre. His words were in vain; the spiritual pretensions of a few people excluded many true pupils of Rudolf Steiner from anthroposophical work within the Society. Polzer drew the consequences and left the Society to its oppressive fate that was determined by this style of leadership and the sleepiness of many members. On the death-day of the man he respected, D.N. Dunlop, he resigned from the G.A.S. on 30 May 1936.

Towards the end of the century then, the symptomatologically very noteworthy fact became clear that Polzer's spiritual effort for freedom in the G.A.S. leadership, which, for example, reached its climax in his bold speech in Dornach in 1935, had again been rejected. At the same time, the impression was given to the membership of the G.A.S. that Rudolf Steiner would have said that 'many friends from the first period of anthroposophical activity are among us again', that is, would definitely be active again within the G.A.S. Could one, for example, honourably count *Polzer* among these friends without at the same time taking seriously the grounds that led him to leave the Society in 1936? These grounds lay in the delusional 'esoteric' pretensions and in spiritual centralization, both of which were rampant. After 1935 these had not faded but had fatally increased.[684]

Could these 'friends' simply be enlisted without further ado for the future G.A.S. in spite of their own impulses? In the Catholic Church there is a comparable demand made on individuals through sanctification and beatification. In the future, however, one will increasingly have to wonder how many of those declared holy by the Church actually continued their lives and work completely outside the Ecclesia.

The most illuminating example here is that of Ignatius of Loyola. Rudolf Steiner's spiritual research found his next incarnation as Emmanuel Swedenborg, the significant Nordic seer who no longer had any connection with the Roman Church at all.

It is precisely in an area such as this, which has to do with subtle questions of the formation of individual destiny and of reincarnation that foggy declarations can only be damaging. The more spiritual areas under consideration are, the clearer and more subtle the thinking should also become that seeks to approach it. Above all here, belongs the insight that one should not proceed from a priori presumptions.[685]

A certain provisional peak and culmination of such anti-anthroposophical efforts and actions within the G.A.S. was the declaration, somewhat in the nature of a legacy, which Manfred Schmidt-Brabant presented to the surprised members at the Michaelmas Conference in the year 2000 in Dornach: the Anthroposophical Society had fallen, he said, 'into occult imprisonment'.[*]

This was supposed to explain why the Society had been able to work so little and so ineffectively into the outside world. The mere fact that the President of the G.A.S. made this grave declaration precisely in the year when, according to the plan for the themes for each year, a plan drawn up by Schmidt-Brabant himself, the theme for 2000 was supposed to be the 'Mystery of Freedom', makes this statement of his, to put it mildly, highly questionable. Yet it was immediately taken up earnestly as a great revelation by numerous, and even leading members.

What went on in Dornach in the decades after Polzer's death was very much in the sense of the Roman Catholic politics of information management and declarations.[686] And the enlightenment of the members for contemporary affairs was for long periods very much along the lines of political Freemasonry.[687]

The effectiveness of the Testament of Peter the Great—as a struggle against the spirit of true, individual, spiritual freedom—did not stop at the gates of the G.A.S., as can be seen from the way in which the very definite spiritual impulses of Ludwig Polzer have been fought against, or from the utterance of certain serious dogmatic declarations.

---

[*] See: 'In welcher okkulten Gefangenschaft befindet sich die Anthroposophische Gesellschaft?', *Der Europäer*, Vol. 5, no. 6 April 2001, p. 20ff.

7. A Look Ahead into the Twenty-First Century

It should have been clear from the previous chapter that the long-range impulse in world politics, which is bound up with the Testament of Peter the Great has in no way faded and must be reckoned with in the coming millennium. The further development of the so-called 'New' World Order, which actually builds on antiquated impulses will also continue in the period after the year 2000. A decisive role will be played by *China*, which has been built up economically and technologically for decades, as was the case in Russia at the beginning of the century and especially after the inception of the Socialist experiment. In the global 'balance of power' and the international dialectic, which are based on consciously cultivated world political contradictions, in what is until today—after the termination of the experiment [in Russia]—the only country of world political weight still subject to the ideology of Leninism, China is likely to form a new dialectical counterpole to the West.[688]

It is not unthinkable that the group of dancers (Cossacks?) on Beedham's map (see p. 486) are also to be prompted to do a war dance and that China will be driven into the socio-economic chaos and ideological vacuum in the former Soviet Union *in order to push this chaos into Middle European culture*. Such a perspective is forecast in the thirteenth paragraph of the Testament which speaks of Russia's imperial actions: '[...] and while it pushes its troops of the line up to the Rhine, *these will immediately be followed by a swarm of its Asiatic hordes*'. In the ideological vacuum in the former Soviet empire, besides the forces of the Orthodox Church, Islam should also be able to gain increased access. This might at the same time link up with the decadent impulses of the Roman Catholic Church, as already seems to have begun.[689] All these spiritual and confessional world streams will have *one* thing in common—that despite all their divergences at lower levels they will converge ever more closely on one point: the underestimation or very deliberate rejection of the principle of real individualism that is contained in German Idealism and the spiritual science of Rudolf Steiner as the foundation for the development of the human being to free individuality—cognitively and ethically autonomous. In its conscious or unconscious rejection of this possibility of individual development in freedom, to which those in the Middle European and western Slavic peoples especially incline by nature, the Holy Alliance will in future find countless new partners. And with these it will remain the executor of the Petrine Testament.

*

Let us attempt in conclusion to show the perspectives which are contained in the work of Ludwig Polzer and which at the same time result in
the outlines of *his* spiritual testament. Let us recall his vow in the Wenceslas Chapel in 1932. It was dedicated to serve the marriage that was to
be founded and consolidated between the German Middle European and
the Czech folk element; the seventh paragraph of the Petrine Counter-
Testament (see p. 520) was not to gain the upper hand. Will there be, in
Prague and Moscow or even in St Petersburg today and tomorrow,
people who will be in a position to press forward to the true core of the
German and Czech cultures, people who see in Jakob Boehme, Goethe
and Steiner no less important companions on the path than Hus and
Wycliffe? Then gradually, another figure would rise up before that of the
spiritual figure of Czar Peter: *Dmitri*, the great herald of the still uncorrupted layer of Slavic culture.

And in Middle Europe it will be recognized that with Bismarck,
German culture was diverted onto completely inappropriate paths of
external power politics that have nothing to do with its real nature; that
Wilhelm II led German culture to the abyss into which Hitler then
pushed Germany; then, from behind the shadow of Bismarck, the Middle
European brother of Dmitri will emerge—Kaspar Hauser, the Child of
Europe, the genius (inspiring spirit) of the social form appropriate for the
German nature.

And looking towards the West, one will have to recall the time when
Oxford was not yet the Rome of the Anglo-American will to world
domination and trained Rhodes Scholars, but rather, received pupils from
Prague, the city on the Vltava, while on the line of connection between
England and Bohemia sparks of freedom sprang from Wycliffe over to
Bohemia. Then behind the shades of Rhodes and Woodrow Wilson the
pair of figures James I and Shakespeare can rise anew; in the far West the
genius of Emerson will become a leading figure. If Rudolf Steiner once
characterized the American element as 'the actual radical evil',[690] this is
not to be taken categorically but refers to the dominant elite of the West,
those such as Harriman and Churchill. On another occasion Steiner said
that anthroposophically-oriented spiritual science could also have been
developed by linking to the work of a man such as Ralph Waldo
Emerson.[691]

In this context another comment by Steiner can be mentioned which
he made in a private circle in 1914 and which refers to the post-mortem
collaboration between certain representative individualities from

German-speaking Central Europe and from the Anglo-American West: 'The following spirits now belong to a self-contained community with a high mission: Gladstone, Tennyson, Emerson, J. Joachim, Herman Grimm, Bettina von Arnim, Hallam. The special task of Herman Grimm is to show sceptics [...] the right path.'[692]

The later obscured line between (America/)England-Bohemia lies on a lower layer of Anglo-Saxon culture which stretches over to Middle Europe and which never stood in real opposition to it; it is the western equivalent of the obscured layer of western Slavic culture. If the bridge can be found and walked from Middle Europe eastwards to the Slavic cultural layer of Dmitri and westwards to the Wycliffe/James layer, then the effectiveness of the *seventh* paragraph of Peter's Testament gradually can be overcome; in no other way can this be done.

The overcoming of this paragraph, which was described as the 'central point', 'on which the success of the whole plan depends' represents the 'central point' of Polzer's Counter-Testament that is under discussion here.

The Middle European pillar of this bridge-building to the East and the West must be built on the foundation of true, radical individualism, which hopes to guide peoples to freedom on the basis of the cognitive and ethical liberation of the individual. The material for this foundation has been drawn for 100 years from the stream of spiritual science inaugurated by Rudolf Steiner.

The contribution to humanity of those that belong to the anthroposophical movement will in the coming centuries have to consist in the preparation of the necessary bridge-building materials. In these foundations neither the representatives of the Ecclesia Romana nor those of the Anglo-American Rhodes-Churchill elite should be allowed to integrate their own unusable building materials. When this is called for, then the foundation of the Middle European pillar will be undermined. All the 'best' of Europe and those who trouble themselves about the 'nobility of our souls' are only able to ruin the cast of the foundations of Europe.

Will they be ruined by these power groups; can the 'word' be found again that is to sound to the eastern future from Europe? The 'word' of the true being of man, who is an unmistakable spiritual individuality, each one a species in himself, who in the course of many earth lives expresses itself in different personalities that belong to different peoples and nations?

Without such a true individualism there can be no prospect of any dignified, humane community building. For the communities of the future should be built according to the ideal already foreseen by Friedrich Schiller—'communities of free spirits'. It is to recall this spiritual *freedom* that a capacity for clear thinking is available to the human being, free of desires and emotions, such as was once especially cultivated in Middle Europe; a thinking that can see itself able to rise above the credulous acceptance of declarations to the reasoning comprehension of the facts of the world of the senses and beyond the senses.

Insight into the principle of true, free human individuality will gradually overcome all oppositions of race, religion, nation and gender; only through this will they lose their power and effectiveness. Such insight is the counter to the 'Clash of Civilizations' that is being stirred up, the crashing against each other of the world's religious, ethnic and national power blocs.

*

In the great procession of the cultural epochs, which have not only a form in time, but also relate to specific geographical regions of the Earth, the turn towards the East has begun. This is known in Washington and in Rome. The way to the East, however, still leads *through the heart of Europe*. 'The path of the cultural epoch in which we live,' wrote Polzer in 1928,

> leads from the West to the East through this space. *In it the old must undergo metamorphosis [. . .] All old forces lose themselves on this path to the East, they cannot pass further through this space without renewing themselves out of the spirit.* If they seek to do so, they become forces of destruction and give rise to catastrophes. It is in this space which, from human knowledge, human love, and human courage, that must come about which may then proceed in a healing way towards the East.[693]

For such a fundamental insight there is hardly any understanding even today in those leading circles that seek to set the pace and course of modern developments, despite the continual catastrophes of modern times.

When one looks at the endeavours that have been made since Polzer's death to find a suitable contemporary social form in Europe, then as we have seen, it has been first and foremost the special interests of the West and the South [the Church of Rome] that have been powerfully at work on the construction of the European house—and they are still at it. The efforts of these elite circles are, however, marked by the fact that they proceed from the illusion that they believe they should be able to work towards the East through the European space with all the old forces untransformed, without spiritual renewal and without radical metamorphosis. The catastrophes which we have, for example, witnessed most recently in the shattered Yugoslavia reveal the enormous powers of destruction which, in reality, *were bound to* exist in the political endeavours of the elites, insofar as they were built on the above-mentioned illusions.

One can look at the present elite-driven politics of the EU which are determined to remake the broken nation states into a super-nation state—federal or centralized and consider the expansion of the EU towards the East. Such a policy must—with the best will in the world—continually produce destruction after destruction as long as it is based on old forces. The destructive force will work through many masks: nationalism, racism, despotism, war. Or consider today's 'globalization', in which the global economic impulses that are *supposed* to be determining the world economy are in fact tyrannized by the interests of the Anglo-American superpower—a blatant caricature of the true world economy needed in the modern age.

Rudolf Steiner once said that from his time onwards real power would pass into the hands of ever fewer individuals.[694] An aristocracy of power relationships would develop as a counter-pole to the simultaneous, growing need for democracy. He laid out a perspective in which precisely those people who from today onwards interest themselves in certain spiritual affairs, will show little inclination to trouble themselves with great political and economic developments. Then the question arises: will the few in power also be 'the best of Europe'? A glance at the history of this twentieth century shows that, on the contrary, many of these few, it seems, gained power in accordance with the principle that 'the truly worst are selected to rise to the top'.

Will it be otherwise in the twenty-first century? Will not only spiritually oriented people reincarnate but will they also be able to become as influential in the great affairs of civilization and culture as the architects of the New World Order were in the twentieth century? One can only hope so. Let us take a brief look at this real hopefulness.

★

For 1000 years the East of Europe took a separate path. Pope Nicholas I prepared the schism of 1054; the individuality that was working in him and which later reincarnated in Helmuth Moltke the Younger wants to help to bind again what he once had to separate for the sake of world historical necessity.[695] He should become a powerful agent for the realization of that part of Polzer's Testament which relates to the marriage between the Germanic and Slavic cultures.

Many other bridge-builders are likely to step forward in support; the 'four times twelve' of whom Rudolf Steiner spoke at the end of his lecturing activity will hardly allow themselves to be disturbed in their work by those seeking to execute the Petrine Testament. They will scarcely subscribe to the error that one has to involve oneself with as many spiritual and political streams as possible, which would only hinder them step by step on their free progress along the path of what they have recognized to be true. They will much rather seek the impossible—to unite the greatest possible openness for what lives and works in humanity today, with spiritual constancy.

Rudolf Steiner once spoke of the double-domed buildings that would rise up everywhere across Europe in the twenty-first century.[696] The lost word of humanity will sound out from them anew. Ludwig Polzer-Hoditz will be among the architects of such buildings—he from whom these words stem, which are meant for him as well as for the other 47,[*] and the many helpers who will accompany them:

> *Great spirit in the spheres*
> *Who was our teacher*
> *On the earth:*
> *We turn to you*
> *In our distress of spirit and soul*
> *With the light that you lit for us,*
> *With the love that you*
> *Gave to our souls,*
> *With the will, which we*
> *Seek to empower*
> *For the work at the end of the century.*
> *To the spirit of eternal being*
> *To the spirit to which you made sacrifice*
> *We dedicate our thinking and being.*

The architects of a truly new European house will find helpers in the anthroposophical movement: in all those who seek to connect with these true continuers and bearers of the impulses of Rudolf Steiner.

We shall close by recalling some other words from Ludwig Polzer. They were spoken at the inauguration of the new Prague branch room in 1936:

> Since the lifework of Rudolf Steiner came to its sudden end, we shall have to bear his work ever more quietly, intimately ... Our souls have shown themselves too weak to fight for a new social order in the present. We want to nurture spiritual wisdom so that it can soon unite itself with the fire of

---

[*] See p. 374: '...4 × 12 individuals ... would be necessary...'.

enthusiasm. So that it can fuse itself with real Michaelic courage in the service of truth [. . .] We must feel ourselves in this creativity linked with all those who have worked and suffered so that continuity during the time without the Mysteries will not cease.

Will there be enough 'fighters' on the European construction site for the new social order of the future to be able to transmute old, unusable and destructive forces into that which is truly new? Let us hope so.

VI. APPENDIX

The Testament of Peter the Great

Text: Sokolnicki version (1797)

Printed from the article in French by Harry Breslau, Historische Zeitschrift, 1879. German version by Ludwig Polzer-Hoditz.
Harry Breslau: The Testament of Peter the Great. In: Historische Zeitschrift, published by Heinrich von Sybel. New series, Vol.5 (Vol. 41 of the entire series), No. 3, p.385ff., Munich 1879. Printed and published by R. Oldenburg. It is only necessary to reproduce here the text by Sokolnicki, since, according to the thorough work by Breslau, it was the original, and above all, because it is here much less a question of the history of the development of the Testament and more of its actual political effectiveness in the destiny of Europe.
   Ludwig Polzer-Hoditz

On the Testament of Peter the Great, see also Erdmuth Grosse, Das Wirken der okkulten Logen, Basel 1986
   The author

★

Peter I's plan for the expansion of Russia and the subjugation of Europe.

1. Nothing is to be neglected in order to give the Russian people European forms and habits: in this sense, to win over the various Courts and especially the scholars of Europe, either through appealing to their interests or from philanthropic or philosophical principles or other motives in order to achieve this goal.
2. The State is to be maintained on a permanent war footing in order to keep the soldiery warlike and the nation always ready to march at the first sign.
3. All possible means are to be employed to expand towards the North along the Baltic Sea and towards the South.
4. The jealousy of England, Denmark and Brandenburg against Sweden is to be aroused, whereby these powers (their eyes will be closed) will be blind to our encroachments against this country, which will eventually be subjugated.
5. The House of Austria is to be interested in driving the Turks out of Europe, and under this pretext our own army is to be developed and outposts on the Black Sea established. Thus, advancing continuously, we shall expand as far as Constantinople.

6. Anarchy in Poland is to be promoted and maintained; the parliament and especially the election of the kings are to be influenced and every opportunity made use of to fragment and finally utterly subjugate it [Poland].

7. A close alliance is to be entered into with England and direct relations maintained by means of a trade treaty, allowing [England] to exercise a kind of domestic monopoly within [Russia] which, unnoticed, will lead to a connection between [Russian] nationals and English merchants and sailors, which will bring in all kinds of goods, in order to accomplish the improvement and enlargement of the Russian fleet with the help of which focus must be kept on the achievement of mastery in the Baltic and the Black Seas. (This is) a key point on which the success of this entire plan depends.

8. At any price, whether by force, or by cunning, a hand is to be kept in European disputes, and especially in those of Germany.

9. The appearance of alliance with Austria is to be maintained and even the smallest influence made use of to involve it [Austria] in ruinous wars in order to weaken it by degrees. Sometimes it can even be supported and aid given, but within the [Holy Roman] Empire enemies of Austria should always be created so that the jealousy of the princes is awakened against it . . .

    N.b.: This article will be easier to achieve because the House of Austria has until now not ceased to allow itself to be enticed by the plan to control a [the] universal monarchy or at least to re-establish the Empire in the west and must above all, to this end, subjugate Germany.

10. German princesses must always be sought for Russian princes so as to multiply connections in this way through family relationships and communities of interest and gain influence everywhere within the [German] Empire.

11. The influence of religion among the non-Uniate Greek Catholics who are distributed in Hungary, Turkey and the northern parts of Poland is to be used and the most cunning means employed to declare [Russia] their protectors and to gain a title of right to priestly supremacy: under this pretext and in this fashion Turkey must be made to submit and Poland conquered; the conquest of Hungary would then be child's play in that Austria would be promised compensation in Germany, while the remaining part of Poland, which would be able to maintain itself neither by force nor by its political connections, would itself bow before the [Russian] yoke.

12. From then onwards every moment is valuable: everything is to be

prepared in secrecy in order to deliver the great blow; it must be executed with an order, a foresight and at a speed which will not give Europe time to think. One must therefore begin, very secretly and with the greatest circumspection, to propose separately to the Courts, first of Versailles and then of Vienna, to share the domination of the world with one of them. It should be brought to their attention that Russia already controls the entire Orient de facto and would only still have to gain the *de jure* title to it, whereby this proposal would not at all seem suspicious to them. It is on the contrary without doubt that this proposal will not fail to flatter them and unleash a war to the death between them. In view of the connections and extensive relations between these two rival Courts and natural opponents and of the necessary interest of all European Powers to participate in these disputes, this conflict would soon have to become a general war.

13. In the midst of this general embitterment Russia will ask for help, first from the one and then from the other of the warring Powers. In order to give them time to exhaust themselves and to gather its own forces, Russia will, after inclining this way and that, finally decide in favour of the House of Austria, and while it pushes its troops of the line up to the Rhine, [Russia] will immediately have these followed by a swarm of its asiatic hordes. Along with the progress of these hordes through Germany, two large fleets would set sail, laden with such asiatic hordes, one from the Sea of Azov and the other from the port of Arkhangelsk, and accompanied by the fleets of the Black Sea and the Baltic Sea, would appear unexpectedly in the Mediterranean and in the ocean in order to disgorge these wild nomadic peoples, greedy for loot, and flood Italy, Spain and France with them. They would massacre one part of the population, enslave the other in order to populate the empty regions of Siberia and render the rest unable to throw off the yoke.

In the text published by M. Lesur in Paris in 1812 there were fourteen paragraphs. The thirteen paragraphs of the Sokolnicki text are the same as those of the Lesur text apart from some unimportant differences. Lesur only has another paragraph inserted as paragraph eight, which reads:

He [Peter] recommends to all his successors to grasp the truth that trade with India means world trade and that he would be the true ruler of the world who has exclusive control of this trade with India. Therefore, no opportunity is to be lost to make war upon Persia and hasten its degeneration in order to press forward to the Persian Gulf and via Syria, re-establish the old trade with the Levant.

From Conversations With Rudolf Steiner

The following reproduces Polzer's diary entries which have been circulating in typescript format for the past two decades. Doubts were always expressed about their authenticity, especially in relation to the Kaspar Hauser text, the 'end of November 1916' dating of which appears problematic, as Polzer did not meet Rudolf Steiner between September 1916 and May 1917, which naturally does not exclude the possibility that in November 1916 he wrote down notes of conversations that had taken place earlier. Also, the original entries have disappeared or were destroyed by Paul Michaelis (see n. 674). The author does not see in these circumstances even any approximately sufficient grounds for alleging that the documents are inauthentic or falsified, a charge which is sometimes levelled at Paul Michaelis without, thus far, any concrete evidence. Fig. 38 shows extracts from the beginnings of Polzer's diary entries from 1923–1925. Evidently, he had the handwritten entries typed and then in his own hand wrote the Roman numerals I to III above the entries and the exact dating in the left-hand margins. The addition of the Roman numerals and the dating in arabic numbers—following a detailed comparison with corresponding numerals and numbers in Polzer's handwritten archive—must be regarded as authentic, that is, as having been written by Ludwig Polzer. The fact of these handwritten numerals and dates has been passed over by those who have put forward the falsification theory.

Conversations I to III were made available to the author in typed form via Dr E. Hermann of Heidelberg; he made no further comment on them. The typescript bears the title: 'Aus den Aufschreibungen des Grafen Ludwig Polzer-Hoditz nach Gesprächen mit Rudlf Steiners'. [From notes made by Count Ludwig Polzer-Hoditz after conversations with Rudolf Steiner]

The communications about the mission of Kaspar Hauser (titled IV by us) with the dating 'End of November 1916' come from the archive of Paul Michaelis. On his Kaspar Hauser drama, see p. 429.

After the appearance of the first edition of this book, new accusations of falsification were made, and were put about notably by Heinz Matile and Andreas Meister. The reader will find a discussion of these claims on p. 530ff.

The square brackets below [ ] contain additions by the author, unless otherwise indicated.

I.

1.1.1923

At noon on New Year's Day after the fire, [Polzer asks] in Villa Hansi: 'How could that have happened?'

[']There is too great a difference between [the members'] souls. They want to see and hear everything and be present at everything but they do not want to wake up. So they have to be awakened by catastrophes and personal sufferings. It is not karma that is prevalent here but only the members' lack of wakefulness, and human envy which works even into the physical.

[']The possibility was given to us of having the Place of the Word, but the Place of the Word can only be when it has its counterparts, its living image in the human heart, in conscientiousness for the Word, that means, when the human being not only listens but wants to bear responsibility, and can bear it as a human being who takes responsibility for himself before the Word of the world. That was the meaning of the Building. Word and answer, Logos and Man.

[']In Ephesus we had the secret of the Incarnation of the Word before us. It had to be destroyed; otherwise the counter-forces would have able to develop a significant centre for their activity there, for the envy of the Gods was effective as far the atmospheric level. But here, there is a reversal [i.e. in Dornach—*transl.*]. The Gods were looking down expectantly to the Place of the Word, but the human beings were not there who could protect the Building. A possibility was given, but there was no answer from mankind; only envy was not silent.

[']Look, Hadrian also bore within himself the thought of a Building of the Word but it could only be like a caricature of the Word, as he wanted to save the old Mysteries. He sought honourably for a renewal of the Mysteries and even came near to Christ. That is why he even went to Egypt, far beyond Edfu up the Nile. Egypt caused memories to rise up in his soul but they blinded him with the power of the sentient soul's world of images. Antinous sacrificed himself [for Hadrian] but he could give him no more answers from the other side. You should try to occupy yourself with Hadrian and in doing so, think about Egypt. There is the important terraced temple of Hatshepsut where you have, deep inside it, a holy grotto with a representation of Isis and the boy Horus, which works like an archetypal image of the Virgin and the Jesus child. Hadrian too came to this grotto and indeed, immediately after [visiting] On. Here [in the holy Isis grotto of Hatshepsut] there was repeated what he had once experienced more than 1000 years before, when, in the time of the Thutmoses Pharaohs, in the blossoming of the culture of Raphael-Mercury-Hermes, the first female Pharaoh reigned and built her wonderful temple. At that time he went as a High Priest of Amun-Re in the entourage of Queen Hatshepsut to the city of On when the Queen brought the architect from the site of the oracle of the Sun initiates. On was founded by Manu and

was the first Sun Oracle of the southern stream [from Atlantis—*transl.*].
The Greek heroes were drawn from here. The course of the Holy Grail
later returned to Europe via On. Akhenaten was also initiated to a certain
degree in On. He could not gain the highest degree as he was an epileptic
and through this knew directly what was to be gained through initiation.
Here we have the high point of history. The Mercury–Hermes Mystery
was taken up by the initiates of the Sun Oracle. Through this, everything
has this tremendous cosmopolitan character, from On to the sources of
the Nile, from the Tigris and the Euphrates over to Alexandria. And it is
also at this time that Moses emerges and takes with him the secret of
Osiris, the secret of the Cosmic Word and from then on, Isis remains
silent. Knowledge of the senses grows and what was a cosmic cultus
becomes a pompous ceremonial cult which found its shadow image in
today's externalized Church of Power.[']

II.

11.11.1924

Arrived in Dornach today. When he learned that I was in D., he had me
called. His atelier had been transformed into his sickroom. At that time he
was sitting at first in an easy chair. We spoke of my father. Then about the
issue of the Michael School and about the Esoteric Circle. To my
question as to how I should hold the Class Lessons in Vienna and Prague,
he answered affectionately: 'Do it as you wish.' With that, I am taking on
a very responsible task. The continuity of the ME [= Mystica Eterna: a
ritual body instituted by Rudolf Steiner before the First World War and
connected to certain freemasonic rituals] has been preserved and transformed in accordance with the times. After a long silence, I asked R.
Steiner whether he was also thinking of establishing a master class in the
sense of the old esotericism. He gave me more or less the following
answer:

> The classes for the members of the General Anthroposophical Society are,
> after the establishment [of the master class], to be put into the hands of Frau
> Ita Wegman. A Class II for Section leaders and Section members as well as
> for lecturers and active members who take initiatives, which has yet to be
> set up, I shall have Frau Doctor [Steiner] lead. Then there will be a final
> class III, which I shall establish and lead as a kind of master class.

He then spoke about details and the number of members of the three
Classes. Class I: numbers unlimited. The texts will, similar to the weekly

verses, go through the course of the year and from the yearly rhythm will speak more directly to the spiritual individuality, so that from the *Übe-Geist-Besinnen* [Work at Spirit-Sensing] an experience of spirit and participation of the human destiny stream can result in responsible consciousness.

Class II: 36. Here will be accepted those who have had spiritual experiences as members of Class I. Moral qualities will be of decided significance here.

Class III: 12. These will then be the esoteric Vorstand. This Class III, the so-called master class, will have a purely ritual character which will be celebrated at three altars at the same time. We turn to the corresponding archangel beings in Class II and in this Class III, we turn directly to the Spirit of the Earth, the Christ Being.

Then he was silent again for a long time in deep contemplation. Then suddenly his face was overshadowed by deep concern, and R. Steiner sighed, breathing heavily. We spoke about the Christmas Conference and the Constitution of the High School. Further, he spoke about the tasks of Albert Steffen, Frl. Vreede and Dr Wachsmuth, whose tasks lay purely in administration. 'They have the places appropriate to them in the Sections.' Then we spoke about his brother and sister. Before I left, he kissed me again on the forehead.

III.

3.3.1925

Count Polzer-Hoditz' last visit. Sickroom. [This heading was added by the copyist]:

After certain difficulties in the Society were spoken about—for example, amongst other things, the early death of Sophie Stinde, whose place in the Johannes Building Association I could have taken so that a certain continuity could have been preserved vis-à-vis the western Slavs—in relation to the activity of Joh.[ann] Sobieski—, the conversation moved on, via Nero-Crown Prince Rudolf, Agrippina and Seneca to Crown Prince Rudolf and Empress Elisabeth. Hadrian and his intermediary role [middle position in time?] between the mad Caesars were also spoken of again. When I asked the Herr Doctor why he always pointed me to these connections, he replied:

> Because they have directly to do with you. But you have never wanted to know anything of it. Always keep this in mind : the Jesuits have deprived

humanity of religiosity, of devotion; they are identical with the power of the Roman State. The battle—that is to say, the sin against the Holy Spirit is the means of power by which they seek to enforce their domination—the only sin which the scriptures say cannot be forgiven. Yet still the spirit cannot be entirely eradicated. But only a few will carry it over into the future.

This [Jesuit] stream can also be felt in the [Anthroposophical] Society and he hoped to have paralyzed it through the Christmas Conference for it was not without reason that he had sought to safeguard a certain parity of the male and female spirit within the Vorstand, as the tendencies were still there from ancient times that would exclude the female spirit.

I drew attention to that already in the early days when I spoke about the Temple Legend. But it was not understood and is still a significant undercurrent in the Society. The battle against the spirit has always lain and will always lie in the background of all outer events. You must have a very fine sensitivity in your fingers for this, or better still, you must have developed a very fine nose. And certainly the nose in particular can be a very special indicator for the spiritual researcher. And among painters and poets, if they are really painters and poets, we find exemplary noses in which we can read not only character, maturity and greatness but much more, the life of this individuality in past ages. Now that is the case, but not every poet has to be a reborn Giotto. Fra Bartolomeo di Marco was indeed a significant poet-painter who took forward the School of Giotto and [who] is that individuality who was in a western region for the first time in Alexandria and was the bishop who had Hypatia killed. He came from Mystery circles in Mexico and played a great role in the event that related to the Mystery of Golgotha like a counter-picture. This stream too had to be absorbed by us and is like the earthly basis of the spirit triangle in the pentagram.

Then we spoke about the activities of Roman Catholic and western lodges and with great earnestness Herr Doctor emphasized that three problems were to be solved, the result of which would be of very special importance for the future,

1. The question about the two Johns [John the Baptist and John the Evangelist—*transl.*].
2. Who was Demetrius? [Czar Dmitri of Russia 1605–1606—*transl.*]
3. Where did Caspar Hauser come from? In all these it is especially important that one's gaze is not directed towards the death of the subject but towards the birth. Where did they come from and with what tasks? The individuality hidden behind the veil of Kaspar Hauser is a being [who has worked] inspiringly into Rosicrucian connections

from the beginning and had incarnated on 29 September 1812 as the son of the Grand Duke Karl of Baden and his wife Stephanie de Beauharnais. This individuality had an important task of esoteric Christianity to fulfil.

For the Russians there appears behind the image of Demetrius the great Jesus Imagination, the imagination on which the Eastern Christian Church has remained fixed. Western occultism tries to drive this Imagination from the world and replace it with a false one: Christ is to appear as the Lord of the Earth, but as Ruler, as tyrant. Eastern occultism wants to do away with the Jesus Imagination and make people forget it. Schiller wanted to portray all this in his drama *Demetrius*, the importing of the false image by the Poles, that is, by the Roman Church. And that is why Goethe's confusion was so great when he lost Schiller and why the *Demetrius* could not be completed. Blavatsky also stood in this struggle between the western and eastern lodges. We all stand in it now.

It is quite unessential to ask who Demetrius was, who Kaspar Hauser was, for such a question leads away from the actual event. It is not who Demetrius was, who Kaspar Hauser was that is important, but: What was intended through them? What was intended through them?—that is what should occupy us for in such a direction of enquiry we shall always find a key for the understanding of many difficulties.

Pay attention to what comes towards you as a question and how a question is formulated. More reveals itself of the being of a personality in this than in all other outer gestures, deeds and words. It is all about how a question is put. In this also lies the decisive significance of the question from Frau Dr Wegman, when she asked me about the new esotericism. She did not just want to link on to the old, but she asked me the decisive Parzival question about a new esotericism. Only through this question, put in this way, did it become possible to establish the Michael School on Earth. In this School lies the kernel of the future as possibility. If this were only understood by the members, as a possibility. When and wherever you hold Class Lessons, always keep in mind that during the Class Lesson it is not a matter of reading out a lecture in a didactic manner but rather that you are taking part in an act, you have to accomplish an act which can place us in relationship with the Mystery stream of all ages.

IV.

[November 1916]

Those circles which conceal everything and today still try to conceal what happened in connection with Kaspar Hauser's destiny are those members of western lodges and of the Jesuits who have worked together in the top positions of their organizations for more than 150 years, but demonstrably since January 1802. They therefore do not want exposed what they have staged as an experiment, as an elaborate attempt, through their experiment, to separate that individuality from his task; to hold him in a twilight zone. The I of this being was not to be allowed to penetrate its body, it was to remain outside it in a twilight zone, neither purely spirit nor purely earthly man. It was to be led away from its task and remain as though in spiritual exile. That means to form a body but not to be able to take hold of it as an I. But the experiment did not succeed and therefore Kaspar Hauser had to die. They had to experience how, through their experiment, exactly what they had striven to prevent was brought about: the awakening of the individuality. Yes, that it became aware of reincarnation and karma. But that was exactly what was not supposed to happen.

South Germany should have become the new Grail Castle of the new Knights of the Grail and the cradle of future events. The spiritual atmosphere had been well-prepared by all those personalities whom we know as Goethe, Schiller, Hölderlin, Herder etc. Kaspar Hauser was to have gathered around him all that lived in this spiritual atmosphere thus prepared. But that was not wanted by those circles [western lodges and S.J.—*Paul Michaelis*]. They could not allow an awakening Middle [Middle Europe—*transl.*] if they were not to relinquish their power and their designs on power. Goethe's kind of spirit frightened them, Napoleon forced them towards each other and into an alliance for global dominion in ideology and economy. Napoleon had already thwarted their efforts; it was Napoleon, basically, who forced the two streams into an alliance. Since then, the tasks of the two realms have been clearly delineated but all the more effectively directed towards their clearly defined goal of world domination. Ideological and spiritual affairs were given over exclusively into the hands of the S.J.; economic matters were the preserve of the Anglo-American lodges, the lodges of the West. But these plans will increasingly lead to tragic conflicts and catastrophes because they do not reckon with the human being and with human development. What was intended for Kaspar Hauser was shattered by human beings. On these planned ruins the principle of black-and-white could gain dominion. The principle of black-and-white, however, is something that constructs, but in an exclusive fashion.

Here also lies the tragedy of Bismarck, who was indeed able to provide a model of a federal state, the construction of a true federation in the Middle [of Europe—*transl.*], but not the Idea to carry it, which could have made such a form of the State seem necessary and justified. That was what Bismarck was also seeking in Frankfurt [at the Frankfurt Parliament

1848–49—*transl.*], the Goethean spirit—that which Kaspar Hauser would have enabled to live in southern Germany but was not alive. It was in Frankfurt where Bismarck actually encountered the principle of black-and-white and everything that then bound him to the King of Prussia. From then on began the era of lawyers, but politics is not a legal problem.

On the Claims of Falsification Asserted by Matile and Meister

Heinz Matile, the President of the Albert Steffen Foundation has published, together with Andreas Meister, a kind of synopsis of all previous falsification theories. The text bore the title 'On the So-called "Writings of Ludwig Polzer-Hoditz after Conversations with Rudolf Steiner".' It can be found under 'Texts about Albert Steffen' on the website of the Steffen Foundation as a .pdf file
(www.steffen-stiftung.ch/pdf/ludwig_polzer.pdf).

Matile and Meister take up my statement about the conversations which I discuss on p. 522ff. of this book in which I argue that the authenticity of Polzer's notes has not been disproven. They claim: 'It is for the historian to determine the authenticity of sources.' This is true only insofar as the serious historian only uses documents the authenticity of which he can adequately vouch for. If someone claims these documents are not authentic or even falsified, it is naturally for *that person* to prove his case.

What proofs do Matile and Meister have to present? First, they take a closer look at the handwritten numerals of Polzers which I have published and compare them with those which can be found on the copies of the notes of the conversations (see Figs. 38 and 39). The authors opine:

> Polzer-Hoditz clearly wrote the number 2 differently. In his handwriting the lower line of the number appears with a swing (often with a small curve at the bottom left), while the number 2s in the handwriting on the papers under discussion show a marked horizontal straight line. Also, the number 9 shows a clearly different entry point [...] Polzer-Hoditz's handwriting always has the 9 closed at the top.

The discrepancy between the two variations of the numbers 2 and 9 they consider to be a proof 'that the dating was in fact not done by Polzer-Hoditz'. If this last point were true, then the typewritten notes would not be marked by Polzer's datings and would then in fact lose an important element that upholds their authenticity.

But the matter is not so simple. A serious graphological analysis can never restrict itself to only two or three pages, in this case, to the examples of handwriting published by me without any intention that they should serve as proof of anything. What Matile and Meister did not consider is that people often write numbers in different ways. This was also the case with Polzer. Below are illustrations of numbers from his handwritten archive which correspond very precisely to those in the notes:

Examples of the number 2

a) with a straight lower line

b) with straight and curved lower lines in one and the same dating

Examples of the number 9, open above

The graphological number 'proof' presented by Matile and Meister thus fails to stand up. For them, it was the first and most important 'proof' of a formal kind of the lack of authenticity of the notes.

With regard to the *content*, they then comment on Hadrian, Steffen, the Anthroposophical Society and Kaspar Hauser. We shall examine these comments in order.

1. Hadrian

Matile and Meister consider it impossible that Polzer can have received from Steiner a direct karmic indication with regard to this personality *before* his Hadrian dream of 1928 (see p. 245f.) Otherwise, he would never have been able to say: 'I had never before thought of Hadrian.' They point to the notes of the conversation of 3 March 1925: 'When I asked the Herr Doctor why he always pointed me to these connections, he replied: "Because they have directly to do with you. But you have never wanted to know anything of it."' Matile and Meister do not consider these sayings to be authentic, for they find: 'Polzer-Hoditz was certainly not a man who simply forgot what Rudolf Steiner said to him.' In saying this, they know more than Polzer himself. He writes in his auto-biographical text, written in drama form, *Schicksalsbilder aus der Zeit meiner Geistesschülerschaft* [Images of Destiny from the Time of my Spiritual Pupilship] amongst other things about two of his conversations with

Rudolf Steiner. On the conversation in September 1924, which does not figure in the notes under discussion (by Matile and Meister) but which Polzer mentions in his written memorial for Ita Wegman (see p. 582ff.), we read:

> He: About personal matters of your destiny / I did not want to say anything to you, / because it once seemed to me / that you shied away from such knowledge, / so as to experience your destiny in complete freedom.
> I: What I said to you at that time was not meant in this sense. It was diffidence that restrained me.

This dialogue might have taken place in the conversation of March 1925 (see above, p. 525f.); Polzer might then later in his review have brought it forward by a few months. As always: he assumes in each case that Steiner was actually trying to give karmic indications, which Polzer did not take up. The conversation at New Year 1923 was just such a case: '*You should occupy yourself with Hadrian and in doing so, think about Egypt.*'

It is not the case, as Matile and Meister simply assume, whether Polzer 'forgot', but that he apparently did not like to relate *to himself* indications that Steiner had actually made. His statement from 1928 can also be interpreted in this light: 'I had never thought of Hadrian before.' It does not at all prove, as Matile and Meister assume without further ado, that Polzer could never have heard of Hadrian from Steiner, but that he had never *referred what he had heard to himself*.

2. Albert Steffen / Fra Bartolomeo

The passage in the conversation of 3 March 1925 raises the greatest questions. After only an indirect allusion to Albert Steffen, this deals with the Renaissance painter Fra Bartolomeo (1472–1517). The fact that in a letter to Marie Steiner on 27 February 1925 Rudolf Steiner spoke of a clear karmic relation of Steffen to Giotto (1266–1337) (published today in GA 262) is of course not compatible with an incarnation of Steffen as Fra Bartolomeo. As both Steiner and Steffen saw it, Steffen had not been Fra Bartolomeo, quite independently of what was said in the conversation about the karmic background of Fra Bartolomeo.

The claims of inauthenticity by Matile and Meister here are the weightiest, indeed, basically the only ones of real relevance. However, in the discrepancy of this important passage I can see no proof that the notes were *falsified*. It could be a case of Polzer not having recalled something exactly, of confusing the contents of a conversation that included a complex of facts, which he possibly first recorded only many years later or had recorded by his friend Paul Michaelis.

★

On the letter by Rudolf Steiner to Marie Steiner on 27 February 1925 to which Matile and Meister refer with great emphasis, I would like to make the following remarks with regard to the deeper implications of the karmic revelation expressed in the letter: Marie Steiner was the first and only person to whom Rudolf Steiner spoke about the Giotto background of Albert Steffen. After Steiner's death, she indicated this to Steffen, basing herself on the letter of 27 February 1925. He immediately understood this and confirmed it on the basis of his own insights. Marie Steiner then read the letter to him.[*]

This letter of 27 February 1925, which includes the indications relating to Steffen, played an important role in the legal case which had to be brought in 1948 by the Nachlassverein [(Rudolf Steiner) Estate Association] founded by Marie Steiner before her death against the G.A.S. (then presided over by Albert Steffen), because the G.A.S. had been disputing the Nachlassverein's perfectly existing rights to the literary estate of Rudolf Steiner; the Nachlassverein won the case in 1951. The letter includes, namely, words which clearly document Rudolf Steiner's high estimation of Marie Steiner's capacity of judgement. The letter was therefore also laid before the judge, but with the karmic indication relating to Steffen redacted (see *Nachrichten der Rudolf Steiner Nachlassverwaltung*, No. 4, October 1952). One can still see today the evidence of the redaction on the original. There was no lack of tragedy in the fact that the heirs of the literary estate of Rudolf Steiner had to be called by Marie Steiner to fight against Albert Steffen for her rights with, amongst other things, a letter that touched on Albert Steffen's karmic past into which, next to Rudolf Steiner, she had been the first person in the anthroposophical movement—besides Steffen himself—to have insight.

A similar tragedy overshadowed the karmic observations that Polzer published in his book *Das Mysterium der europäischen Mitte*. Both Marie Steiner and Albert Steffen misjudged the significance of this work.

To the tragic conflicts within the G.A.S. was added, not least, at the deeper level, karmic knowledge that became *personal*, the sharing of karmic information that was *not worked through* properly, or quite simply, karmic *speculation*. How far Steffen himself became the victim of karmic knowledge which was taken too personally is shown by his behaviour at the outset of the legal case, which had such a deleterious effect on the progress of the anthroposophical cause in the world: Steffen strongly criticized the representative of the Nachlassverein, Dr Paul Jenny, for

---

[*] Communicated to the author by Heinz Matile on 15 January 1992.

having laid before the judge Rudolf Steiner's letter of 27 February 1925, which contained the passage about Steffen, the redaction of which he evidently had not been informed. Marie Steiner had assured him that it would not be published before his death, but she had left behind no instruction to this effect. Paul Jenny wrote to Steffen on 24 June 1952:

> You stopped me and spoke to me at the exit of the courtroom after the hearing at the Solothurn Higher Court on 17 June, not on behalf of the anthroposophical cause—as I might have expected in that moment from the President of the Anthroposophical Society as the person most concerned with the case—but for the sake of your own person, in relation to the letter of Rudolf Steiner to Frau Marie Steiner of 27 February 1925. (loc.cit., p. 78)

With regard to karmic *speculations*, certain speculations about Steffen's karmic background may be mentioned in this context, which have only been put to rest by a definite interpretation of the Bartolomeo passage from the Polzer/Michaelis notes and which were only silenced because the relevant passage from the letter of 27 February 1925 was published in full for the first time in 2002, in the 2nd edition of GA 262. Had this passage been published in 1967 in the 1st edition, four years after Steffen's death, all the speculations about Albert Steffen in connection with the Bartolomeo passage in the notes under discussion here would have been superfluous. The Bartolomeo passage would also have been commented upon accordingly in the first edition of the Polzer biography.

3. Anthroposophical Society

Here too, Matile and Meister only regard as valid those viewpoints which accord with *their* personal notion of Steffen's 'esoteric' function in the Vorstand. They cannot consider it possible that for Steiner, the tasks of three Vorstand members, namely, Elisabeth Vreede, Guenther Wachsmuth and Albert Steffen, 'lie entirely in an administrative capacity'. That Steiner never named a 'successor', yet Steffen remained only the acting President [*der stellvertretende erster Vorsitzender*] of the Vorstand confirms that he too regarded this office as having a purely administrative function.

Paying no attention to this, Matile and Meister simply and indignantly assert: 'And now we are expected to believe that half of the Vorstand's tasks are supposed to be administrative!!'

4. Kaspar Hauser and genetic 'proof' of his non-noble lineage.

Firstly, it can be acknowledged that in fact there is a justifiable question as to why *the same* three tasks which had been left for the members like a legacy by Steiner, as recorded by Polzer in his notes of the conversation of 3 March 1925, were not included in his memorial text for Ita Wegman in 1943 (see p. 582ff.); the Kaspar Hauser indication, notably, was omitted in 1943. I am not in a position to give a clear answer to this question.

But when Matile and Meister believe that this discrepancy is also evidence of falsification then they are leaving the ground of scientific enquiry for which they make such strenuous claims.

They descend straight into an abyss of pseudo-science when they wish to 'protect' Rudolf Steiner from claims that 'he had said Kaspar Hauser had been the Crown Prince of Baden'. They see their justification for this in the publication by *Der Spiegel* in 1996 of a genetic analysis of blood flecks on underpants that supposedly were worn by Kaspar Hauser. This dubious analysis has itself since been clearly disproved! See: http://www.anthroposophie.net/bibliothek/bib_kasparhauser.htm

Conclusion: Even if the history of the emergence of the notes of the conversations between Polzer and Steiner and the form of those notes have not until today been able to be clarified thoroughly, and even if particular details of their contents raise questions that cannot easily be answered, to ascribe to them categorically 'the nature of falsification' and especially to insinuate that Paul Michaelis, who inherited Polzer's estate, had 'impure intentions' and worse, is still, in both scientific and human terms, frivolous behaviour.

The Struggle Over Polzer's Book in 1928

The following documents, published here for the first time, only came to light after the first edition of this book. See p. 256ff.

Letter of Marie Steiner to Polzer

Dornach, 12 March 1929, Haus Hansi

Honoured Count Polzer,

The deep pain, which I felt in the whole affair surrounding your book, especially when I put myself in your position, has always been an obstruction when, in my hectic life, I wanted to answer your letter. I would have preferred to have let the whole matter rest; only the mention of my name obliged me to write. This discomfort caused me to remain silent for so long previously and realize that silence is also consent, something which Dr Steiner had always opposed. I have always mentioned that we had a conversation on one occasion in which, amongst other things which occupied most of the conversation, you said something about your book which to me was not yet at all clear—I was just no longer sure when this conversation had taken place because it had left me with no clear impression at all of what you were intending to say in your book. That sentence—'but it should not be to the detriment of Dr Steiner'—which you yourself in your letter mention came from me, after I had asked the question whether you would bring forward something about karmic relationships [...] gives the clearest explanation of my standpoint. But now something is taken out of Dr Steiner's Karma Lectures, which, according to Dr Steiner's will, ought only to be studied in connection with all his lectures; and everything that you yourself bring about karmic relationships is brought in connection with Dr Steiner; it works back onto him. It has therefore become the opposite of what I agreed and expected to be able to check. I find the matter exceedingly awkward and painful, and so I have written this letter to you out of a feeling of anguish but also out of necessity. How I would have liked to remain silent.

With friendly greetings,

When I had written the enclosed letter, I received Count Polzer's February letter to the Council of the Anthroposophical Society. It now seemed to me that what I had written before now no longer quite corresponded to the situation. But I decided to send it together with the comments which I still had to make to the Council on the letter.

Dornach, 20 March 1929

Polzer's Letter to the Council [Vorstand] of the G.A.S.

Stuttgart, 12th February 1929

To the Vorstand of the General Anthroposophical Society, Dornach

I want to provide the following information and observations in connection with my book *Das Mysterium der europäischen Mitte.*

I have seen that on 27.12.28 Herr Dr von Grunelius, acting in the interest of the Orient-Occident Publishing Company in response to Frau Dr Steiner's objection, had to arrange for the cancellation of the delivery, as the objection, communicated by Herr Steffen or Herr Leinhas related to the lack of written permission for the printing of quotations from the manuscript of a lecture transcription.

By mutual agreement the publishing contract was therefore annulled on 7 February.

Since Frau Dr Steiner in her letter of 12.1, which a few days later was posted to Prague and reached me on 12 January at Aspang Post Office in Mariensee, refers to 'some' Vorstand members and the letter relates to an intervention in the distribution of my book, I cannot therefore consider the letter as a normal private communication.

However, the letter does not deal directly with infringement of copyright—this remains only in the background—but mainly complains about the context in which the quotations appear. Even Herr Dr von Grunelius told me that in conversation with him, Frau Dr Steiner had especially complained about the context in which the quotations appear. In this way 'some Vorstand members' have complained about *the meaning and the independent work in the book.* These are circumstances which lead me to direct some more observations to the Council of the Anthroposophical Society.

First, I must return to the development [of the book] and to what I did in order to act morally, legally and correctly before I handed the book over to be printed. Following the death of Herr Dr Steiner, after I had gradually looked over my own situation within the Anthroposophical Society, I resolved to write about Austrian affairs and Rudolf Steiner's position with regard to those. My specific work always lay in this area and I experienced much of what Herr Dr Steiner said and did in this sense.

Gradually, the thought structure of the book came about. In 1927 I then first wrote seven articles and sent them to Herr Steffen in the summer of 1927. After a short while, the articles were sent back with a friendly accompanying letter. When I then visited Herr Steffen in autumn 1927 and asked him whether he wanted to print the articles in the *Goetheanum*, he told me that he would rather not do that but that I might like to write a book about it.

Now, I felt I should lecture on the content of the book in Dornach before its publication, and I chose to do this at the 1927 Christmas Conference.

I reproduced the content of the book in three lectures there. I did that out of a sense of courtesy which seemed to me necessary and to correspond to trust, and not as the result of any idea that I would need any kind of prior approval for the writing of the book. I did not want to speak on the theme earlier in another place before I had done so at the Goetheanum. I then gave the lectures in Vienna and Prague in the course of 1928.

Soon after Christmas, I visited Frau Dr Steiner and told her that I wanted to write a book on the theme of the lectures, for which I would need approval to print two lectures [by R. Steiner] and some quotations which were connected to the theme of the book. Somewhat later, in March I believe, I then wrote a letter to Frau Dr Steiner to which I appended transcripts of the two lectures and for which I requested permission to have printed [in the book]. By the end of April I had received no answer, so I regarded permission as having been given.

However, I did not wish to satisfy myself with this silent approval but wanted to speak to Frau Dr Steiner herself, so, to *this* end, I travelled to Dornach and was received by Frau Dr Steiner on 5 May.

As all the other Vorstand members except for Frau Dr Steiner had heard my lectures and were familiar with their content in Dornach, no one can imagine that I wanted to keep anything from Frau Dr Steiner; nor could I imagine that she knew nothing at all of them.

In fact, I told Frau Dr Steiner on my visit on 5 May everything that was necessary for permission for publication of lectures and quotations. At that time, Frau Dr Steiner related to me in great detail and with a lively interest matters relating to a person in the Anthroposophical Society, matters that were of a more private and family nature and which had actually nothing to do with me. Because of this, the more—as it seemed to me—important matter of my book, which contained my anthroposophical life task and on account of which I had travelled to Dornach, receded into the background, whereas I, on the contrary, had been expecting an interest in it.

The conversation about it was indeed brief, but touched on everything to the extent that I was able to feel justified in terms of morality and correct behaviour.[1]

Frau Dr Steiner asked me whether I had read through the transcripts of the lectures carefully, which I said I had; then she asked me whether I spoke directly about the incarnation of [Crown Prince] Rudolf of Austria, which I affirmed and added that I would present some quotations.[2] Then Frau Dr Steiner said that one had to be careful with regard to the public. I replied that since the death of Herr Dr Steiner I did not consider great caution and anxiety to be right,[3] and already standing in the doorway—Fräulein Hacker was waiting outside to be received—Frau Dr Steiner then said to me: one would therefore have to take care because something in the spiritual world could perhaps still fall on Dr Steiner. I was still able to say that in the case of the book I did not believe this could happen.[4]

After this conversation, I was bound to feel that since Frau Dr Steiner had raised no direct objections, she had given her permission for publication.[5]

I could not imagine that Frau Dr Steiner could take the position that written permission would be necessary, which I was later told was the justification for cancelling distribution.[6] I did not in the slightest conceive of the possibility of a need for a kind of prior censoring because of the context in which the quotations were to be used, as this was not at all Rudolf Steiner's way. But if Frau Dr Steiner had asked me at that time to show her the printed sheets, I would probably have complied with the request on the grounds of my understanding that there was a really friendly relationship between us.

I could also not imagine that Frau Dr Steiner would simply let me leave the conversation with such an unexpressed thought, namely, that I would need to take steps other than the ones that I had already taken.

I was therefore justified in believing that I had met all the requirements of moral and correct behaviour in order to have my book published.

From the letter written to me on 12 January 1929 it does not directly follow that Frau Dr Steiner is referring to an infringement of copyright[7], since she does not want to take the position of denying my request and of asserting the need for written permission and for prior censorship.

When, within the Anthroposophical Society, one no longer regards oneself as being in a relationship of trust with an older member, then the one real bond within the Society since the death of Herr Dr Steiner is no longer there.

In discussions with Herr von Grunelius, however, Frau Dr Steiner took the view that permission had not been given;[8] the other objection, that relating to ignorance of context, had to be without effect as far as the publisher and the contract were concerned. But the affair is thus consequently made into a legal matter,[9] which is significant for the publisher and must naturally be taken into account.

I have to understand the situation which resulted through all this as follows: that although Herr Steffen and Frau Dr Steiner had had almost a year to deal with the matter, nothing happened.[10] The affair was trivialized; it was regarded as not worth the effort of troubling oneself with. It was taken up *belatedly* and in an unclear fashion, damaging the publisher and myself.

The effect of a combination[11] of copyright and the censorship pretensions of 'some Vorstand members' is that of a silent but effective concordat between Vorstand authority and State legislation.

From the censorship pretension[12], a kind of 'imprimateur', as with the Catholic Church, it is no longer very far from the 'Index'. The only difference is that the possibility of executing such a pretension was not followed up, since Frau Dr Steiner did not find the time within such a long period to read a letter from me, and the Vorstand,[13] that is, Frau Dr Steiner and Herr Steffen, who both knew of the matter, had almost a year to address it and despite their neglect, then did so in a way that was delayed and damaging to others.

I must also lodge the complaint that Frau Dr Steiner thinks that she can judge the situation after a mere cursory glance through the book with which I occupied myself intensively for so many years on the basis of Rudolf Steiner's guidance.

The factual points which Frau Dr Steiner makes to me in her letter I must say are incorrect, while I have to regard the moral instruction with its hardly tactful reference to the strictness of Herr Dr Unger in comparison with myself as insulting and as showing little understanding for different destinies. I am simply not Dr Unger and certainly have a very different task from him.

When the basis of trust, the one effective power that holds things together, is abandoned in this way, when the life work of an older member is so trivialized, indeed, one can even say, taken with such a lack of seriousness as to be insulting,[14] then one naturally cannot believe that it can be taken seriously when 'individual Vorstand members' belatedly oppose the public appearance of the book and then, when something has to be done about it, they have to resort to combining the issue with an alleged infringement of copyright, which is then pushed out from the background into the foreground.[15]

What has showed itself again is that since the death of Herr Dr Steiner, there is no possibility of a central, initiative-taking leadership and that no Vorstand can operate with such comprehensive pretensions as has happened in this case. When similar pretensions *do* exist, then the Index, censorship, concordats, behind-the-scenes manoeuvres, and worse practices will gradually be resorted to.

However, since the death of our great teacher, the anthroposophical movement has actually gone far beyond the boundaries of pettiness and will not allow itself to be constrained by them.

I feel myself justified in writing precisely about Rudolf Steiner's position within old Austria and precisely as his contemporary who lived through such events [in Austria]. The communications about karma were there [in the book] to be studied and shared as I attempted to do.[16]

Furthermore, I thought to be able to forge the right way forward through the use of the quotations, but naturally, other paths can also be taken. I also feel myself justified in the way I proceeded on the basis of what Rudolf Steiner said about these events; therein lies precisely the living work with the concrete karmic communications, the most important for our time, that Rudolf Steiner gave.[17]

Individual cases can always only be worked with in terms of destiny, never in an academic context. Work on an individual case must relate to the destiny of the person doing the work, because no one has the universality that Rudolf Steiner has and we, on the other hand, especially in this area, should [not] fall into normal academic scientific methods.

In regard to the relationships I have worked on, I *also* feel that I am a guardian of the work of Rudolf Steiner.

These are the external circumstances related to the book. There are, however, deeper aspects which led me to write the book as I did, and also deeper reasons for the opposition to the book. I shall refrain from presenting these here.

At any rate, it is my conviction that an ever-more evident anxiety, perhaps fear, has no place in the Anthroposophical Society. It would be the worst thing that could be conceived since the death of Dr Steiner.

In conclusion, I must repeat, as I say in my first letter, that in this matter I have a good conscience which is based on Rudolf Steiner.

Ludwig Count Polzer-Hoditz

Handwritten marginal notes by Marie Steiner:

1. related to the historical [lectures]
2. this is pointing to negativity in my behaviour
3. he therefore had to protect himself
4. could only relate to the phys. world, for I *never* say such things; it's not my way.
5. It follows from this that the question was no longer put. It had already been indicated in writing that silence was interpreted as approval & had been acted on accordingly.
6. I did not say so—If I made the statement mentioned in the letter, 'that nothing should fall back on Dr St.', it follows that I must have received the printed sheets.
7. I never did so
8. on the use of the karma content, in order to support his own ideas
9. did not happen from my side
10. Utopia
11. Duties of responsibility
12. Use for printed works strictly prohibited!
13. But I waited for the manuscript or the printed sheets
14. it *is* taken seriously
15. by whom?
16. !
17. !

The Political Memorandum from the Year 1930

I. Helplessness in Europe and useless efforts to provide solutions

Much has been said in Europe about the decline of western culture. The difficulties of daily life, especially in Middle Europe, have increased immeasurably. The means applied to relieve these difficulties have only worsened them. The way out, which is sought through loans, [the Young Plan] works like a lethal poison in the social organism. Life problems are seen only as financial and juridical issues. The dominant habits of thought, which unleashed the world war, damaging the peoples of Europe merely to serve the interests of some shadowy state mechanisms, have not changed; nothing has been learned. The same thinking operates today on a continental scale that operated earlier on the level of states. Hence the call for a supra-state mechanism, which would, however, only make the powers of the state still more destructive of life.

Today, Europe stands between America and Asia as in 1914, Middle Europe stood between the western states [England and France] and Russia. England vacillates undecidedly between America and Europe. Its position has become quite uncertain.

Pan-europa, in the way it has been conceived, can at best become the image of a superstate, an organized theatre of war for a mighty conflict between America and Asia. It remains in debt to America and thereby has become an organ of American will. The possibilities for the lives of the European population who are not dependent on the State will therefore inevitably be further constricted; the peoples of Europe will be sold and sacrificed.

All the hopes that the European peoples place on America are equally illusory, as were many of those that were heard in Middle Europe during the war. If one does not wish to accept the role of a slave, all the accommodation to America and the attempts to gain its favour are useless.

Thinking in an external, mechanical, quantitative manner, minorities cannot succeed against majorities. They must strengthen themselves from other, stronger habits of thought than those prevailing hitherto. This is not only necessary to uphold themselves, but also to heal and uphold the whole of humanity.

Everywhere, out of spiritual helplessness calls for a dictator are rising. People hope for healing only from power and external order. However, power that only orders is never productive. It merely leads to more great catastrophes. There is little call for spiritually productive ideas. People have sunk so deep into materialism that in terms of ideas, they only understand how to proceed from external quantitative success and do not learn from failure.

And yet the way to save European culture and culture itself has been evident since 1917; the words of rescue have already been spoken, but people did not want to listen. Middle Europe's capitulation was also cultural.

This Memorandum was written with the intention of recalling those words at this time of Europe's dire need.

Dr Rudolf Steiner, who died on 30 March 1925 at the Goetheanum in Dornach near Basel, gave the impulse for a threefolding of the social organism at a time when more could have been saved than can be saved today.

However, it is never too late to translate this idea into action. Each day that is neglected, the scale of the catastrophe approaching humanity increases. If leading figures do not give up their old habits of thought, more and more will they become tools for destructive forces.

In Russia, where there was no fear of the final consequences of these old habits of thought, their destructive force shows itself clearly enough; but people in the West do not wish to look at Bolshevism from this viewpoint.

II. *The necessary new shape of Europe required by the development of mankind*

The rescue of European culture and with it the most important part of humanity is impossible if, on the one hand, the will for a free spiritual life not privileged by the State, and on the other hand, the will for a world economy independent of political and state life do not become fact.

The initiative for the transition to these conditions would have to come from the part of Europe that is most under threat, that is, from Middle Europe. Through such an initiative, Middle Europe could render a more real service to the rest of Europe than by fulfilling the terms of the Young Plan and could thus win back the lost sympathies of the peoples of Europe.

a) Cultural life
In order for civilization to thrive and prosper, the starting point for human culture has always been in the cultural or spiritual life; this requires freedom, for the unconditionality of which, people still have little

understanding due to their concerns for comfort and due to their anxieties. In the spiritual life competition is necessary and every form of democracy is ruinous.

The hierarchical ordering of the spiritual life will be accomplished without force when freedom is prevalent.

In the cultural life a people's national capacities and characteristics show themselves. A people must inevitably lose its individual creative force when instead of real freedom, there is only the collective freedom of political groups. State patronage within the cultural life hinders every necessary step of human progress. Under State patronage the only kind of cultural life that can develop is a distorted one, which can be placed in the service of personal gain and political, collective polarities. This holds back the culture of the spirit, and the culture of the soul cannot keep up with the pace of technical development. Human beings then fall into the servitude of mechanical forces; their brutality increases while their soul strength declines. This leads to illnesses that show themselves in forms of insanity which are increasing but are still hidden today in many ways. Excessive exploitation, which shows itself everywhere in economic life, reaches even into people's inherited and developed cultural capacities and competencies. The education of children, the healing of the sick, and the practice of jurisprudence have been brought to a shockingly low level through the combination of cultural forces with the power of the State.

With an elemental power young people are beginning to ask questions about the meaning of life, and those in leading circles can provide no satisfactory answers. Agnosticism is the only refuge which remains open to the helpless.

b) Economic life

The economy will never be able to recover in Europe when the single States of Middle Europe organize their economic affairs along political boundaries. The more they do this, the more hopeless the economic situation will become. The economy must be freed from the sovereignty of single political states, also in the interest of the good standing of the States themselves, and be subject to an economic council in which men with economic experience communicate with each other, advising each other associatively and making free decisions.

One who observes economic life attentively today will recognize how economic life, following its own needs, always seeks to overcome the hindrances which States—only on grounds of prestige—put in its way. To awaken consciousness of the need to follow reason in this sphere, not to hinder it but to promote it through the dismantling of power, is a human duty.

The first fundamental principal for this economic council must be not to allow any political ideas to interfere with economic necessities. Purely economic decisions must not be subject to the approval of any political bodies and must themselves not be thought out in a legal fashion, that is, one informed by power.

It would then have to be shown that the economic life with its three factors—production, circulation and consumption—can only benefit the welfare of the whole community when it has a purely economically opportunistic, non-political leadership.

Economic life must never be organized in a hierarchical manner. Associative foundations of the various branches of the economy on the basis of free agreements and mutual understanding will finance themselves not on the basis of the gold standard but on the basis of inalienable but non-State means of production in their own circles of activity. Means of payment would circulate within the various associative economic groups.

The most damaging combination of political State forces and economic forces lies today in the chamber of commerce system. This is also true of the cultural life: e.g. the medical doctors' chamber.

A prosperous economy free of politics will not be attainable if political boundaries are allowed to remain with regard to the economy.

Middle Europe's weak political power has made it a scourge of its own populations due to it being bound to the economy, which today stands under foreign control. Under these circumstances obtaining in Middle Europe, the organs of the political State were bound to become mere executive organs of foreign political domination.

c) State Security

The only justified obligations of the political State are those of the police and the military. The sovereignty of Middle European states must be restricted to these. The life of the State will thus form itself conservatively, in accord with its own nature. The past years have shown this. In this sphere of the State democracy is justified.

III. Possibilities of realization

First there is the necessity that Middle Europe, which has the task of caring for the national element communally in mutual complementarity, to give the the impetus for realization of new, practical and spiritual ideas.

Human beings all over the earth have in fact been waiting for this without being conscious of it. But we have heard from Middle Europe only pretensions to power and [territorial] possession. There has been the effort of the minority to force its will, externally and quantitatively, on the majority. That was the real cause of hatred.

European culture and civilization can never be saved by means of old worn-out social institutions.

Never can that most unspiritual concept of the State, Communism, which is actually nothing new but something extremely old, bring European people anything but destruction.

As things stand today, never will the necessary impulse of the removal of State authority from the cultural and economic spheres be taken up by a State. The League of Nations, which is in reality a league of states, can therefore achieve nothing.

Preparations for the new should never simply be thrown open straightaway for public discussion.

The beginning of the new social order, that is, the last possibility to save European culture, and with it that of humanity, from the most colossal catastrophes, could only come about if a few leading figures from all the Middle European states were to meet and join together unofficially—men with a higher level of insight into the most pressing necessities—and beyond all formalities of state, diplomacy and bureaucracy, were able to discuss a free, common will impulse. These would then have to work within their States in accordance with this goal.

If this does not happen, then only after the most dreadful catastrophes, to which the largest part of the European population will fall victim, will the thoughts laid down in this Memorandum nevertheless come about in later times.

How this path to a really new social order is to be taken is something which must be left completely free for each state in Middle Europe to determine. The differentiation of possibilities and capacities within the various Middle European states would be shown to advantage precisely through this.

Accordingly, each state would make the transition in accordance with the differentiated talents of its population and therefore could serve the whole if it remained oriented to the overall perspective indicated.

There is no more damaging delusion than to seek to force the whole of multi-faceted humanity to conform to an intellectually and externally organized social template.

However, if moral and practical ideas were to stand behind an eventual armed struggle that was fought for them, then this struggle would be backed by something spiritual and worthy of human beings, which would effectively contribute to a successful outcome in the interests of the whole of mankind.

Ludwig Polzer-Hoditz

Exoteric and Esoteric Christianity

The Hadrian Essay of 1930

Destinies of Peoples and Individuals
in the Roman-Greek Middle Ages and the Present

(From: *Die Drei*, February 1930)

Anthroposophy tells us that folk spirits are not the abstractions of which one normally speaks. For conventional thinking at the present time, a people [*Volk*] is only a sum of individuals with particular characteristics and a common mother tongue. This abstract concept of a people is shown by events to be untenable when considered with the logic of facts, but the necessary consequences of life are not drawn from it. Because people cannot decide to recognize spiritual being, and because they shut themselves off from spiritual scientific methods, often out of fear, they cannot at all arrive at a concept of a people [*Volk*] that is based on reason. If one really wants to grasp what a people is, one can only do it when one raises oneself to the supersensible, for in the physical earthly realm there are only single, variously formed individuals. The facts show that the earlier separation of peoples is disappearing more and more, and the outer physical characteristics increasingly differentiate themselves; mixings and blendings of peoples have become extraordinarily complex. Also, languages, which have become ever more abstract, increasingly lose the characteristic of being spiritual expressions of the different folk-individualities.

The awkwardness which is felt when 'peoples' are spoken of is especially evident in the case of social and political thinking. One can bind human beings together abstractly in a State when they are limited within boundaries by legal force, but one should then know that this State is a union which has to be regarded as nominalistic, in the sense of the old mediaeval philosophical disputes, and that it will then always be a vain effort to bring this intellectual-abstract union into any kind of congruence with what a people really is. A people can never be regarded in the sense of Nominalism but only in the way one understood Realism in the Middle Ages. There were at that time still individuals who knew that the real does not exhaust itself in the naturalistic and the physical but has a spiritual background that is one of beings. A people is therefore a spiritual being of a higher order than the [individual] human spiritual being; it leads a group of human beings in spirit and soul and is unattainable by conventional knowledge. On the Earth therefore, individual human beings can only be brought together in a State by force and human intellect. Peoples cannot be limited in an earthly way by human beings; this is why the abstract, nationalism of the State, as it is understood today, is so foolish, restricting and ruinous for the development of mankind. The professorial phrases of [Woodrow] Wilson about the liberation of peoples could only result in the further oppression of human beings and lead the modern abstract bureaucratic States into forms even more hostile to life. If people want to achieve what they said they wanted to achieve with the phrase of 'peoples' liberation', they must actually begin by liberating the individual. The effect of collective freedoms is to work against freedom.

Peoples arise and fade through the ingress and egress of spiritual beings, and folk spirits act in accordance with the spiritual intentions of the world spirit; they are themselves differentiations of the world spirit. They lead human souls into a particular relationship with earthly folk souls and withdraw again to take up other tasks when their relationship with a people has fulfilled its task and is no longer needed in the evolutionary process. One speaks then of the decline of a folk community.

The problem of ethnic minorities which is so politically fraught will never be solved in the manner resorted to at present. The boundaries of the State, as they are meaninglessly maintained and even increased today, contributing to the sickness of mankind, can in the present time in which territorial dominance is being increasingly dissolved, never really comprehend peoples and never really benefit the life of peoples. This manner of collaboration, as it is practised today, will bring about the very downfall of the worthiest folk communities. The national element is very closely bound up with the spiritual life, and this endures, if it is to develop itself in a beneficial manner, because it has its impulses in the human being himself and not in a rigid separation of arbitrary, merely geographically created groups. The national characteristics of a people seek to perfect themselves through the national characteristics of other peoples in the free engagement of individual men and women. To shore up the cultural life for the power motives of abstract collective relationships through protectionist tariffs or to privilege it bureaucratically can only lead to ruin. In the cultural life, which the national element bears, an unrestricted free competition should prevail; only then can national characteristics show themselves in their true creativity for the general benefit of mankind. Because there is no courage, even in liberal circles, for such real freedom in the cultural life, mindlessness and chaos prevail in the political world. The current methods of separation and privileging promote only a withering of soul and spirit.

The history and sudden decline of two peoples which were flourishing in the time before the Mystery of Golgotha are especially interesting to consider from a spiritual-scientific viewpoint, because their destinies are deeply bound up with the growth of Christianity. Both the Greeks and the Celts experienced a sudden fall after a high cultural blossoming; the folk spirits that led them, Rudolf Steiner told us in a lecture cycle held in Christiania [Oslo] in 1910, took on special tasks within Christianity after it had emerged. The folk spirit of the Greeks took over the leadership of exoteric Christianity, while the folk spirit of the Celts assumed the leadership of esoteric Christianity. If we want to understand Christianity's path of development after its almost unnoticed entry into mankind's evolution, then we must keep this spiritual fact in mind. Christianity, which did not work through the power of a new teaching but proceeded from the cosmic deed on Golgotha, could not enter so easily into the sense-based consciousness of the individual, as it was a supersensible event within the Earth's cosmic body at the time of the deepest darkness of the human spirit vis-à-vis the spiritual worlds. Its destiny differed among the individual peoples [of Europe]. The history of peoples at that time becomes more understandable to the spiritual gaze through Christianity, and the destiny of Christianity itself becomes more understandable when one sees it in terms of its effects on the various peoples.

If the Mystery of Golgotha is understood as the fructification of mankind by a supersensible element, then history will also be able to reveal its karmic background to human understanding. It will show how one has to speak not only of a karma of human individualities, but of a karma of peoples, of the earth and of the whole of humanity. It will further show how the human being has to live out not only his own individual karma but is also entrusted by higher beings with special tasks for the karma of peoples and of mankind, and such tasks cross their own individual destinies many times, indeed, they can even be in contradiction with them. The human being is to be trained for independent collaboration within the world spirit. This will then for the first time give to the world body its true meaning and thereby contribute to the understanding of the riddle of the human being. This meaning was implanted into the body of the Earth on Golgotha in the greatest Mystery in the whole development of the Earth so that the human being could come to know his true destiny.

Through such understanding of human destiny in human lives which follow on after each other, the destinies of peoples and the destiny of the entire human race can become comprehensible. In world history that is cognized by the inner powers of destiny shines the light with which the way into the future can be illumined, and when the guidance of mankind can be shaped through such knowledge, the tasks of new cultural periods can be fulfilled; then the saying that one can learn nothing from history will be transformed into the sentence: 'The true history of mankind must become our master that guides us into the future.' In the way history is pursued scientifically today, it can be of no positive value in life. The great energy which is spent on collecting facts and interpreting documents will only show itself to have not been in vain for the life of the future if the spirit enlivens this work, supplements it and thereby makes it meaningful. One will then recognize, for example, how the history of the Jews actually tells us how that human body was prepared over generations by divine spiritual influences, which was to provide the bodily sheath for the Christ Being for three years, from the Baptism in the Jordan until the Mystery of Golgotha. We shall recognize the Romans as the people, who, without understanding Christianity, nevertheless provided for it the first, exoteric foundations for its propagation. The Greeks had to sacrifice themselves as a people because their folk spirit had to take on the wisdom-filled guidance of esoteric Christianity in earthly happenings. The Celts were given up as a single people because their folk spirit had to take care that the contents of the esoteric mystery of Christianity were not lost in the age in which a consciousness of gods which still saw the facts of nature as proceeding from divine beings had to fade away. To maintain the spiritual continuity, a spiritual leader-being of the rank of folk spirit had to subordinate himself to the Time Spirit until the latter would say: 'It is time to appear.'

The preparation of the physicality for the Deed of the Christ Being could not simply take place and just as little could Christ consciousness find its way into human beings in any simple, straightforward manner. There first had to be a duality, an exoteric outer form of propagation and an esoteric way of working that had to remain outwardly hidden.

In the first period of Christianity the greatest of all antitheses in human development appeared—that between the Roman spiritual direction, which founded the Imperium, and the supersensible Deed of Christ. This led to the well-known cruelties of the persecutions of Christians which stemmed from the same hatred of the spirit as that which exterminated the being of the Mysteries. Everywhere in the world where the Romans went, these tendencies to extermination showed themselves. The present, violent, revolutionary movements are the repetition of this mood; they also work in the sense of a struggle against the spirit and have also placed the powers of the State in their service.

The Jews had a secret teaching which was protected in the Mysteries and which pointed towards the Mystery of Golgotha. The messianic message of the Sun which, when they fulfilled it, they did not recognize, was something perceived by the Roman nature as something alien and hostile. The gradual annihilation of the Jewish State was therefore intimately linked to the extermination of the Mysteries.

The Imperium borne by the Roman people, like its present successor, had a destiny that continually had to bring it into conflict with Christianity. Christianity, which entered into mankind almost unnoticed by the learned in contemporary Rome and by all those leading personalities in the Roman State, soon became a great problem for the Empire.

Light can best be shed on the understanding of Christian development in the first Christian era when one pays special attention in a spiritual scientific sense to the transition from the nature of the old Mysteries to exoteric Christianity. We shall be able to get to know this era best and most understandably through individual human destinies. Christianity was what gripped people religiously in place of the nature of the old Mysteries; it was the fulfilment of these Mysteries, and was therefore a mystical fact. When the old consciousness of the Gods disappeared in the human soul and Mystery wisdom was lost, traditional, external symbolic cults and decadent, increasingly declining ceremonial rituals maintained themselves in many parts of the world. The Romans, who especially had lost all inner connections to the Gods, were therefore the leading people in that cultural epoch. Yet they still recognized the traditional powers of these old divine worlds of the various subject peoples and made political use of these. It was only then actually that what is called politics began, which today has wholly fallen into decadence.

In the transition from the being of the Mysteries to exoteric Christianity, the Greeks played a special role, karmically. The sober Romans needed Greek art, the Greek sense of beauty and Greek wisdom. The male spirit, which was coming to personal autonomy in this era, needed inspiration from the divine nature forces of the female spirit. The wisdom of the Gods had placed the duality of the male and female spirit in the two leading peoples of the cultural epoch; they were to complement each other.

The turning point of time required a stronger emphasis on the male principle, that which goes out into the external world in order to become independent and autonomously conquer the earthly forces. The Greeks were therefore overcome outwardly, but they had the task to provide cultural inspiration within the structure of Roman power until the onset of the power of the Mystery of Golgotha. The polarity between the Roman nature and the Greco-oriental nature, between the masculine and feminine spiritual principles, showed itself from this time onwards in the struggles between the ruling families and the democratic State-building elements. The polarity, which was then still represented in the two peoples, the Romans and the Greeks, became more inward. With the progress of Christianity, the dualism which in the early Christian era was still represented by the two peoples necessarily took on inward forms, and showing itself more socially, later led to the split between the community of the Empire and the community of the Church. This split was a necessity because it was recognized that the Roman Caesars' pretensions to divinity, which were still dominant as the after-effect of past stages of development, were something impossible. It was also known at that time that the spiritual world had to work into the human social order, shaping it; people in those days had neither the great superstition of modern cleverness—that the spiritual world does not exist—nor the superstitious arrogance that thinks itself capable of creating social institutions on the basis of a one-sided, merely earthly intellectualism.

★

In the time of the Antonines in the middle period of the Greco-Roman epoch, we find a Roman Emperor whose personal destiny was deeply bound up with the transition from the being of the Mysteries to exoteric Christianity. Emperor Hadrian was both Roman and Greek, unlike any of his predecessors. His destiny brought him into close contact with the folk spirits of those peoples who were deeply bound up with the growing Christianity. In the destiny of this Emperor one can clearly follow the transition of the folk spirit of the Greeks from one task to another. Hadrian, who repeatedly wandered on foot across his great Empire, has been judged by history both favourably and unfavourably. Spartianus, who wrote a biography of him 200 years later, in the time of Diocletian, refers to his good and bad qualities in no particular order. There are writings about him by the monk John Xiphilinus in the eleventh century who included extracts from the histories of Cassius Dio that referred to Hadrian. In recent times Ferdinand Gregorovius has written about Hadrian and his times with exactitude and great industry on the basis of the sources available to him, and I have made use of his historical work in these considerations.

All historians agree that this Emperor combined in himself a high level of Greek culture with a kind of universal geniality, that he administered the Roman Empire wisely, was distinguished by a great love of peace and had within him a great urge to travel. His era and that of his immediate successors were preceded and followed by difficult times—before him the era of the Caesars of the first century; later, after Marcus Aurelius, the incursions of the barbarians, which gradually destroyed the great Empire. Hadrian is one of those historical personalities about whom the external writing of history can gain little clarity; he presents it everywhere with riddles that it is not in the position to solve. It is always especially interesting for spiritual science to consider such personalities. Hadrian believed, as Gregorovius writes, in the script of the stars, in the power of oracles, he received signs of his future imperial dignity from the books of the Sibyls, as an astrologer he researched his own future and directed his operations in accordance with what he had read in the starry script. Even people of culture still believed in those days on the once high science of astrology, of the starry script, although this had already become decadent at that time.

The age of the instinctive Intellectual-Mind Soul was in full bloom, and this could only develop at the expense of older capacities. This applied principally to those peoples who were then carrying the main thrust of that cultural epoch, that is, to the Greeks and especially to the Romans.

Some historians consider Hadrian to have been an atheist; others see him as the most pious Emperor. Gregorovius comes to no firm conclusion; on the one hand, he has to admire him in this regard, but then refers to qualities of the Emperor that are not in harmony with it, so that he finally has to confess with regard to Hadrian's religion: 'The religion of this riddle of a man is a mystery for us.'

From the perspective of spiritual science, one can understand that when looking at personalities such as Hadrian, one cannot begin with the current concept of the 'religious'. The cult of the Emperor was then in reality the religion of the State in which Hadrian had to, and wanted to, find himself; he *lived* in a very real way, not only in abstract concepts and principles in the transition to a new world order. What was working within him was the ancient culture, which was once reality in the Orient, and also that in his soul into which he was born as a Roman. The forces of the Sentient Soul and those of the Intellectual-Mind Soul were struggling with each other within him, as is understandable for that era of the Turning Point of Time.

It is very hard to understand such facts of soul development today because people always assume that the thought life of people in that Roman epoch was just like that of our time. The thought life at that time was still close to that of the epoch when people could actually perceive thoughts just as people today can perceive something external, such as a symphony. Plato, Aristotle and others were perceivers of thoughts; they did not at all create them from within out of the efforts of their own souls. Only after Golgotha, in the time of Hadrian, did people experience thoughts first as thought-inspirations stirred by the spirit; only slowly came awareness of the subjectivity of thinking and then, finally, the free creation of thoughts by human beings.

Hadrian's double nature shows itself especially in the fact that he was really a Roman and a Greek. He thus incorporated the Greco-Roman cultural epoch in a very real way within his individuality and moreover, was living in the time in which the transition was beginning from the ancient being of the Mysteries to exoteric Christianity. Only within a polarity, a duality, can the Mystery of Golgotha be recognized as a supersensible event for the awakening of the potential of the Son of God in the Son of Man through the Christ Spirit. The twofold basis was expressed through peoples, through the Romans and through the Greeks. The Jews disappeared very soon as a unitary people after their mission to prepare human physicality to receive the Christ had been fulfilled. One can say that the duality, between which the concept of the Son first had to ripen cognitively as the middle term, would in the fourth cultural period be placed by Gods into peoples [the Greeks and the Romans—*transl.*], but must later be brought by human beings themselves into the process of forming society and that finally, out of this internalization will come Christ consciousness, that is, the understanding of threefoldness, which is at the same time oneness.

Hadrian himself represents the duality in his double nature. He already anticipates in the middle of the Roman-Hellenistic era what in the later age of the Consciousness Soul will emerge ever more clearly in the individual human being, namely, the Parzival nature and the Amfortas nature. Hadrian naturally represented this double nature in a very different way from a modern person; he experienced it in a very elemental fashion out of the natures of the two peoples. This double nature worked much more strongly at that time than it can today. As he learned much from the Mysteries, he was actually able to live out this double nature of his Roman-ness and his Greek-Oriental soul. He was divided between *Stoa* and *Gnosis;* he could find full satisfaction in neither of these philosophies and that is why he sought out the Mysteries. It has not been established historically whether he was initiated in Mysteries other than those of Eleusis, but it is very likely. The growth of rational intellect at that time among the more cultured peoples had turned them away from Mysteries, oracles, and all mysticism: the Oracle of Delphi had been silent since the days of Nero. Trajan showed some interest again in the old Greek wisdom, and Hadrian sought to re-enliven it, for he could not really be a Stoic. During his reign, one can speak of a revival of the cults of the Gods, which he brought about. He felt the need for a spiritual enlivening of Roman rationalism. One spoke at that time of demons becoming priests at the Oracles, and that was indeed often the case due to the decay of the Oracles, but it had nothing to do with the original thing itself. From his perspective, which is often that of the modern period, Gregorovius can hardly speak otherwise than of the 'stupidity' of the people with whom Hadrian had to deal. Habits of thought in the nineteenth century were even further from any consciousness of 'gods' than at that time in Rome. And yet today, true spiritual experience has once again come very close to mankind, and people are again beginning to entertain doubts about the splendour [of modern civilization—*transl.*] to which mankind is supposed to have been brought. The writer Pausanias was certainly right when he called Hadrian the most god-fearing Emperor. Even if he had only built temples out of an artistic sensibility, there was a religious yearning in that sensibility that stemmed from imaginative pictures that had already become uncertain. In Hadrian there were no longer any real pretensions to divinity; on the contrary he seems to have felt that he had the duties of a divine stewardship. This was understandable for a Greek-oriented spiritual seeker on the Caesars' throne; in feeling it, he was in his soul also in tune with the times. Inwardly, he was torn between two worlds—the declining Greek world with its Gods disappearing from the sight of the soul, and the rising Roman world. His attempt to unite Hellas and Rome, which could not be immediately accomplished, shows something of his sense that a harmonizing of these two cultural principles would be necessary in the future. Christianity, which was working within mankind, shows itself in his unconscious, instinctive search for the 'Son'. As he could not find Him, he fell into externalities, but he is therefore one of those personalities that incorporate world forces, which is why Rome today is still filled with memorials to him; his mausoleum—Castel Sant'Angelo— played a later role in the history of Christianity and at its top is a statue of the Archangel Michael.

Destiny ruled when he came to power in the Great Roman Empire. His adoption by Trajan is shrouded in darkness. To succeed at all, it must have been on Trajan's deathbed. Trajan did not like Hadrian's political direction; he was completely different from Hadrian, who was too Greek and oriental for him. Trajan therefore feared Hadrian's influence on the Roman Empire. One can feel the powers of destiny clearly at work then, when Hadrian mounted the throne of the Caesars, probably at the urgings of the ladies Augustina Plotina, Trajan's wife, and Matidia, Trajan's niece, and perhaps also that of his guardian, Trajan's adjutant, Licinius Sura. That women should have played a great part in his adoption is understandable from a spiritual scientific perspective since there lies in every woman, and especially in that era, which was still so close to the Sentient Soul epoch, the 'inwardness' of the East. Hadrian was certainly a Roman and thus bore in himself the strong, male spiritual principle that was striving for autonomy, and which at that time was already beginning to make itself independent of the inspiration of the female spiritual principle and wanted to see in the woman only the housewife and mother, but Hadrian's soul had such a great inclination to what was Greek and oriental that women recognized this.

At the present time, the word 'oriental' can hardly be used without giving the impression that one means by it something inferior, barbaric or something from an Arabian fantasy. Here, it is used to denote what was once deep nature wisdom in Asia and represented the powers of human origins, which must again be recognized as such. It signifies that which is closely bound to the eternally valid elements of the ancient Mysteries. The Romans, who had a special task in the fourth cultural epoch, despised oriental cultures as well as the Germanic cultures of the North as barbaric. This habit of despising the East was taken over from the Romans by their successors and has been passed on down to us; the East was increasingly identified with paganism and was finally stamped by an intellectual arrogance as something that had been conquered. As the ancient Romans called the peoples they conquered 'barbarians' and had to be hostile to all their Mysteries, one heard during the world war the population of Middle Europe described as 'barbarians' by their enemies. But times will change. It is the Middle European population that bears capacities and spiritual seeds within itself which the future needs. They will be able to come forth until finally, these peoples have purified themselves from all Roman and Western influences and have accepted other social forms. Spiritual scientifically, it can be said that in the people of the West and in those who are in their service in Middle Europe, Roman souls have incarnated who in the Roman era represented something that was especially strongly Roman. In every European woman today there still lives a deep inclination to the primeval culture of peace that was once permeated by wisdom and upheld by the divine. European culture has fallen into complete alienation from spirit; a large number of human beings, human products and social institutions will therefore have to go under before a new culture can bloom.

Under Trajan the Roman Empire reached its greatest expansion. The cultural epoch was nearing its mid-point, and it therefore had to show what it could achieve on the basis of the forces of the Intellectual-Mind Soul. The time of the Antonines was the blossoming of this cultural period; it was represented by Trajan, Hadrian, Antoninus Pius, and Marcus Aurelius. An interesting geographical fact is connected with this. There began, already in the reign of Trajan, a pulling back from Europe towards the ancient primeval Indian source of many cultures. The Roman Empire had already almost conquered all of Europe. Now, on the ground of these conquests and consolidations of power, the yearning arose, at first manifesting itself through weapons, violently, to reach back to the East. Trajan sought to reach India but could not succeed. In the middle of the Post-Atlantean Age, in the Greco-Roman cultural epoch, in which the human personality became conscious of its I, with this achievement, it now wanted to return to its spirit-filled origin. Almost 2000 years later, this would be attempted by force but only attained economically for a short period. The effort is now being made to bolster this tottering economic success by forceful ecclesiastical endeavours. But the path of culture can only be taken when a spiritual understanding of the destinies of individuals and peoples has grown from newly blossomed Mysteries in Middle Europe, which correspond to the development of the Con-sciousness Soul. The Middle European region has the same significance for the modern western world as Greece once had for the Roman world, and the whole Balkan peninsula will one day have for the fifth cultural epoch a significance similar to that which the Italian peninsula had for the later fourth cultural epoch.

Hadrian recognized that he would have to consolidate his Empire and benefit it artistically, and did exactly the opposite of what Trajan had done. He immediately abandoned the conquests in Parthia. The Roman military party was therefore hostile to him from the outset, but also in this case we see destiny at work, for the Senate itself took on to remove his opponents. Just as later, the love of truth was Julian the Apostate's striking characteristic, with Hadrian it was his love of peace, which lay deeply grounded within his nature and was even stronger than his feeling for beauty and artistic creativity. A Late Greek with an oriental element was now on the throne of the Roman Caesars. Hadrian sought to harmonize his pronounced double nature in the Mysteries, but could not find what he needed because at that time he could only have found it in Chris-tianity. But the seeds of exoteric and esoteric Christianity lay unfertilized, as though sleeping, in his double nature. Because he united in himself the Roman and Greek natures, the folk spirit of the Romans was working within him and also the folk spirit of the Greeks. In Greece and in Asia he built new temples and rebuilt old ones and everywhere instituted rational administration. The effects of the oriental Mysteries of Light and the Egyptian Mysteries of Man are revealed in these two directions of his actions. He thus worked for the foundations of an exoteric Christianity, which would first be borne by the Roman Empire, and for an esoteric Christianity, because he recognized that the Mysteries were in need of protection and he saw in art the most suitable means to do this. Through Hadrian, the Greek folk spirit as leader of exoteric Christianity was able to bring this into Roman culture. There had to be a human individual in physical incarnation at that time who would build the bridge between Romans and Greeks. The transition had to be prepared on the physical plane and then be accomplished through a human being. That could only happen through a Roman in whose soul were living very deep elemental connections to the being of the Greek people, who was representative of the Roman culture and who had comprehensive capacities for action. Since both the former Greek folk spirit and the Roman folk spirit, as Rudolf Steiner told us, became the educators of the Time Spirit [*Zeit-geist*—transl.] of our present cultural epoch, that had to be recognizable in Hadrian's destiny and deeds.

One who looks at contemporary events not just with his head but with his heart, will be able to discern in those events the education of our Time Spirit by those two Time Spirits. The Time Spirit of our cultural epoch, who wishes to make inner freedom a reality, had, as spiritual science says, still a third educator in the Time Spirit of the Egyptians; much in our fifth cultural epoch is therefore repeated, in a metamorphosed way, from the third cultural epoch. These three educators did not, however, act like so many foolish human teachers do today who seek to educate their pupils to be just like them, but they taught in such a way as to enable something quite new to flow from the spiritual world into the development of mankind and form itself.

With Hadrian, who lived in such a decisive era when so much that was important for humanity played itself out, that Christianity began to become exoterically independent, many later developments were anticipated in seed form. Hadrian was already working in a cosmopolitan manner. He was the first Roman Emperor who moved beyond the differentiation of peoples and who put Rome and the provinces on an equal footing. His endeavours and deeds also show his sense that development in the future would take place in the North. He even saw that the future of the Roman Empire would depend more on the North than on the East. His love belonged entirely to the East, but his duties he saw more in central Europe. One can almost say that the Greek-inclined part of his soul sensed the future task of Middle Europe, which he was unable to achieve in his time through the binding of Rome and Hellas. The Danube basin was a region he was concerned about. He sought to better conditions in Pannonia, Dacia, and Moesia through improvements in administration. So he sensed the future in Europe but he also knew that this Europe needed Greek wisdom and beauty, and that the spirit of past ages which still moved in Greece needed to be brought to Europe just as much as Roman might. Hadrian therefore recognized that the course of the Roman destiny led not towards the orient but to the Germanic and Celtic lands of the occident, and in doing so, he grasped the geographical problem of the development of mankind in the middle of the post-Atlantean age. He said to himself that the future would depend on the Rhine and then on the Danube, for the course of development would turn in that direction. As one can see from the actions of his government that he knew how to weigh up the future correctly, so his awareness of his own time was such that he also knew how to do justice to the past of human development. *The* province of the Roman Caesars was Egypt. That this was so is grounded, in terms of destiny, in the fact that the leading people [*Volk*] of the previous cultural epoch had been the Egyptians and that the most prominent Egyptian souls had mostly reincarnated in Roman bodies. The path of inner cultural progress, that is, of the education of the human race, went from Egypt to Rome. Egypt therefore became intimately bound to the Roman Empire in later times. Its wealth made it the private domain of the Caesars; no one was allowed to go there without the Emperor's permission. The Egyptian Time Spirit had to be active not only in the Roman period, but *beyond* it, down to our own cultural epoch. One must not lose sight of the fact that the Greco-Roman period stands in the middle of the post-Atlantean age as a whole and that on both sides of it, the epoch that preceded the Greco-Roman period will show itself again in the epoch that succeeded it. With the beginning of the Roman age, mankind bound itself to the forces of the earth, lost the sight of the gods and after exiting the Greco-Roman period, from the fifteenth century onwards had to find its way out of the darkness of the earth forces to conscious experience of the spiritual.

Hadrian's journey to Egypt became a tragic destiny for him. The letter, which he wrote from there to his brother-in-law Servianus, the authenticity of which has certainly been doubted, reveals that he was not impressed by conditions in Egypt and at first experienced great disappointment. Yet later, he seems to have been gripped by the remains of the religious cultic magic of the once so deep Egyptian wisdom. He saw a magnificence which still worked its effect on him from out of the ruins and which the original size of the buildings powerfully confirmed. He was driven by it to get to know the wonders of Egypt deeper in the interior of the country. The mysterious Nile had a great attraction for Romans and Greeks in those days; it gave rise to vague memories of their former destinies. Hadrian encountered his personal destiny in a tragic manner on his own journey up the Nile when, in a mysterious way, at Besa, near Hermopolis, he lost his beloved Greek youth, Antinous. He died in the waters of the Nile and it is assumed that he killed himself in an act of self-sacrifice in order to fend off something that was threatening the Emperor. Hadrian was overcome by the death. For the modern way of thinking, which has no understanding of the conditions of people's souls at that time, the problem of Antinous is unfathomable. The way in which Gregorovius writes about it is unacceptable, in spiritual scientific terms; he writes: 'The most bizarre intermezzo of all journeys on the Nile gave to the disappearing paganism and to the art of antiquity its last ideal figure.' And yet, in this statement one can sense a solution to the problem. Even if Gregorovius sees nothing of spiritual symptomatic nature in this event on the Nile and makes his sentence merely information about a purely external fact, the expression 'bizarre' shows how he sees the event, so the fact—which had its own deeper background—is that Antinous was later really worshipped as a god. Collections in Rome and other cities show the most various busts of Antinous. For those who have learned to experience karmic relationships in human development, this Antinous event on the Nile, which modern historians dismiss with a kind of embarrassment and sarcastic remarks, is no trivial matter. One has the feeling that something revealed itself there and has been preserved in history, which, in the future when carefully researched, will throw new light on the formation and fulfilment of destiny.

Hadrian felt the past and the future at work in the present. He felt that he had the task of bridging over great world polarities which first showed themselves to him as the Roman nature and the Greek nature. In that he recognized the future in Europe and also took care over the adminis-tration of the European West as far as Britain, he was also working in a way in the service of the Celtic folk spirit. His wanderlust was in reality the outer expression of his search for a satisfactory understanding of life. He hoped to find this in the beautiful images of art, in association with his love of peace. But the love of peace which imbued this emperor, who travelled restlessly through his great Empire, could not prevent him from having to lead one of the bloodiest wars of extermination. It was a destiny judgement of world history which was incumbent on him to carry out. The fanatical resistance of the Jews against the incursions of the Romans, who had begun to build the city of Aelia Capitolina with a temple to Zeus on the site of the city of Jerusalem that had been destroyed by Titus, forced Hadrian to wage war. The enormous opposition between Jahve and the Greek god Zeus, whom the Romans venerated outwardly without having any inner connection to him went on regardless of the fact that the Mystery of Golgotha had already taken place and that the Turning Point of Time had occurred.

There were two factions among the Jews, the appeasers and the zealots. The former, as Gregorovius writes, were to have negotiated with Hadrian in Egypt in order to keep the peace, although the zealots wanted to know nothing of it. The negotiations must have been just as fruitless as the illusory attempts of those in the world war who thought that the western will to exterminate Middle Europe could be overcome by the usual kind of negotiations. In these modern events Roman events were repeating themselves in new forms. It would be interesting to follow the personalities who were negotiating with Hadrian at that time in their later lives to see whether their experiences were transformed in the deeds of their later deeds for they certainly played a role again in the events in our time. Hadrian would have liked to avoid the war, but the karma of mankind led to a different course, and he could not see through this because he found himself in a situation of inevitability that had developed over a long time. Rabbi Akiba and the people's hero Bar Kokhba, who was held to be the national Messiah, were not prepared to negotiate with the Romans. It is clear that the Messiah, who was still awaited, was conceived entirely externally and thus a decadent self-destructive nationalism developed. In their campaign against the Jews, the Romans did everything to wipe out the last traces of the Mysteries. The secret teachings of the Jews, which were communicated in the messianic message, were to be annihilated with all their bearers; nothing was to be left of this messianic gospel of the sun. At the time of Hadrian the nationalist fanaticism of the Jews was in almost every respect only an externalized racial fanaticism. The priestly nobility of the Sadducee caste ruled the Jews' religion forcefully; these priests had a horror of any Mysteries and were only puppets of the Roman State. The connection between Roman culture and the monotheistic Jahve principle constituted a precondition for the possibility of the later spread of exoteric Christianity. From the perspective of external state politics the Roman Empire could never tolerate a Jewish State between its greatest provinces, Egypt and Syria. Its extermination in the war was a certainty as this priestly national community was under Roman domination and by that time had already lost the spiritual foundations of its Mysteries. It had therefore already become to a degree Roman and alienated from its own folk being. It could no longer defend itself spiritually but only through fanatical violence and pitted against the great Roman world empire, its downfall was certain. Jewish culture was no more suited than Greek to form a State in the Roman fashion; its unity was only possible as a priest-led community with the Mysteries in the background and never as a juridical, democratic community. In democracy the Greeks too died as an independent, autonomous community of people. In this last war against the Jews in Hadrian's reign, two very differently constituted peoples were fighting each other, both of which were in reality hostile to Christianity—the struggles of parties and the State never have anything to do with Christianity—and into which the Christ Event entered very concretely. As a people, the Romans were carrying the main current of the development of mankind appropriate to the fourth cultural epoch, while the Jews belonged to the third cultural epoch and represented a stream that had remained behind; as a unitary national community, they were bound to be overcome by the Romans. In this, one also sees how the politics of the Romans, despite Hadrian and despite Julian the Apostate later on, had as its main mission to prevent the emergence of the esoteric side of Christianity which was living in the old Mysteries. Rome already sensed at that time that in the Sun-nature of Christianity something was living that would gradually destroy the Empire. An oracle prophesied in the later Antonine period that Rome was fated to decline because it had lost the primeval wisdom. Therefore the Romans were on the alert to Christianity, and various Caesars continually tried to come to terms with it somehow, because they sensed in it a power with which they had to reckon. Persecutions of Christians and attempts to come to terms with Christianity therefore went on in parallel. Constantine, who established the exoteric Christian State, wanted to counter this prophecy of the downfall of Rome, so, contrary to the will of the gods, he had the Palladium, the symbol of the ancient, primeval wisdom, transferred from Troy to Constantinople with solemn cultic ceremonial and used it as the foundation for the building of the city. He wanted to preserve in Constantinople the eternal impulse of primeval wisdom which the Romans had lost and could no longer attain. Thus developed out of the uniting of the Roman nature with exoteric Christianity the first external foundations of a dualism, which later resulted in the division of the eastern and western churches. This dualism, which has worked on into our own time was the constant cause of countless conflicts and wars. The other dualism, which developed in Middle Europe between the Empire and the Church was the expression of the right path of human development. The division of the Church between East and West was an event that resulted from spiritual confusion and which was therefore bound to work itself out in lasting external conflicts. These conflicts remain permanent, because Churches, just like abstract States, can do nothing other than fight each other. States and Churches are institutions of conflict. Neither nations nor religions based on spiritual foundations can make wars; by contrast, every nominalistic collectivity bears the being of war within itself. The dualism of Empire and Church, if it had been rightly understood, would have led to the internalizing of the spiritual struggle within the individual human being. The meaning of this dualism was the harmonious binding of the world body with the world spirit through the knowledge that the male and female spirits in each single human being, whether in the body of a man or a woman, must come into balance, because only in this way can the Son of God be born in each human being. The conflicts of the great world polarities must be fought out within the hearts of every single human being. To externalize these conflicts and to maintain them permanently through States and Churches has been a false path in development during the last few centuries. Dante had already conceived of the Holy Roman Empire of the German Nation as a spiritual institution and therefore justified its expansion over the whole of Europe.[*]

At the beginning of our reckoning of time, the Jewish community had arrived in a condition which is characterized by the denial of the Mystery of Golgotha; it did not comprehend the ultimate event, which was taking place in its midst. One can experience today a similar denial in official Germany: Rudolf Steiner brought his message about the Mysteries and about Christ to German culture; it was to take its start from Middle Europe. Official circles in all areas of life have responded to it as the Jews responded to Christ. But just as Christianity established itself, at first exoterically, despite the persecutions, so will esoteric Christianity do the same, despite denials and denunciations from the side of the power-mongers concerned for the Empire.

The more the Germans become aware of their own inner being, the more therefore that they are comprehended by the forces of the Consciousness Soul, then the more they will recognize that they do not constitute a territorial dominion in the modern sense but that they can only develop themselves culturally and socially out of a sense of being a spiritual community. Just as the growing forces of the Intellectual-Mind-

---

[*] Dante (died 1321) would not have been familiar with the concept Holy Roman Empire *of the German Nation,* which only came into usage from 1512 but in his *De Monarchia* (written somewhere between 1308 and 1321) he did indeed strongly support the Holy Roman Empire (Middle Europe and Italy) and the claims of the Emperor vis-à-vis the Pope. See also p. 333. [*transl.*].

Soul in the time of the fourth cultural epoch led on to territorial dominions and the Romans were the representative people in that process, so the growing forces of the Consciousness Soul in our time will again dissolve territorial dominions. The tendency towards this can already be seen in contemporary phenomena. It will have to be recognized after the catastrophic events of the future, if human culture is to be maintained at all.

Rudolf Steiner wanted to call leading personalities in Middle Europe to recognize this in 1917 with the first outline of the threefolding of the social organism. The coming conflicts and confusions will violently demolish territorial boundaries if they cannot be brought into mobility by the exercise of reason. The facts show again and again that efforts to make of the Germans a powerful, unitary, territorial State on juridical and democratic i.e. Roman foundations are in vain. This Roman idea of territorial dominion gradually spread in the post-Roman period to all the other European peoples until our time. Germans and Slavs suffered especially under these legalistic, intellectual forms which are utterly foreign to their nature. Everywhere in history from the ninth century onwards we encounter the sufferings of these peoples, the real causes of which they could not make known to themselves. Everywhere there lived in the souls of these Germanic and Slavic peoples the search for other forms of community, which they were unable to find, and when these ideas were brought to leading Germans by Rudolf Steiner, they failed to translate them into action.

In the year 63 BC Judaea was made part of Roman Syria by Pompey. Through its influence in Judaea, Rome did what it needed to do there in order to become the real ruler over the Jews. Herod was only able to assert his rule with the help of the Romans. We find similar aberrations among leading circles in Germany today to those in Herod's State in Judaea. The German people [*Volksgemeinschaft*] had its mission in spiritual life. The present German State is just as dependent on the Anglo-American economic imperium—it is its instrument—as Herod and the priestly caste of the Sadducees were dependent on the Roman State. Ultimately, the Jewish State had to fall in accordance with the Roman State principle, after it had done its duty, which was to extinguish the Mysteries of Judaism.

Emperor Hadrian, a man who recoiled from war, was placed in this tragic human destiny by higher beings. He became the executor of a terrible judgement of destiny, and his personal destiny was crossed by this destiny of mankind.

After the end of the Jewish State, the Christians separated their destiny from that of the Jews. Christianity, then, found itself between two conflicting forces—those of the Romans and the Jews. It is also Christianity's destiny in our time to come between two powers into the clamps of encirclement.

As servant of the Greek folk spirit, Hadrian actually helped exoteric Christianity to cosmopolitan independence by this war; also, one can recognize how he was the personality who stood in the service of the former Greek folk spirit that became the leader of exoteric Christianity.

The main stream of human development came from Egypt in the third cultural epoch and flowed to Romans, as the representative people of the next epoch. When this people's own forces became lamed, exoteric Christianity came forward as the supporting power of the imperium. The Christ impulse itself forged a path to Middle Europe, to peoples who had the predisposition to understand esoteric Christianity in the future and through this to attain to an understanding of the Son that can shape really new worlds. These peoples also bore in themselves the forces to overcome the Roman Empire ultimately, in whatever form it reappears. Hadrian could not bring the empire to any consciousness of esoteric Christianity and could not therefore illuminate the abyss between the two sides of his dual nature; he stood torn between spiritual poles. He lived out his last years in concerns for the future of the beauty and wisdom of the world and sensed that ancient Rome and everything that it sought to continue would be judged and finally be transformed into a scene of devastation. Such was the concern in the depths of his soul at the end of the life of the wandering emperor. It showed itself especially in his anxieties about the succession, when his adopted son, Lucius Aelius Caesar suddenly died on 1 January 138. He called a few respected senators to him and spoke in favour of adoption and against bloodline succession. The Roman Empire was then to owe him two of its best rulers, for he adopted Antoninus Pius and demanded of him that he in turn pick Marcus Aurelius for his own successor by adoption. After this, he soon died, as Gregorovius writes, in the arms of that truest of men, Antoninus Pius.

The church cult, which stemmed from the Mysteries and which, despite its pagan hostility, was taken over by exoteric Christianity, comprehended in its modified form the soul life less and less and entirely lost any spiritual vision, which was replaced by dogma. Jurisprudence and democracy increasingly took hold of Christianity and founded a democratic, abstract order of Church and State. Exoteric Christianity and the Roman democratic State system went hand in hand and gradually falsified the dualism of the ecclesiastical and imperial communities which should have developed in a spiritual way in accordance with human soul development.

Despite the differences in the activities of the Greek and Celtic folk spirits as Christianity spread, the cooperation of the two also showed itself. The esoteric content of Christianity lost itself in the East as a consequence of the exoteric task of the Greek folk spirit, which bound itself to the Roman in vague, mystical feelings and entirely externalized itself in cultic ritual. A few sporadic remnants of Christian memories of the Mysteries could still be found in the Balkans, for example, in the traditions of the Bogomils and in old wall paintings which had been preserved in many monasteries despite the attacks of the Turks. In the West exoteric Christianity everywhere came up against, on the one hand, ancient, still existing Mystery centres—those which had not been destroyed by the Romans—and on the other, the area of activity of the Celtic folk spirit, which had been entrusted with the mission of esoteric Christianity. The Mystery of Golgotha had been perceived in those places in the macrocosm, and the leader of esoteric Christianity had to supervise the sight of the passing of Christ from the macrocosm into human souls. In other words, esoteric guidance by the Celtic folk spirit consisted of the accomplishment of the transition from the culture of the knights of Arthur to the culture of the knights of the Grail. This transition having been accomplished, esoteric Christianity, bearing the results of it, slowly moved into the middle of Europe into contact with exoteric Christianity, in order to unite with this. Christianity was then, in new Mysteries, gradually able to awaken to individual consciousness that which in ancient times the East had enabled people resting in the maternal bosom of Nature's wisdom to experience of spirituality.

In the middle of Europe in the third cultural epoch, a future-oriented, anticipatory, post-Atlantean development of humanity encountered Atlantean Mysteries. Legend tells of how king Gilgamesh of the Babylonians travelled to the west in order to solve the riddle of immortality after he had become aware of the fact of death. He hoped to find the solution in the Atlantean Mysteries, in the region of today's Burgenland. His initiation into the tasks of the post-Atlantean age failed. Before the Mystery of Golgotha a connection to the secrets of Atlantis that was appropriate to the time was not possible. Out of the harmonized polarity of esoteric and exoteric Christianity, Mysteries will arise from which spiritual guidance for humanity will emerge that will be able to bring the results of the Atlantean age into harmony with the needs of post-Atlantean times. The anthroposophy of Rudolf Steiner, the wisdom suitable for the male and female spirit alike, is the necessary foundation for such re-emerging Mysteries. Through this, understanding with the East will be able to be found in cultural life.

The Jews were as a people the link between the Egyptian-Chaldean and the Greco-Roman cultural epochs; the Germanic tribes and the western Slavic peoples were similarly placed between the Roman-Greek culture and the Consciousness Soul people of the later period, the fifth cultural epoch. From the Jews came the first Christians. From the Germans will come Michaelic people who will build a new, universally human spiritual community in Middle Europe, under the leadership of Michael, the Time Spirit of the fifth cultural epoch.

The Germans, who today are falling back into a one-sided emphasis on race on Roman state foundations, play in the present the same role as the Jews before the fall of their last State, which was dependent on Rome.

In the last three to four centuries a significant power shift has occurred in Europe. The Roman Empire, which repeated itself in the Holy Roman Empire of the German Nation, slowly released itself from Middle Europe; it declined there and re-consolidated itself in the British Isles as an economic empire. London became the capital of this power, corresponding to the increasingly awakening forces of the Consciousness Soul, as in the second third of the fourth cultural epoch, Rome was the capital of power. The Roman Empire has, with its centre, moved ever further to the West, while esoteric Christianity moves ever more towards the Middle of Europe and to the East. The coming Mysteries will proceed from the polarity between exoteric and esoteric Christianity. The spiritual impulse necessary for this entered into the Middle of Europe through Rudolf Steiner. The region of the Middle will have to be prepared for this, both in the sense of destiny and also outwardly. The polarity between the Middle European region of the spirit and the city of power will bring about this preparation, but in the future a balance will have to be found between them. Like Rome to Greece in the fourth cultural epoch, so stands London to Middle Europe in the fifth cultural epoch. In the fourth cultural epoch the call was: away from the Mysteries to power and Rome. It was a movement towards the West. In the fifth cultural epoch, the call in Middle Europe in the future will have to be: away from Roman power, and back to the Mysteries. This will be connected with a movement towards the East.

Human souls bear the results of one cultural epoch over into the next. The Roman Empire has repeated itself in the British Empire through the Roman souls who have reincarnated in this British Empire; some of the Roman, more Greek-inclined souls will find themselves in the middle of Europe.

The monotheistic Jewish culture with its Mars forces became through its rigidity a servant of Rome. The Germans were, just like the Sadducees, servants of the political Rome, servants of the Anglo-American economic empire and harden themselves in an abstract, nationalistic State. They set themselves against Michael just as the supporters of Akiba and Bar Kokhba set themselves against the message of the messianic Mysteries which had become the central Fact of the Earth.

Like Jehovah and Michael, the ancient Hebrew Mystery stream and the German spiritual stream confront one another. Jehovah led mankind into the Roman shackles; Michael casts these shackles off again. With his inner light Michael wants to illuminate the divine world again for human beings and help them return to the paradise from which Jehovah had to eject them. The impulse which entered with Rudolf Steiner clearly lies in the line of continuity of the main stream of human development between two opposite poles, seeking the Son. When individual soul development began with the lighting up of the Sentient Soul, this stream went out from Egypt's services to humanity and led exoterically to the western spiritual life; esoterically, it led to true Rosicrucianism, in order finally to unite exoteric and esoteric Christianity in the new Mysteries.

Polzer's Dornach Speech of 14 April 1935

This speech was to have been published in 1985 in the appendix to the new edition of Polzer's memoirs; it was suppressed by the leadership of the G.A.S. The author of this biography then made it available to the editor of the magazine Erde und Kosmos, *Hellmut Finsterlin, who published it in 1988; Emanuel Zeylmans also included it in the third volume of his book* Wer war Ita Wegman? [Who Was Ita Wegman?] *(Heidelberg 1992) (George Adams-Kaufmann made a translation of this speech for D.N. Dunlop, who read it shortly before his death on 30 May, 1935.)*

If I actively engage at this point in time in the dispute and in the events in the Society, I do it because, on the basis of my many years of experience and observation I feel not only justified in doing so but also duty-bound to do so. I know that I am confronting a majority that over years, especially here in Dornach has in a certain direction formed a judgement that comes to expression in the *Memorandum*. So I am conscious of the difficulties I am facing here when I counterpose my own judgement to that majority judgement and on the basis of my judgement must say 'No' to what a majority of the Society in Dornach now wants to do. But I rely on the force of the decisive facts with which I acquainted myself over many years because I always met them without sympathy or antipathy and remained open and honest with both parties in the dispute.

So, on an active but neutral basis, I want to say something about that which I feel obliges me to speak just at this point in time and in this situation. First I must refuse that which is always being proposed—that one must just take a side. I therefore protest against being ranked with any side. I must oppose both the frivolous expression 'judgement of taste' [*Geschmacksurteil*] that was used in the *Memorandum* and also oppose the assertion that it was malice that did not allow people to be persuaded by much of what the authors of the Memorandum presented. So I must declare that it was not malice on my part; my method *too*, is to seek the truth.

Since such a voluminous book as the *Memorandum* was deliberately prepared, presented and has its effect, it is incumbent on those who disagree with this Memorandum to speak in more detail than is normal at a General Meeting.

For me the personalities who Rudolf Steiner placed in the Vorstand and in the leadership of the Sections, each in his way, are today still there in place where Dr Steiner put them. That they all have failings along with their distinctions, and have made errors cannot alter my view. That errors were made on the one side as on the other has shown itself in the events that have played out over the last ten years. That these personalities could not find the way to work together showed me furthermore that after the death of Rudolf Steiner the esoteric power of the Vorstand as a whole was not strong enough on the one hand, to overcome external, disturbing influences in the right way, and on the other hand, that there was no personality in the Vorstand who could reconcile the opposing sides. Few consequences were drawn from the death of Rudolf Steiner in terms of knowledge that could have brought unity. Rather, impossible pretensions appeared in relation to the leadership of the High School, first from one side and then, somewhat less emphatically, from the other side. So, in accordance with reason and in view of the absence of a spiritual leader, a new, freer, more ambitious basis for the Society could not be found. But when a challenge, which the death of Rudolf Steiner presented, cannot be met on the basis of reason, then it can work itself out through violent catastrophes—catastrophes which will destroy only the basis of the Society that was possible under Rudolf Steiner, but not the being of anthroposophy. Whatever happens, none of the personalities are relieved of their obligations to remain at their posts.

Soon after the death of Rudolf Steiner I recognized with my own eyes that there was no real will for an understanding to work with Frau Dr Wegman, that such collaboration was not seriously held to be possible by either Frau Dr Steiner or Herr Steffen. When, still in the year 1925 I asked Herr Steffen to take on the Presidency of the Vorstand he said to me: 'I could only work with Frau Dr Steiner, but never with Frau Dr Wegman.' So I saw that right from the beginning there was no sincere will for an understanding; only a will for dismissal was prevalent, and this showed itself especially in the attitude and behaviour of many personalities in Dornach. This mood, which was not spoken of openly but which was prevalent amongst people, was bound necessarily to give rise to all the conflicts and misunderstandings, first in the Vorstand and in Dornach, which then occurred. And they spread very quickly out from Dornach to the periphery and disturbed the work everywhere.

There are many deep reasons for the difficulties in reaching an understanding, which can not be pushed only onto Frau Dr Wegman and Dr Vreede. The Society, which was placed in the service of esotericism, increasingly lost its esoteric character through the dispute. The danger threatened that the Society would increasingly become something completely external, despite the emphasis on and the formation of a completely new dogmatic concept of esotericism.

Since the *Memorandum* quite rightly emphasizes that one has to go back into the past if one wants to understand the disagreements, so I too want to go back but a little further, not only as far as the death of Rudolf Steiner, because the resentment and hostility against Frau Dr Wegman goes back earlier than the death of Rudolf Steiner. This opposition was there already before the Christmas Conference; it was more hidden then. I experienced this personally and was able to observe much in regard to it because I was very often in Dornach at that time, often for long periods, [and] because Rudolf Steiner spoke to me about all the personalities who later came into the Vorstand and about many others. Many will perhaps still be here who heard Rudolf Steiner speaking already in those days of a witch-hunt against Frau Dr Wegman and her activity as doctor and how he then said that this would destroy the Society. Yet he went on distinguishing her and emphasizing the need for her collaboration. I could also confirm that there were personalities (I do not want to name any names) of whom he quite definitely disapproved, who became more prominent in his last years and after his death and who suppressed or tried to suppress those whom he had preferred for many areas of work.

Because I stand opposed to the motions, to justify this opposition I must especially address the deeper causes of these difficulties and move on to the area of esotericism. The *Memorandum* addresses this area, even if in a somewhat primitive fashion, but quite openly. So I too may be allowed to speak quite openly. I even consider what I shall say about this to be very necessary because much in the *Memorandum* is very inaccurately and not clearly expressed and I heard and learned a great deal from Rudolf Steiner in this area and therefore since his death I have remained in my activities always consistent and certain.

First, on the view I have had to come to over the years on the leadership of the High School. For me, Rudolf Steiner is even today still the only leader of the High School, if this still has its esoteric character. The [leadership of the] Section for General Anthroposophy can be occupied by no one and taken on out of an earnest, real responsibility. Because of this, the possibility for the Section leaders to meet esoterically still does not seem to me to be an illusion today *if one of these personalities does not claim the leadership in some kind of succession which is not at all the case here*—Rudolf Steiner did not name a successor. But that this happened after Rudolf Steiner's death I have always regarded as a mistake and said so at the time.

A control of Class affairs after the death of Rudolf Steiner I hold to be possible only if the person who wishes to take on the responsibility to the spiritual world and to Rudolf Steiner and who is carried by the wills of a number of [prominent] individuals communicates this to the leaders of the Sections and speaks with them about it. Through this, I believe, continuity with Rudolf Steiner, which is a condition, would be preserved.

I also once put my viewpoint in a similar way much later to Herr Steffen when it was a matter of permission for Herr Arenson. Such an appointment remains an act that is a case of spiritual destiny. A granting of authorization [to be able to read Class Lessons] because of diligent 'achievements' and the acquisition of a great deal of knowledge would be unacceptable to me; that way, we would very soon be travelling on an entirely external authoritarian path.

Now I must speak about my understanding of the sense in which Frau Dr Wegman was Rudolf Steiner's colleague in the Class. For Rudolf Steiner quite clearly described her as such. I hold it to be insincere simply to identify a colleague in the Class with the secretary in the Vorstand. Such an identification seems to me in this case to be an insult. And there has been no lack of those. It is not unclear to me how Rudolf Steiner understood the term 'colleague' [*Mitarbeiterin*]. The appointment of a colleague, an assistant in founding and working together on the being of a Mystery Centre, as in this case with the Michael School, could only be based on a deep destiny connection of which Rudolf Steiner was very conscious, and which was emphasized by him and to which he wanted to do justice. I have no doubt at all that this is how it was. In doing this, Rudolf Steiner in fact said to Frau Dr Wegman that she stands within a great destiny. Not only Frau Dr Steiner but also Frau Dr Wegman stands with Rudolf Steiner within a great destiny which must be borne with all its burdens and sufferings. But now the colleague and helper is never also the successor-in-waiting; as *wife*, she cannot be. But it is humanly understandable that after the death of Rudolf Steiner Frau Dr Wegman misjudged her task. I cannot accept that one may therefore bring in damning judgements and persecutions and speak of a failure that wipes out everything before it and uses this error to make the earlier, concealed witch-hunt into a formal execution, even a moral dismemberment. I must emphasize that I have never spoken with Frau Dr Wegman about her incarnations and neither has anyone ever said anything to me about them directly. One certainly often heard the Alexander-matter mentioned, especially by her opponents. I also once had a conversation with Rudolf Steiner under circumstances and conditions in which personal matters about incarnations could be spoken of. That was in Berlin, in 1917.

The initiative for the esoteric Michael School came, as Rudolf Steiner said, from Frau Dr Wegman. In taking up this initiative then between him and her the necessary esoteric unity of destiny was created which was the precondition for the Mysteries of the modern age.

Before the war Frau Dr Wegman was a colleague in all the esoteric ritual events. The one was as necessary as the other, like *everything* in the life of Rudolf Steiner.

When Rudolf Steiner came back from England in 1924 he gave various indications that he wanted gradually to give the Class a ritual dimension. It was out of the growing ritualistic dimension of the Michael Mystery that then, at admissions [into the Class] which occurred in September, he spoke of the handshake and the promise, which was also to be given to Frau Dr Wegman. This was an indication that this unity of destiny [between him and her—*transl.*] had a significance for the Michael Mystery. When it is said in the *Memorandum* that Frau Dr Steiner has a position that is not only of symbolic but of real importance—that was indeed known to me—this is self-evident, because it could not be otherwise with a colleague of Rudolf Steiner within the being of the Mysteries. The common founding of a Mystery *demands* the reality of the importance of the colleague, and Rudolf Steiner documented this through his deed. Both with Frau Dr Steiner and with Frau Dr Wegman. Now I must turn to what is said [in the Memorandum—*transl.*] about old and new esotericism. In the Mysteries the experience of death was always represented in some way: Death—entombment—resurrection—association with divine beings—in the most primitive way at first to the grandest, which was given to us in the Class. Rudolf Steiner never had anything to do with an esotericism that divided itself into old and new. On the contrary, from the very beginning, even before the war, he dedicated his forces to the necessary return of the Mysteries, how they must be in the present and in the future. He gave them the content of a spiritual consciousness and a form and praxis necessary for the present in that he brought to humanity the wisdom of anthroposophy which is of equal significance for the male and the female spirit. This was bound up with the need to express this duality in the ritual representation of anthroposophy therefore a female colleague was indispensable by dint of her gender. During the Class Lesson we are not only experiencing the didactic reading of a lecture but a ritual operation which can bring us into relationship with the Mystery streams of all ages. When we give up this consciousness and do not always remain wakeful, we forsake that which Rudolf Steiner brought to the Earth as a heavenly institution.

I know that mistakes happened; they happened on both sides. Everyone is subject to them. But for me they are no reason to stop recognizing what can never be extinguished and will continue. Quite apart from outer achievements, which for me are not at all so different in the individual Sections in their significance for humanity, I must reject tendentious criticism. The outrageous, moral calumnies which have for years been cast especially at Frau Dr Wegman in public gatherings and printed in pamphlets I must regard as directed against Rudolf Steiner's will. It almost seems at times, when one has experienced much of what went on before the Christmas Conference and feels it still working on now, as if a hidden mostly unconscious resentment against the last years of Rudolf Steiner was making itself noticeable, the victim of which has especially been Frau Dr Wegman. Such resentment against Dr Steiner showed itself even earlier.

It is also very clear to me that Frau Dr Steiner, who worked for so long with Rudolf Steiner is spiritually the one who has advanced the most. But a sincere, friendly will for an understanding was lacking. That has nothing to do with outer achievements, as the expression 'achievements' is itself something philistine and very inappropriate for *inner* affairs of the soul, for inner 'achievements'. But these play a very great role in esotericism, and because of them, it is *not the head alone that practises esotericism*. Through constant critical speaking and enquiring into methods, it can happen that one remains stuck intellectually with methods, fearful of their results and over-sensitive about life and destiny or repressed in a philistine manner.

I want to mention another fact which shows how much has gone on in this area. At the opening of the Rudolf Steiner Hall in London, when I went there on occasion together with Dr Unger, he urged me to help him so that the Mystery rites which Rudolf Steiner formed anew before the war could be continued. He even went into details about it with me and held it to be an absolute necessity for the Society. At the time I had to avoid the issue in my reply because Frau Dr Steiner had told me shortly before in a conversation that it would present great difficulties, especially in Dornach.

From what has been said thus far I see the need for me to oppose the motions of the Working Group of Co-workers at the Goetheanum. It is for me an impossibility to grant to a part of the broken Vorstand the right to put all the blame on the other part and on the basis of repeatedly uttered concepts that have for a long time now become slogans, such as 'method', 'lack of method', 'forming a judgement', 'achievements', to proudly state that 'we are the only ones justified and capable of continuing Rudolf Steiner's work, we are the ones who have the right methods, the others have no method; who is not with us is against us; you must decide whether you are going with us or whether you are going under with the others.' This is what one hears continuously. It is not possible to use authority to divide anthroposophers into black and white and then to deny the alleged blacks access to the Goetheanum, as Dr Vreede says, with the power of the key. With this, the atmosphere of the Mysteries would be increasingly suppressed in the second Goetheanum Building and would withdraw. Then would also fall ever more heavily on the Vorstand the responsibility for so much harm to the health, souls and bodies of old, faithful anthroposophers, caused by the dispute and proceeding from it but it would not only fall on that part which the *Memorandum* solely blames.

Since 1 January 1927 when Herr Dr Boos disturbed a Class lesson in a violent manner and indeed almost forced Frau Dr Wegman from the podium, I knew that if that could not be made good again peaceably within the Class itself by the whole Vorstand, the General Anthroposophical Society would fall into decay, become superficial in an intellectualistic manner despite the increasing participation at conferences, and that it would more and more lose its original character.

The Memorandum was intended to point the direction for forming a judgement in the decisions that were to be made at the General Meeting. That was the actual reason why it was written. Through the fact that it is a piece of propaganda—it says in the introduction itself that it does not wish to be non-factional—it works destructively, fanatically and manipulatively. The best I can say about it is that it is a 'fable convenue'. It also shows how since the death of Rudolf Steiner, what he indicated to us notably in his last years has been exactly that which has been lacking and systematically ignored: to research history not only from the sources but to foster an approach to history that can be read in the spirit on the basis of repeated earthly lives. Despite dangers and errors through which each of us will have to go and which today no one should be allowed to condemn in an authoritative manner, this history will be written.

Let us look at what has gone on in the Society these last ten years. It began with a war of letters, then the letters became ever more voluminous; they grew into pamphlets and finally into books. If this were to be continued by both sides in an outwardly, self-opinionated fashion, it would fill bookshops and archives. But that would only be the proof that Rudolf Steiner was not understood, that the Society had fallen into error, the centre remained empty and that people on both sides were making themselves sick with such literature. Do we really think that we are on the right path when such propaganda grows and grows? Do we believe that in this way we will be able to enter rightly into the next century, when we fill archives in this manner? Do we really believe that at the turn of the century what is printed will play such a great role? Do we believe that with such propaganda, with such combative moods we can create the calm needed for the real work? The agreement that was present at the Christmas Conference in 1923 was only a pretence; it was in reality a unanimous declaration of will. Rudolf Steiner said *beforehand* what would happen with the Sections, by whom these would be led, and of what personalities the Vorstand would be composed. Today it appears as if one laid claim to trust beforehand without saying the most important things beforehand, which then would happen.

The first Goetheanum was built as a Mystery Centre; it was taken from us because inside it we spoke purely intellectually. There was no one there who could have protected it. Rudolf Steiner was not allowed to protect it because he gave it to mankind as a test of our maturity. Then Rudolf Steiner laid the Foundation Stone in the hearts [of the members]. The Foundation Stones, which rest in strong hearts, are no longer bound to one place and one building. They must become the Foundation Stones for the Mystery Centres of the future in various places. Those who will plant the seeds for these Mystery Centres can only be called to do so directly by the spiritual world through their destiny. This calls above all for esoteric courage, not subordination and constrictions.

The second Goetheanum was built entirely for the public, to work as 'the little book' from outside, as it is called in the fourth apocalyptic seal [shown in the Munich congress of 1907]. But the continuation of the Mysteries will come from the little book from inside. The most important challenge to the anthroposophical movement and Society is therefore: trust in people, not resentment of them. Trust that would first have to be given from Dornach, not trust that is first demanded by Dornach. Trust responds when it is first given and if Rudolf Steiner can speak through the five Section leaders but not when one has to read moral sermons in almost every newsletter, without regard for how the situation has changed, and between the lines pretensions to leadership are raised up—all of which must wound many souls who are closely bound to Rudolf Steiner. Rudolf Steiner will not speak if Frau Dr Wegman and Frau Dr Vreede are excluded.

Rudolf Steiner alone can unite all anthroposophers of the past, present and future, not a sharpening of statutes and anathemas against independent action, when destinies collide and it is hard for people to find agreement. The motions and the *Memorandum* are a sign of weakness, which will unleash violence.

But if agreement cannot be reached in the Vorstand then there only remains the possibility that the Sections at the Goetheanum all stay open and the General Anthroposophical Society constitutes itself on completely free foundation without central control of admissions. After ten years of dispute in the Vorstand and in the Society, the exclusion of such a large part of the membership, among whom are old members valued by Rudolf Steiner, can never be good for anthroposophy.

The trust which was given freely and as a matter of course to the spiritually universal leader and teacher would now in the time without a leader have to be given to the power of anthroposophy itself and to the people it embraces and will be embraced by it. This would be expressed in the Statutes in that the formation of groups and the admission of members would, correspondingly, have to be left in full confidence to the leaders of the groups. Not only to those who say 'yes' to everything and subscribe to conditions.

Another decision can be reached formally through legalistic cleverness, but this would not be Rudolf Steiner's way. There can be no question of advancing esoteric pretensions, such as the dismissal and appointment of Section leaders, under the cover of aggressive majority voting.

I think that even financial catastrophe for the Goetheanum will not be avoided if the call for greater freedom is not met with reason.

On the Matter of the Class

The following 'personal information' from Polzer's literary estate has been included in the appendix to the second edition. It was enclosed by him in his handwritten memoirs. Its content is not only of historical interest. Even though the Class texts and mantras are published today (GA 270, 1–IV, and the Perseus Verlag edition of 2011), the facts and viewpoints expressed by Polzer can be of value to the meditant of these texts and mantras.

Thomas Meyer

Personal information—not to be passed on

1 December 1935

Only for members of the Michael School

In the interests of the School it seems to me necessary to make some comments again in order to render the agitations which some have been stirring in relation to the matter of the Class at least somewhat less effective.

Understandably, younger Class members who are not very familiar with the beginnings of the School and of the esoteric work of Rudolf Steiner can easily be made uncertain by inaccurate, bogus arguments. These give rise to a great variety of erroneous *opinions* which disturb the work in the Class because they are incompatible with the spiritual substance of the Class and with the preconditions for participation in it.

A key argument which is now made against the Class Lessons which I have been holding for more than eleven years, in order to disturb this work, runs rather like this: 'Whoever wants to have the Class as Herr Dr Steiner held it should do so in the national society [*Landesgesellschaft*]; who takes part in Class Lessons in the Free Groups, cannot be admitted to Class Lessons in the national society. Count Polzer does not hold the Class as Rudolf Steiner did.'

Against this it must be said: Herr Dr Steiner did not always hold the Class in the same way. From February until 2 August 1924 he did not make the sign nor the seal of Michael before and after the Class Lesson, nor did he speak the mantric words about the connection to the Rose Cross Mystery through the Michael seal. He only did this after his return from England in September at the Repeat Classes.

At that time, in September at admissions of new members he also began to have them make to himself and Frau Dr Wegman the promise of faithfulness to the Michael School. In doing so, he showed that he wanted to give the Class, as he announced in the last Lesson, on 2 August, before his departure for England, more of a cultic nature.

He further demonstrated that the Michael School stood in a unitary whole with the esotericism given by him before the war by speaking the mantra which he spoke every time before and after every Class already on 30 September 1923, before there was a Class, for the first time at the start of an esoteric Rosicrucian lesson held in Vienna. Also, the connection between the Michael seal with the saying Rosae et Crucis verse and the words spoken to it show unequivocably the unity of the esotericism and Mystery schooling he represented.

Never has a mantric word been spoken in the Class by me which did not come from Rudolf Steiner. That the holding of the Class should be conducted in as a mobile a way as possible and not allowed to be fixed in any outwardly dogmatic manner would have to be clear to every esotericist who does not want the Michael Mystery to go the way of the Roman Church, which led to the dogmatic disputes at its Councils.

An unmistakable indication for me of the correctness of what has been said above are the words which Rudolf Steiner spoke to me on 11 November 1924 when I asked him how I should hold the Class. He replied emphatically: 'Do it as you wish.' This answer is, as I learned to understand more and more, the only one possible in the Michaelic sense, since Rudolf Steiner had agreed that I should take on this task with the Class. But this, which I have often mentioned before, is deliberately ignored by many.

In the present time, since the death of Rudolf Steiner the Mysteries can certainly not be concealed any longer, but the living, and not just the intellectual but also ritual, continuity with the Mystery content that he gave must be fostered in order to share this with those who did not know Rudolf Steiner but who seek to connect with him esoterically and not only intellectually.

The call to the brethren[*], the speaking of individual mantras, which Rudolf Steiner did on such occasions are not ritual acts which deviate from the spirit of his ritual acts. It is certainly not in his spirit and not Michaelic to make of the Class Lessons simply a dogmatic reading out loud.

---

[*] At the cultic operations of the ritual lessons (FM) at the beginning of the last century Rudolf Steiner called on the 'Brothers of the Previous Era, the Present and the Future'. See for example GA 265, p.158. This call was to be understood as the sign of historical continuity of all spiritual striving.

The objection that is often made that I do not hold the Class as Rudolf Steiner did is therefore untrue in the spiritual sense and only formally partly correct. This formal correctness is entirely at one with the majority decision—which corresponds to merely formal, juridical laws—by means of which the dismissals and exclusions were pronounced at the last General Meeting in Dornach at Easter and through which the General Anthroposophical Society has become something other than the one that was founded by Rudolf Steiner.

It must again be emphasized that in Prague there is in Rudolf Steiner's sense no 'Zemska Class' and no 'Jednota Class' but only the Class which Dr Eiselt holds and the Class which I hold. There can never be any exclusive claim on the Michael School by an external group of the Society [?, extra handwritten words in the margin]

I cannot therefore go along with those who say that members who take part in the Jednota Class cannot take part in the Zemska Class and vice versa. For my part, I must leave it entirely to the conscience of the older Class members how as individuals they relate to that. Instructions that do not stem directly from Rudolf Steiner I cannot regard as valid.

I hereby declare that I have been holding the Class for eleven years with the knowledge and agreement of Rudolf Steiner and thus maintain direct continuity. I further believe that it is impossible to bypass Frau Dr Wegman in matters of the Class because this goes against the will of Rudolf Steiner, who expressly stated: 'Frau Dr Wegman will lead the Class with me.' In avoiding her, one departs from the stream of the continuous being of the Mysteries, into which Rudolf Steiner alone could lead us.

If exoteric 'opinions' were to become determinant in the Class, then the content of the esoteric Mystery would soon be lost in such a community. As an instrument of the spiritual world on Earth the Michael School can never have anything to do with intellectual opinions, which have the character of an external association.

In Memoriam Frau Dr Ita Wegman

Wiesneck, End of March 1943

Shocked by the unexpectedly sudden death of Frau Dr Ita Wegman, I take up my pen.

In a few days I will enter my 75th year; every further month of life is a gift of destiny. Before I leave this earthly life, I feel obliged to write down the truth about a most important event on my esoteric path of development. It was in 1935 when I intervened in the destiny of the Society in order to try to maintain the unity of the Vorstand. This event is so deeply bound up with the destiny of Frau Dr Wegman that I want to write something about it in more detail. It is not intended as a justification but as a contribution to the history of the Anthroposophical Society. In such a sacred cause one does not write disputations. But I must say something through which one can throw some light on events which for the consciousness of many friends lie in darkness, and were the cause of many misunderstandings and of harm to the work of Rudolf Steiner.

After the fire of the first Goetheanum Building on New Year's Eve 1922/23, Rudolf Steiner saw no other possibility of continuing his work than to make the sacrifice of taking on himself the leadership of the Society which had formed itself for his life's work. This new formation of the Society was accomplished at the Christmas Conference of 1923/24. Rudolf Steiner established a Vorstand [Executive Council] which through this establishment became an esoteric Vorstand because he was able to perceive the individuals in it in their destinies and capacities. He designated himself as the First President, Albert Steffen as the Second President, Frau Dr Wegman as the Recorder, Marie Steiner and Fräulein Dr Vreede as council members, Dr Guenther Wachsmuth as Secretary and Treasurer.

Dr Rudolf Steiner was well aware of the talents and failings of these personalities and at their appointment he emphasized that he had to choose such personalities as were normally resident in Dornach, who thus were available for him at any time; he could have chosen other personalities from the periphery. The Vorstand had its esoteric nature through his appointments and his presence.

Sections were created for the various areas of work. Dr Steiner himself took on the Section for General Anthroposophy and Pedagogy. Frau Dr Marie Steiner received the Section for Eurythmy and Speech Formation, Herr Albert Steffen the Section for Literature, Frau Dr med. Ita Wegman the Medical Section, Frl. Dr Vreede the Section for Astronomy and Herr Dr Guenther Wachsmuth the Section for Natural Science. A Section for the Plastic Arts was also created for Miss Maryon, although she was very ill and died on 2 May 1924. Rudolf Steiner did not fill that post again.

The principal change was according to Rudolf Steiner's will that from now on only that would be spoken as was demanded by the spiritual world, without compromises. Until then that had not been the case. Rudolf Steiner said repeatedly that from now on a new impulse, a new attitude and stronger spiritual courage would have to take hold of the Society The great significant Conference was closed with a convivial evening in the lecture room of the Schreinerei.

At the beginning of February something extraordinarily meaningful now occurred as the first result of this new foundation. Frau Dr Wegman took the initiative and asked Rudolf Steiner to establish an esoteric institution again. Straightaway Rudolf Steiner willingly responded to this initiative and founded the Michael School on Earth, of which he said it was a heavenly institution, willed by the spiritual world. 'The time had come.' He designated Frau Dr Wegman as his colleague and deputy in this esoteric area. With this, difficulties, as yet unspoken, immediately began in the Vorstand. Outwardly, one noticed nothing. On 15 February Dr Steiner held the first Lesson of the Michael School, in the Schreinerei. Before this a few members, as was necessary, applied in writing for membership in the School. They received their own cards with their names on.

A lofty esoteric mood and joy went through the entire Society. In other locations too new life and new hopes began. National societies and new independent branches formed. Rudolf Steiner worked restlessly and made trips to various cities. There was an especially strong reaction in England to the call to human souls which went out from Dornach. Preparations were made in Dornach for the Michaelmas Conference in September, which was to have an especially rich programme. I too travelled there for the conference although I had often been in Dornach in the months before and had also taken part in the agricultural conference in Koberwitz.

On [24] September I received a telegram from my brother that my mother was dying. Before my departure Rudolf Steiner received me in his atelier. He seemed to me to be unsatisfied with how things were developing in Dornach and Stuttgart. When I expressed my joy about the growth of the activities within the Society, he made a dismissive gesture with his hand which astonished me at the time but remained unforgettable for me. He gave me permission on that occasion to hold Class Lessons in Vienna. I held the first on Michaelmas Day.

On 11 November I was again in Dornach. Rudolf Steiner was ill. He sent for me, was sitting in an easy chair, looked very bad and seemed quite exhausted. I asked him then how I should go on with the Class Lessons and received the answer: 'Do it as you wish.'

My two sons who had been working continuously in Dornach since 1920 and since the fire had been keeping watch on the land and in the Schreinerei told me later that without wanting to eavesdrop, they had heard through the wooden walls how in rehearsals and in sittings of the Vorstand one or the other Vorstand member opposed Rudolf Steiner. Frau Dr Wegman never did that. When I was in Dornach in November I noticed very clearly how among a few members there was an atmosphere hostile to Frau Dr Wegman, although Dr Steiner always gave her signs of his greatest confidence in her, expressed it openly and wrote in various articles. One felt already during his illness that various intrigues directed against Frau Dr Wegman were going on. At first, however, I could not really make out what this meant. We all counted on Rudolf Steiner's recovery and thought that he would put everything in order again as he had always done before.

A few years before all these events Herr Roman Boos had fallen into a abnormal mental condition and since then had been outside what was going on in Dornach. He no longer visited Rudolf Steiner, although he was often seen on the Goetheanum property. Rudolf Steiner handed him over then to Dr Kolisko for his care, but Roman Boos withdrew himself from this. Scarcely had Rudolf Steiner died than Roman Boos reappeared and began to engage actively in the movement.

Already during the Funeral solemnities open conflict broke out between Marie Steiner and Frau Dr Wegman. The aggressive party was Frau Marie Steiner, while Frau Dr Wegman was conciliatory and made her points calmly.

Now two very active parties formed within the membership in Dornach. This division spread only slowly into the periphery [of the movement]. Everywhere there the whole Vorstand enjoyed the sincere trust of the membership. At first, I felt more drawn to Marie Steiner, the wife of the Doctor, as I did not know Frau Wegman well at that time and enjoyed friendly relations with Frau Marie Steiner. On 3 March I was again with Dr Steiner in his atelier which had been made into his sickbed in the Schreinerei. He sent for me; he was lying in bed and spoke in a heavy voice. He wanted to speak to me about something regarding my sons. He always spoke to me about the work very directly. On the day of his death, in the morning at 10 a.m. on 30 March I received a letter from him which he had written on 25 March. A few hours later news of his death came in a telegram to Herr Dr Eiselt.

I write that because it is necessary to understand why I felt obliged, after Rudolf Steiner's death, to make efforts to prevent a threatening split in the Vorstand which he had established and in the Anthroposophical Society.

I then came to Dornach often and spoke to individual members of the Vorstand. The Vorstand as a whole ignored me. I hoped it would call me to hear what Rudolf Steiner spoke to me about in his final period and what authorization he had given me. It later became very clear that all the Vorstand members were quite uninformed about it.They felt a certain awkwardness with me because they sensed that Rudolf Steiner had spoken to me about many things and also about members of the Vorstand. They also thought perhaps that I would have pretensions about joining the Vorstand. I was not thinking of it, because in 1915, when he offered me the post in the Goetheanum Building Association that was vacant after the death of Fräulein Sophie Stinde, he then came to the same view as me that I would be more important for the movement in Austria and Hungary. A symptom made me very clearly aware of this embarrassment, which the Vorstand showed to me before the death of Rudolf Steiner. Apart from the members of the Vorstand and the head of the construction team working on the second Goetheanum, no one else was allowed into Dr Steiner's sickroom except me. When I was called on 3 March, Herr Dr Noll came to me beforehand and somewhat agitated, asked me not to add to interference with the doctors' prescriptions and arrangements! I was really very surprised by this unreasonable demand which seemed to suggest a belief that there was some kind of plot between Dr Steiner and myself. Since Frau Dr Wegman, as the doctor in charge, was always around Dr Steiner, I suspected that I was overestimated by the Vorstand. Because no one except the afore-mentioned people were allowed into the sickroom, my being allowed in was estimated too highly; it was not wanted that I should confront the whole Vorstand.

It was later in 1925 when Herr Albert Steffen told me that he could only work correctly with Frau Marie Steiner and not with Frau Dr Wegman. I had on occasion to meet with Frau Marie Steiner in connection with Rudolf Steiner's literary estate; as an Austrian, I had offered to deal with this, and I was on good terms with her, but always felt there was something that distanced me from her, especially because of her often great unfriendliness towards my wife.

It was probably incorrect that at first, I joined those who objected to Frau Dr Wegman continuing the Leading Thoughts in the *Goetheanum* magazine. I knew that these Leading Thoughts would be written by others, because Frau Dr Wegman was insufficiently fluent. It would probably have been better to give her time and to support her with trust.

But both women wanted [...] to speak to me individually in order to justify to me their awareness of the trust Rudolf Steiner had placed in them to continue his work. In no way did I doubt this justification with regard to their areas of Section work. One day Marie Steiner showed me the last letter Rudolf Steiner had written to her. I read it through in front of her. Then Frau Dr Wegman called me. She had a whole pile of papers before her; there may have been some old documents among them. I felt rather awkward. She took out two papers and gave them to me. I read—it was Rudolf Steiner's handwriting. The content was superb, somewhat difficult to understand quickly; I could not repeat it. There was a lovely, complex interlaced drawing as a heading above the sentences. I was shocked in a way; it made a great impression on me. The letter which Frau Marie Steiner had read to me was written with much affection but contained nothing at all of an esoteric nature. It showed how Rudolf Steiner had affectionately struggled to say something to her that he knew she could not understand: 'You have always understood me.' Between the lines, so to speak, he was asking her also to understand that his task on Earth was too multi-faceted to be linked esoterically with her alone. Such exclusivity was not possible for him. He could not restrict himself in his mission on Earth in a 'bourgeois' way. His destiny stood beyond what was customarily 'bourgeois'.

A real cause of the strife—perhaps most significant—was that various papers and documents from Dr Steiner's writings and possession were in Frau Dr Wegman's keeping. Frau Dr Steiner saw all this as left to her and thought that she alone should be allowed to have it at her disposal. But it is certain that Frau Dr Wegman only took what Dr Steiner had personally given her. As he had also done with the cross that he wore on his breast, so will it have been with other things. Rudolf Steiner certainly did not allow the denial of his right to take certain things from those he owned and present them to his faithful colleague.

It happened one day that Dr Roman Boos burst in on Frau Dr Wegman aggressively in order to take certain documents. He was, however, unable to get away with anything. Frau Dr Wegman had, as I heard later, taken care ahead of time to secure the most important documents.

Now I must speak about something else that Frau Ita Wegman told me personally. Soon after Rudolf Steiner's death, Frau Marie Steiner came to her and wanted to know whether Rudolf Steiner had told her something about incarnations that concerned Frau Ita Wegman. She hesitated somewhat and then Marie Steiner opined that it must be possible among esotericists to come to an understanding of such things. When Frau Wegman then spoke, Marie Steiner stood up and left without a word.

My wife told me that she visited Frau Marie Steiner the day after the death of Rudolf Steiner. It was rather hard for her; she wanted to show how painfully, along with the others, she was feeling the loss of the Doctor and so wanted to show her sympathy. How the visit turned out shocked her, as she found Marie Steiner in a condition of soul that was full of resentment and complaint. She even made agitated remarks about Rudolf Steiner's brother and sister. When my wife was on her way back and met Frau Dr Wegman, she received only warm, affectionate words. So different were the soul constitutions of the two women.

Much later, it was perhaps 1937 [January 1939] I experienced a dream. It seemed to me that the dream had something to do with an event within the tragic conflict in the Vorstand. One comes to deeper insights into questions of historical destiny only slowly, through constant effort to penetrate reality. I found myself in the sacristy of a church or chapel. A very friendly cardinal came to me with whom I could make myself understood pleasantly and peacefully through the eyes and facial gestures. Then I felt, as though from behind, another clergyman push forward who raged against the cardinal. I did not see the latter [second clergyman] at all. A frightful dispute went on between the two. I heard a voice say to me : 'This second one is from the monastery at Santiago de Compostela.' I felt inwardly calm, standing above the dispute. I was once told that important documents were stolen from the monastery at Santiago by the Arabs and were recovered from them after the battle of Granada; but they did not find their way back to the monastery. The esoteric situation called for them to be preserved elsewhere. They were supposed to be the writings of Aristotle. I write this with all due caution, but I want to mention it because it approached me externally and internally.

The misunderstandings became ever greater, the forms of the conflict ever more impossible for an esoteric Vorstand.

Until then Rudolf Steiner's assistant in his esoteric operations had been his wife. After the establishment of the Michael School Frau Dr Wegman became his assistant. The times demanded that women be allowed into the Mysteries. That was the great difficulty in occult development that had to be overcome. It required sacrifices and suffering. We stand within these today.

The fight against Frau Dr Wegman took forms which bordered on the demonic. The battering ram for this was Herr Dr Roman Boos. He took it to the peak. I was there at the time.

Frau Dr Wegman was holding a Class Lesson. By chance I was sitting near the front that day and could see everything. Frau Wegmann [sic] had just begun. Dr Boos rushed forward from behind onto the podium with a pale, distorted expression and began in accusing words to speak against Frau Dr Wegmann [sic]. It was an attack of the worst kind, a disturbance of a ritual act. After this event, at which other members of the Vorstand behaved weakly, I knew where my place was. Despite this incident, the persecution continued, and Dr Roman Boos was again used as the battering ram.

In the following years General Meetings were always an opportunity to attack Frau Dr Wegman in the worst manner. In Vienna and Prague it was possible to maintain the balance and peaceful work until 1935. The national Vorstand in Vienna, which was appointed at Michaelmas 1923 in the presence of Dr Steiner continued until the General Meeting in Dornach in 1935.

For the General Meeting in 1929 [1930] I had worked out a proposal which I wanted to bring. Before I write about this, I want to relate an episode that I experienced soon after the death of Rudolf Steiner. I was staying then at the home of Count Lerchenfeld, where Frau von Vocano was living. A lot of Society politicking always went on there. Frau v. Vocano was fanatically opposed to Frau Dr Wegman, although she had tried to draw Frau Dr Wegman into her circle before Rudolf Steiner's death. One evening I noticed some politicking was going on in the house. Herr Dr Unger had come from Stuttgart. I decided to go that evening and visit Herr Steffen. Until 1935 I was always on friendly terms with him. He opened the door and was somewhat surprised that I had come at such a late hour. The doors of the hall had been left open to his study, and he called into there: 'Herr Dr Unger, do you mind if I let Count Polzer in?' but did not wait for the answer and I went in and greeted Herr Dr Unger, who looked rather embarrassed. I had come just at the moment when Dr Unger had asked Herr Steffen a question and Herr Steffen had not yet replied. Now, Steffen said to Dr Unger: 'I shall think over the proposal you have put to me and then give you my answer.' Dr Unger then soon left. Steffen told me that Dr Unger had brought the wish from some ladies that Frau Marie Steiner should take over the Section for General Anthroposophy and also the esoteric work. 'What do you say to that?' Since I knew that Herr Steffen, as the appointed Vice-President, after the death of Rudolf Steiner, entertained the pretension of now becoming the President, I replied that the [post of leader of the general] anthroposophical Section was the preserve of the President and that Frau Marie Steiner had repeatedly declared that she would not take on the post of President. It was therefore clear again that on both sides, by Frau Marie Steiner and by Steffen, it was declared that there was no will to become President and yet there were pretensions. In Steffen's case it also happened that on every occasion he threatened to withdraw altogether. For me this was a symbol of indecision, this constant saying No and then Yes. Albert Steffen also said to me that older members often came to him and said that as a younger member, he knew nothing of what Rudolf Steiner had given and instituted esoterically before the War, and that therefore it was only possible for Frau Marie Steiner to continue at the centre of the movement's esoteric work.

Later, I felt in this a rejection of what Rudolf Steiner did at the refounding of the Society at Christmas 1923/24. This was even brought in connection with the sickness that showed itself soon afterwards. To Steffen's complaint about being told he did not know of Rudolf Steiner's esoteric work before the War, I merely said I would be happy to go to Frau Marie Steiner for him and ask her to tell him all about it and to give him the necessary documents and papers. To this, Steffen only said he thought that Frau Marie Steiner was very reticent about it and easily suspicious.

The next day, I went to see Frau Marie Steiner. I told her why Steffen was so unsure and that he had often been reproached by older members because of the esoteric issue and that it would be necessary, in order to give him certainty, for her to tell him about it and give him what he needed at least outwardly in the esoteric sense in order to be able to cope with these attacks. Frau Marie Steiner replied that she did not want to burden Albert Steffen's freedom with it. So I saw that between Marie Steiner and Albert Steffen there was not the trust that is necessary between members of an esoteric Vorstand in such a difficult situation. I was very depressed and made no further attempts to facilitate an agreement. The conflict went on from General Meeting to General Meeting.

Now I come back to the proposal which I had prepared for the General Meeting of 1929 [1930]. I had made two written copies of it, in which I said that the individual leaders of the Sections should restrict themselves to their own Sections and for the time being leave the Section for General Anthroposophy unoccupied. The general affairs of the Society should be dealt with in an office only as a matter of administration. No Section leader should wish to place himself above other Sections. No tone of authority should prevail between individual Section leaders. If this could be done [i.e. as Polzer proposed—*transl.*], then help would certainly come from the spiritual world in the foreseeable future. The pretension of carrying on the work in such a way that the President or another member of the Vorstand in Rudolf Steiner's place would oversee it must be set aside. It would be a presumption because no one could claim to act on the basis of such a universality of knowledge. That was more or less the content of my proposal. I did not want to appear suddenly at the General Meeting with this proposal before I had spoken about it personally with Frau Marie Steiner and Herr Steffen. Both Albert Steffen and Frau Marie Steiner were very guarded about it, and Albert Steffen was deeply offended. So I realized that Albert Steffen really thought that he, as President, could represent a Society that had earlier been led in such significant way. I left the two copies of the proposal in the hands of the two named personalities and did not appear at the General Meeting which lasted for more than twelve hours. From this time onwards until 1935 I took no further part in General Meetings.

At the beginning of March 1935 a confidential letter arrived in Vienna from the Vorstand in Dornach addressed to Dr Lauer. He was to test the waters for a motion by the Working Group which had formed in Dornach with the intention of excluding Frau Dr Wegman and Frl. Dr Vreede from the Vorstand. He was supposed to gather votes for this motion. Dr Lauer read out the letter to the Vorstand of the Austrian national society. The effect was shattering. Like a bolt of lightning splits a tree, so was the Vorstand split apart, which until then had always worked together, friendly and united. In my soul I had the impression of an elemental catastrophe in the enormous agitation which now showed itself. Until then, we had been 'in Austria' and now we were seized by powers of destruction. Dr Lauer, Dr Thieben and Herr Breitenstein declared themselves for the motion; Herr Alfred Zeissig, Prof. Halla and I were opposed. Now I resolved to go straightaway to Dornach in order to ask Herr Steffen not to proceed with his intention to have the motions printed in the *Goetheanum* Newssheet before the General Meeting. Time was pressing; I left the next day. Herr Steffen was astonished when I showed up. I immediately gave him a warning, saying that this exclusion would be the end of the Society and the feud in the Vorstand would go on. Albert Steffen was extraordinarily embarrassed and hesitant. He told me only that I might like to speak to the gentlemen in the Working Group, thus pushing the matter onto them, and also said to me that he himself was not free in his decisions. Inwardly indignant, I rejected that energetically. This Working Group that had been thrown together on several occasions had nothing to do with Dr Steiner's institution. It consisted only of younger, very partisan members. Some of them were motivated by economic viewpoints. I felt this unreasonable suggestion to be offensive and told him that I had only come to speak to him as President of the Vorstand. In the last ten years therefore Albert Steffen had not found it possible so to secure himself in his position through spiritual production and purposeful conduct that he enjoyed freedom and trust from others. I left on the next day, but went first to Frau Dr Wegman and told her that I would speak against the motions at the General Meeting.

In Vienna a General Meeting of the Austrian national Society was called which went very badly. Dr Thomsche acted like a Jesuit, and Herr Baltz like a malicious fanatic. I obtained a text with some 50 signatures against the motions in order to forward to Dornach. From the Vienna Vorstand Prof Halla travelled to Dornach to support me. A few friends travelled with me from Prague. To my great sorrow my dear friend Dr Hans Eiselt was completely under the influence of Herr Steffen and voted for the motions. But we remained friends; he did not join in the personal attacks against me.

Before my departure I spent almost three weeks at Mariensee at the estate of Frau Dora Schenker and went only briefly, when it was necessary, to Vienna. I wanted to prepare myself in the rural peace of the woodlands there and wrote the speech which I then gave ad-lib in Dornach. It was however to be kept for the future [and so I] gave the text to Dr Wachsmuth in the moment when I went up to the podium.

The motions were published in the newssheet of the magazine *Goetheanum* before the General Meeting; it was also communicated that prospective speakers should declare their intention to do so in advance. Fourteen days before my departure for Dornach I had an experience in the night and heard a voice say: 'Ask to speak in Dornach, otherwise you will not be able to speak.' I therefore telegraphed my intention to speak against the motions. The speakers were due to speak in order, according to the dates on which they had sent in the declarations of their intentions to speak. After another nocturnal experience with Dr Steiner, my decision to intervene against the motions was confirmed. In this, he put to me the question whether I knew the Jesuit in the Society who worked in destructive ways. So it was the Jesuit spirit! This indication became for me a guideline for my later observations within the Anthroposophical Society and outside it; the fight against the Anthroposophical Society, the struggle against the spirit always lay and still lies in the background of all inner and outer events, especially since the Thirty Years' War. Since then it has been my aim to penetrate this in detail. That nocturnal experience before the General Meeting showed me how I should work in order not to lose my connection with the great teacher. It oppressed me that Schiller's *Demetrius* remained uncompleted and I could not still my longing that it should be rewritten on the basis of anthroposophical knowledge. The last address held by Rudolf Steiner, in which he drew attention to the great esoteric problem of the two Johns was also a task which he left to us. It occupied me more and more. The third task seemed to me to be the relationship between the I of Jesus to Christian Rosencreuz—all tasks which Rudolf Steiner left us before his passing. In all of them one had the opposition of the S.J. to overcome.

Easter 1935! Two times 33 years since my birth and since the last Vatican Council in Rome!

When I came to Dornach, Frau Dr Wegman told me that the British and the Dutch would not come. They had been so harshly attacked in earlier General Meetings despite their faithful and self-sacrificial events which they put on there at the initiative of Rudolf Steiner and his work. In Dornach these undertakings were regarded as competition for the Goetheanum and opposed. So I knew that I would have to speak against a very large majority. Never had I seen the Goetheanum as full as at that time. The auditorium and the stage were filled, the smallest space used and occupied with chairs. There must have been 1500 [c. 1800] members present. A large proportion of them were from the immediate environment and from Dornach and Arlesheim. Only Albert Steffen and Dr Wachsmuth were sitting at the Vorstand table; Frau Marie Steiner was listening from behind the curtains, sitting on an easy chair. The agenda had been limited to a short time. If I had not applied to speak so early, I would not have been able to say what I wanted to say. After a sparing introduction Steffen spoke and raised the question of trust. The motions were presented, and a few speakers spoke about them briefly. I got up to the lectern after 11 o'clock. I was very calm and yet, while speaking, I was carried by the audience. I felt an inner satisfaction that despite the great pro-majority there was repeated applause. After the first quarter of an hour my mouth was so dry that I asked for a glass of water. The interruption was only very short. Dr Wachsmuth, who brought me the water, made an inappropriate joke in that, smiling to those roundabout, he put the bottle under the lectern. At the part where I said that soon after the death of Rudolf Steiner Steffen indicated to me that he could only work with Marie Steiner, he jumped up and wanted to know the date of that day. I could only say that I had not made a note of the day and that it was quite unimportant as the fact showed itself right after Rudolf Steiner's death. I went on calmly and in almost 40 minutes was able to say everything I intended. After that, a few spoke briefly who only spoke very personally against me. Soon after 12 o'clock the General Meeting was paused until 3 o'clock in the afternoon. During the lunch break, they armed themselves against me and discussed how to oppose me. As the main speaker, Dr Erhard Lauer got up and felt himself obliged to wave a wooden Michael sword against me in a slanderous manner. Then the closed session was ended and the local authorities allowed entry for the voting. The majority for the motions was very large [1691]; against were only a few more than 100 [76 against; 53 abstentions]. The General Meeting was already closed at 5 p.m.

Thirty-three years from the beginning of Rudolf Steiner's anthroposophical activity, the last endeavour of his life [the Anthroposophical Society with the esoteric Vorstand instituted by Steiner], on which he placed such great hopes, was buried.

I spent the evening very pleasantly at the Clinic in Arlesheim at Frau Dr Wegman's with a few friends and thought about what Rudolf Steiner had said in the lecture of 20.2.1920 in Dornach: 'Nothing real of course comes from majority decisions, only a dominant phrase.' The esoteric character of the Vorstand was forfeit. With this, the time of my work at the Goetheanum in Dornach was over. A new, very rich period of work began in which I felt very free. I resigned from the Austrian national Society, holding all authorizations, including the esoteric, direct from Dr Steiner.

In the first night after this, what had for me been such a significant day, I had an experience which shook me very much. A huge storm went through the land, and a high, mighty, iron tower was swaying. I was afraid that at any moment it might crash down. Then I heard a voice like thunder which shouted a message to me that sounded peculiarly satisfying to me. It was so wonderful, as if what I had done had been approved from the other side of the world. Courage for life and work were given to me through it.

Soon afterwards, the Vorstand in Dornach sent me a written demand that I return the texts of the Class Lessons and cease my reading of the Lessons. I replied only briefly I could not acknowledge any esoteric character in the present tripartite Vorstand and that it was not justified in seeking to take from me an authorization that stemmed, not from it, but directly from Rudolf Steiner. I came to an understanding with Frau Dr Wegman and agreed to send on to her all applications for membership for her attention. The hope that the exclusion of the two Vorstand members would have served the Anthroposophical Society was not fulfilled. The struggle in Dornach did not quieten down, the Society was divided in two. One could still speak of an anthroposophical movement but no longer of a Society.

It was only after these events I became really close to Frau Dr Wegman and enjoyed her warm, calm manner of being. In her company one felt a connection to esoteric-ritual being. At first there were often opportunities to meet her, either in Arlesheim or at the Summer Schools in England, [I] recall beautiful days with her in Paris. One memory comes to mind. It was after the assassination attempt against Rudolf Steiner in Munich. Then he said to me: if the Germans no longer want me, then I shall go to others.

Now Rudolf Steiner has taken his dear colleague with him into the spiritual world. In a faithful, devoted way she spent the years after his death tirelessly in the service of her medical Section and of the clinics and institutions she had called into life, honoured by her colleagues. Despite all the unjust persecutions, she walked on through life with courage. Her deep and close bond of destiny with Rudolf Steiner is, for people who are of goodwill esoterically, a certainty.

Reminiscence of Ludwig Polzer-Hoditz by Rudolf Herman

My friend Antonin Geryšer—later Director of Weleda in Prague—and I regularly travelled in the years 1930–33 from Pardubice to Prague in order to attend anthroposophical lectures and to take part in Class Lessons. It was our wish to make contact with the Count and invite him to Pardubice. My friend Geryšer could not summon up the nerve to speak to him, but on my urging him, he managed it and asked if the Count would not have an opportunity to visit us. The answer was: 'One opportunity is not possible. I have many invitations from many different places, and so I shall have to fit it into a fixed schedule.' And so a definite schedule was arranged.

Our branch had concerns about how to organize the Count's stay. It was agreed that the Count would stay in our house—Rybalkova 1361, Pardubice—with Miss Valentová. Mrs K. Geryšerová was given charge of catering for him—her menus still survive. For lectures a room was made available in our house. His visits then came often. Each time he came I was always waiting for the Count at the railway station—he always came with a rucksack on his back. I accompanied him on his walks in Pardubice. To the lectures and the Class Lessons which he read to us, members came from various towns and cities in eastern Bohemia and Moravia—Vysoké, Myto, Slatiňany, Zelezny Brod, Olomouc, Brno. They were unforgettable experiences. He also held public lectures at the Veselka Hotel in Pardubice which were well-attended. My friend Geryšer translated them superbly into Czech. Among the themes were: 'The Spiritual Background in the History of the Czech People'. It is interesting that the Count very often concerned himself with our history. So I am of the opinion that in his earlier incarnation he was connected to our people.

Notes and References

Abbreviations for the most frequently cited sources in this book in the order of their appearance in the text:

AP = Arthur Polzer-Hoditz, unpublished memoirs, in the years 1939ff., hand-written, 5 vols.; *eine Lebens- und Familienchronik von den Ursprüngen des Geschlechtes bis zum Jahre 1917* [a Chronicle of Life and Family from the origins of the family until the year 1917]. For the story of the development of these writings see Part IV, Chap. 44 'Die Letzten Jahre' [The Last Years]. Note no. 2.

LP = Ludwig Polzer-Hoditz, *Erinnerungen an Rudolf Steiner* [Reminiscences of Rudolf Steiner] 1937 in an edition of 200 copies under the title *Erinnerungen an den grossen Lehrer Dr. Rudolf Steiner—Lebensrückschau eines Österreichers*, [Remi-niscences of the Great Teacher Dr Rudolf Steiner—Life Review of an Austrian] published in Prague; New edition, from which subsequent quotations are taken, Dornach 1985.

These reminiscences by Polzer are usually referred to in the text as 'Prague Reminiscences' or 'Prague Notes'

JP = Memoirs of Julius, Ritter von Polzer in 1904, written and typed by him. The unpublished typescript has 69 pages. Note no. 8.

LPK = '*Koncept für später zu schreibende Erinnerungen*' [Notes for reminiscences to be written later] Handwritten notes from the year 1924, 129 pages, unpublished. Note no. 27.

LPT = *Der Kampf gegen den Geist und das Testament Peters des Grossen* [The Struggle against the Spirit and the Testament of Peter the Great], 2nd ed., Dor-nach 1989 (under the altered title *Das Testment Peters des Grossen. Der Kampf gegen den Geist*).

APK = Arthur Polzer-Hoditz, *Kaiser Karl—aus der Geheimmappe seines Kabinettschefs* [Emperor Karl—from the Secret File of his Cabinet Director], Vienna 1928, 2nd ed., 1978.

LPM = *Das Mysterium der europäischen Mitte—eine welthistorische Schicksalsbetrachtung* [The Mystery of the European Middle—A Consideration of World-historical Des-tiny], Stuttgart 1928.

LPE = Handwritten notes begun in April 1939 with the title: *V. Mein letzter Lebensabschnitt—die Zeit nach dem Tode Dr Rudolf Steiners 1925* [The Last Phase of My Life—the Time after the Death of Dr Rudolf Steiner 1925], 309 pages. Unpublished. Main source for Part IV.

All quotations in chapters in Part IV without note numbers were taken from this source.

LPS = *Seelenbilder aus der Zeit meiner Geistesschülerschaft*—Dreizehn szenische Bilder aus dem Nachlass, mit einem Vorwort von Th. Meyer [Soul Images from the Time of My Spiritual Pupilship—13 Scenes from the Literary Estate, with a Foreword by T.H. Meyer], Basel 2000.

GA = Rudolf Steiner, Collected Works, Dornach/Switzerland; with subsequent bibliographical numbers.

Loc. cit. = in the place cited.

Op. cit. = in the work cited.

Translations of English and French quotations are, unless otherwise stated, by the author.

Part I

1. Before 1173 the Aargau district belonged to the Counts of Lenzburg, and from 1415 to the Swiss Confederation.
2. AP. All quotations in Chapter 2 are taken from this source.
3. Robert Zimmermann, *Studien und Kritiken zur Philosophie und Äesthetik*, Vol. 1 Vienna 1870, p. 205ff.
4. Lecture of 14 October 1909, today in GA 58.
5. Steiner wrote to Wilhelm Hübbe-Schleiden on 16 August 1902: 'I would like to do everything to bring the Theosophy of the present into the stream that lies in your words: "This path into the spiritual realm leads today through the intellectual realm." ' *Letters*, Vol. 2 1892–1902, Dornach 1953.
6. LP, p. 22f.
7. AP.
8. JP. All quotations in this chapter, unless indicated otherwise, are from this source.
9. JP.
10. 'Marie—a Story of Viennese High Society', quoted in LP, p.19. See also note 16.
11. AP.
12. AP.
13. JP.
14. AP.
15. Munich should be mentioned as the fourth city, where Polzer came into close touch with the spiritual science of Rudolf Steiner. He had already *discovered* it, however, in Vienna.
16. '*In Mussestunden*', [In Leisurely Hours] Novellas by Ludwig, Ritter von Polzer (Ludwig Polzer's grandfather), Vienna 1874; reprint Basel 2009; 'Reiseer-innerungen', p. 229f.—The Council was officially opened on 8 December 1869.

Part II

17. LP, p. 23.
18. That this was possible at all is—especially in relation to Ludwig Polzer's childhood and youth—thanks to Arthur Polzer, in whose unpublished memoirs (AP), which are already a main source for Part I of this book, one finds a plenitude of concrete details and descriptions of background for what his brother Ludwig reports of his youth in a more essential and symptomatic form. The flow, approach and styles of the fundamentally different autobiographical accounts of the two brothers complement each other in the most beautiful way! In view of the strong bond between the two very different brothers Part II of

this book will naturally pay a certain amount of attention to Arthur Polzer's development.

19. AP.
20. LP, p. 19.
21. AP.
22. AP.
23. JP.
24. AP.
25. It was founded by the Order of the Teutonic Knights. The west entrance featured a statue of Mary, which is considered to be one of the most important works of early Gothic sculpture in Austria.
26. AP.
27. LPK.
28. LP, p. 23f.
29. LP, p. 23f.
30. LP, p. 23f.
31. LP, p. 24f.
32. LP, p. 24f.
33. LP, p. 24.
34. All quotations from Arthur Polzer in this chapter are from AP.
35. AP.
36. LP. p. 23.
37. Gerhard Tötschinger, *Auf den Spuren der Habsburger*, Vienna 1992, p. 167.
38. AP.
39. Two brothers of Grandmother Karg and Uncle Max had already served in the garrison there. The Kargs had a house in Modern, in which Mathilde had also lived for a while.
40. AP.
41. LPK.
42. AP.
43. The date of the Emperor's birth was to play a role in Ludwig Polzer's life many times thereafter: on 18 August 1900 he went for the first time to Heiligenkreutz in Bohemia, the hometown of his wife Berta; on 18 August 1906 he and Berta signed the contract to purchase Schloss Tannbach; on 18 August 1911 he heard with Berta the first lecture of Rudolf Steiner's Munich cycle, which was of decisive importance for his further connection to spiritual science.
44. See Rudolf Steiner's lecture of 27 April 1924 (in GA 236) which also deals with the destiny of Crown Prince Rudolf.
45. See : Immanuel Geiss, *Der Berliner Kongress 1878*, Boppard am Rhein, 1978.
46. Lord Salisbury was an exponent of the British doctrine of the global pre-ponderance of Britain (and America) which brought together personalities like Lord Rosebery and Cecil Rhodes.
47. Arthur Polzer writes in his book about the Emperor Karl (= APK), p. 234f. quoted from the English version *The Emperor Karl*, London & New York 1930, p. 161f.:

On the Serbian side the murder was represented as the act of some young Bosnian hot-heads who had no connection with the Serbian government. Concrete data to contradict this assertion were lacking. It is only recently that we have gained light on the obscurity of the murder. The Vienna publicist Leopold Mandl, in a series of articles in the *Wiener Achtuhr-Abendblatt* established, on the evidence of officers of the 'Black Hand' and certain Serbian emigrants who were concerned in the murder and for whom he found a refuge in Vienna that the Russian General Staff not only was aware of the design to murder the Austrian heir-apparent but had even given encouragement to the execution of the plan [...] It is proved today that the Colonel Dragutin Dimitrijević, head of the information section of the Serbian General Staff, known as 'Apis' on account of a white patch in his otherwise black hair, the soul of the secret organization 'Union or Death', founded in 1911, systematically organized the murder of the Archduke, in conjunction with Major Tankosić [...] It is also proved that Pašić [the head of the Serbian government] did *not* warn the Imperial and Royal government as asserted by the Serbian Government.

The threads of the assassination also lead to London and are linked to that international Freemasonry that is *oriented towards power politics* (as distinct from a purely humanitarian Freemasonry). The bomb-thrower Čabrinović and Franz Ferdinand's murderer, Gavrilo Princip indicated that they had been given their task by Freemasons. See: Karl Heise, *Entente Freimaurerei und Weltkrieg* (Entente Freemasonry and the World War), 2nd edition Struktum, p. 74ff.

The unsigned Foreword to the first edition of Heise's book is by Rudolf Steiner. It states: 'The foundations of certain items of knowledge became— through secret societies in the Entente countries—the driving forces behind a political conviction that was preparing the world catastrophe and influencing world events.'

Whoever allows himself to be put off by the label 'conspiracy theory' from looking into such facts for himself may have his reasons for doing so, but by averting his gaze, he will gain no insight into the more complex structures of world events. As with every theory, in the case of a conspiracy theory it is simply a matter of whether it rests on solid facts or is just a mere thought-out construction. This can never be decided generally but only assessed case by case in accordance with the actual phenomena.

48. What played itself out in the '90s of the twentieth century and at the beginning of the twentieth century in Croatia, Bosnia-Herzegovina and Serbia is nothing but a black flood of the mad consequences of Austria-Hungary's *failure* 100 years ago to solve the nationalities problem that had been put to it by world history. A recent result of this anti-human line of development of merely apparent solutions is the separation from Serbia of Kosovo, the Serbian national shrine—the Field of Blackbirds. This can only provoke further conflicts.

49. By 'root race' is meant in Theosophical terminology a great epoch such as the Atlantean; the 'Aryan root race' is the fifth of seven root races. A root race consists of seven 'sub-races'. We live today in the fifth sub-race of the fifth root

race; or, in the fifth post-Atlantean epoch, Steiner sometimes characterized it as the Anglo-Saxon/Germanic epoch, which points to the necessary collaboration between the two peoples in our time; in the view of the western brotherhoods this collaboration is to be replaced by the domination of the Anglo-Saxon, today the American, element. The sixth sub-race belongs to Slavdom. Anyone who makes problematic associations with the term 'Aryan' root race might like to reflect that this root race originated in the fifth Atlantean epoch—that of the original Semites (*Ursemiten*).

50. LPT, p. 106f.
51. Loc. cit. p. 114.
52. Ludwig Polzer-Hoditz, 'Die Okkupation Bosniens und der Herzegovina 1878', in *Anthroposophie—österreichischer Bote von Menschengeist zu Menschengeist*, No. 16, 15 June 1923.
53. Quoted from Ludwig Polzer-Hoditz, *Das Mysterium der europäischen Mitte*, Stuttgart 1928, p. 48.
54. LPT, p. 51.
55. It is noteworthy that the day on which the Dualism was proclaimed was 8 December, the day of the Immaculate Conception of Mary. Through this dualistic structure the Catholic Church was able to exercise much more influence in the Empire than it could with the Orthodox Slavs.
56. AP.

Part III

57. LP, p. 40.
58. LP, p. 40f.
59. LP, p. 42.
60. LP, p, 40f.
61. All following quotations from Arthur Polzer are from AP.
62. LP, p. 41.
63. LP, p. 25.
64. LPK.
65. LPK.
66. All citations in this chapter, if not otherwise indicated, are from LPK.
67. Family chronicle.
68. LP, p. 21.
69. See note 66.
70. LP, p.21.
71. 23.11.1908, in GA 108.
72. This lecture is not in Steiner's Collected Works (GA). It was published for the first time in *Der Europäer* magazine, 2nd Year, No. 9 and No. 10/11 July–Sept. 1998. Steiner later said to Polzer that none of his lectures until then had been so well-transcribed as that one.
73. LP, p. 21.
74. See note 66.
75. GA 119.

76. GA 103.
77. GA 129.
78. AP.
79. LPK.
80. LP, p. 36.
81. LPK.
82. LPK.
83. LP, p. 33f.
84. LP, p. 33f.
85. LP, p. 33f.
86. LPK.
87. AP.
88. LP, p. 39.
89. LP, p. 39.
90. LPK.
91. Polzer had the election results published.
92. LPK.
93. GA 138.
94. GA 139.
95. LP, p. 38.
96. LP, p. 44.
97. LP, p. 45.
98. LPK.
99. GA 146.
100. LP, p. 39.
101. LPK.
102. LPK.
103. LPK.
104. LPK.
105. LP, p. 38f.
106. GA 147.
107. LP, p.38.
108. LP, p. 38.
109. LP, p. 45f.
110. LP, p. 45f.
111. LPK.
112. LP, p. 47f.
113. GA 148.
114. LP, p. 48.
115. 3rd edition, Potsdam 1989. Riemeck's book gives, amongst other things, an excellent overview of the history leading up to the First World War.
116. LPK.
117. GA 153.
118. See Rudolf Steiner lecture of 19.10.1914, GA 287.
119. See also note 47.
120. AP.

121. AP.
122. Cf. end of note 47.
123. AP.
124. LPK.
125. GA 135.
126. For these events and the historical position and significance, see: *Helmuth von Moltke—Dokumente zu seinem Leben und Wirken* (untranslated), 2 vols., Basel 2nd ed. 2005/07.
127. In *Anthroposophie, österreichischer Bote von Menschengeist zu Menschengeist*, 15 June 1922.
128. LP, p. 53f.
129. LP, p. 53f.
130. LPK.
131. LPK.
132. LP, p. 56.
133. On 17 May 1915 Steiner also gave this lecture in Linz. Polzer had again obtained his permission for it to be transcribed by a parliamentary stenographer. Steiner corrected the text. The first part of this lecture was published for the first time in *Der Europäer*, Year 12, No. 2/3, December/January 2007/08, p. 27ff. The lecture of 18 May in Polzer's private house is published in GA 159.
134. LPK.
135. LPK.
136. LPK.
137. LP, p. 60.
138. LP, p. 61.
139. LP, p. 61.
140. GA 24.
141. Cited in Christoph Lindenberg, *Rudolf Steiner—Eine Chronik*, Stuttgart, 1989, p. 374.
142. LP, p. 61f.
143. LP, p. 65f.
144. LP, p. 64.
145. LPK.
146. GA 174.
147. Ludwig Polzer-Hoditz, *Betrachtungen während der Zeit des Krieges*, Linz 1917, p. 15ff.
148. LP, p. 68f.
149. LP, p. 69.
150. In GA 174a.
151. LP, p. 71f.
152. Quoted from Roman Boos, *Rudolf Steiner während des Weltkrieges*, Dornach 1933, p. 56.
153. See note 152.
154. APK, p. 438.
155. LP, p. 72.
156. LP, p. 73.

157. LP, p. 73f.
158. Today this can be found in GA 24, p.339f. Also in APK, p. 613, where the Memorandum was first published.
159. Steiner speaks here of England, but when one adds America to it, then one can say: the global politics pursued by the West today are still directed in line with this programme, as anyone could show to those needing evidence not least after the 1989 turning point when certain murderous attacks were made on particular central European personalities who were to be excluded, such as the CEO of Deutscher Bank, Alfred Herrhausen, or the head of the Treuhand industrial enterprise [agency for the privatization of East German State enterprises— *transl.*], Detlev Karsten Rohwedder. For more on this, see Part V, p. 472ff.
160. LP. p. 127.
161. LP, p. 83.
162. In GA 24.
163. Still very relevant words today! Above all, when it is recalled that the interests of the Anglo-American form of the state has hardly changed since Steiner's time!
164. A Bosnian Muslim living in Croatia would have to be free to associate with his people and with his religion without these associations colliding in the slightest degree with his legal-political citizenship within a particular state. And instead of this, what is placed in the world today [1993]? The Anglo-American Vance-Owen plans, which threaten to perpetuate the perverse mixing-up of economic, political and cultural affairs to the disadvantage of millions of people. It is also no accident that it is precisely the territory of the former Danube Monarchy that is the worst afflicted by the perpetuation of this perversion—it was the Danube Monarchy with its multi-ethnic mix that was, so to speak, foreseen by world history as the practice arena for the development of the threefolded form of the state in Europe ...
165. LP, p. 74f.
166. LP, p. 74f.
167. APK, p. 505f.
168. APK, p. 505f.
169. Cited in Lindenberg, op. cit., p. 386.
170. Jürgen von Grone, 'Gedanken zum 100. Geburtstag von Otto Graf Lerchenfeld' in: *Mitteilungen aus der anthroposophischen Arbeit in Deutschland*, Christmas 1968.
171. Friedrich Rittelmeyer, *Meine Lebensbegegnung mit Rudolf Steiner*, Stuttgart 1970, p. 87.
172. APK, p. 505f.
173. APK, p. 522.
174. APK, p. 522.
175. LP, p. 85f.
176. APK, p. 518f.
177. APK, p. 502f. Karl's son Otto von Habsburg (died in 2011) held to faith in the spiritual life of the Catholic Church, although he was familiar with the thought of threefolding, especially that of a free spiritual life, perhaps even first from Arthur Polzer's book about his father.

178. LP, p. 76f.
179. LP, p. 86.
180. LP, p. 78.
181. LP, p.78.
182. LP, p. 86.
183. Fred Poeppig, 'Eine Erinnerung an Graf Lerchenfeld', in *Mitteilungen aus der anthroposophischen Bewegung*, publ. by J. Streit, March 1967, No. 40.
184. GA 174.
185. LP, p. 72.
186. In the lecture 'Die Notwendigkeit der Erhaltung und Weiterentwickelung des deutschen Geisteslebens für die europäische Kultur' [The Need for the Maintenance and Further Development of German Spiritual Life for European Culture] which Polzer held on 20 March 1919 in Vienna.
187. Cited in Steiner's lecture of 11 Dec. 1916, in GA 173. In 1894 Rosebery became Prime Minister for a short time.
188. Steiner spoke in public for the first time about the Testament of Peter the Great on 9 Dec. 1916 (GA 173) in the *Zeitgeschichtlichen Betrachtungen* lectures.
189. GA 174.
190. Anthony C. Sutton, *America's Secret Establishment*, Billings (USA 1986). See also: Webster Tarpley & Anton Chaitkin, *George Bush The Unauthorised Biography*, 1991. See further: Guido Giacomo Preparata, *Conjuring Hitler—How Britain and America Made The Third Reich*, London/Ann Arbor (USA 2005).
191. See Steiner's lecture of 20.10.1909 (GA 58).
192. GA 202 [Emphasis THM].
193. Crucial in Clinton's political career was his advancement by Skull and Bones member Averell Harriman and his widow Pamela Harriman, formerly married to Randolph Churchill, the son of Winston Churchill.
194. APK, p. 533 [Emphasis THM].
195. APK, p. 534f.
196. APK, p. 19. The words 'states for Socialist experiments' do NOT appear on the map. Arthur Polzer would however know from his brother that 'desert' actually refers to such experiments, as they were also referred to by C.G. Harrison.
197. GA 174a.
198. LP, p. 87.
199. LP, p. 88.
200. LP, p. 90.
201. LP, p. 92.
202. LP, p. 92f.
203. LP, p. 290.
204. LP, p. 92f.
205. LP, p. 94.
206. GA 273.
207. LP, p. 96.
208. LP, p. 96.
209. LP, p. 97.
210. LP, p. 299.

211. LP, p. 288.
212. LP, p. 297.
213. LP, p. 97.
214. 'Rudolf Steiner indicated ... that this ruler was the last initiate on the imperial throne [of the Holy Roman Empire]'. See Hanna Krämer-Steiner, *Geistimpulse in der Geschichte des tschechischen Volkes*, Stuttgart 1971, p. 82. This was an oral communication to the group of friends in Prague, probably in connection with Steiner's visit to Karlstejn Castle in June 1918.
215. LP, p. 98.
216. Oral communication to the author from Julie Nováková, the daughter of Julie Klima.
217. LP, p. 100.
218. LP, p. 101.
219. Unpublished typescript.
220. Unpublished typescript.
221. Unpublished typescript.
222. LP, p. 102.
223. LP, p. 102.
224. LP, p. 102.
225. In GA 24.
226. GA 338.
227. Whoever believes that things are different today is recommended to take a look at chapter 4 of Part IV of this book.
228. LP, p. 107.
229. LP, p. 110f.
230. LP, p. 111.
231. LP, p. 118.
232. LP, p. 113.
233. LP, p. 112.
234. LP, p. 112.
235. LP, p. 105.
236. Not perhaps by chance did Russian President Boris Yeltsin see his ideal statesman in Peter the Great. Western support for Yeltsin should also be seen from this perspective.
237. LP, p. 114ff.
238. LP, p. 116.
239. LP, p. 116.
240. LP, p. 117.
241. LP, p. 119.
242. LP, p. 119f.
243. LP, p. 122.
244. LP, p. 170.
245. LP, p. 171.
246. LP, p. 169.
247. LP, p. 170.
248. LP, p. 171.

249. LP, p. 171f.
250. LP, p. 172.
251. LP, p. 173.
252. Quoted from Lindenberg, op. cit. p. 454f.
253. LP, p. 173.
254. LP, p. 175.
255. Friedrich Hiebel, *Entscheidungszeit mit Rudolf Steiner*, Dornach 1986, p. 45f.
256. LP, p. 174.
257. LP, p. 118.
258. LP, p. 179.
259. LP, p. 136.
260. LPT, p. 95.
261. LPT, p. 96.
262. LP, p. 177.
263. LPT, p. 141.
264. LP, p. 177.
265. Friedrich Hiebel, op. cit. p. 98.
266. LP, p. 177.
267. LP, p. 178.
268. Cited in Lindenberg, op. cit. p. 491.
269. LP, p. 178.
270. LP, p. 179.
271. LP, p. 180.
272. GA 305.
273. GA 348.
274. See also: R.N. Coudenhove-Kalergi, *Aus meinem Leben*, Zurich 1949. Support for Coudenhove from Church circles soon showed itself through the Austrian Federal Chancellor Seipel: 'Through Seipel the movement had established a strong foothold in the Catholic world.' (p. 122) The later Pope Pius XII also declared in May 1933 when he was still Cardinal Secretary 'his frank sympathies for Pan-europa'.

On the other hand in 1922—the year of the West-East Congress—Coudenhove became a member of the Grand Lodge of Vienna (Humanitas). There exists a document of the Grand Lodge of Vienna from 1925 in which the Grand Master Dr Richard Schlesinger expresses his warm support for the 'Pan-europa Idea' of 'Brother Coudenhove' and his efforts to realize it.

In October 1926 the first Pan-europa Congress was held in Vienna, 200 metres from the Music Society Building where the West-East Congress had been held and attracted a similar number of visitors. Otto Zuber reported in Quatuor Coronati, the Yearbook of the Association of Freemasons:

> The first European Congress met from 3–6 October 1926 in the huge Marmorsaal of the Vienna Concert Hall. More than 2000 delegates attended, representing 24 nations. The echo of the Congress resounded round the world. All the world's newspapers were talking about this first congress of European unity as the beginning of a new politics. Millions put

their hopes in Pan-europa and believed now in the possibility of realizing it. It became the new idea and great hope of the younger generation. When opposition became too great because of his belonging to Free-masonry, in 1926 'the Count of Europe' asked to be released from the League.

(I thank Markus Osterrieder of Munich for these indications regarding Coudenhove's links to Freemasonry).

From the *Dictionnaire de la Franc-Maçonnerie* (publ. by D. Ligou, Paris 1987) we learn in relation to Coudenhove's position with regard to Freemasonry on p. 94: 'The author of the idea and the movement of the Pan-european movement, Count Richard Coudenhove-Kalergi was a member of the lodge Humanitas [in Vienna] which opened up for him a path to celebrity. *So as not to be inconvenienced in the propagation of his ideas he had to ask to quit the lodge, which request was granted him.*' [Emphasis THM].

275. On 5 November 1919 Churchill said in his speech in the Lower House:

> We will ... prevent Russia, as far as we can, from throwing herself into German hands and making an arrangement with Germany, which, as we all know, if it became effective would confront our children, and possibly even ourselves, with a repetition of that same evil deadly equipoise of gigantic Powers, with the marshalling up against us of that same for-midable danger which plunged the world in disaster in August, 1914.

Polzer commented:

> Churchill said that this connection [between Germany and Russia] would mean the repetition of the war; he should have said, more correctly, that then the world war which had been long prepared by England and had been fought to the end with such great sacrifices would have been in vain for this connection was precisely what England had wanted to prevent through all its machinations in the Balkans and finally through the world war itself.

(*Politische Betrachtungen* [Political Observations] Stuttgart 1920, p. 51).

276. GA 219.
277. LP, p. 189.
278. To my knowledge, Steiner used this expression only in the Nero-lecture of 27 April 1924, GA 236.
279. Emanuel Zeylmans van Emmichoven, *Wer war Ita Wegman?*, 3 vols. Heidelberg 1990ff., Vol. 1, p. 148.
280. Ibid. p. 124 and elsewhere.
281. LP. p. 183.
282. Polzer's notes on this survived only in the form of a typescript which comes from Paul Michaelis, a friend of Polzer's old age, and bears a few dates in Polzer's handwriting. Graphological examination does not clarify whether this hand-writing actually is Polzer's; but still less can a falsification of these dates be deduced. Michaelis burned Polzer's original notes. On the question of the

genuineness of these typescripts of Polzer's notes, which only came to light in the 1970s and have been repeatedly subject to doubt ever since, see also p. 530ff.

283. LP, p. 186.
284. LP, p. 187.
285. LP, p. 186.
286. LP, p. 187.
287. LP, p. 188.
288. LP, p. 188ff.
289. LP, p. 188ff.
290. LP, p. 188ff.
291. LP, p. 195.
292. In issue 16, 15 June 1923.
293. GA 223.
294. LP, p. 195.
295. Hiebel, op. cit., p. 154.
296. Ernst Lehrs, *Gelebte Erwartung*, Stuttgart 1979, p. 259.
297. LP, p. 197.
298. *Helmuth von Moltke 1848–1916, Dokumente zu seinem Leben und Wirken*, publ. by Thomas Meyer, Basel, 1993, Vol. 2, p. 295f.
299. LP, p. 197.
300. LP, p. 197.
301. GA 233.
302. GA 126.
303. LP, p. 197.
304. A phrase of R. Steiner's from 12 August 1924, in GA 240.
305. LP, p. 197.
306. LP, p. 310.
307. See Steiner's lecture of 18 July 1924 in Arnhem, in GA 240.
308. Ita Wegman noted on the back of a notepad Steiner's words to her in the last period of his illness that 'his illness was peripheral' (*seine Krankheit sei periphärisch*). Communication of E. Zeylmans to the author.
309. LP, p. 198.
310. LP, p. 199.
311. LP, p. 199.
312. LP, p. 199.
313. LPK. See the abbreviated list of sources at the beginning of these Notes.
314. LP, p. 200.
315. LP, p. 200.
316. LP, p. 200.
317. LPE. See the source abbreviations before the notes. In LP, p. 38, it is stated slightly differently: 'When I visited him on 11 November in his atelier at the Goetheanum which had become a sickroom, he told me that my father had received impulses from the School of Chartres in the eleventh century.'
318. LP, p. 201.
319. See the notes of the conversations with Steiner in the Appendix p. 522ff. In the

somewhat poetical style of the Images of the Soul, according to Polzer, on the occasion of the conversation in September 1924:

> About personal matters of your destiny I did not want to say anything to you, because it once seemed to me that you shied away from such knowledge so as to be able to experience your destiny in complete freedom. 'Then the following was said: Me: "What I said to you at that time was not meant in this sense. It was diffidence that restrained me." Him: "When the right time has come, you will experience much. Personalities will appear in your life and then the spiritual world will provide the right instruction. You will not be forgotten. I hope to see you again here soon. Have a good trip." ' (loc. cit., p. 30f.)

320. LPS, p. 202.
321. See note 319.
322. LP, p. 204.
323. LP, p. 204.
324. LP, p. 205.

Part IV

325. LPE.
326. Lili Kolisko *Eugen Kolisko—Ein Lebensbild*, private printing 1961, p. 104.
327. LPE.
328. LPE.
329. *In memoriam Ita Wegman* [actual title: 'In memoriam Frau Dr Ita Wegman'], see Appendix. Rudolf Steiner's last letter to his wife, dated 27 February 1925; in GA 262.
330. See note 324.
331. See note 329.
332. See note 329.
333. LPE.
334. LPE.
335. LPE.
336. LPE.
337. Emphasis THM.
338. Michael Freund, *Deutsche Geschichte*, Munich 1979, p. 1134.
339. LPE.
340. See Irène Diet, *Jules und Alice Sauerwein und die Anfänge der anthroposophischen Bewegung in Frankreich*, 1998, currently out of print.
341. LPE.
342. November issue, 1925.
343. LPE.
344. LPE.
345. LPE.
346. LP, p. 205.
347. LPE.
348. LP, p. 216ff. According to Rudolf Steiner James I was the actual inspirer of the

group of personalities named by Polzer here and to which Jakob Balde also belonged. See Richard Ramsbotham, *Jakob I, Inspirator von Shakespeare und Bacon—ein Beitrag zur Autorschaftsdebatte um Shakespeare*, Basel 2008; Richard Ramsbotham, *Who Wrote Bacon?—William Shakespeare, Francis Bacon and James I A Mystery for the Twenty-first Century*, London 2004.

349. See note 348.
350. In GA 158.
351. LPE.
352. LPE.
353. In the lecture of 23 Sept 1924, GA 238.
354. LPE.
355. LPE.
356. LPM, p. 153.
357. LPE.
358. LPE. Emphasis here THM, and in previous quotes from this source.
359. LPE.
360. GA 121.
361. LPE.
362. LPE.
363. The book appeared in a second edition in Berlin in 1932 with the main title: *Glanz und Untergang Roms* [The Glory and Fall of Rome]. The following quote here is from p. 145ff.
364. See note 363.
365. In a lecture of 17 April 1917, GA 175.
366. See Polzer's article about this journey in the *Goetheanum* 26 August 1928.
367. See note 366.
368. On the attempts to revive the political ideas of 'the Holy Roman Empire of the German Nation' in the 1990s, see p. 488.
369. LPM, p. 198.
370. LPM, p. 198f. Emphasis THM.
371. Polzer's London lecture appeared in Sept. 1928 in the *Österreichischen Blättern für freies Geistesleben*.
372. Emphasis THM.
373. LPM, p. 194. Emphasis THM.
374. LPE.
375. Emphasis THM.
376. Emphasis THM.
377. LPE.
378. LPE.
379. LPE.
380. LPE.
381. All quotes in this chapter, unless otherwise indicated, are from LPE.
382. Emphasis THM.
383. Emphasis THM.
384. Emphasis THM.
385. Cited from Coudenhove, op. cit, p. 137f.

386. Coudenhove, op. cit, p. 159.
387. Diary entry from 1930.
388. See note 387.
389. According to the Young Plan, Germany, to which was ascribed the main guilt for the war, was obliged to pay reparations of 34 billion gold marks until 1988. The Young Plan was abandoned at the Conference of Lausanne in 1932.
390. Emphasis THM.
391. Emphasis THM.
392. A. Reuveni, *In the Name of the 'New World Order'*, London, 1996, chap. 7.
393. LPE.
394. LPE.
395. See note 387.
396. LPE.
397. LPE.
398. LPE.
399. LPE.
400. See note 329.
401. LPE.
402. LPE.
403. Speech to the General Meeting 1935. See Appendix.
404. LPE.
405. See note 387.
406. LPE.
407. The quotations in this chapter, unless otherwise indicated, are from LPE.
408. Emphasis THM.
409. Emphasis THM.
410. See note 387.
411. A formulation used by R. Steiner in a lecture of 13 January 1917 (GA 174). The text reads: 'Naturally, one does take things seriously in life when one allows one's sight to be dulled by all kinds of sympathies and antipathies. One must hold oneself more or less objectively with regard to them, then the world current will bring one what is necessary for understanding.'
412. See note 381.
413. Emphasis THM.
414. Hildegard Wiegand, *Der Kampf mit dem Tarnhelm—Erlebnisse aus der Geschichte des Königs Jakob I. von England und seiner Mutter Maria Stuart und ihres Vetters Francis Stuart* [The Struggle with the Tarnhelm—Experiences from the History of King James I of England and His Mother Maria Stuart and her cousin Francis Stuart] Stuttgart, 2nd ed. 1968.
415. Emphasis THM.
416. Emphasis THM.
417. Cited from Polzer's lecture notes.
418. See the corresponding texts in GA 265.
419. 14 January, in GA 174.
420. Emphasis THM.
421. LPE.

422. Rudolf Steiner warned on 11 April 1924 (GA 270, Vol. I):

> Those who represent the principle of the Roman Church will do what they can in the near future to make the single States of the former German Empire autonomous and out of these autonomous States, with the exclusion—I am only relating this—of the pre-eminence of Prussia, to re-establish the Holy Roman Empire of the German Nation which naturally, when it is set up by such splendid forces, [NB Steiner was here being ironic—*transl.*] will seek to extend its power over the neighbouring lands roundabout. For—so say those involved—it is necessary for us by this means to root out thoroughly the worst, most dangerous movements that exist today. And—these people add—if the re-establishment of the Holy Roman Empire of the German Nation were not to be successfully achieved, and it will be successful—so these people say—if it were not achieved, then we shall find other means to root out thoroughly the most contrary, dangerous movements of the present time, and those are the anthroposophical movement and the movement for religious renewal.

(In GA 270/I.) It has not yet been possible to locate Steiner's source for this, but it was certainly one to be taken seriously. The same destructive impulse for the restoration of the Holy Roman Empire of the German Nation made itself evident once again at the beginning of the 1990s. Cf. Part V, ch. 2.

423. Emphasis THM.
424. GA 13.
425. See Steiner's lecture of 7 November 1917, in GA 73.
426. Emphasis THM.
427. Emphasis THM.
428. LPE.
429. Emphasis THM.
430. Cf. ch. 24, p. 157.
431. See note 329.
432. See note 329.
433. Emphasis THM. This citation is from the reproduction of the text in Zeylmans op. cit., Vol. 3, p. 262.
434. Supplement to the *Goetheanum* for members of the G.A.S.
435. Zeylmans, op. cit. Vol. 3, p. 329.
436. Ibid., p. 159.
437. Emphasis THM.
438. See Appendix.
439. Emphasis THM.
440. Emphasis THM.
441. See note 329.
442. From a typescript in Lauer's archive. A slightly modified version of Lauer's remarks in indirect speech appeared in the Newssheet (*Nachrichtenblatt*) for 19.5.1935.
443. See note 329.
444. See note 329.

445. This was said by Steiner in a lecture he gave on 20.2.1920 (GA 196). Emphasis THM.
446. Polzer also described this dream in his little book *In Memoriam Ita Wegman* but referred to the ritual nature of the event less intimately.
447. Emphasis THM.
448. See note 329.
449. Private notes of Z. Šmídova which were put at the author's disposal by Zdenek Vana.
450. 19.11.1917, GA 178.
451. *The Mitteilungen für die Mitglieder der Anthroposophischen Arbeitsgemeinschaften in Deutschland*, published by J. von Grone, (No. 1, July 1935) carried an obituary of Dunlop by Stein.
452. Emphasis THM.
453. Emphasis THM.
454. By L.A. Langeveld, *Der Graf von St Germain* [The Comte de St Germain] The Hague, 1930.
455. Isabel Cooper-Oakley, The Count of St Germain, New York (new ed.) 1970.
456. Wolfgang Menzel, *Roms Unrecht*, Stuttgart 1873; cf. also *Geschichte der neueren Jesuitenumtriebe in Deutschland*, Stuttgart 1873.
457. See especially Steiner's lecture of 23.12.1917, in GA 180.
458. August Bernhard Hasler, *Wie der Papst unfehlbar wurde*, Munich, 1979, p. 79.
459. Hasler, op. cit, p. 34.
460. Op. cit., p. 39.
461. See note 460.
462. Op. cit., p. 50.
463. See Renate Riemeck, *Glaube—Dogma—Macht. Geschichte der Konzilien*, Stuttgart, 1985, p. 298.
464. Hasler, op. cit., p. 154.
465. Emphasis THM.
466. Emphasis THM.
467. See note 16.
468. He added it to his notes from 1939 (LPE) as a two-sided typescript with the superscript: 'Personal communication—not for distribution—for members of the Michael School only.' He wrote by hand a motto at the top of the paper: 'The Goetheanum is wherever work is done in the spirit of Rudolf Steiner.'
469. See note 468.
470. Emphasis THM.
471. See note 468.
472. Emphasis THM.
473. See the corresponding descriptions by Steiner in GA 109.
474. GA 149.
475. Emphasis THM.
476. *Antoninus und der Grieche. Roman aus der Zeit des römischen Friedens* [Antoninus and the Greek. A Novel from the Time of the Roman Peace], Stuttgart, 1935.
477. Ernst Wettreich.
478. Emphasis THM.

479. Emphasis THM.
480. Emphasis THM.
481. In exercising his veto, Franz Joseph was reacting to the refusal of the College of Cardinals, headed by Cardinal Rampolla, to allow a Catholic funeral service for Crown Prince Rudolf.
482. Emphasis THM.
483. In an unpublished typescript with the title 'Impressions of a Trip to Italy'. On this trip, see also Johannes Tautz, *Walter Johannes Stein—eine Biographie*, Dornach 1989; Engl. version: *Walter Johannes Stein—A Biography*, London 1990.
484. Emphasis THM.
485. According to *Reclams Lexikon der Heiligen* the 4 July was dedicated to the Bohemian national saint and first Abbot of the Benedictine monastery of Sázava (beginning of the eleventh century) in which the heritage of Cyril and Methodius (the Slavonic liturgy) continued to be nurtured. Polzer confuses him with the similarly named Hussite leader Andreas Prokop (died 1434) which he discussed with Major Snítil. My thanks to Markus Osterrieder for drawing my attention to this confusion.
486. Emphasis THM.
487. 'Bedeutendes geist-symptomatisches Geschehen im Herzen Europas' [Significant spiritually symptomatic events in the heart of Europe] in *Anthroposophische Arbeitsberichte*, Vol. 1, Prague January 1938.
488. 3rd ed., Stuttgart 1977.
489. Emphasis THM.
490. GA 112 [In English: *The Gospel of St John and Its Relation to the Other Gospels*].
491. GA 23.
492. Emphasis THM.
493. This diary entry (25 August 1938) clearly shows that Polzer understood the real nature of the deeper sides of Nazism. His initial 'happiness' about the 'apparent defeat of the ecclesiastical Jesuit tendency' put a strain for a while on his relationship with Hüttl, his friend in Bratislava, whose daughter Zdena Šmídova wrote: 'After the Anschluss something very unpleasant happened. My father received a postcard from the Count which included the words: "We are all now very happy". This was a great blow for my father at the time. He walked up and down in his room agitated and said over and over: "How can an anthroposopher, such an honourable man, go so astray?" ' It was during the war years, after the death of Hüttl's son Josef in 1941 that Polzer visited Hüttl in Bratislava 'in order to apologize to him for his error'.

   The relevant passage in the first of Nietzsche's *Untimely Meditations* reads:

> Of all the negative consequences [...] which have followed the last war with France perhaps the worst is a widespread, indeed universal, error: the error, committed by public opinion and by all who express their opinions publicly, that German culture too was victorious in that struggle and must therefore now be loaded with garlands appropriate to such an extraordinary achievement. This delusion is in the highest degree destructive [...] because it is capable of turning our victory into a defeat: into the

defeat, indeed the extirpation, of the German spirit for the sake of the 'German Reich'.

494. LPE.

495. Rudolf Steiner had indicated to Polzer the importance of studying the problem of Demetrius [Dmitri], as well as certain other matters, on 3 March 1925. This is the first reference to Polzer's actual engagement with this multi-faceted issue.— See also: Peter Tradowsky, *Demetrius im Entwickelungsgang des Christentums*, Dornach 1989.

496. Cited from Emil Bock, *Wiederholte Erdenleben*, Frankfurt-am-Main 1981, p. 77—emphasis THM.

497. Emphasis THM.

498. Renate Riemeck op. cit. p. 168.

499. Unpublished typescript by Menny Lerchenfeld for relatives and friends.

500. Emphasis THM.

501. Emphasis THM.

502. Emphasis THM.

503. GA 4.

504. Emphasis THM.

505. Cited from Polzer's dream diary, in which he wrote down his dreams from 1933 to 1941.

506. See note 329.

507. Gregorovius, op. cit. p. 154.

508. Loc. cit. p. 155.

509. Emphasis THM.

510. Emphasis THM.

511. Oral communication of Erika Warnke to the author.

512. Family chronicle.

513. LPM, p. 153.

514. LPM, p. 137.

515. Werner Richter, *Kronprinz Rudolf von Österreich—Geschichte eines übergrossen Erbes*, Zurich, 1941.

516. Richter, op. cit. p. 324.

517. See Steiner's lecture of 6 November 1917 (GA 178) in which he explains certain aspects of the background to the assassination of the Empress.

518. Lecture of 1 July 1924, GA 237.

519. Lecture of 3 August 1924 GA 287.

520. Lecture of 15 January 1917, GA 174.

521. According to Stuart Perowne, *Hadrian—sein Leben und seine Zeit*, Munich 1966.

522. See: M. Bockholt/E. Kirchner, *Rudolf Steiner's Mission and Ita Wegman*, Rudolf Steiner Press, 1977. Also, E. Zeylmans van Emmichoven, *Wer war Ita Wegman?* [Who Was Ita Wegman], op. cit.

523. See note 329.

524. See note 329.

525. Zeylmans, op. cit., Vol. 3, p. 113.

526. See note 329.

527. In 1950 Paul Michaelis circulated a version of Polzer's text *In memoriam Frau Dr*

Ita Wegman (in what follows: 'In memoriam Ita Wegman'). Michaelis supplemented it with Polzer's speech from 1935, with various extracts from Polzer's diaries (some of which are now no longer extant) as well as with certain ritual texts from Steiner which Polzer occasionally used to open Class Lessons that he held. Michaelis gave the text the title: 'The Spiritual Background of the Speech Given by Count Ludwig Polzer-Hoditz at the General Meeting of 14 April 1935' and sent it to certain selected individuals. He says in the Introduction to the text which he had put together:

> At the end of March 1943, immediately after the death of Frau Dr Ita Wegman, Count Ludwig Polzer dictated to me as the first version of the 'Spiritual Background' his 'In memoriam Ita Wegman'. Due to the conditions of the time, this version was only given in a coded form and only for three friends. In accord with the Count's intentions, I have now supplemented the 'Spiritual Background' with some notes from his diaries as he had intended.

The Michaelis version of 'In memoriam Ita Wegman' differs in various places from the version typed by Erika Warnke, cited in this book, and presented in the appendix. It is shorter here and there, less detailed in a few places, and includes some extracts from Polzer's conversations with Steiner. The differences in the texts of these two versions threw into doubt, at least in the view of Emanuel Zeylmans, the personal integrity of Michaelis who, to Zeylmans, seemed to want to create the impression that 'this had all been written down by Polzer'. Zeylmans made the still heavier assertion that the text had been 'circulated [by Michaelis] in 1950 with dishonest intentions'. (Zeylmans, op. cit., Vol. 3, p. 405f.)

But what do the textual differences prove? Could Polzer not actually have had the intention to extend the first version, as Michaelis says in his introduction? Erika Warnke, at that time a recent member of the G.A.S., who typed up the first version was, according to some people, unable to make any copies of this text; however, there was at the time a deep relationship of trust between Polzer and Michaelis; Michaelis was also Polzer's esoteric pupil. It is therefore very likely that Polzer was really thinking of expanding his text about Ita Wegman and put papers at Michaelis's disposal which the latter, after Polzer's death, put together 'in accord with the Count's intentions'. Against the authenticity of the second version circulated by Michaelis, Zeylmans brought only the following argument: 'Already the first sentence [in Michaelis' version] : "[. . .] Count Ludwig Polzer dictated to me [. . .] his *In memoriam Ita Wegman*" is contradicted by Polzer's opening words [in the Warnke-version included in the Appendix]: "[. . .] I take up my pen".' But this argument would also have to be applied against the Warnke-version, for Husemann's secretary would have been able to note that Polzer had *dictated* to her the sentence 'Shocked by the unexpectedly sudden death of Frau Dr Ita Wegman, I took up my pen' just as he had all the other sentences of the text. (The actual opening sentence 'Shocked by . . .' follows his introduction word for word just as in Michaelis' version!) The assertion that the Michaelis version does not have to do with text by Polzer (and that it was assembled by Michaelis after Polzer's death), as well as the further claim that Michaelis had 'circulated [his version] with dishonest intentions' can at the present point in time be regarded as unfounded.

Similar unfounded claims have been made from other directions in relation to the authenticity of the typescripts of Polzer's diary notes from the years 1916–1925. On this, see the appendix p. 530ff. of this book.

528. Letter to Menny Lerchenfeld of 15 October 1943.

529. See note 528.

530. See note 528.

531. Riemeck, op. cit., p. 177.

532. Emphasis THM.

533. Paul Michaelis in the introduction to the Polzer texts compiled by him 'Die geistigen Hintergründe der Rede des Grafen Ludwig Polzer-Hoditz ...' See also note 527.

534. See note 533.

535. See: Anthony C. Sutton, op. cit., *America's Secret Establishment*, Billings (USA) 1986, p. 166ff.

536. On 7 May the Russians occupied Arthur Polzer's house in Baden and remained for the following three years. They confiscated, amongst other things, Arthur's autobiographical writings, notably those from Vol. VI, which dealt with the period from 1917 onwards.

537. From information supplied by Maria-Christine Koutny—the niece 'Christl' with whom Polzer went to Venice in 1933—Berta had her leg amputated on 24 July; she then died from the consequences of the operation.

538. Arthur Polzer's death occurred at 4.15 p.m. due to heart failure.

539. Maria-Christine Koutny reports that the family had to leave the villa in Baden in pouring rain, with baskets full of bed linen. They found temporary shelter in the hall of a doctor until, in mid-May, they found a fine apartment in which Arthur Polzer-Hoditz died in July.

540. Ferdinand Wantschura 1867–1968.

541. Polzer had in the meantime evidently therefore been informed of the death of Julius.

542. Death came at 6.20 a.m. Emil Hamburger wrote to Polzer's grandson Christ-ward in Dornach: 'For me he is the truest pupil of Herr Dr Steiner that I know and my dearest friend.' In the end Polzer wanted to be buried at Gutau, where Berta also lay. The authorities did not allow it, so he had to be buried in Vienna. His niece Christl went from cemetery to cemetery in order to find a place for his grave. Finally, one could be found in a row at the Central Cemetery for ten years. At the burial (apparently on 16 October) there were 'very many people' there. Trucks came, carrying the coffins, but that of Ludwig Polzer was missing. The time for the burial was delayed for several hours in great heat, despite the late time of year. When it then finally took place, seven people were present. Polzer's mortal remains rest today at the Vienna Central Cemetery, Section II, Group 23.

543. '[...] and lived his last hours in continuous meditation', according to a letter from Johannes Eyb, of 25 February 1947. Apart from Emil Hamburger's letter

to Christward Polzer on 16 November 1945, Eyb's is the only surviving document about Ludwig Polzer's last hours. Eyb's letter was addressed to *Hans-Erhard Lauer*, who had asked after the circumstances of the deaths of various anthroposophical friends.

544. Under the title *Ich zähmte die Wölfin—die Erinnerungen des Kaisers Hadrian* [I tamed the Wolf—the memoirs of Emperor Hadrian] Stuttgart 1977.

545. In *Mémoires d'Hadrien*, suivies de 'Carnets de notes de Mémoires d'Hadrien', Paris 1974, p. 342. Emphasis THM.

546. Loc. cit., p. 330.

547. See Rudolf Steiner's lecture of 7 March 1914 in GA 152.

Part V

548. See L.L. Matthias, *Die Kehrseite der USA*, Hamburg 1985, p.107ff. Also Article 51, added at the same time, which guaranteed to each member the right to 'individual or collective self-defence' was later claimed as justification for many aims that served special interests.

549. Loc. cit. p. 118.

550. Loc. cit., p. 124.

551. Churchill's statement here came from a speech he gave in Harrow on 1 Dec. 1949. See *Speeches of Winston Churchill*, Vol. 7, New York 1974, p. 7902.

552. Zurich speech 1946, 19 September 'Memorial in celebration of the 25th anniversary', publ. by the President's Office of the City of Zurich and the Swiss Winston Churchill Foundation.

553. Coudenhove, op. cit., p. 259.

554. Loc. cit. p. 158.

555. *Speeches of Winston Churchill*, [op. cit.] New York 1974. Emphasis TH Meyer. In his Zurich speech Churchill did indeed speak of the 'constant aim' to 'build and fortify' the UN within which 'world concept' the United States of Europe was to be integrated as a 'regional structure'. But he refrained from speaking at that time of an 'authoritative, all-powerful world order' or of an 'effective world government', as he did in London. He apparently did not want to upset his audience 'in' Europe...

556. See R.N. Coudenhove-Kalergi, *Eine Idee erobert Europa*, Munich/Vienna/Basel 1958, p. 311f.

557. Robert Eringer, *The Global Manipulators*, Bristol 1980, p. 20.

558. Matthias, op. cit., p.146ff. On 17.1.1992 an article appeared in the *International Herald Tribune* by Roger Morris, a former State security adviser to Johnson and Nixon. Morris wrote: 'In the early postwar years U.S. officials "exaggerated Soviet capabilities and intentions to such an extent [...] that it is surprising anyone took them seriously."' (Translated from the German)

559. Loc. cit. p.149ff. The discussions in Washington were attended, Matthias suspects, by the German generals Speidel and Heusinger. Behind the threat of the termination of Marshall Aid, about which Matthias has nothing to say in any detail, may have been Averell Harriman. From April 1948 Harriman as special representative of the US government, based in Paris, was in charge of

coordinating the roll-out of the Marshall Plan in Europe. His biography shows him to have been the ramrod of the Marshall Plan. See R. Abrahamson, *Spanning the Century—The Life of Averell Harriman*, New York 1992, p. 427. It is also noteworthy that Harrison's interests, which he pursued under the cover of European reconstruction, were seen through by the Russians months before his arrival in Paris. At the UN Conference at Lake Success the Soviet delegate described him as a 'warmonger', while Pravda called him a plutocrat and representative of a ruling class which was striving to attain 'the global and economic supremacy of the United States'; a capitalist whose goal was 'to exploit the critical situation in Europe in order to enrich himself'. Finally, the accusation was made against him that it was important for him that West Germany should be transformed into an anti-Soviet bridgehead because this would guarantee a position of strength for Brown Brothers Harriman & Co.—the international private bank, to which George Bush's father [Prescott Bush] and Robert Lovett also belonged—'as also for Harriman's other interests in these regions'. Harriman had been ambassador to Moscow in 1942.

560. See note 559.
561. See note 559.
562. Matthias, op. cit. p. 159.
563. Loc. cit., p. 160.
564. Dean Acheson was not like Harriman a member of Skull & Bones, but of Scroll & Key, another Yale University Society; Acheson's brother-in-law William Bundy was another Bonesman. Along with John McCloy, High Commissioner for Germany 1949–52, and the lawyer Robert A. Lovett, Acheson and Harriman belonged to the six 'Wise Men', who were regarded as the main architects of 'the American Century'. See: W. Isaacson and E. Thomas, *The Wise Men*, New York, 1988.
565. Quoted in Robert Eringer, op. cit. (front cover). Translator's note: From the context of this statement in his novel *Coningsby* (pp. 251–252.), it is clear that Disraeli actually said this through the mouth of the character Sidonia in order to alert his readers to the fact that in his (i.e. Disraeli's) view, the world is in fact governed secretly by Jews, a 'fact' of which he was proud.
566. *Lexikon zur Geschichte der Parteien in Europa*, Stuttgart, 1981.
567. Coudenhove, *Eine Idee erobert Europa*, op. cit., p. 317.
568. *Geschichte*, No. 1, 1991. In March 1952 Stalin had made an offer with regard to the reunification of Germany; this envisaged Germany as being neutral and not integrated in a western military alliance; there was also a debate about reunification at the Foreign Ministers' Conference in Berlin in January 1954 prior to West Germany joining NATO. In the West, there was no will to respond to Moscow's renewed call for a reunified Germany that should be 'democratic and peace-loving'.
569. Emphasis THM.
570. According to Schickel (loc. cit.), the 1955 'Intelligence Report' had already stated: 'The report also included an amazingly prescient electoral prognosis: "Experience of a regime that depends strongly on Marxist symbols, antagonism

against a command economy and the suppression of workers by the [German] Unity Party might certainly have called forth anti-Marxist tendencies among groups of East German workers that could contribute in the election to the detriment of the SPD".' (translated from the German)

571. *Frankfurter Allgemeine Zeitung*, 10.9.1981.
572. *Aus Politik und Zeitgeschichte*, 14.4.1984. The study was by Volker Rittberger. Emphasis THM. *In America*, no less an example than that of the CIA throws an interesting light on the methods of the use of the parallel long-range programme as strategic necessity:

> A controversy developed between the Department of Defence and the CIA with regard to the Soviet armaments programme. According to the Democrat Senator Broxmeyer, the CIA presented a study according to which the Soviet Union had only increased its defence expenditures since 1976 by about 2% p.a. [...] President Reagan had repeatedly justified his calls for new weapons on the grounds of Soviet military armaments. (Radio DRS, 20.11.1983).

Two years later, 'the CIA had discovered that the Soviet SS 19 multiple warhead missile was less dangerous than originally supposed'. (*Zofinger Tagblatt*, 20.7.1985). From these statements it can be deduced that there must have been other reasons for the intensification of the western arms build-up than the apparent threat from the Soviets. These other reasons no doubt partly reflect the interests of the arms industry; partly, they have to do with the American decision to take down the entire socialist system. The pressure that first indicated this was applied in the Carter era in the mid-1970s; it came to full expression at the beginning of the 1980s, for example in the statement by Richard Pipes referred to below (note 573). The destabilization of the SPD [Social Democratic Party of Germany] in the [Helmut] Schmidt era, the financial support given to the CDU as well as to the rightwing of the SPD and FPD [Free Democratic Party] at the beginning of the 1980s by the Flick conglomerate must all be seen in relation to the demonstrable US intention at that time to bring down the Soviet system, for in order to realize this goal, a pro-nuclear armament government had to be in place in West Germany.

573. *Newsweek*, 3.3.1981. Quoted in *Der Plan Euroshima*, publ. by G. Neuberger, Cologne 1982. Emphasis THM. The arms build-up forced on Germany also has to be seen in the context of this statement. The theatre chosen for nuclear war, should it occur, was Europe. See also the observations in note 572. Richard Pipes, a Harvard Professor, was regarded as an expert in the history of Eastern Europe, which he discussed in numerous publications.
574. *Time*, No. 48, 1981.
575. *Das Parlament* 16.7.1983.
576. *The Daily Telegraph*, 23.9.1983.
577. New York 1989, pp. ix, 15.
578. Markus Göldner, *Politische Symbole der europäischen Integration*, Frankfurt 1988, p. 82. Emphasis THM.
579. Heiligenkreuztal, 10th ed., 1987.

580. Philippe Chenaux, *Une Europe Vaticane?*, Brussels, 1990, p. 35.

581. William L. Shirer, *The Rise and Fall of the Third Reich*, London 1998, p. 234. The two quotes in the next paragraph are from: Gordon Zahn, *German Catholics and Hitler's Wars*, New York 1962.

582. Chenaux, op. cit. p. 251.

583. See note 582.

584. Otto von Habsburg, *Zurück zur Mitte*, Vienna/Munich, 1991, p. 238 'If Europe is to be healed, it must return to its Christian roots', declared Habsburg in his book *Macht jenseits des Marktes* [Power Beyond the Market] Vienna 1989, p. 247 in which he also opines: 'The substance of God's grace can still give us much even today.'

   In his book *Die Reichsidee* [The Idea of the Reich] (Vienna/Munich 1986) the same Habsburg expressed the following thought about the 12-star symbol:

   > Responding to the motion of Ingo Friedrich from Mittelfranken and with the support of the majority of the European Parliament, the EC Commissioner Ripa de Meana proclaimed the twelve yellow stars on the blue ground to be the definitive flag for the Community. *It is not only Christian circles who see in the flag the starry crown of Mary, who rejoice in this news, but also all those who believe in a greater Europe.*

   It is noteworthy that most books by Habsburg were published by the same Amalthea Verlag (originally in Vienna) that published Arthur Polzer's book about Otto von Habsburg's father, Emperor Karl. It must be presumed that Otto von Habsburg had precise knowledge of this work by Polzer, in which the idea of threefolding is outlined.

585. *Time International* 24.2.1992.

586. See note 585.

587. Margaret Thatcher, *The Downing Street Years*, London 1993 p. 461.

588. Loc. cit. p. 463. How naive Thatcher was about long-range American plans is shown in her comment to Gorbachev: 'The United States ha[s] never shown any desire for world domination' (loc. cit. p. 462). Churchill, the man she so much admired, would have known better.

589. Mikhail Gorbachev, *Glasnost—das neue Denken*, Munich 1989, p. 42. (translated from the German). Emphasis THM. The Socialist experiment had found a special kind of backing in the East, which appears to have repeated itself in the termination phase of the experiment. The painter Nicholas Roerich, who was connected to 'Mahatmas' in Tibet, and his wife Helene Roerich, the founder of Agni Yoga, reported that Lenin was acting with the approval of their teachers, who even bestowed on him the title 'Mahatma Lenin'. N. Roerich also had connections to President Roosevelt, with whom he corresponded. The pyramid on the dollar bill is supposed to have been instigated by Roerich. He is also supposed to have conceived, via Secretary of State Cordell Hull, the United Nations. Roerich—and indeed also his 'Mahatmas'—were convinced that 'only a world government can remove the causes of armed clashes and act as an impartial judge'. (A. Thomas, *Shambhala*, London 1977). In May 1987 and

October 1989 Gorbachev met the son of Roerich, 'the fulfilment of a long-held wish'.

Gorbachev's Roerich connection could have led him on to engage with the West in the very unusual way he did. On Roerich see also: S.O. Prokofieff, *The East In The Light Of The West*, Forest Row, 2010 and further literature referred to therein.

590. Thatcher, op. cit., p. 774.
591. Thatcher, op. cit., p. 477. Emphasis THM.
592. Matthias, op. cit., p. 126. Apparently, Truman did not literally say this. See the debate between Arthur Schlesinger Jnr. and Noam Chomsky about this: http://www.commentarymagazine.com/article/trumans-speech-noam-chomsky/
593. Habsburg, op. cit., p. 13f.
594. *Die Zeit*, 29.5.1987—Sommer, publisher of *Die Zeit* was connected to the 'Atlantic Bridge' group [*Atlantik-Brücke*]. That his editorial here was a conscious attempt to distract readers cannot be excluded.
595. FAZ 26.5.1989: 'In his third speech on American security policy and policy towards the East in two weeks Bush mixed praise for Gorbachev's politics of reform with western self-consciousness in view of the general turning towards democracy throughout the world. "We live in a time when we are witnessing the *end* of an idea ... the final chapter of the Communist experiment." '
596. Hamburg, April 1989.
597. Op. cit. p. 309.
598. See *Der Spiegel*, No. 13 and No. 14, 1989.
599. Henrich, op. cit., p. 278.
600. On the ecclesiastical experiment, which began in the late 1970s and lasted about ten years, to absorb parts of the anthroposophically oriented world picture into Catholic spirituality, see Thomas Meyer, *The Boddhisattva Question*, London, 2nd edition 2010. In the attempt by particular Catholic circles to assimilate anthroposophical thinking, the former anthroposopher Valentin Tomberg (1900–1973) played a key role. He converted to Catholicism in the 1940s. A work by Tomberg was provided with an introduction by the former Jesuit, Hans-Urs von Balthasar, upon whom John Paul II had sought to bestow a Cardinal's hat shortly before his death in 1988. On the stance of the present Pontiff [John Paul II] with regard to Anthroposophy, see also Pietro Archiati, 'Zur Gegendarstellung Prof. Spaemanns', *Das Goetheanum*, 17 Jan. 1993.
601. From the viewpoint represented here, the moral engagement of the representatives of the Lutheran Church or of the Leipzig conductor Kurt Masur, especially on the critical 9 October 1989, lose nothing of their lustre. It was *decisive* for the victory of the 'revolution', however, that it received a green light from Moscow before it began. Was Gorbachev's visit to East Berlin for the 40th anniversary of the GDR on 6 and 7 October not an open encouragement to gentle 'pressure from below' in the GDR? It is noteworthy that already in 1983, in the 500th anniversary year of the birth of Martin Luther, and in the same address to the Bundestag in which he pleaded for the reunification of Germany, Helmut Kohl also emphasized that: 'The commemoration of Martin Luther and the question of what he means for today and for the future brings Germans

together this year.' (*Das Parlament*, 16.7.1983). Did Kohl then already glean how important the Lutheran element in the GDR was to become? In 1989 it helped those in Washington and Rome, in consultation with Moscow to push open the unlocked gates between East and West gently and peacefully ...

602. Ekkehard Kuhn, *Gorbatschow und die deutsche Einheit, Aussagen der wichtigsten russischen und deutschen Beteiligten*, Bonn 1993, p. 44.

603. Loc. cit. p. 43. In Gorbachev's presence, N. Portugalov, Gorbachev's adviser on Germany, said:

> It was this order, initiated by Gorbachev [...], that was outstanding [...] The military were very indignant about it and tried to exert influence. I still remember it: there was the Commander of our Army Group in the GDR, Army General Snedkov. He wanted to make a mountain out of every molehill, [said] how dangerous things would be and that we would lose our rights and so on; *nothing whatsoever was acted upon. Gorbachev remained firm.* [Emphasis THM.]

604. p. 37. It should be noted that *Forum* is, according to its masthead, the official information organ of the Council of Europe.

605. *Rom macht mobil für ein 'christliches Europa'*, Typescript of a documentary broadcast by Saarland Radio, 1991.

606. Loc. cit. p. 39.

607. At the end of 1987 at the annual conference of the World Bank and the IMF, and in front of journalists from all over the world, Herrhausen proposed consideration of a partial remission of the debts of the most heavily indebted countries. 'Take the next helicopter and get out of Washington, you will be shot here' was how Herrhausen himself described his feelings in the US capital later. See G. Wisnewski, W. Landgraeber, E. Sicker, *Das RAF-Phantom*, Munich 1992, p. 154.

608. Magazine of *Süddeutsche Zeitung*, 27.11.1992.

609. *Das RAF Phantom*, p. 172. (Translated from the German) It should not be concluded that the CIA is the only significant instrument of covert power projection; just as little is Skull & Bones the only occult political group in the USA. The more such organizations and groups become known, the more other such associations or brotherhoods will grow.

610. See note 609.

611. Loc. cit. p. 197f. (Translated from the German)

612. See note 611.

613. Loc. cit. p. 190 http://www.prouty.org/comment11.html. When one considers that in the '*Atlantik-Brücke*' [Atlantic Bridge], an influential private political lobby group in Bonn where top German and American industrialists and secret servicemen meet, it is easy to understand how well-informed leading circles in America were about German plans at the time of the Wende were. The *Atlantik-Brücke* is also a German subsidiary of the *American Council in Germany*.

614. There are good grounds for believing that the shots fired from Bad Kleinen in June 1993 were the work of the German federal secret service in order to 'make

clear' to citizens how acute, contrary to the claims of the authors of *Das RAF Phantom*, the danger from the core group of the RAF still was. The investigations in this case too, which were also sloppy and amateurish, only lend yet more weight to the arguments of the book's three authors. See their second book *Operation RAF—was geschah wirklich in Bad Kleinen?* [Operation RAF— What Really Happened in Bad Kleinen?] Munich 1994.

615. Gerhard Wisnewski, 'Herrhausen wurde nicht ermordet', Magazine of *Süddeutschen Zeitung*, 27.11.1992.

616. See note 615.

617. The Testament restricted itself to the Greek Catholics [i.e. Orthodox], but the essential point here is that it is the confessional element of *Catholicism* which is to be used for political purposes.

618. Emphasis THM.

619. Quoted from the FAZ, 13.1.1990 (Translated from the German).

620. *The Economist*, 1–7 September 1990. For the map, see also T.M. Boardman, 'Die neue Weltordnung' in *Goetheanum*, 14.8.1994 and Terry Boardman, *Mapping The Millennium—Behind the Plans of the New World Order*, Forest Row 2013. With regard to the Gulf War, two episodes may be mentioned: 'On 25.7.1990, one day after the CIA had reported Iraqi troop movements towards the Kuwaiti border, the US ambassador April Glaspie told Iraq's Saddam Hussein according to an Iraqi account of the conversation that was never denied: "We have no opinion on your Arab–Arab conflicts, such as your dispute with Kuwait." ' (Die Wochenzeitung, 14.1.1994) When Hussein, who had also been armed by the West invaded Kuwait on 2.8.1990, 40,000 American soldiers received their marching orders. See further: Karlheinz Deschner, *Der Moloch—zur Amerikanisierung der Welt*, Stuttgart 1992, p. 331ff.

621. See note 620.

622. *Foreign Affairs*, Summer 1993.

623. http://www.hks.harvard.edu/fs/pnorris/Acrobat/Huntington_Clash.pdf Huntington's article appeared in German in *Die Zeit*, 13.8.1993.

624. Huntington, who evidently knew of Beedham's map, also has St Petersburg at the eastern edge of the western region; the frontier runs through Yugoslavia, with Croatia in the West, and Serbia and Bosnia in the East. For Huntington, Islam belongs in the sphere of the East.

625. The Encyclical, with a commentary, is included: Before New Challenges to Mankind—*Sozial enzyklika Centesimus Annus Papst Johannes Pauls II.*, Freiburg, 1991.

626. Loc. cit., p. 15.

627. Emphasis THM.

628. Loc. cit., p. 51.

629. Loc. cit., p. 56.

630. Loc. cit. p. 126,

631. *Die Weltwoche*, EEA supplement to No. 47, 19.11.1992.

632. *Wochenbericht*, the Julius Bär Bank 7.5.1992.

633. *Die Welt*, 21.12.1992.

634. *Out of Control—Global Turmoil on the Eve of the 21st Century*, New York, 1995

p. 230. Brzezinski reverently refers in a footnote [p. 166] to the ideas of Huntington which he got to know before the publication of Huntington's essay.

635. Brzezinski, op. cit. p. 221.

636. Loc. cit. pp. 221–222.

637. See note 626.

638. Loc. cit. p. 130.

639. *Die Welt*, 6.5.1994.

640. Robert K. Massie, *Peter the Great—His Life and World* (1980); German edition, Koenigstein, 1980. By 1990 the German edition had sold 30,000 copies. Massie is also the author of a large work on the period before the First World War, *Dreadnought—Britain, Germany and the Coming of the Great War* (1991). The author presents a picture of a war into which the participants had stumbled, and does not mention the western activities, including those in the Balkans, that led to the war.

641. See Carroll Quigley, *The Anglo-American Establishment*, New York, 1981; also M. Barkhoff, 'Der Lehrer des Präsidenten', in *Das Goetheanum*, 17.1.1993.

642. *Der Spiegel*, 23.5.1994.

643. John Morrison, *Boris Jelzin*, Berlin 1991, p. 50.

644. Loc. cit., p. 57 (Translated from the German).

645. Emphasis THM.

646. *Neue Zürcher Zeitung*, 17.6.1992.

647. On Bush, see Konrad Ege, *George Bush—der neue Präsident*, Cologne 1988. On Bush's Yale Club, Skull & Bones, Ege writes (p. 22f.):

> For Bush, the relationships he made in Yale went beyond his friendships with other students from wealthy families. Like his father, he was a member of Skull & Bones. According to the University's archivist Kelley, this society, in existence since 1832 [1833] has been 'perhaps the most famous secret society in the United States [. . .] Its purpose and programme were not disclosed at its founding nor have they been since.' To uncover this purpose, however, despite all the secrecy in the windowless Skull & Bones headquarters, does not require much imagination. In a series of initiation rituals, which include the mutual revelation of their sex lives, the Bonesmen (only 15 are inducted in any one year) create intimate personal relationships which are maintained for life. Bush profited from this: a Bonesman helped him into the oil industry after his years at Yale, and Bonesmen supported his campaign for the Presidency in 1980. Soon after being sworn in as Vice-President in 1980 Bush invited the Skull & Bonesmen and their wives to a dinner at his new villa in Washington.

On the deeper background to this Club see p. 216ff.

648. *The Economist* on 2 July 1994 carried an article about Russia with the title 'Imperial Russia' and a picture of Peter the Great, under which were the words: 'All Russians for Peter the Great'. It was well-known in certain western circles who the prepared marionette was.

649. The first Jesuit priests arrived in North America in 1634, soon after the Pilgrim

Fathers, and in 1640 first baptized native Indians. They founded schools for whites and Indians and established a Jesuit College in New York. According to Fülöp-Miller (p. 423), a seminar was instituted in Georgetown, 'the first Catholic institute in the territory of the United States; from there they cast the net of their teaching activities to Virginia, Delaware, New Jersey and Pennsylvania.' The principle in the American Constitution of the universal freedom of worship stems from their influence. See René Fülöp-Miller, *Macht und Geheimnis der Jesuiten*, Wiesbaden, 1960.

650. By this is meant the impulse of the Consciousness Soul, which is connected to a special degree with the Anglo-American peoples and which can free the human being in his thinking from the compulsions of the instincts and emotions. In this Consciousness Soul is rooted the possibility for really free acts of will. The individual, who is ultimately to cultivate the Consciousness Soul entirely out of his own forces can draw, as it were, extra invigoration for this from the specific element that is spread throughout the English-speaking peoples. On the 'Consciousness Soul', see R. Steiner, *Theosophy—An Introduction to the Supersensible Knowledge of the World and the Destination of Man*, GA 9.

651. See paragraph 12 of the Testament.

652. If this begins to change here and there, it can be hoped that wakefulness in relation to contemporary processes will become more infectious than is currently the case. A negative indication of the declining political consciousness after Steiner's death are the diverse links that some individuals, even if only a few, among Steiner's pupils had to Nazism, as has been documented several times in recent years.

653. A complete list of such assertions—of the kind one knows of from Rome—would be long. We limit ourselves in what follows to a few, especially conspicuous examples of this kind.

654. This 'failure' relates not to the possibility for the individual to take up the Christmas Conference impulse, but to the spiritual binding power that it could have had *for the whole Society*.

655. Emphasis THM.

656. Cardinal Franz König, a Viennese cleric close to Opus Dei said: 'In the following period it was the conferences of European bishops of 1977 and 1980 which took up again and made known the European thought, the idea of European spiritual collaboration.' (See: *Europa und die Folgen—Castelgandolfo-Gespräche 1987*, Stuttgart 1988, p. 16.)

657. In a lecture of 29.10.1981 in St Gallen. In the same lecture an alleged statement by Otto von Habsburg was passed on: 'Without threefolding, Europe will not move forward.' What von Habsburg—if he really made this statement—and for whom a 'Christian' Europe and the Pope were dear to his heart—actually meant by 'threefolding' must remain an open question.

658. Emphasis THM.

659. To avoid misunderstanding: it is not the strivings of Europe's 'best' that are directly under discussion here, but rather, the solidarity with these 'best' suggested by Schmidt-Brabant in 1979. Such solidarity with the representatives of the Catholic Church or with the *present leaders* of European institutions can

never be in the interests of a true representation of the viewpoints of anthroposophy.

660. 2.11.1992.

661. Oral communication from a participant at the General Secretaries' Meeting in
Dornach, spring 1994.

662. In a Michaelmas lecture in Dornach with the theme 'The Idea and Task of a
New Western Culture'; published in M. Schmidt-Brabant, *Idee und Aufgabe
Europas*, Dornach 1993.

663. Loc. cit., p. 17.

664. GA 338. In this Dornach lecture too by Schmidt-Brabant there was a reference
to Europe's 'best'; this time it was to 'the honoured friends in the *Club of Rome*'.
(Loc. cit., p. 23).

665. See note 664.

666. Due to the limited number of places at the Goetheanum, a selection had to be
made from among all the members of the Class, as also at both previous Class
Conferences, ultimately by the Vorstand of the G.A.S.

667. In the Michaelmas newssheet 1993, No. 185.

668. The expression 'ritual-cultic' [*rituell-kultisch*] appeared in a lecture, which was
held in the Foundation Stone Hall, given by Schmidt-Brabant on 6 July 1990 to
members of the freemasonic research lodge *Quatuor Coronati*. See note 688.

669. *Was in der Anthroposophischen Gesellschaft vorgeht—Nachrichten für deren Mitglieder*,
12.5.1991, p. 102.

670. It may be recalled that Pius IX too did not simply launch the Dogma of
Infallibility himself but got certain people to suggest it 'as coming from
themselves'; it could therefore appear as if, quite selflessly, he only wanted to
satisfy an *objective* wish. Even if, in our case, a corresponding wish were actually
present, merely creating the impression of being able to satisfy that wish *in
Steiner's sense and in his name* is as tasteless as it is 'Jesuitical'. In a private printing
for some anthroposophical friends, titled *Anthroposophical Society, Anthroposophical Movement and the Millennium*, the author of this biography criticized
the attempt to launch the experimental balloon of the '2nd Class' at the 1993
Michaelmas Conference. In that paper he contrasted Polzer's call for spiritual
decentralization and only *administrative* centralization with the current growing
tendency for a pretentious spiritual centralization. (The main part of this text is
included in the collective volume *Anthroposophische Gesellschaft an der Jahrtau-
sendschwelle*, Dornach 1994.)

671. On the honour done to Santiago by the visit of the Pope Cardinal Franz König
wrote (*Europa und die Folgen*, op. cit., p. 16): 'The spiritual situation and the
atmosphere at that time [the time since the 2nd Vatican Council] has been
clearly expressed by none other than Pope John Paul II during his pilgrimage to
Santiago de Compostela in a declaration:

> I, John Paul, son of the Polish Nation, who has always on the basis of his
> origin [...] regarded himself as European, as Slavic among the Latins, as
> Latin among the Slavs, I, successor to Peter at the See of Rome, I, Bishop
> of Rome and Shepherd of the Universal Church, call to you, ancient

Europe, from Santiago, full of love: Find yourself again, be yourself again. Reflect on your origin, re-enliven your roots [...] The other continents look to you and hope *to hear from you the answer of James* [...] [Emphasis THM]

With these words during the Europa celebrations in 1982, John Paul II, who wanted to bind the Slavic peoples to the decadent Latin-Roman element, sought to monopolize Santiago de Compostela and bind it too into the Church's purposes. This, seen from the spiritually real standpoint, is the result of the 'honouring' of Santiago with the papal visit.

672. *Was in der Anthroposophischen Gesellschaft vorgeht—Nachrichten für deren Mitglieder*, 5.12.1993. From the report by Frauke Elsner, one can see how far the conference also stood in the sign of the question of Europe, which had earlier been raised in the same manner by the Catholic Church (and by the Council of Europe, cf. p. 475): 'Could what this James' Way once was for Europe be a sign for us today and help in a certain sense in building the European community of the future?' Another correspondent wrote: 'All the lectures were a call to awaken to the historical spiritual consciousness of Spain, which is rooted in the Mysteries of the Grail and of St James.' Cf. note 671.

673. Emphasis THM.

674. According to a written communication from Paul Michaelis to Erika Warnke on 21 Feb. 1968, Michaelis had 'handed over to the Vorstand everything when four years ago in the clinic I began to think about preparing myself for the journey. I only burned the very private diaries. All of them!' On 25 April 1972 he wrote to Herr Geiger in Wiesneck: 'What could be guaranteed as "authentic" I already handed over to the Vorstand in Dornach seven years ago. The exceptions were a few existing mantra texts and corrections by R. Steiner to two of his lectures and letters which have also since been published [...] and then will be handed over to the Vorstand.' It is not certain that the two files mentioned by Schmidt-Brabant refer to the materials from Michaelis; also, Ilona Schubert, Polzer's former daughter-in-law had, according to a personal communication with the author, lent Schmidt-Brabant via her son some important writings [by Polzer], and they were not returned before her death.

675. See Appendix, p. 577.

676. See Appendix, p. 571.

677. Ludwig Polzer-Hoditz, in a letter to the Vorstand of the G.A.S. 30 June 1929.

678. Emphasis THM.

679. *Was in der Anthroposophischen Gesellschaft vorgeht—Nachrichten für deren Mitglieder*, 19.12.1993. A certain peak in relation to the launching of 'spiritual-scientific' declarations may be seen in the following announcement from the same article of December 1993: 'The present Vorstand knows itself to be united with them [the members of the original, founding Vorstand] and with the other, deceased Vorstand members, whether they are in the spiritual world or are again in earthly bodies, in working for the true spiritual form of the Christmas Conference'.

680. Emphasis THM.

681. Loc. cit. 10 January 1993.

682. See note 681.

683. The last question on the 7th day of the Conference was: 'Can the world Society [of the G.A.S.] become *the* [author's emphasis] true community of free spirits?' This question implies, among other things, the following: If it could be so, then all those who do not belong to the G.A.S. find themselves outside the community of free spirits. The form of the question itself already shows the same kind of universalist pretension that one is used to from the Ecclesia: *extra ecclesiam nulla salus*—no salvation outside the Church ...

684. It may be pointed out here that, besides Polzer, this would naturally apply to many other individualities who were pupils of Steiner who would be just as affected by the falsely posed question with regard to the return of the 'friends'. But the unreality of this question is particularly clear in the case of Ludwig Polzer.

685. The absence of preconceptions belongs to the fundamentals of spiritual scientific thinking and knowing. See Rudolf Steiner's basic philosophical works *Truth and Science* (GA 2) and *The Philosophy of Freedom* (GA 4).

686. Two examples of the repeated manner in which Schmidt-Brabant appropriated documents and papers may be adduced here: at the end of the 1970s he had the Albert Steffen Foundation hand over around 70 lever-arch files (which included correspondence by Steffen as President of the G.A.S.) which were to be kept in the G.A.S. Vorstand archive; the then head of the Steffen Foundation, Friedrich Behrmann, was promised access to them at any time if they were to be stored definitively at the Goetheanum; later, copies were requested—in vain. Behrmann's successors were still not allowed access in 1994. Later, 'a decisive agreement was reached on access to the files in question'. On 10.1.1986, the day after the death of Kurt Franz David, the secretary to the Vorstand, David's writing desk in the Glass House by the Goetheanum was broken open on instruction 'from above'; the papers that should have been there—David occupied himself among other things with the question of opponents—were removed. The list would go on.

687. Those 'best' men of Europe—the ones who are obligated to European and international politically oriented Masonry—can be glad about this state of affairs at the present time. In this context it is not without interest that on 6.7.1990, on the occasion of an annual conference of the Quatuor Coronati 'Research Society' at the Hotel International in Basel, Schmidt-Brabant held a unforeseen lecture, and indeed, it followed on from a guided tour round the Goetheanum—in the same Foundation Stone Hall in which the same personality was to speak in the winter of 1993/94 on the meaning of Santiago de Compostela without drawing the members' attention to the systematic occupation of the area by the Church. Schmidt-Brabant spoke on 6.7.1990 about 'the Future of Freemasonry in the Light of Anthroposophy'. What is noteworthy about this is not the fact in itself, but that up in the G.A.S. there was no discussion of it, nor about whether it makes any sense to engage with Masonry *in such a way*.

After the outbreak of the First World War, Rudolf Steiner himself abruptly dropped the contacts that had existed until then with traditional Masonry, although these had always been *only of an external kind*. According to the witness of Marie Steiner, 'Rudolf Steiner declared the [...] working circle, which had met under the name 'Mystica aeterna' was terminated and as a sign of this, tore up the relevant document.' (GA 265, p. 114). The *political* element within western Masonry had developed particular interests which were incompatible with the general-human aims of spiritual science. The approaches made to the *Grand Orient de France* in the last two decades by certain personalities in the G.A.S. would therefore be welcome solely under the condition that within this traditional Masonic brotherhood of the West exclusively general-human goals were being pursued.

688. Cf. Anthony Sutton, *America's Secret Establishment*, p. 180.

689. In connection with the UN global food conference in Cairo—the International Conference on Population and Development, 5–13 September 1994.

690. GA 181. A lecture of 30.7.1918.

691. See Wolfgang Schuchhardt in *Erziehungskunst*, Nov. 1981, p. 654.

692. Oral communication of May 1914, from the diary of Herman Joachim. Cf. also Thomas Meyer (ed.), *Der Briefwechsel Ralph Waldo Emerson/Herman Grimm und die Bildung von Post-mortem Gemeinschaften*, Basel 2007.

693. LPM, p. 198f.

694. 6.11.178, GA 178.

695. See Th. Meyer (ed.) *Helmuth von Moltke, Dokumente seines Lebens und Wirkens*, Basel 2nd, enlarged edition 2007, GA 286.

696. 7.3.1914, GA 286.

List of Illustrations

Illustrations 1, 20, 35, and 47:
Archive of Basel University Library

Illustrations 3, 5–12, 13 (lower), 14–16, 18, 19, 22 (lower), 27, 33:
Unpublished memoirs of Arthur Polzer (= AP)

Illustrations 28, 29, 32 (lower), 36, 37, 42, 43 (upper) 46, 49, 52, 53, 57, 63:
'Meine Lebenserinnerungen in Bildern' von Ludwig Polzer-Hoditz (unver-
öffentlicht)
[My Memoirs in Pictures, by Ludwig Polzer-Hoditz (unpublished)]

Illustrations 17 and 23:
Anna Polzer, Tannbach

Illustration 30:
Verlag am Goetheanum, Dornach

Illustrations 40 and 41:
Goetheanum Archive, Dornach

Illustration 43:
Menny Lerchenfeld, Munich

Illustration 62:
Christiane von Königslöw, Dortmund (Photo: Anneliese Kretschmer)

Other illustrations are from the archive of Perseus Verlag (publishers).

Index of Names